Restoring Vintage Boats

Frontispiece: Maldon oyster smack
Boadicea built 1808 and rebuilt for
the third time by Michael Frost
1964–72.

This book is dedicated to *Boadicea CK213*

RESTORING
VINTAGE BOATS
John Lewis

International Marine Publishing Company
Camden, Maine

By the same author

A Ship Modeller's Logbook
Small boat conversion
A Taste for Sailing
Small craft conversion

ISBN 0 87742 054 8

Library of Congress Catalog Card No. 75-4329

© John Lewis 1975

Set in Monophoto Imprint and printed in Great Britain
by Jolly & Barber Ltd, Rugby, Warwickshire, England
Published in the United States of America by
International Marine Publishing Company, Camden, Maine, 1975

Contents

6 **Introduction**

11 HMS *Victory*
13 Problems of decay
15 Mystic Seaport
19 The *Wasa*
21 Locating vessels for restoration

23 **Fishing boats**

25 Maldon smack *Boadicea CK213*
47 Thames bawleys
51   Leigh bawley *Bona*
55 Zuiderzee botter MK 63
69 Friendship sloops
75   Friendship sloop *Estella A*
76   Friendship sloop *Chrissy*
79 Noank sloop *Emma C. Berry*
   Inshore boats :
87   Winkle brigs, Shetland boats, gun punts
90   *Emma Goody*, a miniature bawley
93   Gun punts
97   Building a wildfowling punt
105   Grand Banks dories

107 **Trading vessels, fishing schooners and sailing barges**

109 Schooner *Kathleen & May*
118 Schooner *L. A. Dunton*
120 Schooner replica *Bluenose II*
124 Swedish galleas *Solvig*
128   *Solvig* : survey report
135 Thames sailing barges
135   Sailing barge *Kitty*
142 The Norfolk wherry
142   Norfolk wherry *Albion*

146 **Yachts**

148 The Broads One-Design *Flittermouse*
153 Auxiliary schooner *Heartsease*
156 Cruising ketch *Armorel*

164 **The restoration of steam launches and steam engines**

164 Steam engines and boilers
166   Basic steam engine repair and overhaul
168   Boilers
170   The pros and cons of coal and oil firing
171   Wood firing
171 Steam launch *Hero*
177 The steam launches of the Windermere Nautical Trust
179 Steam launch *Dolly*

181 **Surveying**

183 Bibliographical references
185 List of maritime museums (including details of restored ships on display)
188 Acknowledgements
189 Index

Introduction

There is today a growing awareness that our natural resources will not last for ever. This awareness has shown itself in various ways, not least in the desire of many thinking people to preserve and restore nice old things, such as furniture, houses, vintage motor cars and even old boats.

In the past, old fishing boats and their like have often been preserved and restored because their owners could not afford to build anew. The preservation of the knowledge of how these old boats were built and worked is a different matter. In 1910, the Society for Nautical Research was founded in London 'to encourage research . . . into matters relating to seafaring and shipbuilding'. The society's greatest achievement has been to pave the way for the establishment of the National Maritime Museum at Greenwich and the raising of the money for, and the supervision of, the restoration of HMS *Victory* at Portsmouth.

Every year, nearly half a million people visit HMS *Victory* in the precise trim of the time of Trafalgar, and just as many visit the USS *Constitution* in Charlestown, restored to the condition of her launch in 1797. Likewise, crowds flock to look at *Wasa*, the 62-gun Swedish ship which was lifted after 300 years from deep mud at the bottom of Stockholm harbour. They go to Bristol to look at Brunel's iron ship *Great Britain*, which was towed half way across the world on a pontoon to come to rest in the dock in which she had been built. They visit Greenwich to see the *Cutty Sark*, the last survivor of the clipper ships. They go to Enkhuizen in Holland to see the collection of Zuider Zee sailing craft and to Mystic Seaport in Connecticut to inspect every kind of craft from a Friendship lobster sloop to a great three masted whaler. Amongst the visitors is a growing proportion of people with a serious interest in these old craft, including some who may themselves be involved in actual ship and boat restoration.

It is more than worth while for any one who is considering restoring an old boat to look at such ships as the *Victory* or the *Constitution*, quite apart from looking at small craft at Mystic or Enkhuizen or elsewhere. Though such massive restoration and conservation projects are beyond the means of any private individual, there is much in the work that has been done to these ships that could be useful to any restorer. In particular, the methods used to combat and eradicate decay in the timbers are an essential part of any restoration work and the quality of workmanship that has given such distinction to these restorations is an inspiration and an example to everyone.

The *Victory* is the great classic of ship restoration. The work done on this eighteenth century man o' war has been chronicled by Arthur Bugler, who for many years as Constructor to HM Dockyard, Portsmouth, was responsible for all major repairs to *Victory* after 1945. His two-volume work, *H.M.S. Victory, Building, Restoration and Repairs*, should be read by every restorer of old boats.

Colchester smacks: they are both about the same age. The one on the left is in the final stages of dissolution. *Iris*, built at Brightlingsea, has been beautifully restored by Charles Harker. (Left: *photo Keith Mirams*.)

US frigate *Constitution* (1797), the
oldest naval vessel afloat, lying to her
moorings in the river off Charlestown,
Mass.

Maritime museums
1 Grand Banker *L. A. Dunton* at
  Mystic Seaport, Conn.
2 Grand Banker *Lettie G. Howard*, at
  South Street Museum, New York.
3 A boeier and a Friesjacht at the
  Zuiderzee Museum, Enkhuizen.

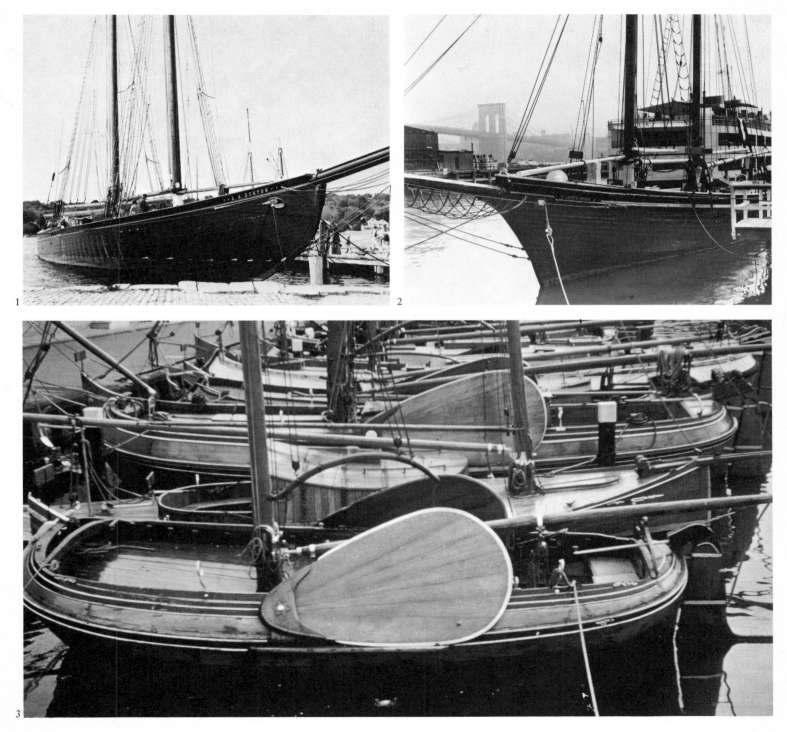

HMS *Victory* in HM Naval Dockyard, Portsmouth. (By permission of The Commanding Officer, HMS *Victory*.)

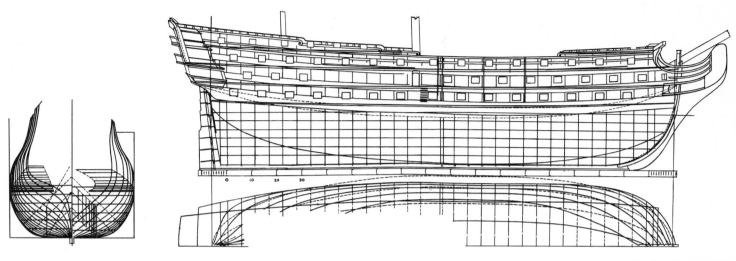

HMS *Victory*. Lines in 1765. The open-galleried stern was altered before Trafalgar. *(Courtesy Society for Nautical Research.)*

HMS *Victory* with part of stern post removed. The figure of the shipwright gives some indication of the scale of such a restoration. (By permission of the Commanding Officer HMS *Victory*.)

HMS *Victory* This is clearly not the place to describe *Victory*'s heroic exploits or even to give a detailed chronology of her various refits and alterations. The bare facts are that *Victory* was designed by Thomas Slade, Senior Surveyor to the Navy, on the lines of the *Royal George* which had capsized and sunk off Spithead. It was a clever design and *Victory* sailed remarkably well for a ship of her class. Her 151ft keel was laid down at Chatham in July 1759. Her building was a leisurely affair for the war with France was coming to an end. Peace was in fact declared at the beginning of 1763 and *Victory* was not launched until 1769. This prolonged building may well have contributed to her long life for it gave her oak timbers time to season. Like all ships of her class, her hull was very closely framed, in places not much more than one inch separating one frame from the next. The oak for *Victory* was in fact felled in 1746, thirteen years before her keel was laid, and came, so it is said, from 3,000 trees.

The building of great wooden ships in the eighteenth century was carried out with few mechanical aids apart from fairly primitive hoists and slings. The shipwrights worked in pairs. This was essential in the handling of large timbers, but there are some jobs on even quite small boats that need a second pair of hands. (Clenching fastenings is just one of these tasks.) The boring of holes for treenails and bolts was done by specialists who used augers. The shipwright used the adze and the axe for trimming all large pieces of timber.

The restoration of HMS *Victory* began in 1922 and was completed in 1928. She was chocked up so that her waterline became level with the dock's sill. She was next secured in a cradle. Then began the job of stripping out all visibly decayed timber and all the structural additions, and refitting her to the condition she was in at Trafalgar. In 1928, she looked as if she would stand for another thousand years but, because of post-

HMS *Victory*

1 The planking round the stern is laminated with five laminates, giving 9in thickness.
2 The starboard side of the lower deck, looking aft, showing decay of the beam ends.
3 Shipwright using an adze on new floor timbers.
4 The bows, portside forward, showing results of decay *(Polyporus sulphureus)* and death-watch beetle in deadwood and cant timbers. (By permission of the Commanding Officer, HMS *Victory*.)

1 Adult death-watch beetle
   Xestobium rufovillosum (much
   magnified). Its real size is just over
   $\frac{3}{16}$in in length. *(Photo Rentokil
   Laboratories Ltd.)*

2 The effect of the gribble *(Limnoria
   lignorum)* on ships timbers. The
   holes are about $\frac{1}{10}$in diameter.
   (Photo Rentokil Laboratories Ltd.)

war shortages of timber, much unseasoned oak and Douglas fir had been used in her reconstruction. Within three years the widespread presence of decay and wood borers was confirmed.

Remarkable to relate, dry rot *(Merulius lacrymans)* was not found at that time in *Victory*'s hull. Wet rot *(Polyporus xantha)* was found to be active at the ends of various fir beams that had been fitted into the boom decks. Much worse than this, however, was the death-watch beetle *(Xestobium rufovillosum)* which was found to be active in many of the oak timbers. The death-watch beetle is rarely found in old craft. The probable reason for this is that once fungal decay has got a hold, the timbers are destroyed before the beetle (whose eggs are often laid in decaying wood) will have had time to complete the life cycle of several years.

The solution to the wet rot problem was to remove any decayed timber and then to dry out the ship with adequate ventilation. To get rid of the death-watch beetle, the hull was sealed up and fumigated with methyl bromide. The gas was delivered from pressurized cylinders through pipes to different parts of the ship. Methyl bromide penetrates well and will kill all beetles and grubs in a 4in × 4in timber. Also, it can be dispersed easily. It took three fumigations to reduce the beetles to what seemed to be manageable limits. Most of the death-watch beetles were almost certainly in the timber that was used in the restorations and they were already in the timber before it was put into the ship.

In the 1950s, a full structural survey was carried out which revealed that the frames, floors and planking below the water-line were in a very poor way. The area round the stern was in a desperate state, mainly from the ravages of the death-watch beetle. The repairs continued over the next ten years. This time, however, whenever timbers were to be enclosed, Burma or Indian teak was used instead of oak. Also, fungicides were now available so all timbers were sprayed before being fitted. Oak was used only for timbers and the kelson which were exposed on two sides to the air. Also – and this is something which every restorer of old boats should take note of – any sawdust, shavings or dirt which had lodged between the timbers was removed by a vacuum cleaner. If such rubbish is left behind, it will usually become sodden in a seagoing vessel and is liable to become a breeding ground for woodlice if nothing worse. If this rubbish does not become damp, it can become a source of another danger: fire. A painter using a blow-lamp started a fire in this way in one of the cabins of the *Victory* in February 1973, which goes to show that they had not used their vacuum cleaner quite as thoroughly as they might have done.

Between the time that HMS *Victory* was launched and when she was finally taken out of the water, she had had three major refits which were almost the equivalent of rebuildings. These refits always involved cutting out decayed timbers. To get at and to remove decayed timbers was almost as skilled a job as shaping them in the first place. The shipwrights took much trouble in the ripping down (ie dismantling) to preserve the timber that was to be taken out and to avoid damaging too much of the lining or planking. They would extract a hanging knee or a frame which was partly decayed with as much care as a dentist takes out a tooth. The decayed area of the removed member would then be cut right back, new wood scarphed into the old and the whole refashioned and refitted. In removing these

HMS *Victory*. This rigging plan (as she was rigged
in 1805) was followed in the restoration.
(Courtesy of Her Majesty's Stationery Office.)

timbers, their fastenings had either to be driven out or cut. If
it was not practicable to back out the bolts, iron-cutting saws
would be used behind the timbers to cut the bolts, thus freeing
the timbers. Treenails of course presented no problem. Whenever possible, the iron or copper bolts were driven out after the
end which was clenched on a roove had been cut off with a cold
chisel. The object of this was that the same fastening could be
used again, but if on the same timber a deeper recess had to be
chiselled out to receive the roove and the new clenched end of
the now shortened bolt.

In January 1974 when I last visited HMS *Victory*, restoration
work was still going on with the almost complete new framing
of her stern. A lesson had been learned over the years and oak
had been replaced with teak. This is restoration for preservation
rather than for slavish duplication. The same lesson was learned
at Mystic Seaport where teak was used in place of softwood for
the stanchions in the newly restored Noank wet-well smack
Emma C. Berry.

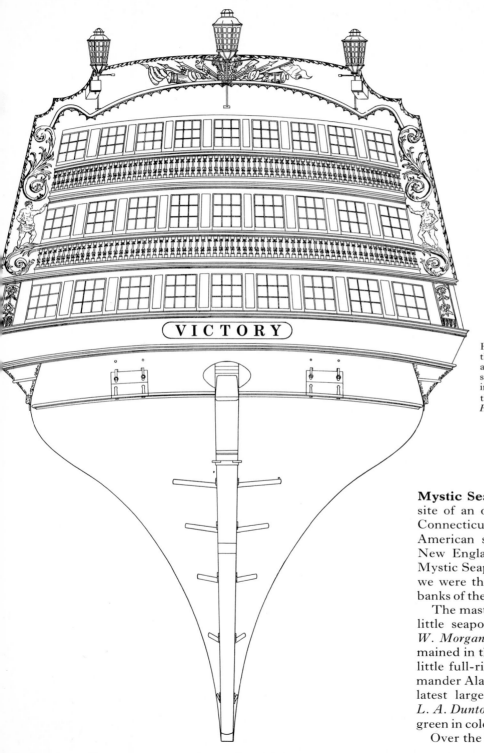

VICTORY

HMS *Victory*. The closed stern of the time of Trafalgar. The balustrades are only decorative and do not provide stern walks. By 1960, this stern was in a bad state owing to the ravages of the death-watch beetle. (*Courtesy of Her Majesty's Stationery Office.*)

Mystic Seaport Mystic Seaport was founded in 1929 on the site of an old shipyard, on the banks of the Mystic river in Connecticut, with the intention of showing something of American seafaring traditions and particularly those of the New England coast and its whalers, sealers and fishermen. Mystic Seaport is a captivating place. It was in the late fall that we were there and the maples and dogwood that clothed the banks of the river were blazing with autumn colours.

The masts of three large ships showed above the roofs of the little seaport village. These ships were the whaler *Charles W. Morgan*, which was built at New Bedford in 1841 and remained in that most arduous of seafaring trades until 1921; the little full-rigged training ship *Joseph Conrad*, in which Commander Alan Villiers sailed round the world in 1934–6; and the latest large acquisition, the Grand Banks fishing schooner *L. A. Dunton*, in course of restoration, hog-backed and a bilious green in colour.

Over the last forty years a large collection of ships and boats

HMS *Victory* : examples of decay and
beetle damage.

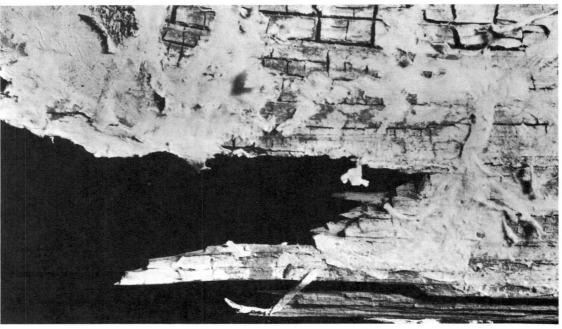

Decay by wet rot fungus, *Poria
vaillantii*.

Decay by dry rot fungus, *Merulius
lacrymans*.

16

Decay by wet rot fungus, *Polyporus sulphureus*.

Adults of the death-watch beetle *Xestobium rufovillosum* on infested oak timber. *(Photos : The Forest Products Research Laboratory.)*

The *Wasa's* stern which, because of the corrosion of the iron fastenings, had largely fallen away.

The *Wasa* had double galleries. Between the two tall windows a pair of cherubs support a sheaf of corn – the symbol of the name of the ship. The initials G A R S on the broad crossbeam above the coat of arms stand for Gustavus Adolphus Rex Succiae.

The height of the aftercastle was 20m (65ft). Drawing by Gunnar Olofsson. *(Courtesy of the Swedish National Maritime Museum and Warship Wasa.)*

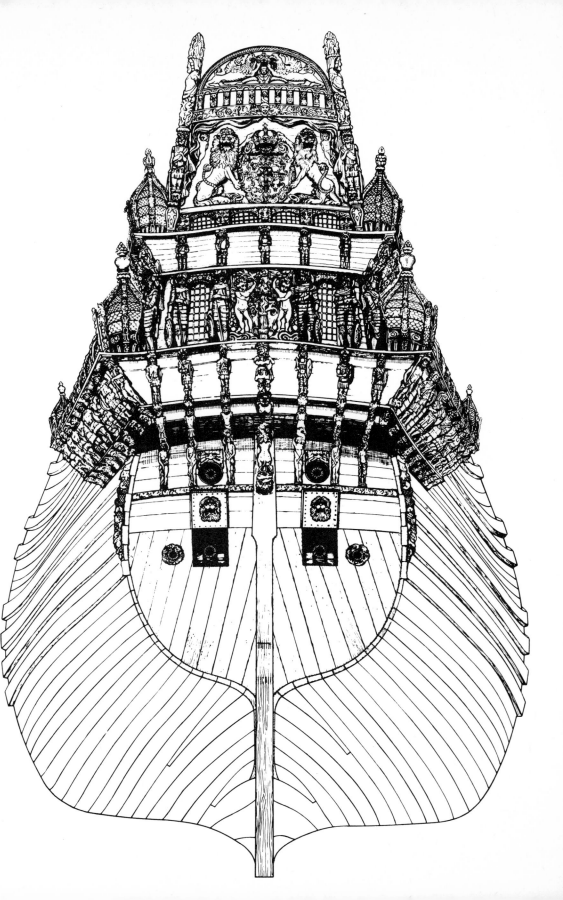

has been assembled and restored. As a setting for the ships, Seaport Village has been created with various workshops including a smithy, a ropewalk and a hoop shop for making casks. To these are added stores, houses, a little pub, appropriately called Schaefer's Spouter Tavern, and a minute Methodist chapel. Many of these have been transferred to Mystic from other sites. Mystic Seaport must be one of the few maritime museums in the world with its own shipyard. Here, they rebuild and preserve their historic vessels. The place is full of life, staffed by young men, some of them University graduates, working as shipwrights, painters and riggers.

John Gardner, the assistant curator for small craft studies, told us much about their work. He said: 'At the Museum here, we are involved in the restoration of old boats for exhibit purposes, but that is far from being the same thing as the restoration or reconditioning of old boats for use. And the building anew of old types for present day use is something quite different still. A good museum restoration attempts to put a boat back in its original condition as near as possible, yet the boat, if it is a small craft type, will generally be exhibited indoors or under cover so it will not be subjected to the effects of weather or the rigors of use. The emphasis then can be upon *appearance*. If an old boat is to be reconditioned for use, it may be expedient to make certain changes and additions to strengthen it, sister frames, additional fastenings and the like, which would not be permissible in a good museum restoration.' These observations are very pertinent to our subject.

My visit to Mystic Seaport had been primarily to look at two recently restored fishing boats, the Noank wet-well smack *Emma C. Berry* and the Friendship lobster sloop *Estella A*. The Noank smack had been restored in the museum's own shipyard, the *Estella A* by Newbert & Wallace's boatyard at Thomaston in Maine. They are both superb restorations and provide an interesting comparison to Michael Frost's restoration of the Maldon oyster smack *Boadicea*.

A visit to Mystic Seaport is an inspiration to those interested in ships and the sea. To anyone hopeful of restoring an old boat, Mystic Seaport is brimful with knowledge, both practical information in the shipyard and research material in the G. W. Blunt White Library, which has a large collection of ships' plans as well as a great number of manuscripts and books on American maritime history.

An interest in ship and boat restoration need not end above the waves. Even below there are lessons for the boat restorer. For hundreds of years divers have been bringing up amphorae and other artefacts from wrecks in the Mediterranean and elsewhere. Haphazard treasure-hunting is now being superseded by an interest in the ships themselves.

It is worth considering some of the problems of nautical archaeology and the work involved in the restoration of very old craft which may have been lifted from the seabed. Such restoration is nearly always for display purposes, though one little steam launch is now in commission after eighty years deep down in Ullswater in the English Lake District.

The rapid development of underwater exploration is due to the aqualung, which was perfected by Jacques-Yves Cousteau and Emile Gagnin. Wrecks have been discovered in many parts of the Mediterranean and around the coasts of Europe. These wrecks have provided through analysis and survey much information about old craft, their size, the woods of which they were built and how they were fastened.

Wasa The actual raising from the depths of water, mud or sand of hulls that may be largely complete is something quite new. So far, the most successful resurrection of an old ship from the depths is the raising of the Swedish 64-gun warship *Wasa* from the bottom of Stockholm harbour. *Wasa* sank in sixteen fathoms on her first sail across the harbour on 10 August 1625. She was caught by a squall, heeled over with her gun ports open and capsized, drowning forty or fifty people. Over the years efforts were made to raise her. The divers succeeded in bringing up many of her guns, but finally she sank into the mud and there she was left for nearly three hundred years.

In 1956, a Swedish Admiralty engineer, Anders Franzen, after much research located the position of the wreck. Naval divers confirmed that Franzen's wreck was the *Wasa*. Her hull planking was in very good order even though nearly all her iron fastenings had rusted away, but *Wasa* was fastened mainly with treenails. The forecastle and the poop had gone, the counter and the stem head also were missing. The planks at the stern had been iron-spiked and, as the iron had rusted, so they had fallen into the mud where the divers found them.

The task of lifting this precious nautical relic was considerable. As she lay, it was estimated (in fact underestimated) that *Wasa* had a dead weight of 670 tons. Divers using high-speed jets of water dug six tunnels underneath her. This was so that the lifting hawsers could be taken under her hull. *Wasa* was raised very slowly by the salvage company who used two large pontoons, each of which could lift 1,200 tons. To achieve this lift, the pontoons were filled with water until their decks were awash. The lifting hawsers were then tightened up and the pontoons were pumped dry.

With her decks 25ft below the surface, *Wasa* was towed into shallow water. The divers now had to make her watertight. All the seams had to be caulked, the gun ports closed and a coffer dam built across her stern. In addition, her bulwarks had to be repaired and about 5,000 bolt holes had to be plugged. All this had of course to be done under water.

On 24 April 1961 *Wasa* came to the surface. All the timbers, as soon as they were exposed to the air, were wrapped in plastic

Swedish 64-gun ship *Wasa* after 336 years at the bottom of Stockholm harbour. *(Photos courtesy of the Maritime Museum and the Warship Wasa.)*

1 View showing how divers boarded up the stern.

2 Beak head and figurehead are missing.

3 Lower gun deck looking towards bow. Tons of mud have been shifted.

1

2

3

sheets to prevent the wood from drying out, and sprinklers were placed around and inside the ship. The pumps kept the level of the water down in the hull and *Wasa* was gently edged into the dry dock.

The work of restoration then began. One hundred and twenty tons of ballast and probably as much again of mud were cleared from her decks and holds. One of the reasons *Wasa*'s hull was in such good shape was the lack of wood borers in the cold and only slightly saline Baltic waters. The teredo worm and gribble cannot live in water with less salinity than 16–20 parts per 1,000.

The laborious business of washing the wood for six months to clear it of minerals, humus and discoloration was then followed by two years of spraying with a special conserving fluid made up of a mixture of carbo-wax and glycol (polyethylene glycol 4,000). After that, bit by bit the ship is being reassembled and reconstructed. Over seven hundred pieces of carving and sculpture have been recovered and have to be put back in their proper places. Amongst them is the figurehead of a lion which weighs several tons and is now once again in place.

To come down to practical possibilities: let's consider what craft are suitable and *available* for restoration. The most easily found are old yachts, both large and small, and the most viable

are those that have led a reasonably sheltered existence on freshwater rivers and lakes and have wintered under cover. In the USA, the Maine Antique Boat Society boasts of a little fin-keel sloop, *Aspenet*, which was built by George Lowley in 1896. In England in a boatyard near Acle on the Norfolk Broads, there is a Broads One-Design called *Flittermouse*, built in 1900. She was one of the first of the class ever built and for some years she lay neglected in a Norfolk barn. Both *Aspenet* and *Flittermouse* look like new – but not new modern yachts, for they do not build boats like fine pieces of cabinet making today.

In one afternoon's exploration in Broadland I came across one yacht that had been built in 1850, another between 1870 and 1880 and two others before the turn of the century. In addition, I found a pre-1914 Danish Pilot Brigantine and a magnificent great racing schooner that had been built in 1903. Both the latter craft were being restored.

The search for old fishing boats and other working craft is likely to be more time-consuming. For instance, old fishing boats, which are now all under power, are plentiful in Scandinavia and can be found elsewhere in Europe. If they can be found in reasonable condition, they are in many ways an easier proposition for restoration than a complicated finely constructed yacht.

In the United States, most fishing boats were worked until

they fell apart or were bought up many years ago and converted into yachts. A recent letter to the author from Charles Minor Blackford, who once owned a converted skipjack and now lives at Crystal River, Florida, throws some light on this problem. Even though he is talking mainly about conversion (to yachts) rather than restoration, much of what Mr Blackford says has some bearing on the restoration of small craft. He writes:

'. . . it is my opinion that in this country (except perhaps in New England) convertible hulls are difficult to find at a price that would compensate for the cost of conversion. One can pick up a good yacht, especially in the larger sizes for far less . . . in regards to converting bugeyes, skipjacks and sharpies from work boats to yachts, one's main difficulty is looks. They are all shallow hulls so, to get cabin room, they have to be high and ungainly wind-catchers. As they are light displacement vessels the high houses slow them down to windward and in coming about. As that type of craft is designed for oystering and crabbing, their freeboard is low, using high bows as reserve buoyancy in head seas.

'As I have said, work boat hulls are not often available. The cost of building is so high that what hulls are left are used until they wear out. If anything the trend is the other way and the fishermen buy old yachts and convert them into work boats. Around here, all the alongshore fishing-boats and shrimpers are converted yachts . . . There is only one work boat schooner left on this coast and she is now used as a home by her owner. He has to hide out in the Ten Thousand Islands to get away from all those who wish to buy her. She is an Appalachicola boat. I have known her since '31 and she was at least thirty years old then and had no caulking until several years later . . . A man here has taken off the lines of his grandfather's Appalachicola-built schooner from a half-model and is reproducing her in ferro-cement.'

Minor Blackford goes on to describe the Appalachicola shoal draft fishing schooners.

'Appalachicola used to be the most important boat building centre on the Gulf of Mexico. The craft were mostly similar to Chesapeake Bay craft, but sometimes had a touch of French from the Louisiana boyous. They were noted for building craft so tight that they needed no caulking. I have seen them at least twenty or thirty years old and still un-caulked. Appalachicola was an ideal place to build boats. They had live oak trees from the swamps, long leaf pine from the backwoods and imported a kind of mahogany from Cape Sable, known as Madeira or 'horseflesh', which got harder and stronger with age. They used black mangrove for trim and rail cappings. These builders were famous for their snapper smacks that fished the Campeche Banks off Mexico.

Mr Blackford also makes an interesting point about the sail plans of fishing boats:

'I have discovered than an alteration of the sail plan (particularly if it is a sloop) of a converted work boat is generally necessary. The main boom has to be shortened and the gaff peaked up higher so as to get more speed to windward and less un-needed power.'

Because of the difficulty of finding old workboat hulls, there has been a marked return to some of these old types of vessel in modern reconstruction. Minor Blackford's mention of the ferro-cement replica of the Appalachicola schooner is just one example. The most striking work in this direction has been the establishment on the coast of Maine of the Friendship sloop model, though only as yachts and not as fishing boats.

This leads to the question of building to the lines of old craft, or even actually constructing a replica of some famous ship. Recent examples are the schooner yacht *America*, the Nova Scotian fisherman *Bluenose II* and the Pilgrim Fathers' *Mayflower*, though this was only the replica of a type and not of a precise ship. Various versions of Joshua Slocum's *Spray* have been built and, at the time of writing, the National Maritime Museum at Greenwich is building a replica of the *Faeringen Fra Gokstad*, the smallest of the three boats discovered in the Gokstad ship when it was excavated from a burial mound alongside Oslo Fjord in 1880.

The building of replicas of particular historic craft may well be useful for museum and other commemorative reasons. Whether there is any other justification for them is hard to say, except perhaps to see how they work. One thing however is certain: no replica of an old sailing ship, fishing boat or yacht is going to behave in exactly the same manner as the original. Michael Frost made this clear when he rebuilt his old Maldon smack *Boadicea* (see p 25). In that case it would have been a much simpler task to have built a new smack alongside the old one, but the shape would not have been exactly the same so the performance under sail would almost certainly have been different.

The building to a type, rather than the attempt to make an exact copy of an old craft, is another matter. If the type was as healthy a little sea boat as a Friendship sloop, there is everything to be said for such revivals.

Whether one is restoring a little steam launch or a 130ft schooner, or building a facsimile of a Chesapeake Bay skipjack or a Morecambe Bay prawner, there is a lot of hard work ahead and to compensate for that, the immense satisfaction of doing a job well. There are the additional pleasures of what one learns at every stage of such labour and also the pleasures of research.

Fishing boats

Introduction The inspiration for this book lies in Michael Frost's restoration of the Maldon oyster dredger *Boadicea*. Michael Frost has inspired others to restore fishing vessels. Today on the Blackwater river in Essex, where *Boadicea* has dredged and fished for the last century and a half, there are more than a dozen oyster boats, smacks and bawleys sailing about, restored to their original form, many of them trawling and dredging under sail.

The task of restoring and rerigging these old fishing boats

every year becomes more difficult, for the abandoned hulls have all fallen apart and, as the old men who sailed and worked them die out, the harder it becomes to find out exactly how they were fitted out and worked. To put something of this on record, Michael Frost has written in his book on the vessel how for a quarter of a century he trawled for fish and dredged for oysters from the little *Boadicea*. It is a detailed and engrossing account of how these fishermen went about their business. At the end of that twenty-five years, he set to work to rebuild his old

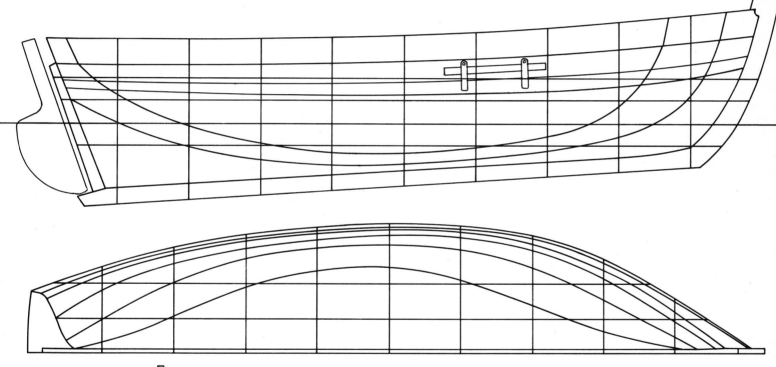

Maldon oyster smack *Boadicea*, built 1808. Lines drawn by Peter Brown, February 1974.

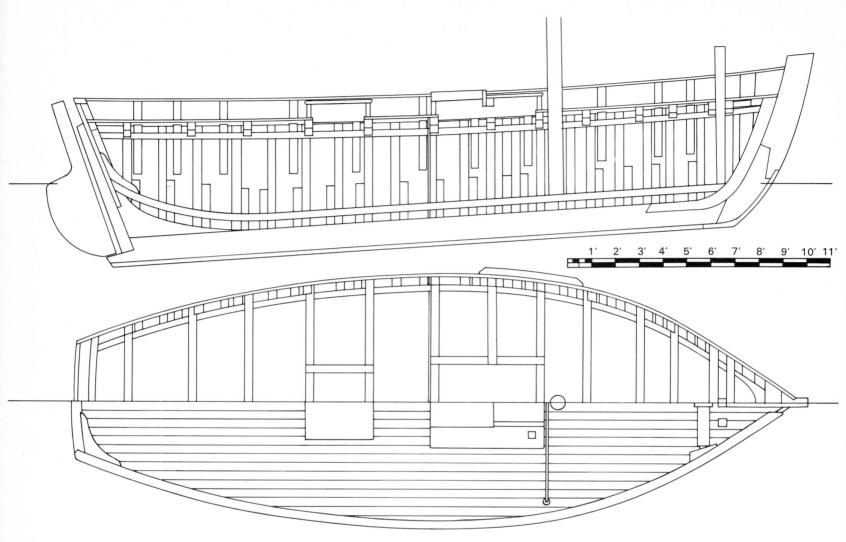

boat. The account of that restoration follows this introduction.

The most likely way to locate an old fishing smack is to find one that has been converted into a power boat for commercial use, or has been turned into a yacht. The seventy-year-old Leigh bawley *Bona* was such a conversion, with a great wheel-house which her restorers ceremonially burnt as an offering to whoever the gods are who bless the work of boat restorers. The three other types of restored fishing boats described here are a Dutch Zuiderzee botter with a wet fish well, a clipper-bowed Noank mackerel and lobster fisherman from Connecticut, also with a wet fish well, and a couple of little Friendship sloops that fished the lobster grounds of Muscongus Bay on the coast of Maine.

Small inshore working vessels such as fishermen use to tend their oyster layings, collect mussels, inspect their inshore lobster traps or use for line fishing vary from locality to locality. The types have often persisted because of their suitability for local conditions. An English east coast winkle brig and a small Shetland boat are taken as examples of traditional types worthy of preservation or restoration.

Finally, two flat-bottomed types of boat, an American fishing dory and an English east coast duck punt, types which were more often than not built by amateurs, their construction being very simple and their materials cheap. Yet both boats are uniquely suitable for their jobs. The high sided dory, looking for all the world like a paper boat, is a great load carrier – it needed to be to carry two or more tubs of 500 fathoms of baited line; the east coast duck punt is long and low and sleek, yet stable enough to carry a gun firing $\frac{1}{2}$lb of shot at a time. Though the main purpose of these skiffs was wildfowling, they were widely used for eel fishing. Anyone who can saw a plank or hammer a nail can build one. The life of such softwood boats is limited, so it is a case of preserving the type rather than the individual boats.

The transom sterned Maldon smack
Boadicea CK213

LOA 30ft
LWL 24ft
Beam 10·3ft
Draught 4·6ft
Depth in hold 4·6ft
Gross tonnage 10·8
Built 1808

When Michael Frost bought *Boadicea* in 1938, she was possibly the oldest working sailing craft in Europe.

Boadicea was built in 1808 by James Williamson of Maldon, Essex; she was originally clinker-planked on cut frames. For the first seventeen years of her life she worked out of Maldon, Bradwell and Burnham, dredging for oysters. In 1825, she was bought by John Pewter of Tollesbury and she worked from this little Essex village for the next hundred years, changing owners in 1871. In 1890 the Binks family, who then owned *Boadicea*, had her largely rebuilt by Aldous of Brightlingsea, who replaced her clench planking with 1½in thick carvel planking. In 1917, E. W. French of West Mersea bought her and kept her at work until 1938 when he sold her to Michael Frost, who had just qualified at Guy's Hospital. He sailed and trawled and dredged from her until 1963 (with a break during the war years).

By the end of 1963 it was clear that *Boadicea* needed a major refit and some drastic repairs to her keel. Michael Frost brought her into Frost & Drake's yard at Tollesbury and it was to be nearly nine years before she was afloat again.

'After twenty-five years of happy and very cheap sailing, I felt I owed something to the smack. These years of work have been my attempt to make her as near time-proof as possible. It is a small return for the pleasure she has given me.'

Michael Frost's words explained it all. Discussing the problems of rebuilding such a craft, he went on to say, 'When I started on this, I did not know anything of shipwright's work, but I soon learned. After all, I was working on the boat in a shipwright's yard and when they discovered that I was really serious about doing this rebuilding job they helped me in many ways and with much advice. There was nearly always someone working near me, and if I was about to do something wrong or something like that, they would stop me at once.'

In his twenty-five years with *Boadicea*, Michael Frost has trawled and fished the Blackwater winter and summer. *Boadicea* has crossed the North Sea to Holland and had to be man-hauled up the Middelburg canal to Veere, for she has never let her purity be defiled with an engine.

'I have nearly turned her over twice,' Michael Frost said, 'once when she touched when being driven hard, the other time when some youngsters said it was not possible to ship a solid sea into the stay sail. In trying to show them it was possible, I thought she was not going to right herself, but she did, with her decks full and a lot of water down the hatches.' After that he put another ton of ballast into her.

When I first saw *Boadicea* she was sitting on the bank alongside Frost & Drake's yard at Tollesbury. The restoration of her hull was finished and she looked like a brand new boat. But no new fishing boat or yacht has been built to these lines for a century or more. *Boadicea* is tubby and rounded yet all her lines are sweet. It was easy to believe him when her owner said she was very handy and perfectly balanced. We climbed aboard. Standing on deck I could see that her new transom was very slightly askew, as her previous one had been for the last hundred years. Below decks, looking at her varnished timbers and superb workmanship, I could feel the love that had gone into the rebuilding of the little ship. Also there was something in her atmosphere that showed that this was not a new ship but still the old *Boadicea*, if a *Boadicea* rejuvenated.

Michael Frost said, 'Once I had decided that rebuilding was necessary it would have been far easier to have taken off her lines and built a new smack alongside, but that was not the point. This is still the same *Boadicea*, whose ways under sail I have got to know. So many people who have boats get rid of them every few years, before they get to know them properly. After twenty-five years I was beginning to feel I did know *Boadicea*.'

The third rebuild of *Boadicea* One of the first things that Michael Frost did when he bought the *Boadicea*, nearly twenty-five years before he started on her third rebuild, was to strip out the lining. Behind the lining and filling the space between the frames was an awesome black compost made up of water, sawdust, shavings and mud, the whole lot swarming with woodlice.

After clearing away this mess, washing out the boat and drying the sodden planks and timbers with a blowlamp, it was possible to see what the inside of the ship was like. The soft surfaces of the planks and the frames were infested not only with woodlice but also with some kind of wood grub. More use of the blowlamp and liberal applications of Cuprinol made the smack smell sweeter but never really eradicated the woodlice. There was a certain amount of rot around the iron fastenings, particularly in the oak frames and keel. The belief that hot-dip galvanized bolts would be any better was dispelled on discovering that some galvanized mild steel bolts, that were put in in 1948, had rusted away to nothing in a dozen years, even though at either end they appeared in perfectly good shape.

The main problem in rebuilding an old ship like the *Boadicea* is to prevent her from going out of shape, not only when she is

Boadicea nearing the end of her
rebuild at Tollesbury, 1971.

Boadicea on ways: G-cramps kept
behind to prevent slipping on slope.
Boadicea was hauled up by a winch (1)
and held in position by an anchor (2)
and cramps (3).

out of the water but even more so when the old keel is taken out
and a new one put in. With *Boadicea*, this problem was finally
resolved by reframing and flooring the boat *inside* her old skin
and then supporting her weight on two massive but temporary
bilge keels, fastened through the old skin to temporary frames
inside. Michael Frost took no short cuts. To saw out six frames
to shape and to fit two twelve-foot bilge keels, which were only
to be used until the new keel was in position, gives some idea of
the care that went into retaining the shape and the characteristics
of this beautiful little ship.

The choice of material in this restoration was governed by a
wish to make *Boadicea* as near trouble free as any boat could be.
Her keel and bottom planking is now of greenheart, the hardest,
most durable, most rot-resistant wood there is. She is framed in
English oak, her transom, coamings, hatch covers and rail are of
teak, her topside planks are 1½in larch. Her fastenings, after
much trial and error, are of monel metal and each 4in nail cost
5p.

Michael Frost brought *Boadicea* into Frost & Drake's yard
in the first week of November 1963 to have some major repairs
done to her keel, which had been damaged when hitting some
obstruction. To begin with she lay in the rill by the road. He
little realized, so he said later, that by the time the necessary
repairs were completed there would be practically nothing left
of her existing hull. She was slipped the following day, sheer
legs were rigged and her mast was lifted out and put into store
with the rest of the gear. The ballast was taken out and laid on
the ground alongside her. By the end of the first week she had
been 'skidded off' to the side of the dock. This was done by
supporting the vessel in a cradle and then sliding her over
greased 'ways'.

Now that the smack was on dry land it was possible to see how
much damage there was to the keel. It looked as if at least the
after half of it would have to be replaced. The yard began work
by chipping out all the concrete and then removed her kelson.
For some time before this Michael Frost had been collecting
grown oak crooks and bends in preparation for the repair work.
These were now delivered to the boat yard. The yard immediately set to work on them, making new floors to replace the
existing ones before they could start on the keel repairs.

By the end of January, all the new floors aft of the bulkhead
were fitted and in place, but not fastened. The men in the yard
were not sure that a whole new keel would be needed and were
in favour of scarphing in a new length at the after end; Michael
Frost had come to the conclusion that it would be better to put
in an entirely new keel. This latter decision was a turning point
in the restoration of the old smack and the point of no return.

The yard realized what might be involved in this work and
probably realized that they were dealing with a perfectionist, so
that the *Boadicea* might end up with a complete rebuild – as in

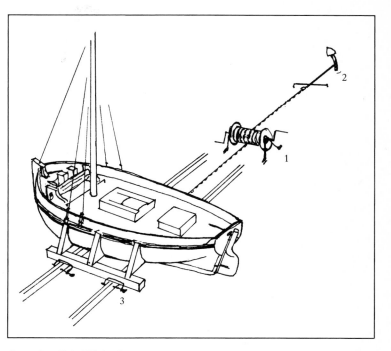

fact she did. This they were not prepared to take on. However,
they came to a friendly arrangement that if Michael Frost would
do the work himself the yard would help in any way it could.
Its help in fact proved invaluable. Michael Frost wrote later
about this:

'During the whole rebuild I almost never asked any of
them how to do things as I did not wish to be a talkative
nuisance, but even so they always knew what I was doing, and
Sid in particular could be relied on to be in the background if
I was on the point of making some irretrievable mistake. I
think he planned the whole rebuild in parallel with me, and
had already worked out each step in detail before I came to it.
He never offered advice until the last moment, but then
would ask me what I was going to do about such and such,
and I would realise that this was a complication which I had
completely overlooked.'

The yard's proposition that Michael Frost should do the
work, but with any help they could give him, at least relieved
the financial burden of such an operation. Whatever the cost of
the materials, these could be met as they occurred – and if they
occurred too frequently, the rate of progress could be slowed
down.

So, singlehanded, Michael Frost set to work on what
amounted to the entire rebuild of *Boadicea*, though he was

certainly not aware of this at the time. He had been conscious that the yard had been reluctant to fit the new floors forward of the bulkhead. They had started to fit the first floor forward of the bulkhead but it was all askew because of a new frame that had been put in twelve years before which was in the way. To get the floor in at the right angle to the line of the keel meant that this frame would have to be cut out and replaced by another one some 4in aft. After some thought, he realised that to let the job begin going awry at such an early stage would be hopeless and there was no alternative but to scrap the frame.

The plan of the operation at this stage was to cut out all the old floors and replace them with new ones. These would be fitted to the old keel but not fastened to it. The garboards would then be cut away, so leaving the keel free of fastenings and free to be taken out.

In the plan for the keel replacement there had been no intention of replacing any of the old frames. However, this one awkward frame by the bulkhead was so much in the way that it had to come out and be replaced. When the new frame was in and fastened, it was obvious that the old frames beside it were not good enough to leave and he decided to have new frames throughout. He still supposed that the old skin could be saved, however.

Each of the new frames took the leisure time of a week to finish. By the time Michael Frost had twelve frames in position and fastened, he realized that each pair was not truly lining up. These twelve new frames had been fitted, six on each side, with one to each deck beam and one in the space between the beams. He had been following the line of the deck beams, which he had assumed to be at right angles to the centre line of the boat. In fact, the beams had been fitted in quite an arbitrary manner, wherever there was space for them between the existing frames and stanchions. They were no fairer than the floor that was askew. This mistake meant that in the end he had to fasten the three forward frames on each side slightly out of alignment, which also meant that later on he could not lap the two forward deck beams to the frames and so could not fit hanging knees.

He at last understood that each floor and the accompanying pair of frames formed a single unit which had to be fitted at the same time and properly lined up before either floors or frames were fastened. In the case of these twelve frames and their accompanying floors they were made to fit as units, but only after quite a lot of trimming to make them lie flush. From this time onwards, he ceased to rush at the job and stopped worrying about visible signs of progress each weekend. *Boadicea* was to have the refit of a lifetime. He had set himself on a perfectionist course.

The seventh pair of frames were matched up with the appropriate floor. He remarked that he had now begun to enjoy the work itself, quite independently from the pleasure that the completed job gave him. This attitude of mind, the pleasure in good workmanship and particularly the satisfaction in doing a job properly, carried Michael Frost right through the restoration of *Boadicea*. Old Joshua Slocum must have felt like this when he rebuilt *Spray*. He communicates his pleasure in every sentence of that famous description in *Sailing Alone Round the World*. Slocum also said something that had a bearing on the restoration of *Boadicea*: 'Now, it is a law in Lloyds that the *Jane* repaired all out of the old until she is entirely new is still the *Jane*. The *Spray* changed her being so gradually that it was hard to say at what point the old died or the new took birth, and it was no matter.'

The way that the correct shape for each frame and floor was achieved was by splitting the old frames out with a chisel and making a cedar wood pattern for the new one. The pattern was made up of short lengths of $\frac{1}{4}$in cedar which were shaped and then clamped to the next length and finally fastened together with short straps of scrap wood. This pattern was then marked out on one of the bends and the yard cut it out on their bandsaw. The bends for the frames were still wringing with sap, for all the dry oak bends had been earmarked for the floors. The use of this green wood was the cause for some anxiety, for on a previous occasion, when Michael Frost was helping Donald Rainbird on the smack *Mayflower*, they had put in some green frames and, although they had been fitted most carefully, within a month or so they had shrunk woefully, coming away from the planking and leaving an awkward gap. While he was thinking in terms of only one new frame, he decided to overcome the problem by fastening it temporarily to let it dry out and then, later on, take it out and refit and fasten it permanently. When it became a case of replacing all the frames this was obviously impractical and, as a possible method of overcoming this shrinkage, the fitting surface of each new frame was coated with roofing bitumen. During the rebuild he used many tins of this messy stuff. Michael Frost decided to go ahead and make, fit and fasten each frame to the old planking of the hull – but in each case coating with bitumen the surface that abutted the planking. It seemed possible that the planking would act as a splint for the new frames and would help them to keep their shape as they dried out. This in fact worked out. In that first, very dry summer of the rebuilding, all the frames dried out and none of them drew away from the planking.

Michael Frost, like many another restorer, learned as he worked. For instance, in making the floors he discovered by trial and error that the first step was to make the floor and fit it in its proper place closely to the hull and at right angles to the keel. The patterns for the frames had to be made to lie flush with the floor. To do this he fastened small stops, which were made of little square blocks of wood. These were fastened at about fifteen inch intervals to the planks in a vertical line. The pattern

was replaced accurately at these stops each time it was offered
up. The first frames which were fitted amidships had a more or
less square cross section. The further forward the frames were,
the more diamond-shaped the cross section became. Also, the
planks which had crossed the frames amidships at right angles
were beginning to lie at a more and more acute angle to the
frame. He began to mark on the cedarwood pattern not only
the edges of the planks but also the bevel of the fitting surface at
each station. He marked also the angle at which the plank
crossed the frames. With this careful preparation of the pattern,
he found he could roughly shape the frame at his home (some
miles from the boatyard). When he brought it down to the
smack there was usually no more than an hour's work to achieve
a precise fit, so that it was ready for fastening.

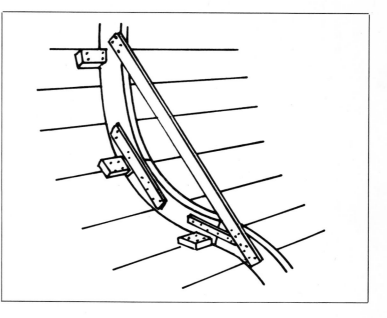

Transferring lines of pattern to oak bend The procedure
for transferring the marks on the pattern to the oak bend was as
follows: the angles of each plank as marked on each pattern
would be recorded with a bevel gauge on a small length of wood.
The pattern would then be taken over to the pile of oak bends
and the most suitable one would be picked out. The line of the
fitting surface of the pattern would then be marked on the oak
bend, parallel with the grain but so placed that the frame when
cut would be free from flaws and sap-wood and would have
enough wood to allow for the cutting of the bevels. This was
not as easy as it sounds and involved turning the 4in plank over
and back at least half a dozen times. When the line was finally
decided, it was clearly marked in and all the mistakes and false
lines planed off – for obvious reasons. When the fitting surface
had been marked in, the inner lines could be measured off and
marked in without difficulty. The yard men would then help
him to lift the oak plank over to the saw bench; if it was a heavy
bend (some of them weighed 5–600lb) it took four or five of
them to cope with it. After it was lifted on to the bench it might
need two of them behind the saw to take the weight as the plank
came through. In the front there would be one on either side to
carry the weight, with the sawyer in the middle. The sawyer
took little or none of the weight but was responsible for steering
the plank so that the saw blade passed slowly and precisely down
the line on the frame. Often the sawyer would make a rough cut
to reduce the bulk and the weight of these hefty pieces of
timber. They would then check the pattern against the lines to
ensure that no distortion had occurred during the first cut. If
any had, the line would be corrected and the frame would be
given its exact cut.

The use of the bandsaw The sawing of such bends needs
much experience. The procedure they followed was that as
soon as the bend had been put into position on the saw bench
the saw would be started and the sawyer would steer the plank

gently round the curve. After they had cut about twelve inches, one of the men behind the saw would tap a wedge into the cut, repeating this every foot. This was to prevent the cut closing and jamming the saw. Even so, the saw often jammed. The electric power would be turned off and the bend would be joggled back until the saw blade was free, then sawing would begin again.

When the frame was cut out it was checked with the pattern and if necessary the fitting edge was retrimmed. While the saw was still running the waste wood would be cut up into logs for burning. Any useful offcuts would be returned to the stockpile.

When the frame had been cut and brushed free of sawdust, in company with its pattern it was loaded into the back of Michael Frost's car for him to complete the rough fitting at home. It is astonishing how large an oak bend an ordinary family car can carry!

The rough fitting of a frame This began with the marking in of the plank edges on the oak and also the angles at which the planks crossed the frames. The depth of the bevel would then be cut in with a saw at each station and the excess wood trimmed away with an adze. The flat surface to fit the flat inner side of each plank would then be finished with a plane.

The inboard bevel (ie the inside face of the frames) to match the one on the fitting surface was then adzed off to a fair curve and the whole frame was planed smooth. Any knots would be cut away and faced with graving pieces cold-glued in. When these had set, the frame was again trimmed up and finally given a flowing coat of Cuprinol. It was now ready for taking back to the smack for the final fitting, bitumen coating and fastening.

The final fitting of a frame This was done by first wetting the planking with Cuprinol and then carefully lowering the frame into position and rubbing it slightly to mark the spots on the fitting surface where it touched. It was then lifted out and the marked spots trimmed away with a plane. In order to handle these awkward, heavy frames a small G-cramp was screwed to each end to provide hand holds. The frames were of course fitted from inside the smack, which was still sheathed in her old planking, with deck still in position. Thus it was both geometrically and practically impossible to make the frames so that they fitted hard up against the deck as well as hard against the side of the keel. It would have been possible to cut holes in the deck so that the head of the frame could poke through while it was being joggled into position, with its foot against the keel, but in the end the frames were made 3in short, and they thus butted hard up against the deck with a 3in clearance of the keel at the foot. This gap was later to be filled with a short floor which passed across the keel and was scarphed to the upper surface of the two frames which formed the pair. Any weakness that this construction might suggest was more than compensated for by

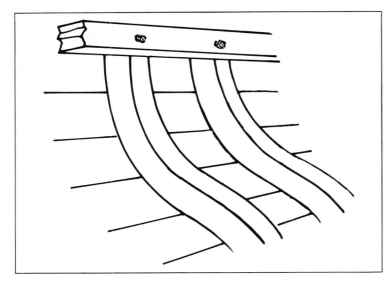

Frames: inboard face bevelled to lie parallel with skin.

the 'long' floors which lay beside the frames and were side-bolted to them.

When each frame had been fitted to the restorer's satisfaction, it was taken out and holes for the fastenings were drilled through the planking from the inside. A matchstick was pushed through each hole to make it easier to find from the outside. The fitting surface of the frame was then given a coating of Cuprinol and a liberal covering of bitumen. It was then put back into position and held securely in place by driving in two wedges between its foot and the keel.

The fastening began at the top, using 4in flat point nails. After the nails were driven, the heads were driven in ¼in further using a punch. This drew the frame hard down against the planking – much closer than if this further driving in of the nails had not been done.

To fit these frames, the shelves that supported the deck beams had to be cut away. This meant that some thought had to be given to the replacement shelves and how they were to be fitted. As for the replacement shelves, Michael Frost had found that the plank-on-edge shelf which he had helped put in *Mayflower* not altogether satisfactory because he thought the space behind the deep shelf could not be reached for painting etc. So he decided on a shelf with a 3in square section. Remembering the difficulty they had bending *Mayflower*'s plank-on-edge shelves he bought some Canadian rock elm which was still green, and, using *Boadicea*'s hull as a former, he clamped it round the outside of the bulwarks just above the deck level. Canadian rock elm is not as durable as oak or pitch pine but it is a wood that will bend easily and will also hold fastenings well. Because of its possible lack of durability, it was soaked in green Cuprinol.

Throughout the rebuilding of *Boadicea* (and this would apply to the restoration of any large craft) there were three programmes to be tackled at the same time. Future needs for as much as a year ahead for material had to be anticipated and wood ordered so that it would be seasoned by the time it was needed. At the same time Michael Frost was working on wood he had bought months before. Between these two extremes was the kind of wood which was bought and rough fitted and bent while it was still green. This would then be left to season for some months until it was time to complete the fitting and fastening of it.

The work of fitting the frames continued until all except the front three pairs were fastened. In due course these would have their heels fitted to the new apron. Also, they would have to be out of the way when the bow planking was cut away so that the new kelson and deck shelves could be poked through into position. The old apron had reached only as far as the forefoot. In order to strengthen the bows for the period when the smack would be without a keel it was decided that the new apron

should be in the form of a grown crook. This would extend the apron back under the kelson to which it would be securely fastened. The forward frames would then be fitted on top of it and bolted to it. It was going to be a pretty solid assembly.

There were going to be some problems about that apron. It was obviously going to be a very heavy piece of wood to work, for it needed to be quite wide at the head. There would have been some difficulty in actually finding a suitable oak bend – even if it was still in a green state. If it was green, only one face of the apron would be exposed to the air and so be able to dry. Wet rot was a real and unpalatable possibility if a piece of green oak was going to be used in that way. In the end a fine seasoned oak bend was found, intended for Guy Harding's yard at Wivenhoe, and Michael Frost was able to buy this, subject to one trial cut to make sure that it was suitable. By an odd coincidence, this bend had been ordered for the bow of the author's sloop *Patient Griselda*, which Guy Harding's yard was building. By mistake it had been cut too short, which delayed *Patient Griselda*'s building but benefited *Boadicea*. It was a delay in a good cause.

Before fitting the forward frames, the old bitts had been removed. The next thing to do was to remove part of the foredeck, the breasthook, the apron and the forward deck beam. The apron came away very easily.

Fitting the apron The after face of the stem post and the upper surface of the keel were cleaned down so that precise patterns could be made for the new apron. The only pattern that mattered for the first sawcuts was that of the fitting surface of the stem and of the keel. *Patient Griselda*'s intended stem post was set up on the saw trolley and the first cut of the fitting surface was made. The wood was beautifully clean and the bend was accepted for *Boadicea*'s apron. The second cut was made for the lower face which was to fit against the keel. The same day the bend was delivered to the smack. The next part of the cutting presented a problem. The frames, despite the weight of the oak bends, had all been cut by the fine-bladed bandsaw, possible because each had a flat surface where it had been cut into a 4in plank.

With the apron the problem was different. Every inch of wood was important so, to avoid any waste, the bend had been left 'in the round' apart from cutting in the fitting faces. Thus it was still a great lump of wood and, worse still from the sawyer's point of view, it had no flat surfaces to rest on the sawing bench. There was no alternative but to cut in the other faces by hand.

So the bend was set up in front of the smack's bow and secured in position by shores fastened to the rails. The inside face was now cut by the use of a two-handed crosscut saw. Whilst Michael Frost and a friend were making rather heavy weather

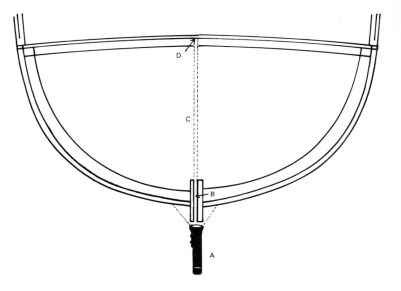

of this, some of the yard men came over to see what they were doing. After watching their efforts for a time the yard men told them that what they needed was a pit saw. This was the kind of saw that they used in the old sawpit days. The yard still had their old pit saws and one of the men went over to the store to collect one. This turned out to be a long, slender saw, similar to a length of bandsaw blade but with a handle at each end. It of course had to be worked by someone at each end. It cut only on the pulling stroke. After sharpening it, Michael Frost and his friend spent a satisfying hour finishing the long cut, with a tool designed to do exactly that kind of work. The oak was tough and hard but the saw was sharp, cut well, and was easy to use.

This underlines the difficulties an amateur craftsman faces. Not only does he often not know how to tackle the job but, as often as not, he struggles with the wrong tools. The proximity of a helpful boatyard made life a lot easier for *Boadicea*'s owner.

After the inboard face of the apron had been cut with the pit saw the sides were trimmed with an adze. With the help of the templates it was rough-shaped in a few hours. To get the apron in place inside the smack a tripod was borrowed from the yard and erected over the smack's bows. The apron was then lifted by a tackle over the smack's bows and lowered into position. Fitting a massive piece of wood like this into the smack needed some kind of system. The one Michael Frost worked out was to fix an eyebolt to the heel and from this a block and tackle to a deck beam above. To lift the apron out they pulled up the heel and then raised the head with the tripod tackle.

A short piece of wood was then placed under the heel to act as a skid and the inboard tackle was eased off for the heel to rest on it. Whoever was inside the smack would call out to the one on deck to ease off the tripod tackle. As this happened the man inside would haul the apron aft, clear of floors and frames. The apron was then turned over and trimmed wherever necessary and then swung back and replaced on the skid.

In order to lift it back into place the tripod tackle was used to lift the head forward and upwards at the same time as the heel was guided over the skid by hand. The heel tackle was then used to pick up the heel so that the skid could be removed. The apron was next lowered into position. The same procedure of wetting the inside surface of the boat with green Cuprinol was used so that any high spots on the apron would be marked each time it was offered up.

As soon as the apron fitted exactly, it was given a coating of Cuprinol and the fitting surfaces were covered with bitumen and placed into position. Using the old holes in the stem as guides, it was drilled and drawn down firmly into place, using mild steel service bolts. The old planking was fastened to it with flat points and the excess bitumen cleared away. The top

horizontal surface of the apron was then faired up to follow the line of the floors, so that the new kelson would fit closely to it.

Drilling the keel Before the kelson could be put into position there was a problem to be faced of how the new keel could be drilled. The keel was 15in deep but only 4in wide so the drilling had to be very accurate. In the stern where the deadwood lay on top of the keel the bolts were 4ft long. Forward they were about 2ft in length. There were two aspects to the problem. First, when the kelson was in position it would not be possible to see if the direction line of the drill was right. Second, there was not enough space below the deck aft to take the drill.

The short holes forward did not present much of a problem. It was decided to drill through the new floors and the old keel before the kelson was put in. Later, when the kelson had been fastened down, Michael Frost drilled it from underneath through the holes which he had drilled in the old keel and the floors.

The problem of the 4ft-long holes aft was solved without too much difficulty. By good fortune, the new floors had not fallen exactly on the old keel bolt holes. By shining a torch through these holes from underneath it was a simple matter to mark the centre line of the light spots made by the beam of the torch on the underside of the deck. The lines were joined up with pencil lines; then, by measuring the distance from the old keel bolt holes to the centre of the new floor alongside, the correct point could be marked on the deck head. Holes were drilled up through the deck. By standing on the deck and using an eight-foot auger it was possible to drill the new holes accurately down the centre of the new floors, the deadwood and the keel. As a

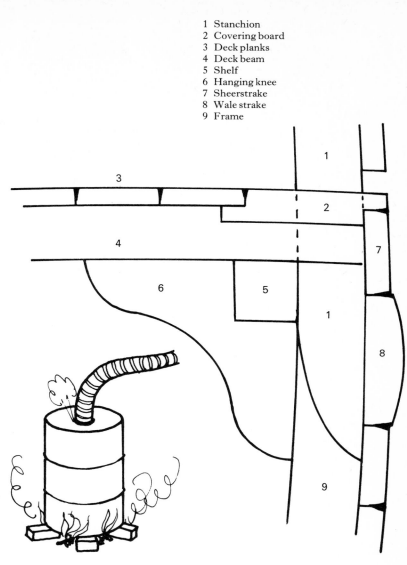

further check, a helpful friend stood outside on the saltings, at the far side of the little rill, astern of *Boadicea*'s berth. The friend conned the auger, giving appropriate directions with cries of 'Down wood up' or 'Up wood up' which was the Tollesbury boatyard's manner of speech and referred to the direction of down or up Woodrope Creek.

All the holes were drilled in one afternoon with only one of them slightly out of alignment.

The kelson The kelson was cut from a well seasoned 4in oak plank. It was 8in wide amidships and tapered fore and aft. The yard cut the tapers in and planed it. Early in the new year (of 1965) a hole was cut in the bow planking and another in the transom to let the kelson in and to allow for its spare length to project outboard. Once bent into position along the top of the floors the spare length would be drawn inside the hull. The kelson was launched through the bows and a hole was cut in each garboard so that a couple of heavy joiner's cramps could be put through to the lower edge of the keel and used to draw the kelson down. The kelson, under this pressure, bent down easily for about six inches. Further pressure brought little further gain. Indeed it seemed likely that if further pressure was applied the oak would break rather than bend, so it was left under pressure for a week. At the end of that time it still showed no signs of bending so the only thing to do was to steam it. The local sailmaker made up a canvas tube fifteen feet long. This was slipped over the middle part of the kelson. The ends were closed up and steam was led in from two improvised oil drum boilers outside the smack. The steam was produced by filling two 5-gallon oil drums each about one third full of water, fitting a hosepipe into a hole in the top and making a tight fit with wedges, oakum etc. After that, a fire was lit under each drum.

After two hours' steaming, the kelson bent under only moderate pressure. Twelve hours later, when the cramps were loosened, the kelson showed no signs of straightening. The canvas tube was cut away and the kelson was then cramped down again. It was only roughly in place now and there was still the final fairing up of the floors to be done so that it would lie truly in position. When that was done, it was given a coating of bitumen.

Stainless steel fastenings For the fastenings, Michael Frost had decided (quite wrongly as he discovered later) to use high grade chromium-cobalt stainless steel. He had already bought enough rod to make all the bolts, and the nuts and washers had been made of the same material. The kelson was fastened with dump bolts through the 'short floors' and the frames were dump-bolted to the 'long floors'. These fastenings were put in as securely as possible because they would later have to carry

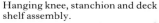

Steaming: oil drum and hose. For steam, a fire was lit under an old oil drum containing about a foot of water, chocked up on bricks and with a flexible hose leading to the steam box.

Hanging knee, stanchion and deck shelf assembly.

the weight of the smack while the old keel was taken out and the kelson was acting as her temporary backbone.

Fitting the deck shelves The next action was to unclamp the deck shelves from the outside of the hull and fix them into position. These were poked through the same hole in the bows that had been used for the kelson. The frame heads were faired to receive the shelves, which were also fastened with stainless steel bolts. To do this, holes had to be cut in the sheer strake so that G-cramps could be used to pull the shelves home. Up to that moment it had been hoped to preserve the existing planking but, with all the holes that had been cut in it, it now looked a hopeless proposition. At last Michael Frost accepted the fact that he would have to replank throughout, but he still intended to preserve the existing deck.

The unsightly holes in the smack's topsides not only looked awful but let the weather in, so patches of roofing felt were laid over them. This made the boat look even worse. Her owner began to be very sensitive about her appearance.

Fastenings To return to the matter of fastenings: though Michael Frost had spent a small fortune on his stainless steel bolts, he had failed to find anyone to make the large nails that would be needed. A chance encounter with an old friend sent him off to Stone's, a firm at Deptford in south-east London who were the largest manufacturers of nails and rivets in Britain. Stone's manager said that they could easily supply his modest needs but said also that they were not happy about his choice of metal. They would make enquiries in their metallurgy department.

The next day Michael Frost heard from Bill Read, a scientist friend, that there was a snag in the use of cobalt-chrome stainless steel. The durability of all stainless steels apparently depends on a protective film of oxide; when not exposed to the oxygen in the air, they soon lose this film and then corrode as rapidly as mild steel – which corrodes *very* rapidly.

In the end, after much discussion with Stone's and the inspection of a certain door knocker that had been exposed to the wind and the rain for thirty years, monel metal was chosen for the nails though iron would have been a less expensive solution. Wrought iron is a pure metal and does not produce internal differences of electrical potential.

The old iron fastenings of *Boadicea* had stood up to the years and, though slightly rusted at the exposed ends, were solid and sound inside the wood. In contrast, the new hot-dip galvanized mild steel keel-bolts which had been put into *Boadicea* during her repairs in 1948 were now (fifteen years later) very badly corroded. But pure iron has to be imported from Sweden and is relatively expensive.

Monel metal is made up of 70 per cent nickel and 30 per cent copper. It appears to be almost indestructible. It is difficult to work but if properly heat treated can be forged satisfactorily. It is, however, very expensive. To put the matter into proportion: even when using monel metal for the fastenings, the bill for the fastenings for *Boadicea*'s rebuild came only to about half the cost of the timber.

At one stage Michael Frost considered using treenails, which are wooden pegs of cleft oak, well dried before being driven home so that they make a tight fit when a craft is in the water. The snag with treenails is that to be effective they require a very tight and accurate fit between the pieces of timber that are to be fastened together. He doubted his ability to achieve this. He considered copper to be too weak and bronze too crystalline.

Monel seemed to be the only easily available metal with a history of fifty years' reliability, which was the time of proven worth that he considered essential for everything that went into *Boadicea*'s rebuild.

Breasthook assembly Once the matter of the fastenings had been sorted out, work was started on the breasthook assembly. A suitable knee was discovered at the timber yard. The breasthook is an important part of the hull structure; it holds the topsides, the deck and the stem together. A pattern was made, the knee was cut to shape and a platform rigged up in the bows on which the breasthook would rest whilst it was being fitted. It took a day to fit the breasthook, including cutting rebates on each side to take the 8in × 3in knightheads. The knightheads are the foremost stanchions and pass through the breasthook to meet the after face of the apron.

At each end of the breasthook the first deck beam, which takes the forward thrust of the bitts, was lap-jointed to it. Immediately aft of that, the ends of the breasthook were lap-jointed to the first forward frame on each side and the deck shelves fastened to the under surface of the breasthook, thus completing this massive and immensely strong assembly. The second deck beam which lies just aft of the bitts was then fastened.

At this stage the smack had been reframed, refloored, fitted with a new kelson, apron, breasthood and shelves. Also, the forward two deck beams and the knightheads were in position. From the beginning Michael Frost had worried that during these early stages of the rebuild, he might lose the shape of *Boadicea*'s hull. If he did this, he felt, the whole reconstruction would have been worthless, for as he later remarked, 'When all was said and done the only thing which was likely to remain after the rebuild was the unique shape, which in my view was pricelessly valuable. If I lost that, I might as usefully have torn the hull to pieces and thrown the bits away.'

Maintaining the hull's shape In spite of the work that had gone into the smack there was still the possibility that when the keel was taken out her bows, with the heavy apron-cum-breasthook assembly, might sag, so further steps were taken to strengthen her.

To make the midship section completely rigid, where the former bulkhead (a flimsy affair) had been a new framework was built up. This consisted of a lower bearer cut from a 15in × 3in iroko plank, fitted on edge to the frames which would carry the bulkhead and be bolted to them. A similar bearer was put in at the next pair of frames forward to take the place of the side thwartship locker. This was likewise bolted to the frames. Next, the hanging knees at the bulkhead deck beam were renewed and two temporary struts were fastened between the deck beam above and the bearer below. This made the midship section as rigid as was humanly possible.

Temporary bilge keels To take the weight of the hull when the old keel was taken out of her, two 12ft-long bilge keels were made from 4in elm plank. These were bolted to the hull through three temporary frames to avoid having bolt holes through the permanent frames. When bolted home the bilge keels seemed fairly rigid, but to give them added support a hanging knee was fitted at each end. These were made from rough offcuts and no time was wasted in making them look smart. When they were fastened, the bilge keels seemed quite rigid enough to carry the smack's weight safely. The thoroughness of this operation calls for some applause.

A dozen elm chocks 2ft long by 12in square were placed under the bilge keels so that the weight of the smack was just taken off her proper keel. This transfer of weight appeared to have no effect on the hull, so the wedges were hardened up to make sure that the weight was evenly distributed.

Even so, Michael Frost was not too happy; it seemed to him that there was much too much unsupported overhang, so he rigged up a rough cradle at the bows and another at the stern, then erected shore legs to take the weight.

He found that by driving wedges under the shores he could lift either bow or stern. This meant that if there was any sag or movement in the hull's sheer when the keel was out, the position of the two ends or the middle could be adjusted independently.

To discover whether there was any sagging or hogging, two chains and bottle screws were fixed on her centre fore and aft line. One was set up on the deck from the stem to the stern post and one inside from the forefoot to the after end of the kelson. They were both taken up bar-tight. The smack was now in a pretty harsh straitjacket, so the sooner the keel was out the better.

Both garboards were cleared away and for the first time the full width of the old keel could be seen. The old keel must have been her second one and was long-spliced to the previous one which had been cut away so only the part that occupied the rebates in the floors remained.

To arrive at the line of the fitting, the upper edge of the new keel, a pattern was made in $\frac{1}{4}$in deal planks. When this pattern was completed its upper edge had a curve which dipped 3in below the straight line and was a fair curve from stem to stern.

The new keel The new keel had been lying at the timber yard for some weeks. It was a 16in-wide plank of greenheart, 4in thick and 30ft long. It was a magnificent piece of wood and had come off the saw with almost a satin finish. It was lying on its side with a number of weights on its middle, for it had arched up about 4in.

To remove the old keel, the service bolts which held the keel to the short floors were removed so that now the keel was held to the smack only by the lap joint at the stem and the tenon at the stern post. Two simple sawcuts dealt with those. The wedges under the keel were removed, a screwdriver was put into the bow sawcut and levered gently. The keel moved slightly and continued moving. In three or four minutes it freed itself of the rebates and the bitumen that had been holding it and dropped gently to the ground. *Boadicea* had shed her second keel and sat there unconcernedly waiting for her third.

The cutting of the greenheart for the new keel presented great problems. Seasoned greenheart is so hard that it is practically impossible to cut it. Unseasoned greenheart can be cut but it moves in an alarming manner.

After some discussion about the use of the bandsaw, the yard decided to use a hand-held circular saw to cut the first 3in depth of the curve and then cut the last inch with a hand saw. After they had cut about three feet, the whole plank began bending away from the cut and the cut itself was creaking loudly. A cramp was put on and they continued cutting, adding further cramps at about three-foot intervals. They finished the 3in cut without further trouble and then started with the hand saw on the 1in cut, shifting the cramps as they worked. When they had done, the cut surface of the curve had drawn out to a straight line and the whole 16in plank had taken up an equal curve in the opposite direction.

The jacks would force this back into shape when it was placed under the smack. As for the sideways curve, which the weights had not cured, this was straightened out by putting an eyebolt at each end and using a chain and bottle screw, pulling against a fulcrum in the middle. When they drilled the holes for the eyebolts, moisture ran out of the holes and continued for several hours.

The greenheart keel was loaded on to a trolley and trundled over to the smack. The keel was rolled under her and with jacks at bow and stern was driven up into place. The fit was not too bad, being not more than half an inch out at the worst station. It took a week of evening work to make the fit perfect. A length of twine was laid along the top surface of the keel before it was driven up under the boat. If the twine was gripped it showed the station was gripping; if not, there was still a space. This final trimming of the keel's upper side was a slow job, but each night the smack was safely sitting on her new keel.

There was one moment of near disaster. The new keel was resting on two iron tanks alongside the dock. In the dock was a largish yacht cradled on the slipway trolley. Now greenheart is not only a very hard wood, it is also very slippery. As Michael Frost was working at the extreme end of the keel, the other end began to slide. It was clear to him immediately that if the greenheart log took charge it would plunge into the dock and bring down the yacht's cradle and the yacht with it. Visions of this impending calamity made him drop his plane and hang on for dear life. It was a losing battle so he yelled for help, which arrived just in time. It would have been a crippling disaster both to him and the yard if it had happened. Obviously, the sooner the lively piece of greenheart was bolted on to *Boadicea* the better for everybody. The trimming was soon completed and the hand-held rotary saw was used to cut the rocker in the bottom of the keel. (The rocker is the downward and upward curve to the lower edge of the keel.) The bottom of the keel was planed smooth and then the greenheart was rolled back under *Boadicea* and driven back into position.

However, this was not the end of it. Though the new keel was a good fit it was a bit askew with a list to starboard. So the following weekend it was dropped out once more and about a quarter of an inch was trimmed off from the starboard side of the top surface. That cured the list.

The offcut end of the keel was fashioned into the lower part of the deadwood. For the upper part, an original piece of the old deadwood which was perfectly sound was retained. When the deadwood had been fitted properly, the keel was dropped for the last time. All the fitting surfaces were coated with bitumen and it was driven back into position to stay there. The holes were drilled for the keel bolts which were drawn down as tight as possible. Wedges were driven under the new keel to take the full weight of the smack, so that the temporary bilge keels could be taken away the following day.

The next day the bilge keels were stripped off and the temporary frames were split and taken out. The chains were loosened and finally the cradles, fore and aft, were knocked away. The most difficult part of the restoration work was finished. *Boadicea* had her new keel.

Stem and stern assemblies The next two major jobs were the new stem post and the transom and stern post. The stern offered the simpler job, so as an apprenticeship for the more difficult job it was tackled first. *Boadicea*'s stern post is outside the transom. The lower part had been cut away in order to put in the new deadwood. The upper part was held up only by the old transom so they could come away together. The edges of the transom were freed by cutting the plank ends aft of the new fashion frames, which had been fitted to lie flush against the transom but had only been fastened to the planking. The transom was now only supported by the taffrail and the deck ends. It was a simple matter to free it from these.

The transom The new transom was made from $2\frac{1}{2}$in teak planks, grooved and filleted. The fillets were of greenheart cut across the grain. These teak planks were fastened to the new fashion frames, but the excess length was not trimmed off yet

so that the end grain should not be exposed, as summer was approaching. They would only be cut away when the new topside planking was ready to be fixed to them. When the teak planks had been fastened to the fashion frames, they were drilled at 6in intervals and $\frac{1}{2}$in monel metal dump-bolts were driven through the whole depth from top to within three or four inches of the bottom of the bottom plank. Before driving the monel bolts in, tiny holes were drilled through the bottom plank into the bottom of these holes to let the air out when the bolts were driven home, to avert the danger of bursting the planks. Finally, the transom was supported inside by a 4in oak stern knee fastened to the kelson.

With the transom in position the stern post could be fitted; this was cut from 4in × 12in greenheart tenoned into the keel. It was dump-bolted into the deadwood and also secured to the end of the kelson by a slanting monel metal through bolt. It was also through-bolted to the head of the stern knee. This was an assembly fit to match the bow.

Michael Frost wrote about the matter of weight and strength. He said:

'The problem of achieving adequate strength was with me constantly, and I tried to visualise all the strains to which the hull could be subjected. I had often worried when sailing the boat hard and in the rebuilt hull I intended to have a margin of strength if it was at all possible. I tried to achieve a good "finish" but did not regard it as being a primary consideration. There is a view that boats sail better when they are lightly built, but this I do not accept. Light construction may be necessary to counteract the top-hamper of the Bermuda rig, but with gaff rig I would not regard it as being either necessary or desirable. The *Boadicea* carries nearly half her weight in ballast, and I thought I had wide margins of weight to play with, and I set out to make good use of them.'

The stem post To begin with, Michael Frost tried to make the new stem post out of a 5in-thick baulk of greenheart by bending it under steam to the shallow curve needed. However, after twenty-four hours in the steam box the wood was just as intractable as when he started. It would not bend at all, so that idea was abandoned. He was loath to abandon the greenheart for *Boadicea* had suffered from areas of softness in her old oak stem, so he decided on a scarphed greenheart stem with one scarph at about waterline level.

This presented no problems. When the new stem was set up and bolted to the apron he began cutting the rebates for the planking. In this very hard timber, cutting rebates was a tedious job and took four weekends to complete. He was then ready to begin planking up.

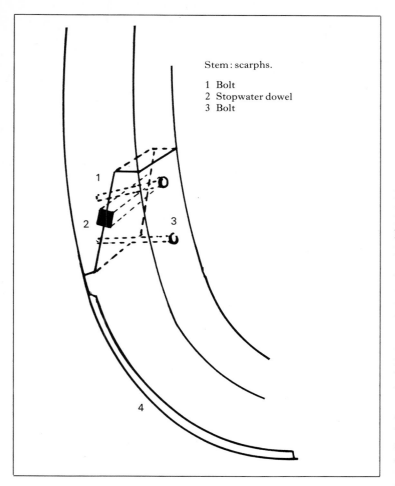

Stem: scarphs.

1 Bolt
2 Stopwater dowel
3 Bolt

The planking For the lower planking (up to the turn of the bilge) $1\frac{1}{4}$in-thick greenheart was used. The sawmill had cut the planks with some difficulty. The saw blade would only cut about five feet before it became blunted. The first five feet appeared to give no trouble at all then quite suddenly the blade jibbed and began cutting away at an angle of 45°. The sawyer switched off the power immediately but not before the plank was badly scored. The blade was changed and the same thing happened after a further five feet. This sequence continued right through the sawing operation. Otherwise, the greenheart gave no trouble. When the planks were planed, an extra $\frac{1}{4}$in had to be taken off to remove the score marks, which was probably just as well as even a $1\frac{1}{4}$in greenheart plank takes a bit of bending. The difference in behaviour between the greenheart keel and these planks was probably due to the fact that the keel log was a good deal greener than the one from which the planks were cut.

As these boards had caused so much trouble in the sawing, it was decided to make accurate patterns for each plank from thin deal and to shape the greenheart planks from these. The first plank to be fitted was the garboard. When fitting each plank, the bottom half of the old plank above was cut away. This permitted the use of wedges to force the new plank down tight against the one below. When the plank was cramped into position, Michael Frost climbed down inside the boat to inspect the fit. Wherever it needed adjustment he would write instructions on the inside face of the plank.

In addition to the fit of the edge of the plank, the bevel for the caulking had to be cut in. This was nearly as much trouble as the fitting of the edges. When everything was fair all the frame surfaces would be coated in bitumen, the plank would be dressed with Cuprinol and then clamped back into position for fastening. Where there were butts, the planks were scarphed with a 12in-long flat scarph, both ends of which were through-fastened to frames.

Fastenings For the fastenings, $\frac{1}{4}$in diameter 4in monel metal nails were used. Both the greenheart and the oak of the frames was so hard that holes had to be drilled to the depth of the nail. This in no way affected their holding power. To avoid bending the nails, a punch was used instead of hitting them direct and this proved completely effective.

Above the turn of the bilge $1\frac{1}{2}$in larch was used for the planking. Handling this was child's play after the greenheart. The fastenings for this were the same 4in monel nails.

At this stage the overlapping transom planks were cut off flush with the fashion frames. The $2\frac{1}{2}$in oak wales had been cut and bent round the hull while still green and then left there to season. A year later, when it was time to fit them, they were dry and gave no trouble. These were fastened with 5in by $\frac{5}{16}$in nails.

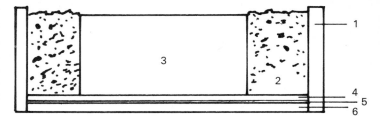

The sheer strakes were made of 1¾in larch and went in easily after the covering boards had been raised. The heads of all the fastenings were sunk ½in and covered with wood plugs cold glued into position. The plugs for the fastenings were turned out of greenheart for the greenheart planks and from iroko (a hard closegrained wood) for the larch planks. The caulking was of oakum and the seams were splined. The splines were cut from larch.

The deck It was not until the covering boards were up that Michael Frost decided to rebuild the deck, thus coming at last to a complete rebuild of *Boadicea*.

In case of this possibility he had earmarked two stacks of good oak sweeps. These were oak planks that had some curve in them. All the deck beams could be cut from one stack, the covering boards and capping rails from the other.

The beams were of 4in oak, cut to a moulded depth of five inches. The covering boards were 2½in oak, cut to a moulded width of eight inches. The deck planks were to be of 1¾in larch, so the covering boards were rebated for both the sheer strake and the deck planks. This plan of action was largely fortuitous but it proved a very good method, greatly increasing the strength of the hull. This method also provided support for the ends of the deck planks.

When the covering boards were fitted they were pierced for the stanchions. These were of oak, 4in-sided, they were not caulked but sealed on each face with larch wedges set down as hard as possible.

Coamings The coamings for the main hatch and the cuddy top were made of 2½in teak. The bits were of 5in oak. For the windlass, it was possible to use the original barrel, pawl box and pawl ring. It was mounted on new oak chocks. The original anchor davit and gammon iron and staysail horse were also retained.

Channels and chainplates The channels were cut from 4in-thick greenheart. The four chainplates Michael Frost and a friend forged from ½in monel metal. This was done in the White Colne blacksmith's shop on a Boxing Day. Mr Tatum, the blacksmith, kept an eye on the work. His advice was basically to hit the monel metal whilst it was hot. The forging was completed by Boxing Day evening. The chain plates were then drilled and finally annealed.

Fastenings All the bolts in the hull were made up from monel rod with the heads threaded on and then spread so that they would not unscrew. A quotation for making thirty 2in plate washers was for the outrageous sum of £75, with Michael Frost supplying the metal.

With the facilities of a local small engineering plant he made all thirty washers in under one day. After that he did all the metalwork himself, though monel metal is not easy to work and needs frequent annealing.

Ballast East coast smacks were usually ballasted down with concrete and pig iron. Michael Frost was loath to bring pig iron in contact with the new oak floors as oak and iron do not agree, and decided to use lead instead which, though much more expensive, is easy to cast.

As there was a deep space between the topsides of the floors and the planking below, slats were fastened on the sides of the floors and the ballast was hung in the space between them.

Each pig had to be cast to fit. By using garden earth in a wooden box, with a wooden model of the lead pig, it was quite easy to make accurate moulds. All this lead Michael Frost cast by his fireside during winter evenings, using a large iron ladle in which to melt the lead. The lead was melted from sheet or ingots (NOT lead pipes which might contain water and explode). The melting was done over an ordinary dog grate in the sitting room of Michael Frost's home. The mould was placed just outside the sitting room window, so he scuttled back and forth between fireplace and window sill using a smaller ladle. Each time he lifted a ladle full of melted lead, his wife added ingots to the lead that was heating. In order to get enough heat out of the fire, a length of hose was fitted into the back of the domestic vacuum cleaner and the jet of air directed on to the fire, which was roaring like a blacksmith's forge.

The mould was made up from ½in deal planks knocked together to make a shallow open-topped box. The bottom was covered with a sheet of asbestos and then a thin sheet of metal. The model (ie the facsimile of the piece to be cast) was laid on the bottom of the box, but first wrapped in newspaper and then surrounded with ordinary garden earth which was tamped down firmly.

Any rough spots on the pigs were trimmed off with a chisel while the lead was still very hot. It was as easy as cutting cheese. When the pigs had been fitted into the hull they were sealed into position with hot bitumen.

By April 1971 the rebuild was virtually finished and *Boadicea* was ready to return to the water. Such work that still had to be done was little more than normal fitting out, except for the building of a new rudder and hanging it on new gudgeons and pintles.

The rebuilding of *Boadicea,* as Michael Frost said, needed to be seen in perspective. This smack, much loved by a succession of owners, has a long record of extensive renewals. The records in the Colchester Customs House say that in the 1830s John Pewter claimed he had virtually rebuilt her hull. When the planking came off her this time, it was possible to see what had been done. In the 1880s, fifty years after Pewter's first replanking, the elder Mr Binks had given her new planking once again and also a new keel and stern post.

In the 1930s Manny French had taken the whole deck off her and had a number of new frames fitted. On this final occasion Michael Frost rebuilt her throughout except for that one small part of the deadwood. What is clear from his account is the care he took to retain her shape, which he regarded as beyond price. He could probably have built three new smacks in the time it took to rebuild *Boadicea.* But, even if the most careful measurements had been taken, these would not have been *Boadicea.*

Boadicea's former owner, the elder Mr Binks, had a son, Isaiah, who was still alive in 1951. Michael Frost visited him and heard much about the old smack and of the care the elder Mr Binks had lavished on her. Writing of this visit to Isaiah Binks, Michael Frost said:

'His father had always maintained that no other smack was in the same class, and had given her the new keel and skin. He, Isaiah, had sailed her until he became the oyster company foreman. She had always been well kept, but where most boats had money spent on them because some return was expected, the *Boadicea* was different. Each of her rebuilds had been a simple acknowledgement, and had not involved any thought of exacting something from her.'

This is what boat restoration is all about.

It has not been easy to establish the exact sequence of work involved in the rebuilding of *Boadicea.* The reason for the difficulty in resolving a neat and tidy sequence was because the work developed in at least two different streams. The obvious stream was the actual work on the hull itself, the other was the anticipatory work such as sawing and shaping timbers, preforming shelves and wales etc whilst they were still green so that by the time they were ready to go into the boat, possibly twelve months or more later, they would be both preformed and seasoned.

Sequence of actual work on the hull

1 To gut the inside and to remove the flooring from cabin and holds: in the case of *Boadicea* all the lining had been removed years before and all the mess behind it. This of course would have to be the first part of the job in most restorations.
2 The loose ballast was taken out.
3 The concrete in the bottom of the boat was chipped out with a cold chisel. This is a wearisome job but if the boat is going to be entirely rebuilt, there is no need to take undue care to avoid damaging the hull structure.
4 The kelson was removed.
5 The floors were removed one at a time and new floors were cut and carefully fitted and temporarily fixed with service bolts to the old keel and flat nails to the skin.
6 The old frames were taken out, again one at a time, and were replaced by new frames, temporarily fastened to the old skin. Amongst these frames was the fashion frame for the transom. The frames were 4in with a moulded depth of up to six inches at the turn of the bilge.
7 'Short floors' were made to join the base of the frames together and fitted with service bolts.
8 The apron, forward deck beams, breasthook and knightheads were taken out. A new apron was then fitted.
9 The floors and short floors were faired up and the kelson was fitted and fastened to the short floors with dump bolts after the garboards had been cut. The garboards had been cut to allow cramping the kelson into position. Thus far, the work on *Boadicea* had taken fourteen months.
10 The new breasthook, knightheads and first forward deck beam were fitted and fastened. Chains had been stretched and fastened fore and aft along the length of the deck and also along the top of the kelson. The object of this was to indicate, if either chain went slack, that hogging or sagging had occurred.
11 The shelves of 3in × 3in Canadian rock elm were fitted. The problem of getting the shelves to shape had been solved by cutting them when the timber was green and then clamping them round the *outside* of the boat. They remained in that position for eighteen months until Michael Frost was ready to fit them inside the boat. To do this holes were cut in the old transom so that the excess length could project outboard until they had been drawn close to the frames and fastened down. Some cutting to fit was necessary at the stern.
12 Before the old keel could be dropped out, the weight of the smack had to be taken up somehow. This was done by fitting 2ft-deep temporary bilge keels which were 4in thick and 12ft long. These were fitted very accurately to the old skin and were fastened to three service frames on each side.

13 A pattern was then made for the new keel. This was done by offering up a $\frac{1}{4}$in thick deal plank to the old keel and very carefully scribing, then cutting rebates round each floor. The chief reason for this was that the original keel was anything but straight along the top.

14 The new keel was made from a heavy plank of greenheart, 30ft long, 4in thick and 15in deep. Seasoned greenheart is fearsome stuff to saw. This log was shaped to the keel pattern and it was placed on rollers ready to be rolled under the boat as soon as the old keel was taken out.

15 The service bolts and the wedges were removed from the the old keel and, with only the slightest persuasion, out it fell.

16 The new keel was rolled into position. By this time it had developed both a slight droop and a twist, which was to complicate the fitting somewhat. The rollers were on planks a few inches clear of the ground to allow for car jacks to be slid underneath. When the keel was in position it was jacked up. Because of the droop and twist there was still quite a lot of marking and cutting to do. This marking was done by laying a length of whipping twine along the top of the new keel. The string was necessary as the keel had to be bent into position. The middle floors touched at first but did not necessarily touch when the ends had been bent up. It took a full two weeks to fit the new keel with precision. It was then through-bolted to the kelson.

17 During all this time an anxious watch had been kept on the chains but they had shown no movement. There had been no sagging or hogging. All the extraneous work of fitting the bilge keels to their service frames had proved its worth. The most difficult part of the job was over.

18 The old transom and the top half of the stern post were then cut away and the new transom of $2\frac{1}{2}$in × 12in teak was nailed into position on the new fashion frame (which was fastened to the old skin). These planks were not cut to shape at this stage but overlapped the ship on each side. The new stern post was not put in, nor for that matter was the old one taken out, until the new keel was fitted.

19 The new stern and stem posts were then fitted and *Boadicea* had her new backbone and framing complete. The work at this stage had taken twenty months.

20 The next stage was the planking, which began with the garboards.

21 *Boadicea* was planked from her garboards up to the turn of the bilge in $1\frac{1}{8}$in greenheart and then up to the sheer strake in $1\frac{1}{2}$in larch. The overlapping transom planks were cut at this stage. The wale strakes were $2\frac{1}{2}$in oak.

22 After planking, the seams were caulked with oakum and then splined.

23 The completion of the planking, including the deck, with all inside framing completed, brought the time of the operation up to two and a half years.

24 There were various extraneous reasons why the later stages took so long that had nothing to do with *Boadicea*.

25 *Note about the fastenings* The choice of monel metal was arrived at only after rejecting a quantity of stainless steel bolts which, Michael Frost discovered, rust when away from air (ie inside wood) as fast as galvanized steel. The only sensible alternative to monel metal is plain honest iron which lasts indefinitely inside wood and is prone to rust only when it comes in contact with the air; here, particularly in oak, it blackens and rots the wood eventually.

26 Using the best possible timber, the next consideration for a hull structure that would last indefinitely was to try and prevent rot where one piece of wood abutted another. Every fitted surface was coated with bitumen and a very messy job that must have been. Before this, all the wood was treated with green Cuprinol and given a coat of metallic pink primer, except where it was to be bright-varnished. Here, colourless Cuprinol was used and the timbers were given two coats of varnish. There were problems of handling the timber once it had been delivered. Shelves and wales had to be clamped to the ship in a green state, ready to be used a year or so later when they would have had time to season and to take up their final shapes. If attempts were made to cramp seasoned timber into sharp curves it would almost certainly break.

27 *Ballast* Smacks are usually concreted in their bilges and, contrary to the opinion held by most boat surveyors, rot is rarely found below the concrete. Michael Frost decided to go one better than concrete and fill the bottom of the hull with bitumen. This should not only hold the ballast in position but also be resistant to damp and water. The only thing bitumen is not resistant to is diesel oil or petrol, so in case an engine was ever installed in *Boadicea* the bitumen was painted with metallic primer and then given a coat of white paint.

28 *Spars* *Boadicea*'s mast and bowsprit were in poor shape though the boom and gaff were sound. Michael Frost bought a larch tree with the bark still on it. He cut off 34ft of it and with a drawknife stripped the bark. He then, using a spar gauge, trimmed it to eight sides, then to sixteen sides, and then to thirty-two sides and finally rounded it off.

Traditionally, the cheek pieces for the hounds should have been elm, but he still had some greenheart left so he used that, letting the pieces into the mast by $\frac{1}{8}$in.

The bowsprit was a simple spar without cranse irons, also made of larch. The spars were treated with boiled linseed oil after final cleaning up.

Boadicea under sail after her rebuild.

Boadicea under sail after her rebuild.

I seem to have sailed in most of these restored vessels in the autumn. It was a still, grey morning in mid September when Michael Frost picked me up from the hard at West Mersea and rowed me down to Mersea Deeps where *Boadicea* was lying. Her mooring was between Old Hall Point and Cobmarsh. She looked as pretty as a toy with her bright garden-gate green topsides, white bulwarks and varnished rail. He rowed me round the smack so that I could photograph her from various angles and then we climbed on board to join his wife Martha and their small daughter.

Whilst I went down to the cuddy to put a new film in my camera Martha and Michael began to cast off the sail tiers. As I came up on deck, Michael said to me, 'Just take the peak halliard while I hoist the throat.' As there is a 4 : 1 purchase on the peak and a 3 : 1 on the throat, this is a leisurely procedure.

As soon as the mainsail was set, Martha let go the mooring and *Boadicea* gathered way. There was the faintest of winds from the east and for a moment it looked as if we would not weather *Shamrock,* a large converted Colchester smack that lay just up stream of us. Michael took a sweep, stuck a rowlock in the taffrail and started to scull. *Boadicea* responded like a dinghy. She had this affinity in her lightness on the helm and in other ways as well.

The wind was fitful, but slowly strengthened as we sailed close-hauled down to the Nass Beacon. Michael handed the tiller to me. It took a little while to get the feel of the boat. The end of the tiller is not much more than a foot above the deck. On the port tack one could sit on the gunwale, but on the starboard tack, because of the 14ft beam trawl stowed in the scuppers, one had to perch on top of that or sit on the deck. While I was trying to get comfortable, Michael walked aft and said, 'This is how the fishermen usually steered', and stood with his legs on the lee side of the tiller, his knees bent, both hands resting on his knees and his head thrust forward. 'Like this, they could keep an eye on everything that was happening, and if you are standing you can keep warm. Once you sit down, you begin to freeze.'

I tried the position with more or less success. 'Of course, on a hot summer's day they might flop down on the deck, but once the trawl was shot they left the helm and steered on the trawl.'

Boadicea sailed easily and well both on and off the wind. Her one eccentricity, which she had kept after her rebuild, was that on the starboard tack she tended to pay off and on the port tack to come up into the wind.

'She always has had this difference when sailing on different tacks', Michael said. 'It must be due to differences on the port and starboard sides of her underwater shape. Anyhow, I think she could do with a bit more ballast; her rebuilt hull, in spite of the greenheart, must weigh quite a bit less than her old water-soaked timbers.'

As we left the Nass Beacon astern, the sun came out. Michael drew the dinghy alongside and I climbed into it. He cast off the painter and *Boadicea* drew ahead. This was so that I could take photographs of her under sail. He made several runs past me. The *Boadicea* was carrying only a little pocket handkerchief of a storm jib which in all but very light winds is the jib normally used for dredging or trawling. She looked a pretty sight with her freshly tanned red mainsail contrasting with her stone coloured decks and green topsides. When I had exhausted my film Michael brought the *Boadicea* up into the wind and hove to. She lay quietly with a barely perceptible pitching motion. I rowed the dinghy up to her and climbed on board. The dinghy was an interesting little boat that Michael Frost himself had designed and had had built some years ago. She had a hull shaped like a miniature smack, but he said she would have been a better boat with a rather flatter floor.

As soon as I was back on board, we broke away from being hove to and had a close-hauled sail out towards St Peter's Chapel-on-the-Wall, on the Bradwell shore. We came about and took another long tack over towards Brightlingsea, for a while chasing and overhauling a red-sailed schooner. The wind freshened as we took a final tack out beyond the Bench Head Buoy. *Boadicea* romped along, with water swirling through her lee scuppers and every so often a dollop of spray wetting her foredeck.

Our run home against the ebb tide was a splendid series of surging rushes. The smack yawed a bit and, for one unused to her ways, her tiller needed constant attention.

Michael Frost described to me the way the fishermen when working the vessel had absolute control of her from one position. This was at a point close to the mast on the starboard side and just aft of the staysail horse.

'Look,' he said, 'here is the topping lift within easy reach of the three essential halliards: the peak, the staysail, and the jib. You only have to take one step forward to reach the jib outhaul on the starboard bithead. These really are the only ropes that matter. The unimportant ones are all kept out of the way somewhere else.' He put his hand on the fall on the throat halliard and said, 'One does not have to worry with this at all, while working the vessel. If the breeze is anything like fresh an extra reef is put in the mainsail directly after heaving to, but this will be slipped out for the sail back at the end of the tow. The throat is not interfered with either for putting the reef in or for slipping it out.

'From time to time while working the trawl one needs to make small adjustments to the amount of sail set, in order to regulate the speed at which the smack is towing. Most of this is done by raising or lowering the peak. When the peak is run right off so that the gaff points downwards by about 45°, the pull of the mainsail is reduced by more than half. The other big

adjustment is raising or lowering the staysail, and usually if the staysail is run down the peak is set up a little to compensate for this considerable loss of sail.

'When the staysail is down the smack will stay quietly hove to with the storm jib sheeted to weather, but if the staysail is up the jib is not enough to hold her hove to and the staysail itself must be sheeted more or less to weather according to need. Then on occasions the storm jib is allowed to draw. Either way the hove-to smack loses all of her forward movement.'

We went through these manoeuvres and I made a note of where the various halliards were made fast. The jib halliard was made fast to the starboard forward cleat on the bulwark stanchions and the purchase to the pin rail on the port shrouds. The jib sheet was made fast to the forward bollard on either rail, level with the windlass. The staysail halliard was made fast to the cleat on the fore side of the mast, six inches below the boom jaws. The staysail has a standing sheet secured to a ring on the staysail horse. The peak halliard is made fast with a figure of eight and a half hitch to the starboard end of the fife rail and the throat halliard to the port end of the fife rail.

44

The fall-ends of both peak and throat halliards are secured to the throat bolt on the gaff and go aloft with the sail, and the halliards are stowed by hauling down on the fall end and then taking a half hitch round the standing part. The coil is then looped back and forth through the V gap between the two ropes and the coils are pushed through in the same direction as the half hitch is made. The main sheet is made fast with a half hitch to itself just above the cringle of its fair lead.

As he walked back to the tiller, Michael pointed out to me that from a working point of view the topping lift is possibly the most important rope in the whole rig, to the extent that if the lift is to leeward of the mainsail the vessel is almost unworkable. A fisherman keeps the position of the topping lift in mind all the time, and if need be will drop the gaff while wending so as to get the lift on the right side of the sail.

Wending a smack is quite unlike coming about in a yacht. It is a much more agreeable and unhurried business. In a yacht, all the sheets lead to the cockpit where the crew and the helmsman fall over each other as they heave away on an array of winches, trying to make every sheet bar taut. In a smack there

is no cockpit. The tiller is left almost to its own devices except that the fisherman pushes it over to leeward and makes it fast with a piece of cod line. He then potters forward to go through the motions of freeing the lee side jib sheet, holds the sail back if necessary, and then when she is on her new tack makes fast the sheet to the opposite bollard. When the jib is sheeted he steps back and frees the staysail from its bowline, the sail sliding across the horse and filling on the new tack. The other bowline is then made fast. These bowlines consist merely of a short length of rope spliced round the forward shroud, one on each side. The fisherman then walks aft, frees the tiller if need be, or if the smack is on course leaves well alone.

That afternoon we did not shoot the trawl for the wind was against the tide, an impossible situation for a sailing trawler. When a smack is trawling she is hove-to, and all the wind does is to neutralise the drag of the trawl along the seabed. The tide then drives the boat broadside with the trawl towing after her.

'We shall shoot our trawl tomorrow,' Michael Frost said to me as we rowed ashore. The *Boadicea* was back at work, a monument to her owner's devotion, skill and labour.

Thames bawley *Bona* sailing out of
the Blackwater.

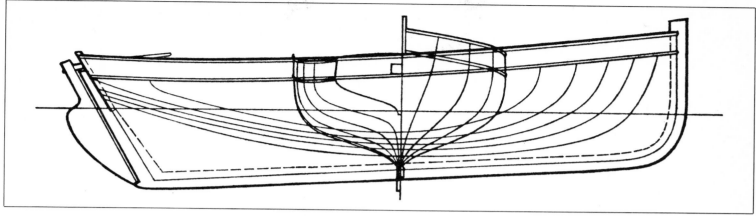

Harwich bawley *Maud*. Lines.
(Courtesy of the Science Museum.)

Thames bawleys

Little has been written about bawleys, unlike the East Coast smacks. Frank Carr described the handling of a bawley's sails some forty years ago in his pleasantly nostalgic book *Vanishing Craft* (1934). Dixon Kemp wrote about them in his *A Manual of Yacht and Boat Sailing* which was first published nearly a century ago. There is one set of plans available of a bawley which were taken off a Harwich boat by the late W. M. Blake. Photographs of these can be obtained from the Science Museum, London, where there is a model of a bawley, showing its gear.

Bawleys were primarily shrimpers. The Leigh bawleys fished for shrimps in the river Thames from Sea Reach to the Nore. The Harwich bawleys fished for shrimps off the Naze, round the Cork Sand and down the Wallet. In the winter, between November and February, if they were not whelking, they used to so 'stow boating', that is fishing with a stow net, a net with a fine mesh in the form of a very long conical bag.

The term 'bawley' means boiler boat. The first brick boiler was put into a small shrimp boat in the 1860s. Brick boilers were soon superseded by copper boilers. The bawley rig is wonderfully handy for the job for which it was designed. A loose-footed mainsail with a short luff and a 25ft gaff banging about overhead, a gigantic topsail above that, and two headsails, might fill most yachtsmen with dismay. Yet there are few modern yachts that could do half the manoeuvres that a bawley would take in her easygoing stride. With her flowing lines and her long straight keel, the bawley will sail herself on most points of the wind. At the stern of the steerage well there is a pin rack so that the tiller can be pinned in any position and the boat can then sail herself on whatever course is set.

A bawley must not be sailed with her sails sheeted in hard. She just will not go unless her sheets are free. Off the wind a bawley is faster than most smacks of her size, but to windward

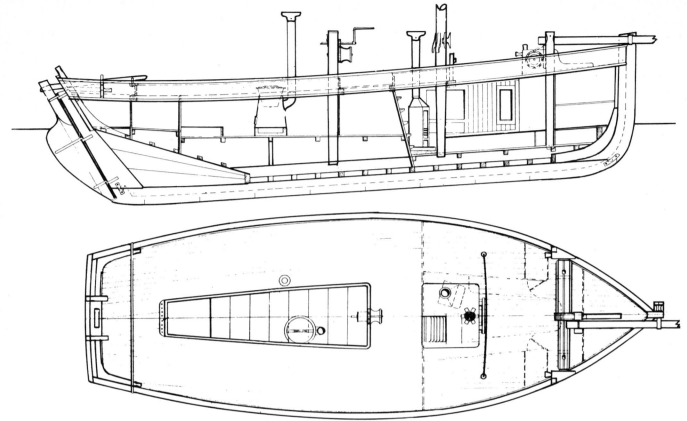

the smacks have the edge on her. The virtuosity of the bawley's sail plan is made possible by a single line, the brail. This line is fastened to the throat, runs down to a cringle on the leech of the mainsail and up to a block at the throat on the other side of the sail and so down to the pinrail. The main sheet is eased off, the brail is hauled down and the sail is bunched up to the throat. Immediately, about three-quarters of its power is taken out of the sail. The topsail can still be left in position over this much reduced mainsail. Alternatively, and this can be done by smacks that carry their mainsails on booms, the tack of the sail can be hauled up so reducing the sail's area by about a third.

The lead of the mainsheet is rather curious. An iron horse is fitted across the stern of the boat between the steering well and the transom. The heavy mainsheet double block travels on this horse; the block has its pin projecting from each side of its shell. A single block is shackled to the clew cringle and another single block is fastened to the first reef cringle. The sheet leads from the double block up to the lower block, down to the double block, up to the upper block, and down to the double block to be belayed to the projecting pin on this block.

Reefing the bawley is a simple operation. The boat is brought head to wind, the main sheet is eased off, the upper block is raised to the cringle at the second line of reef points, the lower block is brought up to the first line of reef points, the tack cringle at the first line of reef points is hauled down and made fast and the reef points are tied.

Vangs were not set up on a working bawley since when going to windward they tended to pull the peak end of the gaff downwards, thus causing the mainsail to bag. Vangs were used off the wind when racing.

Dixon Kemp writing about Thames bawley boats in 1895 described them as '. . . exceedingly handy little vessels, and may be seen in great numbers in the mouth of the Thames and the Medway, and more especially in Sea Reach. For knocking about in all weathers in these waters it would perhaps be impossible to find a better type of boat. During the last fifteen years, the bawley has grown considerably in size. The size of boats ten or twelve years ago was about 22ft × 8ft, with a draught of about 3ft: they were clinker built of oak, very strongly put together and were fitted with fishwells. The more modern boats however are carvel built and "dry-bottomed", that is fitted without fishwells.' Dixon Kemp shows the sail plan and lines of a 32ft bawley built at Erith on the Thames, with a shorter topmast than later became customary.

Harwich bawley *Maud*, LOA 37 ft 0in,
built by J. & H. Cann of Harwich.
This model was one of the sources of
information in the restoration of *Bona*.
(*Photo Crown copyright.*)

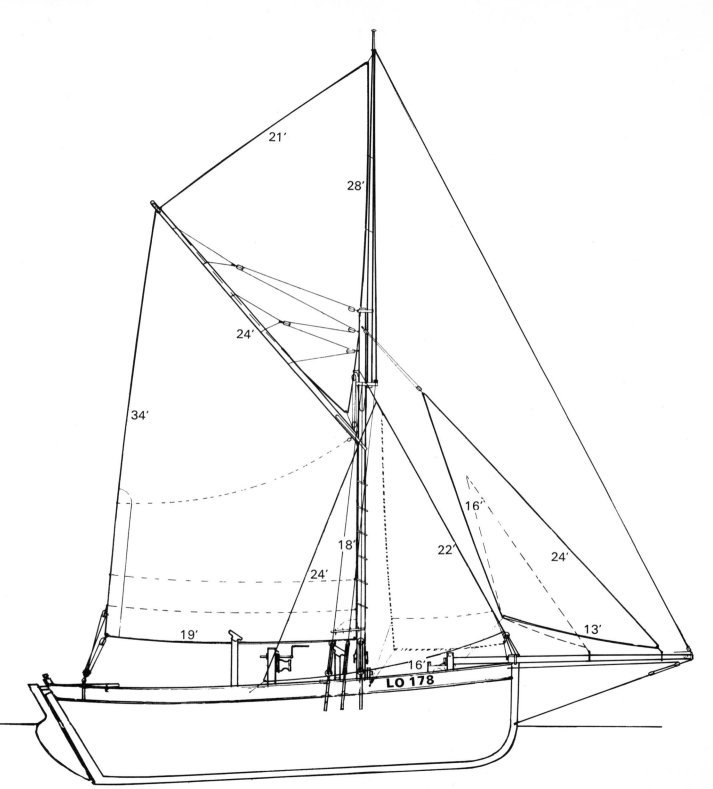

Bona's sail plan, modified from that of the Harwich bawley *Maud*.

21′

28′

24′

34′

18′

16′

22′

24′

24′

19′

13′

16′

LO 178

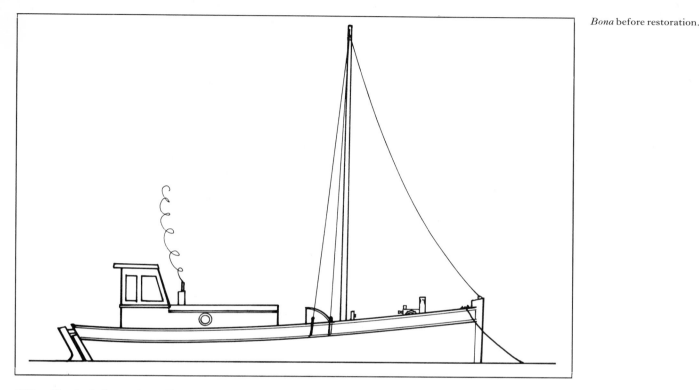

The Leigh bawley *Bona*

LOA 36ft 0in
LWL 34ft 0in
Beam 12ft 11in
Draught 4ft 6in
Depth in hold 5ft 0in
Gross tonnage 14·05
Net tonnage (without ballast) 9·62
Built 1903

The Leigh bawley *Bona* was restored to her original rig and deck fittings in 1970–1 at Brightlingsea by Stephen Swann and three friends. After sailing her for a season they proceeded with further restoration work on the hull. *Bona*'s latest owners were curious about her antecedents and learned a certain amount from her registry papers at the Customs House, Mark Lane, London E1.

According to these records, this bawley was built for Charles Kirby of Leigh at Brightlingsea in 1903 and was first registered in December 1903 with her home port as Leigh. Her registration number was LO 178, in 1928 changed to LO 99. In 1910, *Bona* was bought by Abraham Thomas Kirby of Leigh and she

changed hands again in September 1926, when Arthur Myatt of Southend bought her, but retained R. Kirby and later George Robinson as skippers. She changed hands again in 1936 when the registry papers came to an end. All this time she was trawling and stow boating.

The reason for the bawley's curious name was given to Stephen Swann by Mr T. R. Kirby of Southend, who said that in the years 1898–1900 his grandfather, then a young Leigh fisherman, served as a crew aboard Prince Louis Abruzzi's yacht, which was named *Bona*. Charles Kirby, this bawley's first owner, was the son of Prince Louis' yacht hand and he named his bawley after the Abruzzi yacht.

As far as *Bona*'s new owners could discover, there had been no fully rigged bawley sailing in the Thames estuary or out of Harwich or Brightlingsea since before World War II. For their restoration, the only material they had to work on were the Science Museum plans of the Harwich bawley, which was one foot longer, one inch wider and with six inches more moulded depth than *Bona*. In addition to this, they had the advice of one or two veteran bawley men at Leigh to help them in drawing out plans for Bona's restoration and rerigging.

When they purchased *Bona* she had a raised coaming and an ugly wheelhouse aft. Both the coamings and the wheelhouse had been built on to the original hatch, so it was a simple matter to unbolt the wheelhouse and knock down the built up coamings. Stephen Swann afterwards said 'The wheelhouse was burnt in one piece, complete with glass in the windows, as a kind of sacrifice, or perhaps as a tribute to old 'Bona' Kirby, who had had the bawley built nearly seventy years ago. After this bonfire they were left with a large gaping hole in the deck. This was just as well, for down below crouched the forty year old Thorneycroft diesel engine. The local marine engineers came into the picture by offering them £50 for it – and lifting it out for them. With the engine out of the way and the hatchways open to the sky, all the linings were taken out and the frames and planking were washed down with caustic soda, as still happens when smacks change from spratting to shrimping. She was thoroughly cleaned out, allowed to dry and then painted.

Bona had been solidly built with heavier scantlings than a Colchester smack of her size but she had no hanging or lodging knees. With a transom stern, she had none of the drawbacks of a counter with almost certain rot in the rudder trunk.

Bona's deck beams forward were in good shape but some of the half beams in the way of her long hatchway needed replacing. Whilst this was being done both hanging and lodging knees were fitted. The rest of her framing and her backbone were not too bad. Her apron is still good but her stem needed replacing.

Bona's worst feature was her deck planking. This was very worn in places and in spite of cleaning down to the bare wood and oiling the planks and recaulking the seams it still leaked badly. It was decided to sheathe the deck in ¾in marine ply covered in fibreglass (GRP) which would have the effect of stiffening her up considerably. The reason for using marine ply was the simple one of cost. To replank the deck with 2in fir planks would be quite a costly business. With a worn and moving deck it would be useless to put GRP straight down on to it, hence the marine ply.

The bulwark rail was in good shape forward of the mast but had to be renewed on both sides aft of the mast. This was done in oak, bought off a Colchester coffinmaker. The last two stanchions were rotten so they were cut off flush and replaced by dummies. The bitts were in quite good shape though the head of the bowsprit bitt was worn and is to be renewed in time.

Practically the only interference with tradition is that the main hatch has had two beams built across it and is covered with tongue and groove planks with a flush sliding hatch over the steerage. A green hatchcloth was laid over the planking and battened down. Two flush skylights were cut in the new cabin roof. Thus she remains to all intents and purposes a work boat and will be used for fishing, if not for shrimping, for the shrimps, once so plentiful hereabouts, have now deserted these waters.

Spars The mast was in her when they bought her and is still in good condition. The story of how *Bona* got her spars is worth retelling. There were no pine trees long enough or otherwise suitable for this job nearer than the Forest of Dean in Gloucestershire. Various barge owning friends down at Maldon needed new sprits and bowsprits so a lorry was chartered to bring a load up to Maldon. At Maldon, *Bona*'s new spars and a tree for a mainmast for another smack were loaded aboard the barge *Marjorie* and sailed round to Brightlingsea. The spars were towed ashore by the Pyefleet Oyster Company's boat *Peewit*. They were then adzed and planed down to size. Cranse irons were not fitted to the bowsprit because they were not originally used for fastening stays to bowsprits. Instead, a shoulder was cut in the spar and soft eyes were worked in on the wire. These were then parcelled and served and knocked on to the bowsprit with a mallet.

The shrouds and forestay were in position and in good condition. Topmast cross trees were fitted to the mainmast and the long topmast; backstays and forestay were next made up. Because they got in the way, bawleys, never used these backstays when working, though they did when racing.

Bona's remaining rigging was of 2in hemp. Her topmast is 26ft overall and her gaff 25ft overall. From the deck to topmast head is 51ft. Her total sail area is 1,036sq ft:

mainsail 450sq ft Admiralty flax no 3 (weighs 2cwt)
foresail 192sq ft   ,,   ,,   ,,
jib   170sq ft 14oz Canadian cotton
topsail 224sq ft ,,   ,,   ,,

The sails were made in his spare time by Jimmy Lawrence, the skipper of the barge *Marjorie*, and are probably the first complete set of bawley sails to be made for forty or even fifty years. When fully stretched, they will be dressed with Kanvo, a patent red-brown dressing.

Painting *Bona*'s new owners burnt off the bawley's topsides down to bare wood, primed her and then gave her four undercoats and finally a coat of gloss black, but she opened up so much that they changed to a dark grey and this seemed to improve things.

I first visited *Bona* on a warm misty morning in October whilst the restoration was still in progress. Stephen Swann met me on the hard at Brightlingsea and rowed me out into the fairway.

'We anchored in the Pyefleet for the night. You can see her now.' He pointed to the shore of Mersea Island across the water. The bawley is an unmistakable craft with its loose-footed boomless mainsail that hangs down from a long low-peaked gaff like a great theatre curtain.

'I don't know what on earth they are doing', Stephen muttered, resting on his oars. The bawley's antics did seem curious, for she was sailing round and round in a very tight circle. We learned later that the crew was trying to sail out the anchor, which must have fouled an old mooring.

As we waited for the bawley to pick us up, Stephen told me something of the vicissitudes of buying and restoring old fishing boats. *Bona* had been advertised for sale at £1,600 but this was about twice the amount of money they had, so they offered the owner £800 for her, and that subject to survey. To their surprise, he agreed. The surveyor's report implied that he would not have touched the bawley with a barge pole. Armed with this bleak document they went over the ship themselves. I can well imagine that bawley's owner's feelings as he read the surveyor's report and listened to the mutterings of these young men as they poked and prodded about below decks. 'Beam ends a bit ropey . . . soggy carlines . . . how many timbers do you think we will have to replace?' Or 'Goodness, look at her shelf!' leading to the final insult when the owner quite reasonably pointed to the motor, saying 'Look at that lovely motor, I have stripped her right down and rebuilt her', only to hear them reply in unison, 'We will chuck that thing out as soon as we buy her, *if* we buy her.' The engine was a heavy old 30hp Thorneycroft diesel about the size of a kitchen table and weighing the-Lord-knows-how-many tons. Another hundred pounds sterling was knocked off as a result of the survey and, as they sold the engine for £50, including its removal, and also finally sold the propeller and stern gear for a few more pounds, they got their almost unique bawley hull, which was in quite good shape, for not much more than £600. Their heaviest expense after that was for the sails which cost them between £200 and £300.

Apart from burning off all her paint and cleaning her out, the only structural work they did at the beginning was to remove the large wheelhouse and rebuild the hatches. The mast was in good shape but she lacked a topmast and bowsprit. These were the spars that came from the Forest of Dean.

The tide was on the ebb, so to prevent us being carried seawards, Stephen Swann slowly paddled against the stream. For a few minutes a moored coaster hid the bawley from our view, then she appeared sailing close-hauled towards us. She was a pretty sight, even though she was not setting her topsail, a sight that had not been seen on the Colne or the Blackwater for many years. In 1914 there were still seventy-two sailing bawleys at work, but by the 1940s they had all gone out of business or had fitted diesels and left their sails at home. This bawley's hull was painted grey with black bulwarks and the characteristic bawley outline treatment of the transom, with 'Bona Southend' boldly painted across the black strake at the top of the transom.

In spite of her 36ft length *Bona* seemed quite a little boat. The luff of her mainsail was a good deal less than that of my own 6-tonner but I had not got a menacing 25ft gaff to contend with. As she came up on us the crew brailed up the mainsail, let go the jib sheets and backed the foresail. *Bona* hove-to peacefully. We came alongside and scrambled aboard. The low freeboard aft of bawleys and most fishing smacks makes this a much easier operation than boarding any modern yacht of comparable size.

The first thing that would strike one about the bawley is her great beam and her uncluttered decks. Though she has no lifelines, as one would have on any seagoing yacht, yet with her substantial bulwarks and her refusal to heel over much there is a feeling of security on those wide decks. Also, the fact that the bawley has a loose-footed sail and no boom allows for a wonderfully clear deck, particularly when the sail is brailed up.

Up in the bows is the windlass stretching right across the deck. It provides plenty of power for pulling in the $\frac{5}{8}$in chain and the 56lb fisherman anchor. Just aft of the mast is a small raised coach roof with a curved-back scuttle leading down to the cuddy. Aft of that is a long tapering hatchway, tapering aft to the steering well. Unlike the east coast oyster smacks, where the helmsman stands on deck, the bawley's helmsman stands in this well, or sits on the deck with his feet dangling in the well.

The forepeak of *Bona* was fitted out with two comfortable bunks with good sitting headroom. A half bulkhead separated the forepeak from the rest of the interior of the boat which was open for its full length aft. There was plenty of room for scrambling about, but very little headroom. The floor sloped steeply towards the stern and the headroom became that much less. A coal stove was fixed just aft of the bulkhead on the starboard side.

In the brief sail that we had she seemed a uniquely attractive craft, sailing beautifully off the wind. Her hollow bow cut through the water and she left hardly any disturbance. Her performance to windward with her great gaff sagging away to leeward was not so good, though I imagine the increased leading edge that her topsail would give her would make quite a difference. In fact the bawleys were often worked in the same way as a Thames barge, with their topsails set and their mainsails brailed up.

The following year Stephen Swann's original partners went their own ways and his cousin Peter Allen became a co-owner. The two of them looked critically at *Bona*'s hull and decided she deserved, and in fact needed, a more complete restoration than had originally been considered. She was, after all, seventy years old. Even though solidly built, her lack of lodging knees and hanging knees, and her vestigial apron, left little to keep her in shape. With her stem post in a poor way, she was in danger of falling apart. She needed not only a new stem assembly, including a proper apron, but a new kelson and at least half a dozen new frames on each side.

They berthed *Bona* at the St Osyth Boatyard which then had an owner sympathetic to old boats and their far from wealthy owners. They found another friend in Pat Brace who owned a

Hyacinth after her refit at West
Mersea, built by Aldous in 1901, now
belonging to Mrs Molly Kennett.
(Photo Keith Mirams.)

small timber yard at High Ongar. He produced six fine grown oak crooks for new portside frames. These when shaped were 4in × 4in. He also provided them with an 8in × 8in oak log for their kelson.

They set to work and strengthened her shelves in the way of the chainplates and replaced her planking with about 40ft of larch where it was overworn and in one place where she had sat on her anchor. The keel was in fair order so they fitted a new iron shoe to it and put in the new kelson. They had four galvanized steel webs made up, which were dump-bolted to the top of the kelson and through-bolted to the frames. The object of this was to strap the fore part of the ship together. 'Probably not necessary', Stephen Swann remarked, 'but we had used four stainless steel bolts (they cost £12) to fasten the 12in × 12in apron. They were guaranteed the best quality, EN 58 J – whatever that means – but one hears of stainless steel corroding...'

In November 1973, *Bona* was moved to her home port of Brightlingsea to a site alongside the hard which the local council leased to the Colne Smack Restoration Society for a very reasonable rent and a lease of 21 years.

There was still much to be done, including fitting eight new frames in her starboard side and new 1½in planking on both sides at the turn of the bilges where the existing planking was badly worn (rather than decayed) after a lifetime of lying about on Southend Beach. New covering boards, new stanchions and the new bulwarks will also be completed. When that is done *Bona* will be fitted out and sailed and fished each summer and further repairs and preservation work will be carried out each winter. Replanking the deck will be one of the first jobs.

I think this approach to restoration has much to recommend it. *Bona*'s owners had her sailing with the minimum of work, and then after one season they set to work on essential structural replacements. After a couple of years' work she will be sailing again with additional work going on every winter. Looking after an old boat like this is a never ending job. The pleasures of summer sailing and fishing are repaid by the winter's work.

There are three other bawleys that have been or are being restored. One is the *Doris*, owned by Nicholas Harding and restored by Frost & Drake at Tollesbury on the Blackwater River. (This is the yard where Michael Frost did his restoration of *Boadicea*.) *Doris* is a beautiful bawley and reputed to be a very fast sailer. At Maldon, at the head of the same river, David Patience has started work on a little clinker-planked bawley, which is over a hundred years old.

A third, *Auto-da-Fe*, is being restored on the River Orwell near Ipswich. Whether this completes the roll call of bawleys that are once again sailing, I hesitate to say.

Zuiderzee botter MK 63

LOA 13·50m
Beam 4·20m
Draught 1·00m
Sail area 40sq m (mainsail and staysail)
Large jib 25sq m
Small jib 15sq m
Built 1912

This fishing botter was built by de Haas at Monnickendam for Jan Uithuisje for fishing out of the island of Marken where she was registered. MK 63 was worked by the sons and grandsons of Jan Uithuisje until 1956 when she was sold out of the fishery trade and used as a yacht. She was left moored in the river Vecht some kilometres inland from Muiden. Her last commercial voyages were delivering hay when, unlike a stackie, (that is a Thames barge with a haystack on deck) she would be steered by tiller lines by the helmsman standing on top of the stack. The sail would be reefed and the boom raised to clear the stack. In light winds or going to windward, another sailing botter would take her in tow.

When in 1962 Peter Dorleyn, a young artist and art master from Amsterdam, found MK 63 she was partly under water and in a sorry state. Her mast was rotten, all her other spars and gear, including her leeboards, were missing. There were holes in her deck, her topside planking from midships aft needed replacing and practically every frame and floor was more or less rotten. However, she still retained her lovely lines and had not been sheathed in steel plates, as so often happened in later life to these fishing boats.

The first thing Peter Dorleyn did was to pump her out, using a powerful sand pump for the job. To his surprise, she came to the surface within half an hour. Her timbers and floors were buried beneath a layer of mud so the next job was to clean this away. MK 63 remained afloat with periodic bailing and in this condition Peter Dorleyn, using his other botter, towed her to Spakenburg, to the yard of the Nieuwboer brothers. Peter Dorleyn had bought this other botter a year or so before and was running her as a charter boat. Her registration letters and number BU 29 refer to the municipality of Bunschoten. Spakenburg comes under this district.

Peter Dorleyn's plan was to restore MK 63 and run both boats for charter. He was then living and working in Amsterdam; Spakenburg is only 35km away at the southerly end of the Ijselmeer. During the next two years, whilst he was working on MK 63, he was still sailing BU 29, but she was an older boat than MK 63 and in less good condition. She was built in 1891.

Side, deck and sail plans of Zuiderzee fishing botter, LOA 13m, beam 4·5m and draught 1m.

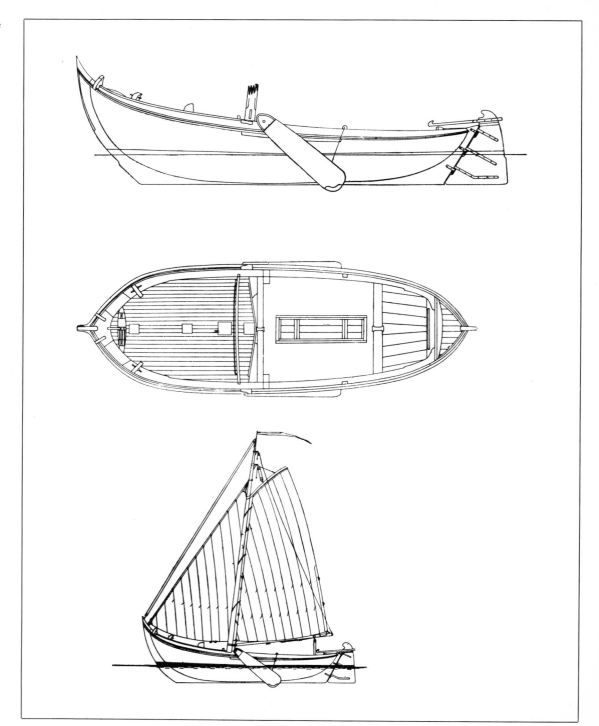

Zuiderzee fishing botters
Fishing botter under full sail.
(*Photo Peter Dorleyn.*)

When BU 29 was nearly twenty-five years old and her topsides were going, like many other old Dutch fishing boats she was sheathed with galvanized steel plates. By the 1960s these plates were eaten away with rust and the planks behind the plates were in an advanced state of decay. In contrast, MK 63 had had much of her topside planking replaced while she was still fishing. This must have been about 1950. In spite of her long neglect she was potentially a much sounder craft. It was these factors that decided Peter to set about her restoration.

He was fortunate to have such friends as the Nieuwboer brothers who allowed him to use all their yard equipment, including bandsaws and planers. During his long summer holidays from teaching Peter worked as a shipwright for the yard, and then, as soon as the day's work was completed, would set to work on his own boat and put in several hours' work before falling exhausted into his bunk. After the holidays, he continued to come over from Amsterdam every weekend to carry on the restoration work.

The first job he did was to raise the sides of the fish well, which were too low and allowed water to slop over the top into the cockpit. These botters all had fish wells. The sides of the botter below the waterline were perforated to allow free passage of water into a sealed-off area between the floors to the fish well amidships.

Marken fishing botter MK 63 bow
and foredeck.

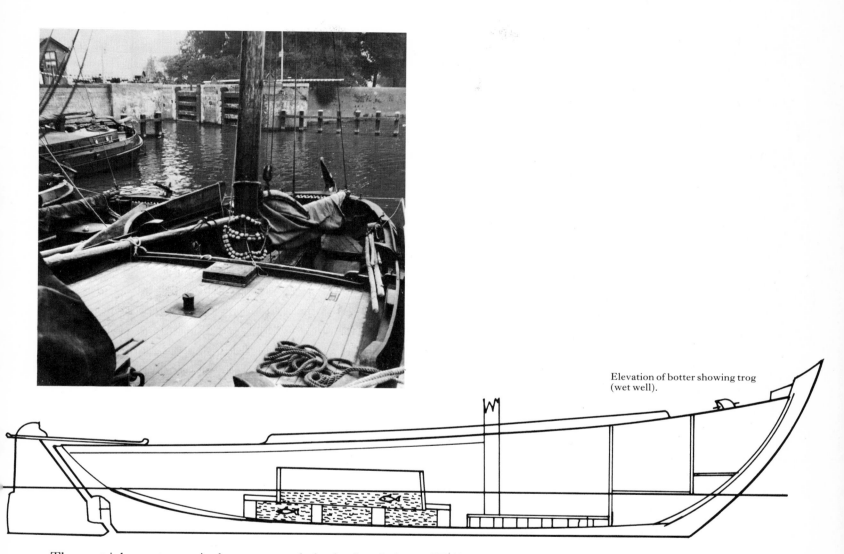

Elevation of botter showing trog
(wet well).

The next job was to repair the numerous holes in the pitch pine decks. These were temporary repairs, for ultimately he was to strip the deck and completely replank it in teak as he was unable to buy the pitch pine traditionally used in Holland. Within a few weeks of towing MK 63 to Spakenburg he had a stroke of luck and was able to buy the sails, masts, spars, leeboards and other gear of another botter that was being broken up. Within eighteen months MK 63 was sailing, though he continued to work on her restoration. He used this secondhand gear for the next seven years, when he finally replaced the masts, spars, leeboards, sails and all the rigging. The new mast had been used as a spar for a derrick on a steamer. It was a heavy pole of Riga pine which he had to adze and plane down to size.

Whilst MK 63 was at Spakenburg, she could be hauled up into the shipyard so that work could be done below the water-line. Here, he started to replace various floors and frames which were originally fastened to the bottom planking with treenails. For his replacement Peter used bolts, drift bolts and spikes. One of the biggest jobs in the restoration was the replacement of the heavy timbers up forward that served for both frames and floors. Five of the floors in the fo'c's'le had to be replaced and three of the old floors were doubled up and side-bolted together. The heavy timbers up forward that run from gunwale to gunwale were made up in each case of three grown crooks scarphed together.

In 1965, Peter Dorleyn moved to Hoorn to a new art teaching

The construction of a fishing botter.
Drawing by Peter Dorleyn.

1 Tiller pinrack.
2 Belaying pins.
3 After well, for bailing the bilge.
4 Forward well, for bailing the bilge.
5 Floor (timber).
6 'Zitter' (frames resting on deck above floors).
7 Trog or fish well.
8 Perforated plates to allow passage of water for the fish well.
9 Leeboard fair lead.
10 Rubbing strake for leeboard.
11 Timberhead for support of leeboard.
12 Hollow wooden shovel or scoop for bailing.
13 Foredeck beam shelf.
14 Stove and iron backplate.
15 Sleeping platform.
16 Lining.
17 Tar bucket.
18 Stockholm tar bucket.
19 Windlass.
20 Cable hatch.
21 The 'crop' (wide covering board).
22 The four armed grapnel anchor.
23 Bollard or staghorn.
24 Wale strake.
25 Single cleat for the topping lift, on the starboard side of the mast just below the gooseneck.
26 Downhaul for tack of mainsail.
27 Parrel lines.
28 Reef line.
29 Boom.
30 Outhaul with violin block.
31 Mainsheet.
32 Foresail.
33 Belly rope of foresail.
34 Washboard to which horse for the foresail sheet is fastened.
35 Tricing lines.
36 Jib sheet.
37 Bezaan.

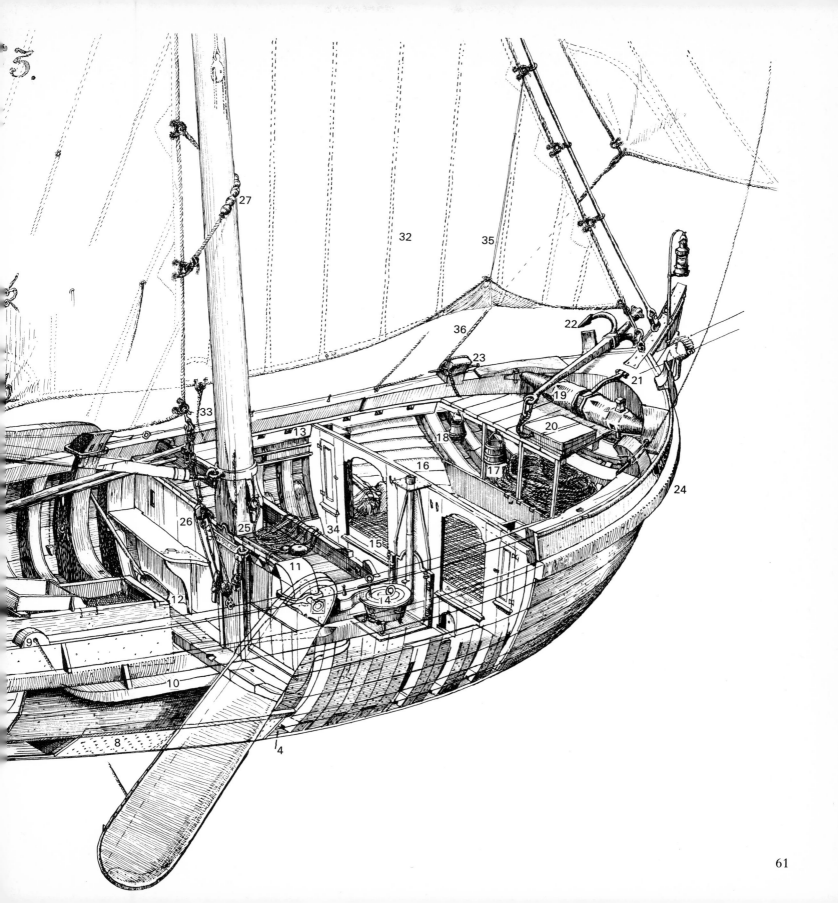

Construction details. Drawings by
Peter Dorleyn.

1 Washboard and horse for foresail
  sheet.
2 Scupper.
3 Stern thwart and horse for
  mainsheet.
4 Stern locker.
5 Lodging knee and belaying pin.
6 Mainsheet block.
7 Main beam.
8 Mast case.
9 Mast step.
10 Floors.
11 'Zitter' (grown crook frames that
  rest on top of the deck above the
  floors in the open part of the
  vessel or alongside the floors).
12 The frames.
13 Hanging knees.
14 Lodging knees.
15 Shelf.
16 Gunwhale.
17 Threshold (to the fo'c's'le).
18 Eyebolt to take mast locking band.
19 Treenails.
20 Drift bolt.

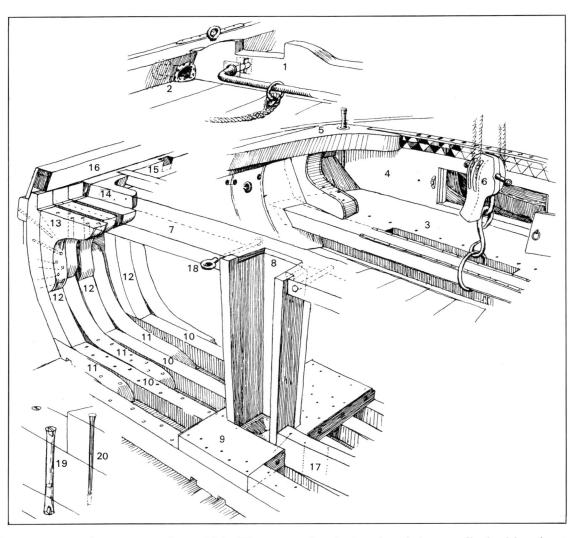

job and a new home. Spakenburg was too far away, so he brought his MK 63 over to Hoorn and at the same time he sold BU 29, his first botter. He found coping with two ships too difficult.

There is no shipyard today at Hoorn and as the Ijselmeer is not tidal everything has to be done whilst the vessel is afloat. No longer were the bandsaws and other mechanical tools of Nieuwboer's yard to hand. Every piece of timber (and some of the frames were huge) had to be cut by hand.

As MK 63 had had much of her topside planking replaced, there were only three strakes from midships aft on each side that needed renewing. Oak was used for this as for everything else, except for the deck and the spars. The planks were 4cm thick. They were fitted, tarred and then caulked with oakum and payed with Tencofix Dik, an effective substance that is used for the undersealing of motorcar bodies.

The windlass was rebuilt and slowly the frames were replaced. This presented a fastening problem when the boat was afloat. It was simple enough to cut away or even to pull out the rotten old frames, for many of the fastenings had corroded away to nothing between frame and planking. The old fastenings in the planks were punched out and the holes filled with wooden plugs. These were cut off flush inside the boat. Templates of hardboard were cut and the angles of the bevels marked using a carpenter's bevel, an indispensable tool that looks like a hinged setsquare. The frames would be cut and offered up

The doorway into the fo'c's'le.

The fo'c's'le showing traditional decoration.
1 The bread cupboard.
2 The compass.
3 The water cask.
4 The mast case.

several times until they fitted exactly. They were then coated with tar and fastened.

The fo'c's'le When Peter Dorleyn bought MK 63, her fo'c's'le was a bare, empty space. A little research was needed here. After inspecting various old craft and then finding some photographs of the interior of a botter in the Netherlands Open Air Museum, Arnhem, he was able to establish fairly conclusively what this fo'c's'le must have looked like in 1912. The Zuiderzee botters normally had their fo'c's'les divided athwartships by a bulkhead perforated with two doorways. The area forward of this bulkhead had a floor raised by about 65cm. This was used for storing nets and sometimes as a sleeping platform. Forward of this was a cable locker. In the after cabin were port and starboard benches on which the crew could sit or sleep. Between the two doorways was the coal stove. Peter found a little round cast iron stove mounted on cabriole legs. Earlier fishing boats had an open fireplace, backed with an iron plate set between two classical half round pillars and with a canopy leading up to the deck head and the chimney.

The botter's tremendous sheer means that there is good headroom forward but little at the after bulkhead. The doorway to the open after part of the botter on the starboard side of the mast is only waist high (1m). One has to double up to pass through it. The restoration of the fo'c's'le of MK 63 has been beautifully done. Peter Dorleyn has painted the traditional triangular red and white pattern over the doorway and along the front of the side benches. On the dark green double stable doors he has inscribed this little verse.

Ik vaar op alle winden
En wend het roer gezwind
Naar 't Harde, Ketel, Urker Val
Daar waar ik het meeste vangen zal
Dat is des vissers wensch.

(I am sailing in all sorts of winds
And turn the helm quickly
Towards Harde, Ketel, Urker Val
Where I can make the biggest catches
That is the fisherman's wish.)

(Harde is where Lelystad now is, Ketel is the mouth of the river Ijsel and Urker Val is a deep near the old island of Urk.)

Dutch fishing craft have a number of idiosyncratic features. Their blocks, for instance, are quite unlike those used in other northern European vessels.

1 The zwaardtalie and the vioolblok (violin block), which is shaped as it is because it carries two sheaves, one below and larger than the other. Thus the ropes can lie parallel and not get mixed up with each other.

2 The botter-fokblok (the botter foresail block) is so shaped that the top of the foresail cannot twist or turn, the head of the sail having two cringles.

3 The hakblok or staartblok is the mainsheet block. The sheet is turned round the hak (tail) and finally half-hitched to the pin which protrudes on either side (like a bawley's mainsheet block).

4 The luff and leech ropes of both jib and bezaan are held apart by an angle spreader before coming together in a cringle, to which the jib halliard is hooked.

5 Botter's masthead.
   1 Hemel boender (sky-brush).
   2 Mast kloot (mast ball).
   3 Scheerhoutje (frame for vleugel)
   4 Vleugel (pennant).
   5 Masthead.

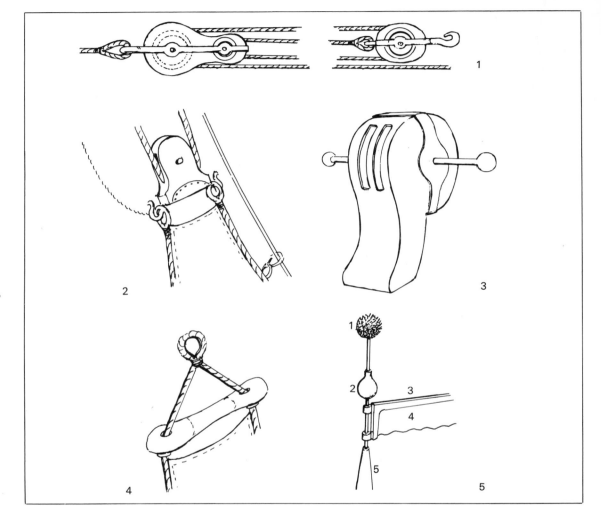

Timber As all fishing boats and most yachts in Holland are now built of steel, good timber is difficult to buy. A fortuitous gale in North Holland blew down a number of oak trees and Peter Dorleyn was able to buy his timber as it lay. It was of course green but it was autumn felled, for the gale was in November. This provided a number of grown crooks for frames, heavy wale strakes and some planking.

The new spars were of Oregon pine except for the curved gaff which traditionally is always made of ash. The blocks are also of ash.

Ironwork All the ironwork had eventually to be renewed, but this was not necessary until MK 63 was based at Hoorn. Here there is a good blacksmith, in fact two good blacksmiths, who are brothers. So new ring bolts, hooks (these are much used on fishing botters, where such things as shackles are not seen), new cranse irons, gudgeon pins and pintles etc were made up.

The ground tackle consists of a very heavy grapnel with four hooks and a normal fisherman's anchor for less rigorous conditions. Coir cable is used for both anchors.

I first saw Peter Dorleyn's botter at Hoorn on the Ijselmeer on a warm day in September. This particular botter, MK 63, was lying between a straight-stemmed Plute and a fully decked, round-bowed Aak in a trot of old Zuiderzee craft beneath the walls of the sixteenth-century Hooftoren. It was an appropriate setting for these lovely old boats. Hoorn was the birthplace of the great navigator Willem Schouten, the first man to

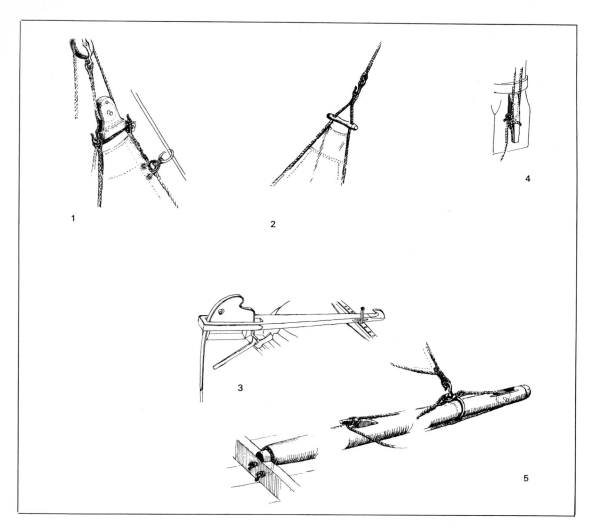

Blocks and gear on botter.
1 Botter fokblok at the head of the foresail, which prevents the head of the sail from twisting.
2 The headropes of the bezaan sail, separated by a length of ash.
3 The tiller can be pinned in position.
4 The single main halliard belayed to a cleat on the mast.
5 The jib outhaul.

double Cape Horn, which he named after the old Zuiderzee port.

There are still thirty-five botters and five Vollendammer Kwakken (which are like big botters), six Weiringer Aaken, one Plute and one Schouw sailing round the Ijselmeer. And this takes no account of Staverse Jolen and the many Boeiers that are still to be seen on these inland waters. Holland is the home of ship restoration.

Most restorations show evidence that they are restorations and not the original thing by their over elaboration, or their over perfect finish, in the same way as restored vintage motorcars have more gleaming brass and more bright yellow paintwork than they ever had when they were first built. Peter Dorleyn's botter is an exception. She does not look like a restored ship but like a working fishing boat that has had an owner who has loved

her well. MK 63 has not had her topsides and timbers scraped down to the bare oak for, however handsome that may look, it was not the way the Marken botters were treated. Her topsides and timbers, impregnated with tar, are a rich dark colour yet smooth and clean. At the bows, a splash of vermilion and apple green on her top strake frames her registration numbers. It was not the fashion at Marken to name the fishing boats, though Zuiderzee ports reacted in different ways to this problem. Geometrical bands of red and white along the coaming at the after end of the cockpit and above the door into the fo'c's'le are the only other visible signs of decoration.

Her closely planked foredeck is a silvery grey in colour. The cockpit, which is the whole of the vessel aft of the mast, has a fish well amidships. Aft of that is the engine box, housing a

Sail plan of Marken botter MK 63 with detail of reefed foresail. The head of the mast has a tapered metal case, above which the vleugel flies, supported on a frame (scheerhoutje) to keep it clear of the halliard blocks. Above the masthead is the hemel boender, the sky scrubbing brush.

Drawings by Peter Dorleyn.
1 The jib (kluiver).
2 The foresail (fok).
3 The mainsail (grootzeil).
4 The bezan (bezaan).
The perforated plates for the fish well can be seen below the leeboards.

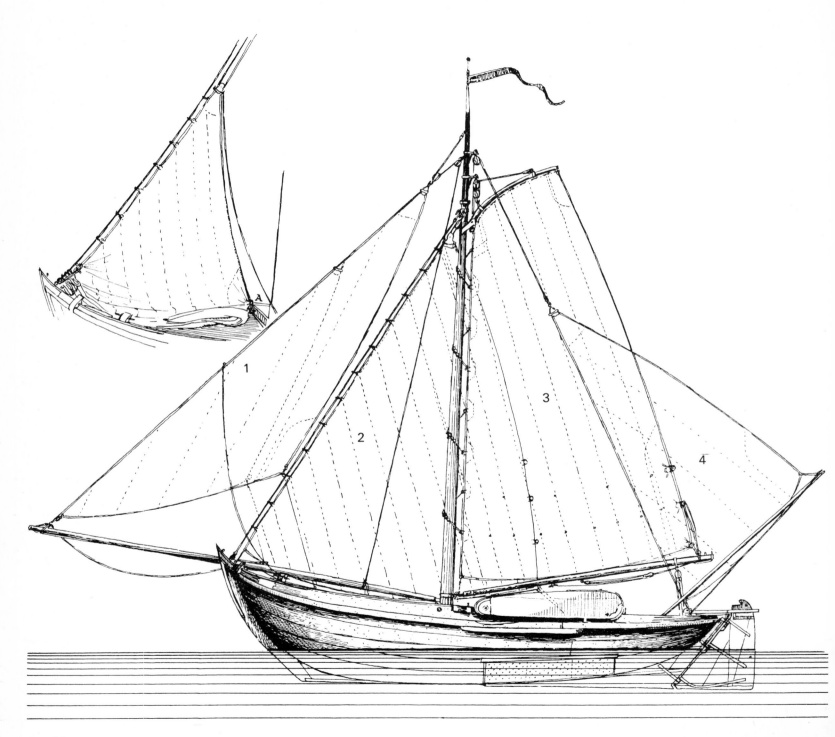

30hp Ford petrol engine that was installed in 1930. From about that time most sailing botters were built with auxiliary engines, so though the retention of this venerable piece of machinery may be an anachronism for a boat built in 1912 it was used for a quarter of a century. Also, its usefulness for charter work was a factor that may have helped to outweigh historical exactitude.

The botter is a wonderfully simple craft to work. She has no standing rigging apart from a forestay. The great heavy mast is very strongly housed in a tabernacle at the break of the fo'c's'le. The running rigging for the mainsail consists of a single topping lift with 2:1 purchase and a single halliard which does duty most efficiently for both peak and throat. The end is made fast to the curved gaff about three-quarters of the way along the spar. It leads through a double block on the mast, which is in the position of the normal throat halliard block, down to a block on the gaff at the throat, back up to the double block and to a cleat on the starboard side of the mast. This gives a 3:1 purchase. When the sail is hoisted, it sets perfectly as soon as the throat block comes hard up against the double halliard block. This is a great help in the dark, for as soon as the blocks bang together the fisherman knows his mainsail is properly set.

The main sheet is hooked on to a ring that travels on a horse in front of the bench at the back of the cockpit. Just above this bench is a pin rail fitted with iron pins for pinning the tiller when the helmsman is needed to help with the trawl or for any other duty.

The staysail and jibs have normal single halliards leading to cleats on the port side of the mast. The large overlapping staysail has an additional line fastened part way along its foot, called the 'belly' rope, for hauling the after part of the sail round the mast when going about. The foresail sheet runs on a horse fastened on the fore side of the wash board that prevents water on the foredeck slopping into the cockpit.

The bowsprit is a relatively light spar. In harbour it is stowed fore and aft in the open part of the vessel. When in use it slides through an iron ring which has been served and parcelled and which is fastened to the starboard side of the stem post. It has a sheave at its outer end and an iron ring outhaul (traveller) which hooks on to the tack of the jib. The jib sheet is made fast to one of the forward stag horns.

Another light spar is rigged like a spinnaker pole to hold out the clew and sheet of the bezaan. This is a triangular sail set from the stern of the botter. The sheet is made fast to one of the iron pins in the gunwale opposite the end of the pinrack. The foot of the bezaan spar is normally chocked into the after side of the aftermost *dekenpoot* (the frames that sit on top of the deck over the floors). In the case of MK 63 the foot of the bezaan spar rests against the after side of the engine housing.

Botters were very heavily built to stand up to rough usage. Their normal working life was expected to be about twenty

Botter MK 63. Details of the stemhead.
1 Solid iron bar forestay.
2 Gammon iron.
3 Iron eyebolt on stem post, to which is attached the trawl warp when using the dwarskuil.

years. Their construction had certain defects that led to the corrosion of fastenings and to wet rot in the timbers. For instance, there is no covering board on the gunwales so the joints between timbers and planks are exposed to the weather. Damp is certain to penetrate, with obvious results, but as the timbers were so massive there is room for a fair amount of decay before the ship falls to bits. When these botters were treenail and *iron* fastened, the fastenings lasted much better than galvanized mild steel.

Botters do not have pumps. They carry instead a couple of hollow shovels or scoops. There is a bilge well just aft of the mast and another at the after end of the cockpit. The bailer scooping the water out of the bilge straight into the fish well can clear the bilges surprisingly quickly.

Botters are of course fishing boats, but since the building of the Afsluitdijk which converted the Zuiderzee into a fresh water lake the whole pattern of fishing has changed. After the closing of the dyke, only eel and pike-perch remain. From April to October the botters fish for eel with a beamless trawl and also with lines and fish traps; in the winter they fish with dragnets for pike-perch. Since 1970, the use of the trawl has been prohibited in the Ijselmeer.

When the Zuiderzee and the Waddenzee were one huge, shallow tidal basin several types of trawl were used for catching fish. There was the *dwarskuil* (the transverse trawl, so named because the botter sails crabwise) which was towed from a spar set outboard from the vessel. This method, also called the *wonderkuil* because it was a wonder how much you can catch with this trawl, was widely used. When towed between two

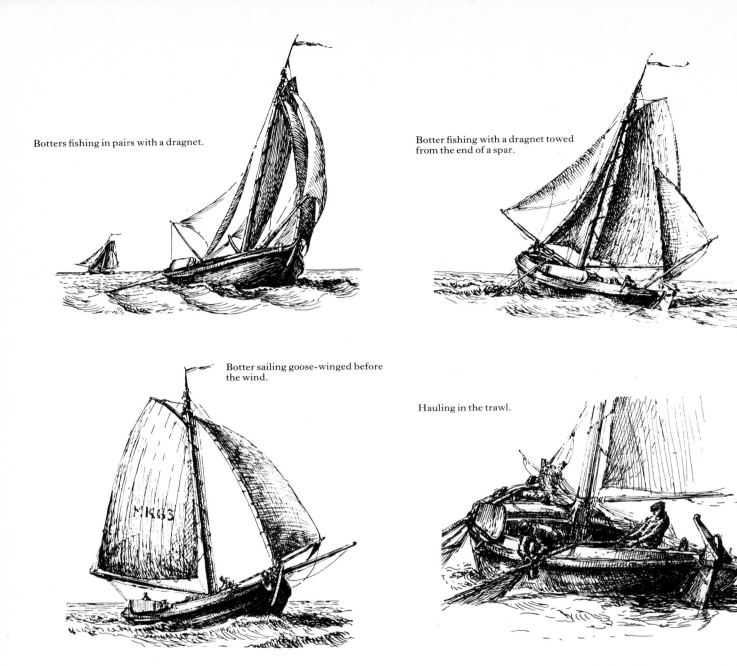

Botters fishing in pairs with a dragnet.

Botter fishing with a dragnet towed from the end of a spar.

Botter sailing goose-winged before the wind.

Hauling in the trawl.

botters the same trawl was called a *moordkuil* (the murder trawl), so named because of the number of young fish killed by this method.

There was also the *kwakkuil*, only used by Kwakken in the summer time. Here two large spars, one on each side of the vessel, spreadeagled the mouth of the trawl on the sea bottom, though only the spar on the weather side actually rests on the bottom. The *kwakkuil* was used for catching shrimps and eel. *Sleepnetten* (dragnets) which had heavy weighted ground ropes were used for catching sole, plaice and flounder. The botter fishermen used various other methods such as the *staande netten* which were long walls of netting buoyed and anchored;

and they also used different kinds of fish trap, particularly for catching the much prized eel.

There were no oysters in the Zuiderzee, but mussels were dredged up by Zeeland fishermen who used to work over the Kreupel sandbanks north of Enkhuizen.

Peter Dorleyn's interest in the fishing botters extended to how they were used, just as much as to how they were built. The result of his research into their fishing methods can be seen in a little book called *Het Botslepen* published by the Zuiderzee Museum. The results of over ten years of his restoration work can be seen in MK 63 as she lies alongside the jetty at Hoorn or sails over the short waved seas of the Ijselmeer.

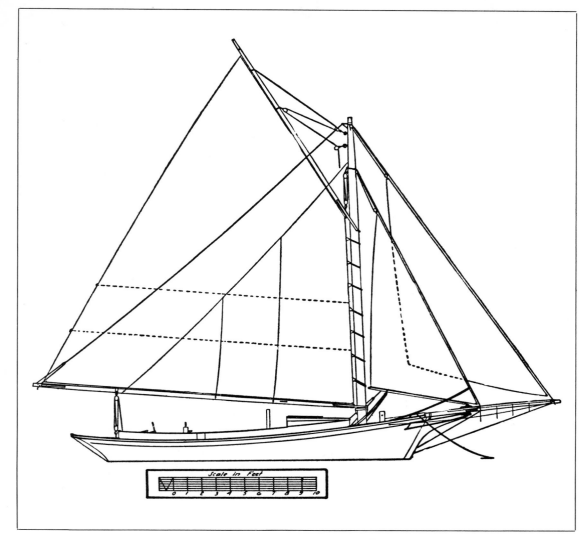

Sail plan of working Friendship sloop in last stage of development. Drawing by Howard I. Chapelle.

Friendship sloop: spar and sail plan.

Mast 26ft 3in.
  Foot 7in square.
  6in dia at hounds.
  4in dia at head.

Boom 22ft 10in.
  3in – 2½in.

Bowsprit 12ft 6in.
  3ft 6in.

Staysail boom 6ft 9in.

No shrouds on bowsprit.

Standing rigging ¼in wire rope.

Mainsail.
  Head of sail 14ft 0in.
  Diagonal of sail 24ft 6in.
  Foot of sail 22ft 0in.

Staysail.
  Luff 15ft 8in.
  Leech 12ft 9in.
  Foot 7ft 6in.

Jib.
  Luff 19ft 6in.
  Leech 13ft 10in.
  Foot 10ft 0in.

Friendship sloops

Most efforts at restoration of old boats are a matter of a single craft being brought back to its original condition: a *Cutty Sark*, a *Constitution* or a *Boadicea*. The Friendship sloops have a different kind of story. It all began at a little harbour in Maine that had the Indian name of Meduncook, which apparently and poetically means 'place by the tide, where the sun shines over the islands and warriors make beautiful canoes'. About the turn of the eighteenth century Meduncook became Friendship, named so it is said after some visiting vessel of that pretty name.

Around 1880, a thousand or so men were engaged in fishing from the neighbourhood of Friendship, along the sea shores and through the islands of Muscongus Bay. The local fishing ports were Friendship, Bristol and Bremen. Most of the men went lobster fishing, seine netting and line fishing for cod in the summer, and in the winter became boatbuilders, either building their own boats or helping such professional boatbuilders as Wilbur Morse. The red oak and the white pine for these boats could be cut by the builder on the mainland and towed over to the islands, usually to the sawmills of Bristol. Most of the sloops they built were centreboard boats, but by the 1890s these began to be replaced by deep keeled hulls. Topsails and two headsails replaced the bald headed sloop rig so that the typical working

Friendship sloops.
1 *Galatea*, LOA 25ft 0in, built by McKie Roth for John Kapelowitz in 1964. (*Photo Diane Beeston.*)
2 *Ellie T*, LOA 25ft 0in, owned and built from the lines of *Pemaquid* by John Thorpe in 1961. (*Photo Carlton Simmons.*)

Friendship sloop became a cutter. And the sails were mostly sewn by women.

Between 1885 and 1915, over one thousand Friendship sloops were built in the Muscongus Bay area. Between 1915, when power driven craft began to replace sail, and 1961, barely another dozen were built for fishing.

Howard I. Chapelle, writing in 1965, said 'While all interested in American small craft have probably heard of the Friendship sloop . . . the type was gradually disappearing. Then a group of Friendship citizens began to arouse interest in the revival of the local craft. Not only this but a strong effort was made to retain the purity of design and construction of the type. Now, within a few short years, enough interest has been aroused to create a whole squadron of Friendship sloops.'

One of the first to arouse this interest was Bernard Mackenzie. He found *Voyager*, his Charles Morse-built Friendship sloop, on a wintry afternoon in 1951 in a boatyard at Onset, Mass. In 1960, in a handicap race in Boston Harbour, *Voyager*, in a run before the wind, showed her heels to the entire fleet of spinnaker-carrying modern boats. She blew out a jib but Friendships can stand up to their canvas. Her great gaff mainsail carried her home in first place just as it had driven *Voyager* home to market

2

in her work days. The idea of the Friendship sloop Regatta was born on that windy September afternoon. Fourteen sloops took part in the 1961 regatta. In 1973, there were fifty-three Friendship sloops taking part, most of them modern copies of the old design.

There is some argument as to the exact origins of the Friendship sloop. According to Chapelle, who probably knows more about the history of American small craft than anyone else living, the design is based on the Muscongus Bay sloops which had clipper bows and were either carvel or clinker planked. These were centreboard boats twenty-eight foot overall which

were used for hauling lobster traps. Chapelle mentions further influences on Friendship sloops such as Edward Burgess's Gloucester fisherman *Fredonia*, which had a cutaway underbody and easy sections which led to the Gloucester sloops. The marriage of the Muscongus Bay and Gloucester sloops produced the wholesome little Friendship type.

Wilbur Morse, who set up a boatbuilding shop in Friendship in 1882, said, with a refreshing lack of modesty, 'A Friendship sloop is a sloop built in Friendship by Wilbur Morse!' Morse's records were destroyed by fire, but it is known that he built between four and five hundred lobster boats, many of them the

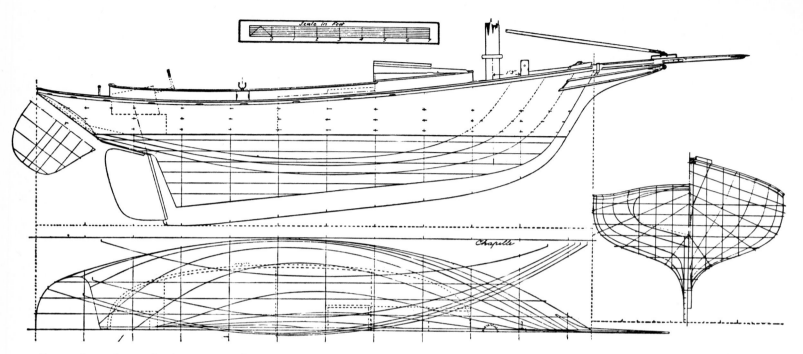

Lines of *Pemaquid*, a small working Friendship sloop, built by Abdon K. Carter about 1904 at Bremen, Maine. Drawing by Howard I. Chapelle.

clipper-bowed smacks that we now know as Friendship sloops. Wilbur Morse built his boats of pine and the local grey oak, which belongs to the family of red oaks. This use of grey oak accounts for the poor lasting qualities of the Friendship sloops when taken to warmer climates. American white oak is very rare in Maine and was imported only for expensive yachts. Wilbur Morse claimed that he had dreamed up his ideal boat, the little Friendship sloop, while fishing on the Grand Banks.

According to Winfield Lash, the boatbuilder of Hatchet Cove, the true Friendship is based on a model of a thirty-seven foot boat that is in his possession, and was made by Wilbur Morse. Mr Lash says: 'A Friendship sloop must have the hollow bow and the hollow garboards of the model. The drag and the rocker of the keel must be the same. She must have an overhanging counter with a transom which does not drag in the water, and the buttock lines must not be flat, but curve slightly upwards to meet the counter. The prismatic coefficient and waterline must not vary from the model.'

Winfield Lash concludes this somewhat dogmatic statement with: 'A Friendship sloop whether larger or smaller than the original thirty-seven-foot sloop built from the model, must preserve these proportions.'

No doubt the type developed through trial and error, for they were built by several other local builders including different members of the Morse family.

However the Friendship sloops evolved, they are characterful little ships with their sharp entries and high freeboard forward.

They are seldom stopped by a sea and are dry ships in a sea-way. Their relatively large beam gives them a comfortable, stable working platform and the low sides and narrow side decks make easy the lifting of dredges, trawls and lobster traps. They have no selfdraining cockpits; the water goes into the bilges and is pumped out.

Friendship sloops were usually ballasted with rocks and pebbles. The mast is set far forward leaving plenty of space aft for working. Friendship sloops will handle under a mainsail alone, but like any craft of their type will not stand being pinched when going to windward.

The Friendship sloops have survived and have been well worth reviving because they are a healthy, seaworthy type of sailing boat and because they are things of beauty – and by beauty I do not refer to their intricately carved trail boards and gold-leafed transoms, but to their beauty of line, so that, from no matter what angle one sees them they look right. That this elegance should belong to a very cheaply built work boat is an additional satisfaction.

In 1961, the Friendship Sloop Society was formed. The Society has two hundred members who between them own 137 registered Friendship sloops. The Society is much more than a regatta affair. Its basic purpose is to promote an interest in the skilled craftsmanship that produced these interesting boats. Nearly all the current Friendship sloops are modern boats built as faithfully as they can be to the original lines and varying in size from about twenty-one foot overall up to forty-

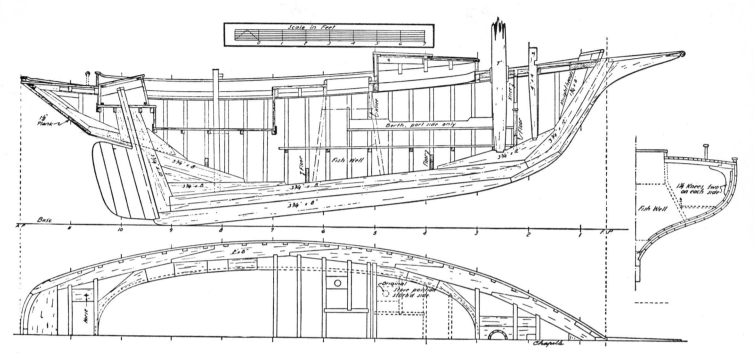

four foot overall. However, there are among these boats almost a dozen genuine restorations including *Amity*, a Wilbur Morse boat built in 1900, *Voyager* built in 1902, *Dictator* in 1904, *Golden Eagle* in 1910 and *Chrissy*, built by Charles Morse in 1912. And there is *Estella A* at Mystic Seaport. The *Estella A* is the only one of these old boats to have the original open well. None of the restored or new vessels are workboats, for they have all been converted into, or built as, yachts. Maybe 'yacht' is not the right word for these old clipper-bowed cutters. Perhaps 'family' boats would be nearer the truth, for a Friendship sloop is not regarded as a status symbol but rather as a much loved and particularly beautiful member of the family.

The boats are also very much of the place. Friendship itself is a neat little town of white clapboard houses which, if they do not have the superb elegance of the old captains' houses in the main street of neighbouring Thomaston, still have a pleasant, trim, lived-in air about them. They line the long metalled road that leads down to the harbour. The wharves and jetties are still piled high with the slatted wooden lobster traps and other gear, including the individually coloured buoys, with which the fishermen mark their traps. The harbour is sheltered by Friendship Long Island from the wilder waters of Muscongus Bay, except when the wind is in the south-west. Friendship is actually on a promontory between two rivers, the Meduncook and the Medomak. Of its population of 832, over 150 are registered as lobstermen. It is an enchanting place and the people match their surroundings.

Friendship sloop *Pemaquid*. Construction plan drawn by Howard I. Chapelle. *Pemaquid* was steered originally by a tiller. Scantlings taken from *Charm* and fitted to *Pemaquid*.

Friendship sloop scantlings 25ft 0in between perpendiculars.
1⅛in coamings.
1¼in × 2in deck.
⅞in × 2½in rail cap.
1½in × 1½in rail.
Deck beams side 1⅞in, mould 3in.
Crown of deck 4in in 8ft 6in.
¾in × 4in ceiling.
Frames 1¾in × ⅞in on flat side spaced 10½in.
Four floors sided 1½in moulded 8in.
1in plank.
Keel and stem post and stern post sided 3¾in.
Iron fastened keel bolts ½in and ⅝in galvanized rod.
Other bolts ¼in and ⅜in galvanized rod.
Boat nails 1¾in and 2¼in.

Estella A, LOA 34ft 6in, built by
Robert McLain in 1904, rebuilt by
Newbert & Wallace at Thomaston,
alongside the *Emma C. Berry* at
Mystic Seaport.

For the purposes of this book I have taken the rebuilding of two of the older boats, the *Estella A* which has just been entirely rebuilt at Newbert & Wallace's yard at Thomaston, some twelve miles from Friendship, and *Chrissy*, owned by Mr Ernst Wiegleb of Pleasant Point, for nearly thirty years and twice rebuilt by him.

Friendship sloop *Estella A*

LOA 34ft 6in
Beam 11ft 8in
Draught 5ft 8in
Built 1904

Estella A is on permanent show at Mystic Seaport. She cost $450 to build when she was launched and was the first Friendship sloop to be built on Bremen Long Island with auxiliary power. She had a 9hp 2-cylinder Knox engine with clutch and reverse gear, which was manufactured at Rockland, Maine. The *Estella A* was ballasted with pig iron instead of the customary stones. She was built by Rob McLain for Jack Ames of Matinicus during a very severe winter when there were twenty-two inches of ice in the channel. In her construction she had no screw bolts but was iron spiked. These spikes were driven through the timbers and clenched. To save costs, the size of the boat timbers and planks were standardised and brought over from the mainland already cut to stock sizes:

5in stock oak was used for stem, keel and stern post

3in stock oak was used for the deck beams

$1\frac{1}{2}$in × $2\frac{3}{4}$in oak was used for the frames which were bent on the flat side

$1\frac{1}{8}$in stock white pine was used for planking, topsides and bottom

$\frac{7}{8}$in stock white pine was used for the ceiling.

The deck planks, 2in wide, were sprung into position parallel with the rail and the seams caulked with cotton by means of a caulking wheel. They were not pitched or puttied but were finally painted white. The reason for not covering the cotton was that it made it a simple matter to caulk in extra lengths of cotton if the deck sprang a leak.

Contrary to normal American boat building practice, the cabin sides and coaming were not stepped on the deck but ran inside the carlings. The cabin top was made of wide tongue and groove close grained white pine planks and painted white. In fact *Estella A* was painted mostly white, except for her grey platform and cabinsole. The coamings, cabin sides and rail were given an oil finish. This was made up of a mixture of 3 quarts of boiled linseed oil, 1 pint of turpentine and 1 pint of pine tar (ie Stockholm tar). These surfaces darkened to a silky black.

The bitts were capped with sheet copper. Her standing rigging was simple, consisting of two forestays and two pairs of shrouds, each pair looped over the masthead and seized at the hounds. They were hardened with lanyards and deadeyes to iron chainplates bolted to her topsides.

Estella A worked as a freight carrier from 1930 to 1935. Before that she was a lobsterman and fishing smack. Her cockpit had no seats but was fitted with 'kid' boards to divide it up; part of it could thus be used as a fish hold. Her cuddy had three berths, two facing forward, one aft, and an oven stove facing inboard. She had tiller steering and carried two jibs and a main, but no topmast or topsails.

By 1970, after lying at Mystic for many years, *Estella A* returned to Maine for a major refit. A low-loader delivered her to Newbert & Wallace's yard at Thomaston. She was going to be almost entirely rebuilt before she returned to her berth at Mystic Seaport two years later.

Estella A was badly twisted so the first job was to chock her up and straighten her out. Then patterns were taken of her sections at 4ft intervals and moulds were made and fitted inside the boat. Three or four planks were removed from each side and ribbands were fastened to the moulds. This basic former was then braced to overhead beams.

Everything was rotten. She had come to the end of her life and needed a complete rebuild. The midship section was taken out first, the old frames were removed and new ones of white oak were cut, steamed, fitted and fastened to the ribbands. This was repeated for each section of the boat.

Estella A had been coppered at the waterline round the bow. When the copper sheets were removed the stem fell out. The new stem was made up of white oak, a grown crook being scarphed into straight grained timber. (Mr Roy Wallace explained this by saying it was almost impossible to buy suitable grown crooks.) The *Estella A* has no apron; the planking is rebated into the stem post.

When the shipwrights started to cut the horn timbers (the frames supporting the overhang of the short counter) the transom in its turn nearly fell off, so that it had to be chocked up into position until new horn timbers and a new stern post were fitted to the old keel. This was a lead casting with an oak false keel on top of it. Part of this false keel was the only piece of old timber to remain when *Estella A*'s refit was finished. The reason the false keel had survived was that the whole of the top surface was cemented over. As in the English East Coast smacks, rot rarely occurs under the cement.

Mr Wallace pointed out that the curve of the transom was not there for looks but for strength. A planked and framed transom, such as the Friendship sloop has, would develop after four or five years an inverse curve of as much as $1\frac{1}{2}$in even if made quite flat in the first place. The pressure of the topside planking

Friendship sloop *Chrissy*. LOA 29ft 8in,
built by Charles Morse in 1912.
Owned and restored by Ernst Wiegleb.
(*Photo Boutillier*.)

would cause this. This, of course, would not apply if the transom was made up of 3in planks, edge fastened. Even so, these would look better if they were curved slightly.

The *Estella A*'s covering boards had been made up of short lengths of pine planking, shaped only on the outside and left straight on the inside. These boats were cheaply built and the builders resorted to any expedient that would save either labour or material, within the limitations of making good seaworthy boats.

When her new backbone was in position, with new stem and stern posts, horn timbers, and framing and deck beams, the planking could commence. *Estella A* is now bronze screw fastened, which today is normal practice in the USA. The completion of the restoration followed normal boatbuilding practice and *Estella A*, still the same fishing boat she was seventy years ago, is now good for another seventy.

Mr Wallace almost repeated the words Michael Frost used when he had finished rebuilding *Boadicea*. 'I could have built three or four sloops in the time it took to restore the *Estella A*.'

Estella A (she was named after her first owner's little daughter, Estella Ames) is back at Mystic Seaport, lying alongside the Noank sloop *Emma C. Berry* and looking very trim. They make a pretty pair, the 34ft 6in white Friendship sloop in contrast with the dark green topsides of the 47ft Noank fishing boat.

Friendship sloop *Chrissy*

LOA 29ft 8in
LWL 25ft 0in
Beam 9ft 4in
Draught 5ft 0in
Sail area 450sq ft
Topsail 100sq ft
Built 1912

Chrissy was built by Charles Morse (Wilbur Morse's brother) at Friendship in the year that Woodrow Wilson was elected President of the United States and Arizona and New Mexico were created States of the Union. Down east in Maine, the life of the fishing communities was still much the same as it had been for the previous half century, though by this time quite a number of lobster boats had installed auxiliary gasoline engines.

Chrissy (then called *Sonny*) was still in the shape of a working boat when Mr Ernst Wiegleb bought her from Mr J. W. Belano of Port Clyde in 1945, but she had been badly neglected during the war years and needed a lot doing to her. Mr Wiegleb started work on her. She was leaking badly, particularly through the rudder box. He tried to patch this up without much success. In 1949, as his time was limited (he was still fully engaged on rail-

road construction work), he placed *Chrissy* in the hands of Wilbur J. Morse's boatyard. Mr Morse fitted a new keel, a new stern post, several new frames and replanked her below the waterline with white pine. He also cured the rudder box leak. *Chrissy* had originally been planked in oak. A new and enlarged cuddy was built and fitted out with berths and a coal stove. A water closet was also installed.

After launching *Chrissy* Mr Wiegleb put in 4,200lb of scrap iron, made up of old bridge bars cut up into short lengths. This overballasted her.

Between 1949 and 1965 various improvements were made to *Chrissy*. In Ernie Wiegleb's competent hands she proved to be a good sailer and had a consistently successful record in the annual Friendship regatta. She missed the first regatta but after that had 10 firsts, 3 seconds and 1 third in 18 races.

By the summer of 1969, *Chrissy* was fifty-seven years old and was in need of major structural repairs. In the fall of the same year, after making contact with a rocky ledge off the end of Crotch Island, *Chrissy* was hauled out and Ernie Wiegleb, now retired from his railroad construction, set to work on her. He cleared the cabin, shifting all the bulkheads and then stripped the ceiling. This showed that most of the frames were rotten, with badly corroded fastenings, and that much of the original oak planking was in a very poor way. He said to me later, 'I guess the boat was held together by her reputation!'

Chrissy had been reframed so often that there was little space between the old frames to insert new ones. There was nothing for it but to rip them all out, with the exception of five white oak ones that had been put in some ten years earlier. These were still quite sound. To keep the shape of the hull, Mr Wiegleb fixed braces under the main deck beams at either end of the cabin where the bulkheads had been.

The new frames were cut from $1\frac{1}{2}$in × 2in white oak spaced 9in apart. After some discussion about fastenings with Mr Wallace (of Newbert & Wallace's Yard at Thomaston), Ernie Wiegleb abandoned the idea of galvanized screws as being too short lived and decided on bronze screws and bronze holdfast nails.

It was at Newbert & Wallace's Yard that I finally got the answer as to why screws were the normal method of fastening 'down east'.

'Labour costs, that's all', Roy Wallace had said. 'Of course copper nails and rivets are better, but they take that much longer to fix and are occupying two men at the same time, one to hammer, one to hold the dolly.' Mr Wallace then added this rider about the use of power driven screw drivers. 'People tend to use these impact wrenches nowadays to save time. What usually happens is that the screw is driven in and then held spinning in its hole, destroying the wood round it and so weakening its holding power. Bronze screws are all right – after all

you use them for the hoodends – but they need careful driving in.'

To make sure that he did not lose the shape of the hull, Ernie Wiegleb worked on 18in wide sections, starting at the bow. He stripped out the frames, drove out the fastenings and cleaned up the planking, removed any butt pads, and plugging the holes left by the spikes. He then gave the whole area a good coating of Cuprinol and bent and clamped the timbers into position. To this end, he cut a series of slots in the planking which was later to be removed. He could then get a proper hold for his clamps.

The frames were steamed for at least two hours, or until they would bend easily. The steam was provided by water, heated in an old oil drum by an equally ancient oil burner. A jig for bending the frames was made on a wide 2in thick oak plank, with 1in diameter steel rods, which were set along a predetermined curve, taken from the old frames. The two ends of the curved timber were held together by a wooden strap.

The midships frames, which were an **S** shape, were made in two pieces, placing their overlapping ends side by side. The reason for making them in two pieces was that the deck was still in position and there was not enough room to bring a full length frame into the boat and then bend it to shape. Also, in the case of an **S** bend, because of the shape of the boat it was impossible to retain the two straps that held each bend in position. When making these frames in two pieces the overlap was about 10ft. One plank at the turn of the bilge and another about two planks above the garboard were removed. This made it possible to clamp the frames into position where the curves were most acute. Where the curves were greatest, a sawcut inside the curve helped to avoid any fractures.

At the stern post, where the curves were very complicated, Ernie Wiegleb laminated stern frames, springing each thin lamination into position and gluing it. In all he fitted sixty-six new frames into *Chrissy* and fastened them with bronze holdfast nails except where he was able to use the old screw holes, when he used Everdur bronze screws. The plank butt pads were also screw fastened.

To strengthen the lapped frames, 4in × 1in bilge stringers were fitted. *Chrissy* originally had only four floors. Mr Wiegleb replaced these with twenty timbers each 1¾in wide and high enough to act as bearers for the cabin sole and cockpit platform. Between these floors 1,200lb of lead ingots were stowed, for *Chrissy* was now to be given an outside lead keel weighing 2,000lb.

When the Morse boatyard replaced the old keel for Mr Wiegleb in 1949, they made it with an outside shoe (of oak) which was 6in thick aft and tapered up to 2in thick forward. The width varied from 10in to 7in. He now calculated the dimensions for a ballast keel, which worked out at 9ft 4in from the forward end aft. He drew the bolts and cut off this length of the shoe. Using this as his guide, he made up a box to fit around it, allowing enough space for shrinkage. The box was made of 2in pine, caulked with asbestos and coated inside with waterglass. He then buried it in the ground to save the need for bracing it. The mould was shaped to give the correct angle of the fore and aft slope to the bottom of the keel. The lead was melted in a pot, which was set up close to the mould, and piped into it. To do this a valve was opened and the lead allowed to run in until the level of the hot metal came up to marks inside the mould.

Though *Chrissy* has 1,000lb less ballast than she had originally, with the lowering of the weight it has proved enough, with her inherently stiff hull form, for the boat to carry all sail, including her topsail, in an eighteen knot breeze.

With the new keel and all frames and floors in position, *Chrissy* was ready for her new planks. These were fastened and dowelled. After planing and sanding, a professional caulker was called in to caulk the garboards and the rest of the seams. He used cotton and a polysulphide seam compound.

Ernie Wiegleb said that he reckoned he had put in over 3,000 fastenings and dowels and also had plugged about 1,500 old nail holes. He filled all the small spaces between floors and frames with Marine Tech, an epoxy compound. The deeper spaces on either side of the stern post and between the horn timbers had been filled in originally with pitch. This had to be chipped out in order to reach the defective frames. Pitch is a good preservative (see *Boadicea* pp 25–46) but Mr Wiegleb could not find anyone in the neighbourhood of Friendship who sold pitch, so, after further discussion with Roy Wallace, he used a special cement called Sakrete at the bow and stern posts and melted down the pitch he had chipped out and used this around the horn timbers.

The next job was to fit new covering boards. For this Ernie Wiegleb used black locust. It is a very strong wood and once it has been cut is not liable to rot. The covering boards were made up from relatively short lengths, cut to the shape of the boat and scarphed together. When the covering boards had been fastened down the deck was planked with narrow planks caulked with cotton and the polysulphide compound.

Finally, the inside of the boat was ceiled, leaving a 1in airspace between ceiling and sheer clamp. After that, it was just a matter of putting back the bulkheads, bunks etc, laying the floorboards and completing the cockpit. This hangs from the carlings, supported by bronze rods and longitudinal stringers. The engine is under the cockpit and is mounted on 2in-square floors.

Ernie Wiegleb rowed me out to *Chrissy* as she lay at her moorings off Pleasant Point, a few miles from Friendship. She looked a handsome old boat. Her dark powder blue topsides were set off by her white decks, cabin trunk and coamings.

'Lots of people think blue is an unlucky colour for a boat', Ernie Wiegleb said. 'One old fisherman refused to come out with me. "Darned if you will ever get me into a blue boat", he roared. He never did come out in her. Never will now. He died last year.'

Chrissy still showed some slight evidence of hogging. 'Morse managed to get some of that out of her in 1949', Mr Wiegleb said as he rowed me round the sloop. As we came up under her fine elliptical transom, her great beam was suddenly evident. I remarked on this and Mr Wiegleb replied, 'About right for east coast boats. We reckon it should be three beams to her overall length, so we've got a few inches in hand.'

Stepping on board gave evidence of her stiffness. She hardly moved as I walked along her side decks. With the mast almost up in the eyes of the boat there was little room on her foredeck, but her long bowsprit took care of her headsails. The staysail was set on a boom that pivoted from halfway along the bowsprit, just above the end of her fiddlehead.

Chrissy was most efficiently laid out on deck with a large Gibb 2-speed winch set amidships for the main sheet, for the anchor cable or for any other purpose. Her sheet winches were all single speed and were made for *Chrissy* by a friend of Mr Wiegleb's in return for his making up a complete set of rigging for a 37ft yawl.

Her deck layout was some way removed from the humble little fisherman she had been for the first thirty years of her existence, yet it did not need much imagination to restore her to that role.

We sat in the cockpit talking about *Chrissy*'s racing successes, then Ernie Wiegleb said, 'You know, these little boats have some basic weaknesses. One was that they were always built of green timber. A second was, at least in *Chrissy*'s case, they had a basically weak structure, with only four floor timbers in her whole length. Also, I have never seen any knees in them.'

'Hanging or lodging knees?' I asked.

'Both', he replied, 'though I think Chapelle shows them in his drawings of a Friendship sloop in his book about small American sailing craft. I must admit that *Chrissy*'s decks were stiffened up with a heavy horizontal shelf into which were driven 12in long $\frac{3}{8}$in galvanized nails. They had all corroded between the planking and the frames or between the frames and the shelf, so the moment these fastening had gone the value of the shelf had gone also. I retained this type of construction only from the stem to the forward heavy cabin beam. Aft of that, I I used bronze rods, threaded each end, horizontally to the frames and bronze bolts were driven vertically through the carlings. The original galvanized 12in nails caused the oak to rot, hence the use of bronze. Bronze rods, threaded in the same manner, were also used along the side decks as tie rods. They were spaced at 18in centres.' He paused as a lobster boat went by, rocking us in its swell. 'Another thing, no ventilation behind the ceiling. Planked right up to the deck.' He moved across the cockpit and lifted up the lid of a hatch over the counter. 'Come and look in here', he said. I peered down at the framing and rudder box. 'That's what Morse called the Friendship sloop's built-in weakness. That rudder box. There is no means that I know of getting at the caulking inside it. Once it goes, you've got a leak with you for ever. When I first had the boat I tried to cure it by lining it with copper and turning over the ends of the copper sheet. It cured the leak, but within a year, as a result of electrolytic action, all the galvanized fastenings near it failed and the back of the boat nearly fell off. Morse put this right in 1949. The bronze rudder shaft is inside a bronze tube bent to a C shape to clear the propeller. All the fastenings are bronze.'

These swingeing criticisms lost most of their sting by the tone of voice in which Ernie Wiegleb expressed them. It was almost as if he was expressing the endearing failings of a beloved mistress.

We rowed ashore. *Chrissy* swung away from us, unmoved by her owner's strictures but obeying the natural laws of wind and tide. She looked good for another half century and perhaps yet another rebuild.

Noank sloop *Emma C. Berry*

LOA 47ft 0in
Beam 14ft 0in
Draught 6ft 0in
Built 1866

The *Emma C. Berry* is afloat at Mystic Seaport. Maynard Bray, the shipyard supervisor, and his team of shipwrights under the direction of Arnold Crossman, have done a superb restoration job on this old fishing boat. The detailed story of the restoration has been told by Willits D. Ansel (*The Restoration of the Smack Emma C. Berry* – see Bibliographical References). Mr Ansel has not only written and illustrated this account, but was also one of those who worked on the Noank sloop. It would be pointless and invidious for me to repeat or even paraphrase all that Will Ansel had to say about the restoration work on the *Berry*, but there are certain points about the boat that he amplified when we were talking together that offer interesting comparisons not only with the Friendship sloops, but also with the English East Coast smack *Boadicea* and the Dutch Zuider-zee fishing botter *MK 63*.

The *Emma C. Berry,* as her lines show, is a handsome vessel; her restoration has triumphantly revealed the beauty of this very old boat. If the *Emma C. Berry* is typical of the Noank sloops, they must rank amongst the most beautiful craft that have ever fished inshore waters.

Noank sloop *Emma C. Berry*.
1 Bow and trail board.
2 Looking forward showing flush gratings over fish well.
3 Looking aft showing access hatch to fish well and companionway.
4 Transom of the *Berry*.

1

2

The *Emma C. Berry* was built over a hundred years ago at Noank, Connecticut, which is some four or five miles downstream from Mystic Seaport, at the mouth of the Mystic river. The Noank sloops fished not only the local waters up to Cape Cod but even worked down the Gulf coast. This particular boat was designed and built by R & J. Palmer though the actual work was subcontracted to James A. Latham. She was designed to be a sloop-rigged well smack and was intended for the mackerel fisheries. These boats were used either for line fishing or trolling. They rarely trawled but did use seine nets. The bulk of their fish was caught by hook and line. The local fish merchants at New London were reluctant to accept the catches from the otterboard trawls, complaining that the fish caught in this manner were often damaged. The line fishermen used to work from the starboard side of the vessel, using a weighted hook called a jig (hence the expression jigging) baited with strips cut from the belly of a mackerel. Behind each fisherman was a barrel into which he dropped his catch. In a good day he might fill a dozen or so barrels. In 1886, the *Emma C. Berry* was converted into a schooner for greater ease of handling. When she was not mackerel fishing, the *Berry* was probably lobster-catching, which, by the time she was launched, had become a

thriving trade. She fished throughout the year. Her wet well would be essential for this work. Being a relatively large smack, and larger than most of the lobster boats, she worked out as far as Martha's Vineyard and beyond these customary grounds to Nantucket Island. She probably also freighted the catches of some of the smaller boats to New London or even to New York.

Emma C. Berry worked her home waters from 1866 to 1894 when she was sold to a fisherman down in Maine. Here she continued in the lobster trade. About 1900 she was fitted with a petrol engine of an unspecified make. She continued to earn her keep but like any wooden built ship she was deteriorating. In 1924 her owner decided her useful days were over and abandoned her on some mudflats near Stonington. A couple of years later, however, a new owner, Mr Milton Beal, discovered her, liked the look of her and considered she was still capable of earning a few dollars as a freight carrier. To this end, her hull was stiffened with several new frames of birch, her wet fish well and perforated planking were removed and she was replanked in the way of the well with cedar.

Seven years later the *Emma C. Berry* was again abandoned, this time because of the Depression, yet once again she was rescued because of her good looks. Her new owner was Mr

3

4

Slade Dale, who bought the old smack for use as a yacht. Mr Dale took the *Berry* south to Virginia where, at a shipyard in Norfolk, she was replanked with white cedar cut from trees in the sadly-named Dismal Swamp. Later she had new masts stepped (she was still sailing as a schooner). At the same time her decks were given new beams and were replanked and some new frames, a new apron and new horn timbers were fitted. The *Emma C. Berry* continued to sail the eastern seaboard until she had reached her hundredth year. Three years later, in 1969, Mr Dale presented her to Mystic Seaport.

By this time, she was really beginning to look her age.

When Arnold Crossman and his small team of shipwrights started work on the *Emma C. Berry*'s restoration, they were faced with a 47ft wooden vessel that was over a hundred years old, had had her rig altered quite early in her career, converting her from a sloop to a schooner, and had undergone at least one if not two major rebuilds. When her masts were taken out of her, her ballast removed, and she had been slipped, it appeared that her stem, stern, keel, outside cedar planking and deck structures were relatively sound, but there was much else that was not. Her keel was hogged by about three inches amidships.

The main objective of the restoration was to restore *Emma C.*

Berry to her original appearance, that is to that of a Noank well smack of the 1860s. The secondary objective was that all work and choice of materials should help towards a long life for the boat rather than faithfully duplicating the materials used in her when first built. In the 1860s economy was an important factor for in those days the Connecticut fishermen were not rich men.

'It was obvious', Maynard Bray said, 'that this restoration would be quite a long job. In fact, it took two years – four times as long as it had taken to build the ship in 1866.'

The *Berry* was chocked up so that her waterline was level and her keel straightened out. To protect both the smack and her restorers from the weather, a temporary shed was built round her. The first job they did on the boat was to strip off the bulwarks, which were in a very poor way. Most of the stanchions and the covering board were rotten. The deck was good in parts though, wherever it was pierced by masts, knightheads or bitts, water had lodged and decay had set in. Practically all the frames were rotten and many of the deck beams had gone at the ends.

The central deckhouse which had been fitted over her enlarged main hatchway had no place in a Noank well smack, so this also was removed.

The restoration of *Emma C. Berry* at
Mystic Seaport. *(Photos courtesy
Mystic Seaport Photographic Library.)*
1 The starboard side bulwarks were
the first to go.
2 Stripping off some of the outer
planking showed that many of the
frames had wasted away.

3 Fitting new frames.
4 Stripping inside lining revealed
further rot in the frames.

Reframing Before the frames and the floors could be examined properly the kelson had to be shifted. The frames in the *Emma C. Berry* were mostly of white oak, though there were the birch frames that had been put in during the 1920s. They were all showing signs of fungal decay, particularly where they abutted the planking. Many of the 4in galvanized steel spikes had corroded right away. Some of the frames were doubled. These were side fastened with galvanized steel bolts which were heavily corroded. These fastenings were clearly not original, for when the *Berry* was built she must have been treenailed and spiked with black iron.

These old frames were removed in much the same way as Michael Frost did in *Boadicea,* by cutting and splitting them, then gently levering them out, taking great care not to draw the fastenings through such planking as they were hoping to preserve. When these fastenings had not corroded away but were stuck fast in the frames, they were cut with a hacksaw and then driven out through the planking. The holes were plugged and dowelled, the dowels being set in epoxy resin.

The original frames were either fashioned from large grown oak crooks or they were steam bent. Such grown oak crooks today could not be found in the neighbourhood of Mystic, so composite frames were made up from straight grained white oak. For ease of working, these were doubled from two 2$\frac{3}{4}$in planks, making a width of 5$\frac{1}{2}$in which was the width of the original frames. Each half of the frame was cut from three pieces scarphed together. By using a stretched line from the top of each frame to its partner on the opposite side of the boat and dropping a plumb line from the centre, the exact position of each frame was established. From these points (on the keel and at deck level), a batten was then pinned to the inside of the planking and the position of the centre line of the frames was chalked in. As the new frames were to be doubled this chalk line provided the line where they were abutted. Patterns from thin sheets of cedar were then scribed in the normal manner for both the insides and the outsides of the double frames. The cutting of any bevel was made relatively easy by setting the bandsaw table to whatever angle the bevel gauge suggested. Then, as in *Boadicea,* it was a matter of offering up. The planking against which it was to lie was heavily chalked and only when chalk rubbed off on the whole face of the frame was it ready for final cutting on its opposite face, to give it a moulded depth of 4$\frac{1}{2}$in (see *Boadicea* p 30).

Protection against rot When the frame was finally complete, it was taken out and a hole bored into the grain at the top, where it came up against the covering board. A 6in hole with a $\frac{1}{2}$in diameter was drilled, filled up with linseed oil, and then plugged. The theory (and it is an old if not proven one) is that the oil slowly seeps down through the grain of the wood and prevents rot. All the other surfaces were coated with Cuprinol. One would have thought that this pentachlorophenol preservative, instead of the linseed oil, would have been more usefully poured into the little reservoir.

The frames were clamped into position. Holes were drilled through the planking into the frames for 3$\frac{1}{2}$in no 16 bronze screws which were countersunk and dowelled. To speed up all this screwing, an electric impact screwdriver was used. The frames were bolted together with $\frac{3}{8}$in bronze carriage screws. Where frames came up against floors, they were side-bolted.

The floors Six of the floors in the *Emma C. Berry* were sound enough to be left in position but eight needed replacing. The new ones were cut from relatively small grown crooks of either hackmatack or white oak. The floors had been fastened to the keel with iron drift bolts which had corroded away to nothing. The decayed floors were removed and the iron drift bolts in the keel were drilled out to a depth of about six inches and the holes plugged with cedar set in epoxy resin. Likewise the iron spikes in the planking were driven out and the holes plugged. Patterns were fitted and made and the most appropriate crooks were cut to approximate size. They were offered up in the same manner as the frames and finally shaped to an exact fit. They were then side-bolted to the adjacent frames and each bolted to the keel with 12in × $\frac{3}{4}$in bronze bolts. The head of the bolt was countersunk so that the bolthead was below the level of the top of the floor. Where the kelson was resting on the floors, the keel bolt pierced the kelson as well as the floors.

Stem The stem post was sound but the apron had decayed extensively and was replaced by a large crook of white oak.

Kelson The forward 6ft of the kelson had been replaced some time previously. The mast step rested on this. Both the mast step and the end of the kelson had decayed, causing undue pressure on the keel at this point. This had been the cause of badly leaking garboards.

The remainder of the kelson, which may have been original, had of course been removed before the old frames and floors had been ripped out. When the new frames and floors were fitted, the kelson was replaced and through-bolted to the keel.

A new 7ft length of 5in × 14in oak was cut to overlap the old kelson and the new apron inside the stem. It was then through-bolted to the keel making a very strong assembly. The mast step, of white oak, was fastened down with coach screws to the new part of the kelson. It was laid in white lead and, like all these timbers, liberally coated with Cuprinol.

The shelf In British boatbuilding yards they call it 'the shelf' and on the north-east coast of the USA they call it 'the sheer

5

6

5 The frames were made up of short
  lengths of white oak and doubled.
6 Laying the deck.
7 New timber to support mast step
  scarphed into kelson.
8 New hackmatack floors were fitted.

clamp', which is a more sensible name. Either way it is a heavy plank, comparable to a gunwale in an open boat, that runs from stem to transom and supports the deck beams. It is fastened to the frames. For some odd reason the *Emma C. Berry* had no shelf. She did however have a horizontal 2in × 8in plank bolted to the deck beams opposite to the chain plates and her ceiling was much heavier than usual. It was of 2in cedar planks, spiked to the frames, and with caulked seams. It had to come out so that the shipwrights could get at the rotten timbers that lay behind it.

New shelves were put in as soon as the *Berry* had been re-framed. The shipwrights again turned to a restoration expedient by doubling up two thicknesses of 1in longleaf pine because, of course, it was much easier to bend a thinner plank. These planks were 8in wide from the bow to two-thirds of the distance aft, then fining off to 5in wide. They were not steamed or shaped but sprung into position with wedges, which were driven between the bottom of the shelf and a block of wood clamped to a frame. By the same method, but clamping the blocks to the deck beams, they drove the shelf hard up against the frames. When the inner thickness of the shelf had been fastened it was doubled up in the same manner with staggered butts, the inner layer being first Cuprinoled and then painted with red lead.

The ceiling was fitted next, leaving a 1in gap below the shelf for ventilation. It was of 1in southern cedar and caulked with cotton in the seams and at the butts. The top three planks were sprung into position but, with the changing shape of the hull, the remainder had to be spiled and shaped. The shelf and ceiling were then given a coat of varnish. The hull planking and the ceiling were fastened to the frames with no 16 bronze screws, countersunk and dowelled. This may not be the best shipbuilding practice but it was done for two reasons. One was for the lasting qualities of bronze, the other for the relative ease of unscrewing rather than having to draw out an iron spike or drill out a treenail, or cut and draw out riveted copper nails, let alone the impossibility of drawing holdfast nails. Michael Frost's solution of monel metal nails for the *Boadicea* would certainly be longer lasting but was probably more expensive.

Before fitting the covering board, new pieces had to be scarphed into the ends of all the deck beams. The new covering board was sawn to the shape of the hull from a number of lengths of 2in longleaf pine. These were fastened to the deck beams at each joint. Long cedar plugs called stopwaters were driven into these joints. They were of $\frac{1}{2}$in diameter and were used also in all scarphed joints. The making of these stopwaters, as described by Will Ansel, is of interest. He writes that they must be a tight driving fit. The drill used for boring through the seam is also used to make a die from a piece of hardwood, such as seasoned oak. After shaping, the stopwater is driven through the die which smooths and rounds it. It is then ready to be driven home along the seam or scarph.

The *Emma C. Berry* had seventeen stanchions on each side. These all had to be renewed. The new ones were made of 3in × 4in teak, tapering at the rail to $2\frac{3}{4}$in. They pierce the covering board and project downwards some 20in. They are not caulked but (again like *Boadicea*) have wooden wedges of pitch pine or cedar driven home on each side and cut off flush with the top surface of the covering board. These stanchions are about thirty inches apart and are screwed to the planking, the screws being driven in from the outside. They are thus easy to remove, and though teak was never used in the east coast fishing boat construction it was used in the reconstruction to give the stanchions a long life.

The bulwarks were planked in cedar, three planks of $3\frac{1}{2}$in width to each side, the lowest being $1\frac{1}{4}$in thick, the upper two 1in thick. The planks were capped by a rail of yellow pine $1\frac{1}{2}$in thick and $5\frac{1}{4}$in wide. This was sawn to shape and given beaded edges. The rail was screwed to the top of the stanchions and also to the top plank of the bulwark. The taffrail was two planks wide, sawn to shape with lodging knees at either quarter.

The new kingplank down the centre of the foredeck was made up of two wide planks of 2in yellow pine. A $13\frac{1}{2}$in diameter hole was cut in these for the mast. The kingplank was penetrated also by the samson (pawl) post, which was of longleaf yellow pine, 5in × 8in at deck level tapering down to the foot which rests on the apron and is side-bolted to a floor and to a deck beam by means of bronze bolts. The seams at the deck are caulked in the usual manner. The after end of the bowsprit is mortised into the samson post, just clear of the deck, so that water will not lodge there. Its top is capped with sheet lead. The same kind of capping is used for the windlass bitts and the mooring bitts aft.

The samson post carries the pawl for the windlass which is set just aft of it. The windlass drum is supported by the bitts. These are of $2\frac{1}{2}$in yellow pine, tenoned into the kingplank and pierced and locked below deck by pine treenails. Hackmatack knees, bracing the forward side of the bitts, take some of the forward strain when breaking out the anchor. Shaped pieces on the after side take any strain in the opposite direction. These are fastened down with coach screws to the kingplank and to a deck beam below.

The aft mooring bitts (or bollards) are of teak and are pierced fore and aft with oak pins to prevent lines from slipping off. Below decks they are stepped on a thick hardwood pad which is fastened to two frames with coach screws. The bitts are also through-bolted to a deck beam forward of them and to short false beams aft.

The fish well The perforated planking and fish well had been removed from the *Berry* nearly fifty years ago. However, after talking to Mr Milton Beal who had owned her in the 1920s, and with additional advice from Howard Chapelle, the well was re-constructed. It is quite unlike the botter's fish well (see p 59). Its sides slope inwards up to the deck, and the deck opening has no coamings so that the fish can be shovelled in without any ledge in the way. The fish well is about 7ft square at the base and 3ft square at the deck. The boat's planking would be perforated to admit the sea which of course fills to the level of the waterline.

When *Emma C. Berry* was converted for general cargo, her well had been taken out and the hatchway increased in size. In the restoration this was reduced to the original size and the fish well was rebuilt. Considerable care was needed to make it watertight, with wedges, caulking and cedar stopwaters in all seams. The well was framed with heavy square oak timbers and planked with baulks of pine, caulked on the inside. These timbers were drift-bolted to each other and to the corner post. As the *Berry* was never actually going fishing again, it was thought that a single hole would be enough to fill the well. Whenever they wanted to get at the inside of the well, for re-caulking it etc, a bung could be put in the hole and the well pumped dry.

Apart from the one over the fish well the *Berry's* existing deckhouses were used, but as a result of the memories of Mr Beal a small access hatch was constructed just aft of the fish well. A flush grating covered the well.

Finally, the smack had to be painted. Her colour scheme is based on the records and memories of Noank fishermen. Her topsides are painted a deep forest green which was and still is common in New England for fishing vessels. Her rail is also the same dark green. Her bulwarks are black on the outside with a yellow bead separating them from the sheer strake. This yellow line, a vestigial reminder of the gold leaf that ships of the line once used, runs out along the top of the trailboards to the billethead. There is no boot topping, the dark green reaching to the waterline. Below the waterline the *Emma C. Berry* is painted with red copper anti-fouling as was the inside of the fish well. On the green transom her name and port of registry are painted yellow and the nameboards are outlined in yellow.

On deck, the inside of the bulwarks, the covering boards, the bitts, samson post, hatches, tops of the wheel box, deck house and companionway are grey, but the hatch coamings and sides of the other deck structures are forest green. The deck is treated with the boiled linseed oil-turpentine-Stockholm tar mixture. Most of the ironwork is black. The bowsprit inboard is black and white from the billethead outwards. The mast is treated with boiled linseed oil and turpentine and painted white from the crosstrees to the mast cap. The topmast is painted white.

The *Emma C. Berry* was put back in the water on 7 May 1971. The only work still to be done was below decks. This included the completion of the fish well, the ceiling and the bulkheads. She had also to be ballasted and her mast stepped.

The smack hardly made any water but she floated high until 7¼ tons of lead ingots were stowed in her bilges. The mast with standing rigging was then stepped with the help of a steam crane and wedged into position. The shrouds and forestays were set up and her standing and running rigging was completed. (Mr Ansel has two most informative chapters in his book about the making of the spars and the rigging for the *Emma C. Berry*.)

Externally, the restoration of the *Emma C. Berry* was complete. The crowds at Mystic Seaport may flock to look at the classic nineteenth century whaler *Charles W. Morgan*, or the *Joseph Conrad* which is the little full rigged ship that Alan Villiers sailed round the world, or the Banks fishing schooner *L. A. Dunton*. They can have them. The two small fishing vessels the *Emma C. Berry* and the *Estella A* are the ones for me, though the beamy little Long Island Sound oyster sloop *Nellie* is worthy of their company.

Inshore boats:

Winkle brigs, Shetland boats, gun punts

Winkle brig is a name given to a small open sailing boat of a type used on the rivers Colne and Blackwater in Essex for tending the oyster smacks and for collecting cockles and winkles. Charles Harker, who sailed these rivers, said of these little boats: 'A brig should be gaff rigged and not gunter rigged and should set a foresail on a short steel bumkin. There seems to have been some variety in hull forms, but I think the true brig is probably very beamy, flat in the floor and built with two or three grown oak frames (about 2in sided) on each side of the boat, to strengthen the hull which was otherwise steam-timbered. The oyster men probably picked up old barge boats, rigged them with this almost universal rig and then used them to potter about the oyster layings.'

The winkle brigs were obviously general purpose workboats and there are still several of them sailing round the Essex rivers. Anyone who saw the film of Paul Gallico's *The Snow Goose* will remember the little sailing boat in which the character played by Richard Harris went off to Dunkirk. It was actually Janet Harker's winkle brig *Joy*, which began life as an oversize barge boat, 15ft long. The normal barge boat was 14ft overall.

These little winkle brigs are the antithesis of the modern sailing dinghies, which are designed to plane downwind or to sail close to the wind and need sitting out to keep them upright. Designed and rigged as they are, such dinghies are useless as workboats. This factor was brought home to me by Ruari McLean who keeps a little Shetland boat at Carsaig on the

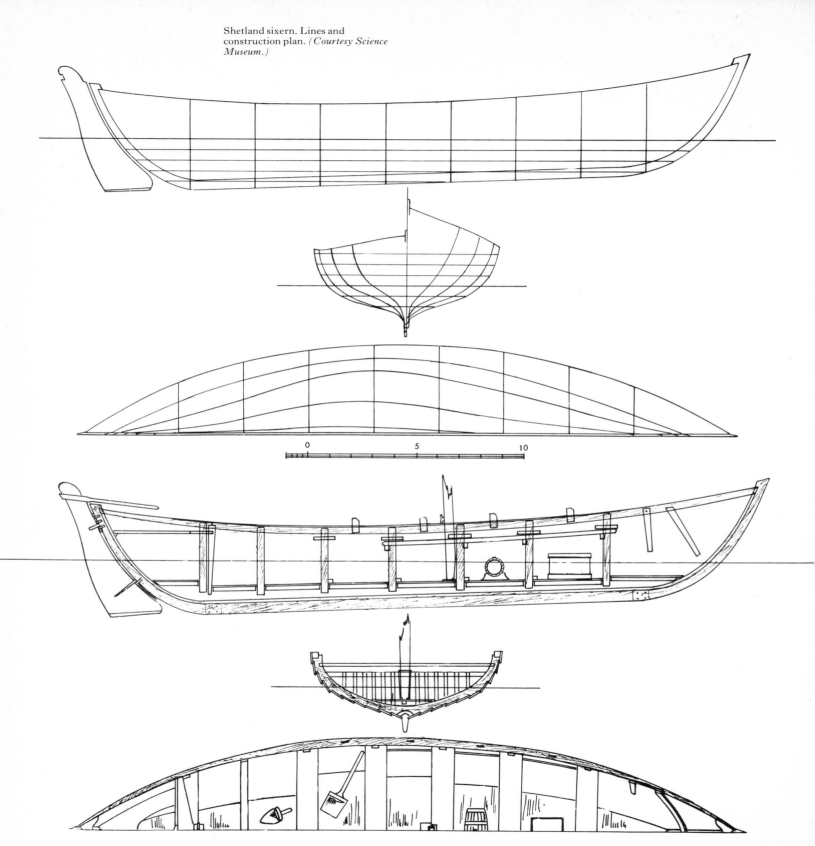

Shetland sixern. Lines and
construction plan. *(Courtesy Science
Museum.)*

Shetland Sixern. LOA 37ft 0in, built
at Lerwick in the Shetland Islands
(as was this beautiful model).
Double-ended, clinker-built of
Norwegian fir, and iron fastened.
(Photo Science Museum.)

Shetland foureen. LOA 14ft 0in.
Sail plan of lug sail for use when
handling lobster traps.

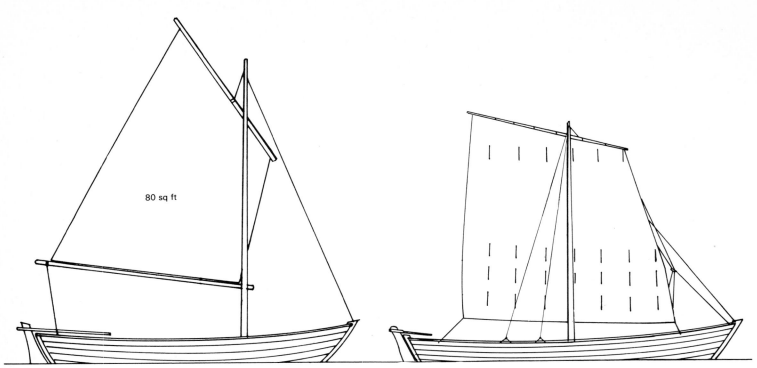

80 sq ft

island of Mull. This traditionally designed hull, 16ft long, was built by J. A. Sutherland, boatbuilder at Lerwick. It is smaller than a 'sixern' and might be called a 'foureen', that is, a four-oared boat. She is fitted with a high peaked gunter lugsail and a foresail. Ruari has a few lobster pots at Carsaig which he needs to tend from the boat and he found her sail plan quite unmanageable for his purpose. After some discussion I drew out a standing lugsail for him. Taylor's at Maldon, after a further modification, made the sail for him. The transformation of this tippy and, at least for these purposes, unhandy little boat was extraordinary. She now became quite docile and, as the helmsman had only one sheet to tend, very easy to handle as well. She was reverting to type and doing the kind of traditional work for which her type of boat was built.

The sixern was the forerunner of this design. It was a six-oared yawl made at Lerwick in the Shetlands. They were used for long line fishing and also for net fishing, when the net was pulled in over a 'hailing kabe' or mongoggle stepped in the gunwale. They were double-ended boats built of Norwegian fir and iron fastened. The mast was stepped just forward of amidships and carried a large dipping lug with four rows of reef points. Foureens were built for inshore fishing.

Emma Goody, a miniature bawley

It was during the winter of 1968 that two young men of Essex, Stephen Swann and Paul Rogers, set about finding a traditional small sailing boat for trawling on the Blackwater and Colne estuaries. This was to be the first stage of a love affair with traditional fishing craft that led to their fine reconstruction of the Thames bawley *Bona* (see p 51).

At this stage in their careers their financial resources were very limited, so all they could hope for was to find an old clench-built hull of traditional form that was going cheap. After some searching, they found at Maldon in Essex a bruised and battered old CB boat lying upside down on a concrete ramp. It looked a poor thing and had grass growing in the lands of the planking and daylight showing through the topsides. As Stephen later remarked, 'She looked more like a window box than a boat.' Her owner gladly parted with her for £25. She had one thing in her favour and that was she was the right shape for their purpose; broad beamed and transom sterned, she was a good traditional boat.

It was quite clear that in her opened-up condition she was not seaworthy, so they did the sensible thing and allowed her to fill up with water and to sink in a shallow spot. They left her to soak and then about a week later raised her, pumped her out and set out to row from Maldon to Brightlingsea, which is a very long row. They arrived there fourteen hours later, tired from both rowing and bailing.

They moved the hull to a dry shed and after allowing it to dry out burnt off every morsel of paint and sandpapered the hull smooth. They then gave the whole hull a coat of raw linseed oil. The hull needed some caulking, for which they used Sealastic, and one crack had to have a plywood tingle. After that they primed and painted the boat, giving her grey topsides, a

Winkle brig *Emma Goody*, showing loose-footed mainsail, stepped topmast and topsail.

Winkle brig *Joy*. Janet Harker taking
Richard Harris on a trial sail during the
making of the film *The Snow Goose*.
(*Photo Essex County Newspapers.*)

black wale, a white rubbing strake and boot topping, and a blue transom. Below the waterline she was brick red.

The rig and sail plan were based on that of the old Peter boats that were used on the Thames during the nineteenth century for shrimping and spratting. This sail plan gave her two head-sails, a loose-footed gaff sail and a topsail set on a topmast that could be housed when it came on to blow. It was basically the bawley rig, for it was clear in which direction their thoughts lay. They were in fact producing a miniature bawley.

They bought two scaffold poles for their mast and bowsprit and another pine pole for the gaff. The mast step, as it was in the boat when they bought her, was too far forward, so they made a new step by making a one inch high box on the thwart at the fore end of the CB case. The foot of the mast was tenoned into this thwart and rested inside the box. The thwart was reinforced by 4in × 2in posts stepped on the forward end of the CB case.

The original hull was completely open, so fore deck and after deck were put in, supported on oak beams rounded on the top. The decks were then planked in tongue and groove pine. Oak bitts 2in × 2in were fitted through the foredeck to the kelson, with lodging knees on the deck. They were also through-bolted to one of the deck beams.

The spars were stepped and, nicely varnished, look handsome. Both Stephen Swann and Paul Rogers had spent a lot of time working on smacks and barges and had worked also as riggers of those craft. After such experience the rigging of this little bawley was a simple task.

They took their sail plan to Mr Taylor of Maldon, who had a lifetime's experience of making sails for the east coast smacks and barges. He entered into the fun of the thing and made a pretty set of canvas sails for them for a mere £50. The main and staysail were tanned in the traditional colour but using a modern preservative called Kanvo. The mainsail ran up the mast on metal mast hoops, bound against chafe with codline. Vangs were fitted to her gaff, though when set up they tended to drag down the end of the gaff and so spoil the set of the sail. They later found the same problem with *Bona*, their full sized bawley. Up to this stage, the restoration and rigging of this little craft including the price of the sails had cost only about £110 and this included the purchase price.

The little boat's gear was completed with anchor, cable, sweeps, a vertical bilge pump and a 6ft beam trawl. All that was now left for them to do was to find her a name and then to try her out. As for naming, such workboats were often called after the fisherman's wife, but as neither Stephen nor Paul were wed they had to look elsewhere and finally picked a name off a tomb-stone in Lexden churchyard. The name was *Emma Goody* and it suited the boat. I will leave Stephen Swann to describe *Emma Goody*'s first sail out to the fishing grounds:

'Our net and trawling gear was shipped and early one July morning we set all sail and raced out to the grounds. *Emma Goody* (with her official registration number CK 48 showing proudly on her mainsail) was fishing under sail alone with no aid at all from any mechanical device. She was an anachron-istic link in a tradition that went back many hundreds of years.

'With the Inner Bench astern we put *Emma Goody* before the wind under easy sail and shot the trawl. She slowed until she was just sailing faster than the tide and with her helm lashed she would sail herself.

'We had reckoned on leaving the net down for half an hour, but curiosity soon got the better of us. The suspense was killing and after about twenty minutes we hauled our net.

'It's bloody heavy, I thought, as Paul and I heaved it alongside. The cod end was opened and the contents slid into the bottom of the boat. About a thousand crabs, half a ton of jellyfish and assorted weed was all that we had caught. Still cleaning up, we sailed to the Bench Head, shot the net and began to trawl into the Blackwater. This time we kept the net down for exactly half an hour.

'The wind was piping up and a nasty little sea was running; *Emma Goody*, lying to her net, rode it like a gull. We were under half the mainsail and the jib.

'Again we hauled our net, a tricky operation with this sea running, our efforts were rewarded. Three prime soles, a plaice and a small skate had been caught by a boat towing a beam trawl under sail.'

One of the reasons for including this description of the miniature bawley is to give an indication of some of the attitudes that are part of the boat restoration idea. In this case, Stephen Swann and Paul Rogers wanted to recapture the feeling of working a trawl under a traditional sailing rig that was uniquely effective for such a purpose. The loose-footed mainsail for instance was almost an essential in a small fishing boat, to allow for adequate space for handling the trawl.

They proved their point and within a couple of years, in collaboration with two other friends, they were putting this exercise into full scale effect by acquiring and restoring the bawley *Bona* to full working trim.

Gun punts

There is more than one way of researching any problem. In the matter of the restoration or the building of replicas of old boats, one may be able to refer to published plans and other printed information. This would certainly apply to many old yachts but the approach may not serve so well for small, local types of work boat, for instance the duck punt or gun punt, which as its

Colonel Hawker's gun punt, LOA
21ft 4in. Engraving from *Instructions
to Young Sportsmen in all that
Relates to Guns and Shooting* (1838).

Solid stem piece, to close front of punt, and elevate gun for rough weather, or shooting over mud.

Circular stick, to keep down butt of gun, in rough weather.

Trap-hatch, to ship and unship, for sculling or setting. But for one who can *paddle*, the places for the two trap-hatches should be cut nearly amidships, instead of aft.

DIMENSIONS OF PUNT

	Feet	Inches		Feet	Inches
Length, from stem to stern . . .	21	4	Height, a'stern	0	11
Ditto, at bottom. . . .	20	6	Height of bulwarks, forward .	0	4
Width, at gunwale . . .	3	8	Ditto, aft, gradually declining to	0	2
Ditto, at bottom. . . .	3	0	Gradual rise of decks to bulwarks	0	2
Spring, fore and aft . . .	0	1½			
Kammel	0	1	Bottom, ½ in. plank; sides ⅜ in.; all to be made of		
Height, at bow	0	6	oak, except decks of withey or Norway deal.		

name implies is used for wildfowling. These little boats varied in design from builder to builder, river to river and country to country. The first printed description that I know of a gun punt is in Lt-Colonel Peter Hawker's famous book *Instructions to Young Sportsmen in All That Relates to Guns and Shooting*, first published in 1830. It ran quickly through seven editions; an eighth edition, enlarged and illustrated, was published in 1838. In this edition Hawker describes in some detail the characteristics of what he considers to be the ideal punt. I referred to this book more than once when I had my punt built, but the hard core of my research was done in many hours of conversation with three Manningtree wildfowlers, the two Porter brothers, Lun, Bill who actually built my punt, and their Uncle Dod Porter, who was not only a very experienced punt gunner but also knew much about the use of all kinds of firearms.

The main reason for building this punt was to follow stage by stage the methods these wildfowlers used in building their craft, so this is neither a restoration or a replica but the last example of a traditional punt built by the Porters, for both brothers and their uncle are now dead.

On the banks of the river Stour, as on many other Essex, Suffolk and Norfolk rivers, for centuries past men have been building punts to enable them to fill their pots in wintertime by wildfowling and in summer by line fishing and babbing for eels. Simple methods were used to construct these able little craft (they had to be able, for on great open estuaries like the Stour and the Blackwater vicious seas can be whipped up all too quickly). The methods of building these punts were handed down from father to son, none of whom were known as boatbuilders. The Porters and the Lucas's at Manningtree, and many others elsewhere earned their living as fishermen and as wildfowlers and maybe a few other things as well. The duck punt was a necessary part of their livelihood and, of necessity, they built it themselves.

Manningtree gun punt, LOA
20ft 0in, built by Joe Lucas in 1971.

For anyone unfamiliar with wildfowling, perhaps I should explain that the fowler when stalking his prey at night lies on his stomach with his legs extended and propels himself along in this uncomfortable position with small ash paddles which are little more than extensions of his hands. When within seventy or eighty yards of the duck he will sight his gun, give a smart rap with the toe of his boot on the floor boards and, as the startled fowl rise off the water, he will let fly with his six or seven ounces of shot. If he is lucky he may kill as many as a dozen birds, though an average shot will only bring down three or four. For travelling to and fro to the feeding grounds the fowler rows his punt using six foot spruce oars and sitting on a low, flat stool.

The form of duck punts varies on the different English rivers and is in marked contrast to the boxlike scows used in America for punt gunning. Some English punts are completely open, others more or less decked in. The Stour punts have more decking on them than any other variety that I have seen. The punts built by the Porters and the Lucas family at Manningtree were beautiful craft, long and slim, low on the water and as buoyant as can be, with the slightest suggestion of reversed sheer.

A duck punt is a lovely craft to row. What is usually an irksome business in a yacht's tender becomes a major pleasure in one of these long, well balanced skiffs. These little craft can also be fitted with a sail, usually set on a sprit. With an oar as a combined rudder and drop keel, they can be sailed well if you know how to handle them. They are very fast off the wind.

Though duck punts are intended primarily for wildfowling they make a useful and weatherly craft for general use on rivers and estuaries. In a winter some twenty years ago I had a duck punt built for me for just such a purpose. When building a punt there are a number of factors that should be considered if it is going to be used for its proper purpose of wildfowling. There are indeed as many factors as a gunmaker such as Purdey has to

95

Open Blackwater punt with shooter
paddling with short weighted
paddles.

consider when building a pair of twelve bores for a Texas oil
king or any other rich man who wishes to make an impression
on the Scottish grouse moors.

The first thing to be considered when building a punt is the
gun. Dod Porter said about this 'I don't recommend too heavy
a gun. You can buy guns that will fire half a pound of shot or
over, but you will find them spiteful. From using such big guns,
I have seen fellows with broken collar bones and busted jaws.
No, I prefer a lighter gun, about six foot six inches on the barrel
and firing no more than seven ounces of shot. As to whether
they are breech loading or muzzle loading, that's a matter for
the gunner to decide. If his pocket isn't very deep, he'll get
himself a muzzle loader. The old muzzle loaders only take
about two and a half minutes to reload and that is plenty quick
enough, for after your first shot you will have quite a wait before
the duck settle on the water again and you can get near enough
for another shot.' Mr Porter had much more to say in the same

vein, ending up with the remark that muzzle loading punt guns
could still be picked up for a song.

Having decided on the gun, the next consideration was the
weight of the fowler and after that the length of the fowler's
arms, for this span governs the width of the boat. After some
deliberation, I and Bill Porter, who was building the punt,
decided on the dimensions shown in the plan as being suitable
for me or for any other eleven stone man who was 5ft 10½in tall
with an armspan of 5ft 6in. Having got this far, I turned to
Colonel Hawker's book to see what he had to say about punts.
He began his observations by saying:

'All gunning punts should be as flat as possible in the
bottom (except having the necessary 'kammelling' (rise in
beam) to give them life; by which they draw far less water,
and are so stiff, that it becomes impossible to capsize them.
The most destructive gunning punt for *one* hand that I had

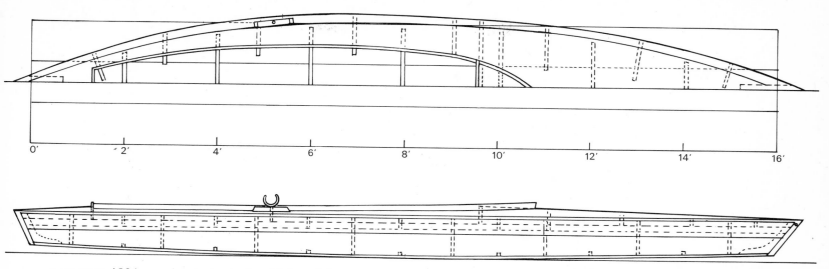

Construction plans of 16ft gun punt designed by W. G. Porter of Manningtree in 1951.

0' 2' 4' 6' 8' 10' 12' 14' 16'

seen up to 1824 was about nine inches high and drew scarcely two inches of water, with a man and his gun. This punt should be full three feet broad, from about a yard before the stern, decked all the way from the gunning bench to the bow; and so sharp forward that when required the bow may be shoved for several feet up the edge of the ground.'

Colonel Hawker continues:

'There is not a boat builder in a thousand who knows anything about punts, as the best gunners generally make their own and keep the secret to themselves. The best way, therefore, is to get an able gunner to find *head*, and a good inland carpenter to find *hand and tools*. I could never get a punt that would answer until I did this.'

Hawker designed and had built various punts which he claimed were more seaworthy than other contemporary ones, for they had more beam and more 'flam' (by which he must have meant 'flare'). One of his punts was highly commended by Sir William Symonds RN, the great naval architect and Surveyor to the Navy. Hawker says of this punt:

'She must be decked over in every part, excepting just room enough for the shooter to lie to his gun, and the man to work the birds . . . The deck should be the lightest possible board, and covered all over with strong canvas; which helps to strengthen it, and renders it doubly waterproof. The only parts of the deck requiring strong support are the front, where a man has to stand, if he loads the gun afloat; and the place where is fixed on the light metal tholes (rowlocks). The space left open must be surrounded with bulwarks.

'This punt should be rounded athwartships about an inch and sprung fore and aft at least three inches. Mine is about

four, by which she has more life in a sea, and I put on a little wooden shoe, just under her bow, which holds her steady when you run her nose aground and saves her from rubbing when landing on a gravelly shore. I have of course a defense of thin sheet copper.

'Except for a few little cross-pieces of well-seasoned oak, each floor and timber should be formed all in one, with a piece of tough hoop ash which must be well boiled in a large copper, or steamed over a fire in a wooden funnel . . . the sides must of course be filled up with angle-pieces, where sides and bottom meet.

'Light bottom boards are of course required, in order to protect the timbers etc. The sides, amidships on this plan, being so very low may be "flammed" out as much as you please; because they are not more than two or three inches above the water. About eight inches above the surface of the water is the best height for the gun, in dark nights, or in a dead calm; but in rough water, the higher the gun is fired, the more birds you will kill.'

Colonel Hawker concludes his remarks by discussing at length a spring recoil for a stanchion-mounted gun, but says in reference to punts in general that rope breechings are 'now adopted by all launches in the new school'. There is much else of interest in this utterly fascinating book.

Building a wildfowling punt

We built our punt in an old stable near the water at Manningtree. We had two 3ft wide trestles, each 2ft 3in high, and a building horse which was made from a 2in plank placed on edge, 18in long and 9in high. We started with the bottom planking. We took three white wood bottom planks for the punt.

Gun Punt
Stemhead is made from a grown crook with rebates for both side and bottom planking.
Knees are made from grown crooks with a waterway at the chine and a notch cut in the top for the gunwale.

Knees at stem and stern are toed in (and not at right angles to the centre line).

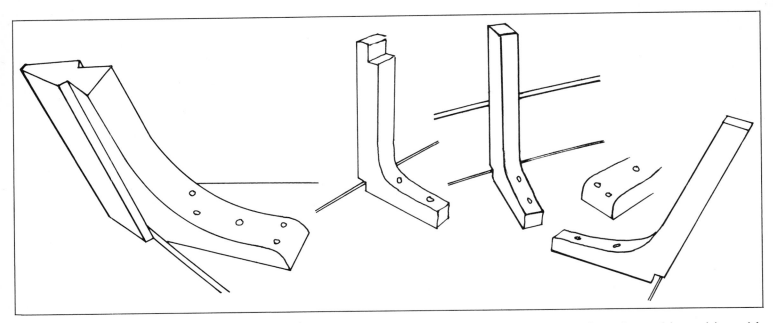

These were each 16in long, 1in thick and 11in wide before planing. These were laid flat on the trestles with the edges butting cleanly. Timber can be saved by projecting the middle plank a foot or so beyond the outer ones. This spare timber can be used for bearers etc and bottom boards. Temporary straps were next fitted across these three planks, the planks being first tightly cramped together with two large sash cramps. If these are not available, one can use a Spanish windlass. Before the straps were fixed, the centreline of the boat was marked in chalk. This can most easily be done by stretching a line between two nails, chalking it, and then flicking it. This line was then ruled in by pencil against a straight edge. Next, we marked in 2ft stations, starting from the centre and at right angles to the centre line. Working from our plan, we marked off the widths of the bottom at each station, then took a long straight edged spline of about 18ft in length and clamped it into position. When the curve of this looked fair, we drew in the outline of the bottom. We had to use tacks where the clamps would not hold. This procedure we repeated on the opposite side and then sawed the bottom to shape, cutting the wood clear of the outline for final fairing up with a plane.

After the bottom planks were faired up, the floor timbers were prepared. These were cut from 1in oak plank, 12in wide and 36in long. The widest floors (ie those amidships) were given a $\frac{5}{8}$in rocker (rounding) and the other floors were rounded in proportion. When the floors had been cut the midship floor was fitted over the centre station. Both the underside of the floor and the bottom planks, where the floor abuts, were given a thick

coat of white paint. They were then clamped in position with G-cramps. We drilled through the floor and the planks, working from the centre outwards, using a $\frac{1}{8}$in drill, and fastened up from underneath using $2\frac{1}{4}$in copper nails and a 7lb weight for steadying.

To fair up the floor, we gave it a $1\frac{3}{4}$in flare amidships in a perpendicular height of 11in. Using a bevel plane, we planed the sides of the bottom to the correct angle to match the flare on the first floor. We then cut the ends of the floors off $\frac{5}{8}$in short of the side of the boat to allow for waterways. This completed the bottom of the boat.

Stem and stern posts The stem and stern were cut from a $2\frac{1}{2}$in thick grown oak crook, having already marked the rabbet line on this. We then cut out the toe, fitted it into position, and marked on the underside the angle of the rabbet. This was taken from the angle of the punt's bottom planks. We marked in the same angle at the top then saw cut down the rabbet lines to meet these angles. We used a rabbeting plane and planed down to the angle lines. Finally, we squared up and cleaned off with sand paper. At the stem the perpendicular height was $8\frac{1}{2}$in and the rake from the vertical $7\frac{1}{2}$in.

The knees The knees for our punt were cut from grown oak crooks 1in thick. There were eight knees a side, so in all sixteen knees had to be cut. They were $1\frac{3}{4}$in wide and 11in in height. We used grown crooks, but if they are not available the alternative is to laminate or to use marine plywood. The knees were

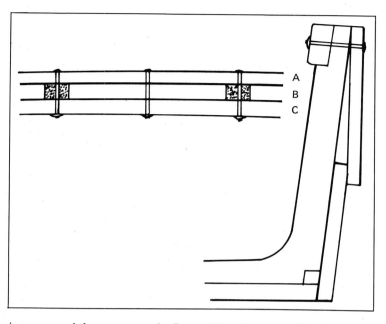

Section and plan of gunwale.
A Planking.
B Timberheads.
C Gunwale.

interspaced between each floor. The knees amidships were almost vertical; forward they had much more flare; aft only a little more.

Stem and stern knees The stem and stern knees were then put into position and fastened. We laid a line across the top of the stem and stern knees and down the length of the punt to make sure that they were in line. When lined up, they were nailed and rooved into position (or the nails could have been clenched). We drilled fastening holes before fitting the knees. When positioned, we clamped with G-cramps and marked the exact position. We then removed them and painted the bottom liberally with white lead, painting also the bottom plank on to which it abutted. We then put them back on the marks, checked for position, and clamped down. Finally, we drilled through and then drove the nails up from underneath.

Planking the sides of the punt We next lifted the punt on to the building horse. She had a 2½in spring or rise at either end. We marked the centre of the horse and put the centre of the boat over it, placing a 2½in chock at either end, 8ft from the centre line; the chocks were no wider than the horse and were nailed down on to it. The bottom of the boat was screwed down on to the horse, one screw at 1ft aft of the centre and the second screw 2ft forward of the centre. We slid the trestles underneath so that we had a firm platform on which to work.

Elm was used for the bottom strakes and white pine for the top strakes. The strakes were ½in thick and, as we could not get planks for the full length of the boat, they were about 9ft long and 8in wide and scarph jointed. The aft starboard side bottom strake was temporarily fastened in position and the curve of the bottom scribed along it. It was then removed and the profile of the bottom cut to shape. The top edge was marked in a straight line from 5¾in high at the stern to 7in high amidships. It was then offered up again and we marked in the bevel at the stern post. The plank was cut to this line and reclamped at the stern and bent round the midship timber, which was held in position by a heavy weight resting on its toe. It was then clamped at its forward end. To hold these bottom planks in position sash cramps are best used, stretching to the other side of the boat. The top of the plank was then lined up on the midship and stern post markings (7in high amidships and 5¾in at the stern), making sure that the plank reached the ends of the bottom planks and that it covered the edge of the bottom planking of the boat. We then trued up the bevel at the end of the plank. This is most easily done by taking a pair of dividers or a compass and running the one point down the line of the bevel on the stern post and at the same time making a parallel line by the other point on the edge of the plank. The next thing we had to do was to climb under the boat and run a pencil line along the inside of the bottom plank where it overlapped the bottom of the boat. We then marked the top line from the marks on the midship knee and stern post, undid the cramps, trued up the bevel at the end of the cramp and cut the bottom to the line scribed to it, just leaving the line showing. We then offered it up again, using the top line as our datum line. We offered up

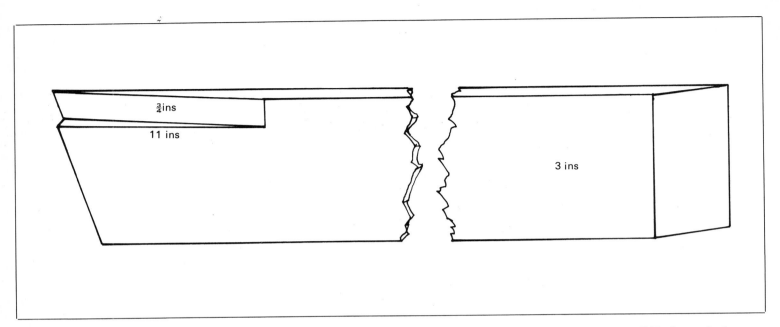

this same plank on the opposite side to make sure the work was true. It fitted perfectly so we unclamped it, placed it on top of another plank and traced round it with a pencil. We then cut out the duplicate.

Rabbets At bow and stern the upper strakes fit into rabbets cut along the top edge of the lower planks. Both the lower and upper planks had to be joined by scarphs. We allowed a ¾in overlap and cut back for 11in. The best way to do this is to put in a saw cut at the side and then to take out the unwanted wood with a skew plane. It can however be sawn out. The end scarph which is 3½in wide from the outside was then cut. The scarph should overlap from forward. We planed this scarph almost to a feather edge.

Next we fastened and fitted the two bottom strakes to the stern post and to the edge of the bottom, nailing at 4in intervals using 1¼in copper nails driven into the holes already drilled. We fitted the two forward bottom strakes in the same manner and fastened up the scarphs with 1in nails and ¼in rooves, putting eight fastenings in each scarph and two chine fastenings. To fit the top strakes, we took the bevel at the end and made our first cut, dropping the board into the rabbet and clamping into position at the stern. We bent the board round to a fair fit and clamped it into position. The board should take up its proper line. We marked with a pencil inside over the top of the lower strake, then took off the board and scribed a cutting line ¾in below the line that we had just drawn. We sawed the board to shape then clamped it back into position. We measured up the

height for the top strake at the stem post (8½in from the bottom line and 11in amidships), then stretched a piece of string from a nail in the stern post at the 8½in mark and round the outside of the plank to the midships mark (11½in), marking this line in by pencil at 2ft intervals. We bent a spline round these marks and ruled in the cutting line, next removing the plank and sawing it to the line, just leaving the line showing.

Fitting timbers When the bottom strakes were fitted, but before the top strakes were nailed into position, we fitted and fixed the timbers, cutting their bottoms to the flare of the bottom strakes. The after pair were fixed at right angles to the strake and not to the boat's centreline. They thus have a toed-in appearance. The first and third pairs forward were also at right angles to the sides. An additional reason for this is that they should not act as water traps below the covered deck.

The top planks were then fastened and the timbering was completed. The timbers were cut down to the sheer line and filling pieces were fitted inside the timbers along the sheer. These were 1½in deep and ran the full length of the sheer. They help to provide something on which to nail the capping rail. Next, breast hooks were fitted fore and aft. These should be of oak from grown crooks but can be laminated. With breast hooks and filling pieces in position, we clamped the gunwale on to the inside of the heads of the timbers. The gunwale was 2in deep. We marked on each timber a line under the bottom of the gunwale, then removed the gunwale and cut a notch into the timber head to receive half its width. We fitted the gunwale into position in these notches and through-fastened, drilling from the outside through the top strake and the filling piece, timberhead and gunwale. Copper nails 2½in long were needed for this, and were rooved in the ordinary way. The gunwale provides considerable strength.

Before decking in the punt fore and aft we painted the inside. With the deck on, it would be virtually impossible to do this. We used tar varnish for the bottom boards, and metallic pink priming, grey undercoating and grey enamel for the rest.

The mast step was fitted across two of the floor timbers. It was made up from a piece of 2in × 4in oak. A tenon was cut in it to receive the foot of the mast and a ¼in hole drilled through the bottom of the tenon for drainage. The rowlocks were set into the gunwale with a raised oak strip to take the necessary wear and tear.

Decking The Manningtree punts have a longer foredeck than most. This decking was supported by 1in square oak beams, rounded on their undersides and half checked into the gunwales. The planking we used was tongue and groove white pine, ⅜in thick and 3in wide. The stern deck is quite short but the decks help to make these punts seaworthy and are also useful as a place for stowing gear away from the spray and the rain.

The main beam that supports the gun was cut to shape, with a camber of about 2½in, and fitted. The forward beam of the after deck was the next to be fitted. Lines were stretched from the centre of the gun beam and the after deck beam to the stem and stern posts; this gave the amount of camber each beam would need. The beam was half-dovetailed into the gunwale. The side decks were made up from 9in planks, ½in thick, cut to shape and supported by small knees.

The decks were then canvased, following the normal procedure. We used unbleached 6oz calico in 3ft widths, laying it down on a sticky mixture of paint, varnish and turpentine. We drew the canvas hard down over the edges of the boat, tacked it in position and then fixed the rubbing strakes and the coamings over the calico. The spare calico that showed below the rubbing strakes was trimmed off with a sharp knife. Coamings 4in × ¼in thick were fitted inside the side decks and overlapping the fore and aft decks.

A hole was drilled through the stem post to take the recoil rope of the punt gun, ½in round bronze strip was fitted as stem and stern bands, and protection pieces of brass sheet were nailed down fore and aft. We then completed the painting, tar varnishing the bottom strakes and the bottom of the boat.

The floorboards were of 5⁄16in deal and rested on the floor timbers. When rowing the punt, the punt gunner sits on a little square stool about 12in square and 3in high.

Following local practice, we made our oars from pine. They were 6ft long, 4½in wide and were painted the same muddy grey as the rest of the punt. The punt was now ready for rowing, but had no equipment for shooting or sailing. And that was how I used her.

Sir Ralph Payne-Galwey showed two plans of gunning punts in *Shooting : Moor and Marsh*, of which he was co-author with Lord Walsingham. The book was published by Longmans Green in 1886. Sir Ralph elaborated these plans ten years later, with detailed instructions for the building of single and two-man gun punts. This was in his *Letters to Young Shooters*, third series, published in 1896 by Longmans Green. His designs differ in one or two respects from the Manningtree punts. His punts have only one strake on each side, with a maximum height of 8in. He fits battens over his bottom seams and a chine timber along the full length of each chine. Sir Ralph, a tremendous authority on every aspect of game shooting and wildfowling, was no boatbuilder, but his punts were soundly constructed, if somewhat overtimbered. He gives sail plans for both sprit and leg-of-mutton sails. He fits his mast off centre, clearly intending to use the sails for work and not just for racing as they do at Manningtree. In place of a bench on which to sit when rowing, he uses an ammunition box with a padded top. He refers to rowlocks as 'rowing spurs'. His final observation about fitting the gun is worth repeating. It was: 'Your *life* depends on a *sound* breeching rope.'

These books, long out of print, are hard to find though the National Central Library should be able to produce them. The British Museum Library certainly has copies. They are packed with useful information, not only about building gun punts but on wildfowling in general.

As I never fitted a gun to my punt, I will leave it to Dod Porter to describe the general arrangement of the punt fitted out for wildfowling. At the time Bill Porter was building my punt, his Uncle Dod was using a punt that was nearly fifty years old. Dod described this punt's equipment in these words:

'Starting from the stem, you will notice a length of Italian hemp rope passing through a hole in the stem post and finishing off with a single eye spliced in on one side and three or four eyes spliced in on the other. These are the breechings for the gun. The single eye is for the bolt to go in and should be left on the side of the bolt which is passed through a hole in the gun stock, which should be between two feet and two feet six inches from the breech of the gun. The bolt is then passed through one of the eyes on the right side of the gun and forms the front breechings which take up the recoil of the gun.

'Another smaller and lighter length of rope is attached to the bolt and passes through two screw eyes on the gun beam. These are the back breechings and take the strain of the gun going forward after the recoil has been taken by the fore breechings. It is important that these breeching ropes are watched for wear and chafe.'

The Manningtree punters have always preferred very short paddles to the poles that punters in some other areas use. The paddles are 2ft 6in long, weighted at the bottom with a strip of lead, and are used with the handles just clear of the water. They always have a hole in the top of the blade with a piece of hambro line passed through it and made fast to the inside of the punt. This is in case the punt gunner has to let go his paddle in a hurry to take a shot at some duck that may suddenly have become aware of him. These little paddles are by no means easy to use and certainly make the novice's wrists ache. Dod Porter remarked, 'When rowing we always put a leather washer under the rowlocks. Any punt gunner would regard it as a crime if he made the slightest sound when rowing down river at night in search of duck.'

The punt's equipment, apart from the little stool, is completed with anchor, cable and mop. The anchor cable should be made of good quality cod line and about 10 or 12 fathoms in length. The anchor, or grapnel, need not be heavy, 7lb would be ample. Payne-Galwey had this to say about anchors: 'I should have lost my life ten times over had I not *always* my anchor ready to hand in my gunning punt.'

The mop should have a head of worsted, never of cotton. It is essential to be able to mop out the punt before one has to lie in it and cotton is useless for this. I remember another of the Manningtree punt gunners, Joe Lucas, saying 'Old pullovers and jerseys, they are the things for mops. They will absorb water better than anything you can buy.'

The punt was given several coats of grey paint ('The same colour as a kittiwake's back' as Payne-Galwey said). The calico, even when painted, has a less reflective surface than wood so it helps to make the wildfowler and his punt that much less obvious.

Charles Harker, who restored the little Colchester smack *Iris*, was also a punt gunner. His description of the open Blackwater punts makes an interesting comparison with the decked Manningtree punts. In a recent letter, he wrote:

'We used to work out of Tollesbury with the *Iris* as base vessel and take a single punt and a double punt when there were three of us. The single punt is completely open and double-ended. She was built at Maldon and I bought her for £5. This punt we used to haul on deck when sailing down the river to the birds. The double punt, which like the Manningtree and Norfolk punts is decked in fore and aft, was towed astern. I had a muzzle-loading gun (in the single punt) which fired ½lb of shot. The breech rested in a chock on the punt's thwart, whilst the muzzle lay in a small groove on the stem. The breech rope, which was hemp, had an eyesplice in one end and which was secured through itself round the thwart, passing through a notch on the gun's breech and its end made fast to the thwart again. The muzzle was kept just a ½in inboard of the stem, so that if you rowed into the cant edge (the edge of the mudbank), you did not get the muzzle end blocked up with mud. This could have been disastrous!

'The gun on the double punt was slightly bigger and fired about 9oz of shot. This gun was secured to the punt in this manner: two small mushroom shaped trunnions were fitted over the gunbarrel about two-thirds of the length of the barrel from the muzzle. The breech rope had two eyesplices which fitted over these trunnions whilst the forward end looped over the stem and was seized together. The gun could be elevated or depressed by means of the forward rest which had a long handle like a billiard cue rest. The foredeck sloped forward so all one had to do was to push or pull the rest to raise or lower the muzzle.

'In the single punt, the muzzle end rested on a rowlock which was mounted on a threaded spindle. There was a large sheave on the bottom of this and an endless rope passed round this and led aft to the gunner's hand, the gunner being able to alter the gun's elevation at will. In fact little adjustment was needed, for the gun was laid to shoot a pattern of shot which began to strike the water at sixty yards. The punt gunner always tried to get as close as this to the ducks.'

Charles Harker concluded the notes in his letter with these evocative words:

'I have wonderful memories of setting out from Woodrope Creek late on a Saturday night, sailing the *Iris* up to Osea Island on the flood tide, and launching the punt about midnight under a full moon to paddle all the way up the Strumble to Goldhanger. We never made any really big shots – my best was ten Widgeon in St Lawrence Bay one December afternoon. The whole set up of smack, punt, gunpowder and smoke, and aboard the *Iris* a coal stove roaring away in the fo'c's'le, was pure magic.'

Wildfowling still goes on at Manningtree, with various members of the Lucas family still active as punt gunners. While writing this book, I returned to Manningtree and renewed acquaintance with Mr Joe Lucas after a fifteen-year gap. He showed me a 20ft gun punt he had built a couple of years before. She was a handsome craft, with more freeboard and relatively less beam than the older punts. Her bottom was sprung 2½in forward and 1½in aft with a 1in rocker, flattening out fore and aft. Joe Lucas said, 'The reason that flattens out is because we made the bottom up from three 11in planks. If we had planked her bottom with 3in planks, we could have carried

Gun punts and dories.
1 Breech rope secured round thwart
  in open punt.

River Stour, Essex, wildfowling punt

Dimensions
Length 17ft 1in OA
Breadth 3ft 1½in OA
Length (bottom) 16ft 0in
Breadth (bottom) 2ft 9½in

Timber

Quantity		Type of wood	Where used
3	16ft × 1in × 11in	whitewood	bottom
2	9ft × ⅜in × 7in	elm	bottom strakes
2	8ft × ⅜in × 7in	elm	bottom strakes
2	10ft × ⅜in × 7in	spruce	top strakes
2	8ft × ⅜in × 7in	spruce	top strakes
4	9ft × ⅜in × 8in	whitewood	floorboards
3	7ft × ⅜in × 9in	whitewood	fore and stern decks
2	17ft × ⅝in × 1¼in	spruce	gunwales
2	17ft × ⅜in × 1¼in	whitewood	filling pieces
2	17ft × ½in × 1in	elm	rubbing strakes
1	3ft × 1in × 12in	oak	floors
2	2½in	oak crooks 120°	stem and stern posts
5	1in	oak crooks 100°–105°	side knees

Oars 6ft × 2½in × 8in pine

Fastenings required
Copper nails

2¼in (or 2½in)	1lb
2in	2lb
1¾in	1lb
1½in	1lb
1in	1lb

Copper rooves

¼in	½lb
5/16in	½lb

12in × 12in of 21 gauge (G.B.) or 22 gauge (U.S.A.) copper sheet.

Galvanized nails

1½in	½lb
1in	½lb

1 pair rowlocks, medium
1 pair rowlock plates
1 anchor
3½ fathoms of 1in bass line

that rounding right through to stem to stern.' I asked him if they ever caulked the bottom seams of their punts.

'Never,' he replied, 'when we could buy good seasoned white wood, we used to leave a space wide enough so you could slip a penny through it – a real penny. When they were put in the water they took up. But since the last war, we've always cramped them up tight. By the time we'd finished building, they would have opened up, but once in the water they take up. This punt was built in white wood throughout. No need for elm bottom strakes now we have stopped going out after fowl when there is ice on the river!' He paused, then said, 'Elm was always used for the bottom strakes but was never used for the bottom planking, as it made the punts too heavy.'

Joe Lucas left me standing on the causeway. Wading through soft mud, he collected another punt for me to look at. She was a pretty little thing, noticeably lower and wider than the one we had been looking at. She was 17ft long and 3ft 5½in wide with 10½in freeboard.

'Forty years old, this one. She belongs to my cousin. She's a good old punt, but a good bit wetter than this new one of mine. You see, the river's more open now, most of the marsh grass has gone and there is less protection.'

As we walked up the causeway, a redshank rose in front of us.

'I am glad they are still here,' I said, 'are there plenty of fowl on the river?'

'Plenty,' Joe answered, 'plenty now it is getting colder.'

The punt gunners will soon be about their business.

1

2 Dory at Mystic Seaport.
3 & 4 Dories at St John,
        Newfoundland.
5 Double punt on the Blackwater.

Lines and elevation of dory.
Fourteen-foot Banks dory built by
Higgins and Gifford, Gloucester 1881.
Lines drawn by Howard I. Chapelle.
LOA 18ft 1½in.
Length of bottom 14ft 0in.
Beam 4ft 11in.
Depth 1ft 8¾in.

Table of offsets in feet, inches and
eighths to inside of plank.
Construction: tholes, ¾in diameter,
are made from oak or locust.
Drawings by H. I. Chapelle.

Inshore boats: Grand Banks dories

The simplest boats for amateurs to build are flat bottomed craft, hence the tradition for this type on the east coast of the USA and Canada where in colonial times there was a shortage of trained shipwrights. The type also existed in the shallow waters of the east coast of England and in the Netherlands. In addition to the gun punts, other types of punt were built for fishing, reed cutting and for shooting from shoulder guns. Larger flat bottomed craft, usually rigged with a single lugsail, were also widely built and used for marsh work and fishing in the east coast estuaries between the Medway and the Wash. I owned an example of just such a craft, which was known as a Medway punt. She was a very stable little boat. The flat bottomed Dutch craft were so numerous and so much more sophisticated they would need a book of this size to do them justice.

In the USA, the traditional flat bottomed types are many and various, ranging from primitive square-ended scows and punts to fifty-foot sharpie schooners. The most noteworthy type, however, is the Grand Banks dory. The dory was developed to be carried aboard the Banks schooners and then, once on the fishing grounds, to be used for long line fishing. Without any gear aboard a dory floats high in the water looking for all the world like a paper boat. With gear aboard, it rows easily and will sail downwind. When dories were stacked on the decks of the schooners, the thwarts were taken out and the little boats were placed one inside the other, with as many as ten or a

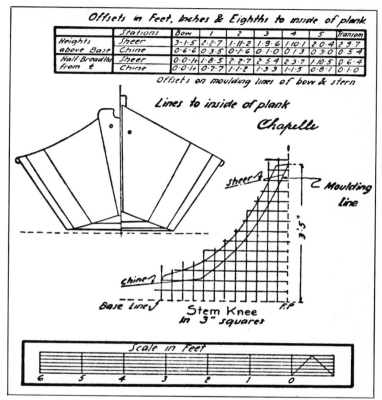

Offsets in Feet, Inches & Eighths to inside of plank								
	Stations	Bow	1	2	3	4	5	Transom
Heights above Base	Sheer	3-1-5	2-2-7	1-11-2	1-9-6	1-10-1	2-0-4	2-9-7
	Chine	0-6-6	0-3-5	0-1-6	0-1-0	0-1-3	0-3-0	0-5-4
Half-Breadth from ₵	Sheer	0-0-1½	1-8-5	2-2-7	2-5-4	2-3-7	1-10-5	0-6-4
	Chine	0-0-1½	0-7-7	1-1-2	1-3-3	1-1-5	0-8-1	0-1-0

Offsets on moulding lines of bow & stern

Lines to inside of plank

Chapelle

sheer

Moulding Line

3'5"

chine

Base Line

Stem Knee in 3" squares

F.P.

Scale in Feet

6 5 4 3 2 1 0

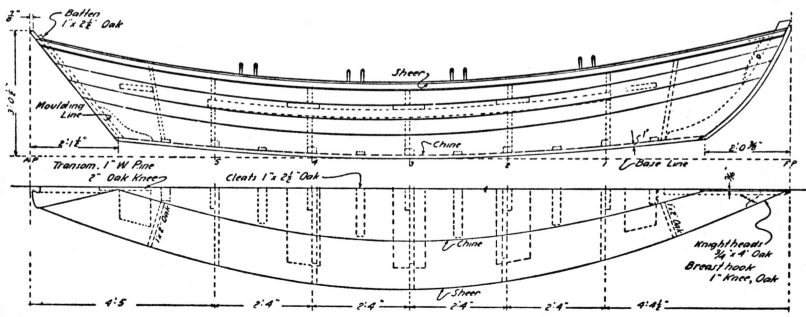

Batten 1"x 2½" Oak

Sheer

Moulding Line

Chine

3'0⅝"

2'1¼"

2'0⅞"

A.P. 5 4 3 2 1 Base Line F.P.

Transom. 1" W Pine
2" Oak Knee

Cleats 1"x 2½" Oak

Chine

Knightheads ¾"x 4" Oak

Breasthook 1" Knee, Oak

Sheer

4:5   2:4   2:4   2:4   2:4   4:4⅛

Details of dory construction.
Stem post overlaps planking.
Set of galvanized iron frame clips:
ten sets needed.
Dory lap-joint for planking.

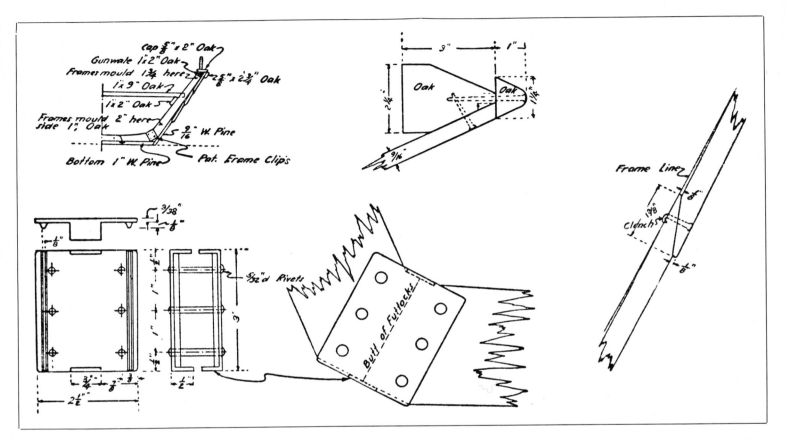

dozen in a stack. They were built all along the north-east coast from Massachusetts to Nova Scotia.

The dories were strongly but lightly built, with cedar or white pine side planking and oak bottoms and timbers. They were light enough to lift aboard easily. They were constructed with four wide planks on each side. These planks were not of the usual clinker built overlap but had a diagonal half lap; they still build them like this today. Unlike the practice in the building of most American flat bottomed boats, their bottoms are planked fore and aft. The seams of the bottoms are grooved and splined and joined together by cross timbers. There is a considerable spring in the bottom – as much as a 6in rise forward and a 5in rise aft in the larger (16ft) dories. The building of the dories follows very much the lines of the duck punt except that no rabbets are cut in the stem. Instead of a one-piece stem post made up from a single grown crook, the stem assembly here consists of a grown crook to which the planks are fastened and then cut off flush with the forwarded edge. A covering stem piece is then fitted to this 'apron' to cover the plank ends.

The transom is very narrow. To facilitate lifting, a loop of rope is passed through two holes in the transom and another loop through two holes in the bow.

Another marked departure from English punt building procedure was the use of galvanized iron frame clips to join the floor timbers to the side timbers. These clips took the place of grown knees. The fastenings were galvanized iron nails which were clenched.

The three or four thwarts rest on a shelf that does not run the full length of the boat. Double wooden thole pins were used for rowlocks. The dories rowed with one or two pairs of oars, depending on their size. When sailing under a loose-footed spritsail they were steered like the duck punt, with an oar. The mast was stepped through the forward thwart into a pad of hardwood fastened across two floor timbers.

Howard I. Chapelle, the American naval historian, has written at length and in detail about dories (see Bibliographical References) as well as about practically every other kind of traditional American sailing craft. His books are essential reading for anyone seriously interested in the wider historical aspects of small craft restoration.

106

Trading vessels, fishing schooners and sailing barges

Introduction The restoration or rebuilding of vessels of over 100ft in length or 100 tons burden is a considerable and expensive undertaking. However, such restorations and rebuildings are done. Some are done by private individuals blessed with enough wealth to make such an activity possible. Other restorations are carried out under the auspices of such bodies as The Marine Historical Association in the USA, which is responsible for Mystic Seaport and all the vessels there; or in Britain by the Maritime Trust which is now responsible for the maintenance of the *Cutty Sark*, the frigate *Foudroyant* (which with the exception of the USS *Constellation* is the oldest ship afloat) and various other vessels including the last British wooden topsail trading schooner, the *Kathleen & May*.

Mystic Seaport apart, there are numerous other centres in the USA and Canada that have preserved small trading vessels. At South Street Seaport Museum in New York City there is the *Lettie G. Howard*, a beautiful clipper-bowed New England banks schooner. *Lettie G. Howard* was built in 1893 at Essex, Mass. for owners at Beverley, Mass. The schooner fished off the New England banks until 1901, when she was sold to owners in Pensacola, Fla. From here she fished in Mexican waters. She was rebuilt in 1923. In 1966 she was bought by the Historic Ships Association and two years later by the South Street Seaport Museum. The *Lettie G. Howard* is a handsome ship and has been very well restored. She lies at one of the jetties in New York's South Street Museum in the Fulton Street area on the East River near Battery Point. She makes an interesting comparison with the later banks fishermen such as the *L. A. Dunton* at Mystic Seaport or the *Sherman Zwicker* at Boothbay Harbour, Maine.

There are numerous other small trading vessels preserved on both the east and west coasts of North America. On the west coast in San Francisco Bay there is the *C. A. Thayer*, a three-masted lumber schooner, and also the famous German pilot boat *Wander Bird* which is being privately restored. Up in Vancouver BC, the Royal Canadian Mounted Police 104ft vessel *St Roch* rests under cover. *St Roch* was the first vessel to navigate the North-West Passage in both directions.

One could go on adding to an evergrowing list. At long last, people have realized that these modest trading vessels are as much a part of their history as *Victory* and *Constitution*, let alone any Wren church or Brownstone house.

There has also been a recent resurgence of building replicas of famous old ships, beginning with *Mayflower II* which is berthed at Plymouth, Mass. This movement has continued with various other copies, including one of the schooner yacht *America* and another of the famous Canadian Grand Banks fisherman *Bluenose* at Halifax, Nova Scotia.

Bluenose, built in 1921, was the pride of Canada and for

Lettie G. Howard, built 1893.
1 Her clipper bow and staysail boom.

seventeen years was the undefeated winner of the International Fishermen's Races. Her replica will make an interesting comparison with the New England dory fisherman *L. A. Dunton* at Mystic Seaport.

Among the other trading vessels described here are *Solvig*, a Swedish galleas, *Kitty*, a Thames sailing barge, and *Albion*, a Norfolk wherry. The ketch-rigged galleases were as common in Scandinavian waters as the brown-sailed barges were on the London river. Neither type is now trading under sail but their hulls can still be found afloat, converted to power and often used as yachts. The wherries of the Norfolk rivers and the shallow broadlands of East Anglia are a unique type of vessel, cat-rigged and with a huge black mainsail. *Albion* has been rescued and preserved by the Norfolk Wherry Trust. The restorations of *Solvig* and *Kitty* have resulted from private endeavour.

Lettie G. Howard

2 Deck: looking forward, with companionway to fo'c's'le.
3 Looking forward from just aft of the mainmast.
4 Wheel and main boom crutch.

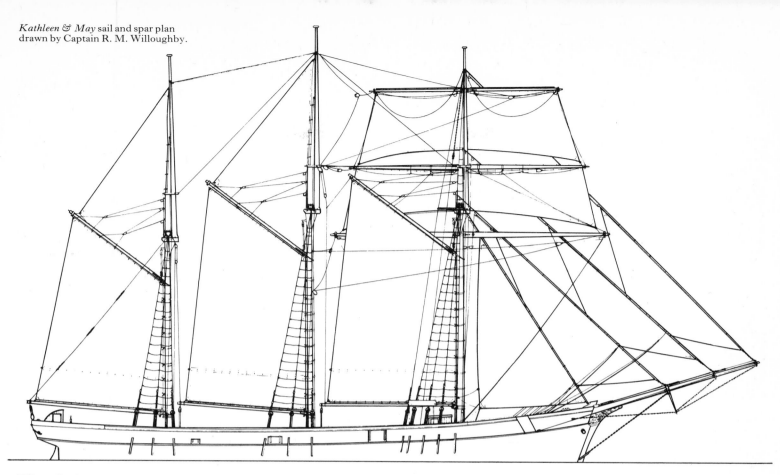

The Schooner *Kathleen & May*

LOA 98ft 4in
Beam 23ft 3in
Draught 10ft 0in
Gross tonnage 140·51
Net tonnage 92·76
Built 1900

Kathleen & May was built by Ferguson and Baird at Connah's Quay on the river Dee in North Wales. She was named *Lizzie May* after the daughters of her first owner, but her name was changed in 1908 to *Kathleen & May* when she was sold to new owners in County Cork. In 1931 she was bought by Captain Tommy Jewell and his father William, both of Appledore near Bideford in Devon. Here, the thirty-one-year old schooner was refitted, her square yards and topsails removed and her topmasts shortened. With the installation of an 80hp Beardmore engine she became a motor sailer with a fore and aft rig, and very well she did under it.

With the outbreak of war her days might well have been numbered, as for two years *Kathleen & May* was sailing the Western Approaches to Southern Ireland. She risked being sunk by enemy action or suffering an even more ignoble end. Captain R. M. Willoughby, who made the first report to the

Maritime Trust of the vessel's condition in 1970, remarked with some acerbity: 'The ship is a splendid example of the coasting schooner and has survived because the Admiralty decided that she was not in good enough condition to serve as a balloon barrage vessel during the last war, which is very fortunate as all the vessels they commandeered became total losses through neglect.' In a more mellow tone, Captain Willoughby continued: 'Captain Jewell, who owned her for over thirty years, must take the credit for her eventual survival.'

Kathleen & May had a further twenty years of useful trading before Mike Willoughby surveyed her in 1970. In 1952, she had been fitted with a new 133bhp 4-cylinder Crossley diesel; she had a 6hp Lister as a donkey engine working the winch; she was equipped with radio receivers and her sails were fitted with Appledore roller reefing gear. She was a thoroughly efficient little auxiliary schooner and served Captain Jewell well for another eight years. In the autumn of 1960, Captain Jewell put the *Kathleen & May* up for sale. Her trading days were over. She changed hands several times but not until 1965 did she find a sympathetic buyer. This was Captain Paul Davis of Llantwit Major in South Wales. By this time *Kathleen & May* was showing signs of her five years of neglect. However, Captain Davis sailed her from Southampton Water round to Barry docks and then set to work on her restoration, at the end of two years taking her across the Bristol Channel to Appledore.

Kathleen & May.
1 Deck and deck beams.
2 Deck from bow.
3 Waterways repairs
4 Forepeak painting

3

4

111

Captain's cabin.

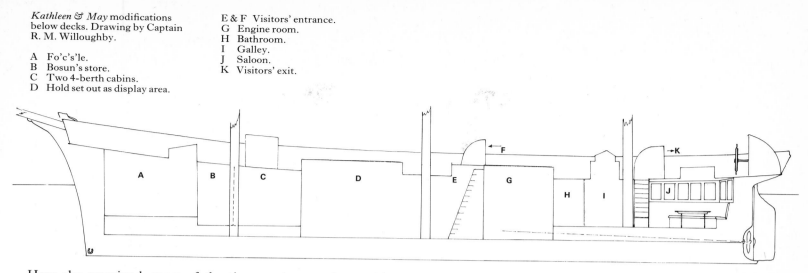

Here she remained, most of the time resting on the muddy bottom of the River Torridge and floating only at high tides. For four years Captain Davis worked away on her restoration. He sank his life savings into the work and put in countless hours of work. He had reached the end of his resources and was on the point of chartering the *Kathleen & May* to a film company, who planned to alter the ship beyond recognition. This was in January 1970, when the Maritime Trust came on the scene and asked Captain Willoughby to do his preliminary survey with a view to their buying the vessel.

Mike Willoughby's report was hopeful. The main fabric of the hull appeared sound but there was rot in the counter, the stem was badly cracked, the ends of the deck beams were suspect, the bulwark stanchions needed renewing, and so on. The masts and all the rigging would have to be renewed. The happiest note in the report was about the captain's quarters. Of this he wrote 'The after accommodation is in beautiful condition and is the result of some very hard work by the owner. It is a perfect example of the living quarters of the period and is absolutely original.'

Captain Willoughby's first estimate for a rebuild was £25,000. In June 1970 the Maritime Trust bought *Kathleen & May* from Captain Davis. Towards the end of July she was slipped at the Bideford shipyard to have certain very necessary work done below the waterline, including the scarphing in of a 16ft 6in length of keel, fitting a steel shoe to the keel, and replacing the false stern post. A new stem post was also fitted and one of the forward floors taken out and replaced by a new one to take the strain of the new stem post. Three hundred feet of the seams were caulked and payed and the hull was cleaned down and coated with Bituguard. When she was refloated she made no water.

The problem now facing the Maritime Trust was whether to restore the *Kathleen & May* into full commission so that she could be kept sailing, or to rebuild her insofar as it would be necessary to keep her afloat as a permanent exhibit. It would have been tempting to commission her so that she could return to her proper element, but the arguments against this were that it would cost more, the running costs if she was actually sailing

would be much greater, and there would be the risk of losing this irreplaceable vessel. Mr Basil Greenhill, the present director of the National Maritime Museum and a member of the Ship's Committee of the Maritime Trust, favoured the static solution. Mr Greenhill had been involved at the very beginning in the negotiations to purchase the *Kathleen & May* from Mr Davis.

The problem of the cost of the restoration of the *Kathleen & May* was overcome when Mr Y. K. Pao, the governing director of the Hong Kong firm of World Wide Shipping, decided 'to become a godfather to the project'.

If the ship was to be moored permanently, clearly it was important for the public to have easy access. Appropriate though it would have been to leave the schooner at Appledore, a port with which she had been so long associated, a suitable site was not available. After some discussion it was agreed that the *Kathleen & May* should be kept afloat permanently in the conservation area of Sutton Harbour in Plymouth, berthed just in front of the handsome old Three Crowns Inn and close to the Customs House. Meanwhile, Captain Willoughby was preparing drawings of the *Kathleen & May*'s spars, rigging and sail plan. On 25 February 1971, his work sheet showed:

1 *Work in progress*
Wood treatment of interior of hull
Making good deck planking and caulking
Making new after dolly winch
Caulking ship's sides
After hatch being repaired and fitted
Three lower masts being installed
2 *Work completed*
Windlass rebuilt
New main fife rail completed, fitted to deck; new deck
  planking fitted where soft and then caulked
Hanging knees chipped and painted
Engine room casing removed and new deck fitted
Hatches caulked
Three yards, three topmasts, bowsprit, mizzen boom, and
  three gaffs installed

Kathleen & May
1 Repairing bows.
2 Scarphing stem post.
3 Flat bilges.
4 Caulking.

3

4

3 *Drawings*
  Details of three lower masts
  Details of three crosstrees
  Details of foreyard truss and sling

4 *Orders in hand*

	£ p
Richardson & Starling: wood treatment materials	202·21
Clark & Carter: all spars	6,255·12
Hall's Barton Ropery: wire and terylene ropes	2,409·00
Bideford shipyard (approx)	2,000·00
additional work (approx)	1,000·00

  Negotiating with Mashford's, Plymouth for
      towing from Appledore
      rebuilding stern
      repairing bulwarks and waterway

5 *Alterations*
  New lower masts are being made to the correct height
  All sheets reduced to 3in from 4in
  All lower shrouds reduced from $3\frac{1}{4}$in 6 × 19 to 3in 6 × 19

A month later his next sheet showed:

1 *Work in progress*
  Wheelhouse removed
  Deck under repair
  Three lower masts completed – crosstrees being built
  Caulking starboard side of ship
  Whaleback removed and deck being renewed where rotten

2 *Work completed*
  Forward hatch rebuilt and fixed to deck
  After hatch repaired and fixed
  New half-circular companion ladder made and fixed
  Deck in way of after hatch and skylight repaired
  All deck seams, butt joints etc now watertight
  Chainplates renewed and fixed for all three masts
  Donkey engine removed, new cylinder head fixed and engine
      ready for fixing on deck
  Forward deckhouse removed
  Deck renewed where rotten
  Foremast partners renewed
  New mizzen partners fixed

3 *Orders*
  Tender documents sent to Mashford's for all spar ironwork?
  Dinghy ordered – standard schooner boat £265

4 *Remarks*
  With the progress made by Vladimir (member of the crew
  still working aboard), and his ability to get help, both part
  time and from local sources, it is becoming apparent that
  Mashford's will only have the bulwarks to do.
      It is then a question of stepping the masts and rigging the
  ship. In view of the urgency to have the ship earning, it is

Kathleen & May.
1 Passing Drake's Island.
2 Setting up rigging.

suggested that some of this might be contracted out to Mashford's.

The ship should be ready for the sea passage by the end of April.

The trip round to Plymouth was made without incident and *Kathleen & May* was put into the hands of Mashford Brothers at Cremyl, which lies across the Tamar Estuary from Plymouth. Captain Willoughby's final instruction sheet to Mashford Brothers was concerned mainly with the conversion of the hold into a display area.

Kathleen & May is a very closely framed vessel, with double oak frames each 5in × 7in, interspaced with only 4in gaps. Her planking is 3in thick pitch pine and the thickness of her pine ceiling in her hold varies between $2\frac{1}{2}$in and $3\frac{1}{2}$in, to withstand the wear and tear of cargoes such as coal, stone or brick.

This cargo hold now makes an effective display area, renovated in a sympathetic manner by the National Maritime Museum, with some superb schooner models. The most evocative part of this rugged little schooner is the accommodation at the after end of the vessel with a small saloon and cabins for captain and mate leading off to port and starboard respectively. There is an open firegrate, a tapered mess table with flaps and a bench built round three sides of the table. Above this bench are deep cupboards with panelled doors and a narrow ledge with a balustrade rail. An oil lamp swings below the skylight and in the stern of the saloon is a carved wooden plaque with the prayer 'God protect the *Kathleen & May*'.

Mashford's completed their work on the hull, stepped the masts, and towed *Kathleen & May* across the Tamar to Sutton Pool. On 16 September 1971 Mr Pao opened her to the public. The total cost had reached nearly £70,000. The breakdown of costs may be of use to anybody who thinks of undertaking a comparable restoration; to have made this schooner fit for sea-going use would have added considerably to this figure.

Bluenose II going to windward. This copy of the legendary Grand Banker was launched in 1963. (*Photo Nova Scotia Communications and Information Centre.*)

Kathleen & May – costs to end October 1971

	Rebuild costs £	Other costs £
Bought from Captain Davis		8,570
Consultants' fees, surveys, expenses	1,453	
Work at Bideford Shipyard	8,267	
Masts, ironwork, rigging rope	13,511	
Tow: Bideford to Plymouth		1,244
Work at Mashford's to September 1971	7,283	3,485
Timber preservation	201	
Wages and sundries: refit crew	7,885	
Wages and sundries: permanent crew		3,384
Miscellaneous	127	579
Insurance		445
	38,727	17,707

Total costs at end October 1971   **£56,434**

Estimated outstanding at end October 1971

Mashford's 9/71 and 10/71	say	10,000
Gangway and platform	say	1,000
Electrical installation	say	750
Miscellaneous	say	500
		12,250

Total including estimated outstanding costs   **£68,684**

The *Kathleen & May*, now beautifully restored, lies alongside Guy's Quay in Sutton Harbour, in Plymouth. This in itself is a hallowed spot, for it was from Sutton Pool that the Pilgrim Fathers sailed for New England. *Kathleen & May*, with her fine sheer, is a lovely little vessel. She evokes the days of coastwise sail more than any ship I have ever seen. Her restoration is a tribute not only to the Maritime Trust's act of faith in buying her but to Captain Paul Davis who first tried to save her, and to Captain Tommy Jewell who sailed her to every kind of little port between Oban on the west coast of Scotland, southern Ireland, and the London river.

Grand Banks fishing schooner *L. A. Dunton*

LOA 124ft 0in
Beam 25ft 0in
Depth in hold 11ft 6in
Designer Thomas F. McManus
Builder Arthur Storey
Built 1921

The fishing schooners of New England and Nova Scotia are legendary. They were the fastest, most weatherly and indeed most able sailing fishing boats ever built. They had need to be, for they used to fish all the year round beyond Cape Sable and out to the fishing shoals of the Newfoundland Grand Banks and on the dangerous Georges Banks off Cape Cod. The type evolved over the last quarter of the nineteenth century and was perfected in the first quarter of the twentieth century. They were designed by such men as Thomas F. McManus, Starling Burgess, and the Canadian William J. Roue.

The *L. A. Dunton* was one of Tom Macmanus's designs. She was named after the sailmaker at Boothbay in Maine and was built in Essex, Mass. She sailed out of Gloucester to the Banks for the first fourteen years of her working life. In 1935 she was sold to Canadian owners and was based at Grand Bank, Newfoundland. The *L. A. Dunton* crossed the Atlantic at least once with a cargo of salt cod for Portugal. In the late twenties an auxiliary engine was fitted and her rig cut down, but she was still primarily a sailing vessel. The *Dunton* was launched in the same year as *Bluenose*, but would have long outlived that famous vessel even if *Bluenose* had not been wrecked in 1946. The *Dunton* was planked in 3in white oak, whereas *Bluenose*, like all Canadian vessels, was softwood planked.

In 1960, the *L. A. Dunton* (then nearly forty years old) was sold to another firm in Grand Bank for use as a general cargo carrier, serving various small ports in Newfoundland and Nova Scotia. By this time, she had been converted into a ketch and her bowsprit unshipped. A 160hp diesel had been installed in what was once the captain's cabin. She was now a motor vessel with steadying sails. At the same time, her arrangements below decks were altered to allow for more cargo space and her fore-hatch was enlarged.

In 1963 the *L. A. Dunton* sailed into Mystic Seaport. She had come to her last resting place. The job of restoring the old vessel was begun in the autumn of that year. Apart from her foremast, she needed a complete new set of spars. Her original spars were of pine, the replacements are fir. A new mainmast 88ft 6in long, two new topmasts, new gaffs and new booms (the main boom is 75ft long) were made at Mystic Seaport with all the ironwork being made there in the blacksmith's shop. The distance between the truck of the main topmast and the deck is 113ft.

The old vessel is badly hogged. It is difficult to eradicate this but it is being concealed slowly by adjustments to the rail and the sheer strake.

After ten years' work, there is still much to do to the *L. A. Dunton*. She was never one of the most beautiful of the Gloucester Schooners but she is one of the few that have survived. The *Dunton* was planked and framed in white oak. Her decks are planked in pine.

On deck she carries her nests of 14ft dories, ten of them in all, from which all the line fishing was done. The *Dunton* carried a crew of twenty-two men, sixteen of them bunking down in the tapering fo'c's'le forward. Everything tapers in that fo'c's'le, including the bunks and the table where they had their meals. Cooking – they lived entirely on fish – was done on the range in the fo'c's'le.

The *L. A. Dunton* is an apt counterpart to the small fishing vessels at Mystic Seaport, the Cowhorn, the Stamford oyster boat, the Noank well smack and the Friendship lobster boats. They all stand as reminders of New England's oldest industry.

Grand Banks fishing schooner replica
Bluenose II

LOA 143ft 0in
LWL 112ft 0in
Beam 27ft 0in
Draught 15ft 10in
Displacement 285 tons
Sail area 11,690sq ft
Mainmast (Douglas fir) 22in diameter at deck level, 96ft 3in
Main topmast 58ft 0in
Overall height of main and topmast 125ft 10in
Foremast (Douglas fir) 19in diameter at deck level, 84ft 0in
Fore topmast 45ft 0in
Overall height of fore and topmast 102ft 6in
Topmasts 11in at heel to 8½in at truck
Bowsprit 34ft 0in, projecting over bow 17ft 6in
Fore boom 32ft 10in
Fore gaff 32ft 11in
Main boom 81ft 6in
Main gaff 51ft 0in
Built 1963

The replica of the legendary *Bluenose*, the most famous of all Grand Banks schooners, was launched from Smith & Rhuland's yard at Lunenburg just seventeen years after the original *Bluenose* had struck a reef off Haiti whilst trading in the West Indies. The building of the second *Bluenose* was commissioned by the Halifax family firm of Oland & Son. Until 1970 she was

Grand Banks Knockabout schooner
refitting at Lunenburg, NS, 1943.
1 Looking forward.
2 Bow of *Delawana II*.
3 Foremast and winch.
4 Foot of mainmast and break in
   deck.
5 Looking aft, windlass in foreground.
6 A stack of dories under cover on
   port side.

engaged on charter work, but by this time her softwood hull was showing signs of being in need of drastic repairs. Olands' sold her for $1 to the Nova Scotian Government who, after an appeal had brought in sufficient funds, set about giving her a major refit. The estimate for the refit was $175,000, so what the cost of building such a schooner would be now I hesitate even to guess.

The original *Bluenose* had been launched from the same yard in 1921. She was designed by a local naval architect, William J. Roue, but whether it was due to his draughting skill or to the vagaries of wooden ship building, Roue never succeeded in producing another vessel that could beat her.

While I was serving in the army in Canada in 1943, I visited Lunenburg and had a lengthy conversation with a shipwright called Carl Zinck who had worked as a foreman in the gang that built the original *Bluenose*. It was his theory that in the framing of her hull her bows came out fuller than Roue had intended. It was, so Carl Zinck said, that extra buoyancy up forward that made her such a fast craft.

It was not until thirty years later that I had confirmation of

5

6

Carl Zinck's theory. In August 1974 Mr David Keith, who lives in Westport Nova Scotia, told me exactly what had happened. And this was that the builders had positioned her moulds incorrectly. In doing this, they placed her stations too far forward by one station, so that the fifth station back from the bow came in the fourth place and so on. David Keith went on to say 'Mr Roue, the designer, wanted them to tear her down and start all over; but they felt she was too far along and it would cost too much to do that. He was very displeased, and refused to have anything more to do with the project, disclaiming any responsibility. In the race, the extra fullness gave her buoyancy and she coasted over the water, making less effort than plough-ing through the waves. Mr Roue acknowledged his design. Later another schooner was built to beat the *Bluenose* from a Roue design. Built in Shelburne, N.S., she was named the *Haligonian*. In fact, the lines were the *Bluenose* lines, and they were followed exactly – without the increased sheer in the bows or the extra fullness forward. History shows that the *Bluenose* was far superior. I suspect that the new *Bluenose* was built according to the plan and thus her hull is a replica of *Haligonian* rather than the original *Bluenose*.'

No duplicate can ever perform in exactly the same manner as the original. It would have been interesting to have been able to compare the performances of the two vessels. Report has it that *Bluenose II* would have been no match for the original schooner, though it is claimed that she has logged 18 knots for 1½ hours with all sail set in a 55mph wind.

It is of course impossible to say just how the two vessels would have compared. Modern sailors are not used to racing these great fishing boats. David Keith concluded his remarks

with 'The big schooners needed a lot of wind to get going . . . the old salts knew how the vessels reacted in a blow and were not afraid to crack on the canvas. Angus Walters (skipper of the original *Bluenose*) took the wheel on one of *Bluenose II*'s first sails in Lunenburg and put the lady through her paces. The vessel got herself laid down to her work and sailed like the old original.'

The scantlings of *Bluenose II* follow those of her predecessor. They are:

   keel: oak, 12in sided
   kelson: spruce
   stem post: oak, 12in sided
   stern post: oak, 12in sided
   frames: oak and birch, 9in × 10in doubled, spaced 27in apart
   planking: 4in thick oak below waterline, and Douglas fir elsewhere
   ceiling: 4in thick
   deck beams: 9in × 9in spruce
   deck planks: 4in pine.

Bluenose I, in her twenty-year racing career under the hand of her famous skipper Captain Angus Walters of Lunenburg, defeated the American schooners *Elsie, Henry Ford, Columbia* and *Gertrude L. Thebaud* as well as a number of Canadian vessels. In her final race, when she defeated the *Gertrude L. Thebaud*, she was eighteen years old.

There are those that say that the Gloucester schooner *Columbia* was more beautiful than *Bluenose*, and others that the *Mayflower* was a faster ship. The former point is a matter for debate; the latter cannot be proved, for *Mayflower* was debarred from racing by the Canadian Race Committee because she had

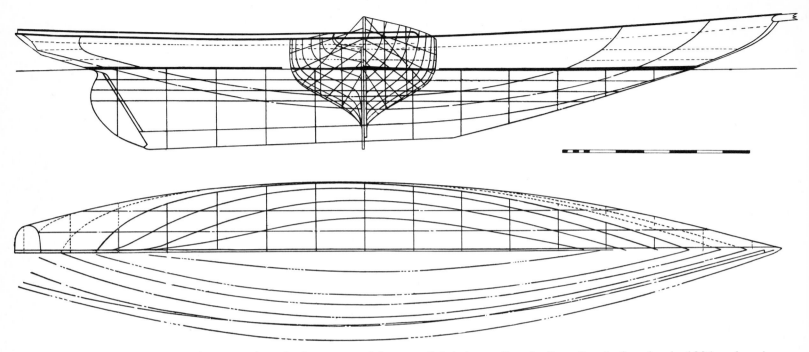

been built primarily as a yacht, even though she was used for some years as a fisherman.

Bluenose II is certainly as handsome as the original. She has had her extensive refit at Lunenburg, where she will remain, to remind future generations of the power and beauty of these great fishing boats.

Every summer, *Bluenose II* cruises the Nova Scotian coast acting as a sailing ambassador, taking parties of guests on sightseeing tours, and sailing by private charter.

Swedish galleas *Solvig*

TM 100 tons approx.
LOA 67ft 8in (20·62m)
Beam 20ft 4in (6·19m)
Draught 6ft 6in (1·98m)
Engine 2-cyl. 86hp June Munktell semi-diesel

The galleas is the traditional small trading vessel in use in the Baltic; Chapman shows a ketch rigged galleas in his *Architectura Navalis* (1775). The main difference from the modern sailing galleas is a very long pole bowsprit and a square topsail on her mainmast. As a result of some relaxation by certain Scandinavian countries of the rules about the need for serving in sail, which governed entry into their mercantile marine, a number of galleases have come on the market over the last few years.

Solvig is a galleas built at Raa in Sweden in 1926 and registered at Gothenburg. When Peter and Janet Light found her she was still trading. She had a bald-headed ketch rig and a short bowsprit, but for propulsion in her latter years had relied mainly on her massive June Munktell semi-diesel, built by A. B. Jonkopings Motor Fabrik. To start its enormous flywheel, it needed compressed air cylinders and a Calor gas blowlamp to heat up the hot bulb. Sometimes it would start spinning the wrong way, so at a critical point it had to be caught and reversed. The engine has no gear box but drives a variable-pitch two-bladed propeller, a common practice among Baltic traders and fishing boats. Her fuel tanks carry 500 gallons of diesel oil, giving her a cruising range under power alone of over 800 miles. *Solvig*, in spite of her diesel engine and her inadequate rig, was still an impressive vessel. With her bluff bows, deep bulwarks, catheads and stern davits, she certainly looked as if she belonged to the last century. From her davits, she carried a fourteen foot clinker built boat. There was one anachronism and that was a wheelhouse built of wall board that looked like a beach hut.

Peter Light had been a sailing barge skipper for ten years though he came from a family with no seafaring connections. The days of the trading sailing barges were coming to an end, so after a short spell of skippering *Memory* for the East Coast Sail Trust he bought a big smack which he restored and ran as a charter boat. He was an east coast pioneer in this charter work.

Solvig
1 Working the windlass.
2 Wide side decks and high
  bulwarks.
3 Peter Light found the windlass in
  a shipbuilder's yard.

126

After a few trips across the North Sea, he realized he needed a larger craft to make the chartering business pay.

After considering one or two Thames barges, on the advice of some friends who had been in Sweden he went off to the Baltic in search of a trading vessel. At Fiskebakschiele he found *Solvig* and, after prolonged negotiations, bought her for a reasonable sum. He then sailed her back to Maldon and spent the winter on her restoration. Before he left Sweden he had to find a windlass, for her last owner in a moment of mental aberration had sawn off her previous windlass and thrown it into the Baltic, remarking that he had no need for it as he never anchored. After scouring various shipbreakers' yards, Peter Light found a windlass to replace the missing one.

The first part of the restoration work consisted of removing the unsightly wheelhouse and also a donkey motor winch which was used for loading cargo. The wheelhouse had been built up over the coach roof of the after cabin, which was still in place. A sliding hatch was made and fitted into this coach roof and the deck was made good where the wheelhouse had rested. The covers of the main hatch were fastened down and canvased over and another sliding hatch, and a skylight, were fitted here. This skylight, which had come from some stately yacht, had for many years been used as a cucumber frame. However, after the moss and lichen were removed the teak frame came up like new.

Below decks there were bulkheads at either end of the main hold. In this large open area Peter Light built accommodation for twelve people. The work was done in the simplest possible manner, using tongue and groove pine for bulkheads, for his intention was to take charter parties from youth clubs and similar organizations. Before this could be done the sole had to be raised about eighteen inches to make for greater floor space and also to make space for about seven tons of pig iron ballast. The new hemlock planking was then sanded and varnished. The skipper's quarters aft and the fo'c's'le for the crew were retained though the aft cabin had to be panelled out afresh. A galley was fitted up and water tanks with a total capacity of 400galls built in.

For her first season, *Solvig* sailed under her bald-headed rig of two pole masts, a stump bowsprit and an old and patched suit of sails. The mizzen mast proved to be rotten and had to be replaced. The new larch mizzen mast came from Sutton Hoo near the Saxon ship burial mounds. *Solvig* was steered by a miserable little wheel which was all right when motoring but had insufficient leverage when sailing in anything more than a fresh breeze. Janet Light found a barge steering wheel which had been used as a decoration over someone's fireplace; this wheel was man enough for the job.

The following year, *Solvig*'s restoration work was completed by a re-rig and the addition of a topmast on her main, a new bowsprit and jib boom, and a new set of sails made for her by

Arthur Taylor & Co of Maldon. With her glossy black topsides and this tall rig, *Solvig* was a handsome sight. Her topsail was in truth closer to Thames barge practice than to any Baltic style of sail, but Peter Light had learned his sailing in Thames barges and their topsails were not only regarded as their most important sail but were designed, like everything else on a barge, for ease of handling. A purist might well have fitted a square topsail on the main and dispensed with the fore and aft topsail.

Solvig may not be an exact reconstruction of a Baltic sailing galleas but she is near enough in spirit to warrant inclusion here. To tackle both the restoration and the sailing of a vessel of *Solvig*'s size, one must have both handled and worked as a shipwright aboard large vessels. Peter Light with his experience as a skipper of Thames barges and with the work that he did in restoring his heavy smack was fully able to cope with such a vessel. This is not the kind of craft for anyone of limited strength and experience, for the gear is heavy and the behaviour of a boat of this size is in no way comparable to that of a small yacht.

Solvig is a relatively old vessel. In 1972, in her forty-sixth year, she was surveyed before passing to new owners. The survey was done by Peter Brown and Geoffrey Baverstock of the firm of J. Francis Jones & Partners. The survey looked intimidating but in fact, as their general notes stated, they considered the galleas to be in a satisfactory condition considering her age. This detailed survey is printed here to give some idea of what one has to look for in such a vessel as this, and so that anyone who has not had the experience of a surveyor's report should not be too intimidated by their painstaking fault finding.

Survey of 100 ton TM Auxiliary Gaff Ketch *Solvig*

Yacht on slipway.

GENERAL NOTES

Solvig is a Baltic trading ketch typical of her kind, which had been converted to pleasure use. The construction follows traditional lines, being pine planking on sawn oak frames; the backbone is of beech and oak, with iron fastenings, the whole forming a robust and picturesque craft of great potential.

Bearing in mind that *Solvig* was built for commercial use in 1926 her general condition is considered satisfactory. There are some defects, none of which are particularly serious.

Subject to the defects set out in the following report being properly set to rights, and given adequate maintenance and handling, the vessel *Solvig* would be considered in satisfactory structural condition and suitable for sea sailing in weather and conditions suited to her age, size and type.

Survey No S.1749

NB   Unless otherwise stated structural items and members when mentioned under the headings below were examined where accessible and appeared in satisfactory material condition so far as could be ascertained without opening-up. They were also considered of adequate scantling and material bearing in mind the type and class of vessel, her age, type of building and standard of maintenance. For convenience the items inspected are listed alphabetically below.

Anchors Two anchors seen both traditional fisherman type of adequate sizes for the vessel. The second anchor was rather rusty.

Apron The stem is backed with an apron of oak in satisfactory condition.

Ballast The whole of the ballast is carried internally, and is in the form of cast iron pigs stowed in the bilge. Where access was gained to the bilge, ballast was found stowed and in satisfactory condition.

Batteries In engine room annexe.

Beams Generally of oak or pine. Those in the original accommodation were of oak. The beams used over what is now the main saloon are the old hatch strongbacks and are of pine. Bearing in mind the massive scantlings of the beams they were found to be for the main part in satisfactory condition, some surface softening and erosion being noted but not of a serious nature. The 4th beam from forward in the fo'c's'le is in need of attention at the outboard ends, both to P. and S. where small areas of decay are evident. The transom beam needs attention at the outboard end to P. where a small area of decay is in evidence. Half beams fitted under side deck, tie-rods are fitted in association with these beams and no signs of undue strain or movement were apparent.

Bilge Access to the bilge is difficult due to the fact that the sole is fixed and immovable for most of its area. Where access was gained the bilge was found in satisfactory condition.

Blocks Traditional ironbound blocks of ash or elm. All found in acceptable order.

Bobstay Chain fitted with dolphin striker, satisfactory.

Booms Main boom of tubular steel, some minor surface rusting but satisfactory. The boom is slightly bowed but not to any serious extent.
   Mizzen boom solid pine, satisfactory.
   Boom ironwork – iron, some rust but in acceptable condition.

Bowsprit Solid pine in good order.
   Jib boom in satisfactory condition.

Solvig : hauling up the mainsail.

Breasthook Oak on main shelf. The breasthook has deteriorated, generally being soft and eroded over most of its area. To P. the aft end is rotten and showing slight signs of fungal attack. It is recommended that the breasthook is repaired by cutting away the affected timber and either replacing with new wood or a strap steel breasthook.

Bulkheads Variously constructed. Those in the new accommodation are of T. and G. pine. All found in acceptable order.

Bunks The original bunks are still in place in the fo'c's'le and master cabin aft. Those in the aft cabin are pilot berths under the side decks. An additional double berth has been formed across the stern. Bunks in the new accommodation are generally in pairs constructed satisfactorily from pine.

Bulwarks Pine, iron fastened to oak stanchions. Generally found in acceptable condition. Some attention is needed at the butt joints and one or two planks which are loose. There are minor splits and areas of softening, none at present serious.

Bulwark capping Pine, found throughout in good order.

Bulwark stanchions Heavy sectioned oak stanchions are fitted through the deck. Minor deterioration is noted at deck level and also the heads of the stanchions are set out below. The stanchions are numbered from forward.

S. side
No 3 – rot at deck level and on the outboard face.
No 5 – rot at deck level.
No 6 – rot at head.
No 7 – deterioration at deck level and head.
No 9 – deterioration at deck level.
No 10 – rot at head.
No 11 – rot outboard at deck level.
No 13 – rot at the head.
No 14 – badly split.
No 15 – rot at the head.
No 17 – the head is split and deteriorating.
No 19 – at deck level rot on the outboard face.
No 23, 24 and 25 – are soft at the outboard corners at deck level.

P. side
No 1 – very soft at the outboard corners at deck level.
No 9 – rot at the head.
No 10 – rot at deck level and the head.
No 11 – deterioration at the head.
No 13 – rot at deck level and the head.
No 14 – outboard corner at deck level is softening.

No 15 – Outboard face both at deck level and the head is deteriorating.
No 16 – Head is soft.
No 17 – Outboard corners at deck level and the head are rotting.
No 20 – deterioration at deck level and the head.
No 21, 22, 23 – the outboard corners at deck level are softening.
No 24 – shows a bad shake.
It is recommended that the affected timber at each stanchion is cut away and either replaced by new timber or filled with marine glue or pitch.

The covering board may be affected to a minor extent in way of the stanchions and should be treated as mentioned above.

Cabin trunkings Generally of oak with some pine. Constructed on bedlogs bolted on deck and through carlines. The lower edge of the trunkings against the deck show signs of water softening and leaks are evident below decks through the fastenings in the bedlogs and carlines. It is felt that these leaks may well be combated by the fitting of reasonably sized quadrants at the trunking to deck joint, any soft timber being cut away and repaired. The quadrants should be set down on plenty of mastic and secured by screws vertically into the deck and horizontally into the trunking, not diagonally into the joint.

Cable $\frac{5}{8}$in chain. The cable is generally rather rusty but adequate in strength.

Carlines Oak mentioned above there is leakage through the carlines in way of the cabin trunking fastenings. The surface of the carlines particularly in way of the old hold shows some surface erosion but not to any extent which would affect the structural strength. There are two small areas of rot in the carlines in the aft cabin both to P. and S. against the aft corner posts. This affected timber should be cut away and made good.

Caulking Oakum. The bottom shows signs of over-caulking and approximately 10% of the bottom is in need of attention, particularly where the over-caulking is very bad, and also where the seams are open and the stopping is missing. The garboard seam to P. in particular needs completely recaulking and re-stopping; also the rebate seam on the stern post to S. This is tingled over at present with lead but is leaking badly. Many of the butt joints in the planking are tingled over; several were examined and the caulking was found to be waterlogged, but attention to this is not considered vital at present.

Catheads Fitted P. and S. of oak. Both show numerous splits, shakes or cracks and the S. one is very loose and in need of refastening. Due to the general condition of the catheads it would be advisable to replace these with new members, preferably giving a greater outreach than those fitted at present.

Ceilings Throughout the vessel is lined on the inner faces of the frames with pine which restricts inspection access to the structure behind.

Chainplates External steel straps, very rusty as are the fastenings. Strength is considered to be adequate at present.

Cleats Massive mooring cleats are fitted on the inner faces of the frames on deck.

Coachroofs Coachroofs of pine over the deckhouses, over the fo'c's'le, the old hold, engine room and aft cabin. The roof over the accommodation formed in the old hold consists of the old hatch covers fitted over the original strongbacks and canvas covered. This canvas is not secured to the structure below and is a potential source of trouble. The roof over the aft cabin is not canvas covered and areas of rot were found, particularly in way of the skylight to P.; this roof has deteriorated generally and is in need of renewal.

The canvas over the other coachroofs was generally found to be in exceptionally poor condition and in need of immediate renewal.

Corner posts Apart from the aft pair of corner posts to the aft cabin other corner posts were found in satisfactory order.

The corner posts to P. and S. in the aft cabin were both found to be rotten, particularly at their lower ends. This rot has also affected the adjacent structure such as carlines and repairs should be carried out in the near future.

Covering board Oak. Generally found in acceptable condition apart from a small area of rot in way of the 4th stanchion from forward. This rot should be cut away and a graving piece fitted.

Davits Wood stern davits are fitted on the aft rail. Both were found to be rotten at the scarph joint and no reliance should be placed on these davits before repairs have been carried out.

Decks Pine. Seams are payed with marine glue. There are signs that the decks leak and attention should be given to the caulking and paying, particularly in way of the butt joints, some of which are waterlogged.

Doors The doors generally are showing signs of age, but are in acceptable condition. The P. door post to the aft cabin is rotten at the bottom and should be repaired. This rot may also affect the lower edge of the cabin sides.

Engine Not covered under terms of survey. It was noted that a twin cylinder 86hp diesel engine manufactured by A. B.

Jonkopings Motor Fabrik is fitted. The installation of the engine appears to be sound and satisfactory.

Engine room Immediately forward of the master cabin. The engine room is extensively lined with steel or tin sheets, probably an insurance requirement against fire risk when the vessel was in trade. These sheets have rusted and deteriorated extensively. It is recommended that the worst of these are replaced.

Fastenings The vessel is iron-fastened. Numerous fastenings were examined and all were found in acceptable condition. There are no signs of extensive rusting.

Floors Apart from the frame heels the vessel is fitted with some heavy sectioned wood floors in good condition. There are some steel strap floors fitted in the after body which are structurally satisfactory but are rusty.

Frames Very heavy sectioned double oak sawn frames. Where accessible these were found to be in satisfactory condition apart from the frame head in the forepeak which is rotting at the head to S. This rot should be cut away and made good.

Gaffs Both main and mizzen gaffs of solid pine in satisfactory condition apart from the main gaff jaws which are broken and poorly repaired by a steel strap. It is recommended that the gaff jaws are renewed.

Gammon iron Steel straps, satisfactory.

Gas installation The Calor gas bottles are carried in a deck box and are piped to the cooker below, satisfactory.

Hatches Oak, all accommodation access hatches without exception are in need of renovation. They show movement at the joints and a general lack of maintenance. The sliding hatch over the main cabin access is softening and should be renewed.

Hawse Fitted P. and S. the hawse pipes are very rusty and the covering board, knightheads etc. in way of the pipes are eroding badly, particularly at deck level. It is recommended that the hawse pipes are removed, affected timber cut away and the hawse pipes are refitted and secured by oak wedges, and any voids made good with marine glue or pitch.

Hog Oak, satisfactory where seen.

Horse A tubular steel horse is fitted across the foredeck between frame heads for carrying the staysail sheet.

Keel Thought to be beech. The keel is heavily hogged probably about 7in. As these vessels are frequently built with some hog in them and there are no signs of straining or structural movement due to hogging this is not considered a serious matter.

Approximately 35ft from the stem there is a very deep shake on the underside of the keel, approximately 3ft long which should be cleaned out and any soft wood removed and filled against the entry of water.

On the P. side approximately 10ft from the stem a graving piece has been fitted in the past. This is missing and needs replacement.

A false keel approximately 3ft in depth is fitted on the underside of the keel. This is broken and missing for approximately two-thirds of its length and should be renewed.

Knees Oak lodging and quarter knees. Generally show minor surface erosion but satisfactory apart from the pair in the forepeak against the first beam which are in very poor condition and rotting. These knees should be renewed either with new timber or strap steel knees.

Hanging knees are fitted in way of the beams of wrought iron, satisfactory.

Knightheads Oak P. and S. in way of the hawse pipes. Both show vertical shakes and the P. one is softening in way of the shakes. Both are eroding at deck level and renovation is recommended.

Light boards Carried on iron stanchions through the bulwark rail. Need attention to P.

Masts Main mast and top mast of solid pine, found in satisfactory condition. Chafe of the main mast is evident where the gaff jaws work but not to any serious extent.

Mizzen mast solid pine. The mast has a permanent set aft but otherwise satisfactory.

Planking Pine, approximately $2\frac{1}{2}$in in thickness. The general condition of the hull planking is as expected in a vessel of this type and age, showing surface unevenness, minor surface softening and erosion with minor deterioration in way of some of the butt joints and fastenings. Apart from the points set out below the planking is considered to be in acceptable condition but it should be borne in mind that some work will be necessary on the hull during the future years, probably at yearly intervals to keep the vessel in a seaworthy condition.

P. side underwater
As mentioned under Caulking the garboard seam is very poor and needs attention. Several of the butt joints are tingled with lead, where examined the butts were found to be water-soft. Repairs are considered necessary at the butt at waterline approximately 8ft from the stem and 21ft from the stern, also at waterline. Additional repairs should be carried out approximately 12ft from the stem, 4 planks below the waterline where there is an extensive shake and softening for approximately 2ft.

S. side underwater
General condition as on the P. side. The rebate seam against the stern post should be recaulked being at present tingled and in poor condition. There is deep scarring approximately 18in below the waterline extending from approximately 12ft to 24ft from the stem. Repairs should be carried out in the garboard plank approximately 6ft from the stem where a graving piece is missing, and approximately 15ft from the stem 18in below waterline where there is a deep scar and erosion approximately 1ft in length.

P. Topsides
General condition is as above. There are very deep scars in way of where the anchor flukes have chafed against the vessel. It is recommended that these are filled and the whole area where chafe can take place is covered with a steel plate.

In way of the forward main chainplate there is a soft area in the sheer strake. The butt joint in the 3rd plank down from the sheer strake in way of the aft gangway is soft and deteriorated.

The butt joint in way of the new planking in the sheer strake in the midbody is soft. These areas are at present not serious enough to warrant repairs but should be watched for further deterioration.

S. Topsides
Planking is scarred in way of the anchor similar to the S. topsides and should be treated in a similar fashion.

Repairs should be carried out in the following places. 9ft aft of the stem in the planking next to the sheer strake there is a soft area which needs a graving piece. 12ft aft of the stem in the sheer strake there is a small area of rot which should be cut away and renewed. 13ft aft of the stem in the 5th plank below the sheer strake there is a soft area which needs a graving piece, and 18ft aft of the stem in the 3rd plank below the sheer strake there is rot extending for approximately 2ft 6in which should be cut away and replaced with new timber. Other areas which need watching for further deterioration are in way of the 3rd chainplate in way of the bottom fastenings where the planking is softening. 12ft from the stern in the 2nd plank down on the sheer strake there is a soft area. Also 9ft from the stern at the waterline where there is an additional soft patch.

Generally the planking is acceptable but a careful watch

should be kept, particularly in the wind/water region for any further deterioration.

Propeller A 2-bladed variable pitch propeller is fitted on the centreline in satisfactory condition.

Pumps Large diaphragm pattern deck bilge pumps fitted. Found in working order. An additional twin plunger pattern pump was also seen.

Pin rails Fitted against the bulwarks. The forward one to P. is badly rotted on the underside and should be renewed. The aft one to P. is softening but is acceptable at present.

Rigging 7 × 7 galvanized PSWR standing rigging. All found in acceptable order.
Rigging screws Massive steel, satisfactory.
Running rigging Mainly of sisal in acceptable order.

Rubbing strakes Oak capped with iron bin rail satisfactory.

Rudder Oak. Main piece with steel blade. The blade is clad with oak planks which are missing at the heel. It is recommended that the missing timber is replaced on the blade and the existing timber fastenings are checked as they do not appear secure. The lower pintle is badly worn and needs bushing and building up. The false stern post is loose and moves when the helm is turned. It is recommended that the pintles are tightened and additional fastenings fitted if necessary to prevent this movement.

Samson posts Oak fitted against frames fore and aft. The forward samson post to S. is loose and should be refastened.

Seacocks Found in good order.

Shelves Pine. There is slight electro-chemical action in way of the frame fastenings throughout the vessel. This is not serious. The shelf is soft aft against the transom frame, again not to any serious extent.
   There is a small area of rot in the shelf to P. in the pilot berth in the aft cabin. On the S. side in the same place the shelf and some associated blocking is also soft. These areas of rot should be cut away and made good.

Soles Throughout the vessel they were found difficult to lift which restricted access to the bilge.

Steering gear From a wheel on the aft deck by chain and drum, satisfactory.

Stem Oak. It is thought that the head of the stem has been renewed in recent years. The scarph on the outside above waterline is open and should be caulked and stopped against the ingress of moisture.
   On deck the seam between cover board and stem is poor and needs caulking and paying.

Stern post Oak in satisfactory condition. Fastenings through the stern post to the false post outboard should be checked.

Skylights Several skylights are fitted on the coachroofs. Without exception these are in very poor condition and show signs of leakage.

Tanks Inspected as far as practical visually.
   Water tanks are galvanized and appear in good order.
   Fuel tanks which are in the engine room show considerable rust.

Transom Oak found in acceptable order.

Transom frames Oak. The vertical frame outboard to S. shows an area of rot in way of a shake which should be cut away and renewed.

Tierods Fitted under side decks, satisfactory.

Ventilation The ventilation in the old accommodation is poor, particularly in the forepeak where the structure has deteriorated. Ventilation should be provided, particularly in this area.

WC's Two Simpson Lawrence type marine toilets were seen, both in working order.

Wheel Traditional deck steering wheel which is in rather poor condition. It is recommended the wheel is knocked down and reassembled.

Zinc wasting plates Sacrificial plates are fitted underwater. These appear to be working. They should be renewed every other season or two to give protection.

28th September, 1972.   P. S. Brown,
                         Francis Jones & Partners,
                         Yacht Designers and Surveyors,
                         Ferry Quay, Woodbridge, Suffolk.

Lines and sail plan of 50-ton spritsail
barge, redrawn after plans of
Nautilus in the Science Museum,
London.
LOA 77ft 0in.
Beam 18ft 9in.
Draught (laden) 5ft 6in.

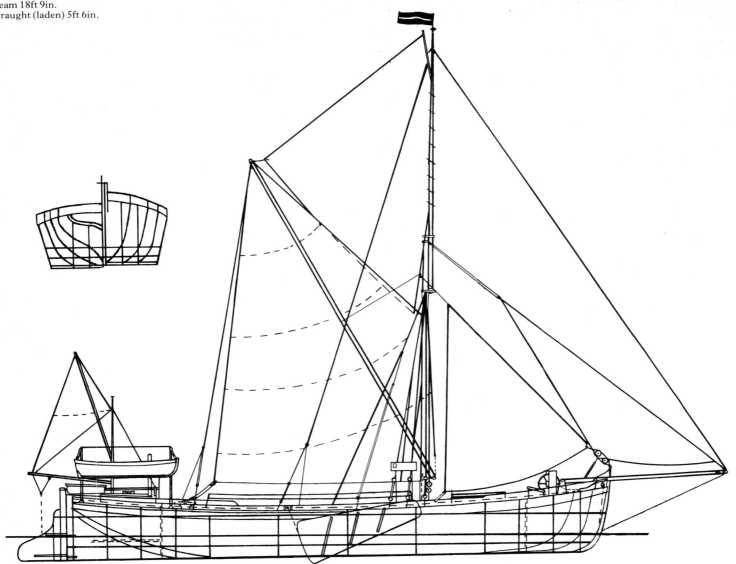

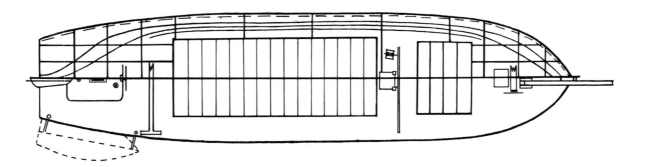

Thames sailing barges

Sailing barges were in their day the most humble, least considered of commercial sailing craft. They were to be found, in their different types, in most of the shallow estuaries of Europe from the Tagus to the Thames. They carried every kind of bulk cargo on coastal passages and up rivers and creeks.

The Thames sailing barge developed during the nineteenth century from a swim-headed lighter, that carried a bit of sail to help push it along, into a highly sophisticated sailing machine. Even though at a first impression the basic shape of a barge may appear to be a bit like a shoebox, further investigation shows considerable subtlety in the lines. The flat bottom, which was so convenient both for cargo stowage and for sitting on the mud, did not make for a weatherly hull. However, her two leeboards and the bite of her long chine gave a surprisingly good windward performance.

The average sized Thames river sailing barge carried 140 tons of cargo and was over 80ft long and 18ft beam and drew about 7ft when fully loaded. The truck of the topmast was some 70ft above the deck. An Oregon pine sprit 56ft long pivoted from the foot of the mast just above deck level. This hefty pole provided the answer to the question how these fairly large sailing vessels were handled and sailed by a crew of two. The sprit provided support for the peak of the mainsail, which never had to be lowered to the deck but was brailed up like a theatre curtain. The topsail likewise remained aloft but could easily be set or furled from the deck.

Races for trading barges on the river Thames were started by William Henry Dodd in 1863. Dodd, a muck-contractor and refuse collector, had made a fortune from his unsalubrious trade and earned the nickname of 'the golden dustman'. Dodd's aim was not only to provide a sporting event but also to improve the design, build, and equipment of the barges as well as the status of the men who sailed them. The races proved a triumphant success.

When the series of sailing barge races started by the golden dustman ended in 1963, exactly one hundred years after they had started, there were few barges still trading under sail. However, there were still a dozen or so that were being sailed as yachts. The owners of these barges arranged a new series of races, four each year, to be held at Southend, in the Medway, the Blackwater, and at Pin Mill on the Orwell. These races continue to this day. Among the most successful barges in these later races have been the *May*, the *Edith May* and the *Spinaway C*. The *May* was built at Harwich in 1891 and is owned by a subsidiary of the sugar firm of Tate & Lyle; she is used by them as a sail training ship. On occasions she still carries a cargo of sugar.

One or two barges have been converted into training ships. A pioneer in their use for this purpose is the East Coast Sail Trust. In 1960, the Trust bought *Memory*. Six years later, the Trust replaced *Memory* by the 150 ton 'mulie' barge *Thalatta*, an auxiliary barge built at Harwich and owned for many years by Pauls' the Ipswich millers. 'Mulie' means that she was mule-rigged, that is, with a standing gaff on her mizzen mast. The first objective of the East Coast Sail Trust is to provide educational and adventure cruises for boys and girls, the second is to preserve at least one sailing barge in seagoing condition.

In 1970 there was only one Thames barge still trading under sail alone. This was the *Cambria*, owned and skippered by Captain Bob Roberts. In the October of that year the Maritime Trust bought *Cambria* from Bob Roberts. She is to be kept in her original trading state and will eventually be placed in a suitable berth on the Thames. *Cambria* is a fine seagoing mulie barge with a steel hull 123ft long and 21ft beam. She was built for F. T. Everard & Co at Greenhithe in 1906.

Old Thames sailing barges can still be bought. A few of them have been kept in use as yachts or houseboats by private owners. They look as if they might be an appealing proposition for restoration, for they are big enough to live in and yet when trading they were handled by a crew of two. To deal with the latter point first; they need to be handled by an experienced professional skipper and mate. As for the restoration, this can be a very big undertaking. After the restoration, which could easily cost a fortune if the work has to be entrusted to a shipyard, there is the annual cost of maintenance, slipping the barge and so on to be reckoned with.

Some people are capable of both sailing a barge and doing most of the restoration work themselves. John Fairbrother, the owner of the barge *Kitty*, is such a person. As soon as he had left school he joined a barge as mate. This was Cranfield Brothers' *Spinaway C*, in which he served under Bill Polly who came from a famous Ipswich barging family. *Spinaway C*, though she is no longer trading, is still winning races. She was built in Ipswich in 1899 with a net tonnage of 57 tons, some 8 tons less than *Kitty*, whose restoration we are going to consider in some detail.

Thames sailing barge *Kitty*

OAL (bowsprit end to aft of rudder blade) 110ft 0in
    (between stem post and transom) 82ft 0in
Draught (unladen) 3ft 8in
Draught (laden) 6ft 6in
Net tonnage 65
Built 1895

Kitty was built at Gashouse Creek, Harwich, for Horatio Horlock of Mistley. She worked between Mistley and the

London river carrying barley, malt and cattle feed. In 1933 she
was sold by the Horlocks to Francis & Gilders of Colchester
who used her for the general carrying trade. It was soon after
this that Frank Carr, in his book *Sailing Barges*, described
Kitty as 'one of the finest barges in the large fleet owned by
Francis & Gilders'.

In 1955 *Kitty* was no longer a paying proposition, so her
sailing gear was removed and she was sold to Browns' of
Chelmsford for use as a timber lighter in Heybridge Basin. In
1964 John Fairbrother and two friends formed the Maldon
Yacht & Barge Charter Co Ltd and bought *Kitty* for a modest
figure as a bare hull.

Secondhand spars, sails, rigging and leeboards were found
without much difficulty at various barge centres. The objective
was to restore her to the working condition of a well kept
trading barge, so no cabin trunks or deckhouses were built. The
only external differences visible on deck are the skylights in the
main hatch and also the companion way, which has been cut
through the hatch covers on the port side. Otherwise, the
original hatch covers are still in use and *Kitty* from a few yards
off looks just like a trading barge.

Inside the barge, the first major job was to refloor her from
end to end. The old flooring boards were so rotten they had to
be shovelled out. Deal boards were bought (£125 worth), impregnated with anti-fungal solution and laid on the original
timbers. Some of these timbers were a bit soft but did not need
immediate replacement. The massive kelson which is about
16in square and stretches from bow to stern, was a pitchpine
log and absolutely sound.

Even though a barge is a square sectioned flat bottomed
vessel, its construction is quite complicated. A Thames barge
is built in a most idiosyncratic manner. So idiosyncratic, in fact,
that one would think bargebuilders were determined no one
should ever rebuild one. The longitudinal stiffness is achieved
by the heavy kelson, which acts as a backbone and is set on top
of the floor timbers which are spaced at 20in distance from
centre to centre above the relatively insignificant keel which,
though 12in wide, is only 4in thick. This backbone assembly of
kelson, floors and keel is reinforced by two chine kelsons, which
are pitchpine logs running the full length of the chines and
bolted to both floors and the vertical frames. These frames are
also half-dovetailed into the floors and provide the support for
the outside planking. A barge's flat bottom has transverse
floors that are checked into a chine timber that runs the length
of the chine. The side frames likewise are fastened to this chine
timber. Just below deck level the frames are enclosed in an
inner and outer wale, the inner being comparable to a shelf or
sheer clamp in ordinary boat construction. The deck beams are
dovetailed into the inner wale.

The wales in the *Kitty* are oak planks 16in deep on the out-

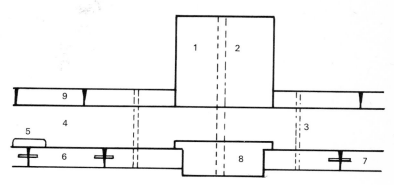

Bottom construction of barge:
kelson and keel. The bottoms of some
barges were sheathed with 1in pine
planking and a layer of 'hair and
blair'.
1 Kelson (pitchpine) 12in × 16in.
2 1in galvanized steel bolt.
3 ¾in galvanized steel bolt.
4 Floor (oak) 8ft × 6in.
5 Limber hole.
6 Bottom (pine) 3in.
7 Dowel.
8 Keel (elm) 12in × 4in.
9 Ceiling (pine) 14in × 3in.

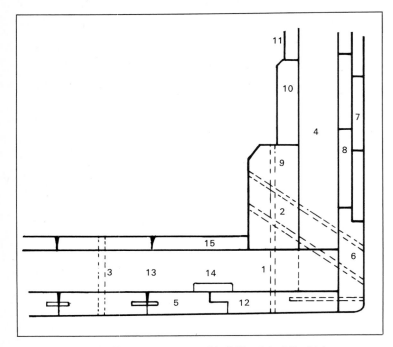

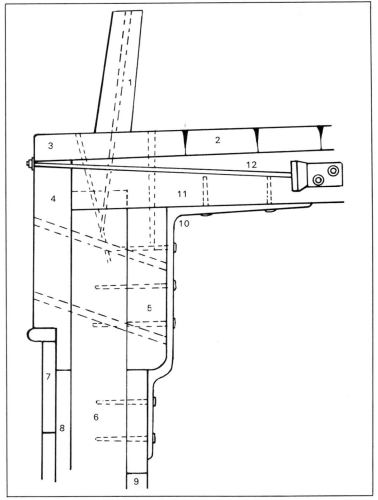

Chine construction of barge.
1 $\frac{7}{8}$in galvanized steel bolt.
2 $\frac{3}{4}$in galvanized steel bolt.
3 $\frac{3}{4}$in galvanized steel bolt.
4 Frame (oak) 6in × 6in.
5 Bottom (pitchpine) 3in thick.
6 Chine (elm) 16in × 3in.
7 Outer planking (pitchpine) 1$\frac{3}{8}$in,
   separated by a layer of hair and
   blair from.
8 Inner planking (pitchpine)
   1$\frac{1}{4}$in thick.
9 Chine kelson (pitchpine)
   16in × 7in.
10 Chine rider (oak) 12in. × 2$\frac{1}{2}$in.
    This runs from transom through
    cabin 12ft along the chine.

11 Ceiling (pine) 2in thick.
12 Lower chine (elm) 16in. × 3in.
13 Floor (oak) 8in × 6in.
14 Limber hole.
15 Ceiling (pine) 14in × 3in.

Barge construction, continued.
The use of tie rods where deck beams
are weak :
1 Rail (oak) 12in × 3in.
2 Deck (pine) 6in × 3in.
3 Covering board (oak) 12in × 3in.
4 Outer wale (oak).
5 Inwale (larch) 12in × 3in.
6 Frame (oak) 6in. × 6in.
7 Outer planking (pine) 1$\frac{3}{8}$in,
   separated by 'hair and blair' from
8 Inner planking (pine) 1$\frac{1}{4}$in.
9 Ceiling (pine) 2in thick.
10 Wrought iron carling.
11 Deck beam (oak) 8in × 8in.
12 Tie rod with 3in washer
    overlapping covering board joint.

side and larch planks 3in thick on the inside. These wales and timber heads are through-fastened with bolts, dumps and spikes. In the *Kitty*'s case, and this would apply to most old barges, the inner wale and beam ends had deteriorated very badly owing to fungal decay. Thus there was virtually no transverse strength left at deck level. To cure this defect, John Fairbrother fitted steel tie-rods. The ties were bolted into steel angle brackets fitted to the beams 3ft inboard. The heads of the bolts fitted over 3in washers that overlapped both the covering board and the top planks. This effectively held the boat together. However, deterioration was continuing, though much more slowly as the deck was tight and no rainwater was getting down below. This deterioration in wales, timbers and chines is typical of barges of this age, but they are so strongly built that they remain quite seaworthy. John Fairbrother plans to replace *Kitty*'s chine timbers in due course, a major operation.

When the lining of the *Kitty*'s hold was removed, some deterioration of the topside planking was visible, yet the planks on the outside were or appeared to be sound. The reason for this is the double sheathing and the 'hair and blair' (a mixture of cow hair and tar) between the planking. Today, shipwrights would use felt. It is almost impossible to remove the inside planking of this double sheathing, so one has to double up from outside.

The two layers of the side planking are of $1\frac{1}{4}$in and $1\frac{3}{8}$in pitchpine fastened with treenails and galvanized spikes. The tar and cow hair is worked in hot between the planks and into the seams. The bottom planking, which runs fore and aft, is of 3in pitchpine, also treated with tar and hair between the seams. It is fastened to the floors with oak treenails driven upwards.

The deck is of 3in Oregon pine, bolted to the deck beams which are half-dovetailed into the inner wale. The seams of the deck are caulked with three strands of oakum and then payed with pitch or marine glue. The barge is further stiffened along the side decks by wrought iron or mild steel angle brackets, called in bargebuilding terminology 'carlings'. These are bolted to the deck beams and to the inner wale.

The stem and apron assembly follows normal wooden ship building practice, except that the plank ends are fastened to the apron, and the stem post, which is of oak 10in sided and 11in moulded, covers the plank ends. The transom is heavily planked with 5in oak planks, fastened to the stern post and the fashion frames.

The barge *Kitty* is lined and floored with heavy planks of Oregon pine fastened with spikes.

The original bulkheads in the *Kitty* were still in good condition and the fo'c's'le and captain's cabin were in fair order. The latter was pleasantly panelled in pine but much of the beading on the panelling had to be replaced. When this was completed and a new table fitted, the skipper and mate had a snug little retreat. A small stainless steel Pither stove replaced the old open grate, which had long since disappeared. Another and larger Pither was fitted in the saloon which filled the after part of the hold. These stoves are kept going all the winter, which keeps the barge aired. Sleeping cabins with twelve bunks, a lavatory and a washroom were partitioned off in the midships part of the barge.

The mast and spars were cleaned up, varnished and stepped. New running rigging was set up and the sails were bent on early in 1965. A new mainsail was bought for £185. At the time of writing, the price would be about £450. By the April of that year, *Kitty* was away on her first charter voyage.

John Fairbrother finally took over the shares of his two original and at the time indispensable partners. At the end of each charter season he set to work on a series of jobs aboard the barge. *Kitty* is getting old, like all the other barges afloat. She was actually over seventy years old when John Fairbrother took her over. She needed a lot done to her. His first major job was to build new bittheads and scarph these into the timbers below deck, which were quite sound. In four successive winters John Fairbrother replaced the rail, capping and covering board. A barge's rail has no stanchions but is of solid oak 3in thick and about 12in high. It is through-fastened with dump bolts to the timber heads below the covering board. The *Kitty* has a bluff bow so, though the timber was green, the bow section had to be steamed. The local yard's steam box was borrowed for this purpose.

The same yard fitted a new stem post to replace the old one which was in very bad condition. As I mentioned earlier, a barge is so constructed that the topside planking is not rebated into the stem post but is fastened to the apron. Thus the re-fitting of a stem post is not a problem and in fact the barge would still remain afloat even when the stem post was removed.

One interesting feature in the *Kitty* is a door, set into the forward bulkhead of the hold, which opened into the fo'c's'le. This door was there so that the mate, who was stowing the large sacks of barley, could stow a few extra in the fo'c's'le to increase the barge's capacity as barley always has to be stowed under hatches and is a bulky cargo. John Fairbrother believes that this door was cut in the bulkhead within a year or so of *Kitty*'s launching.

Today *Kitty* is a fine looking barge. She never had an engine and so is dependent on a tug to shift her out of her berth on the Hythe at Maldon. As a charter barge she is unique, and really gives the feeling of what life aboard one of these sailing craft must have been like, as she works her tides through the swatchways of the Thames estuary or noses her way up the rivers and creeks that lies between Orfordness and the North Foreland. *Kitty* is enjoying an Indian summer and is fortunate to be in such good hands, for not only is John Fairbrother a real 'sailor-

1

Sailing barge *Kitty* at Maldon,
Essex.
1 Bows and winch.
2 *Kitty's* transom.
3 Looking forward, with washboards
   in foreground.
4 Looking aft, showing foot of mast
   and sprit.

3

man' but in every aspect of the vessel, both above and below decks, there is evidence of his skilled craftsmanship. Her saloon and galley, which of course are no part of the restoration, are superbly planned and constructed yet seem utterly appropriate to this lovely old trading vessel.

The Norfolk wherry

In the lowlands of East Anglia there are a great number of shallow, brackish lakes, bordered by reedbeds and linked by artificial channels to rivers that ultimately run into the North Sea. The origin of the shallow lakes lies in the peat diggings of the late Middle Ages. These are the Norfolk Broads, set in a landscape of fens and reclaimed pastureland. It is a watery countryside reminiscent of Friesland, with a vast open skyline broken at intervals by the towers of great reed-thatched flint churches and tall windmills.

Reed cutting for thatched roofs still goes on in the winter when wildfowlers in their gun punts are afloat. In the summer months, these waters are thick with pleasure craft. Of the black-sailed trading wherries that were the main method of transport before the days of the motor lorry there is only one survivor, the *Albion*.

Special conditions have produced specialized craft. The various types of flat bottomed Dutch boats, evolved to sail over the short steep waves of the Zuiderzee or the quieter waters of Friesland, provide the richest variety of such an evolution.

In Britain, the Norfolk Broads provide the only comparable conditions and the Norfolk wherry is the one type of trading vessel that has survived.

In 1949, a group of wherry enthusiasts met in a dark cellar in Tombland, Norwich. This was actually the bookshop of Roy Clark, who was one of the instigators of the Norfolk Wherry Trust. Another at this meeting was Major James Forsythe, who is now the chairman of the trust, and a third and perhaps the most important was Lady Mayhew, for it was Lady Mayhew who provided the hull of a wherry called the *Plane* which her family had used as a lighter in the Norwich river.

The objectives of the trust were to keep at least one Norfolk wherry trading and so to preserve a unique vessel. They had a hull; after their first public meeting they raised £750 and, with this modest sum, they fitted her out.

A wherry is rigged somewhat like a cat boat with her mast right up in the eyes of the ship. A large black gaff sail (*Albion*'s is 1,400 square feet) is raised by a single halliard which leads to a winch just forward of the mast. With a loaded draught of only 4ft, a length of 50ft or more and a beam of about 15ft, these boats were remarkably weatherly, but it was a skilled business to sail a wherry – in fact it was usually a family business, the knowhow being handed on from father to son.

The hull was practically all cargo hold, the forepeak largely taken up with the space for the foot of the counterbalanced mast to swing in when it was lowered or raised. A small, neat cabin was set in the stern with doors leading to a well from where she was steered by means of a 6ft tiller. The Norwich river wherries did not have a well; they were called 'high stern sheet' wherries. Both types of craft had low freeboard and no bulwarks. The narrow sidedecks were left clear so that the wherryman could walk along as he quanted the boat when there was no wind. When the wind was dead ahead, he made fast to the bank.

Since the 1880s, wherries were fitted with a false keel about 35ft long and 18in deep, which helped to make them more weatherly. It was bolted through the main keel with three bolts. The way this false keel was fastened is of some interest, even though it has nothing to do with restoration. On either side of the stem post, two curved pieces of iron stretched up from the false keel to near the stem head to which they were bolted. At the after end of the false keel, there were two holes through which lines were rove and held with stopper knots. These lines led in opposite directions up to the deck.

When approaching anywhere such as Bungay, where the river was shallow, the keel would be slipped, the boltholes plugged and the keel left on the river bank. When the wherry returned, the false keel would be dragged under the vessel and lined up by means of ropes, then drawn up and refastened. A surprisingly small amount of water entered the vessel while this manoeuvre was taking place.

The wherries were picturesque craft, with their black hulls and a white quadrant painted on either side of their stem. The Norwich wherries differed here, having no painted 'eyes'. From the decks upwards, they vie with the old canal narrow boats with their use of colour, with vermilion, dark blue, yellow and white on hatch covers and coamings and on rigging and mastheads. At the masthead a bright red fathom-long pennant flew from a decorative vane. The *Albion* has all this.

Norfolk wherry *Albion*

LOA 58ft 0in
Beam 15ft 0in
Draught 4ft 6in
Registered tonnage 22·78
Payload (tons) 40
Built 1898

When the Norfolk Wherry Trust began to investigate the history of the *Plane*, (Lady Mayhew's wherry), they found that she had been built by William Brighton, a yacht and smack builder with a yard at Lake Lothing on the seaward side of the lock. She was built for W. D. & A. E. Walker, Maltsters, of

Bungay. She was launched in October 1898 as *Albion* – and *Albion* the trust renamed her.

Albion was built from a half model and, unlike any other trading wherry ever built, she was carvel planked. The reason suggested for this was that her lands, if clinker planked, might catch on the sills of the lock. Apparently the Walkers, her owners, had lost another wherry in this way. She earned her keep carrying barley for the Bungay firm for over thirty years though she sank once near Yarmouth Bridge and in 1931 lost her Oregon pine mast. She was sold in that year to the General Steam Navigation Co and, following the company's policy of naming their wherries after trees, she was renamed *Plane*. She continued under sail until 1939 when she was stripped of her gear and used as a lighter. A year or so later, Colmans' bought her.

In November 1949, under the auspices of the Norfolk Wherry Trust, with Jack Cates as skipper and his brother George, known as 'Shackles', as mate, *Albion* was trading again. For two years she was kept going with goodwill freights of grain, timber, building materials, sugar, and even beer to an isolated Broadland pub, but it was a losing battle. There was not enough trade to pay the crew's wages, let alone take care of her upkeep. However, there was a demand for charter work of a somewhat spartan, outward-bound character. With a five month season, *Albion* was kept at work combining charters with a certain amount of trade but not without her share of trouble. She broke her mast racing on Breydon Water in 1952; five years later she sank at Hardley Staithe with a load of sugar beet and in 1959 she sank again. She continued her mixed charter-trading existence up until 1965, when mounting costs brought matters to a head.

The Norfolk Wherry Trust reformed their committee and set about a fundraising operation with some success. Money was now at hand for some very necessary restoration work on *Albion*. Quite a lot of money is needed to keep any relatively large vessel in good order, and *Albion* was no exception.

In 1965, *Albion*'s restoration was carried out under the guidance of John E. Perryman who is not only a successful practising naval architect and surveyor but is also passionately interested in the preservation of old craft. To this end, Perryman has become an authority on the control of decay in old boats.

When *Albion* was slipped, John Perryman found that she was hogged by eighteen inches. By supporting the wherry only at her ends this was reduced to nine inches, but she would not go down any more and the false keel was permanently fixed in position.

The restoration consisted of completely reframing the hull and refastening with galvanized steel spikes. Her new frames were all from oak crooks, locally grown. They are 8in × 4in and doubled. Her stem, stern and keel assemblies are still original, as is about half of her 1¾in oak planking. Her original rock elm garboards are still sound. *Albion* had a new foredeck of pitchpine and a new cabin top fitted. Her tabernacle and shelves are still original.

A new mast of pitchpine and a new gaff have been made. The mast was a gift from a local boatyard. A new sail also was presented to them by one of the Broads boat hire firms.

The actual shipwright's work has followed normal practice for a wherry; in spite of its uniqueness, it is much more like a normal wooden ship than is a Thames barge and its construction is only a variant on the art of smack building.

A most valuable lesson in *Albion*'s restoration can be learned from the methods used to counter fungal decay. *Albion* is being

treated with two different types of fungicides, Brunophen and Woodtreat.

Brunophen is an organic solvent type of preservative and is both fungicidal and insecticidal. It is effective against dry and wet rot, wood destroying beetles, and termites. It is not effective against marine borers.

One of the best features of Brunophen is that it is highly penetrating. It dries quickly and paint or varnish can be applied as soon as the non-corrosive (to metals) solvents have dried out. There are two grades of this preservative No 1 and No 2. No 2 is used on *Albion*.

Brunophen No 2 can be applied by submerging the timber in a container of the preservative for anything from a few hours to some days, depending on the size and the permeability of the timber. It can also be sprayed or painted on. The spraying method is being used in *Albion*, with particular attention to all the joints. For this purpose, special wedge-shaped nozzles are fitted to the spray guns and these are forced into all the joints, and the preservative is then driven in under pressure. It is also freely painted on the surface of the timbers. When the first application has dried, the process is repeated a second time.

One gallon of Brunophen No 2 will treat about 200sq ft of new timber. Infected or partially rotten timber may need twice as much. Protective clothing including Toucan spray masks and goggles should be worn when spraying.

Woodtreat is a new type of organic solvent preservative in the form of a thick creamy emulsion. Woodtreat should be used in confined undisturbed places. On *Albion*, it is being used both to protect new timbers and for eradicating decay in infected wood that is difficult to cut out.

Before an old boat is subjected to this fungicidal treatment, all the surfaces of her timbers should be thoroughly cleaned and all surfaces dried.

In any reconstruction work, John Perryman suggests that the end grain or faying surfaces of scarphs and other joints should be treated with preservative. When using Woodtreat, cover these surfaces with a layer of emulsion ¼in thick, but not if they are to be glued. In that case use Brunophen. All holes bored for nails, screws or bolts should be filled with preservative. Any softwood used in badly ventilated areas or where rainwater might lodge should be coated with Woodtreat, and any hardwood used for replacing frames etc should have its endgrain coated and boreholes filled with Woodtreat. Any new cut ends of timbers that were partially rotten and have had the rotten wood cut away should also be treated with Woodtreat. Where it is difficult to remove an infected timber, give it a liberal coating of the preservative. Wherever possible remove or cut away decayed timber.

The successful penetration of Woodtreat is due to the thick coating of emulsion acting as a reservoir on the surface of the wood. The emulsion consists of oil containing the active preserving ingredients emulsified in a much smaller volume of water. After it has been applied to the surface of the timber, the water evaporates and the mixture of oil and preservatives penetrates the wood. Even if the coating is spread unevenly or put on in bands some inches apart, the same thing happens. Woodtreat can be spread with a rough-surfaced trowel, a wooden batten, or with old worn brushes or even with a lambskin glove. For seams, joints, etc a caulking gun is ideal.

The importance of these preservation treatments in restoration work is obvious. In *Albion*, a programme of treating her timbers is being followed over a three-year period. No doubt such treatment will be repeated from time to time.

Yachts

The first three Broads One-design boats tacking through Lowestoft Inner Harbour in 1901 on their way back to Oulton Broad.
In the foreground is a trading wherry hoisting her mast. (*Photo Ford Jenkins.*)

Introduction The restoration of old yachts, particularly large yachts, is a much more exacting task than restoring old fishing boats. Yachts were built by highly skilled craftsmen, much of whose skill was devoted to a high degree of finish. Fishing smacks, though usually well enough built for their purpose, were roughly built for rough usage. In New England, they were often built by the fishermen themselves.

Anyone setting to work to restore or rebuild a fine old yacht should be prepared to match his joinery skills with those of a cabinet maker. Not all yachts were built to these high standards, but thoroughbreds deserve fine craftsmanship.

The small yachts that have lasted longest are those used on inland waters. One of the reasons for this is that they were usually kept in wet boathouses, not drying out yet protected from the weather. The Norfolk Broads must have more yachts over fifty years old than any other comparable area. Some are much older than this, such as the *Volunteer*, which was built in the 1870s, or the *Dora*, which was built in 1898 and much loved by the Lamb family to whom it belonged for over sixty years; or the *Flittermouse*, one of the original four Broads One-Designs, built in 1900.

The restoration of a boat of the size of a Broads One-Design (which can be lifted on to a trailer and taken to one's home) is within the capabilities of any good amateur woodworker. With larger yachts, different problems emerge, problems of time, cost and accessibility. These seem to multiply many times over with big yachts like the schooner *Heartsease* and the ketch *Armorel*.

The Broads One-Design (The Brown Boats)
Flittermouse

LOA 24ft 0in
LWL 16ft 0in
Beam 5ft 10in
Draught 3ft 0in
Sail area 252sq ft
Built 1900–1

The Broads One-Design, because of their varnished hulls, are always referred to as the Brown Boats. They were designed by Linton Hope in 1900 as a class of keel racing boat, suitable both for the inland waters of the Norfolk Broads and for the troubled waters of the North Sea off Lowestoft.

Linton Hope was a successful naval architect whose designs were advanced for their time. By 1914, Lloyds *Register of Yachts* showed nearly 170 yachts from his drawing board. In the Brown Boats, Linton Hope produced boats that were not only fast but also good seaboats. They are pretty little boats with fine lines, a shallow spoon bow and an overhanging counter. They were originally built by the Burnham Yacht Building Company.

The rigging and sail plan is simple and efficient. They have a stemhead gaff rig, with a mast in a tabernacle, and two sails only, a mainsail and a staysail. All the halliards and the topping lift lead through the foredeck and are made fast below deck. When the yachts are racing, if it is blowing hard, instructions are given for one or two reefs and every boat has to follow these orders.

At one stage, various owners experimented with Bermudan rig but the boats would not point so well. The centre of effort had shifted. Also, the long Bermudan mast was much more troublesome when lowering away for bridges. Today they are all gaff rigged. They are based mostly on Oulton Broad or at Wroxham. The original boats cost £100; today, a new one would cost over £2,000, but they are still being built.

In 1972 Mr Nick Truman, at the Old Maltings Boatyard at Oulton Broad, built and launched No 32 of the fleet. She was built exactly to Linton Hope's design but, of course, from new moulds – the old ones having long since disappeared. Mr Truman has been responsible for the restoration of several Brown Boats. It is a firm rule of the BOD Club that any rebuilding must leave the boats as they were, with no 'improvements' to make them lighter. Amongst those Mr Truman has restored are *Dunlin, Peewit, Dabchick, Snipe, Bittern, Mallard, Shearwater, Widgeon, Gannet* and *Goshawk*. The Brown Boats are all named after birds with the solitary exception of *Flittermouse*; there are plenty of bats in Norfolk, seven different varieties in fact, including the Water Bat (Daubenton's) which on summer evenings can be seen hawking low over the Broads for midges and other insects.

Flittermouse, in company with *Dunlin, Teal* and *Curlew*, made their first appearance on Whit Monday 1901. *Flittermouse* was built for Newborn Garnett who in 1906 sold her to G. A. Wells Beard. In 1908 *Flittermouse* was bought as a wedding present for a young couple, Mr and Mrs W. L. Clabburn. Mr Clabburn raced her regularly for the next fifty years and, even when he was in his eighties, he and *Flittermouse* were still winning races. In 1957 *Flittermouse* was bought by Mr J. Hall and in 1963 was sold to Lord Somerleyton. She was not raced for the next few years but was laid up in a barn until 1970, when she was bought by Mr Tim Whelpton. Mr Whelpton brought *Flittermouse* to his boatyard at Upton, near Acle. The hull had dried out to such an extent that he could see daylight through the shakes in the deadwood. Everyone of her ninety-six timbers was either rotten or broken. Her decks had gone but her Honduras mahogany planking looked sound. *Flittermouse* was lowered into the water and after being allowed to soak for some days was then bailed out and brought into the shed.

Broads One-Design lines and sail
plan. *(Courtesy Charles Goodey.)*
LOA 24ft 0in.
LWL 16ft 0in.
Beam 5ft 10in.
Draught 3ft. 0in.
Sail area 252sq ft.

0' 1' 2' 3' 4' 5'

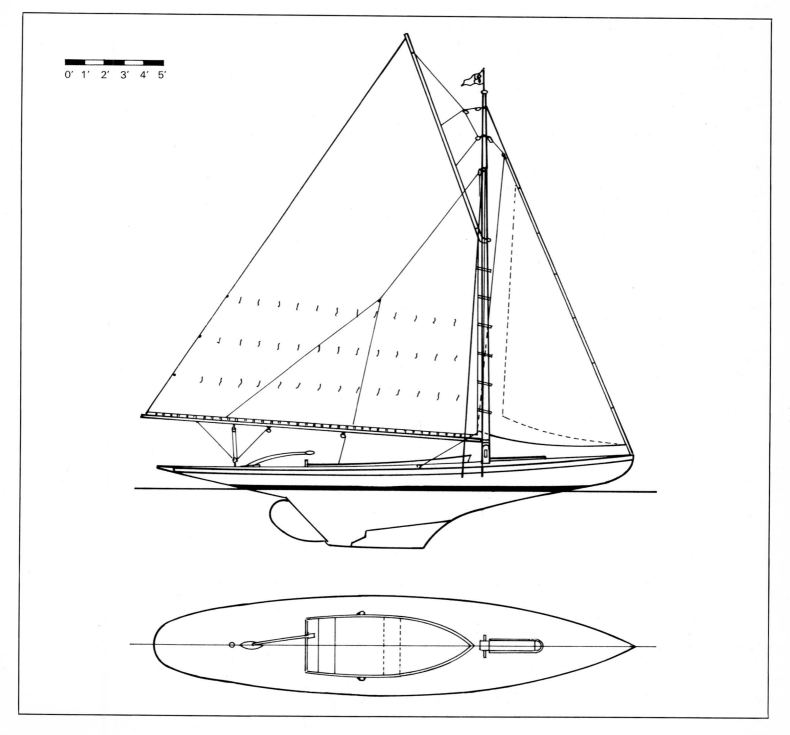

Dunlin, the first of the Brown Boats, coming about off Lowestoft.

Flittermouse (No 3) leading the
fleet of Brown Boats in a race during
Lowestoft sea week.

When the little yacht had dried and had been cleaned out, Mr Whelpton could see that her mahogany planking was still in good condition. All the old fastenings were driven out, ninety-six new oak timbers were fitted and she was refastened. New deck beams were fitted and, to strengthen the old hull, a marine ply deck was fitted and in due course covered with Trakmark. New coamings of teak, new floorboards, new chainplates and stem and keel band, new gudgeons, pintles and rudder completed the rebuild. The old Honduras mahogany hull was sanded down and given many coats of varnish. When Mr Whelpton had finished his work, *Flittermouse* looked as good as the day she was launched; she looked even better, for she now had the mellowness of a fine piece of old furniture.

The Brown Boats may look oldfashioned but they are superbly suited to their environment. As for being good sea boats – in June 1968, during the Lowestoft sea week, they continued racing in heavy weather off Lowestoft whilst the much larger Dragons decided they were better off in harbour. At least half a dozen of the Brown Boats in that race were over sixty years old.

224 ton Auxiliary Schooner *Heartsease*

The problem of restoring a seventy-year old 120ft schooner with an original sail area of 16,000sq ft and no ballast keel (her original keel weighed 62 tons) would be too daunting a proposition for most people. However, *Heartsease*'s new owner, Wing-Commander Gordon Waller, a retired RAAF Officer, is someone who is not easily daunted. Before he bought *Heartsease*, he had rescued a paddle steamer in Australia. This unusual craft is worth more than a mention. She was called *Brothers* and was 110ft long, 24ft beam and drew only 2ft when empty and 5ft when loaded. *Brothers* was a stern-wheeler driven by a double expansion steam engine. She was built to carry timber on the Myall Lakes which lie just inland from the coast of New South Wales, about midway between the north and south state boundaries. The lakes, which are now a national park, are about thirty miles long but have a shore line of nearly 400 miles. Gordon Waller found *Brothers* underwater, even if the depth was only three feet or so. His rescue of this unique craft would make another saga. At least when he found *Heartsease* he had some experience in dealing with relatively large craft.

In *Heartsease,* he began with a fine hull that was sound and beautifully fitted out below decks. *Heartsease* (or *Adela* as she was originally named) had been built for Claud Thornton Cayley, who must have been a very rich man. Cayley was born and educated in Canada. He had inherited his love of yachts from his father, who had been the Vice-Commodore of the Royal Canadian Yacht Club in Toronto. *Adela* was Claud Cayley's third boat. She was designed for him by W. C. Storey and built by Fay & Co of Itchen near Southampton. She was launched in 1903. She was composite-built of teak planking on iron frames. Her 62 ton ballast keel was of lead and she was intended for both racing and cruising. She carried a captain, mate and a crew of twenty-two; there was accommodation in seven or eight cabins for the owner and his guests and room for many more in her huge stateroom, which was the full width of the ship. The quality of the panelling and cabinet work in this accommodation has to be seen to be believed. The stateroom is hung with a green damask with chair-rail high maplewood panelling; both have faded to much the same beautiful colour. The cabins are fitted out in the finest Honduras mahogany.

Adela was none too successful in her first season of racing, but after her head had been raised by ballasting down her stern she proved to be a different ship altogether. She raced with some success against the German emperor's very large schooner *Meteor* and against two other schooners, Mr Max Guilleaume's *Clara* and Lord Iveagh's *Cetonia*; and also against Sir Maurice Fitzgerald's famous yawl *Satanita*.

In 1904, in her second year of racing, she was awarded a cup by the Kaiser at the Kiel Regatta for her performance in coming in second in the main race for the big schooners. Mr Cayley sold *Adela* in 1914. The day of the great and vastly expensive racing schooners was nearing its end and war was imminent. Little seems to be known of *Adela* between 1914 and 1920, but she served in the war as a mine spotting vessel in the English Channel and the North Sea. Gordon Waller wrote:

'It stirs one's imagination to think of this vast and graceful engine-less schooner gliding through these waters, with, one assumes, the White Ensign flying and her masthead man searching for mines instead of for the best racing wind and tide, as was his task during the halcyon days of pre-war yachting.'

In 1920, *Adela* had an auxiliary engine installed and was fitted out for ocean cruising. In 1923, she changed hands again and her new owner, Sir Henry Seymour King, changed her name to *Heartsease*. Except for the duration of World War II, she was in commission until 1951, though she was put up for sale in the spring of 1938 for a mere £8,000. In 1951, she was sold for considerably more than that to someone who wanted to use her as a houseboat. She was stripped of her spars, sails and gear, her lead keel was cut away and all this was sold. *Heartsease* was then put in a mud berth at Tollesbury at the head of a creek on the river Blackwater in Essex. Here she remained with a paid hand living permanently aboard until 1968 when her owner died. Mr Tim Whelpton, boatbuilder and former charter-skipper from Upton on the Norfolk Broads (the owner and restorer of the Broads One-Design *Flittermouse*), and Mr J. H. Russell, a dentist, both members of the Royal Norfolk and Suffolk Yacht Club, bought her with the idea of restoring her and fitting her out for charter work.

Mr Whelpton had *Heartsease* towed up to Lowestoft but her draught was too great for her to be taken up to the yard at Upton on the Broads. Over the next four years some progress was made with the restoration though her hull, deckhouses and everything below decks had been well cared for. Frames and planking were in excellent shape, the only questionable thing being the fastenings where some wastage was to be expected. In the end, the joint owners found that they had not sufficient time to give to this time-consuming job; in November 1971, with some reluctance, they sold *Heartsease* to Gordon and Caroline Waller.

The Wallers obtained the services of John Perryman, the naval architect in Lowestoft, who had considerable experience in restoration work, to examine the practicability of replacing the ballast keel and to design a new sail plan. The problems and expense of fitting a ballast keel finally proved too great and Mr Perryman decided on internal ballast to balance a gaff rig of considerably less area than the original rig. Also, the new masts

Schooner *Heartsease* (originally
named *Adela*) racing with 16,000
sq ft of sail in the Solent before
World War I. *(Photo Beken.)*

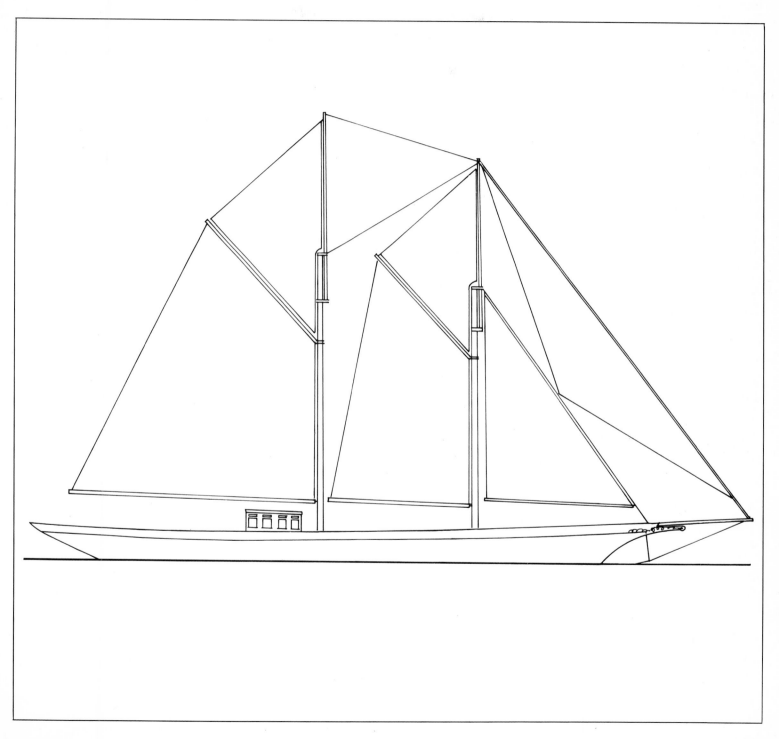

were designed to be shorter and lighter than those originally used.

With her revised sail plan, *Heartsease* will never match her former performance (neither will she have a crew of twenty-four paid hands), but it is a well balanced rig. To match this, she will carry thirty tons of ballast in her bilges. A wood or ferro-concrete shoe may be fitted. The draught will then be reduced from 13ft 6in to about 12ft.

In the autumn of 1972, *Heartsease* was slipped. At last the Wallers could see the beauty of her lines. Her bottom was scrubbed for the first time in twenty years. It took four men using high-pressure hoses only two and a half hours to clean her, for she was copper sheathed. John Perryman surveyed her and put their minds at rest. She was sound – planking, iron frames, fastenings, everything.

The auxiliary power in *Heartsease* used to be a five-cylinder Gardiner diesel, placed four feet above the offset propeller shaft, which it drove by means of a massive chain. This odd installation gave her a maximum speed of seven knots but, though quite efficient, was not suitable for continuous motoring. At some stage the engine was moved from its original position to an in-line position, so taking up part of the accommodation.

Gordon Waller thought round the problem for a while and finally came to the conclusion that a hydraulic drive would not only be more flexible in regard to the position of the engine but would also allow continuous motoring. The engine could therefore be put back where it originally was, up above the propeller shaft. What is more, the original engine room was intact with bearers sitting waiting for an engine and it was separated from the rest of the ship by a soundproof, watertight bulkhead.

By the kind of luck that comes to the venturesome, Gordon Waller found a 160bhp V8 Perkins diesel engine complete with a hydraulic drive installed in the middle of a gigantic pea-picking machine being offered for sale by Birdseye, the canners. He bought it and then took about a month to cut his way with oxyacetylene equipment into the bowels of this Heath Robinson construction, originally built for Birdseye in Niagara Falls. *Heartsease* will have a 26in propeller of fairly coarse pitch working under her port quarter.

Her 4000sq ft of sail is about a quarter of her original racing sail plan but her ballast has been reduced by half and is no longer slung below the keel. This sail plan will lack drive going to windward but should prove quite effective when going before the wind. Anyhow, the cost of 16,000sq ft of sail is too much for anyone to contemplate.

To restore such a schooner as *Heartsease* to her original sail plan is outside the range of practical possibilities, not only because of the initial cost but because of the cost of maintenance and the wages of a large crew.

Gordon Waller's original plan had been to give *Heartsease* a three-masted rig based on that used by Jean-Yves Terlain in *Vendredi Treize* and Mr Perryman suggested giving her the rig of a steam yacht of the period. The Wallers weighed up the practical advantages of such a scheme but in the end chose the more difficult, and to them more satisfying, course of restoring *Heartsease* to something nearer to her former glory.

Cruising ketch *Armorel*

LOA 53ft 0in
LWL 47ft 3in
Beam 12ft 6in
Draught 7ft 4in
Registered tonnage 12·27 (19·59 laden)
Designed and built by C. Sibbick & Co Ltd 1898

Armorel was built at Cowes in the Isle of Wight. C. Sibbick, her builder and designer, was a carpenter by trade with a passion for beautifully built yachts. Sibbick leased a small yard on Cowes waterfront and, so it is said, more or less confined his building activities to yachts he himself designed. These boats are all very well built and shapely for the period. Only a few are still listed in the current Lloyds *Register* (1973). These are *Armorel*, 29 tons TM, *Gwenda*, 7, *Nanette*, 5, *Popinjay*, 15, *Ripple*, 5, *Riva*, 10, *Saunterer*, 16, *Thalassa*, 16, *Wilful*, 8, and *Witch*, 8.

Sibbick's yard was destroyed by fire in 1903 or 1904 and presumably all his records were lost at the same time. When he retired, his yard was taken over by another firm.

Armorel as she is today is a fitting memorial to this perfectionist designer-builder. She was very well built of teak planking, copper fastened to double oak frames. It seems possible but by no means certain that she was built without any external ballast on her keel, but some time in her early life she was bought by a fisherman and converted into a sailing trawler. This conversion completely altered her appearance, for in addition to the removal of any coach roof that she may have had her saloon was turned into a fish well with normal hatch covers. What was even more remarkable was that she was given a false bow with a vertical stem post. This was fitted on to an iron shoe that projected from the original keel like an early ironclad's battering ram. The new bow was planked in larch and scarphed into the original teak planking some ten or twelve feet back from the old bow. The object of this straight stemmed false bow was to enable her to lie more easily to her trawl. It also seems probable that her counter was shortened and she was given a trawler stern, although her owner, Charles Hoskins, does not agree and thinks she is now like she was when launched. She was fitted

Ketch *Armorel*.
1 *Armorel* arriving in Grimsby docks
before her restoration, with her
straight false stem removed.

1

2 Showing her 'trawler' stern and
  high bulwarks.
3 On the Outer Sands at Spurn Head.
4 *Armorel* after her restoration.

2

158

with 24in high bulwarks and her yawl rig was altered to that of a typical west country fishing ketch. In fact, she looked just like a small Brixham trawler. Some years later *Armorel* was rather clumsily reconverted into a yacht but retained her straight stem, her trawler stern and her ketch rig. Her deckhouses and hatches were made of ordinary white pine and her deck was canvased. When in 1965 Charles Hoskins first saw *Armorel* lying in the south dock at Cardiff she looked forlorn. Her previous owner had started to dismantle the false bow because of water between the two skins and the impossibility of getting at the seams on the inner, original planking. He had removed most of the outer planking and had cut away the vertical stem post except for the top three feet. He had not tackled the projecting iron keel. At this stage, he and his children were tragically drowned off Appledore, whilst going ashore in a dinghy.

Charles Hoskins tidied up her stem and then sailed *Armorel* down the Bristol Channel and round the Longships, and roared up Channel and the North Sea before a south-westerly gale. In spite of her looks, *Armorel* could certainly sail. *Armorel* remained afloat at Grimsby Docks for about a year and then was lifted out of the water, placed on a low-loader, and taken to Charles Hoskins's construction works at Humberston. She must have made an impressive sight on this short journey, for she towered above the doubledecker buses. Once she was unloaded at Humberston, a galvanized roof was erected over her with hanging tarpaulins down the sides to protect the ship from the weather.

The restoration It took Charles Hoskins three years of spare time working to complete *Armorel*'s restoration. Though she looked such a woebegone object, her hull was basically in good shape. Her teak planks, her double oak frames and her copper fastenings were all sound. The frames, incidentally, fishing boat fashion, stopped short of the keel but were side-bolted to massive oak floors. Though her copper fastenings were sound, her keel bolts and other bolts in the stem and stern assemblies were of yellow metal. These had all crystallized. One hundred and twenty were replaced by galvanized mild steel bolts. Within the three years that *Armorel* was on the stocks at Humberston, galvanic action had caused such deterioration in the new bolts that the whole lot had to be replaced. This time Charles Hoskins used hand-fashioned iron bolts, brought to red heat and then dipped into black varnish. This old fashioned method and the use of iron rather than steel was completely successful. There has been no further galvanic action.

In the restoration, the first job was the removal of the unsightly bow. This involved cutting away all the remaining timber in the false stem post etc, cleaning up the original teak planking and scarphing in new wood at the point where the false bow had been fitted. This was a wearisome job and Charles

Hoskins had the help of a shipwright. The original teak planks had been reduced to almost half their thickness to receive the ends of the planking of the false bow. The 'battering ram' projection of the false keel had to be cut off flush and in line with her original stem post. This was done with the help of an oxyacetylene cutter. Next, the entire hull was burnt off, sanded and recaulked.

After the old canvas was removed from the deck, it was seen that the decks needed replanking. The old deck was stripped off, revealing sound beams and a sound shelf, but there were several defective lodging knees. These were replaced, fashioned out of oak crooks, and new decks of 2in × 2in Oregon pine were laid down and caulked with oakum and pitch. The covering boards were sound but many of the stanchions were rotten and the bulwarks needed replanking for which larch was used.

The pine planks were 'secret' fastened, ie side fastened, with 4in galvanized rosehead nails. Her caulking seams were $\frac{3}{4}$in deep and $\frac{5}{16}$in wide. These seams were overwide and should have measured only $\frac{1}{8}$in. The caulking consisted of two layers of oakum. The pitch was heated in pails over a Propane gas burner and ladled into the seams, the overflow being scraped off the planks when the pitch was cold.

The teak covering boards were original and were already notched to receive the ends of the deck planks. Notched filling pieces were added on each side of the kingplank for the same purpose.

Charles Hoskins had none of the original plans of *Armorel,* so it was no easy task to restore her to the exact appearance she had when originally launched in 1898. It is almost certain that her bulwark rail would have been nothing like as high as it was after her trawler conversion. Without this high rail, however, she would have had little freeboard, and he wisely retained it and the trawler stern.

A new forehatch cover, a new skylight and a new coach roof over the galley and chartroom were built of mahogany and decked with Oregon pine. A patent caulking compound was used here. It is much easier to use than hot pitch but would have added £200 to the cost of the entire deck had it been used overall.

Below decks The new saloon followed the layout of the previous saloon and was beautifully built. Church pews were used for the port and starboard benches, and the fittings of a dismantled bank, including a fine mahogany counter and chest of drawers, provided other bits of furniture. The large hinged-flap table was part of her original furnishings.

The heads and washroom forward of the saloon on the starboard side have a most ingeniously placed bath. It occupies the passageway to the starboard fore cabin. One steps over one end of it on to a rubber mat in the bottom and stands in the bath to

Armorel.
1 The remains of her false bow and stem post.
2 Remains of after end of false bow planking.
3 Bow after restoration.

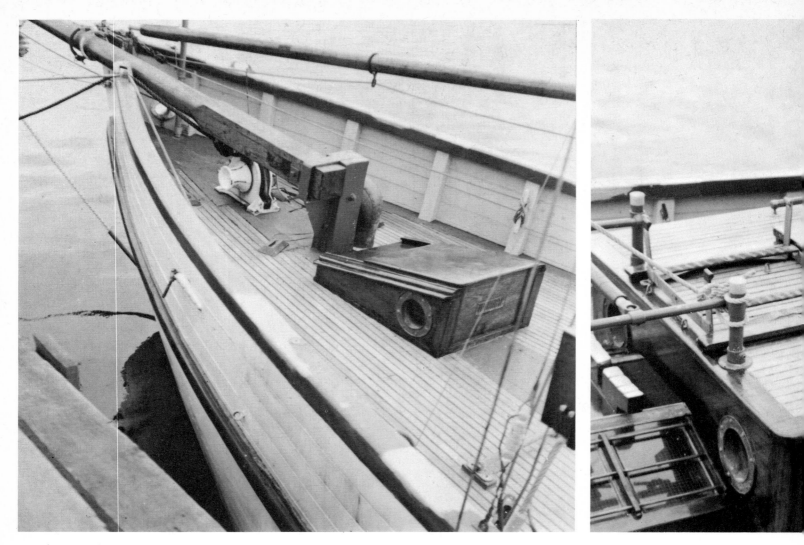

use the wash basin; to go into the fore cabin one merely steps over the other end and goes through a door.

The engine, a 24hp Saab, has a 25in variable-pitch propeller and is situated below the charthouse-cum-galley. The galley, with a large Calor gas stove, is on the starboard side. The chart table, the navigating instruments, RDF and ship-to-shore VHF telephone are on the port side. This equipment consists of a 30A alternator on the engine and a 25A 12V portable generator; a Seafarer echo sounder; a 25W MW radio transmitter (2182 only) with a 150 mile range; a VHF radio telephone (6 channels) with a 25 mile range. There is also a 1·5KW portable 230U generator and, in the bilges, a gas detector.

That part of her bilges below the saloon is concreted, a relic of the time when the saloon was a fish well. In addition to this, *Armorel* carries six tons of inside ballast made up of 56lb and 112lb pigs of iron, and, of course, she has her heavy iron shoe.

On deck, even though *Armorel* is relatively narrow in the beam, there is a feeling of space and security within her high bulwarks. Her staysail is boomed, with a sheet leading to a horse. She has both roller reefing and reef points on her main-sail. *Armorel* stands up to her canvas.

Both her main and mizzen masts were sound and were retained, but her topmast and all her other spars are new, made up from spruce poles. *Armorel* has been entirely rerigged and given a new set of sails, the dimensions of which are:

mainsail	490sq ft	flax
mizzen	190 ,,	,,
staysail	190 ,,	terylene
no 1 jib	230 ,,	,,
no 2 jib	200 ,,	,,
no 3 jib	110 ,,	,,
genoa	900 ,,	,,
mizzen staysail	200 ,,	cotton
spinnaker	1500 ,,	nylon 202.

When Charles Hoskins first completed his restoration he had given the yacht very open scuppers, but so much water came sluicing through them and over the deck that he has now closed the scuppers and limited himself to ¾in drain holes.

The tiller was replaced by the original wheel assembly that was still on board. *Armorel* has four pumps, a 3in brass Whale

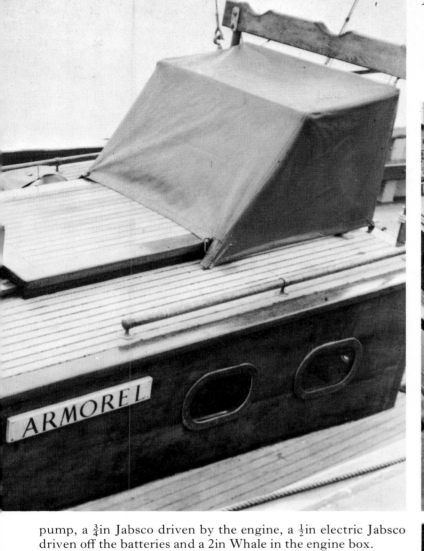

pump, a $\frac{3}{4}$in Jabsco driven by the engine, a $\frac{1}{2}$in electric Jabsco driven off the batteries and a 2in Whale in the engine box.

Armorel has two dinghies, one traditional, clinker built in Honduras mahogany, and another of light GRP. The latter is stacked inside the mahogany dinghy on the centreline of the ship and securely fastened within a galvanized steel tube frame-work. The anachronistic GRP dinghy is there for instant use and can be lifted and chucked overboard like a coracle.

Charles and Carole Hoskins and their small daughter have used *Armorel,* based on Alexandra Docks in Grimsby, as a home for the last three years, but they have also cruised to the conti-nent and even as far as Norway in her. She is a fine ship and worthy of the skill and ingenuity that has gone into her restora-tion. In the summer of 1973 *Armorel* made a very fast passage to Limfjord in Northern Denmark. Charles Hoskins wrote later about this voyage : 'We had a pretty good dusting, the forecast of force 6–8 developed into three vicious lows, culminating in a severe force 9. *Armorel* made relatively easy work of it. In one twenty-four hour spell, under the staysail only, she maintained 6 knots and completed the passage in under three days.'

The restoration of steam launches and steam engines

Introduction Steam propulsion is a subject of infinite depth, variety and complexity, but a first sight of the steam launch *Hero* determined me to include here at least a brief discussion of small steam launch restoration.

Old steam launch hulls, being river or lake craft, have usually been kept under cover and so may not have deteriorated too badly. Whatever the condition of the hulls, it is most unlikely they will still have their engines and boilers. The main problem is how to re-equip such hulls for steam propulsion. Old or dismantled steam engines can still be found but there cannot be many of them about. Probably the best way to find such an engine is to make contact with other steam engine enthusiasts, who may know where the remains of some old engine is lurking. Otherwise, it is a matter of building the engine yourself or finding an engineer who will build it for you.

One or two firms still supply either castings or complete engines. The old established firm of Stuart-Turner have for some years supplied castings for a robust little single cylinder engine (Type 5A) which, with a 2¼in bore and a 2in stroke at 60lb/sq in will develop ⅝bhp at 1,000rpm. This engine stands only 15in high but will drive a 20ft launch. Stuarts are planning to offer the complete engine, slightly modified, under the name of the Cygnet. They are also going to market a 2-cylinder version of the same engine to be called the Swan. This is some indication of the renewed interest in steam propulsion.

David King, a Yarmouth-born engineer, has established himself near Norwich 'for the restoration and manufacture of interesting things – especially those driven by steam'. Over the last nine years, Mr King has built and restored a number of steam engines, ranging from a Mississippi stern-wheel type of engine to a tiny single-cylinder oscillating engine for a 7ft 6in dinghy. David King, on his own admission has been making steam engines 'since he was so high, and making boilers out of treacle tins'.

The Mississippi sternwheeler, *Charlie Allnutt*, is a miniature reconstruction of the real thing. It was beautifully built by David King using an ex-army bridging pontoon for the hull. The stern wheel was driven by a twin-cylinder simple steam engine through chains with a 6 : 1 reduction. Mr King also built the engine for another stern wheeler, the *Phoenix,* for Mr Norman Terry of Redditch. This engine was 14ft long, with 8ft wooden connecting rods (called pitmans in the USA) made of ash and eccentric rods of laminated ash and mahogany. The engine is a simple expansion 2-cylinder slide valve with Stephenson link reverse gear. It has a 3in bore and an 18in stroke. The stern wheel is 5ft in diameter.

At the beginning of 1974, when I first visited David King, he was completing the rebuilding of an old White compound engine, built in 1912, and a water-tube oil fired LIFU (Liquid Fuel Engineering Company) boiler which had been built about 1900. This engine is for a steam pinnace that is being built in Sydney, Australia. Apart from its obvious efficiency, it is a superb example of craftsmanship.

David King is now going into the production of a simple, robust single-cylinder (2½in bore and 3in stroke) slide valve engine which will develop 1½bhp. The engine is 20in high, 12in long and 9in wide. It has an overhung crankshaft and a slip eccentric reverse. (Stephenson's link reverse gear can be supplied if required.) The slip eccentric reverse is simple; David King has planned the whole engine for maximum simplicity. The cylinder and piston are of cast iron; the piston has two rings. The boiler also is simple; it is a finned drum type designed by David King and is fired by Propane gas.

Before completing my description of the restoration of some actual steam launches, I asked Christopher Stirling, a Nottingham steam launch enthusiast who has restored more than one launch, and Keith Cutmore, who has worked in steam and has rebuilt more than one engine, to write a few brief notes on some of the problems that have to be faced in restoring and running marine steam engines.

If anyone has doubts about the growing popularity of the revival of steam propulsion, a glance at the *Steamboat Index* should reassure them. Over sixty launches are listed in Great Britain, and there must be many more than that in the USA.

Steam engines

Some notes by Christopher Stirling, David King and Keith Cutmore

Introduction The restorer of steam engines should have ample machine shop facilities and also be an expert turner, miller, fitter, coppersmith and patternmaker. This accounts for the fact that a large percentage of steam launch owners are either engineers, or own engineering businesses.

Exotic materials were not used in steam engine construction, so no problems arise in that respect. Patience is the most essential quality, with a great deal of practical and theoretical knowledge about the steam engine if anything like a reasonable performance is to be achieved. Of paramount importance is the setting of the valves on the engine. Incorrect valve setting can waste much of the steam produced in the boiler, and the correct setting is by no means easy. If replacing engine valves, it is worth remembering that Churchward, the chief mechanical engineer of the Great Western Railway, is reputed to have said that he had studied steam engine valves for thirty years and still did not know enough about them.

Notwithstanding what I have said here regarding valve settings, the steam engine is essentially a simple contraption (mechanically) and, with a little educated guesswork, even

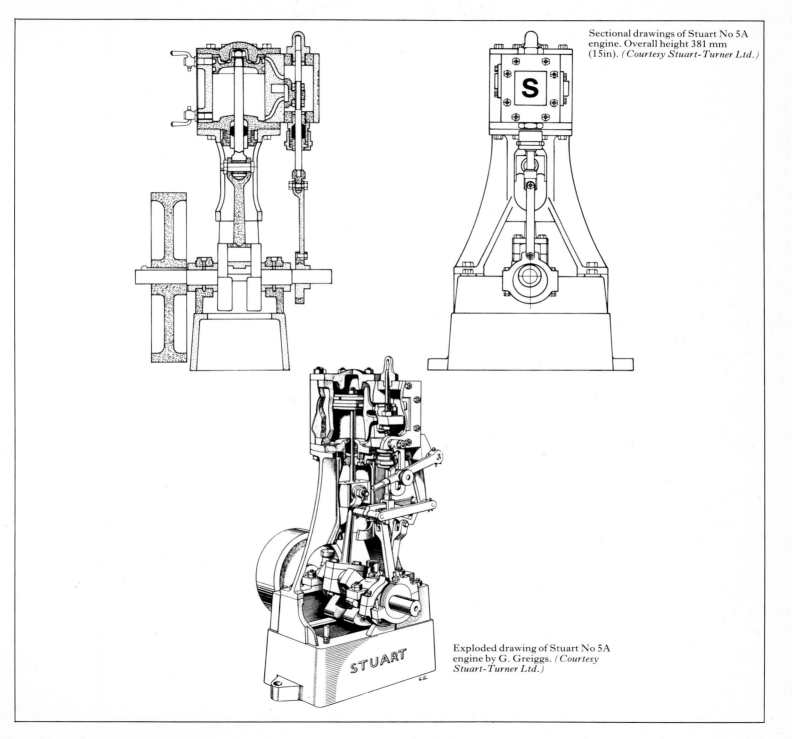

Sectional drawings of Stuart No 5A engine. Overall height 381 mm (15in). *(Courtesy Stuart-Turner Ltd.)*

Exploded drawing of Stuart No 5A engine by G. Greiggs. *(Courtesy Stuart-Turner Ltd.)*

STUART

Steam Engines.
1½bhp single cylinder 2½in bore ×
3in stroke slide valve engine
designed and built by David King.

missing parts can be made. To make a steam engine that will work is not difficult; to make one that works efficiently is more difficult; but to make a boiler is to be bedevilled with problems.

Anyone could make a steam engine with the aid of a small foundry and a jobbing engineer's workshop, for mechanically they are simple. Theoretically, the actual design of steam engines, however, is not, for a thorough knowledge of the behaviour of heat and the expansion of elastic fluids is needed. Putting the Carnot and Rankin heat cycles into practice is not always easy. C.S.

Basic steam engine repair and overhaul The simplest form of traditional steam engine is a single-cylinder type where the steam is admitted to either side of the piston by means of a slide valve. After driving the piston, the steam is released into the atmosphere, or may be exhausted through a nozzle in the funnel to draw the fire. The drawback with such an engine is that it is not self starting, having two dead points in each revolution. Even so, in the early days quite large vessels were fitted with single-cylinder engines, relying on the skill of the engineer to see that the engine did start when required. This drawback can easily be overcome by having two cylinders with their cranks set at 90°, thus giving four power strokes per revolution, and provided the engine is hot and free of condensate it will start as soon as the steam is turned on.

The next stage is the compound engine which extracts much more energy from the steam by expanding it through a series of two or three more cylinders of ever increasing size, to match the increasing volume of steam at the pressure drops. Usually a compound expansion engine exhausts into a condenser which is maintained at a vacuum by the steam turning back into water and an air pump driven from the engine. This has two advantages, firstly the low pressure cylinder is working with a greater effective pressure due to the suction from the condenser, and secondly the steam used by the engine is available as water to be eventually returned to the boiler. The complete steam water cycle of the engine, condenser and boiler becomes almost a closed circuit, the only additional water required is sufficient to make up for wastage from the safety valves, whistle, leakage from glands etc.

The steam pressure required to drive these engines that have been mentioned is usually about 85lb/sq in. It is quite important to keep the run of the main steam pipes from the boiler to the engine as short and as direct as possible. The steam in these pipes must be kept as hot as possible, so heavy lagging is necessary. The value of superheating cannot be overemphasised, provided the engine is designed and lubricated to withstand the higher steam temperatures. Superheating is the reheating of the steam after it has left the boiler. D.K.

166

$\frac{5}{8}$bhp single cylinder $2\frac{1}{4}$in bore $\times$ 2in stroke engine built by Mr A. Atthill from Stuart-Turner 5A castings.

Stuart-Turner 2-cylinder Swan engine (1974).

Most repair work is basic engineering coupled with a certain amount of patience. A workshop with a lathe is essential.

Begin by completely dismantling the engine. It is usually best to start at the top of the engine, first taking off the cylinder heads, followed by the steam inlet and exhaust manifolds, cylinder, piston and piston rod, so working right down to the crankshaft. When the engine is completely dismantled, thoroughly clean all the parts. Rake out all the old gland packing from the piston rod and valve rod glands and examine the glands themselves. Ascertain how much wear has taken place, though it is unusual for the glands to wear. It is usually the packing that goes. If they are badly worn, however, new glands will have to be made. These are usually of the adjustable-flange type, with two studs. They are nearly always made of brass. Also, examine the piston and valve rods to see how worn they are.

The piston and valve rods are the most likely to be worn and pitted, especially if the engine has been laid up for any length of time. The valve rods may be re-machined, but it is sometimes impossible to replace them if they are forged as an integral part with the cross head. They could of course be cut off, machined and re-welded, but the lining up would be no easy task.

So, if the piston and valve rods are badly worn, they will have to be replaced and new ones made. Examine the crankshaft, measuring the main journal bearings (the part of the shaft or axle that rests on the bearings) and crank pin journal. If badly worn they will have to be re-machined, and if they are re-machined it will certainly mean new main and big end bearings will have to be made. If the journal bearings are reasonably true, the bearings themselves can be adjusted by filing the top half of the main bearing shell to bring the surfaces closer together. This must be done very carefully, only taking off a small amount of metal each time, then assembling the crankshaft in its bed, tightening the caps of the bearings and making sure the crankshaft turns freely. If too much is filed off, bearing shims must be inserted. In the case of the big end bearings the same procedure applies. If the big end bearings are badly worn, it is essential to measure the clearances between the piston and cylinder covers at top and bottom dead centres. If necessary packing shims can be fitted between the connecting rod foot and the top bearing brass. In this case only file the lower half of the bearings. This procedure may take some time, but it is well worth all the effort. Make sure that the engine turns freely after the bearings have been filed.

Any tight spots that are left will only cause bearing failure soon after the engine is run. When you are quite satisfied that the crankshaft is properly adjusted, you can then start reassembling the cylinder on to the crank bed. When reassembling the piston on to the piston rod, make certain it fits very tightly and is securely locked. They have a habit of working loose. All new joints should be made from a heatproof material, such as Halite, though it is possible to use oiled brown paper.

The piston and valve rod glands should be repacked with asbestos material impregnated with graphite. Adjust these evenly. After each operation during reassembly, turn the engine to make sure nothing is binding or too tight. All the oil pipes should be cleared and all the oil wicks in the oil cups renewed. Pipe cleaners are very good for this job. Examine all valves. Slide valves should be reground on a surface grinder. It may be necessary to regrind or re-machine the port face. Piston valves may need new rings.

Finally clean up and polish all brass, copper and machined steel work and paint all unmachined castings. K.C. and D.K.

Boilers Boilers are the most difficult things to make or have made. In fact they are not things an amateur should undertake lightly. There is nothing to prevent a private individual building any boiler he likes and blowing himself up in the process. The only British government regulations cover manufacturing premises, steam vehicles used on the highway, or steam vessels licensed to carry passengers for reward.

However, before an insurance company will provide cover for a steam boiler, the insurers will need to be satisfied about its design and construction. Their requirements will overlap some of the Government restrictions. As with road vehicles, a licence will not be issued unless a boiler is insured.

Before starting to build a boiler, one should get in touch with one's insurance company and arrange for their boiler inspector to vet and approve the plans, materials and methods of construction. They are usually helpful and their charges are reasonable. If anyone omits these precautions and builds a boiler, which subsequently blows up and injures or kills a third party, the consequences could be horrific!

The testing is usually quite simple and X-ray inspection is not normally called for. An insurance company, however, does like to be assured of the competence of the engineer who is carrying out the welding.

As for getting boilers made made for one, the big firms of boiler makers are not interested in small one-off jobs. Small firms often have not the testing facilities demanded by the in-insurance companies, so one is caught in a cleft stick. Also, boiler-smiths skilled in the making of small boilers are becoming rare. Despite this gloomy picture, it is possible for the private individual to get small boilers made by one or two private firms, if he can get them sufficiently interested. One firm, Warren Brothers of Swadlincote, at the time of writing, would be willing to make a small boiler – at a price.

D.K. and C.S.

The two main types of boiler are the fire-tube and the water-

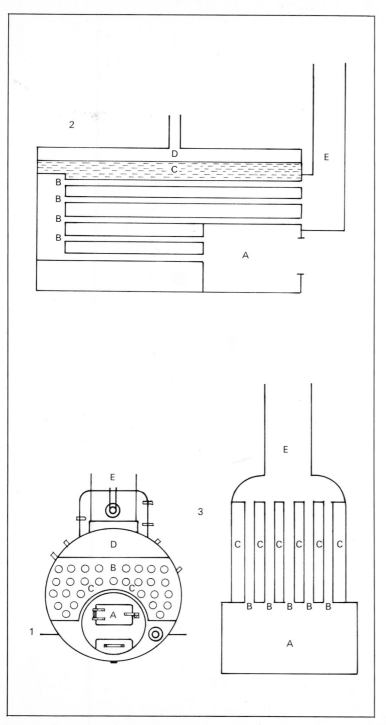

Boilers for steam engines.
1 Cross section of fire tube boiler (Clyde type).
2 Side view: horizontal fire-tube boiler.
3 Vertical water-tube boiler (Merryweather Type).

A Fire box   B Heat   C Water
D Steam   E Funnel.

tube boiler. In the fire-tube (such as the Scotch), the heat, in the form of hot air and gases, is drawn from the fire through tubes which pass through and so heat a circular water tank, nearly full of water. The tank is not quite full, because there must be space for the steam to collect.

The water-tube boiler (such as the Merryweather) was a later development with greater efficiency. As its name implies, water passes through the tubes which are heated by the hot air and gases from the fire. The launch with a water-tube boiler needs to carry less water than one with a fire-tube boiler. The water-tube type is reputed to be safer and is easier to construct.

Scale working drawings of water-tube launch boilers designed to have a working pressure of 200lb/sq in can be supplied by Light Steam Power, Kirk Michael, Isle of Man (the publishers of the bimonthly magazine *Light Steam Power*). Light Steam Power supply over twenty sets of working drawings, including (No 2) Marine Steam Plant, for which they also supply castings. This water-tube boiler has been planned for ease of construction in a home workshop. Light Steam Power also produce drawings for a Lune Valley type of vaporizing burner and for the Merryweather Type B water-tube boiler which can be fired either with solid or oil fuel. The Lune Valley type is a reliable design which incorporates selfcleaning jets and burns paraffin.

The pros and cons of coal and oil firing For convenience, cleanliness and availability of fuel, oil firing has much to recommend it. However, in an old and probably irreplaceable craft, the fire hazards are greater with oil than with solid fuel and must be considered. Also, if the existing boiler is built for solid fuel firing, the combustion space, especially in a small plant, may be insufficient for oil firing. The chief disadvantage with oil firing is the electrical installation necessary to drive the pumps and the burner. I have tried using a steam atomizing burner but, with the small combustion space available in a Merryweather boiler, the results were not very good. In their heyday some steam launches were oil fired, but they were in the minority and were, I believe, at least in Britain, restricted to those built by the Liquid Fuel Engineering Company (the builders of SL *Hero*'s present engine).

Despite the attendant dirt, coal has more to recommend it. It is certainly my own preference (an oil burning steam launch just does not seem right). Coal firing is simple, and once the art of stoking has been mastered there is little to go wrong, unlike the electrics of an oil burning boiler. Most old launch boilers were built for coal firing and so combustion space problems do not arise. The hazards associated with oil just do not exist and the maintenance of supplies of coal need not inconvenience a boat owner if he arranges things beforehand. If he runs out of coal he can manage even on driftwood, which I have done on at

least one occasion. There is a deal of satisfaction in stoking a good fire and it is possible to gain a far greater variation of steam production than with oil firing, especially in the upper end of the boiler's output range.

The LIFU engine was built to run on steam at a pressure of 250lb/sq in and this steam was to be slightly superheated. The Merryweather boiler ran at 125lb/sq in and produced wet steam only. In other words the steam, when collected off the surface of the water, was not passed through a series of tubes exposed to the products of combustion in order to surcharge it with heat.

The advantages of superheating in a small engine are twofold: first, since work equals heat, a greater degree of expansion can be gained from a cylinder full of hot steam before condensation takes place; also the fact that no water is carried over with the steam means that slightly less steam is used for each stroke; second, and this is of great importance with a small engine where conducting areas are large in relation to the capacity of the cylinders, initial condensation is much reduced on entry of the steam into the cylinder. This is due partly to the fact that dry steam is a bad conductor of heat and partly because steam which is raised above its saturation temperature will tolerate a slight drop in temperature but, provided it remains above its saturation point, will not cause condensation upon the cylinder walls. When condensation occurs, the steam remains as water until such time during the stroke that pressure and temperature fall below the level of the cylinder wall condensate; when this happens, the condensate will flash into steam and pass into the exhaust without doing any work at all.

In running a steam launch, one's main thought is to preserve the power plant in as good a condition as possible. This means, basically, keeping the engine well oiled and preventing coal dust, which is remarkably abrasive, from entering the engine. Given this treatment, the engine will run for long periods without needing any work done on it. The weakness in the power plant is the boiler. Most water is unsuitable for boiler feed. Even at moderate pressure, oxygen dissolved in the feedwater will seriously attack the steel plating of the boiler. Even carbon dioxide dissolved in the water can attack boiler plating if conditions are right. If the water is hard the boiler will scale up rapidly; the scale, being a bad conductor of heat, will cause local overheating of the plates. This can eventually lead to the burning of the metal and the inevitable failure of the boiler. If on the other hand the water is very soft, acid corrosion occurs, causing thinning of the plates and the eventual failure of the boiler.

The ideal pH for feedwater is nine, seven being the neutral figure; the water should be slightly alkaline. Sediment in the feedwater, if allowed to build up in the boiler, can cause overheating and failure, so small boilers, if drawing their feedwater from overboard, must be washed out frequently. Even a traction engine with its large boiler should be washed out every hundred hours of steaming. There are warning plates fixed on most traction engines to remind the crew that this must be done.

The ultimate in feedwater would be that used in power stations, which is demineralized, de-ionized and degassed. The price is in the region of 70p per gallon. Ordinary distilled water such as that used for car batteries is not pure enough.

There is no simple answer to the problem of the treatment of the boiler water. Chemical treatment will work providing that the pressures are low (ie below about 150lb/sq in), but the dosage of treatment to be added to the feedwater depends entirely on the chemicals present in the water that is being used. Therefore, to be really sure of the appropriate treatment, each lot of water should be chemically analysed, though this is hardly possible unless one is a chemist. The correct dosage is impossible to ascertain if one is drawing water from overboard where the constituent chemicals can vary not only because the amount of rain the river may be carrying but also in different reaches because of the differences of tributary water.

I ran the steam launch *Hero* at Nottingham on town water and my chemical treatment was made up to suit that, but elsewhere, despite the fact that I had been shown how to analyse the water and had been given equipment for the job, the dosage and the treatment were somewhat haphazard.

If a totally enclosed system is employed, that is if the exhaust steam from the engine is condensed and pumped back into the boiler, then other problems arise. Sediment in the feedwater can be removed by chemical treatment, thus all the problems are solved apart from those arising from the dissolved gases, but the condensate is liable to become contaminated with oil from the cylinders.

Oil in a boiler is a killer, so much so that only one part of oil to a million parts of water is allowable. The oil, if it gets into the boiler, clings to the boiler plates. Oil is a bad conductor of heat and causes the plates to overheat; the oil carbonises and, carbon itself being a bad conductor, the overheating continues with the inevitable result. Thus a suitable method of removing the oil has to be devised.

There are two basic methods of removing oil from a closed system: by filtering, and by separation; neither is 100 per cent effective. By filtering, the contaminated feedwater is passed through some suitable body to remove the oil. The substances used were coke, towelling and sponges. By separation, the oil is allowed to flow into a series of connected chambers where, oil being lighter than water, it settles out on the surface and is skimmed off every now and again. I used the separation system on *Hero*. The chemical feedwater treatment removed any slight traces of oil that were still present in the water.

If a satisfactory method for removing the oil can be found,

condensing has the added advantage of allowing one to get more work out of the same quantity of steam. Since it is exhausting into a vacuum, a fuller expansion of the steam can take place and hence more work is gained.

The remaining problems of running a steam launch are few and trivial; the amount of copper and brass to be polished, the difficulty of finding crews, and the apprehension with which one is greeted by owners of modern fibreglass river craft. As for the maintenance of the hull, it is no different for a steam launch than for any other river craft.   C.S.

Wood firing Wood is the most popular fuel for steam launches in Australia and probably in the USA. It is cleaner to use than coal and on most rivers and lakes is freely available. For it to be successful however, wood firing needs a larger grate than that used for coke or coal. This may be difficult or even impossible with a vertical boiler of the Merryweather type, but it is quite feasible for horizontal boilers. The most satisfactory boilers for wood firing would be the mono-coil once-through type or the underfed horizontal boiler with a completely surrounding water-walled combustion chamber. Both these types need a forced draught and constant stoking. Whenever possible, the wood should be cut up into small pieces of uniform size. The softer the wood, the more ash to clear.

The forced draught can be most effectively achieved by leading the exhaust blast up inside the smoke stack, thus producing an induced draught which creates a suction effect over the whole area of the fire grate. For details, see 'The Firing of small steamboat Boilers', by Sidney Clement (*Steam Boats and Modern Steam Launches* Jan–Feb 1963).

Steam launch *Hero*

LOA 35ft 0in
Beam 6ft 1in
Draught 2ft 3in

I first saw *Hero* floating in the pool at Earl's Court during the 1972 Boat Show. It was like finding a Hepplewhite chair for sale in a supermarket. Her 35ft clipper-bowed hull, built of finest Burma teak, her beautifully striped narrow deck planks, the 'cabinetmade' quality of her lockers and other fittings, and her gleaming two-cylinder compound steam engine with its coal fired Merryweather boiler, elegantly lagged with narrow mahogany planking (a bit like Stephenson's *Rocket*), made the surrounding boats look like a lot of plastic soapdishes.

I followed *Hero* to her base at Tom Trevethick's yard on the Nottingham canal at Lenton. From John Player and Sons, I discovered something of her history.

Christopher Stirling discovered the launch in a Somerset

Steam launch *Hero*.
Hero just after her restoration was completed, with canopy in position, steaming along under her sixty-year-old 2-cylinder compound steam engine. *(Photo John Player and Sons Ltd.)*

Hero without her canopy in Torbay
harbour, steaming under her 10bhp
LIFU engine. *(Photo Bernard
Lake.)*

farmyard. Apart from her teak skin she was in poor condition, but the beauty of her lines was quite obvious. What was equally obvious was that it was going to take a great many man-hours and quite a lot of money to get the launch back to anything near her original condition. Mr Stirling approached John Player and Sons. John Seager, a sympathetic boat-minded public relations chief, was able to persuade his masters that the launch suitably restored, could be used for promotion and public relations. The point he made was that the boat could epitomize Players' old-established tradition for quality yet make an up-to-date contribution to contemporary activities.

Christopher Stirling, the prime mover behind *Hero*'s restoration, made some interesting observations in a letter to the author about the finding and restoration of steam launches. He wrote:

'The main problems of finding steam launches are their age and their limited production in the first place. Even by the outbreak of the First World War, the steam launch was in the decline, due to the development and increasing reliability of the petrol and paraffin engines; and such firms as Thorneycroft who had made their names with their high speed launches had ceased to manufacture steam sets. Also, steam launches were never a very numerous breed, for only a small percentage of the population, compared with today, could afford a boat of any kind, and then the population was only about half what it is now.

'Whilst on the lookout for *Hero*, one or two old steam launch hulls were looked at by Tom Trevethick, but all of them were suffering from the ravages of age and neglect, for none of them could have been less than sixty years old. A couple of locally built boats that had been steam launches, although no longer with steam power, were still in good condition. These were the *San Toy*, about the same size as *Hero*, but with a straight bow, and another and larger vessel with a clipper bow called the *Yoyo*. This was the sum total of steam launch hulls that could be found on the whole of the east midlands waterway system.

'The chances today of finding a steam launch with its engine and boiler is very remote. Most steam launches were converted to internal combustion propulsion when the boilers became worn out. It was cheaper to ditch the old steam plant than to have a new boiler built to order. There are however several launches with their original power plants in them. One of the most noteworthy is a vessel called the *Cygnet* which was built by Thorneycroft in 1873. It is, thanks to its being stored for fifty years or more at Thorneycrofts', completely original.

'The main problems in restoring steam engines is the matter of cost. In any steam engine of great age that has had much usage, the degree of wear may be considerable, necessitating the making of new parts. Should these parts be either beyond the skill of the restorer to produce himself or requiring a machining capability that he does not possess, then it means finding a firm that is willing even to do the job. Then, not only does he have to pay for the job, but also to pay to take the craftsman off production work.'

The launch, not yet named *Hero*, was transported from Somerset to Trevethick's canalside boatyard at Lenton near Nottingham and came under the loving care of Tom Trevethick himself. On a wet and windy day in March, I stood talking to Mr Trevethick alongside *Hero*. The launch was sitting on her trailer, wrapped up in her winter cover.

'It was a good thing they came to me,' Tom Trevethick said, 'because there cannot be many boatbuilders of my age still at work. It is over 55 years since I was apprenticed. In those days we still used to do the kind of work that went into launches like this one.' He paused for a minute to lift up the canopy for the fore part of *Hero*. 'You don't see that kind of work today,' and he pointed to the finely panelled locker fronts. 'Mind you, I didn't do this work myself, but I've good craftsmen here. I could tell them what to do and how it used to be done.'

The name *Hero* and the little roundel are the only concessions to advertising. The name is taken, of course, from that on the sailor's cap on the Players' Navy Cut cigarette packet.

The first sanding down of the hull revealed the name *Avondale*, but it is by no means certain that this was her original name. The launch had previously been owned by Mr Charles Doble of Bletchley boatyard in Buckinghamshire. Mr Doble was at school at Eton from 1961–7 and during those years *Hero* was used as a launch from which the eights could be coached. Before that, and apparently for the whole of her career, she had been based at Windsor and was used for taking trippers up and down the river. From what local watermen said, it seemed that she must have been built in the 1880s by Andrews' of Maidenhead.

When Tom Trevethick got to work on the launch he first set her up on chocks, levelled her up exactly with plumblines at stem and stern post, and fitted battens across her gunwales to help keep her shape and in places to pull her back into shape. He found her carvel planking in perfect order. Her forefoot had to be replaced but the apron, stem and hoodends were sound. The keel and deadwood also had to be replaced. He used seasoned oak for this purpose. Inside, every timber had to be removed, new oak timbers steamed and fitted, and of course the planking refastened. Two heavy larch stringers almost to the full length of the boat were then fitted at the turn of the bilges. Finally, the substantial engine bearers were put in. These consisted of 3in moulded oak floors and two very long fore and aft bearers (they were actually about 8ft long). Thwarts were fitted and panelled with bulkheads and the bow and stern were redecked. The old decks which were rotten had been planked in pitchpine and mahogany. Trevethick used the same style of alternating narrow 2in planks of oak and mahogany. The lockers with their panelled fronts were also made of mahogany. The launch was then caulked and the deck plank seams payed with a patent black stopping.

As originally built, it seemed that the launch had been propelled by a coal fired engine, though it is just possible that, as suggested by her narrow beam of 5ft 4½in, she may have been built as an electric launch. There is no record of this. At some stage in her career she certainly had electric propulsion and, later on, a 2-stroke Stuart-Turner petrol engine was installed. Nothing was left of her original engine bearers, stringers or stern gear.

As one of the objects of the exercise, at least in the eyes of Mr Stirling, was to restore the boat as a steam launch, a steam engine of the right vintage had to be found. To begin with, the nearest they could get to it was a sixty-year old 2-cylinder compound engine, which came from a Mr Harding of Great Hayward Wharf, Sutton Coldfield, near Birmingham. Under the supervision of two of Players' engineers, Mr Leslie Elston and

Steam launch *Hero*. The 10bhp LIFU engine is under the 'skylight'. The vertical Merryweather boiler is coal fired. Ian Abbott is the stoker and Tony Kellett the skipper. (*Photo Bernard Lake.*)

Mr Arthur Smith, this partially built engine was installed. It needed some reconditioning and had to be fitted with a new crankshaft and air pump. It did not prove satisfactory.

Towards the end of 1971 another old steam engine, built in 1911 by the Liquid Fuel Engineering Company (LIFU) at Poole in Dorset, was found in a Rochester boatyard. This engine, which was still in its original packing case, was a much better proposition. It was of better design with low and high pressure piston-valves and it also used superheated rather than wet steam. The new engine had an output of 10hp at 450rpm, working at the high pressure of 250lb/sq in, the equivalent of 250,000btu. In smooth water this engine will drive *Hero*'s slender hull at a respectable seven knots. The boiler is a Merryweather, of the kind originally fitted to fire engines, relying on induced (as opposed to forced) draught. It has a steam output of 350lb/hour and steam can be raised in 25 minutes. It is fired on Welsh steam coal, the best there is for the purpose. *Hero*, when cruising at about six knots, uses about 28lb of coal per hour. Forcing the speed up trebles her coal consumption. The coal box has a cast iron base 14in in diameter, with firebars $\frac{1}{2}$in thick and 1in sided with $\frac{1}{2}$in gaps between them. There is an eight or nine inch space below for the ashpit. The engine and boiler unit sits in the middle of the boat in an area between two bulkheaded thwarts; this 'open engine room' is decked with steel plates. The engine itself is housed under a beautiful little hinged skylight, the glass protected by brass bars. The steering box is just aft of the engine, with the ship's bell mounted on its fore side. The helmsman sits on the side bench both to steer and to handle the engine controls. The fireman remains within the engine area ready to shovel on the coal.

The three-bladed propeller, which was specially made, is 18in in diameter and has the very coarse pitch of 24in. The reason for this is that a steam engine can produce about twice the power of an equivalent diesel, and at far lower revolutions.

Though *Hero* looks very pretty under her blue awning, I think that she is even more handsome without this covering. The shining brass of her funnel and her other fittings, the gleaming mahogany planked boiler and her lovely teak hull make an unforgettable picture. She is a well proportioned little launch and her engine and boiler do not, as so often happens in these small steamboats, look like a cuckoo in a sparrow's nest. She is all of a piece and is a great credit to Tom Trevethick and all those who worked on her.

To get *Hero* under way, the first thing to do is of course to raise steam. The procedure for getting up steam is as follows:

1 Check the water level (the boiler takes from 5 to 6 gallons)
2 Light the fire, using sticks, paper or a firelighter
3 Add coal to the fire
4 Steam pressure begins to rise
5 When 20lb/sq in pressure is showing on the gauge, open the valve (this is a $\frac{1}{2}$in blower wheel steam valve) and inject steam into the funnel; this provides the induced draught
6 Keep adding coal; at the same time lubricate the engine
7 When steam pressure rises to 120lb/sq in undo the drain cocks
8 Turn on the main steam line valve
9 With the throttle valve open, slide valve linkage from mid-gear (neutral) until the engine begins to turn; this will drive the residue of water out of the system
10 When all water has been cleared from the system, turn off (ie close) drain cocks

The boat is now ready to move off. The fireman keeps adding small shovelfuls of coal to the fire. The coal is stowed in two stainless steel bunkers to port and starboard of the engine. To reverse the engine, the valve linkage is slid across. In the centre position it is in neutral and the engine is no longer turning over.

Hero's fame has spread, for the launch was used in the BBC Television serial *The Onedin Line* and was nearly swamped in Torbay. *Hero* is a river launch and not a seagoing tender.

In May 1972, a 24V dc pressure jet burner was fitted to the boiler to convert it to oil firing. On 19 September 1972, *Hero* was being lowered into her moorings at Clayton's Wharf, Nottingham, when the crane toppled over. The jib fell across the stern well, pinning the boat to the canal bottom. Repairs were carried out by Trevethick's boatyard and a new oil-fired patomastic Mk X1 150lb/sq in fire-tube boiler, designed by Perkins Boilers Ltd, was fitted at the same time.

The steam launches of the Windermere Nautical Trust

On Lake Windermere in the English Lake District, a collection of steam launches and other craft has been formed by Mr George Pattinson. These boats range in size from a small cargo steamer called the *Raven* down to a little 18ft steam launch, the *Lady Elizabeth*. This collection of unique vessels is now in the care of the Windermere Nautical Trust with Mr Pattinson, the National Maritime Museum at Greenwich and the Maritime Trust as joint trustees. The objectives of the Windermere Nautical Trust are to preserve and to keep these most interesting boats in commission. They are not being used for taking trippers for joyrides, but the trust will show them to people who may have a serious interest in them, when the museum in the dockyard is opened.

The SL *Lady Elizabeth* is most often seen on the lake for Mr Pattinson uses her for trolling for char. She is driven by a single-

Steam launch *Branksome* on Lake Windermere, driven by a Sissons compound engine. *(Photo Windermere Nautical Trust.)*

cylinder 2in bore by 3in stroke engine of an unknown make, fitted with Stephenson's valve gear. The *Lady Elizabeth* was built at the beginning of the 1890s but her Lune Valley boiler dates from 1905. She is, and always has been, oil fired. Steam can be raised in about five minutes.

The pride of the Pattinson collection is the SL *Branksome*. *Branksome* is a 52ft steam launch, built in 1896 for Mrs Howarth, a wealthy local resident who lived at Langdale Chase. *Branksome* is driven by a Sissons compound engine. She is an exquisite craft, almost exactly in the condition in which she was launched, even having the same leather cushions in the cockpit, the same white rubber mats on the decks and the same original upholstered bench seats with tasselled fringes in the saloon. She also has her original Windermere steam kettle. These kettles are, I believe, unique to the Windermere steam launches. They look like small copper tea urns with a brass tap at the bottom. Inside, they have a coil of copper piping connected to the boiler. The kettles are filled from the top and a stopcock in the steam line is turned on. Within ten seconds one gallon of water is boiling.

Branksome had lain neglected in a dock at Bowness until Mr Pattinson took her over. Restoration was largely a matter of cleaning the dirt and dust of ages out of her, sanding down her teak hull, revarnishing the woodwork and polishing the brass. The engine was in good order. It is fired with both wood and coal and there has been no alteration to the boiler.

The joinery of this craft was impeccable. The alternate narrow vertical planks of oak and mahogany that surrounded her cockpit were similar to those Tom Trevethick put into John Players' steam launch *Hero*. The heads on the starboard hand forward of the saloon were also original with the typical flat mahogany seat of the period. In the galley is a solid marble washbasin with a pottery 'beerpump' handle to pump fresh water.

To complete the picture, the original aprons for the servants were found in a drawer in the galley, as were the original silver tea and coffee pots, milk jug and sugar basin, all engraved with the name of the launch. *Branksome* is a delight to look at, but the restoration work was minimal in comparison with that required by another boat in Mr Pattinson's collection, the Ullswater launch *Dolly*.

SL *Dolly*

LOA 41ft 0in
LWL 36ft 0in
Beam 6ft 6in
Built *c* 1850

Of all the craft described in this book, the steam launch *Dolly* has the most unique history. *Dolly* was built about 1850, probably by Brockbank, the Bowness-on-Windermere boatbuilder. At some stage in her career she was transported to Ullswater, probably by a wagon and a team of horses over the 1500ft Kirkstone Pass. The fact that she came from Lake Windermere is confirmed by photographs of the vessel which were found in the Arthur Fildes Collection in 1972. The name SL *Dolly* and the then owner's name, Alfred Fildes, is written on the back of the photograph.

SL *Dolly* was apparently sunk at her moorings on Ullswater during one of the great frosts of the hard, cold winters of the 1890s. She sank in forty feet of water near Cannon Crag at Glenridding and there she lay for eighty years until some members of the Furness Sub-Aqua Club found her. Her fine-lined hull appeared to be intact. After a discussion with Mr Pattinson the Furness divers agreed to attempt to salvage her for him.

This salvage operation was by no means easy for *Dolly* lay on a ledge near a steep escarpment. If she had fallen off the ledge into the deep water, the salvage attempt would have had to be abandoned. *Dolly* proved to be very heavy as her steam engine and boiler were still in place, but she was slowly brought to the surface by means of buoyancy tanks. The final stages of getting her to the surface were prolonged, for no sooner had she broken surface, and attempts made to pump and bail her out, than she filled and sank again. While still partly underwater, she was towed to Glenridding Pier. She finally came to the surface properly in November 1962. Wonderful to relate, her hull appeared to be virtually undamaged; though her funnel had gone, the brass flare was still there and her engine and boiler were intact. One of her spanners was still resting on top of the boiler. This spanner was used to open the manhole cover on the boiler, which showed a complete absence of rust, scale or pitting of either boiler or tubes. (One problem the Windermere and Ullswater steam launches never had to face was boiler corrosion. The water, taken straight from the lake, is absolutely pure and free from all corrosive minerals.) The firebars were still lying in the stokehole, propped up on end around the engine as might be the practice when the vessel was laid up for the winter.

Though *Dolly*'s hull was undamaged, and her oak rudder was firmly hanging by means of iron pintles and gudgeons, the surface of the deal planking and oak timbers was so soft that a finger could be pushed into it to a depth of a quarter of an inch. Mr Pattinson was faced with a small scale *Wasa* operation in salvaging the vessel. It was fortunate that *Dolly* had surfaced in the moist atmosphere of winter in the Lake District. If she had been brought to the surface at the beginning of a hot, dry summer, there would have been a danger of disintegration as she dried out.

Before restoration could begin, *Dolly* had to be taken to Mr Pattinson's dry dock at Bowness-on-Windermere. She was floated on to a six-wheeled trailer, immense care being taken not to distort her hull in the process. The same night, she was towed once again over the Kirkstone Pass and down to Windermere, retracing the journey she had made nearly a hundred years before.

Dolly was floated off the trailer at the head of Lake Windermere and towed by the little *Lady Elizabeth* to Bowness. This time she hardly made any water at all.

At Bowness, the work of restoration started with the vessel slowly drying out. The remains of any paint on her bottom was stripped off and, as the moisture in the planking and timbers dried out, it was replaced at two-week intervals by the application of various oils and preservatives, though they did not actually use the *Wasa*'s mixture of carbo-wax and glycol. This treatment was continued for six months, by which time her planking and frames were hard and firm. The iron fastenings appeared to be as good as new. Neither planking nor frames needed renewing. This was a restoration that involved the most painstaking preservation and resuscitation of what was already there, not in refastening or in cutting away rotten timber as is so usual when restoring very old boats.

Engine and boiler The single-cylinder steam engine had a 7in bore with a 7in stroke and needed no renewal of parts. The iron return-tube boiler was in fair condition, but at least from the point of view of safety precautions needed overhauling. Mr Pattinson's difficulty here was to find anyone who knew anything about iron-tube boilers, which have a different metallurgical technology to that of the modern steel-tube boilers.

At length, he found a craftsman on the north-east coast of England who had been brought up on iron boilers. He was an octogenarian, a retired owner of a ship repair company near Newcastle-upon-Tyne, who happily came out of his retirement to undertake this job. So the boiler was sent across country to Newcastle.

Dolly's boiler had been designed to run at possibly 60lb/sq in, but with minor modifications to the plain furnace, and after a hydraulic test to about 70lb/sq in, her working pressure was fixed at 35lb/sq in.

The layout of this steam installation is a first class example for a steam launch of the 1850s. Mr Pattinson listed the following points about this installation which he thought might be of interest.

1 The pump located at the fore end of the engine may be operated by hand or connected to the crosshead of the engine for mechanical pumping. This may be used either for pumping cold water into the boiler direct from the lake; or by means of an open bottom single ported cock to pump the bilges fore and aft.
2 The low pressure boiler feed water injector was probably made *c*. 1870 and draws water direct from the lake. The final delivery even when working at 3lb/sq in, achieves an inlet feed temperature of 90°F.
3 The engine valve gear is the Stephenson's link motion type – manoeuvering with a single-cylinder engine can at times be difficult due to sticking on top and bottom centres.
4 The steam exhausts either overboard or to the nozzle at the base of the funnel, by means of a two-way cock, which helps draught.

The 3ft diameter three-bladed left-handed cast iron propeller had her original straight cast blades forged to shape and bolted on to the hub. This clumsy piece of work was quite rustless and, surprisingly, drives *Dolly* through the water with little or no vibration. The propeller shaft was also of iron, with iron half bearings which, like all the other engine bearings, were in good condition with no sign of rust. The shaft had a diameter of 3in. The one thing that *Dolly* did need was a new funnel, though it was possible to use the original brass flare.

Dolly was steered by a wheel forward of the engine, connected by a simple system of ropes and pulleys that led at deck level to an iron tiller. These ropes and pulleys had of course to be replaced.

The suggestion that Brockbank was the builder of *Dolly* is based on her remarkable resemblance to another craft, *The Sunbeam*, that Brockbank built for Joseph Sly, a local celebrity who was a friend of Charles Dickens. It was Brockbank's son who built SL *Branksome*.

Surveying

(For a detailed professional survey of an old vessel, see p 128.) If the boat smells bad, it is probably suffering from wet or dry rot. Dry rot has a pungent smell. If it is an old boat, freshly painted, view it with suspicion. If the bottom of a boat is cemented inside, and it is not a fishing smack, also view it with suspicion. Fishing boats were often cemented as soon as they were built and there is rarely any trouble under the cement. Any rot will be along the planks where they abut the top of the cement.

If the inside of a boat is lined throughout, have the lining removed for inspection. Places where one is likely to find rot are at the timberheads, at the end of the deck beams and the covering board. One or two rotten beams can be dealt with quite easily, but it is a major operation to replace a rotten deck shelf.

The chainplates and their fastenings should be inspected to see if they are badly rusted and to see if there is any corrosion in the fastenings.

Rudder If the rudder is outboard, either hung from a transom or from the stern post as in Scandinavian boats, it is easy to inspect the gudgeon and the pintles. If the rudder is supported in a trunk running up through the counter, then it should be examined carefully. The insides of counters in workboats and yachts are often infected with rot.

The floorboards should be lifted and the ballast moved. Prick with a spike or screwdriver the floors, the kelson, the top of the keel, the mast step and the deadwoods at stem and stern. Look out for heavy shakes in stem and stern assemblies; these may need tying with iron straps. Replacing floors is not too difficult; replacing cut frames is a rather more difficult task.

If the deck or cabin is canvased, and if it is loose or bubbling up, then the canvas should be raised to reveal any possible rot below it.

Spars Longitudinal shakes are not important, providing the wood has not rotted inside the cracks. These shakes should be cleaned out, dried and plugged with soft filling. In addition to a spike for pricking soft or rotten wood, a hammer is a useful tool. A soft tap on good wood gives a sharp note, a tap on rotten wood a more muffled note.

Fastenings If the ship is iron fastened, examine for rot in the timber round the fastenings, particularly in mahogany. Examine for rusty or loose nails. If copper fastened, see that the rooves are hard up against the timbers. If they are not, it may merely mean that the timber has shrunk. If this is the case, the rooves can be hardened up.

Stem and apron Hoodends: examine these to see that the screws are firm. If the screws are of brass, they may well have dezincified and will have to be replaced. If the hoodends are frayed, the stem damaged or the apron has rot in it, one way of dealing with it is to take out the old apron, fit a new apron and fasten the ends of the planks to this. Then remove the old stem and cut off the plank ends flush with the front of the apron and fit a new stem post overlapping the apron by the thickness of the planking, thus providing a rabbet for the hoodends.

Planking and sheerstrakes If these have to be replaced, it is advisable to use freshly felled timber. The planks can then be drawn into position with tackles and cramps. To fasten them to the frames, drill and countersink and drive home flat point iron nails, or copper nails and clench. Examine along the waterline to see if there is any rot. Also examine the garboards for the same purpose.

Floors and frames If floors have to be replaced, the kelson (if the boat has one) will have to be shifted. It will be bolted through the floors to the keel. The frames of most fishing smacks are not checked into the keel but merely butt up to it. These frames are sometimes joined by short floors scarphed into them or heavy floors held up against them and sometimes side-bolted to them.

In taking out old frames, it would be wise to make a template of their shapes before removing them. They can then be chiselled out in small bits. New frames can either be cut from grown crooks or cut from $\frac{3}{4}$in marine ply and laminated, which is certainly not traditional but is an effective method of construction.

Keelbolts One or two of these should be drawn in order to verify their condition. The fact that they look all right at the head means nothing. They may have wasted away in the middle. If the boat has a steam or internal combustion engine there is rarely any rot below it, presumably because of the preserving effect of dripping sump oil.

Decks If the decks are very worn, remove all the planks and any deck beams that look at all suspect, then replace beams and replank the deck with teak or fir. In the case of very old craft a marine ply deck will help to stiffen the vessel. Thin planking can be laid over the ply.

Hull If any major replacements have to be made to the hull of an old craft, it is important to prevent the hull from going out of shape. The restoration of the Maldon smack *Boadicea* is a good example of how this can be done. Before her keel was removed, she was reframed; then, to conserve her shape, temporary bilge keels were fitted to take the weight of the hull while the old keel was being taken out of her. If concrete ballast has to be removed, chip it out with a cold chisel. In the case of a rebuild it does not matter what damage you do, but if it is a matter of replacing a few floors it is worth taking care not to damage the structure of the boat. Also, if major replacements have to be made, the order of the operation should be carefully planned. This is most important in cases where there may be difficulty of access, such as for a beam shelf or a breast-hook.

Rot and decay There are various kinds of so-called wet rot fungi, such as *Coniophora cerebella*, which produces dark stains on the surface of the wood and yellow streaks under the surface. There are also different species of *Poria*, such as *Polyporus sulphureos, Poria vaillantii* and *Poria xantha* which are all forms of wet rot found in old boats. *Polyporus sulphureus* is often found in the heart wood of oak trees. If such infected timber is used in boat building, conditions are usually favourable for the development of the fungus. The only possible treatment is to cut out the infected timber. All these *Poria* species are recognisable by white or cream growths on the surface of the timber, together with fine white strands.

Merulius lacrymans the so-called dry rot, grows in places that are damp and badly ventilated. It is more commonly found in buildings than in boats. It can be recognised by a grey bloom over the surface of the wood, which soon begins to look charred with a surface broken up into a regular pattern of transverse and longitudinal shakes. The spores can reach every part of the boat and its greyish strands can spread over paint and metal in search of bare wood. Without moisture, the fungus cannot live. It also cannot live below water, for it needs oxygen. To deal with dry rot, remove all affected wood and paint the nearby timbers with two coats of an organic solvent based preservative, such as Rentokil Dry Rot Fluid. In addition, fumigate the boat by mixing 9oz of potassium permanganate with one pint of formalin in a bucket and leave in the boat for several days with all the entrances blocked up. Then open up and air for several days. Rot nearly always comes from fresh water, either from condensation or rainwater leaks. Where it is difficult to remove affected timbers that are still structurally sound, drill them in a staggered fashion and force in a fungicide under pressure. Staining under varnish, which is usually caused by fungi, can be prevented by brushing on two coats of an organic solvent preservative before varnishing.

Woodborers Gribble *(Limnoria lignorum)* is a crustacean about $\frac{1}{8}$in long which makes burrows about $\frac{1}{10}$in wide in the planks and timbers of boats. It does not penetrate much below the surface but can cause considerable damage to planking and to rudder trunks. An even worse borer is the mollusc *Teredo navalis*, which is found in some European waters. The teredo, like the gribble, bores along the grain and can be detected, as can the gribble, by hammering and pricking. The bottom of a boat that is badly infested with these borers will have to be replanked. Woodlice may often be found in old smacks. They eat sodden wood. Tar varnish is a better deterrent against wood borers than antifouling. Woodborers flourish in salt water; a boat moved to fresh water will become de-infested of borers, as will one left on shore for some months.

The death-watch beetle *(Xestobium rufovillosum)* which made such ravages to the *Victory*'s structure, is rarely a problem in old boats that are still afloat. It seems that it breeds only in timber that is already suffering from fungal decay. Also, it has such a slow and prolonged life cycle, lasting over a period of several years, that the decayed timber would probably be removed from the vessel before the larvae could do any visible damage. The treatment for dealing with death-watch beetle is described in the Introduction.

In the restoration of any old boat all new timber should be treated with preservatives such as Rentokil Dry Rot Fluid or Brunophen, which have maximum penetration. Or the timbers should be pre-treated with a water-based copper-chrome-arsenate (CCA) preservative, applied by vacuum pressure. This can be done only at special treatment plants and the timbers should be machined, cut and drilled before receiving treatment.

Bibliographical references

Introduction

Bugler, Arthur. *HMS Victory, Building, Restoration and Repair* (London: HMSO, 1966)

Gregor, Hugh. *The SS Great Britain* (London: Macmillan, 1972)

Journal of Nautical Archaeology, Vol 1, published for the Council for Nautical Archaeology (London and New York: Seminar Press, March 1972)

Longridge, C. N. *The Cutty Sark*, 2 vols (London: Percival Marshall, 1953)

The Mariner's Mirror, National Maritime Museum, London, quarterly (published by the Society for Nautical Research)

Morris, E. P. *The Fore-and-Aft Rig in America* (New Haven, Conn.: Yale University Press, 1927; Oxford: Oxford University Press, 1927)

Naish, George P. B. *The Wasa: Her Place in History* (London: HMSO, 1968)

Nautical Museum Directory, 3rd ed (New York: Quadrant Press, 1973)

Rudder Magazine, founded in New York in 1890 (see articles on practical boat building by Charles G. Davis, 1895)

Fishing boats

The Annual Illustrated Catalogue and Oarsman's Manual for 1871 (Troy, New York: Waters, Balch & Co)

Ansel, Willits D. *The Restoration of the Smack Emma C. Berry* (Mystic, Conn: The Marine Historical Association, 1973)

Benham, Hervey. *The Last Stronghold of Sail* (London: Harrap, 1948)

——. *Once upon a Tide*, illustrated by Roger Finch (London: Harrap, 1955)

Brewington, M. V. *Chesapeake Bay Log Canoes and Bugeyes* (Cambridge, Md: Cornell Maritime Press, 1963)

British Fishing and Coastal Craft, Science Museum catalogue (London: HMSO, 1951)

Carr, Frank G. G. *Vanishing Craft* (London: County Life, 1934)

Chapelle, Howard I. *Boat Building* (New York: W. W. Norton, 1941)

——. *American Small Sailing Craft* (New York: W. W. Norton, 1951)

Duncan, Stanley and Thorne, Guy. *The Complete Wildfowler Ashore and Afloat* (London: Barrie & Jenkins, 1911; repr 1950)

Frost, Michael. *Boadicea CK213* (London: Angus & Robertson, 1974)

Hall, Henry. *The Ship Building Industry of the United States*. 10th census report, 1884. Deals with a number of native American fishing boats.

Hawker, Peter. *Instructions to Young Sportsmen in All That Relates to Shooting* (London: Longman, 1838)

Huitema, T. *Round and Flat Bottomed Yachts* (Amsterdam: P. N. van Kampen en Zoon, 1962)

March, Edgar J. *Inshore Craft of Britain in the Days of Sail and Oar*, 2 vols (Newton Abbot: David & Charles, 1970)

Payne-Galwey, Sir Ralph. *Letters to Young Shooters*, 3rd series (London: Longmans Green, 1886)

Roberts, Al (ed). *Enduring Friendships*, published by the Friendship Sloop Society (Camden, Me: International Marine Publishing Co, 1970)

Sedgwick, Whittaker and Harrison (eds). *The New Wildfowler in the 1970s* (London: Barrie & Jenkins, 1970)

Slocum, Joshua. *Sailing Alone round the World* (London: Rupert Hart-Davis, 1948. First published 1900)

Stephens, H. P. *Canoe and Boat Building*, published by *Forest and Stream*, 1885. Covers canoes, fishermen's dories, sneak boxes.

Walsingham, Lord and Payne-Galwey, Sir Ralph. *Shooting, Moor and Marsh* (London: Longmans Green, 1886)

Trading vessels, fishing schooner and pilot boats

Carr, Frank G. G. *Sailing Barges* (London: Peter Davies, 1951; Conway Maritime Press, Greenwich, 1972; 1st ed 1931)

Church, A. C. *American Fishermen* (New York: W. W. Norton, 1940)

Clark, Roy. *Black-sailed Traders* (London: Putnam, 1961)

Greenhill, Basil. *The Merchant Schooners*, 2 vols (Newton Abbot: David & Charles, 1968; 1st ed 1951)

Maltster, Robert. *Wherries and Waterways* (Lavenham: Terence Dalton, 1971)

March, Edgar J. *Spritsail Barges of Thames and Medway* (London: Percival Marshall, 1948; repr 1972)

Martin, E. G. *Sailorman* (Oxford: Oxford University Press, 1933)

Scott, Richard J. *The Story of the Kathleen & May* (London: Ships Monthly & Maritime Trust, 1972)

Yachts

Chapelle, Howard I. *Yacht Designing and Planning* (New York: W. W. Norton, 1936)

Goodey, Charles. *The Brown Boats: The Story of the Broads One-Design*, published by the author, Lowestoft, 1972

Griffiths, Maurice. *Little Ships and Shoal Waters* (London: Peter Davies, 1937; repr Conway Maritime Press, Greenwich, 1972)

Kemp, Dixon. *Yacht Designing* (The Field, 1876)

——. *A Manual of Yacht and Boat Sailing*, published by *The Field*, 1878 and later eds.

Knight, E. F. *Small Boat Sailing* (London: John Murray, 1896)

Kunhardt, C. P. *Small Yachts, Their Design and Construction* (published by *Forest and Stream*, 1885). Shows plans of yachts, sharpies, skipjacks and catboats.

Stephens, W. P. (ed). *Lloyds Register of American Yachts 1897–1932* (London: Lloyds)

Stephens, W. P. *Traditions and Memories of American Yachting* (New York: Hearst Magazines Inc, 1942)

The restoration of steam launches and steam engines

Building a Steam Engine from Castings, by *Exactus*, (Henley-on-Thames: Stuart-Turner, 1974). This book contains a detailed description of building a Stuart No 10 engine which is only 149mm high, but would be useful to anyone building one of their larger engines.

Light Steam Power, monthly magazine (Isle of Man: Kirk Michael)

Reed's Guide to the Use and Management of Yacht, Trawler and Launch Engines (Sunderland: J. Denholm-Young, 1904)

Steam Boat Index (Fareham, Hants: Steamboat Association of Great Britain, 1970)

List of maritime museums

United Kingdom

Angus
Frigate *Unicorn* (restored), Dundee

Avon
Brunel's SS *Great Britain*, Great Western Dock, Bristol

Belfast
Ulster Museum

Cleveland
Maritime Museum, Southgate, Hartlepool

Cumbria
Barrow-in-Furness Museum

The Windermere Nautical Trust, Bowness-on-Windermere
Collection of early steam launches.

Devon
Bideford Museum, Municipal Buildings, Bideford
Brixham Museum, Higher Street, Brixham
Exeter Maritime Museum

Plymouth: *Kathleen & May* sailing trading schooner berthed at Sutton Harbour.

Salcombe: Brixham trawler *Provident* chartered to the Island Cruising Club at Salcombe.

Dumfries
Annan Museum, The Moat House, Annan

Fife
The Scottish Fisheries Museum, Anstruther

Gwent
Nelson Museum, Market Hall, Priory Street, Monmouth

Hampshire
Maritime Museum, Buckler's Hard, Beaulieu
The Victory Museum, HM Dockyard, Portsmouth
HMS *Victory*, HM Dockyard, Portsmouth
Maritime Museum, Wool House, Bugle Street, Southampton

Humberside
Doughty Museum, Grimsby
The Maritime Museum, Kingston-upon-Hull

The Ferrens Art Gallery, Kingston-upon-Hull
Fine collection of maritime paintings.

Isle of Man
National Museum, Bridge Street, Castletown

Kent
The Dolphin Sailing Barge Trust Museum, Sittingbourne

London
The Maritime Trust, 80 Duke Street, W1M DQ
The *Cutty Sark*, Cutty Sark Gardens, Greenwich Pier, SW10
HMS *Discovery*, King's Reach, Victoria Embankment
National Maritime Museum, Romney Road, Greenwich SE10

Science Museum, Exhibition Road, SW7
Fine collection of ship models – mainly mercantile craft.

Norfolk
Maritime Museum for East Anglia, Marine Parade, Great Yarmouth

Northamptonshire
Inland Waterways Museum, Stoke Bruerne

Scilly Isles
Valhalla Maritime Museum, Tresco Abbey
Collection of ships' figureheads.

Suffolk
Christchurch Mansion, Ipswich
Collection of ship models.

Sparrow's Nest Museum, Lowestoft
Collection of trawler paintings.

South Glamorgan
National Museum of Wales, Civic Centre, Cardiff
Collection of ship models.

Tyne and Wear
Museum of Science and Engineering, Newcastle-upon-Tyne

Wirral
Williamson Art Gallery and Museum, Slatey Road, Birkenhead

United States of America

California
Maritime Museum of San Diego, 1306 North Harbor Drive, San Diego, Calif 92101
Barque *Star of India* built 1863 Isle of Man, oldest merchant ship afloat
Ship models etc.

San Francisco Maritime Museum, Foot of Polk Street, San Francisco, Calif 94109
Full-rigged ship *Balclutha* built 1886 Scotland
Side-wheel paddle tug *Eppleton Hall*
Ship models, paintings etc.

San Francisco Maritime State Historic Park, 2905 Hyde Street, San Francisco, Calif 94109
Three-masted schooner *C. A. Thayer* built 1895
Scow schooner *Alma* and various steam vessels.

Connecticut
Mystic Seaport, Mystic, Conn 06355

Washington DC
Navy Memorial Museum Building, 76 Washington Navy Yard, Washington DC 20390
197 years of US naval history.
Ship models, displays, dioramas etc.

Smithsonian Institution National Museum of History and Technology, Washington DC 20560
175 world's finest ship models etc.

Truxtun-Decatur Naval Museum, Room 218, Building 220, Navy Yard, Washington DC 20390

Florida
MGM's *Bounty* Exhibit, 345 Second Ave NE, St Petersburg Fla 33701
Replica of the famous vessel and Captain Bligh's longboat.

Georgia
Ships of the Sea Museum, 503 East River Street, Savannah, Ga 31401
Fine display of ship models.

Hawaii
Falls of Clyde, Pier 5, Honolulu, Hawaii 96819
Full rigged ship *Falls of Clyde* built 1878 Scotland.

Illinois
Museum of Science and Industry, Jackson Park, Chicago, Ill 60637
Lifesize replica of USS *Constitution* gun deck
Ship models etc.

Iowa
Keokuk River Museum, Keokuk River Commission, 226 High St, Keokuk, Iowa 52632
Mississippi sternwheel tow boat *George M. Verity*.

Kentucky
Steamer *Belle of Louisville*, Foot of Fourth Street, Louisville, Ky 40202
Operating June – Labour Day.

Maine
Bath Marine Museum, Marine Research Society of Bath, 963 Washington Street, Bath, Maine 04530
365 years of Maine maritime history
Ship models etc.

Grand Banks Schooner Museum, 100 Commercial Street, Boothbay Harbor, Maine 04538
Grand Banks schooner *Sherman Zwicker* built 1941 by Smith & Rhuland
Wooden steam tug *Seguin*

Fisherman's Museum, Pemaquid Point

Penobscot Marine Museum, Searsport, Maine 04974
Collections ship models, marine paintings etc.

Maryland
US Naval Academy Museum, Annapolis, Md 21402
Over 250 fine ship models.

Chesapeake Bay Maritime Museum, St Michaels, Md 21663

Frigate *Constellation*, c/o Harbormaster Pier, 4 Pratt Street, Baltimore, Md 21202

Massachusetts
Museum of Science, Science Park, Boston, Mass 02114
Ship models, dioramas etc.

Boston Naval Shipyard, Boston, Mass 02129
The USS *Constitution* built Boston 1797. The only frigate still surviving and perfectly preserved.

US Naval Academy Museum, Annapolis

Francis Russell Hart Nautical Museum, 55 Massachusetts Avenue, Cambridge, Mass 02139
Fine display of nautical items, ship models etc
Working drawings of yachts and small craft by twentieth-century designers.

Thomas Cooke House and Museum, Dukes County Historical Society, PO Box 827, Edgartown, Mass 02539
Ship models, pictures, whaling boat and whaling relics.

Marine Museum, Fall River, PO Box 1147, Mass 02722
Ship models, paintings etc.
Kendall Whaling Museum, Sharon, Mass

Museum of the American China Trade, 215 Adams Street, Milton, Mass 02186
Memorabilia pertaining to maritime commerce with the Orient.

The Whaling Museum, 18 Johnny Cake Hill, New Bedford, Mass 02740
Exhibits include half scale model of the barque *Lagoda*, typical of the whaleships from New Bedford around 1850.

Mayflower II, PO Box 162, Plymouth, Mass 02360 (berthed at State Pier)
Full scale reproduction of the ship that brought the Pilgrim Fathers to America.

Peabody Museum of Salem, 161 Essex Street, Salem, Mass 01970
Exhibits include a very large collection of ship models, marine paintings etc.

Michigan
Greenfield village and Henry Ford Museum, Dearborn, Mich 48121
The steamboat *Suwanee*, stern-wheeler constructed 1930, with engines built 1888.
This museum contains many items of nautical interest.

Dossin Great Lakes Museum, Detroit Historical Commission, 5401 Woodward Ave, Detroit Mich 48202
Maritime history of the Great Lakes. Ship models etc.

Minnesota
Julius C. Wilkie Steamboat Museum, Winona, Minn 55987
Sternwheel Steamboat *Julius C. Wilkie* houses a museum of river transportation history.

New Hampshire
Strawbery Banke. Restoration of part of original early colonial settlement at Portsmouth. Dories built here in traditional manner.

Peabody Museum, Rye Beach

New York
Thousand Islands Museum, Riverside Drive, Clayton, NY 13624
Extensive displays of building small vessels. Canoes, skiffs etc on display.

Thousand Islands Shipyard Museum, Mary Street, Clayton, NY 13624
159 vessels on display, including St Lawrence River skiffs, canoes, kayaks and antique power boats. Restoration workshop.

Adirondack Museum, Blue Mountain Lake, NY
Second largest collection of small craft in America, including Adirondack guideboats (lines and plans available), canoes and kayaks.

Whaling Museum, Cold Spring Harbor, NY 11724
Exhibits illustrate the nineteenth century whaling era.

South Street Seaport Museum, 16 Fulton Street, New York, NY 10038
Exhibits include 4-masted barque *Moshulu* and various other vessels including the clipper-bowed fishing schooner *Lettie G. Howard*.

Suffolk Marine Museum, Long Island

Suffolk County Whaling Museum, PO Box 327A, Sag Harbor, NY 11963

Skenesborough Museum, Whitehall, NY 12887
Hull of USS *Ticonderoga* built 1812. Models of lake boats, locks etc.

North Carolina
Blockade Runner Museum, PO Box 386, Carolina Beach, NC 28428
Story of 2,000 ships that attempted to reach North Carolina ports through the northern blockade during the Civil War. Ship models of the fast ships of the time.

Ohio
The *Delta Queen*, Greene Line Steamers Inc, 322E Fourth Street, Cincinnati, Ohio 45202
Sternwheel paddle steam boat built 1936. Cruises mainly on Ohio and Mississippi Rivers. 62 cruises made in 1973.

Pennsylvania
USS *Niagara*, 142 East 3rd Street, Erie, Pa 16500
Reconstruction (1913) of small square-rigged brig, originally built *c.* 1812.

Philadelphia Maritime Museum, 427 Chestnut Street, Philadelphia, Pa 19106
Outstanding display of ship models, paintings etc.
Gazela Primeiro, a sailing ship preserved by the museum, is berthed at Pier 15N on the Delaware River. A 324-ton barquentine used for cod fishing for 90 years, built 1883.

Rhode Island
Revolutionary war frigate *Rose*, 60 Church Street, Newport, RI 02840
Full-sized reconstruction of British 24-gun frigate.

Virginia
Jamestown Festival Park, PO Drawer, J. F. Williamsburg, Va 21385
Replicas of three square-rigged merchant vessels, *Susan Constant, Godspeed* and *Discovery*, that originally landed at Jamestown in 1607.

The Mariner's Museum, Newport News, Va 23606
Extensive nautical collections. Many small craft on large lake near museum.

Canada

British Columbia
Maritime Museum. 1,905 Ogden Street, Vancouver 9
RCMP vessel *St Roch* built 1928. The first ship to navigate the North West Passage in both directions.

New Brunswick
The New Brunswick Museum, St John.

Nova Scotia
Maritime History Department of Nova Scotia Museum, 1,747 Summer Street, Halifax
A large marine library and photograph collection.

Ontario
Marine Museum of Upper Canada, Exhibition Park, Toronto, 2B Ont
Exhibitions include many fine ship models.

Europe and Near East

Belgium
National Scheepvaartsmuseum, Antwerp

Denmark
Fiskeri Sjofartsmuseet, Esbjerg

Handels -og Sjofartsmuseum, Helsinger

Viking Ship Museum, Roskilde

Israel
National Maritime Museum, Haifa

Italy
Museo Storico Navale, Venice

Netherlands
Maritime Museum 'Prince Hendrick', Rotterdam

Nederlandsch Historisch Scheepvaart, Amsterdam

Schokland Museum, Schokland NOP

Zuiderzee Museum, Enkhuizen

Norway
Stavanger Sjofartsmuseum

Norsk Sjofartsmuseum, Oslo

Bergens Sjofartsmuseum

Maritime Museum, Bergen

Portugal
Museum de Marinha, Lisbon

Spain
Museo Maritimo, Barcelona

Sweden
Marinmuseum, Karlskrona

Sjöfartsmuseet, Goteborg

Statens Sjöhistoriska Museum, Stockholm

The *Wasa* Museum, Stockholm

West Germany
Deutsches Schiffahrtsmuseum, Bremerhaven

Altona Museum/North German State Museum, Altona, Museumstrasse 23, Hamburg
Museum of Hamburg History, Holstenwall 24, Hamburg

Acknowledgements

I would like to thank all those who have helped me in the production of this book and particularly Mr Willits D. Ansel of Mystic Seaport, Mr Hervey Benham, Mr C. M. Blackford, Commander J. R. Blake RN of SS *Great Britain*, Mr Bob Brewster, Mr Peter Brown, Mr John Burgess, Mr Howard I. Chapelle, Mr David Clarkson of the Yare Valley Sailing Club, Mr Keith Cutmore, Mr Peter Dorleyn, Mr John Fairbrother, Major J. Forsythe, Mr Michael Frost, Mr John Gardner of Mystic Seaport, Mr Colin Glass, Mr David Goddard of the Exeter Maritime Museum, Mr Charles Goodey, Mr Maurice Griffiths GM, Mr and Mrs Charles Harker, Mr Sem Hartz, Mr Brian Hillsdon of the Steamboat Association of Great Britain, Mr and Mrs Charles Hoskins, Dr T. Huitema, Mr David Kasanof of *Classic Boat Monthly*, Mr David King, Mr R. F. Lawrence, Light Steam Power, Mr Joe Lucas, The Maritime Trust, Mrs Diana Matthews of the Windermere Nautical Trust, Mr George P. B. Naish FSA, Mr John MacCormick of the Nova Scotia Communications and Information Centre, Miss C. Janet Palmer, Mr John Perryman ARINA, Mr D. Phillips-Birt, John Player and Sons Ltd, Mr David Proctor of the National Maritime Museum, Mr J. P. Richards of WAGBI, Mr Edwin Rideout, Mr and Mrs Al Roberts, Mr John Scarlett of The Old Gaffers Association, Statens Sjöhistoriska Museum, Wasavarvet, Stockholm, Stuart-Turner & Co Ltd, Mr J. A. Sutherland, Mr Christopher Stirling, Mr Stephen Swann, Lieutenant Commander H. A. A. Twiddy RN, Commanding Officer HMS *Victory* (Ship), Mr Alan Viner of the National Maritime Museum, Mr Roy Wallace of Wallace & Newbert, Wing-Cdr Gordon Waller, Mr T. Whelpton, Mr Ernst Wiegleb, Captain Michael Willoughby and all the various photographers who have been kind enough to lend photographs.

J. L.

Index

Aaken, Weiringer: 64–5
Abruzzi, Prince Louis: 51
Acle: 21
Albion, (Plane): 107, 142–5
Aldous of Brightlingsea: 25, 55
Allen, Peter: 53
America, schooner yacht: 22, 107
Ames, Estella: 76
Ames, Jack: 75
Amity; Friendship sloop: 73
Amsterdam: 55
Ansel, W. D.: 79, 86–7
Appalachicola: 22
Appledore: 109, 113, 159
Apron: 31–2, 34, 39, 52, 81, 128, 139
Armorel, ketch: 156–163
Arnhem: 63
Aspenet, sloop: 21
Atthill, A.: 167
Auto-da-Fe, bawley: 55
Avondale, steam launch: 175

Ballast: 38–40, 72, 76, 78, 81, 87, 127–8, 153, 156, 162
Baltic: 21, 124
Baltic traders: 124
Banks schooners: 9, 15, 87, 105, 119–124
Barge boat: 87, 124
Barry Docks: 109
Baverstock, G.: 128
Bawley: 23–4, 46–55, 93
Beal, Milton: 80, 86–7
Beardmore diesel engine: 109
Belano, J. W.: 76
Bideford: 109, 113
Bilge keels: 27, 35, 39
Bilges: 128, 162
Binks family: 25, 39
Birdseye: 156
Bitts: 34, 44, 75, 81, 86
Bituguard: 113
Bitumen: 28, 32, 37, 40
Blackford, C. M.: 22
Blackwater, river: 23, 53, 55, 93–4, 96, 104, 135, 153
Blake, W. M.: 47
Bluenose: 118, 120, 122–4
Bluenose II: 22, 107, 119, 120, 122–4
Boadicea, Maldon oyster smack: 2, 19, 22–45, 69, 76, 79, 83, 86, 181
Boeier: 9, 65
Boilers: 164, 168–171, 180
  Clyde type: 169
  Coal fired: 170
  Feedwater for: 170–1, 180
  Finned drum: 164
  Lune Valley: 178
  Merryweather: 169–171, 176–7
  Oil fired: 177
  Perkins: 177
  Propane fired: 164
  Wood fired: 171
Bona, bawley: 24, 45–55, 90, 93
Boothbay Harbour, Me.: 107, 118
Boston Harbour, Mass.: 70
Bow, false: 157, 159–161
Bowness: 178–180
Brace, Pat: 53

Bradwell: 25, 44
Bray, Maynard: 79, 81
Breasthook: 34, 39, 100, 130
Breechings: 101–2
Bremen, Me.: 69, 75
Breydon Water: 144
Brightlingsea: 7, 25, 51–2, 55, 90
Brighton, Wm.: 142
Bristol: 6
Bristol Channel: 109, 159
Bristol, Me.: 69
Brixham trawler: 159
Broads One-Design: ('Brown Boats') 21, 146–152
  Bittern, Curlew, Dabchick, Dunlin, Flittermouse, Gannet, Goshawk, Mallard, Peewit, Shearwater, Snipe, Teal, Widgeon: 148
Brockbank, boatbuilder: 179, 180
Brothers, paddlesteamer: 153
Brown, Peter: 23, 128
Browns of Chelmsford: 137
Brunel, I. K.: 6
Brunophen: 145, 182
BU 29, botter: 55
Bugeye: 22
Bugler, Arthur: 6
Bulwarks: 52–3, 82, 86–7, 110–11, 126, 130, 158, 160
Bungay: 142, 144
Bunschoten: 55
Burgess, Starling: 118
Burnham: 25
Burnham Yacht Building Co: 148

C. A. Thayer, lumber schooner: 107
Cambria, Thames barge: 135
Campeche Banks: 22
Cann J. & H.: 49
Canvassing decks: 101, 160, 181
Cape Cod: 80, 118
Cape Sable: 22, 118
Cardiff: 159
Carnot and Rankin: 166
Carr, Frank: 47, 137
Carsaig: 90
Casting: 38, 78
Cates J. & G.: 144
Catheads: 130
Caulking: 40, 75, 78–9, 86, 103, 113, 115, 130, 139, 160
Cayley, C. T.: 153
Ceiling (lining): 25, 76, 86–7, 131
Cemented bilges: 27, 75, 181
Cetonia, schooner: 153
Chain plates: 38, 86, 131, 181
Chapelle, H. I.: 69–73, 79, 87, 105–6
Charlie Allnutt, miniature Mississippi sternwheeler: 164
Charles W. Morgan, whaler: 15, 87
Charlestown: 6, 8
Charm, Friendship sloop: 73
Chatham: 11
Chesapeake Bay: 22
Chrissy (Sonny), Friendship sloop: 73, 75–9
Churchward, G. J.: 164
Clabburn, W. L.: 148
Clara, schooner: 153

Clark, Roy: 142
Clayton's wharf, Nottingham: 177
Coamings: 38, 51, 75, 87
Colchester smacks: 7, 28, 52, 54–5, 102
Colmans (Norwich): 144
Colne, river: 52
Colne Smack Restoration Society: 55
Columbia, Banks schooner: 123
Composite building: 153
Connah's Quay: 109
Constellation, USS: 107
Constitution, USS: 69, 107
Cork Sand: 47
Counter: 52, 72, 75, 79, 148, 156, 181
Cousteau, Jacques-Yves: 19
Covering boards: 33, 38, 76, 81, 86, 131, 139, 160
Cowes: 156
Cowhorn, (Stamford oyster boat): 120
Cranfield Brothers, (millers): 135
Crossley diesel engine: 109
Crossman, Arnold: 79, 81
Crystal River, Fla.: 22
Cuprinol: 25, 30, 37, 40, 78, 83, 86
Cutmore, Keith: 164, 168
Cutty Sark, clipper: 6, 69, 107
Cygnet, steam launch: 175

Dale, Slade: 81
Danish Pilot Brigantine: 21
Davis, Captain Paul: 109, 113, 118
Death watch beetle: 12–13, 15, 17
Deck: 33, 38, 52–3, 76, 81, 84–5, 101, 108, 110–111, 113, 120, 131, 137, 139, 160, 181
Decay in timber: 11–13, 16–17, 25, 31, 52, 67, 75, 76, 81–3, 113, 128, 137, 139, 144–5, 160, 181–2
Delawana II, Banks schooner: 122–3
Dickens, Charles: 180
Dictator, Friendship sloop: 73
Dinghies: 163
Dodd, W. H.: 135
Dolly, steam launch: 178–180
Dories: 24, 104–6, 120, 122, 123
Doris, bawley: 55
Dorleyn, Peter: 55–68
Duck punt: 24, 93–104
Dunkirk: 87
Dunlin: B.O.D.: 148, 150

East Coast Sail Trust: 124, 135
Edith May, Thames barge: 135
Electrolytic action: 79, 159
Ellie T, Friendship sloop: 70, 71
Elsie, Banks schooner: 123
Elston, Leslie: 175
Emma C. Berry, Noank sloop: 14, 19, 74, 79–87
Emma Goody, miniature bawley: 90–3
Emperor, German: 153
Enkhuizen: 6, 9
Erith: 48
Essex, Mass.: 107
Estella A., Friendship sloop: 19, 73–6, 87
Everard, F. T. & Co.: 135

Faeringen Fra Gokstad: 22
Fairbrother, John: 135, 137, 139
Fastenings: 11, 14, 18–19, 25, 27, 33–4, 37–40, 55, 67, 76, 78–9, 83, 86, 90, 99, 100, 103, 138–9, 145, 156, 159, 180–1
Fay & Co.: 153
Ferguson & Baird: 109
Ferro-cement: 22, 156
Fibreglass (GRP): 52, 163
Fildes, Arthur: 179
Fishing methods,
  American: 105, 120
  Dutch: 67–8
  English: 93–4
Fishing, New England: 69, 71, 80
Fish well: 24, 57, 59, 60–1, 66, 80–1, 86–7, 156, 162
Fiskebakschiele: 127
Fitzgerald, Sir M.: 153
Flat bottomed boats: 24, 93–106
Flittermouse, B.O.D.: 21, 148–53
Floors: 28, 32, 34, 39, 55, 79, 83, 85, 98, 131, 137, 181
Francis & Gilders: 137
Franzen, Anders: 19
Fredonia, Gloucester fisherman: 71
Friendship: 69, 71, 73, 76
Friendship sloops: 6, 19, 22, 24, 69–79, 87, 120
Friendship Sloop Society: 72
Friesjacht: 9
Friesland: 142
French, E. W. (Manny): 25, 39
Frost & Drake: 25, 27, 55
Frost, Michael: 19, 22–45, 55, 76, 83, 86
Fungicides: 13, 144–5
Furness Sub-Aqua Club: 179

Gagnin, Emile: 19
Galatea, Friendship sloop: 70
Galleas, Swedish: 124–33
Gallico, Paul: 87
Gardiner diesel engine: 156
Gardner, John: 19
General Steam Navigation Co.: 144
Georges Banks: 118
Gertrude L. Thebaud, Banks schooner: 123
Glenridding pier: 179
Gloucester, Mass.: 71, 105, 123
Golden Eagle, Friendship sloop: 73
Goldhanger: 102
Grand Banks: 72, 118
Great Britain: 6
Greenheart: 35, 37–8, 40
Greenhill, Basil: 113
Greenhithe: 135
Greenwich: 6, 22
Grimsby: 157, 159, 163
Guilleaume, Max: 153

Gulf of Mexico: 22
Gun punt: 24, 93–104

Haas, de: 55
Hailing Kabe (Mongoggle): 90
Hair and Blair: 139
Haiti: 120
Halifax N.S.: 120
Haligonian, Banks schooner: 123
Harding, Guy: 31
Harding, Nicholas: 55
Hardley, Staithe: 144
Harker, Charles: 7, 87, 102
Harker, Janet: 87, 92
Harris, Richard: 87, 92
Harwich: 135
Harwich bawley: 47, 49–51
Hatchet Cove Me.: 72
Hawker, Lt. Col. Peter: 94, 96–7
Heartsease (Adela), schooner: 153–6
Heath Robinson: 156
Henry Ford, Banks schooner: 123
Hero, steam launch: 164, 170–8
Heybridge Basin: 137
Higgins and Gifford: 105
Historic Ships Association: 107
Hong Kong: 113
Hoodends: 181
Hoorn: 59, 62, 64
Hope, Linton: 148
Horlocks: 137
Horlock, Horatio: 135
Horn timbers: 75–6
Hoskins, Carole: 163
Hoskins, Charles: 156, 159, 160, 162–3
Howarth, Mrs.: 178
Humberston: 159
Hyacinth, Colchester smack: 54–5

Ijselmeer: 55, 62, 64
Insecticides: 13, 145
International Fishermen's Races: 107
Ipswich: 55
Iris, smack: 7, 102
Iveagh, Lord: 153

Jewell, Captain T.: 109, 118
Jewell, W.: 109
Jol, Staverse: 65
Jones, J. F. & Partners: 128
Jonkopings, A. B.: 124
Joseph Conrad: 15, 87
Joy, winkle brig: 87, 92
June Munktell semi-diesel engine: 124

Kanvo: 52, 93
Kapelowitz, John: 70
Kathleen & May, schooner: 109–118
Keel: 11, 32, 34–6, 39, 40, 55, 75, 81, 113, 132, 137, 152–3, 156, 159, 181–2
Keel bolts: 34, 181
Keel, false: 142, 144, 160
Keith, David: 123
Kelson, 33, 34, 39, 40, 55, 83, 85, 137
Kemp, Dixon: 47–8
Kennett, Mrs Molly: 55

Ketch rig: 159
Kiel Regatta: 153
King, David: 164, 166, 168
King, Sir Henry Seymour: 153
Kirby, A. T.: 51
Kirby, C.: 51–2
Kirby, R.: 51
Kirkstone Pass: 179, 180
Kitty, Thames barge: 107, 135–42
Knightheads: 34, 39, 81, 132
Knox petrol engine: 75
Kwakken, Vollendammer: 65

L. A. Dunton, Grand Banks schooner: 15, 87, 107, 118, 120
Lash, Winfield: 72
Latham, J. A.: 80
Lawrence, Jimmy: 52
Leeboards: 55, 60–1, 135–7
Leigh bawley: 47, 51
Lenton, Nottingham: 171
Lettie G. Howard, fishing schooner: 9, 107–8
LIFU: 164, 170, 174, 177
Light, Janet: 127
Light, Peter: 124, 126–8
Light Steam Power: 170
Limfjord: 163
Lister 6hp diesel engine: 109
Llantwit Major: 109
Long Island Sound: 87
Lothing, lake: 142
Lowestoft: 146, 150, 153
Lowley, George: 21
Lucas family: 94–5
Lucas, Joe: 95, 102–3
Lune Valley burner: 170
Lunenburg N.S.: 120, 122–4

M.K. 63, botter: 55–68, 79
Mackenzie, Bernard: 70
McManus, T. F.: 118
McLain, Robert: 74–5
McLean, Ruari: 87, 90
Maine Antique Boat Society: 21
Maldon: 25, 52, 55, 90, 127–8, 139
Maldon Yacht and Barge Charter Co.: 137
Manningtree: 94–5, 97, 101–2
Marine borers: 12, 13, 17, 21, 145, 182
Marine glue: 139
Marine Historical Society, The: 107
Marine Tech: 78
Maritime Trust: 107, 109, 113, 118, 177
Marjorie, barge: 52
Marken: 65–6
Martha's Vineyard: 80
Mashford Brothers: 115, 116, 118
Matinicus, Me.: 75
Maud, bawley: 47, 49, 50
May, Thames barge: 135
Mayflower, Banks schooner: 123
Mayflower II: 107
Mayhew, Lady: 142
Medomak, river: 73
Meduncook (Friendship): 69, 73
Medway, river: 105, 135

Medway punt: 105
Memory, Thames barge: 124, 135
Mersea Island: 52
Meteor, schooner: 153
Methyl bromide: 13
Middelburg: 25
Mistley: 135
Monnickendam: 55
Morecambe Bay prawner: 22
Morse, Charles: 70, 76
Morse, Wilbur: 69, 71–3, 76, 78–9
Muiden: 55
'Mulie' barge: 135
Mull, Island of: 90
Muscongus Bay: 24, 69–71, 73
Myatt, Arthur: 51
Mystic Seaport, Conn.: 6, 9, 14–15, 19, 74–6, 79–83, 107, 118, 120

Nantucket Island: 80
Narrow boats: 142
National Maritime Museum, Greenwich, 6, 22, 113, 116, 177
Nautilus, Thames barge: 134
Navigating instruments: 162
Naze: 47
Nellie, oyster sloop: 87
Netherlands Open Air Museum: 63
New Bedford: 15
New London: 80
New York: 9, 80, 107
Newbert & Wallace's Boatyard: 19, 74–6
Newcastle-upon-Tyne: 180
Niagara Falls: 156
Nieuwboer Brothers: 55, 57
Noank fishing sloop: 14, 19, 24, 76, 79–87, 120
Nore Light Vessel: 47
Norfolk Broads: 142, 148, 153
Norfolk Wherry Trust: 107, 142, 144

Oland & Son: 120
Old Maltings Boatyard: 148
Onedin Line, The: 177
Onset, Mass.: 70
Orfordness: 139
Orwell, river: 55, 135
Oulton Broad: 146, 149

Palmer, R. & J.: 80
Pao, Y. K.: 113, 116
Patience, David: 55
Patient Griselda: 31
Patterns: 28–9, 40
Pattinson, George: 177–180
Pauls (millers): 135
Payne-Galway, Sir R.: 101–2
Peewit B.O.D.: 52
Pemaquid, Friendship sloop: 70, 72–3
Pensacola, Fla.: 107
Perkins diesel engine: 156
Perryman, J. E.: 144–5, 153, 156
Peter boat: 93
Pewter, John: 25, 39
Phoenix, sternwheeler: 164
Pilgrim Fathers: 118
Pin Mill: 135

Pit saw: 32
Pitch: 78, 139, 160
Pither stove: 139
Planking: 37–8, 40, 75–6, 78–9, 81–2, 86, 98–9, 100–103, 106, 116, 120, 127, 132, 137–9, 144, 152–3, 156, 159, 160, 181
Player, John & Sons: 171, 174, 178
Pleasant Point: 75
Plute: 64–5
Plymouth, Devon: 113, 116
Plymouth, Mass.: 107
Polyethylene Glycol: 21
Port Clyde: 76
Porter family: 95
Porter,
   Dod: 94, 96, 101–2
   Bill: 94, 96
   Lun: 94
Portsmouth, H.M. Dockyard: 6, 10
Pumps: 21, 55, 133, 162–3
Punt guns: 94–7, 101–4
Purdey, gunmakers: 95
Pyefleet Oyster Co.: 52
Pyefleet Channel: 52

R.C.Y.C., Toronto: 153
Rainbird, Donald: 28
Redditch: 164
Rentokil: 182
Replicas: 22, 94, 107, 120
Rigging: 52, 75, 87, 93, 113, 127, 133, 137, 139
Rig and sail plan: 14, 36, 44–5, 47–51, 56, 64–7, 69, 81, 90, 93, 109, 124, 127, 134–5, 142, 148–9, 153, 155–6, 162
Roberts, Captain Bob: 135
Robinson, George: 51
Rockland, Me.: 75
Rogers, Paul: 90, 93
Roller reefing gear: 109, 162
Roth, McKie: 70
Roue, W. J.: 118, 122–3
Royal George, H.M.S.: 11
Rudder: 39, 52, 133, 152, 181
Rudder box: 76, 79, 181

Saab diesel engine: 162
Sail plans: 50, 66, 69, 90, 109, 134, 149, 155
St Lawrence Bay: 102
St Osyth Boatyard: 53
St Roch, R.C.M.P. Vessel: 107
Sakrete: 78
Samson post: 86–7, 133
San Francisco Bay: 107
Satanita: 153
Scarphs: 36–7, 78, 85–6, 99, 100, 113, 139, 145, 159
Schooner: 105, 107–24, 153–6
Schouten, Willem: 64
Schouw: 65
Science Museum, London: 47, 134
Scow: 105
Sea Reach, Thames: 47
Seager, John: 174
Sealastic: 90
Shamrock, smack: 43

Sharpies: 22, 105
Shelf (sheer clamp): 31, 33, 39, 78–9, 83, 86, 133, 137, 160
Sheer strake: 38, 120
Shelburne, N.S.: 123
Sherman Zwicker, Banks fishing schooner: 107
Shetland boats: 24, 87–90
Shrimpers: 47, 93
Sibbick, C.: 156; Yachts designed by: *Armorel, Gwenda, Nanette, Popinjay, Ripple, Riva, Saunterer, Thalassa, Wilful, Witch*: 156
Sissons Compound engine: 178
Skipjack: 22
Slade, Thomas (Senior Surveyor to the Navy): 11
Slocum, Joshua: 22, 28
Sly, Joseph: 180
Smack, East Coast: 6, 7, 23–47, 75, 102
Smith & Rhuland: 120
Snow Goose, The: 87, 92
Society for Nautical Research: 6
Solent: 154
Solvig, Swedish galleas: 107, 124–33
South Street Seaport Museum, New York: 9, 107
Southampton Water: 109
Southend: 135
Spakenburg: 55, 59, 62
Spanish windlass: 98
Spars: 40, 52, 64, 81, 87, 113, 128, 131–2, 137, 162, 181
Spinaway C, Thames barge: 135–7
Spithead: 11
Spratting (see Stowboating)
Spray (Slocum's): 22, 28
Stackie barge: 55
Stanchions: 81, 86, 113, 130, 139
Steam engines: 164–71
Steaming (steambox): 33, 78, 139
Steam launches: 22, 164–80
Stem: 19, 36, 40, 75–6, 81, 98–9, 106, 113–14, 133, 142, 152, 156–7, 159, 160, 161, 181
Stephenson link reverse gear: 164, 180
Stern: 11–13, 36, 39, 40, 76, 78–9, 81, 98–9, 113, 133, 139, 153, 156, 158–9, 160
Sternwheeler: 153, 164
Stirling, Christopher: 164, 166, 168, 170–1, 174–5
Stockholm: 6, 19–21
Stockholm tar: 75, 87
Stonington, Mass.: 80
Stopwater: 86
Storey, W. C.: 153
Stour, river: 94, 95
Stowboating (spratting): 47, 93
Stuart-Turner Ltd.: 164–5, 167, 175
Steam engines:
  Swan: 164, 167
  Cygnet: 164
Sunbeam, steam launch: 180
Surveying: 53, 128–33, 181–2
Sutherland, J. A.: 90
Sutton Hoo: 127

Sutton Pool: 113, 116, 118
Swann, Stephen: 51–3, 55, 90, 93
Sydney, Australia: 164
Symonds RN, Sir W.: 97

Tagus, river: 135
Tamar estuary: 116
Tate & Lyle: 135
Tatum, Mr (blacksmith): 38
Taylor, Arthur (sailmaker): 90, 93, 128
Tencofix Dik: 62
Terlain, Jean-Yves: 156
Terry, Norman: 164
Thalatta, Thames barge: 135
Thames barge: 52–3, 55, 107, 124, 127–8, 134–42
Thames, river: 47–8, 51–2, 58, 135, 175
Thomaston, Me.: 19, 73–6
Thorneycroft, (boat builders): 175
Thorneycroft petrol-paraffin engine 52–3
Thorpe, John: 70
Tie-rods: 79, 138–9
Tollesbury: 25, 33, 55, 153
Torridge, river: 113
Trafalgar: 6, 11, 15
Transom: 25, 40, 53, 72, 75–6, 79, 87, 106, 133, 139, 140
Trawl, beam: 93
Trevethick, Tom: 171, 175, 177
Truman, Nick: 148

Uithuisje, Jan: 55
Ullswater, lake: 19, 178–80
Underwater exploration: 19
Upton, Norfolk: 148, 153

Vancouver: 107
Vecht, river: 55
Veere: 25
Vendredi Treize, yacht: 156
Victory, H.M.S.: 6, 10–17, 107
Villiers, Commander Alan: 15, 87
Vollendam: 65
Voyager, Friendship sloop: 70

Walker, W. D. & A. E.: 142, 144
Wallace, Roy: 75–6, 78
Waller, Caroline: 153
Waller, Wing Commander Gordon: 153, 155–6
Wallet, The: 47
Walters, Captain Angus: 123
Wander Bird, pilot boat: 107
Warren Brothers (Swadlincote): 168
Wasa: 6, 18–21, 180
Wash, The: 105
West Mersea: 25, 43, 55
Whelking: 47
Whelpton, Tim: 148, 152–3
Wherry, Norfolk: 107, 142–7
White compound engine: 164
Wiegleb, Ernst: 75–9
Wildfowling: 24, 94–104
Williamson, James: 25
Willoughby R.M., Captain: 109, 113, 116

Windemere, lake: 177–80
  steam kettle: 178
Windermere Nautical Trust: 177–8
  Raven, cargo steamer: 177
  Lady Elizabeth, steam launch: 177, 180
  Branksome, steam launch: 178, 180
  Dolly, steam launch: 178–80
Windlass: 53, 62, 86, 126–7
Windsor: 175
Winkle brig: 24, 87, 91–2
Wivenhoe: 31
Wood borers: 21
  death watch beetle: 12, 13, 15–17, 21, 182
  gribble: 13, 21, 182
  teredo: 21
Wood, conservation of: 21, 180
Woodtreat: 145
Wood preservation: 19–21, 137, 145, 180–2
Woodlice: 25, 182
Woodrope Creek: 33, 102
Worldwide Shipping: 113
Wroxham: 148

Yachts: 21–2, 146–63
Yarmouth bridge: 144

Zinck, Carl: 122–3
Zuiderzee: 6, 55–68, 142
Zuiderzee fishing botters: 24, 55–68
Zuiderzee Museum: 6, 9, 68

L'EUROPE

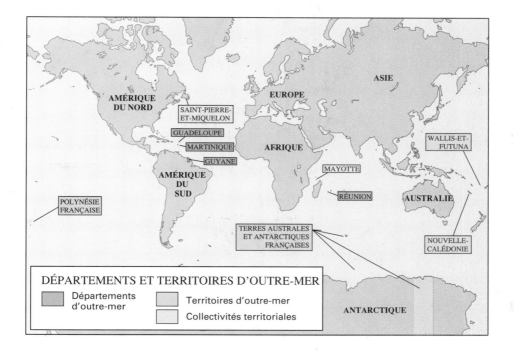

DÉPARTEMENTS ET TERRITOIRES D'OUTRE-MER

Entre amis

Entre amis

An Interactive Approach

Fourth Edition

Michael D. Oates

University of Northern Iowa

Larbi Oukada

Indiana University, Indianapolis

Houghton Mifflin Company Boston   New York

Components of *Entre amis*, Fourth Edition

- **Student Text with Student Audio**
- **Instructor's Annotated Edition with Student Audio**
- ***Cahier d'activités:* Workbook/Lab Manual/Video Worksheets**
- **Instructor's Resource Manual (IRM) with Test Bank and Information Gap activities**
- **Instructor's Test Cassette**
- **Audio Program**
- ***Pas de problème!* Video**
- ***Entre amis* Multimedia CD-ROM**
- ***Entre amis* WWW Site with Web-Search Activities and ACE Practice Tests**

Director of World Languages: Beth Kramer
Sponsoring Editor: Randy Welch
Senior Development Editor: Cécile Strugnell
Senior Project Editor: Florence Kilgo
Senior Production/Design Coordinator: Sarah Ambrose
Senior Manufacturing Coordinator: Florence Cadran
Associate Marketing Manager: Claudia Martinez

Credits for text, photos, realia, and illustrations are found following the index at the end of this book.

Printed in the U.S.A.

Library of Congress Catalog Card Number: 2001131538

Student Text ISBN: 0-618-11502-1

Instructor's Annotated Edition ISBN: 0-618-11503-X

2 3 4 5 6 7 8 9-DOW-05 04 03 02

Contents

Chapitre préliminaire Au départ 1

Pronunciation	Functions	Grammar	Culture
Masculin ou féminin? 4 L'alphabet français 4	Understanding basic classroom commands 2 Understanding numbers 3 Understanding basic expressions of time 3 Understanding basic weather expressions 6	Les nombres 3	*Il y a un geste* Frapper à la porte 2; Compter avec les doigts 3; Comment? Pardon? 5

Chapitre 1 Bonjour! 6

Pronunciation	Functions	Grammar	Culture
L'accent et le rythme 11 Les consonnes finales 11	Greeting others 12 Exchanging personal information 13 Identifying nationality 18 Describing physical appearance 22	Les pronoms sujets 13 Le verbe *être* 14 L'accord des adjectifs 15 La négation 20 L'accord des adjectifs (suite) 22	*À propos 9* Monsieur, Madame, Mademoiselle; Le premier contact; La politesse; Le prénom *Il y a un geste* Le contact physique 10; Le téléphone 10; Assez 22; *Lecture* Manchettes 25

Chapitre 2 Qu'est-ce que vous aimez? 28

Pronunciation	Functions	Grammar	Culture
L'alphabet français (suite) 32 Les accents 33	Asking and responding to "How are you?" 34 Giving and responding to compliments 35 Offering, accepting, and refusing 40 Expressing likes and dislikes 43	Les verbes en -er 36 L'article défini: *le, la, les* 41 Les questions avec réponse *oui* ou *non* 45	*À propos 31* Les compliments; Merci; Le kir *Il y a un geste* Non, merci 30; À votre santé 30; Ça va 34 *Lecture* Seul(e) et las(se) de l'être 49

Chapitre 3 La famille 52

Pronunciation	Functions	Grammar	Culture
L'accent et le rythme (suite) 56 Les sons [e], [ʒ], [ə], [a] et [wa] 56	Identifying family and friends 57 Sharing numerical information 62 Talking about your home 70	L'article indéfini: *un, une, des* 59 Le verbe *avoir* 60 Les nombres (suite) 63 Les expressions *il y a* et *voilà* 67 Les adjectifs possessifs: *mon, ton, notre, votre* 68 La négation + *un (une, des)* 71 La possession avec *de* 73 Les adjectifs possessifs *son* et *leur* 75	*À propos 55* La langue et la culture; Les pronouns *tu* et *vous*; Pour gagner du temps *Il y a un geste* Voilà 54 *Lectures* Maisons à vendre 79 La famille 81

Escale 1   La France dans le monde   84

La France et la Francophonie 84   **L'Hexagone** 84
La France et l'Union européenne 85

Chapitre 4 L'identité 88

Pronunciation	Functions	Grammar	Culture
Les voyelles nasales 92	Describing personal attributes 93 Describing clothing 98 Describing people and things 104 Describing what you do at home 108 Identifying someone's profession 110	Quelques groupes d'adjectifs 95 *Ne ... jamais* 96 Les adjectifs de couleur 100 L'adjectif démonstratif 103 La place de l'adjectif 106 Le verbe *faire* 108 Les mots interrogatifs: *qui, que* et *quel* 112	*À propos 91* Au pair; Le franglais; Les McDo et l'influence américaine; Les cartes postales *Il y a un geste* Bravo! 90; Paresseux 94; Ennuyeux 94; Cher! 101 *Lectures* Offres d'emploi 116 L'accent grave 116

Chapitre 5 Quoi de neuf? 120

Pronunciation	Functions	Grammar	Culture
Les syllabes ouvertes 124	Expressing future time 125 Telling time 130 Explaining your schedule 133 Telling where to find places 138	À + article défini 125 Le verbe *aller* 127 L'heure 130 Les jours de la semaine 133 Le verbe *devoir* 136 Quelques prépositions de lieu 138 L'imperatif 139 Les prépositions de lieu avec une ville ou un pays 141 Les mots interrogatifs *où* et *quand* 143	*À propos 123* Quelques malentendus culturels; Pour dire au revoir *Il y a un geste* La bise 122; Au revoir/Salut 122 *Lectures* Vos vacances à Angers 145 Village natal 147

Chapitre **6** Vos activités 151

Pronunciation	Functions	Grammar	Culture
Les sons [u] et [y] 155	Relating past events (Part 1) 156 Describing your study habits 161 Describing your weekend activities 165	Le passé composé avec *avoir* 157 Les verbes *écrire* et *lire* 161 *Ne ... rien* 162 *Temps, heure* et *fois* 164 Les verbes pronominaux 165 *Jouer de* et *jouer à* 167 Les pronoms accentués 168 Les verbes *dormir, partir* et *sortir* 170 Les verbes *nettoyer* et *envoyer* 171	*À propos* 154 La maison; Relativité culturelle: la maison *Il y a un geste* C'est la vie 155; J'ai oublié! 155 *Lectures* Un homme courageux; Les soldats ont planté des arbres 174 Moi 175

Escale 2   L'Amérique du Nord   **178**

Le français dans l'Amérique du Nord   178
Le Québec   178
Le Maine   180
La Louisiane   181

Chapitre **7** Où êtes-vous allé(e)? 182

Pronunciation	Functions	Grammar	Culture
Les sons [ɔ] et [o] 186	Relating past events (Part 2) 187 Describing your background 194 Stating what you just did 200	Le passé composé avec *être* 188 Le pronom *y* 192 Le verbe *venir* 194 Les prépositions de lieu avec une ville ou un pays (suite) 195 Les mois de l'année, les saisons, le temps 198 *Venir de* + infinitif 200	*À propos* 185 L'amabilité; Une technologie de pointe; La télécarte; Le TGV *Il y a un geste* Je vous en prie 184 *Lectures* Les femmes parlementaires européennes 203 IL 206

Chapitre **8** On mange bien en France 208

Pronunciation	Functions	Grammar	Culture
Les sons [k], [s], [z], [ʃ], [ʒ] et [ɲ] 213	Ordering a French meal 215 Discussing quantities 222 Expressing an opinion 226 Expressing a preference 229	L'article partitif 216 *Ne ... plus* 218 Le verbe *prendre* 220 Les expressions de quantité 222 Le verbe *boire* 223 Les pronoms objets directs: *le, la, les* 226 Quelques expressions avec *avoir* 227 Les verbes comme *préférer* 230	*À propos* 211 L'apéritif; L'art d'apprécier le vin; Tout se fait autour d'une table; Un repas français; Sans façon *Il y a un geste* Encore à boire? 212; L'addition, s'il vous plaît 219 *Lectures* Déjeuner du matin 234 Week-end privilège à Deauville 235

Escale 3   L'Afrique noire francophone   264

La négritude dans l'Afrique indépendante 265   **La femme africaine** 267
Le français en Afrique 266

Chapitre **9**   Où est-ce qu'on l'achète? 237

Pronunciation	Functions	Grammar	Culture
Le son [R] 242	Finding out where things are sold 242	Les verbes en *-re* 243	*À propos* 240
	Describing an illness or injury 245	*Depuis* 247	La pharmacie; Le tabac; Les petits magasins; On achète des fleurs
	Making a purchase 250	Le verbe *acheter* 251	
		Le pronom relatif 256	*Il y a un geste*
			Désolé(e) 239
			Lectures
			Il pleure dans mon cœur 259
			Hystérie anti-tabac; Les mesures du président 260

Chapitre **10**   Dans la rue et sur la route 268

Pronunciation	Functions	Grammar	Culture
La lettre *h* 273	Giving reasons, making excuses 273	Les verbes *vouloir* et *pouvoir* 274	*À propos* 271
	Expressing familiarity and judgment 277	Le verbe *connaître* 277	Conduire en France; Les expressions de tendresse
	Giving orders and advice 281	Les pronoms objets directs (suite) 278	*Il y a un geste* 270
	Describing ways of doing things 287	L'impératif (suite) 281	Chut! 270; Tais-toi! 270; Mon œil! 270; Invitation à danser 274; À toute vitesse 287
		Le subjonctif: bref aperçu 282	*Lectures*
		Les pronoms à l'impératif 285	La France au volant 291
		Les nombres ordinaux 285	Automobiles 293
		Le verbe *conduire* 287	
		Les adverbes 288	

Chapitre **11**   Comme si c'était hier 295

Pronunciation	Functions	Grammar	Culture
Les sons [i] et [j] 299	Describing conditions and feelings in the past 300	L'imparfait 301	*À propos* 298
	Setting the scene in the past 304	*Ne... que* 303	La famille; Les jeunes; Le mariage en France
	Making comparisons 307	L'imparfait et le passé composé 304	*Il y a un geste*
		Le comparatif 308	J'en ai assez 297
		Le comparatif de *bon* et de *bien* 310	*Lectures*
		Le superlatif 311	La grand-mère Aïda 315
			Annonces personnelles 317

Chapitre 12   Les réservations 319

Pronunciation	Functions	Grammar	Culture
Les sons [l] et [j] 323	Making a request 324 Making a restaurant or hotel reservation 324 Making a transportation reservation 335	Le verbe *savoir* 327 Les verbes réguliers en *-ir (-iss-)* 331 L'adjectif *tout* 333 Le futur 336 Le futur avec *si* et *quand* 338	*À propos* 322 Pour répondre au téléphone; La politesse (rappel); À l'hôtel; Mince! *Il y a un geste* Qu'est-ce que je vais faire? 321 *Lectures* L'horaire des trains 340 Séjours organisés au Sénégal 341

Escale 4   Le Maghreb 344

La cuisine maghrébine   345   **La littérature maghrébine**   345

Chapitre 13   Ma journée 348

Pronunciation	Functions	Grammar	Culture
Les voyelles arrondies [ø] et [œ] 352	Describing a table setting 353 Describing one's day 356 Describing past activities 362 Expressing one's will 365	Le verbe *mettre* 353 Les verbes pronominaux (suite) 357 Les verbes *se promener, s'inquiéter, s'asseoir* 360 Le passé des verbes pronominaux 362 Le subjonctif (suite) 365	*À propos* 351 L'étiquette à table; Au menu ou à la carte? *Il y a un geste* Il n'y a pas de quoi 350 *Lectures* Les feuilles mortes 371 Une lettre du Burkina Faso 373

Chapitre 14   Les hommes et les femmes 377

Pronunciation	Functions	Grammar	Culture
La tension 382	Describing interpersonal relationships 383 Describing TV programs 390 Expressing emotion 396	Le verbe *dire* 383 Les pronoms objets indirects 385 Les verbes *voir* et *croire* 391 Les interrogatifs *quel* et *lequel* 392 Le pronom relatif (suite) 394 Le subjonctif (suite) 396 Le pronom *en* 398	*À propos* 380 Qu'est-ce que les Français regardent à la télé?; La télévision française; Les faux amis *Il y a un geste* Je te le jure 379; Quelle histoire! 379 *Lectures* La télévision 401 Au cinéma 402

Chapitre 15   Qu'est-ce que je devrais faire? 405

Pronunciation	Functions	Grammar	Culture
La voyelle [ə] 410	Seeking and providing information 411 Making basic hypotheses 420	L'imparfait, le passé composé (suite) et le plus-que-parfait 411 Le verbe *devoir* (suite) 413 Les pronoms interrogatifs 414 *Ne ... personne* et *ne ... rien* 417 Le conditionnel 420 *Si* hypothétique 423	*À propos* 408 Les accidents de la route; Les agents et les gendarmes; Les contraventions *Il y a un geste* J'ai eu très peur 409; Quel imbécile! 409; Ivre 409 *Lectures* Deux accidents 426 La France nucléaire 427

Escale 5   Les Antilles   430

Haïti   430   **Les petites Antilles**   431

To the Student

Entre amis is a first-year college French program centered around the needs of a language learner like you. Among these needs is the ability to communicate in French and to develop insights into French culture and language. You will have many opportunities to hear French spoken and to interact with your instructor and classmates. Your ability to read and write French will improve with practice. The functions and exercises are designed to enable you to share information about your life—your interests, your family, your tastes, your plans.

Helpful Hints

While you will want to experiment with different ways of studying the material you will learn, a few hints, taken from successful language learners, are in order:

En français, s'il vous plaît! Try to use what you are learning with anyone who is able to converse in French. Greet fellow students in French and see how far you can go in conversing with each other.

Enjoy it. Be willing to take off the "wise-adult" mask and even to appear silly to keep the communication going. Everybody makes mistakes. Try out new words, use new gestures, and paraphrase, if it helps. Laugh at yourself; it helps.

Bring as many senses into play as possible. Study out loud, listen to the taped materials, use a pencil and paper to test your recall of the expressions you are studying. Anticipate conversations you will have and prepare a few French sentences in advance. Then try to work them into your conversations.

Nothing ventured, nothing gained. One must go through lower-level stages before reaching a confident mastery of the language. Study and practice, including attentive listening, combined with meaningful interaction with others will result in an ability to use French to communicate.

Where there's a will, there's a way. Be resourceful in your attempt to communicate. Seek alternative ways of expressing the same idea. For instance, if you are stuck in trying to say, «Comment vous appelez-vous?» ("What is your name?"), don't give up your attempt and end the conversation. Look for other ways of finding out that person's name. You may want to say, «Je m'appelle John/Jane Doe. Et vous?» or «John/Jane Doe» (pointing to yourself). «Et vous?» (pointing to the other person). There are often numerous possibilities!

Use your imagination. Some of the exercises will encourage you to play a new role. Add imaginary details to these situations, to your life story, etc., to enliven the activities.

Organization of the Text

The text is divided into fifteen chapters with a brief preliminary chapter plus five *Escales* that provide a glimpse of some of the many places where French is spoken outside of France. Each chapter is organized around a central cultural theme with three major divisions: **Coup d'envoi, Buts communicatifs,** and **Intégration.**

All presentation material, *Prise de contact* and *Conversation* in the *Coup d'envoi,* and the introduction to each *But communicatif* are recorded on the Student Audio shrink-wrapped with your text. Listen to these to prepare for your French class or to review by yourself afterwards.

> **Coup d'envoi** = *Kickoff.*
> **Prise de contact** = *Initial Contact.* See pp. 7, 29, etc.

Coup d'envoi

This section starts the cycle of listening, practicing, and personalizing which will make your learning both rewarding and enjoyable. You will often be asked to reflect and to compare French culture with your own culture.

Prise de contact is a short presentation of key phrases, often illustrated. In this section you are encouraged to participate and respond to simple questions about your family, your life, or your recent activities.

Conversation/Lettre typically shows a language learner in France, adapting to French culture. You will often find this person in situations with which you can identify: introducing himself or asking for directions, for example. Then you will be asked what you would do or say in a similar situation.

The *À propos* section describes particular aspects of French culture closely tied to the *Conversation.* These cultural sections will help you understand why, for example, the French do not usually say "thank you" when responding to a compliment or why meals are structured in France.

The *Il y a un geste* section is a special feature of **Entre amis** and an integral part of every chapter. It consists of photos and descriptions of common French gestures. The primary purpose of the gestures is to reinforce the meaning of the expressions associated with them that you will learn and use throughout the year.

The *Entre amis* activities give you a chance to speak French one-on-one with another student. You are given a role-playing activity that duplicates a real-life situation (ordering a meal in a café, finding out what your partner did yesterday, etc.). These appear several times in each chapter.

The *Prononciation* section helps you to imitate correctly general features of French pronunciation as well as specific sounds. It is important that your speech be readily understandable so that you can communicate more easily with people in French. The Student Audio also practices the pronunciation lesson for each chapter.

> **Buts communicatifs** = *Communicative goals.* See pp. 12, 34, etc.

Buts communicatifs

As was the case in the **Coup d'envoi** section, each of the **Buts communicatifs** sections begins with a presentation, including key phrases that you will use to interact with your instructor and classmates. Material from the **Coup d'envoi** is recycled in the **Buts communicatifs.** The section is divided according to specific tasks, such as asking for directions, describing your weekend activities, and finding out where things are sold. Within this context, there are grammar explanations, exercises, vocabulary, and role-playing activities. The vocabulary is taught in groups of words directly related to each of the functions you are learning. All of these words are then listed at the end of each chapter in the *Vocabulaire actif* section. Each section of the **Buts communicatifs** ends with an *Entre amis* activity that encourages you to put to use what you have just learned.

Intégration

This final section includes one or more reading selections (*Lectures*). These readings are from authentic French materials, such as excerpts from newspapers, magazines, literary texts, or poems. (The poems are recorded on your student audio.) There are activities both before and after each reading to relate the material to your own experience and to help increase your understanding. In addition, there is an activity that corresponds to a specific segment of the *Pas de problème!* video. A list of all the active vocabulary of the chapter is included at the end of this section.

Escales

Escale = *Stop over.*
See pp. 84, 178, etc.

These five magazine-like sections, appearing at intervals between chapters, will give you an appreciation for the widespread use of French throughout the world. You will be introduced to many francophone countries and will enjoy discovering particular aspects of their culture, such as literature, music, art, festivals, sports, food, and traditions.

Appendices

The reference section contains verb conjugations, an appendix of phonetic symbols, a list of professions, a glossary of grammatical terms, French-English and English-French vocabularies, and an index.

Ancillaries

Cahier d'activités

The *Cahier d'activités* combines Workbook, Lab Manual, and Video Worksheets with answer keys for each section so that you can correct yourself as you progress through the chapters.

The Workbook activities will provide you with additional practice for each section of vocabulary and grammar. A final activity, *Rédaction,* will give you writing practice with pen pals from the francophone countries mentioned in the *Escales*. Step-by-step instructions and suggestions will help you through the writing process.

The Laboratory Manual and Audio Program will combine to help you practice your pronunciation and your listening and speaking skills. You will listen to the recordings and instructions of the Audio Program available to you in CDs or cassettes. The Lab Manual will provide you with cues to answer the questions. In the last activity of each chapter, rhymes, tongue twisters, lively exchanges, and traditional songs will motivate you to speak French.

Following the Lab Manual, activities based on *Vignettes,* short skits featuring an exchange between native speakers, provide additional listening practice. The *Vignettes* are also recorded on the Audio Program.

Video worksheets help you to understand the *Pas de problème!* video (see below). A *Vocabulaire à reconnaître* lists new words spoken in the video and their meaning. The worksheets provide simple activities that reinforce the links between the video and what you learned in your textbook.

Pas de problème! Video

The video *Pas de problème!* was filmed in France. Each module introduces young people, French native speakers from different countries, living in France, interacting with each other, and encountering everyday problems that you may experience if you visit France. Between the modules, the video includes *Impressions,* short sections shot in France and in Guadeloupe, that provide insights into the culture and way of life of people in these countries. The themes presented expand on topics addressed in the video or in the textbook. In Guadeloupe, native speakers express their opinion or talk about their own experience as it applies to the chosen themes.

Entre amis Multimedia CD-ROM

This CD-ROM will be a valuable tool for you to practice each of the fifteen chapters of the textbook. Each chapter has three sections: 1. video-based skill development, 2. language practice, and 3. multimedia presentation. The CD-ROM also includes a grammar reference, a verb conjugation reference, a glossary of grammatical terms, and bilingual French/English and English/French glossaries.

Entre amis WWW Site

You may access this site through the Houghton Mifflin WWW site. Icons in the textbook will cue you in to some of the components. At the beginning of the *Intégration* section, an icon indicates web-search activities you can do by accessing the links described. An icon in the *Escales* indicates that the site has links to French WWW sites so that you can look up more information on topics of the *Escale* you are reading. In addition, the WWW site offers interactive ACE Practice Tests that will enable you to check your understanding of the chapter grammar and vocabulary, as well as Vocabulary Flash Cards and other helpful resources.

Acknowledgments

We, the authors, are deeply indebted to the editorial staff of Houghton Mifflin for giving us the opportunity to develop and produce the text. Their encouragement and guidance made **Entre amis,** Fourth Edition possible.

Michael Oates specifically wishes to thank his wife, Maureen O'Leary Oates, for her patience during the development and editing of **Entre amis.** He is grateful for the support of Joye Lore-Lawson, of Indian Hills CC, and Linda Quinn Allen of Iowa State University. Larbi Oukada also wishes to express his gratitude to the following individuals for their contribution to the renovated *Escales*:

Brenda Bertrand, Associate Faculty, IUPUI
Didier Bertrand, Associate Professor, IUPUI
Obioma Nnaemeka, Associate Professor, IUPUI
Page Curry, Associate Faculty, IUPUI DePauw University
Rosalie Vermette, Associate Professor, IUPUI

We would also like to express our sincere appreciation to the following people for their thoughtful reviews of the fourth edition of **Entre amis.**

Martine Howard, Camden County College, New Jersey
Richard Stroik, University of San Diego, CA
Professor Ray Cornelius, Daytona Beach Community College,
    West Campus, FL
Carolyn Jacobs, Houston Community College Central, TX
Rolande Léguillon, University of St. Thomas, Houston, TX
Mike Zoltak, Spokane Community College, WA
Kara Rabbitt, William Patterson University, NJ
Donald Dziekowicz, St. Thomas University, MN

Entre Amis

Chapitre Préliminaire

Au départ

Buts communicatifs

Understanding basic
   classroom commands
Understanding numbers
Understanding basic
   expressions of time
Understanding basic
   weather expressions

Buts communicatifs

Grasping the meaning of spoken French is fundamental to learning to communicate in French. Developing this skill will require patience and perseverance, but your success will be enhanced if you associate a mental image (e.g., of a picture, an object, a gesture, an action, the written word) with the expressions you hear. This preliminary chapter will focus on establishing the association of sound and symbol in a few basic contexts: classroom expressions, numbers, time, and weather.

1 Understanding Basic Classroom Commands

Dans la salle de classe

■ Listen carefully and watch the physical response of your teacher to each command. Once you have learned to associate the actions with the French sentences, you may be asked to practice them.

Levez-vous!
Allez à la porte!
Ouvrez la porte!
Sortez!
Frappez à la porte!
Entrez!
Fermez la porte!

Allez au tableau!
Prenez la craie!
Écrivez votre nom!
Mettez la craie sur la table!
Donnez la craie à ... !
Donnez-moi la craie!
Asseyez-vous!

le tableau
la craie
la porte
la table

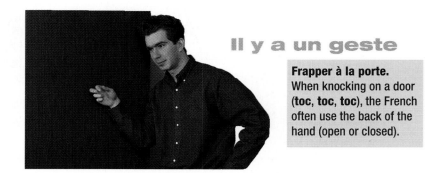

Il y a un geste

Frapper à la porte.
When knocking on a door (**toc, toc, toc**), the French often use the back of the hand (open or closed).

2 Understanding Numbers

0123456789

Il y a un geste

Les nombres

0	zéro	10	dix	20	vingt
1	un	11	onze	21	vingt et un
2	deux	12	douze	22	vingt-deux
3	trois	13	treize	23	vingt-trois
4	quatre	14	quatorze	24	vingt-quatre
5	cinq	15	quinze	25	vingt-cinq
6	six	16	seize	26	vingt-six
7	sept	17	dix-sept	27	vingt-sept
8	huit	18	dix-huit	28	vingt-huit
9	neuf	19	dix-neuf	29	vingt-neuf
				30	trente

Compter avec les doigts. When counting, the French normally begin with the thumb, then the index finger, etc. For instance, the thumb, index, and middle fingers are held up to indicate the number three, as a child might indicate when asked his/her age.

3 Understanding Basic Expressions of Time

Quelle heure est-il?

Il est une heure.

Il est une heure dix.

Il est une heure quinze.

Il est une heure trente.

Il est deux heures moins vingt.

Il est deux heures moins dix.

Il est deux heures.

Il est trois heures.

Masculin ou féminin?

■ You will learn to identify nouns and adjectives in French as masculine or feminine.

Often, the feminine form ends in a consonant sound while the masculine form ends in a vowel sound.

Féminins – consonant		*Masculins* – vowel	
Françoise	Louise	François	Louis
Jeanne	Martine	Jean	Martin
Laurence	Simone	Laurent	Simon
chaude	froide	chaud	froid
française	intelligente	français	intelligent
anglaise	petite	anglais	petit

L'alphabet français

	prononciation		prononciation
A	*ah*	**N**	*enne*
B	*bé*	**O**	*oh*
C	*sé*	**P**	*pé*
D	*dé*	**Q**	*ku*
E	*euh*	**R**	*erre*
F	*effe*	**S**	*esse*
G	*jé*	**T**	*té*
H	*ashe*	**U**	*u*
I	*i*	**V**	*vé*
J	*ji*	**W**	*double vé*
K	*ka*	**X**	*iks*
L	*elle*	**Y**	*i grec*
M	*emme*	**Z**	*zed*

Comment est-ce qu'on écrit **merci?**   *How do you spell "merci"?*
Merci s'écrit M-E-R-C-I.   *"Merci" is spelled M-E-R-C-I.*

4 Understanding Basic Weather Expressions

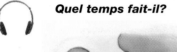

Quel temps fait-il?

Il fait beau.
Il fait du soleil.

Il fait du vent.

Il fait froid.

Il fait chaud.

Il pleut.

Il neige.

Il y a un geste

Comment? Pardon?   An open hand, cupped behind the ear, indicates that the message has not been heard and should be repeated.

VOCABULAIRE

Quelques expressions pour la salle de classe

Pardon? *Pardon?*
Comment? *What (did you say)?*
Répétez, s'il vous plaît. *Please repeat.*
Encore. *Again.*
En français. *In French.*
Ensemble. *Together.*
Tout le monde. *Everybody, everyone.*

Fermez le livre. *Close the book.*
Écoutez. *Listen.*
Répondez. *Answer.*

Comment dit-on «*the teacher*»? *How do you say "the teacher"?*
On dit «le professeur». *You say "le professeur."*

Que veut dire «le tableau»? *What does "le tableau" mean?*
Ça veut dire «*the chalkboard*». *It means "the chalkboard."*

Je ne sais pas. *I don't know.*
Je ne comprends pas. *I don't understand.*

1

Bonjour!

Buts communicatifs
Greeting others
Exchanging personal information
Identifying nationality
Describing physical appearance

Structures utiles
Les pronoms sujets
Le verbe **être**
L'accord des adjectifs
La négation
L'accord des adjectifs (suite)

Culture
Monsieur, Madame et **Mademoiselle**
Le premier contact
La politesse
Le prénom

Coup d'envoi

Prise de contact ## Les présentations

Mademoiselle Becker	***Monsieur Davidson***	
Je m'appelle° Lori Becker.	Je m'appelle James Davidson.	*My name is*
J'habite à° Boston.	J'habite à San Francisco.	*I live in*
Je suis° américaine.	Je suis américain.	*I am*
Je suis célibataire°.	Je suis célibataire.	*single*

Review the Helpful Hints found in the *To the Student* section in the front of your text.

Be sure to learn the vocabulary on the first two pages of each chapter.

Madame Martin	***Monsieur Martin***	
Je m'appelle Anne Martin.	Je m'appelle Pierre Martin.	
J'habite à Angers.	J'habite à Angers.	
Je suis française.	Je suis français.	
Je suis mariée°.	Je suis marié.	*married*

Et vous? Qui êtes-vous?°   *And you? Who are you?*

Conversation

Dans un hôtel à Paris

Deux hommes sont au restaurant de l'hôtel Ibis à Paris.

PIERRE MARTIN:	Bonjour°, Monsieur! Excusez-moi de vous déranger.°
JAMES DAVIDSON:	Bonjour. Pas de problème.°
PIERRE MARTIN:	Vous permettez?° *(He touches the empty chair.)*
JAMES DAVIDSON:	Certainement. Asseyez-vous là°.
PIERRE MARTIN:	Vous êtes anglais?°
JAMES DAVIDSON:	Non, je suis américain. Permettez-moi de me présenter.° Je m'appelle James Davidson. *(They stand up and shake hands.)*
PIERRE MARTIN:	Martin, Pierre Martin. *(A receptionist comes into the room.)*
LA RÉCEPTIONNISTE:	Le téléphone, Monsieur Davidson. C'est pour vous.° Votre communication de Californie.°
JAMES DAVIDSON:	Excusez-moi, s'il vous plaît, Monsieur.
PIERRE MARTIN:	Oui, certainement. Au revoir, Monsieur. *(They shake hands again.)*
JAMES DAVIDSON:	Bonne journée°, Monsieur.
PIERRE MARTIN:	Merci°, vous aussi°.

Marginal glosses:
Hello
Excuse me for bothering you.
No problem.
May I?
there; here
Are you English?
Let me introduce myself.
It's for you.
Your call from California.
Have a good day
Thank you / also; too

Jouez ces rôles. Role-play the conversation with a partner. Use your own identities.

Why does Pierre Martin say **Bonjour, Monsieur** instead of just **Bonjour**?

  a. He likes variety; either expression will do.
  b. **Bonjour** alone is a bit less formal than **Bonjour, Monsieur**.
  c. He is trying to impress James Davidson.

Only one answer is culturally accurate. Read the information below to find out which one.

Monsieur, Madame et Mademoiselle

A certain amount of formality is in order when initial contact is made with French speakers. It is more polite to add **Monsieur, Madame,** or **Mademoiselle** when addressing someone than simply to say **Bonjour.** James Davidson catches on toward the end of the conversation when he remembers to say **Bonne journée, Monsieur.**

Le premier contact
(Breaking the ice)

Pierre Martin asks if he can sit at the empty seat. However, the French are usually more reticent than Americans to "break the ice." This may present a challenge to the language learner who wishes to meet others, but as long as you are polite, you should not hesitate to begin a conversation.

La Politesse

According to Polly Platt, the five most important words in French are **Excusez-moi de vous déranger.** This is a polite way to interrupt someone in France and a valuable formula for students and tourists who need to ask for directions or get permission to do something. Remaining polite, even in the face of adversity, is an important survival technique.

Le prénom *(first name)*

It is not unusual to have the French give their last name first, especially in professional situations. Americans are generally much quicker than the French to begin to use another's first name. Rather than instantly condemning the French as "colder" than Americans, the wise strategy would be to refrain from using the first name when you meet someone. It is important to adapt your language usage to fit the culture. "When in Rome, do as the Romans do."

VOCABULAIRE

La politesse

Bonjour, Madame/Monsieur. *Hello, ma'am/sir.*	Pardon. *Pardon me.*
Excusez-moi. *Excuse me.*	Permettez-moi de me présenter ... *Please allow me to introduce myself ...*
Excusez-moi de vous déranger. *Excuse me for bothering you.*	S'il vous plaît. *Please.*
Je vous demande pardon ... *I beg your pardon ...*	Vous permettez? *May I?*
Merci. Vous aussi. *Thanks. You too.*	Bonne journée, Madame/Monsieur. *Have a good day, ma'am/sir.*

Il y a un geste

Le contact physique. James Davidson and Pierre Martin shake hands during their conversation, a normal gesture for both North Americans and the French when meeting someone. However, the French would normally shake hands with friends, colleagues, and their neighbors each time they meet and, if they chat for a while, at the end of their conversation as well. Physical contact plays a very important role in French culture and forgetting to shake hands with a friend would be rude.

Le téléphone. The French indicate that there is a telephone call by spreading the thumb and little finger of one hand and holding that hand near the ear.

▶ **À vous.** How would you respond to the following?

1. Je m'appelle Alissa. Et vous?
2. Vous êtes français(e)?
3. J'habite à Paris. Et vous?
4. Excusez-moi, s'il vous plaît.
5. Bonne journée.

Entre amis

Permettez-moi de me présenter

1. Greet your partner.
2. Find out if s/he is French.
3. Give your name and tell where you live.
4. Can you say anything else? (Be sure to shake hands when you say good-bye.)

Revieur

L'accent et le rythme

■ There is an enormous number of related words in English and French. We inherited most of these after the Norman Conquest, but many are recent borrowings. With respect to pronunciation, these are the words that tend to reveal an English accent the most quickly.

▶ **Compare:**

Anglais	*Français*
CER-tain	cer-TAIN
CER-tain-ly	cer-taine-MENT
MAR-tin	Mar-TIN
a-MER-i-can	a-mé-ri-CAIN

■ Even more important than mastering any particular sound is the development of correct habits in three areas of French intonation.

1. *Rhythm:* French words are spoken in groups, and each syllable but the last is said very evenly.
2. *Accent:* In each group of words, the last syllable is lengthened, thus making it the only accented syllable in the group.
3. *Syllable formation:* Spoken French syllables end in a vowel sound much more often than English ones do.

■ Counting is an excellent way to develop proper French rhythm and accent. Repeat after your instructor:

un DEUX	*un deux TROIS*	*un deux trois QUATRE*
mon-SIEUR	s'il vous PLAÎT	le té-lé-PHONE
mer-CI	cer-taine-MENT	A-sse-yez-VOUS
fran-ÇAIS	té-lé-PHONE	Mon-sieur Mar-TIN

Les consonnes finales

■ A final (written) consonant is normally not pronounced in French.

François	permettez	s'il vous plaît
Georges	français	trois
Il fait froid	américain	deux

■ There are some words whose final consonant is always pronounced (many words ending in **c, f, l,** or **r,** for instance). ✶

Frédé**ric**   neu**f**   Miche**l**   bonjou**r**

■ When a consonant is followed by **-e** within the same word, the consonant is always pronounced. A single **-s-** followed by **-e** is pronounced as [z]. Two **-ss-** followed by **-e** are pronounced [s].

françai**se**   sui**sse**   américai**ne**   j'habi**te**   je m'appe**lle**

■ When a final silent consonant is followed by a word beginning with a vowel, it is often pronounced with the next word. This is called **liaison.**

vous *(silent)*   vous [z]êtes
deux *(silent)*   deux [z]hommes

Buts communicatifs

1 Greeting Others

le jour° / le matin° / l'après-midi°	*day / morning / afternoon*

Learn all the words in each *But communicatif*.

Bonjour, Madame.
Bonjour, Mademoiselle.

Bonsoir, Marie.
Salut°, Marie.

le soir° / la nuit°   *Hi*

Bonsoir°, Monsieur.   *evening / night*
Bonsoir, Madame.
Bonsoir, Mademoiselle.   *Good evening; Hello*

Bonsoir, Marie.
Salut, Marie.

Remarques

1. **Bonjour** and **bonsoir** are used for both formal (**Monsieur, Madame,** etc.) and first-name relationships.
2. The family name (**le nom de famille**) is not used in a greeting. For example, when saying hello to Madame Martin, one says **Bonjour, Madame.**
3. **Salut** is used only in first-name relationships.
4. **M., Mme,** and **Mlle** are the abbreviations for **Monsieur, Madame,** and **Mademoiselle.**

1 **Attention au style.** Greet each of the following people at the indicated time of day. Adapt your choice of words to fit the time and the person being greeted. Be careful not to be overly familiar. If there is more than one response possible, give both.

MODÈLES: Monsieur Talbot (le matin à 8 heures)
Bonjour, Monsieur.

Marie (l'après-midi à 2 heures)
Bonjour, Marie.   ou
Salut, Marie.

1. Éric (le soir à 7 heures)
2. Mademoiselle Monot (le matin à 9 heures)
3. Monsieur Talbot (l'après-midi à 4 heures)
4. another student (la nuit à 1 heure)
5. your French teacher (le matin à 11 heures)
6. your best friend (le soir à 10 heures)

2 Exchanging Personal Information

Learn all the words in each *But communicatif.*

Pronounce **appelle** [apɛl] and **appelez** [aple].

Comment vous appelez-vous?°
    Je m'appelle Nathalie Lachance.

What is your name?

Où habitez-vous?°
    J'habite à Laval.
    J'habite près de° Montréal.

Where do you live?

near

Êtes-vous célibataire?
    Non, je suis mariée.

▶ **Et vous, Monsieur (Madame, Mademoiselle)?**

Remarques

1. **Je m'appelle** and **Comment vous appelez-vous?** should be memorized for now. Note that in **Comment vous appelez-vous?** there is only one **l**, ✯ while in **Je m'appelle,** there are two.
2. Use **J'habite à** to identify the *city* in which you live.
3. Use **J'habite près de** to identify the city you live *near.*

2 **Les inscriptions** *(Registration).* You are working at a conference in Geneva. Greet the following people and find out their names and the city where they live.

MODÈLE: Monsieur Robert Perrin (Lyon)

> —**Bonjour, Monsieur. Comment vous appelez-vous?**
> —**Je m'appelle Perrin, Robert Perrin.**
> —**Où habitez-vous?**
> —**J'habite à Lyon.**

1. Mademoiselle Chantal Rodrigue (Toulouse)
2. Madame Anne Vermette (Montréal)
3. Monsieur Joseph Guy (Lausanne)
4. Mademoiselle Jeanne Delon (Paris)
5. le professeur de français
6. le président de la République française
7. le président des États-Unis (USA)
8. le premier ministre du Canada

A. Les pronoms sujets

■ The subject pronouns in French are:

singular forms		plural forms	
je (j')	*I*	**nous**	*we*
tu	*you*		
vous	*you*	**vous**	*you*
il	*he; it*	**ils**	*they*
elle	*she; it*	**elles**	*they*
on	*one; someone; people; we*		

■ Before a vowel sound at the beginning of the next word, **je** becomes **j'**. This happens with words that begin with a vowel, but also with most words that begin with **h-**, which is silent.

J'adore Québec, mais **j'habite** à New York.

■ **Tu** is informal. It is used to address one person with whom you have a close relationship. **Vous** is the singular form used in other cases. To address more than one person, one always uses **vous.**

Tu es à Paris, Michel?
Vous êtes à Lyon, Monsieur?
Marie! Paul! **Vous** êtes à Bordeaux!

Note Whether **vous** is singular or plural, the verb form is always plural.

■ There are two genders in French: masculine and feminine. All nouns have gender, whether they designate people or things. **Il** stands for a masculine person or thing, **elle** for a feminine person or thing. The plural **ils** stands for a group of masculine persons or things, and **elles** stands for a group of feminine persons or things.

le tableau = **il**   les tables = **elles**
la porte = **elle**   les téléphones = **ils**

■ For a group that includes both masculine and feminine nouns (**Nathalie, Karine, Paul et Marie**), **ils** is used, even if only one of the nouns is masculine.

Karine et Éric? **Ils** sont à Marseille.

■ **On** is a subject pronoun used to express generalities or unknowns, much as do the English forms *one, someone, you, people.* In informal situations, **on** can sometimes be used to mean *we.*

On est à San Francisco.   *We are in San Francisco.*
On est riche en Amérique?   *Are people in America rich?*

B. Le verbe *être*

Il est à Québec.
Je suis à Strasbourg.
Nous sommes à Besançon.

■ The most frequently used verb in French is **être** *(to be).*

je	**suis**	*I am*	nous	**sommes**	*we are*
tu	**es**	*you are*	vous	**êtes**	*you are*
il	**est**	*he is; it is*	ils	**sont**	*they are (m. or m. + f.)*
elle	**est**	*she is; it is*	elles	**sont**	*they are (f.)*
on	**est**	*one is; people are; we are*			

Review the use of **liaison** on p. 11.

■ Before a vowel sound at the beginning of the next word, the silent final consonant of many words (but not all!) is pronounced and is spoken with the next word. This is called **liaison. Liaison** is necessary between a pronoun and a verb.

Vous [z]êtes à Montréal. On [n]est où?

■ **Liaison** is possible after all forms of **être,** but is common *only* with **est** and **sont.**

Il est [t]à Paris.   Elles sont [t]à Marseille.

3 **Où sont-ils?** *(Where are they?)* Identify the cities where the following people are. Use a subject pronoun in your answer.

MODÈLES: tu (Los Angeles) **Tu es à Los Angeles.**
vous (Québec) **Vous êtes à Québec.**

1. Lori (Boston)
2. Lise et Elsa (Bruxelles)
3. Thierry (Monte Carlo)
4. je (...)
5. Pierre et Anne (Angers)
6. nous (...)
7. Sylvie (Paris)

C. L'accord des adjectifs

Review *Pronunciation*, p. 4.

■ Most adjectives have two pronunciations: one when they refer to a feminine noun and one when they refer to a masculine noun. From an oral point of view, it is usually better to learn the feminine form first. The masculine pronunciation can often be found by dropping the last consonant *sound* of the feminine.

Barbara est **américaine.**   Bob est **américain** aussi.
Christine est **française.**   David est **français** aussi.

■ Almost all adjectives change their spelling depending on whether the nouns they refer to are masculine or feminine, singular or plural. These spelling changes may or may not affect pronunciation.

Il est américain.   Elle est américaine.
Ils sont américains.   Elles sont américaines.

Il est marié.   Elle est mariée.
Ils sont mariés.   Elles sont mariées.

■ The feminine adjective almost always ends in a written **-e.** A number of masculine adjectives end in **-e** also. In this case, masculine and feminine forms are identical in pronunciation and spelling.

célibataire   fantastique   optimiste

■ The plural is usually formed by adding a written **-s** to the singular. However, since the final **-s** of the plural is silent, the singular and the plural are pronounced in the same way.

américain   américain**s**
américaine   américaine**s**

Note If the masculine singular ends in **-s,** the masculine plural is identical.

un homme français   deux hommes français

■ Adjectives that describe a group of both masculine and feminine nouns take the masculine plural form.

Bill et Judy sont **mariés.**

VOCABULAIRE

L'état civil *(marital status)*

With the exception of **veuve(s)** [vœv] and **veuf(s)** [vœf], the spelling changes in the adjectives listed to the right do not affect pronunciation.

Femmes	Hommes	Women/men
célibataire(s)	célibataire(s)	*single*
mariée(s)	marié(s)	*married*
fiancée(s)	fiancé(s)	*engaged*
divorcée(s)	divorcé(s)	*divorced*
veuve(s)	veuf(s)	*widowed*

4 **Quelle coïncidence!** *(What a coincidence!)* State that the marital status of the second person or group is the same as that of the first.

MODÈLES: Isabelle est fiancée. Et Marc?   Pierre est marié. Et Chantal et
   Il est fiancé aussi.   Max?
      Ils sont mariés aussi.

1. Anne et Paul sont fiancés. Et Marie?
2. Nous sommes mariés. Et Monique?
3. Nicolas est divorcé. Et Sophie et Thérèse?
4. Je suis célibataire. Et Georges et Sylvie?
5. Madame Beaufort est veuve. Et Monsieur Dupont?

5 **Qui est-ce?** *(Who is it?)* Answer the following questions. Try to identify real people or famous fictional characters. Can you name more than one person? Make sure that the verbs and adjectives agree with the subjects.

MODÈLE: Qui est fiancé?
   Olive Oyl est fiancée.   ou   **Olive Oyl et Popeye sont**
         fiancés.

1. Qui est célibataire?   5. Qui est veuf?
2. Qui est fiancé?   6. Qui est français?
3. Qui est marié?   7. Qui est américain?
4. Qui est divorcé?

Carte de débarquement *(Arrival form).* When you travel overseas you are usually given an arrival form to fill out. Provide the information requested in the form below.

Carte de débarquement

Nom de famille: _____

Prénom(s): _____

Âge: _____ ans

Nationalité: _____

État civil: _____

Adresse: _____

_____

_____

Code postal: _____

Numéro de téléphone: _____

Motif du voyage: ❏ touristique   ❏ professionnel
                       ❏ transit   ❏ visite privée

Entre amis

Dans un avion *(In an airplane)*

Complete the following interaction with as many members of the class as possible.

1. Greet your neighbor in a culturally appropriate way.
2. Find out if s/he is French.
3. Find out each other's name.
4. Find out the city in which s/he lives.
5. What else can you say?

3 Identifying Nationality

| | Quelle est votre nationalité?° | | *What is your nationality?* |

Learn all the words in each *But communicatif.*

Moi, je suis canadienne.

Et vous?   Vous êtes chinois(e)°?   *Chinese*
              Pas du tout!° Je suis ...   *Not at all!*

Remember to pronounce the final consonant in the feminine (see p. 11).

	Féminin	*Masculin*	
GB	anglaise	anglais	*English*
F	française	français	*French*
J	japonaise	japonais	*Japanese*
SN	sénégalaise	sénégalais	*Senegalese*
USA	américaine	américain	*American*
MA	marocaine	marocain	*Moroccan*
MEX	mexicaine	mexicain	*Mexican*
CDN	canadienne	canadien	*Canadian*
I	italienne	italien	*Italian*
S	suédoise	suédois	*Swedish*
D	allemande	allemand	*German*
E	espagnole	espagnol	*Spanish*
B	belge	belge	*Belgian*
CH	suisse	suisse	*Swiss*
RUS	russe	russe	*Russian*

Remarque   In written French, some feminine adjectives are distinguishable from their masculine form not only by a final **-e,** but also by a doubled final consonant.

un homme canadien   *a Canadian man*
une femme canadie**nne**   *a Canadian woman*

7 **Quelle est votre nationalité?** The customs agent needs to know each person's nationality. Your partner will play the role of the customs agent and ask the question. You take the role of each of the following people, and answer.

Modèles: Madame Jones et Mademoiselle Jones (GB)
—**Quelle est votre nationalité?**
—**Nous sommes anglaises.**

Maria Gomez (MEX)
—**Quelle est votre nationalité?**
—**Je suis mexicaine.**

1. Jean-François (CDN)
2. Monsieur et Madame Smith (USA)
3. Mademoiselle Nakasone (J)
4. Madame Colon et Mademoiselle Colon (E)
5. Mademoiselle Balke (D)

6. Bruno (SN)
7. Madame Volaro (I)
8. Marie-Christine (F)
9. votre professeur de français
10. vous

Ces trois amis habitent à Paris.

8 **Qui êtes-vous?** *(Who are you?)* Assume the identity of each one of the following people and introduce yourself, indicating your name, your nationality, and the city you are from.

MODÈLE: Mademoiselle Brigitte Lapointe/Paris (F)
Je m'appelle Brigitte et je suis française. J'habite à Paris.

1. Monsieur Pierre La Vigne/Québec (CDN)
2. Madame Margaret Jones/Manchester (GB)
3. Madame Anne Martin/Angers (F)
4. Monsieur Yasuhiro Saya/Tokyo (J)
5. Madame Mary O'Leary/Boston (USA)
6. Monsieur Ahmed Zoubir/Casablanca (MA)
7. votre professeur de français
8. vous

D. La négation

James Davidson **n'**est **pas** français. Il est américain.
Il **n'**habite **pas** à Paris. Il habite à San Francisco.

◼ Two words, **ne** and **pas,** are used to make a sentence negative: **ne** precedes the conjugated verb and **pas** follows it.

Guy et Zoé **ne** sont **pas** mariés.   *Guy and Zoé aren't married.*
Il **ne** fait **pas** très beau.   *It's not very nice out.*

◼ Remember that both **ne** and **pas** are necessary in standard French to make a sentence negative.

ne + conjugated verb + **pas**

◼ **Ne** becomes **n'** before a vowel sound.

Je **n'**habite **pas** à Paris.   *I don't live in Paris.*
Nathalie **n'**est **pas** française.   *Nathalie is not French.*

9 **Vous êtes français(e)?** Choose a new nationality and have other students try to guess what it is. If the guess is incorrect, use the negative to respond. If it is correct, say so.

MODÈLE: —**Vous êtes belge?**
—**Non, je ne suis pas belge.**   ou   **Oui, je suis belge.**

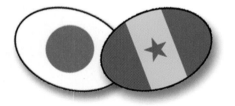

10 **Ils sont français?** Ask your partner whether the following people are French. Choose the correct form of **être** and make sure that the adjective agrees. Your partner will first respond with a negative, and then state the correct information.

Modèle: —**Elles sont françaises?**
—**Non, elles ne sont pas françaises. Elles sont anglaises.**

1.

2. *suisse*

3. *américain*

4. *canadiens*

5. *belge*

6. *marocain*

7. *allemand*

8. *sénégalaise*

Entre amis

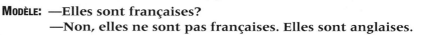

Une fausse identité: Qui suis-je? *(A false identity: Who am I?)*

1. Pick a new identity (nationality, hometown, marital status) but don't tell your partner what you have chosen.
2. Your partner will guess your new nationality by asking you questions.
3. Your partner will guess your new marital status.
4. Your partner will try to guess which city you live in (one that fits your new nationality).

4 Describing Physical Appearance

Learn all the words in each *But communicatif.*

assez = rather

Try to use **assez** and, in the case of a negative, **pas très** to avoid being overly categorical when describing people.

Voilà° Christine.
Elle est jeune°.
Elle est assez grande°.
Elle n'est pas grosse°.
Elle est assez jolie°.

Voilà le Père Noël.
Il est assez° vieux°.
Il est assez petit°.
Il n'est pas très° mince°.

There is; Here is
young / rather / old
tall / short; small
fat / very / thin
pretty

▶ **Et vous?** Vous êtes . . .

jeune	*ou*	vieux (vieille)?
petit(e)	*ou*	grand(e)?
gros(se)	*ou*	mince?
beau (belle)	*ou*	laid(e)?°

Décrivez votre meilleur(e) ami(e).°

attractive or ugly
Describe your best friend.

Il y a un geste

Assez *(sort of, rather; enough).* The gesture for **assez** is an open hand rotated back and forth (palm down).

E. L'accord des adjectifs (suite)

■ The masculine forms of some adjectives are not like their feminine forms in either pronunciation or spelling, and so they must be memorized.

belle **beau** vieille **vieux**

■ The masculine plural of some adjectives is formed by adding **-x.** Pronunciation of the plural form remains the same as the singular.

Robert et Paul sont très **beaux.**

Some nouns form the plural in the same way: **le tableau, les tableaux.**

■ Masculine singular adjectives that end in **-s** or **-x** keep the same form (and pronunciation) for the masculine plural.

Bill est **gros.** Roseanne et John sont **gros** aussi.
Je suis **vieux.** Georges et Robert sont très **vieux.**

Synthèse: L'accord des adjectifs

féminin		masculin	
singulier	*pluriel*	*singulier*	*pluriel*
petite	petites	petit	petits
grande	grandes	grand	grands
jolie	jolies	joli	jolis
belle	belles	beau	beaux
laide	laides	laid	laids
jeune	jeunes	jeune	jeunes
vieille	vieilles	vieux	vieux
mince	minces	mince	minces
grosse	grosses	gros	gros

11 **Oui, il n'est pas très grand.** The French often tone down what they wish to say by stating the opposite with a negative and the word **très.** Agree with each of the following descriptions by saying the opposite in a negative sentence.

MODÈLE: Michael J. Fox est petit.
> **Oui, il n'est pas très grand.**

1. Abraham et Sarah sont vieux.
2. Marie-Christine est mince.
3. Goofy est laid.
4. Alissa est petite.
5. Dumbo l'éléphant est gros.
6. L'oncle Sam est vieux.
7. James et Lori sont jeunes.

12 **Décrivez ...** Describe the following people. If you don't know what they look like, guess. Pay close attention to adjective agreement.

MODÈLE: Décrivez James Davidson. **Il est grand, jeune et assez beau.**

1. Décrivez votre meilleur(e) ami(e).
2. Décrivez votre professeur de français.
3. Décrivez une actrice.
4. Décrivez un acteur.
5. Décrivez Minnie Mouse et Daisy Duck.
6. Décrivez le (la) président(e) de votre université.
7. Décrivez-vous.

Entre amis

Oui ou non?

1. Choose a famous person and describe him/her.
2. If your partner agrees with each description s/he will say so.
3. If your partner disagrees, s/he will correct you.

Intégration

Révision

Ⓐ Il y a plus d'une façon *(There's more than one way).*

1. Give two ways to say hello in French.
2. Give two ways to break the ice in French.
3. Give two ways to find out someone's name.
4. Give two ways to find out where someone lives.
5. Give two ways to find out someone's nationality.

Ⓑ L'Inspecteur Clouseau. A bumbling inspector is asking all the wrong questions. Correct him. Invent the correct answer if you wish. Use subject pronouns.

MODÈLES: Vous êtes Mme Perrin?
Non, pas du tout, je ne suis pas Mme Perrin; je suis Mlle Smith.

Madame Perrin est française?
Non, pas du tout, elle n'est pas française; elle est canadienne.

> Notice that 1 and 2 are plural. Use **nous** in your answer.

1. Vous êtes Monsieur et Madame Martin?
2. Vous *(pl.)* êtes belges?
3. Madame Martin est veuve?
4. Monsieur et Madame Martin sont divorcés?
5. James et Lori sont mariés?
6. Lori est italienne?
7. James est français?

Ⓒ Décrivez trois personnes. Choose three people and give as complete a description as you can of each of them. Include at least one famous person.

MODÈLE: **James Davidson est grand, jeune et assez beau. Il est aussi célibataire. Il est américain et il habite à San Francisco.**

Ⓓ À vous. How would you respond to the following?

1. Bonjour, Monsieur (Madame, Mademoiselle).
2. Excusez-moi de vous déranger.
3. Vous êtes Monsieur (Madame, Mademoiselle) Dupont?
4. Comment vous appelez-vous?
5. Vous n'êtes pas français(e)?
6. Quelle est votre nationalité?
7. Vous habitez près d'Angers?
8. Où habitez-vous?
9. Vous êtes célibataire?
10. Bonne journée!

Pas de problème!

Preparation for the video: Video worksheet in the *Cahier d'activités*.

Complete the following exercise if you have watched the introduction to the *Pas de problème* video (up to 1:44). Give each person's nationality.

Quelle est la nationalité de Moustafa?
Il est tunisien.

Quelle est la nationalité ...

1. de Jean-François?   3. de Bruno?   5. d'Yves?
2. de Marie-Christine?   4. d'Alissa?

Lecture

This first reading is a series of headlines **(manchettes)** taken from the French-language media. It is not vital that you understand every word in order to grasp the general meaning of what you read. The context will often help you guess the meaning.

 Trouvez les mots apparentés *(cognates).* In French and English, many words with similar meanings have the same or nearly identical spelling. These words are called cognates. Scan the headlines that follow and find at least fifteen cognates.

 Sigles *(Acronyms).* Acronyms are used frequently in French. They are abbreviations made of the first letter of each word in a title and may involve the same letters in their French and English forms. However, the order of the letters is normally different because in French, adjectives usually follow a noun, e.g., **la Croix-Rouge** *(the Red Cross)*. Can you guess the meaning of the following French acronyms?

MODÈLE: ONU (a group of countries)
      UN, the United Nations (Organization)

1. OTAN (an alliance)
2. SIDA (a disease)
3. UE (a group of European countries)
4. TVA (a special tax)
5. ADN (a way to identify)
6. FIV (a way to conceive)
7. FMI (lends money to poor countries)
8. VIH (a virus)
9. IRM (a body scan to detect illness)

Manchettes

1. Le président américain propose une réduction des armements classiques de l'OTAN

2. Un homme innocenté par des tests d'ADN

3. Des combats violents se déroulent dans le nord de l'Afghanistan

4. Un Allemand pour remplacer le Français à la tête du FMI?

5. L'indifférence de la Banque centrale européenne accentue la baisse de l'euro

6. Mise au point aux États-Unis d'un test prédicatif pour le cancer héréditaire

7. Le jazz fait vibrer La Nouvelle-Orléans d'un air de Mardi Gras

8. Un observatoire national du SIDA va être mis en place

9. Ottawa a entrepris de renforcer son dispositif de défense dans le Grand Nord

10. UN HÉROS INCONNU: Le général canadien qui commanda deux forces de maintien de la paix

C **Les manchettes.** Read the above headlines and decide which ones apply to any of the following categories.

1. Canada
2. the United States
3. politics
4. health and medicine
5. war and peace
6. money

D **Dans ces contextes** (*In these contexts*). Study the above headlines to help you guess the meaning of the following expressions.

1. armements classiques
2. homme
3. combats violents
4. tête
5. baisse
6. pour
7. nouvelle
8. mis en place
9. renforcer
10. paix

VOCABULAIRE ACTIF

Pour identifier les personnes
Noms

un acteur / une actrice *actor / actress*
une femme *woman*
un homme *man*
un(e) meilleur(e) ami(e) *best friend*
le Père Noël *Santa Claus*
une personne *person (male or female)*
un professeur *teacher (male or female)*
la nationalité *nationality*
un nom *name*
un nom de famille *family name*
un prénom *first name*

Description physique
beau (belle) *handsome (beautiful)*
grand(e) *big; tall*
gros(se) *fat; large*
jeune *young*
joli(e) *pretty*
laid(e) *ugly*
mince *thin*
petit(e) *small; short*
vieux (vieille) *old*

Le jour et la nuit
à ... heure(s) *at ... o'clock*
le jour *day*
le matin *morning*
la nuit *night*
le soir *evening*
l'après-midi *m. afternoon*

D'autres noms
un hôtel *hotel*
une porte *door*
un restaurant *restaurant*
une table *table*
un tableau *chalkboard*
un téléphone *telephone*
l'université *f. university*

Prépositions
à *at; in; to*
de *from, of*
en *in*
près de *near*

Adjectifs de nationalité
allemand(e) *German*
américain(e) *American*
anglais(e) *English*
belge *Belgian*
canadien(ne) *Canadian*
chinois(e) *Chinese*
espagnol(e) *Spanish*
français(e) *French*
italien(ne) *Italian*
japonais(e) *Japanese*
marocain(e) *Moroccan*
mexicain(e) *Mexican*
russe *Russian*
sénégalais(e) *Senegalese*
suédois(e) *Swedish*
suisse *Swiss*

Salutations et adieux
Au revoir. *Good-bye.*
Bonjour. *Hello.*
Bonne journée. *Have a good day.*
Bonsoir. *Good evening.*
Salut! *Hi!*

Pronoms sujets
je *I*
tu *you*
il *he, it*
elle *she, it*
on *one, people, we, they*
nous *we*
vous *you*
ils *they*
elles *they*

État civil
célibataire *single*
divorcé(e) *divorced*
fiancé(e) *engaged*
marié(e) *married*
veuf (veuve) *widowed*

Nombres
un *one*
deux *two*
trois *three*
quatre *four*

À propos de l'identité
Comment vous appelez-vous? *What is your name?*

Je m'appelle ... *My name is ...*
Madame (Mme) *Mrs.*
Mademoiselle (Mlle) *Miss*
Monsieur (M.) *Mr.; sir*
Permettez-moi de me présenter. *Allow me to introduce myself.*
Quelle est votre nationalité? *What is your nationality?*
Vous habitez ... *You live, you reside ...*
Où habitez-vous? *Where do you live?*
J'habite ... *I live, I reside ...*

La politesse
Bonne journée. *Have a good day.*
Excusez-moi. *Excuse me.*
Excusez-moi de vous déranger. *Excuse me for bothering you.*
Je vous demande pardon ... *I beg your pardon ...*
Merci. Vous aussi. *Thanks. You too.*
Pardon. *Pardon me.*
S'il vous plaît. *Please.*
Vous permettez? *May I?*

Verbe
être *to be*

Adverbes
assez *sort of, rather; enough*
aussi *also, too*
certainement *surely, of course*
ne ... pas *not*
là *there; here*
où *where*
très *very*

D'autres expressions utiles
Asseyez-vous. *Sit down.*
C'est ... *It is ...; This is ...*
C'est pour vous. *It's for you.*
entre amis *between friends*
Et moi? *And me?*
Oui ou non? *Yes or no?*
Pas du tout! *Not at all!*
qui *who*
Voilà ... *There is (are) ...; Here is (are) ...*
votre communication de ... *your call from ...*

2

Qu'est-ce que vous aimez?

Buts communicatifs
Asking and responding to *"How are you?"*
Giving and responding to compliments
Offering, accepting, and refusing
Expressing likes and dislikes

Structures utiles
Les verbes en **-er**
L'article défini: **le, la, l'** et **les**
Les questions avec réponse **oui** ou **non**

Culture
Les compliments
Merci
Le kir

Coup d'envoi

Quelque chose à boire?

Vous voulez ...°	*Do you want ...*
une tasse° de café?	*cup*
un verre° de coca°?	*glass/Coca-Cola*
un verre de vin°?	*wine*
une tasse de thé°?	*tea*
Oui, je veux bien.°	*Gladly.; Yes, thanks.*
Non, merci.°	*No, thanks.*
J'aime° le coca.	*I like (love)*
Je n'aime pas le café.	
Est-ce que vous aimez ...°	*Do you like ...*
le café? le coca? le vin? le thé?	

 Et vous?   Voulez-vous boire quelque chose?°   *Do you want to drink something?/Yes, I'd like ...*
Oui, je voudrais ...°

Est-ce que is often placed at the start of a sentence to make it a question.

Conversation

Une soirée à Besançon

Listen carefully to your instructor and/or the Student Audio while the conversation is presented. As soon as the presentation has ended, try to recall as many words as you can.

James Davidson étudie le français à Besançon. Mais il vient de° San Francisco. Au cours d'une soirée°, il aperçoit° Karine Aspel, qui est assistante au laboratoire de langues.

    he comes from / During a party / notices

JAMES: Quelle° bonne surprise! Comment allez-vous?°   *What a / How are you?*

KARINE: Ça va bien°, merci. Et vous-même°?   *Fine / yourself*

JAMES: Très bien ... Votre prénom, c'est Karine, n'est-ce pas?°   *isn't it?*

KARINE: Oui, je m'appelle Karine Aspel.

JAMES: Et moi, James Davidson.

KARINE: Est-ce que vous êtes américain? Votre français est excellent.

JAMES: Merci beaucoup.

KARINE: Mais c'est vrai!° Vous êtes d'où?°   *But it's true! / Where are you from?*

JAMES: Je viens de° San Francisco. Au fait°, voulez-vous boire quelque chose? Un coca?   *I come from / By the way*

KARINE: Merci°, je n'aime pas beaucoup le coca.   *No thanks*

JAMES: Alors°, un kir, peut-être°?   *Then / perhaps*

KARINE: Je veux bien. Un petit kir, pourquoi pas°?   *why not*

(James hands a glass of kir to Karine.)

JAMES: À votre santé°, Karine.   *To your health*

KARINE: À la vôtre°. Et merci, James.   *To yours*

▶ **Jouez ces rôles.**   Role-play the above conversation with a partner. Use your own identities. Choose something else to drink.

Il y a un geste

À votre santé.   The glass is raised when saying *To your health.* Among friends, the glasses are lightly touched as well.

Non, merci.   The French often raise the index finger and move it from side to side to indicate *no.* They also may indicate *no* by raising a hand, palm outward, or by shaking their heads as do English speakers. In France, however, the lips are usually well rounded and often are pursed when making these gestures.

> **Why does Karine say Mais c'est vrai! when James says Merci beaucoup?**
>
> a. She misunderstood what he said.
> b. She doesn't mean what she said.
> c. She feels that James doesn't really believe her when she tells him his French is good.

Les compliments

While certainly not averse to being complimented, the French may respond by playing down a compliment, which may be a way of encouraging more of the same. While Americans are taught from an early age to accept and respond *thank you* to compliments, **merci,** when used in response to a compliment, is often perceived by the French as saying "you don't mean it." It is for this reason that Karine Aspel responds **Mais c'est vrai!** insisting that her compliment was true. It is culturally more accurate, therefore, and linguistically enjoyable, to develop a few rejoinders such as **Oh, vraiment?** *(Really?)* or **Vous trouvez?** *(Do you think so?),* which one can employ in similar situations. In this case, a really French response on James's part might be **Mais non! Je ne parle pas vraiment bien. Mon accent n'est pas très bon.** *(But, no! I don't speak really well. My accent's not very good.)*

Merci

The word **merci** is, of course, one of the best ways of conveying politeness, and its use is, by all means, to be encouraged. Its usage, however, differs from that of English in at least one important way: when one is offered something to eat, to drink, etc., the response **merci** is somewhat ambiguous and is often a way of saying *no, thank you.* One would generally say **je veux bien** or **s'il vous plaît** to convey the meaning *yes, thanks.* **Merci** is however the proper polite response once the food, the drink, etc., has actually been served.

Le kir

A popular drink in France, four parts white wine and one part black currant liqueur, **kir** owes its name to **le Chanoine Kir,** a French priest and former mayor of Dijon. It is often served as an **apéritif** *(before dinner drink).*

▶ À vous.   How would you respond to the following questions?

1. Comment allez-vous?
2. Est-ce que vous êtes français(e)?
3. Votre prénom, c'est ... ?
4. Vous êtes d'où?
5. Voulez-vous boire quelque chose?

Entre amis

À une soirée *(At a party)*

1. Greet another "invited guest."
2. Find out his/her name.
3. Find out his/her nationality.
4. Find out where s/he comes from.
5. What else can you say?

Prononciation

Review the alphabet on p. 4 before doing this activity.

Review what was said about **l'accent et le rythme**, p. 11.

L'alphabet français (suite)

■ English and French share the same 26-letter Latin alphabet, and although this is useful, it is also potentially troublesome.

■ First, French and English cognates may not be spelled the same. French spellings must, therefore, be memorized.

adresse   personne   appartement

■ Second, because the alphabet is the same, it is tempting to pronounce French words as if they were English. Be very careful, especially when pronouncing cognates, not to transfer English pronunciation to the French words.

téléphone   conversation   professeur

■ Knowing how to say the French alphabet is not only important in spelling out loud. It is also essential when saying the many acronyms used in the French language.

le TGV   les USA   la SNCF

▶ **Quelques sigles.**   Read out loud the letters that make up the following acronyms.

1. **SVP**   S'il vous plaît
2. **RSVP**   Répondez, s'il vous plaît
3. **La SNCF**   La Société nationale des chemins de fer français *(French railroad system)*
4. **La RATP**   La Régie autonome des transports parisiens *(Paris subway and bus system)*
5. **Les BD**   Les bandes dessinées *(comic strips)*
6. **Les USA**   Les United States of America *(= Les États-Unis)*
7. **La BNP**   La Banque nationale de Paris
8. **La CGT**   La Confédération générale du travail *(a French labor union)*
9. **BCBG**   Bon chic bon genre *(a French yuppy)*
10. **Le RER**   Le Réseau Express Régional *(a train to the suburbs)*

Accents

■ French accents are part of spelling and must be learned. They can serve:

1. to indicate how a word is pronounced
   ç → [s]: français
   é → [e]: marié
   è → [ɛ]: très
   ê → [ɛ]: être
   ë → [ɛ]: Noël

2. or to distinguish between meanings
   ou   *or*   la   *the (feminine)*
   où   *where*   là   *there*

French names		Examples
´	**accent aigu**	américain; téléphone
`	**accent grave**	à; très; où
^	**accent circonflexe**	âge; êtes; s'il vous plaît; hôtel; sûr
¨	**tréma**	Noël; coïncidence
¸	**cédille**	français
-	**trait d'union**	Jean-Luc
'	**apostrophe**	J'aime

Crème s'écrit C–R–E accent grave–M–E.

▶ **Comment est-ce qu'on écrit ... ?**   Your partner will ask you to spell the words below. Give the correct spelling.

MODÈLE: être
  VOTRE PARTENAIRE: **Comment est-ce qu'on écrit «être»?**
  VOUS: **«Être» s'écrit E accent circonflexe–T–R–E.**

1. français
2. monsieur
3. belge
4. mademoiselle
5. professeur
6. vieux
7. hôtel
8. très
9. téléphone
10. j'habite
11. canadienne
12. asseyez-vous

Buts communicatifs

1 Asking and Responding to "How are you?"

	Questions	
more formal	Comment allez-vous?	
	Vous allez bien?	
first-name basis	Comment ça va?°	*How's it going?*
	Ça va?	

Réponses	
Je vais très bien°, merci.	*Very well; I'm fine*
Ça va bien.	
Ça ne va pas mal°.	*Not bad.*
Oh! Comme ci, comme ça.°	*So-so.*
Oh! Pas trop bien.°	*Not too great.*
Je suis assez fatigué(e).°	*I'm rather tired.*
Je suis un peu malade.°	*I'm a little sick.*

Learn all the words in each *But communicatif.*

Remarque It is very important to try to tailor your language to fit the situation. For example, with a friend or another student, you would normally ask **Ça va?** or **Comment ça va?** For someone whom you address as **Monsieur, Madame,** or **Mademoiselle,** you would normally say **Comment allez-vous?**

Il y a un geste

Ça va. This gesture implies "so-so" and is very similar to **assez.** Open one or both hands, palms down, and slightly rotate them. This is often accompanied by a slight shrug, and the lips are pursed. One may also say **comme ci, comme ça.**

1 **Attention au style.** Greet the following people and find out how they are.

Review activity 1, p. 12.

> **MODÈLE:** Monsieur Talbot (le matin à 8 h)
> **Bonjour, Monsieur. Comment allez-vous?**

1. Paul (le soir à 7 h)
2. Mademoiselle Monot (le matin à 9 h 30)
3. Monsieur Talbot (l'après-midi à 4 h)
4. le professeur de français (le matin à 11 h)
5. votre meilleur(e) ami(e) (le soir à 10 h)
6. le (la) président(e) de votre université (l'après-midi à 1 h)

2 **Vous allez bien?** Ask the following people how they are doing. Be careful to choose between the familiar and the formal questions. Your partner will provide the other person's answer.

MODÈLE: Marie (a little sick)
VOUS: **Comment ça va, Marie?**
MARIE: **Oh! je suis un peu malade.**

1. Madame Philippe (tired)
2. Paul (not too great)
3. Monsieur Dupont (sick)
4. Mademoiselle Bernard (very well)
5. Anne (so-so)
6. votre professeur de français (...)
7. votre meilleur(e) ami(e) (...)
8. le (la) président(e) de l'université (...)

Entre amis

Au café

Practice the following situation with as many members of the class as possible. You are in a sidewalk café at one o'clock in the afternoon.

1. Greet your partner in a culturally appropriate manner.
2. Inquire how s/he is doing.
3. Offer him/her something to drink.
4. What else can you say?

2 Giving and Responding to Compliments

Quelques° compliments   *A few*

Vous parlez très bien le français.°   *You speak French very well.*
Vous dansez très bien.
Vous chantez° bien.   *sing*
Vous skiez vraiment° bien.   *really*
Vous nagez comme un poisson.°   *You swim like a fish.*

Quelques réponses

Vous trouvez?°   *Do you think so?*
Pas encore.°   *Not yet.*
Oh! pas vraiment.°   *Not really.*
Oh! je ne sais pas.°   *I don't know.*
C'est gentil mais vous exagérez.°   *That's nice but you're exaggerating.*
Je commence seulement.°   *I'm only beginning.*
Je n'ai pas beaucoup d'expérience.°   *I don't have a lot of experience.*

Remarque   There are several ways to express an idea. For instance, there are at least three ways to compliment someone's French:

Votre français est excellent.   *Your French is excellent.*
Vous parlez bien le français.   *You speak French well.*
Vous êtes bon (bonne) en français.   *You are good in French.*

3 **Un compliment.** Give a compliment to each of the people pictured below. Another student will take the role of the person in the drawing and will provide a culturally appropriate rejoinder.

MODÈLE: —**Vous parlez bien le français.**
—**Vous trouvez? Oh! je ne sais pas.**

1.   2.   3.   4.

A. Les verbes en *-er*

■ All verb infinitives are made up of a **stem** and an **ending.** To use verbs in the present tense, one removes the ending from the infinitive and adds new endings to the resulting stem. Verbs that use the same endings are often classified according to the last two letters of their infinitive. By far the most common class of verbs is the group ending in **-er.**

For a further explanation of any grammatical terms with which you are not familiar, see Appendix *C, Glossary of Grammatical Terms,* at the end of this book.

parler *(to speak)*	stem	endings
je	parl	**e**
tu	parl	**es**
il/elle/on	parl	**e**
nous	parl	**ons**
vous	parl	**ez**
ils/elles	parl	**ent**

tomber *(to fall)*	stem	endings
je	tomb	**e**
tu	tomb	**es**
il/elle/on	tomb	**e**
nous	tomb	**ons**
vous	tomb	**ez**
ils/elles	tomb	**ent**

■ Whether you are talking to a friend (**tu**), or about yourself (**je**), or about one or more other persons (**il, elle, ils, elles**), the verb is pronounced the same because the endings are silent.

Tu **danses** avec Amy?	*Are you dancing with Amy?*
Je ne **danse** pas du tout.	*I don't dance at all.*
Il **danse** bien, non?	*He dances well, doesn't he?*
Moustafa et Betty **dansent.**	*Moustafa and Betty are dancing.*

■ If you are using the **nous** or **vous** form, the verb is pronounced differently. The **-ez** ending is pronounced [e] and the **-ons** ending is pronounced [ɔ̃].

Vous **dansez** avec Marc?	*Do you dance with Marc?*
Nous ne **dansons** pas très souvent.	*We don't dance very often.*

■ Remember that the present tense has only *one* form in French, while it has several forms in English.

Remember to change **je** to **j'** before a vowel sound. See p. 14.

je **danse**	*I dance, I do dance, I am dancing*
j'**habite**	*I live, I do live, I am living*

■ Before a vowel sound, the final **-n** of **on** and the final **-s** of **nous, vous, ils,** and **elles** are pronounced and linked to the next word.

On [n]écoute la radio?	*Is someone listening to the radio?*
Nous [z]étudions le français.	*We are studying French.*
Vous [z]habitez ici?	*Do you live here?*

VOCABULAIRE

Activités

chanter (une chanson)	*to sing (a song)*
chercher (mes amis)	*to look for (my friends)*
danser (avec mes amis)	*to dance (with my friends)*
écouter (la radio)	*to listen to (the radio)*
enseigner (le français)	*to teach (French)*
étudier (le français)	*to study (French)*
jouer (au tennis)	*to play (tennis)*
manger	*to eat*
nager	*to swim*
parler (français)	*to speak (French)*
patiner	*to skate*
pleurer	*to cry*
regarder (la télé)	*to watch, to look at (TV)*
skier	*to ski*
travailler (beaucoup)	*to work (a lot)*
voyager (souvent)	*to travel (often)*
tomber	to fall

Note Verbs ending in **-ger** add an **-e-** before the ending in the form used with **nous: nous mangeons, nous nageons, nous voyageons.**

4 **Comparaisons.** Tell what the following people do and then compare yourself to them. Use **Et moi aussi, ...** or **Mais moi, ...** to tell whether or not the statement is also true for you.

MODÈLE: Pierre et Anne/habiter à Angers
Ils habitent à Angers. Mais moi, je n'habite pas à Angers.

1. vous/nager comme un poisson
2. James/parler bien le français
3. Monsieur et Madame Dupont/danser très bien
4. tu/étudier le français
5. vous/chanter vraiment bien
6. tu/regarder souvent la télévision
7. le professeur/enseigner le français
8. Karine et James/travailler beaucoup
9. Sébastien/patiner/mais/il/tomber souvent

Non, pas du tout. Respond to each question with a negative and follow up with an affirmative answer using the words in parentheses. Supply your own responses for items 5 and 6.

> **MODÈLE:**   Je danse *mal,* n'est-ce pas? (bien)
> **Non, pas du tout. Vous ne dansez pas mal; vous dansez bien.**

1. Vous *écoutez* la radio? (regarder la télé)
2. Le professeur *voyage* beaucoup? (travailler)
3. Est-ce que je chante *très mal?* (assez bien)
4. Vous *chantez* avec le professeur? (parler français)
5. Vous habitez *à Paris?* (...)
6. Est-ce que nous étudions *l'espagnol?* (...)

VOCABULAIRE

Des gens que je connais bien
(People that I know well)

mon ami	*my (male) friend*
mon amie	*my (female) friend*
mes amis	*my friends*
ma mère	*my mother*
mon père	*my father*
le professeur	*the (male or female) teacher*
les étudiants	*the students*

 Mes connaissances. Tell about your family and your acquaintances by choosing an item from each list to create as many factual sentences as you can. You may make any of them negative.

> **MODÈLE:**   **Nous ne dansons pas mal.**

	chanter bien
	travailler beaucoup
	écouter souvent la radio
les étudiants	étudier le français
le professeur	skier bien
je	danser mal
nous	patiner beaucoup
ma mère	habiter en France
mon père	parler français
mes amis	nager comme un poisson
	voyager souvent
	pleurer souvent
	regarder souvent la télévision

Tu parles bien le français! Pay compliments to the following friends. Use **tu** for each individual; use **vous** for more than one person.

MODÈLES: Éric skie bien.
Tu skies bien!

Yann et Sophie dansent bien.
Vous dansez bien!

1. Alissa est très jolie.
2. Christophe parle très bien l'espagnol.
3. David est bon en français.
4. François et Michel parlent bien l'anglais.
5. Ils travaillent beaucoup aussi.
6. Anne et Marie sont vraiment bonnes en maths.
7. Elles chantent bien aussi.
8. Olivier est vraiment très beau.
9. Luc skie comme un champion olympique.

 Identification. Answer the following questions as factually as possible.

MODÈLE: Qui parle bien le français?
Le professeur parle bien le français.
Mes amis parlent bien le français.

1. Qui étudie le français?
2. Qui enseigne le français?
3. Qui ne skie pas du tout?
4. Qui chante très bien?

5. Qui joue mal au tennis?
6. Qui regarde souvent la télévision?
7. Qui écoute souvent la radio?

Entre amis

Avec un(e) ami(e)

Practice the following situation with as many members of the class as possible.

1. Pay your partner a compliment.
2. Your partner will give a culturally appropriate response to the compliment and then pay you a compliment in return.
3. Give an appropriate response.

3 Offering, Accepting, and Refusing

Pour offrir une boisson°   *To offer a drink*

Voulez-vous boire quelque chose?

Voulez-vous un verre d'orangina°?   *orange soda*

Voulez-vous un verre de (d') ... ?

  bière°?   *beer*

  eau°?   *water*

  jus d'orange°?   *orange juice*

  lait°?   *milk*

Voulez-vous une tasse de ... ?

  café?

  chocolat chaud°?   *hot chocolate*

Qu'est-ce que° vous voulez?   *What*

Pour accepter ou refuser quelque chose°   *To accept or refuse something*

Je veux bien.

Volontiers.°   *Gladly.*

S'il vous plaît.

Oui, avec plaisir.°   *Yes, with pleasure.*

Oui, c'est gentil à vous.°   *Yes, that's nice of you.*

Merci.

Non, merci.

NOTE CULTURELLE
Les jeunes Américains aiment beaucoup le lait. Mais, en général, les jeunes Français n'aiment pas le lait.

❑ *Boisson à l'orange*
❑ *Jus de pomme*
❑ *1/4 Évian*
❑ *Boisson aux fruits exotiques*

boissons

❾ Voulez-vous boire quelque chose? Use the list of words below to create a dialogue in which one person offers something to drink and the other responds appropriately.

MODÈLES: Coca-Cola
    —Voulez-vous un verre de coca?
    —Volontiers.

    coffee
    —Voulez-vous une tasse de café?
    —Non, merci.

1. water	4. wine	7. hot chocolate
2. tea	5. milk	8. beer
3. orange soda	6. orange juice	

Qu'est-ce que vous voulez? Examine the drink menu of **La Bague d'or** *(The Golden Ring)* and order something.

MODÈLES: **Je voudrais une tasse de thé.**
Je voudrais un verre de coca-cola, s'il vous plaît.

La Bague d'or
BRASSERIE ALSACIENNE

Boissons

Vin rouge

Riesling (Vin d'Alsace)

Jus de fruits

Bière (pression)

Café

Thé

Chocolat chaud

Coca-cola

Orangina

Eau minérale (Perrier)

B. L'article défini: *le, la, l'* et *les*

■ You have already learned that all nouns in French have gender — that is, they are classified grammatically as either masculine or feminine. You also know that you need to remember the gender for each noun you learn. One of the functions of French articles is to mark the gender (masculine or feminine) and the number (singular or plural) of a noun.

forms of the definite article	when to use	examples
le (l')	before a masculine singular noun	**le** thé
la (l')	before a feminine singular noun	**la** bière
les	before all plural nouns, masculine or feminine	**les** boissons

■ **Le** and **la** become **l'** when followed by a word that begins with a vowel sound. This includes many words that begin with the letter **h**.

le professeur *but* **l'**étudiant, **l'**ami, **l'**homme
la femme *but* **l'**étudiante, **l'**amie

■ When they are used to refer to specific things or persons, **le, la, l',** and **les** all correspond to the English definite article *the*.

Le professeur écoute **les** étudiants.	*The teacher listens to the students.*
L'université de Paris est excellente.	*The University of Paris is excellent.*

■ **Le, la, l',** and **les** are also used before nouns that have a generic meaning, even when in English the word *the* would not be used.

Le lait est bon pour **la** santé.	*Milk is good for your health.*
Elle regarde souvent **la** télé.	*She often watches TV.*
J'étudie **le** chinois.	*I'm studying Chinese.*

Review nationalities, p. 18.

■ All languages are masculine. Many are derived from the adjective of nationality. All verbs except **parler** require **le** before the name of a language. With **parler, le** is normally kept if there is an adverb directly after the verb, but is normally omitted if there is no adverb directly after the verb.

Ils **étudient le** russe.	*They are studying Russian.*
Ma mère **parle bien le** français.	*My mother speaks French well.*
Mon père **parle** français **aussi.**	*My father speaks French too.*

VOCABULAIRE

Pour répondre à Comment? *(How?)*

très bien	*very well*
(vraiment) bien	*(really) well*
assez bien	*rather well*
un peu	*a bit*
assez mal	*rather poorly*
(vraiment) mal	*(really) poorly*
ne ... pas du tout	*not at all*

11 **Parlez-vous bien le français?** For each language, describe how well you and a friend of yours **(mon ami(e) _____)** speak it.

MODÈLE: l'allemand
Je ne parle pas du tout l'allemand mais mon ami Hans parle très bien l'allemand.

1. le russe   2. l'espagnol   3. l'anglais   4. le français

Remember that **Est-ce que ...?** just signals a question; **Qu'est-ce que ...?** means **What ...?**

12 **Dans la salle de classe.** Practice asking and answering the following questions with your partners.

1. Qu'est-ce que vous étudiez?
2. Étudiez-vous le français le matin, l'après-midi ou le soir?
3. Étudiez-vous aussi l'anglais?
4. Parlez-vous souvent avec le professeur de français?
5. Est-ce que le professeur chante avec la classe?
6. Est-ce que le professeur de français parle anglais?
7. Parlez-vous bien le français?
8. Parlez-vous un peu l'espagnol?

Entre amis

Une réception

You are at a reception at the French consulate.

1. Greet your partner and find out his/her name.
2. Offer him/her something to drink.
3. S/he will accept appropriately.
4. Toast each other.
5. Compliment each other on your ability in French.
6. Respond appropriately to the compliment.

4 Expressing Likes and Dislikes

Qu'est-ce que tu aimes, Sophie?
    J'aime beaucoup le vin blanc°. J'adore voyager.   *white wine*
    J'aime bien danser.
Moi aussi°, j'aime voyager et danser. Et qu'est-ce   *Me too*
que tu n'aimes pas?
    Je n'aime pas le vin rosé. Je déteste le coca. Je
    n'aime pas chanter. Je n'aime pas beaucoup
    travailler.
Moi non plus°, je n'aime pas travailler.   *Me neither*

Et vous? Qu'est-ce que vous aimez?
           Qu'est-ce que vous n'aimez pas?

Remarques

1. When there are two verbs in succession, the second is not conjugated. It remains in the infinitive form.

Mon ami **déteste nager** dans l'eau   *My friend hates to swim in cold water.*
   froide.
Les étudiants **aiment parler** français.   *The students like to speak French.*
Francis **désire danser.**   *Francis wants to dance.*

2. The use of **le, la, l',** and **les** to express a generality occurs particularly after verbs expressing preferences.

Marie adore **le** chocolat chaud.   *Marie loves hot chocolate.*
Elle aime **les** boissons chaudes.   *She likes hot drinks.*
Mais elle déteste **la** bière.   *But she hates beer.*
Et elle n'aime pas **l'**eau minérale.   *And she doesn't like mineral water.*

Qu'est-ce qu'ils aiment? Tell, as truthfully as possible, what the following people like and don't like by combining items from each of the three lists. Guess, if you don't know for certain. How many sentences can you create?

MODÈLES: **Mes amis détestent le lait.**
Je n'aime pas du tout skier.

		skier
		travailler
		la bière
		le français
	adorer	la télévision
mes amis	aimer beaucoup	chanter
le professeur	ne pas aimer vraiment	patiner
je	ne pas aimer du tout	danser
nous	détester	le lait
		l'université
		voyager
		nager
		enseigner

 Vous aimez danser? Use the words below to interview the person sitting next to you. Find out if s/he likes to dance, to swim, etc. Use **aimer** in every question.

MODÈLE: dance

VOUS: **Vous aimez danser?**
VOTRE PARTENAIRE: **Oui, j'aime (beaucoup) danser.** ou
Non, je n'aime pas (beaucoup) danser.

1. sing
2. swim
3. watch television
4. ski
5. study
6. study French
7. work
8. travel
9. play tennis
10. speak French

VOCABULAIRE

Quelques boissons populaires

le café	*coffee*	le coca	*cola*
le café au lait	*coffee with milk*	la limonade	*lemon-lime soda*
le café crème	*coffee with cream*	l'orangina *m.*	*orangina (an orange soda)*
le chocolat chaud	*hot chocolate*		
le citron pressé	*lemonade*		
l'eau minérale *f.*	*mineral water*	la bière	*beer*
le jus d'orange	*orange juice*	le kir	*kir*
le thé	*tea*	le vin	*wine*

NOTE CULTURELLE
La limonade française ressemble beaucoup à la boisson *7-UP.* La boisson américaine *lemonade* est **le citron pressé** en France.
Le café au lait est moitié *(half)* café, moitié lait chaud.

Vous aimez le café? Interview another person to find out which drinks s/he likes or dislikes, then be prepared to report as many answers as you can remember.

En général, les étudiants ... Decide whether you agree (**C'est vrai**) or disagree (**C'est faux**) with the following statements. If you disagree, correct the statement.

> **MODÈLE:** En général, les étudiants détestent voyager.
> **C'est faux. En général, ils aiment beaucoup voyager.**

1. En général, les étudiants n'aiment pas du tout danser.
2. En général, les étudiants détestent la pizza.
3. En général, les étudiants aiment beaucoup étudier.
4. En général, les étudiants n'aiment pas beaucoup regarder la télévision.
5. En général, les étudiants aiment nager.
6. En général, les étudiants aiment skier.
7. En général, les étudiants aiment beaucoup patiner.
8. En général, les étudiants détestent chanter.
9. En général, les étudiants aiment parler français avec le professeur.
10. En général, les étudiants désirent habiter à New York.

 Comment trouvez-vous le café français? *(What do you think of French coffee?)* Your partner will ask you to give your opinion about something you have tasted. Use **aimer, adorer,** or **détester** in an answer that reflects your own opinion. Or make up an imaginary opinion. You might also say **Je ne sais pas, mais ...** and offer an opinion about something else that is related, instead.

> **MODÈLE:** les tamalis mexicains
> VOTRE PARTENAIRE: **Comment trouvez-vous les tamalis mexicains?**
> VOUS: **J'aime beaucoup les tamalis mexicains.** ou
> **Je ne sais pas, mais j'adore les enchiladas.**

1. le thé anglais
2. le chocolat suisse
3. la pizza italienne
4. l'eau minérale française
5. le jus d'orange de Floride
6. le café de Colombie
7. la limonade française
8. la bière allemande
9. le vin français

C. Les questions avec réponse *oui* ou *non*

■ In spoken French, by far the most frequently used way of asking a question that can be answered *yes* or *no* is by simply raising the voice at the end of the sentence.

Vous parlez français?   *Do you speak French?*

James habite ici?   *Does James live here?*

Lori est américaine?   *Is Lori American?*

Hélène danse bien?   *Does Hélène dance well?*

■ **Est-ce que** is often placed at the beginning of a sentence to form a question. It becomes **Est-ce qu'** before a vowel sound.

Est-ce que vous parlez français?	*Do you speak French?*
Est-ce que James habite ici?	*Does James live here?*
Est-ce que Lori est américaine?	*Is Lori American?*
Est-ce qu'Hélène danse bien?	*Does Hélène dance well?*

■ The phrase **n'est-ce pas?** (*right?, aren't you?, doesn't he?,* etc.), added at the end of a sentence, expects an affirmative answer.

Tu parles français, **n'est-ce pas?**	*You speak French, don't you?*
James habite ici, **n'est-ce pas?**	*James lives here, doesn't he?*
Lori est américaine, **n'est-ce pas?**	*Lori is American, isn't she?*
Hélène danse bien, **n'est-ce pas?**	*Hélène dances well, doesn't she?*

■ Another question form, which is used more often in written French than in speech and which is characteristic of a more formal speech style, is *inversion* of the verb and its *pronoun* subject. When inversion is used, there is a hyphen between the verb and the pronoun.

Parlez-vous français?	*Do you speak French?*
Aimez-vous chanter?	*Do you like to sing?*
Êtes-vous américain(e)?	*Are you American?*

Note If the third person (**il, elle, on, ils, elles**) is used in inversion, there is always a [t] sound between the verb and the subject pronoun. If the verb ends in a vowel, a written **-t-** is added between the final vowel of the verb and the initial vowel of the pronoun. If the verb ends in **-t**, no extra **-t-** is necessary.

Enseigne-**t**-il le français?	*Does he teach French?*
Aime-**t**-elle voyager?	*Does she like to travel?*

But:	Aimen**t**-ils voyager?	*Do they like to travel?*
	Es**t**-elle française?	*Is she French?*
	Son**t**-ils américains?	*Are they American?*

FOR RECOGNITION ONLY:

• If the subject is a noun, the inversion form can be produced by adding the pronoun of the same number and gender after the verb.

noun + verb + pronoun

Karen est-elle américaine?	*Is Karen American?*
Thierry aime-t-il la bière?	*Does Thierry like beer?*
Nathalie et Stéphane aiment-ils danser?	*Do Nathalie and Stéphane like to dance?*

Comment? *(What did you say?)* We are often obliged to repeat a question when someone doesn't hear or understand us. For each question with inversion, ask a question beginning with **Est-ce que** and a question ending with **n'est-ce pas.**

MODÈLES: James habite-t-il à San Francisco?

> VOTRE PARTENAIRE: **Comment?**
> VOUS: **Est-ce que James habite à San Francisco?**
> VOTRE PARTENAIRE: **Comment?**
> VOUS: **James habite à San Francisco, n'est-ce pas?**

1. James est-il américain?
2. Étudie-t-il le français?
3. Parle-t-il bien le français?
4. Aime-t-il Karine Aspel?
5. Karine est-elle française?
6. Travaille-t-elle beaucoup?

19 **Une enquête entre amis** *(A survey among friends).* Use the following list to determine the likes and dislikes of two classmates. Be prepared to report back the results of your "survey" to the class. Are there any items on which all the students agree completely?

MODÈLES: skier —**Est-ce que tu aimes skier?**
—**Oui, j'adore skier.**

le jogging —**Est-ce que tu aimes le jogging?**
—**Non, je n'aime pas le jogging.** ou
Non, je déteste le jogging. Je n'aime pas les sports.

1. parler français
2. parler avec le professeur de français
3. voyager
4. regarder la télévision
5. chanter en français
6. la politique
7. l'université
8. étudier le français
9. nager dans l'eau froide
10. travailler beaucoup

20 **Les Dupont.*** Here are a few facts about the Dupont family. Interview a classmate to find out if this information is also true for him/her.

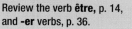
Review the verb **être**, p. 14, and **-er** verbs, p. 36.

MODÈLES: Les Dupont habitent à Marseille.
> VOUS: **Habites-tu à Marseille aussi?**
> VOTRE PARTENAIRE: **Non, je n'habite pas à Marseille.**

Gérard et Martine sont mariés.
> VOUS: **Es-tu marié(e) aussi?**
> VOTRE PARTENAIRE: **Non, je ne suis pas marié(e).** ou
> **Oui, je suis marié(e) aussi.**

1. Martine adore voyager.
2. Gérard Dupont aime la limonade.
3. Les Dupont sont malades.
4. Martine Dupont parle un peu l'espagnol.
5. Monsieur et Madame Dupont aiment beaucoup danser.
6. Les Dupont voyagent beaucoup.

An **-s is not added to family names in French; the article **les** indicates the plural.*

Entre amis

À un bal

Practice the following situation with as many members of the class as possible. You are at a dance and are meeting people for the first time. Use **vous**.

1. Say good evening and introduce yourself.
2. Find out if your partner likes to dance.
3. Ask your partner if s/he wants to dance. (S/he does.)
4. Tell your partner that s/he dances well.
5. Offer your partner something to drink.
6. Toast each other.
7. Compliment each other on your ability in French.
8. Respond appropriately to the compliment.

Intégration

Révision

A **Trouvez quelqu'un qui ...** *(Find someone who ...).*
Interview your classmates in French to find someone who ...

MODÈLE: speaks French   **Est-ce que tu parles français?**

1. likes coffee
2. swims often
3. doesn't like beer
4. sings poorly
5. studies a lot
6. doesn't ski
7. is tired
8. hates to work
9. likes to travel
10. cries often
11. skates

B **À vous.** How would you respond to the following questions and comments?

1. Parlez-vous français?
2. Comment allez-vous?
3. Où habitez-vous?
4. Voulez-vous boire quelque chose?
5. Si oui, qu'est-ce que vous désirez boire?
6. Vous parlez très bien le français!
7. Vous étudiez l'espagnol, n'est-ce pas?
8. Aimez-vous voyager?
9. Est-ce que vous aimez danser?
10. Qu'est-ce que vous n'aimez pas?

Pas de problème!

Preparation for the video:
1. Video worksheet in the *Cahier d'activités*
2. CD-ROM, *Module 1*

Complete the following activity if you have watched video *Module 1.* Decide if the following statements are true or false. If a statement is false, correct it.

1. Jean-François et René jouent au tennis.
2. Jean-François joue très bien.
3. Il regarde Nathalie.
4. Marie-Christine est la cousine de Nathalie.
5. Marie-Christine n'aime pas les mélodrames.
6. Les Français détestent les sports.

Lecture

The following reading selection is taken directly from the *Gab,* a weekly newspaper published in Besançon. It is not vital that you understand every word.

 Étude du vocabulaire. There are words in French that we refer to as **faux amis** *(false friends, false cognates),* since they mean something different from the English word they seem to resemble. Study the following sentences and match the **faux ami,** in bold print, with the correct meaning in English: *understanding, reading, sensitive.*

> **La lecture** est mon passe-temps préféré.
> Florence est timide et très **sensible.**
> Nous aimons les professeurs **compréhensifs.**

SEUL(E) ET LAS(SE) DE L'ÊTRE*
VOUS ASPIREZ À NOUER UNE RELATION SENTIMENTALE DURABLE
Simplement, facilement, vous pouvez connaître quelqu'un
qui comme vous est motivé par une vie de couple stable.

Depuis 1975
ANDRÉE MOUGENOT CONSEILLÈRE DIPLÔMÉE
10 RUE DE LA RÉPUBLIQUE BESANÇON
fait des heureux
Retournez tout simplement le bon ci-dessous, vous recevrez gratuitement sans aucune marque extérieure un exemple de proposition de mise en relation.

JE SUIS
Nom et prénom...
Adresse

....
Âge .... Taille ....
Profession ....

JE CHERCHE
Célibataire ☐ Veuf(ve)☐ Divorcé(e) ☐
Âgé de .... ans à.........
Études souhaitées ....
Profession souhaitée

....
Autres caractéristiques ....

Célibataire ☐ Veuf(ve) ☐ Divorcé(e) ☐
J'aime recevoir ☐ Sortir ☐ Danser ☐
Le sport ☐ La nature ☐ Bricoler ☐
Jardiner ☐ Voyager ☐ La lecture ☐
La musique ☐

Simple☐ Gai(e)☐ Loyal(e)☐ Calme ☐
Amusant(e)☐ Tendre ☐ Sensible ☐
Compréhensif(ve)☐ Affectueux(se)☐
Sincère ☐ Tolérant(e)☐ Conciliant(e)☐
Passionné(e)☐Dynamique☐

Alone and tired of it.   Le Gab n° 648 (Besançon)

Familles de mots *(Word families).* Can you guess the meanings of the following words? One member of each word family is found in the reading.

1. comprendre, compréhensif, compréhensive, la compréhension
2. recevoir, une réception
3. sortir, une sortie
4. lire, un lecteur, une lectrice, la lecture

C **Autoportrait** *(Self-portrait).* Describe *yourself* using five adjectives from the **Je cherche** section of the reading.

Modèle: célibataire, loyal(e), ...

VOCABULAIRE ACTIF

Quelque chose à boire
la bière *beer*
une boisson *drink*
le café *coffee*
le café au lait *coffee with milk*
le café crème *coffee with cream*
le chocolat chaud *hot chocolate*
le citron pressé *lemonade*
le coca *cola*
l'eau *f.* (minérale) *(mineral) water*
le jus d'orange *orange juice*
le kir *kir*
le lait *milk*
la limonade *lemon-lime soda*
l'orangina *m. orangina (an orange soda)*
le thé *tea*
le vin (rouge, blanc, rosé) *(red, white, rosé) wine*

Des gens que je connais bien
les étudiants *the students*
ma mère *my mother*
mes amis *my friends*
mon ami(e) *my friend*
mon père *my father*

D'autres noms et pronoms
une chanson *song*
le jogging *jogging*
la pizza *pizza*
un poisson *fish*
la politique *politics*

quelque chose *something*
quelqu'un *someone*
la radio *radio*
une soirée *an evening party*
une tasse *cup*
la télévision (la télé) *television (TV)*
un verre *glass*

Adjectifs
bon (bonne) *good*
chaud(e) *hot*
cher (chère) *dear*
excellent(e) *excellent*
fatigué(e) *tired*
faux (fausse) *false; wrong*
froid(e) *cold*
malade *sick*
vrai(e) *true*

Pour répondre à un compliment
Vous trouvez? *Do you think so?*
Pas encore. *Not yet.*
Oh! Pas vraiment. *Not really.*
Je ne sais pas. *I don't know.*
C'est gentil mais vous exagérez. *That's nice but you're exaggerating.*
Je commence seulement. *I'm only beginning.*
Je n'ai pas beaucoup d'expérience. *I don't have a lot of experience.*

Articles définis
le, la, l', les *the*

D'autres verbes
chanter *to sing*
chercher *to look for*
danser *to dance*
désirer *to want*
écouter *to listen to*
enseigner *to teach*
étudier *to study*
habiter *to live; to reside*
jouer (au tennis) *to play (tennis)*
manger *to eat*
nager *to swim*
parler *to speak*
patiner *to skate*
pleurer *to cry*
regarder *to watch; to look at*
skier *to ski*
tomber *to fall*
travailler *to work*
trouver *to find; to be of the opinion*
voyager *to travel*

Mots invariables
alors *then, therefore, so*
avec *with*
beaucoup *a lot*
bien *well; fine*
comme *like*
en général *in general*
ensemble *together*

ici *here*
mais *but*
mal *poorly; badly*
peut-être *maybe; perhaps*
pour *for; in order to*
pourquoi *why*
seulement *only*
souvent *often*
un peu *a little bit*
vraiment *really*

Pour demander à quelqu'un comment il va

Comment allez-vous? *How are you?*

Vous allez bien? *Are you well?*

(Comment) ça va? *How is it going?*

Je vais très bien. *Very well.*

Ça va bien. *(I'm) fine.*

Comme ci, comme ça. *So-so.*

Assez bien. *Fairly well.*

Je suis fatigué(e). *I am tired.*

Je suis un peu malade. *I am a little sick.*

Pas trop bien. *Not too well.*

Ça ne va pas mal. *I'm not feeling bad.*

Pour offrir, accepter et refuser quelque chose

Voulez-vous boire quelque chose? *Do you want to drink something?*

Je veux bien. *Gladly. Yes, thanks.*

Volontiers. *Gladly.*

S'il vous plaît. *Please.*

Oui, avec plaisir. *Yes, with pleasure.*

Oui, c'est gentil à vous. *Yes, that's nice of you.*

Merci. *No, thank you.*

Non, merci. *No, thank you.*

Je voudrais ... *I would like ...*

Verbes de préférence

adorer *to adore; to love*
aimer *to like; to love*
détester *to hate; to detest*

D'autres expressions utiles

Comment? *What (did you say)?*

est-ce que ... ? *(question marker)*

n'est-ce pas? *right? are you? don't they? etc.*

Comment est-ce qu'on écrit ... ? *How do you spell ... ?*

Comment trouvez-vous ... ? *What do you think of ... ?*

Qu'est-ce que vous aimez? *What do you like?*

Qu'est-ce que vous voulez? *What do you want?*

Vous êtes d'où? *Where are you from?*

Quelle bonne surprise! *What a good surprise!*

À votre santé! *(Here's) to your health!*

À la vôtre! *(Here's) to yours!*

Au fait ... *By the way ...*

Je ne sais pas. *I don't know.*

Je viens de ... *I come from ...*

... s'écrit ... *... is spelled ...*

même(s) *-self (-selves)*

moi aussi *me too*

moi non plus *me neither*

La famille

Buts communicatifs
Identifying family and friends
Sharing numerical information
Talking about your home

Structures utiles
L'article indéfini: **un, une** et **des**
Le verbe **avoir**
Les nombres (suite)
Les expressions **il y a** et **voilà**
Les adjectifs possessifs **mon, ton, notre** et **votre**
La négation + **un (une, des)**
La possession avec **de**
Les adjectifs possessifs **son** et **leur**

Culture
La langue et la culture
Les pronoms **tu** et **vous**
Pour gagner du temps

Une photo de ma famille

MARIE:	Avez-vous des frères ou des sœurs?°
CHRISTOPHE:	J'ai° un frère et une sœur.
MONIQUE:	J'ai une sœur, mais je n'ai pas de° frère.
PAUL:	Moi, je n'ai pas de frère ou de sœur.
MARIE:	Dans° ma famille il y a° cinq personnes. Ma sœur s'appelle° Chantal et mon frère s'appelle Robert. Mes parents s'appellent Bernard et Sophie.

Do you have any brothers or sisters? / I have

I don't have any

In / there are
My sister's name is

▶ **Et vous?**   Avez-vous des frères ou des sœurs?
Avez-vous une photo de votre famille?
Qui est sur la photo?°

Who is in the picture?

Conversation

L'arrivée à la gare

Lori Becker est une étudiante américaine qui vient en France pour passer un an° dans une famille française. Elle descend du train à la gare° Saint-Laud à Angers. Anne Martin et sa fille, Émilie, attendent° son arrivée.

    year

    railroad station

    are waiting for

MME MARTIN:	Mademoiselle Becker?
LORI:	Oui. Bonjour, Madame. Vous êtes bien Madame Martin?°
MME MARTIN:	Oui. Bonjour et bienvenue°, Mademoiselle. Vous êtes très fatiguée, sans doute°?
LORI:	Pas trop°. J'ai dormi° un peu dans le train.
MME MARTIN:	Mademoiselle Becker, voilà ma fille.
LORI:	Bonjour, tu t'appelles comment?
LA PETITE FILLE:	Émilie.
LORI:	Et tu as quel âge?°
	The child holds up her thumb and two fingers.
MME MARTIN:	Elle a trois ans.
LORI:	Elle est charmante.° Vous avez d'autres enfants°, Madame Martin?
MME MARTIN:	Oui, nous avons six enfants.
LORI:	Comment? Combien dites-vous?°
MME MARTIN:	Six.
LORI:	Mon Dieu°! Vraiment?
MME MARTIN:	Pourquoi? Qu'est-ce qu'il y a?°
LORI:	Euh ... rien°. J'aime beaucoup les enfants.

You're Mme Martin, aren't you?

welcome

probably

too much / I slept

And how old are you?

She's charming.

other children

How many do you say?

God

What's the matter?

nothing

▶ **Jouez ces rôles.** Role-play the conversation exactly as if you were Lori Becker and Mme Martin. Once you have practiced it several times, role-play the conversation using one partner's identity in place of Lori's.

Il y a un geste

Voilà. The open hand is extended, palm up, to emphasize that some fact is evident. **Voilà** is also used to conclude something that has been said or to express that that's how things are.

Why does Lori say **"Mon Dieu!"**?

a. She is swearing.
b. She is praying.
c. She is expressing surprise.

Why does Lori use **tu** with Émilie Martin?

a. They have met before and are good friends.
b. She is speaking to a child.
c. Lori considers Émilie an inferior.

La langue et la culture

Each language has its own unique way of expressing reality. The fact that French uses the verb **avoir** *(to have)* when expressing age, whereas English uses the verb *to be,* is only one of many examples that prove that languages are not copies of each other. Similarly, the expression **Mon Dieu!** *(Wow!)* is milder in French than its literal English equivalent *My God!* The French way is not right or wrong, nor is it more or less logical than its English counterpart.

Les pronoms tu et vous

French has two ways of saying *you.* The choice reflects the nature of the relationship, including degree of formality and respect. **Tu** is typically used when speaking to one's family and relatives as well as to close friends, fellow students, children, and animals. **Vous** is normally used when speaking to someone who does not meet the above criteria (e.g., in-laws, employers, teachers, or business acquaintances). It expresses a more formal relationship or a greater social distance than **tu.** In addition, **vous** is always used to refer to more than one person.

Visitors to French-speaking countries would be well advised to use **vous** even if first names are being used, unless they are invited to use the **tu** form. In the *Conversation,* Lori correctly uses **vous** with Madame Martin and **tu** with Émilie.

Pour gagner du temps
(To stall for time)

A helpful strategy for the language learner is to acquire and use certain expressions and gestures that allow him or her to "buy time" to think without destroying the conversational flow or without resorting to English. Like the cup of coffee we sip during a conversation to give us a chance to organize our thoughts, there are a number of useful expressions for "buying time" in French. The number one gap-filler is **euh,** which is the French equivalent of the English *uh* or *umm.*

VOCABULAIRE

Pour gagner du temps
(To stall for time)

alors	*then; therefore, so*	euh	*uh; umm*
ben	*well*	hein?	*huh?*
bon	*good*	mais ...	*but ...*
comment?	*what (did you say)?*	oui ...	*yes ...*
eh bien	*well then*	tiens!	*well, well!*
et ...	*and ...*	voyons	*let's see*

Euh rhymes with **deux. Ben** [bɛ] is derived from **bien.**

À vous. How would you respond to the following?

1. Comment s'appellent vos parents?
2. Vous avez des frères ou des sœurs?
3. (Si oui) Comment s'appellent-ils (elles)?
4. Où habitent-ils (elles)?

Entre amis

Des frères ou des sœurs?
1. Introduce yourself and tell what you can about yourself.
2. Find out what you can about your partner.
3. Find out if your partner has brothers or sisters.
4. If so, find out their names.

Prononciation

L'Accent et le rythme (suite)

■ Remember: When pronouncing French sentences, it is good practice to pay particular attention to the facts that: (1) French rhythm is even (just like counting), (2) syllables normally end in a vowel sound, and (3) the final syllable of a group of words is lengthened.

▶ Count before repeating each of the following expressions.

Review the *Pronunciation* section of Ch. 1.

un, deux, trois, quatre, cinq, SIX

Je suis a-mé-ri-CAIN.
Elle est cé-li-ba-TAIRE.
Vous tra-va-illez beau-COUP?

un, deux, trois, quatre, cinq, six, SEPT

Je m'a-ppelle Ka-rine As-PEL.
Vous ha-bi-tez à Pa-RIS?
Je n'aime pas beau-coup le VIN.

Les sons [e], [ɛ], [ə], [a], [wa]

■ The following words contain some important and very common vowel sounds.

▶ Practice saying these words after your instructor, paying particular attention to the highlighted vowel sound.

[e] • **é**crivez, z**é**ro, r**é**p**é**tez, **é**coutez, nationalit**é**, t**é**l**é**phone, divorc**é**
• ouvr**ez**, entr**ez**, ferm**ez**, ass**ez**, assey**ez**-vous, excus**ez**-moi
• présent**er**, habit**er**, écout**er**, arrêt**er**, commenc**er**, continu**er**
• **et**

[ɛ] • personne, professeur, hôtel, université, espagnol, elle, canadienne
    • crème, frère, chère, discrète
    • être, êtes
    • anglaise, française, célibataire, laide, certainement

[ə] • le, levez-vous, prenez, regardez, que, de, je, ne, votre santé, me

Note encoré, heuré, femmé, hommé, uné, amié, famillé, entré amis

[a] • la, allez, amie, américain, assez, matin, canadien, quatre, salut, d'accord
    • à, voilà

[wa] • François, moi, trois, voilà, Mademoiselle, au revoir, bonsoir
    • voyage

■ Now go back and look at how these sounds are spelled and in what kinds of letter combinations they appear. What patterns do you notice?

■ It is always particularly important to pronounce **la** [la] and **le** [lə] correctly since each marks a different gender, and the meaning of a word may depend on which is used.

la tour = *tower*	**la tour** Eiffel
le tour = *tour, turn*	**le Tour** de France

Buts
communicatifs

1 Identifying Family and Friends

—Je vous présente° mon amie, Anne Martin.   *I introduce to you*
  Elle a° une sœur qui habite près d'ici.   *has*
—Votre sœur, comment s'appelle-t-elle?
—Elle s'appelle Catherine.
—Et vous êtes d'où?
—Je suis de Nantes.
—Tiens! J'ai des cousins à Nantes.
—Comment s'appellent-ils?
—Ils s'appellent Dubois.

▶ **Et vous?** Présentez un(e) ami(e).

Remarque When you use **qui,** the verb that follows agrees with the person(s) to whom **qui** refers.

Elle a des cousins **qui habitent** à Nantes.

Arbre généalogique d'une famille française

Jean et Monique Martin — Marie et Georges Duhamel

Éric Bernard et Chantal — Michel — Pierre et Anne — Catherine et Alain Dubois

Christophe — Céline — David — Sylvie — Amélie — Benoît — Émilie — Nathalie — Stéphane

VOCABULAIRE

Une famille française

des parents	*parents; relatives*
un mari et une femme	*a husband and a wife*
un père et une mère	*a father and a mother*
un(e) enfant	*a child (male or female)*
un fils et une fille	*a son and a daughter*
un frère et une sœur	*a brother and a sister*
des grands-parents	*grandparents*
un grand-père	*a grandfather*
une grand-mère	*a grandmother*
des petits-enfants	*grandchildren*
un petit-fils et une petite-fille	*a grandson and a granddaughter*
un oncle et une tante	*an uncle and an aunt*
un neveu et une nièce	*a nephew and a niece*
un(e) cousin(e)	*a cousin (male or female)*
des beaux-parents	*stepparents (or in-laws)*
un beau-père	*a stepfather (or father-in-law)*
une belle-mère	*a stepmother (or mother-in-law)*
un beau-frère	*a brother-in-law*
une belle-sœur	*a sister-in-law*
un demi-frère	*a stepbrother*
une demi-sœur	*a stepsister*

Add **arrière-** before **petit** or **grand** to convey the meaning *great:* **un arrière-petit-fils; une arrière-grand-mère.**

Notes

1. Most plurals of nouns are formed by adding **-s.** In compound words for family members, an **-s** is added to both parts of the term: **des grands-pères, des belles-mères.**

2. The words **neveu** and **beau** form their plurals with an **-x: des neveux, des beaux-frères.**

3. The word **fils** is invariable in the plural: **des fils, des petits-fils.**

A. L'article indéfini: *un, une* et *des*

■ The French equivalent of the English article *a (an)* is **un** for masculine nouns and **une** for feminine nouns.

un frère	**un** train	**un** orangina
une sœur	**une** table	**une** limonade

■ The final **-n** of **un** is normally silent. Liaison is required when **un** precedes a vowel sound.

un [n]étudiant

■ The consonant **-n-** is always pronounced in the word **une.** If it precedes a vowel sound, it is linked to that vowel.

une femme   [yn fam]   *But:* une étudiante   [y ne ty djɑ̃t]

■ The plural of **un** and **une** is **des.**

singulier: un frère   une sœur
  pluriel: **des** frères   **des** sœurs

■ **Des** corresponds to the English *some* or *any.* However, these words are often omitted in English. **Des** is not omitted in French.

J'ai **des** amis à Paris.   *I have (some) friends in Paris.*

■ Liaison is required when an article precedes a vowel sound.

un [n]enfant	un [n]étudiant	un [n]homme
des [z]enfants	des [z]étudiants	des [z]hommes

■ In a series, the article *must* be repeated before each noun.

un homme et **une** femme	*a man and (a) woman*
une mère et **des** enfants	*a mother and (some) children*

1 **Présentations.** How would you introduce the following people?

Modèle: Mademoiselle Blondel / F / frère à New York
  Je vous présente Mademoiselle Blondel.
  Elle est française.
  Elle a un frère qui habite à New York.

Review nationalities on p. 18.

1. Madame Brooks / GB / sœur à Toronto
2. Mademoiselle Jones / USA / parents près de Chicago
3. Monsieur Callahan / CDN / frère à Milwaukee
4. Monsieur Lefont / B / fils près d'ici
5. Madame Perez / MEX / petits-enfants près d'El Paso
6. Mademoiselle Keita / SN / cousins à New York
7. un ami
8. une amie
9. votre père ou votre mère

Tout le monde
prend un café.

2 Quelque chose à boire? Order the following items.

Modèle: citron pressé
Je voudrais un citron pressé, s'il vous plaît.

Review the list of **boissons** on
p. 44

1. thé
2. café
3. bière
4. verre d'eau
5. jus d'orange
6. chocolat
7. coca
8. limonade
9. orangina
10. café crème

B. Le verbe *avoir*

J'ai des cousins à Marseille.
Tu as un(e) camarade de chambre?
Nous avons un neveu qui habite
près de Chicago.

I have cousins in Marseille.
Do you have a roommate?
*We have a nephew who lives near
Chicago.*

avoir *(to have)*			
j'	**ai**	nous	**avons**
tu	**as**	vous	**avez**
il/elle/on	**a**	ils/elles	**ont**

■ Liaison is required in **on a, nous avons, vous avez, ils ont,** and **elles ont.**
on [n]a
nous [z]avons

■ Do not confuse **ils ont** and **ils sont**. In liaison, the **-s** in **ils** is pronounced [z] and is linked to the following verb.

> **Ils [z]ont** des enfants.   *They **have** children.*
> *But:* **Ils sont** charmants.   *They **are** charming.*

■ Use **Je n'ai pas de (d') ...** to say *I don't have a ... or I don't have any ...*

> **Je n'ai pas de** père.   *I don't have a father.*
> **Je n'ai pas de** frère.   *I don't have any brothers.*
> **Je n'ai pas d'**enfants.   *I don't have any children.*

3 **Un recensement** *(A census).* The following people are being inter-viewed by the census taker. Follow the model with a partner to complete each interview.

MODÈLE: Mademoiselle Messin / 2 sœurs, 0 frère / Jeanne et Perrine (frères ou sœurs?)

> LE RECENSEUR: **Avez-vous des frères ou des sœurs, Mademoiselle?**
> MLLE MESSIN: **J'ai deux sœurs mais je n'ai pas de frère.**
> LE RECENSEUR: **Comment s'appellent-elles?**
> MLLE MESSIN: **Elles s'appellent Jeanne et Perrine.**

1. Monsieur Dubois / 2 frères, 0 sœur / Henri et Luc (frères ou sœurs?)
2. Madame Bernard / 1 enfant: 1 fils, 0 fille / Christophe (enfants?)
3. Monsieur Marot / 2 enfants: 1 fils, 1 fille / Pascal et Hélène (enfants?)
4. vos parents (enfants?)
5. votre meilleur(e) ami(e) (frères ou sœurs?)
6. vos grands-parents (petits-enfants?)
7. vous (?)

Ils ont une petite-fille
qui s'appelle Lara.

La famille de David. Use the genealogical chart on page 58 to create sentences describing David's family ties.

MODÈLE: **David a des parents qui s'appellent Pierre et Anne.**

 # Entre amis

Ta famille

1. Find out if your partner has brothers or sisters.
2. If so, find out their names.
3. Find out where they live.
4. Find out if your partner has children or other family members living with him/her.
5. If so, find out their names.
6. Introduce your partner to another person. Tell as much as you can about your partner and his/her family.

2 Sharing Numerical Information

Combien de personnes y a-t-il
dans ta famille, Christelle?

Il y a quatre personnes:
mes parents, ma
sœur et moi.

Quel âge ont tes parents?

Ils ont cinquante
ans et quarante-
sept ans.

Quel âge a ta sœur?
Quel âge as-tu?
En quelle année es-tu née?

Elle a dix-huit ans.
J'ai vingt ans.
Je suis née°   *I was born*
en mille neuf cent
quatre-vingt deux.

▶ **Et vous?** Combien de personnes y a-t-il dans votre famille?
Quel âge ont les membres de votre famille? Quel âge avez-vous?

Remarques

1. The verb **avoir** is used when asking or giving someone's age.

   Quel âge **a** ta camarade de chambre?   *How old is your roommate?*
   Quel âge **a** ton petit ami?   *How old is your boyfriend?*

2. In inversion, remember to insert a **-t-** before the singular forms **il, elle,** and **on.**

   Quel âge ont-elles?   *How old are they?*
   But: Quel âge a**-t-**elle?   *How old is she?*

3. The word **an(s)** must be used when giving someone's age.

   J'ai vingt et un **ans.**   *I am twenty-one.*

**VOCABULAIRE
À RETENIR**
**un(e) camarade de
chambre** *roommate*
un petit ami *boyfriend*
une petite amie *girlfriend*

C. Les nombres (suite)

Review the numbers 0–29 on p. 3

30	trente
31	trente et un
32	trente-deux
33	trente-trois
	etc.
40	quarante
41	quarante et un
42	quarante-deux
43	quarante-trois
	etc.
50	cinquante
51	cinquante et un
52	cinquante-deux
53	cinquante-trois
	etc.
60	soixante
61	soixante et un
62	soixante-deux
63	soixante-trois
	etc.
70	soixante-dix
71	soixante et onze
72	soixante-douze
73	soixante-treize
74	soixante-quatorze
75	soixante-quinze

Numbers from 70 to 99 show a different pattern: 70 = 60 + 10; 80 = 4 × 20; 90 = 80 + 10.

76	soixante-seize
77	soixante-dix-sept
78	soixante-dix-huit
79	soixante-dix-neuf
80	quatre-vingts
81	quatre-vingt-un
82	quatre-vingt-deux
83	quatre-vingt-trois
	etc.
90	quatre-vingt-dix
91	quatre-vingt-onze
92	quatre-vingt-douze
	etc.
100	cent
101	cent un
200	deux cents
1.000	mille
1.999	mille neuf cent quatre-vingt-dix-neuf
2.000	deux mille
2.004	deux mille quatre
100.000	cent mille
100.000.000	un million
1.000.000.000	un milliard

Numbers above 101 repeat the same pattern: **cent vingt *et* un, cent quatre-vingt-un, deux cent vingt *et* un,** etc.

■ All numbers are invariable except **un.** Remember to replace the number **un** with **une** before a feminine noun, even in a compound number.

un oncle	trois oncles	vingt et un cousins
une tante	trois tantes	**vingt et une** cousines

■ When numbers from 1 to 10 stand alone, the final consonants of **un, deux,** and **trois** are silent, but all others are pronounced. The **-x** at the end of **six** and **dix** is pronounced [s].

	un	deux	trois				
But:	quatre	cinq	six	sept	huit	neuf	dix

■ Certain numbers have a different pronunciation when they precede a noun:

- The final consonant of **six, huit,** and **dix** is not pronounced before a consonant.

  six personnes   huit jours   dix verres

- When the following noun begins with a vowel sound, the final consonant is always pronounced and linked to the noun. Note that with **quatre,** both final consonants are linked and the final **-e** is not pronounced.

un [n]homme	cinq [k]hommes	huit [t]hommes
deux [z]hommes	six [z]hommes	neuf [f]hommes
trois [z]hommes	sept [t]hommes	dix [z]hommes
quatre [tR]hommes		vingt [t]hommes

- The **-f** in **neuf** is pronounced as [v] only before the words **ans** *(years)* and **heures** *(hours).*

	neuf [v]ans	neuf [v]heures
But:	neuf [f]enfants	neuf [f]hommes

- The final **-t** in **vingt** is silent when the number stands alone, but is pronounced in the compound numbers built on it.

vingt	[vɛ̃]
vingt et un	[vɛ̃ te ɛ̃]
vingt-deux	[vɛ̃t dø]

■ For numbers ending in 1, from 21 to 71, **et** is used. From 81 to 101 **et** is not used.

vingt **et** un   *But:* quatre-vingt-un

■ **Vingt** and **cent** do not add an **-s** if they are *followed* by a number.

quatre-vingt**s** personnes	*But:*	quatre-vingt-un
trois cent**s** personnes	*But:*	trois cent cinq

■ **Mille** never adds an **-s.**

mille personnes   deux **mille** personnes

■ The words **million** and **milliard** are nouns and take an **s** in the plural. If they are followed by another noun, **de** is inserted between the nouns.

deux millions d'euros

Note In France, commas and periods used with numbers are the reverse of the system used in North America.

L'état a besoin de **2.000.000,00** d'euros. (deux millions)

■ There are five pairs of numbers in a French telephone number: **02.42.83.21.14.** The first pair indicates the general area of France.

Les numéros de téléphone. Pronounce the following phone numbers.

MODÈLE: 02.81.88.40.01
              **zéro deux / quatre-vingt-un / quatre-vingt-huit / quarante /
              zéro un**

1. 02.41.93.21.80
2. 04.77.63.06.97
3. 04.42.08.98.89
4. 02.31.86.15.96
5. 04.71.83.61.91
6. 04.67.85.76.90
7. 05.61.10.99.02
8. 02.51.81.95.12
9. 03.88.19.82.43
10. 04.78.87.03.92

 Parlez-moi de votre famille *(Tell me about your family).* Describe the people listed below. Use the model as a guide. If you don't have a brother, etc., say so.

MODÈLE: un frère
              J'ai un frère qui s'appelle Bill.
              Il habite à Boston.
              Il est grand et assez beau.
              Il a vingt-trois ans.

1. une sœur
2. un frère
3. un oncle
4. une tante
5. des cousins
6. une cousine
7. un grand-père ou une grand-mère
8. des parents

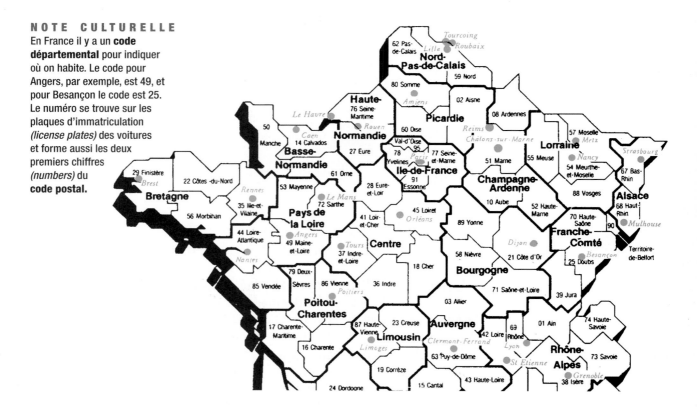

7 **Codes postaux.** The map above shows major cities and the first two numbers of the zip code for several French **départements.** Give the general zip code for the following cities.

Modèle: Nantes
Le code postal pour Nantes est quarante-quatre mille (44000).

1. Dijon
2. Amiens
3. Tours
4. Besançon
5. Angers
6. Le Mans
7. Orléans
8. Nantes
9. Paris
10. Brest
11. Rouen
12. Strasbourg

D. Les expressions *il y a* et *voilà*

Voilà la famille Laplante.
    Il y a combien de personnes dans la famille Laplante?
    Il y a quatre personnes.
    Il y a combien de garçons et **combien de** filles?
    Il y a deux filles mais **il n'y a pas de** garçon.

■ **Voilà** can mean either *there is (are)* or *here is (are)*. **Il y a** means *there is (are)*. While **voilà** and **il y a** are both translated *there is* or *there are* in English, they are used quite differently.

■ **Voilà** and **voici** *(here is, here are)* point something out. They bring it to another person's attention. There is usually an accompanying physical movement—a nod of the head, a gesture of the hand toward the person or object, or a pointing of the finger to identify a specific object.

    Voici mon fils et ma fille.   *Here are my son and daughter.*
    Voilà ma voiture.   *There's my car.*

■ **Il y a** simply states that something exists or tells how many there are.

    Il y a un livre sur la table.   *There is a book on the table.*
    Il y a quatre filles et deux garçons   *There are four girls and two boys in the*
    dans la famille Martin.   *Martin family.*

■ The negative of **il y a un (une, des)** is **il n'y a pas de.**

    Il n'y a pas de voiture ici.   *There aren't any cars here.*

Attention   Do not use **de** if **il n'y a pas** is followed by a number.

    Il n'y a pas trois voitures dans le   *There aren't three cars in the garage;*
    garage; il y a quatre voitures.   *there are four cars.*

■ There are several ways to use **il y a** in a question.

    Il y a un livre sur la table?
    Est-ce qu'il y a un livre sur la table?   *Is there a book on the table?*
    Y a-t-il un livre sur la table?

■ **Il y a** is often used with **combien de.**

    Il y a combien de garçons?
    Combien de garçons **est-ce qu'il y a?**
    Combien de garçons **y a-t-il?**

8 **Lori parle avec Anne Martin.** Complete the following sentences using either **il y a** or **voilà.**

MODÈLE: <u>Voilà</u> ma fille Émilie.

1. _____ deux enfants dans votre famille?
2. Non, Mademoiselle, _____ six enfants.
3. _____ une photo de ma famille.
4. _____ ma mère. Elle est jolie, n'est-ce pas?
5. _____ combien de filles dans votre famille?
6. Où sont-elles? Ah! _____ vos filles!

9 **À vous.** Answer the following questions as factually as possible.

1. Quel âge avez-vous?
2. Combien de personnes y a-t-il dans votre famille?
3. Quel âge ont les membres de votre famille?
4. Combien d'étudiants y a-t-il dans votre classe de français? Combien d'hommes et combien de femmes y a-t-il?
5. Quel âge a votre professeur de français? (Imaginez!)
6. Combien d'oncles et combien de tantes avez-vous? Quel âge ont-ils?

E. Les adjectifs possessifs *mon, ton, notre* et *votre*

—Comment s'appellent **tes** parents?
—**Mes** parents s'appellent Marcel et Jacqueline.
—Combien d'enfants y a-t-il dans **ta** famille?
—Il y a trois enfants dans **ma** famille: deux garçons et une fille.
—Quel âge a **ton** frère? Quel âge a **ta** sœur?
—**Mon** frère a dix-huit ans et **ma** sœur a douze ans.
—Où habitent **vos** grands-parents?
—**Nos** grands-parents habitent à Saumur.

adjectifs possessifs						
en anglais	masculin		féminin		pluriel (m. et f.)	
my	**mon**		**ma**		**mes**	
your	**ton**	père	**ta**	mère	**tes**	parents
our	**notre**		**notre**		**nos**	
your	**votre**		**votre**		**vos**	

■ Possessive adjectives agree in gender and number with the nouns they modify (the "possessions"). **Notre** and **votre** are used for both masculine and feminine singular nouns.

Denise, **ton** père est gentil.	*Denise, your father is nice.*
Alain, **ta** mère est gentille aussi!	*Alain, your mother is nice also!*
Nathalie, **tes** parents sont très gentils.	*Nathalie, your parents are very nice.*

■ In the singular, **ma** and **ta** become **mon** and **ton** when used directly before a feminine word beginning with a vowel sound.

ma meilleure amie   *But:* **mon** amie
ta tante   *But:* **ton** autre tante

■ Liaison occurs if the word following **mon, ton, mes, tes, nos,** or **vos** begins with a vowel sound.

     mon petit ami   vos bons amis
But: mon [n]ami   vos [z]amis

■ As with **quatre,** the final **-e** of **notre** and **votre** is not pronounced before a vowel sound, but the final consonants are linked to the next word.

notre [tR]ami

10 **Qui?** Try to identify people from among your friends and relatives who "fit" the following questions. Use possessive adjectives in each response. Be sure that verbs agree with subjects, and that adjectives agree with nouns.

Modèle: Qui chante bien?
Mes parents chantent bien.   ou   **Notre professeur chante bien.**

1. Qui est grand?
2. Qui parle français?
3. Qui ne skie pas?
4. Qui adore le sport?
5. Qui n'aime pas beaucoup la bière?
6. Qui aime être étudiant(e)?

11 **À vous.** Show a real (or imaginary) picture of your family and point out parents, brothers, sisters, cousins, uncles, and aunts. Give each person's age as well.

Modèle: **Voilà ma sœur, Kristen. Elle a seize ans.**

Entre amis

Dans ta famille

Use possessive adjectives whenever possible.

1. Ask your partner how many people there are in his/her family.
2. Find out the names of his/her brother, sister, etc.
3. Find out how old they are.
4. Find out where they live.
5. Ask if his/her brother, sister, etc. speaks French or studies French.
6. What else can you find out about his/her family members?

3 Talking about Your Home

Habitez-vous dans une maison° ou dans
un appartement°, Lori?   *house*
    Nous habitons dans une maison.   *apartment*

Et combien de pièces° y a-t-il dans votre   *rooms*
maison?
    Il y a sept pièces.

Et qu'est-ce qu'il y a chez vous°?   *at your house*
    Chez moi° il y a ...   *at my house*

Bureau can mean either *desk* or *office.* The teacher's office = **le bureau du professeur. Chambre** normally implies *bedroom,* not *room* in general.

... dans ma salle de séjour.

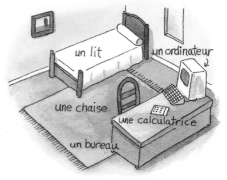

... dans ma chambre.

... dans ma cuisine.

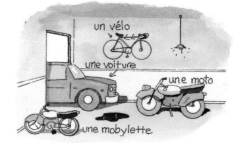

... dans mon garage.

▶ **Et vous?**   Qu'est-ce qu'il y a chez vous?

Les renseignements *(Information).* Olivier is giving some information about people in his neighborhood. Help him to complete the sentences. Use the verb **avoir** and a number. Where no number is indicated, use **un, une,** or **des** as appropriate.

> **Modèle:** Les Dufoix / deux enfants / chat
> **Les Dufoix ont deux enfants et un chat.**

1. Charles / radio antique
2. Je / enfants extraordinaires
3. Les Dubois / trois télévisions / stéréo / ordinateur
4. Madame Martin / mari / six enfants
5. Nous / petit appartement / voiture
6. Mes grands-parents / grande maison / quatre chambres
7. Les Martin / chat / chien / deux réfrigérateurs / cuisinière à gaz / lave-vaisselle
8. Madame Davis / voiture japonaise / vélo français

F. La négation + *un (une, des)*

Review the negative of il y a, p. 67.

■ After a negation, indefinite articles **(un, une, des)** usually become **de (d')**.

Vous avez **un** ordinateur?	Non, je n'ai pas **d'**ordinateur.
Vous avez **une** voiture?	Non, je n'ai pas **de** voiture.
Vous avez **des** frères ou **des** sœurs?	Non, je n'ai pas **de** frère ou **de** sœur.
Y a-t-il **un** lave-vaisselle?	Non, il n'y a pas **de** lave-vaisselle.

Note   This rule does not apply after **être.**

> Christophe n'est pas **un** enfant.
> La voiture n'est pas **une** Ford.
> Ce ne sont pas **des** amis.

■ Also, definite articles **(le, la, l', les)** and possessive adjectives (**mon, ma, mes,** etc.) do not change after a negation.

> Je n'aime pas **le** thé.   Mon frère n'aime pas **notre** chien.

■ When contradicting a negative statement or question, use **si** instead of **oui.**

Il n'y a pas de sandwichs ici.	**Si,** il y a des sandwichs.
Vous n'avez pas d'ordinateur?	**Si,** j'ai un ordinateur.
Vous n'aimez pas le café?	**Si,** j'aime le café.

 Un riche et un pauvre. Guy has everything, but Philippe has practically nothing. Explain how they differ.

> **Modèle:** voiture
> **Guy a une voiture, mais Philippe n'a pas de voiture.**   ☆

1. appartement	4. ordinateur
2. machine à laver	5. amis
3. petite amie	6. chien

14 **Bavardages** *(Gossip).* Someone has made up gossip about you and your neighbors. Correct these falsehoods.

> **MODÈLE:** Monsieur Dupont a des filles.
> **Mais non! Il n'a pas de fille.**

1. Marie a un petit ami.
2. Il y a une moto dans votre garage.
3. Vous détestez le café.
4. Jean-Yves a des enfants.
5. Christophe et Alice ont un chien.
6. Votre voiture est une Renault.

15 **As-tu . . . ?** Your partner will interview you according to the model. If you really do have the item in question, say so. If not, give a negative answer and then name something that you do have.

> **MODÈLE:** une voiture
> **VOTRE PARTENAIRE:** **As-tu une voiture?**
> **VOUS:** **Non, je n'ai pas de voiture mais j'ai une moto.**

1. une maison	4. un ordinateur
2. un chien	5. des amis qui habitent à Paris
3. un cousin à Lyon	6. un frère (une sœur) qui parle français

16 **Une diseuse de bonne aventure.** A fortune teller has made the following statements about you. Affirm or deny them. Be careful to use **si** if you wish to contradict a negative statement.

> **MODÈLE:** Vous n'avez pas de frère.
> **Si, j'ai un frère (des frères).** ou
> **Oui, c'est vrai, je n'ai pas de frère.**

1. Vous n'avez pas de sœur.
2. Vous n'habitez pas dans un appartement.
3. Vous n'avez pas de stéréo.
4. Vous n'étudiez pas beaucoup.
5. Le professeur n'est pas gentil.
6. Vous n'aimez pas étudier le français.

VOCABULAIRE

Les pièces d'une maison

un bureau	*office*	les toilettes	*restroom*
une chambre	*bedroom*	un salon	*living room*
une cuisine	*kitchen*	une salle de séjour	*den; living room*
une salle à manger	*dining room*	un sous-sol	*basement*
une salle de bain	*bathroom*	une véranda	*porch*

À vous. Answer the following questions.

1. Où habitez-vous?
2. Combien de pièces y a-t-il chez vous?
3. Quelles pièces est-ce qu'il y a?
4. Y a-t-il un fauteuil dans votre chambre?
5. Combien de chaises y a-t-il dans votre chambre?
6. Y a-t-il un chien ou un chat dans votre maison?
7. Qu'est-ce qu'il y a dans votre chambre?
8. Qu'est-ce qu'il y a dans le garage du professeur? (Imaginez!)

Entre amis

Une interview

1. Find out where your partner lives.
2. Find out how many rooms s/he has.
3. Ask if s/he has a basement or a porch.
4. Find out if your partner has a refrigerator in his/her room.
5. Find out if s/he has a TV in his/her room.
6. If so, ask if s/he watches television often.
7. Try to find one additional item which your partner has and one item which s/he does not have.
8. Turn to another person and gossip about your partner. Tell what you found out.

G. La possession avec *de*

C'est le mari **de** Mme Martin.	*It's Mme Martin's husband.*
Ce n'est pas la maison **de** René.	*It's not René's house.*
C'est la maison **des** parents **de** René.	*It's René's parents' house.*

■ The preposition **de (d')** is used to indicate possession or relationship. French has no possessive *-'s* ending: *Marie's sister* has to be expressed in French as *the sister of Marie*.

la sœur **de** Marie	*Marie's sister*
la voiture **d'**Alain	*Alain's car*

■ If the "owner" is indicated with a proper name, **de (d')** is used without article or possessive adjective. When the word referring to the "owner" is not a proper name, an article or a possessive adjective precedes it: *The grandmother's room* has to be expressed as *the room of the grandmother*.

la chambre de **la** grand-mère	*the grandmother's room*
la moto de **mon** ami	*my friend's motorcycle*

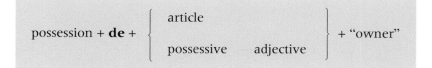

possession + **de** + { article / possessive adjective } + "owner"

■ The preposition **de** contracts with the articles **le** and **les,** but there is no contraction with the articles **la** and **l'**.

Remember that **de l'** could be masculine or feminine.

de + le	→	**du**	du professeur
de + les	→	**des**	des étudiants
de + la	→	**de la**	de la femme
de + l'	→	**de l'**	de l'enfant

C'est une photo **du** professeur.   *It's a picture of the teacher.*
C'est la maison **des** parents d'Éric.   *It's Éric's parents' house.*
C'est le chat **de la** mère de Céline.   *It's Céline's mother's cat.*
C'est la voiture **de l'**oncle de Pascal.   *It's Pascal's uncle's car.*

18 **J'ai trouvé une radio** (*I found a radio*). A number of objects have been found. Ask a question to try to identify the owners. Your partner will answer negatively and will decide who *is* the owner.

Remember to use only **de (d')** with a proper name.

MODÈLE: J'ai trouvé une radio. (Jeanne)
               VOUS: **J'ai trouvé une radio. C'est la radio de Jeanne?**
   VOTRE PARTENAIRE: **Non, ce n'est pas la radio de Jeanne. C'est la radio de Kevin.**

1. J'ai trouvé une voiture. (Madame Dufour)
2. J'ai trouvé une radio. (professeur)
3. J'ai trouvé un chat. (Karine)
4. J'ai trouvé une moto. (l'ami de Michèle)
5. J'ai trouvé un chien. (les parents de Denis)
6. J'ai trouvé une calculatrice. (Frédérique)
7. J'ai trouvé un vélo. (la sœur de Sophie)

19 **Nos possessions.** Complete the following sentences by filling in the blanks.

1. Le vélo _de_ Laurence est dans le garage.
2. La voiture _du_ père _d'_ Anne est bleue.
3. La photo _de l'_ oncle et _de la_ tante _de_ Guy est sur le bureau _des_ grands-parents _de_ Guy.
4. Le chat _du_ frère _de_ Chantal est sur le lit _des_ parents _de_ Chantal.
5. Où est la calculatrice _de la_ sœur _de_ Sandrine?
6. C'est la stéréo _des_ enfants _du_ professeur.
7. La moto _de_ mon frère est dans notre garage.

20 **Où est-ce?** Patrick's family has a number of possessions. Ask where each item is.

MODÈLE: La sœur de Patrick a un vélo. **Où est le vélo de la sœur de Patrick?**

1. Les sœurs de Patrick ont une télévision.
2. Le frère de Patrick a une voiture.
3. L'oncle de Patrick a un chien.
4. Les cousins de Patrick ont une stéréo.
5. Les enfants de Patrick ont un ordinateur.
6. La cousine de Patrick a un appartement.
7. Les parents de Patrick ont une voiture allemande.
8. Le père de Patrick a un bureau.
9. La tante de Patrick a un petit chat.
10. Les parents de Patrick ont une belle maison.

H. Les adjectifs possessifs *son* et *leur*

As-tu une photo de la famille de Léa?	Voilà une photo de **sa** famille.
Où est le père de Léa?	Voilà **son** père.
Où est la mère de Léa?	Voilà **sa** mère.
Où sont les grands-parents de Léa?	Voilà **ses** grands-parents.
Où est la fille de M. et Mme Dupont?	Voilà **leur** fille. C'est Léa!
Où sont les cousins des Dupont?	Voilà **leurs** cousins.

■ **Son, sa,** and **ses** can mean either *his* or *her.* As with **mon, ma,** and **mes,** the choice of form depends on whether the "possession" is masculine or feminine, singular or plural. It makes no difference what the gender of the "owner" is.

son lit	*his bed* or *her bed*
sa chambre	*his room* or *her room*
ses chaises	*his chairs* or *her chairs*

■ **Leur** and **leurs** mean *their* and are used when there is more than one "owner." Both forms are used for either masculine or feminine "possessions."

leur lit   **leur** chambre   **leurs** lits   **leurs** chambres

Note Be sure not to use **ses** when you mean **leurs.**

ses parents	*his parents* or *her parents*
leurs parents	*their parents*

■ In the singular, **sa** becomes **son** when used directly before a feminine word beginning with a vowel sound.

sa meilleure amie   *But:* **son** amie

■ Liaison occurs if the word following **son, ses,** or **leurs** begins with a vowel sound.

	son petit ami	ses bons amis	leurs parents
But:	son [n]ami	ses [z]amis	leurs [z]amis

■ Sometimes the identity of the "owner" would be unclear if a possessive adjective were used. In such cases, it is better to use the possessive construction with **de.**

Robert et Marie habitent avec **sa** mère.   *(Robert's mother? Marie's mother?)*

Robert et Marie habitent avec **la** mère **de Marie.**   *(clearly Marie's mother)*

Synthèse: les adjectifs possessifs				
pronom	masculin	féminin	pluriel (m. et f.)	
je	**mon**	**ma**	**mes**	*my*
tu	**ton**	**ta**	**tes**	*your*
il/elle/on	**son**	**sa**	**ses**	*his/her*
nous	**notre**	**notre**	**nos**	*our*
vous	**votre**	**votre**	**vos**	*your*
ils/elles	**leur**	**leur**	**leurs**	*their*

21 **La chambre de qui?** Clarify the identity of the "owner" in each of the following phrases by completing the following expressions with the appropriate form of de + *article défini.*

MODÈLE: sa chambre. La chambre de qui?   La chambre __du__ frère de Marc.

1. leur photo. La photo de qui?   La photo ____ enfants de ma tante.
2. son nom. Le nom de qui?   Le nom ____ jeune fille.
3. sa moto. La moto de qui?   La moto ____ mari d'Anne.
4. leurs livres. Les livres de qui?   Les livres ____ étudiants.
5. son chien. Le chien de qui?   Le chien ____ oncle d'Isabelle.
6. sa maison. La maison de qui?   La maison ____ ami de Laurent.
7. ses amies. Les amies de qui?   Les amies ____ sœur de Denis.
8. son chat. Le chat de qui?   Le chat ____ petite amie de Jean-Luc.
9. son bureau. Le bureau de qui?   Le bureau ____ professeur.

Comment s'appellent leurs filles?

Be careful to distinguish between **son/sa/ses** and **leur(s)** when asking these questions.

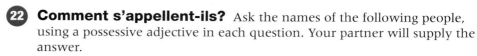

22 **Comment s'appellent-ils?** Ask the names of the following people, using a possessive adjective in each question. Your partner will supply the answer.

Modèles: le cousin de Nathalie? (Stéphane)
> **VOUS:** **Comment s'appelle son cousin?**
> **VOTRE PARTENAIRE:** **Il s'appelle Stéphane.**

les cousines de Nathalie? (Christelle et Sandrine)
> **VOUS:** **Comment s'appellent ses cousines?**
> **VOTRE PARTENAIRE:** **Elles s'appellent Christelle et Sandrine.**

1. le père de Nathalie? (Michel)
2. la sœur d'Éric? (Isabelle)
3. la mère d'Éric et d'Isabelle? (Monique)
4. les frères de Nathalie? (Christophe et Sébastien)
5. les sœurs de Nathalie? (Sylvie et Céline)
6. le chien de Nathalie? (Fidèle)
7. les grands-parents de Nathalie? (Marie et Pierre Coifard; Louis et Jeanne Dupuis)
8. les parents de votre meilleur(e) ami(e)?
9. les amis de vos parents?

23 **À vous.** Ask and answer the questions using possessive adjectives.

MODÈLE: Où est la maison de votre ami(e)?
Sa maison est à Denver.

1. Comment s'appelle votre meilleur(e) ami(e)?
2. Quel âge a votre ami(e)?
3. Combien de personnes y a-t-il dans la famille de votre ami(e)?
4. Comment s'appellent les parents de votre ami(e)?
5. Où habitent les parents de votre ami(e)?
6. Qu'est-ce qu'il y a dans la maison des parents de votre ami(e)?

Entre amis

Ton (ta) meilleur(e) ami(e)

1. Find out the name of your partner's best friend.
2. Find out where that friend lives.
3. Find out three items of information about that friend's home or possessions.
4. Find out three items of information about that friend's family, e.g., names, ages, activities, etc.

Intégration

Révision

A **Ma chambre.** Décrivez votre chambre. Qu'est-ce qu'il y a dans votre chambre?

B **La maison.** Décrivez la maison ou l'appartement de vos parents ou de vos amis. Qu'est-ce qu'il y a dans leur maison?

C **Mon professeur.** Imagine the home, garage, etc. of your French teacher. Make up five different sentences to state what s/he has or does not have.

MODÈLE: **Il y a une moto dans son garage.**

D **Trouvez quelqu'un qui ...** Interview your classmates in French to find someone who ...

MODÈLE: speaks French
Est-ce que tu parles français?

1. has a computer
2. has no brothers or sisters
3. has a dog or a cat or a fish
4. likes children a lot
5. is 21 or older
6. has a sister named Nicole
7. has a brother named Christopher
8. lives in an apartment
9. has grandparents who live in another state or province

À vous. Answer the following questions.

1. Combien de personnes y a-t-il dans votre famille?
2. Comment s'appellent deux de vos ami(e)s?
3. Où habitent-ils?
4. Quel âge ont-ils?
5. Sont-ils étudiants? Si oui, ont-ils une chambre à l'université? Étudient-ils le français ou une autre langue?
6. Avez-vous des amis qui ont un appartement? Si oui, qu'est-ce qu'il y a dans leur appartement?
7. Avez-vous un ami qui est marié? Si oui, comment s'appelle sa femme? Quel âge a-t-elle?
8. Avez-vous une amie qui est mariée? Si oui, comment s'appelle son mari? Quel âge a-t-il?
9. Avez-vous des amis qui ont des enfants? Si oui, combien d'enfants ont-ils? Comment s'appellent leurs enfants? Quel âge ont-ils?

Pas de problème!

Preparation for the video:
1. Video worksheet in the *Cahier d'activités*
2. CD-ROM, *Module 1*

Complete the following activity if you have watched video *Module 1.* Answer the following questions.

1. Comment s'appellent les quatre personnes qui jouent au tennis?
2. Comment s'appelle l'amie de Marie-Christine?
3. Qui est la cousine de René?
4. Comment s'appelle le film d'aventures?
5. Comment s'appelle le mélodrame?
6. Quel film est-ce que Marie-Christine préfère?

Lecture I

You may wish to consult the vocabulary on page 72 when labeling the rooms.

A **Ma maison idéale.** Draw a sketch of a home that would be ideal for you. Then label each of the rooms.

B **Étude du vocabulaire.** Study the following sentences and choose the English words that correspond to the French words in bold print: *square meters, fireplace, planted with trees, in new condition, winter, landscaped lot, approximately, stone, in good taste, on one level, roof, country, house, set up/ready-to-use.*

1. Le **pavillon** est situé à la **campagne** à **environ** 30 kilomètres de Paris.
2. Près de la maison il y a un jardin **arboré** et un beau **terrain paysager** de 300 **mètres carrés.**
3. En **hiver,** s'il fait froid, il y a une belle **cheminée** en **pierre** dans la salle de séjour.
4. La cuisine est **aménagée** et équipée **avec goût.**
5. La **toiture** de la maison est **en état neuf.**
6. Les personnes handicapées n'ont pas de problème avec une maison de **plain-pied.**

C **Les pièces.** Read the ads in order to:

1. identify the number of rooms in each home, and
2. make a list of the rooms that are mentioned.

MAISONS À VENDRE

CADRE EXCEPTIONNEL

Belle maison récente, agréable séjour-salon en L 45 m² environ, cuisine aménagée équipée, 3 chambres, belle salle de bain, garage et jardin, mérite votre visite !

ELLE VOUS SÉDUIRA

Aux portes de Cholet, agréable pavillon indépendant sur 500 m² de terrain, cuisine aménagée équipée, beau séjour-salon avec cheminée, 3 chambres, garage 2 voitures et jardin aménagé avec goût.

DE TOUTE BEAUTÉ

Le charme de la campagne à 10 mn de Cholet, belle cuisine aménagée équipée, vaste pièce de réception 90 m² avec superbe cheminée en pierre, salon d'hiver parfaitement exposé, 4 chambres, 2 s. de b., bureau, grand garage, 1 700 m² de terrain paysager, aménagement de goût et de qualité !

EXCEPTIONNELLE

Plain-pied indépendant, séjour-salon, 2 chambres, toiture état neuf, garage et jardin arboré. Affaire à saisir !

D **Inférence.** Reread the ads to try to determine the following information. Be ready to justify your answers by quoting the reading.

1. the newest home
2. the biggest home
3. the largest lot
4. the home that has been remodeled
5. the name of the closest French city
6. the home you would choose and why

E **À discuter.** Aimez-vous ces maisons? Pourquoi ou pourquoi pas?

F **Comparaisons culturelles.** What similarities or differences between French homes and those of your country can you infer from what you have read?

Lecture II

A **Étude du vocabulaire.** Study the following sentences and choose the English words that correspond to the French words in bold print: *week, live, birth, today, new, is able to, more and more, one out of two.*

1. La **naissance** d'un enfant est une joie pour la famille.
2. Une personne bilingue **peut** parler deux langues.
3. Il y a sept jours dans une **semaine.**
4. **Un** étudiant **sur deux** est un homme.
5. Le **nouveau** professeur est charmant.
6. **Aujourd'hui,** il y a **de plus en plus** d'étudiants qui **vivent** sur le campus.

B **Parcourez la lecture** *(Skim the reading).* Skim the following reading to identify:

1. three types of families
2. the French words for *maternity leave, public day care,* and *nursery school.*

La Famille

À quel âge se marient-ils? L'âge légal du mariage est fixé à dix-huit ans et une jeune fille peut se marier à quinze ans avec l'accord de ses parents. Mais les jeunes se marient de plus en plus tard[1].

	hommes	*femmes*
en 1968	25 ans	23 ans
aujourd'hui	30 ans	28 ans

(d'après le Quid)

De nouveaux modèles de la famille. Le modèle traditionnel de la famille avec un couple marié et des enfants issus du mariage coexiste de plus en plus avec des modèles nouveaux. Avec le développement de la cohabitation il y a une augmentation du nombre des enfants hors mariage[2]: près de 40% des naissances aujourd'hui. Le nombre des divorces (un divorce sur trois mariages en France et un sur deux à Paris) augmente le nombre des familles monoparentales: 9% des enfants vivent avec un seul[3] de leurs parents. Les remariages multiplient les situations où des enfants vivent avec d'autres enfants issus d'un ou de plusieurs[4] mariages précédents: 11% des enfants vivent dans des familles recomposées. *(d'après Francoscopie)*

Si la mère travaille. Il y a, en France, des conditions qui facilitent la situation de la femme qui continue de travailler après[5] la naissance de son enfant. La femme qui travaille peut avoir un congé de maternité où 84% de son salaire est rémunéré. Elle peut rester[6] à la maison pendant[7] seize semaines: six semaines avant[8] la naissance du bébé et dix semaines après. Pour une femme qui a trois enfants ou plus, la période du congé de maternité est plus longue: huit semaines avant et dix-huit semaines après la naissance. Après son congé de maternité, quand la femme recommence à travailler, elle peut confier son enfant à une crèche collective publique ou choisir[9] une autre solution comme le système des jeunes filles au pair. À deux ans, son enfant peut aller[10] à l'école maternelle où il y a souvent un service de garderie le matin à 7 heures 30 et le soir jusqu'à[11] 19 heures. *(d'après La Civilisation française en évolution II).*

1. *late* 2. *out of wedlock* 3. *only one* 4. *several* 5. *after* 6. *remain* 7. *during* 8. *before*
9. *choose* 10. *go* 11. *until*

C **Questions:** Answer the following questions in French.

1. Quel est l'âge légal pour le mariage?
2. Y a-t-il des exceptions?
3. Quel est le pourcentage des divorces à Paris?
4. Est-ce que le nombre de familles avec un parent augmente?
5. Quel pourcentage des enfants n'ont pas de parents mariés?
6. Quelle est la période du congé de maternité pour une femme qui a trois enfants?

D **Comparaisons culturelles.** What similarities or differences between France and your country can you infer from the reading with respect to:

1. the change in family structure
2. maternity leave and day care
3. the average age for marriage

VOCABULAIRE ACTIF

Possessions
un bureau *desk*
une calculatrice *calculator*
une chaise *chair*
un chat *cat*
un chien *dog*
une cuisinière *stove*
un fauteuil *armchair*
un lave-vaisselle *dishwasher*
un lit *bed*
un livre *book*
une machine à laver *washing machine*
une mobylette *moped, motorized bicycle*
une moto *motorcycle*
un ordinateur *computer*
un réfrigérateur *refrigerator*
un sofa *sofa*
une stéréo *stereo*
un vélo *bicycle*
une voiture *automobile*

La maison ou l'appartement
un appartement *apartment*
un bureau *office*
une chambre *bedroom*
une cuisine *kitchen*
un garage *garage*
une maison *house*
une salle à manger *dining room*

une salle de bain *bathroom*
les toilettes *restroom*
un salon *living room*
une salle de séjour *den; living room*
un sous-sol *basement*
une véranda *porch*

La famille
un beau-père *stepfather (or father-in-law)*
des beaux-parents (m. pl.) *step-parents (or in-laws)*
une belle-mère *stepmother (or mother-in-law)*
une belle-sœur *sister-in-law*
un(e) cousin(e) *cousin*
un(e) enfant *child*
une famille *family*
une femme *wife*
une fille *daughter*
un fils *son*
un frère *brother*
un demi-frère *stepbrother*
une grand-mère *grandmother*
une arrière-grand-mère *great grandmother*
un grand-père *grandfather*
des grands-parents (m. pl.) *grandparents*
un mari *husband*

une mère *mother*
un neveu *nephew*
une nièce *niece*
un oncle *uncle*
des parents (m. pl.) *parents; relatives*
un père *father*
une petite-fille *granddaughter*
un petit-fils *grandson*
des petits-enfants (m. pl.) *grandchildren*
une sœur *sister*
une tante *aunt*

D'autres personnes
un(e) camarade de chambre *roommate*
un(e) étudiant(e) *student*
une fille *girl*
un garçon *boy*
une petite fille *little girl*
un(e) petit(e) ami(e) *boyfriend/girlfriend*

D'autres noms
l'âge (m.) *age*
un an *year*
la gare *(train) station*
un membre *member*
une photo *photograph*
un train *train*

Nombres

trente *thirty*
quarante *forty*
cinquante *fifty*
soixante *sixty*
soixante-dix *seventy*
soixante et onze *seventy-one*
soixante-douze *seventy-two*
quatre-vingts *eighty*
quatre-vingt-un *eighty-one*
quatre-vingt-dix *ninety*
quatre-vingt-onze *ninety-one*
cent *one hundred*
mille *one thousand*
un million *one million*
un milliard *one billion*

Adjectifs possessifs

mon, ma, mes *my*
ton, ta, tes *your*
son, sa, ses *his; her*
notre, nos *our*
votre, vos *your*
leur, leurs *their*

D'autres adjectifs

autre *other*
charmant(e) *charming*
gentil(le) *nice*

Verbes

avoir *to have*
passer (un an) *to spend (a year)*

Prépositions

dans *in*
sur *on*

Conjonction

si *if*

Articles indéfinis

un/une *a, an*
des *some; any*

Adverbes

combien (de) *how many; how much*
comment *how; what*
encore *still; again; more*
trop (de) *too much; too many*

Expressions utiles

Bienvenue! *Welcome!*
chez moi *at my house*
chez vous *at your house*
Comment s'appelle-t-il (elle)? *What's his (her) name?*
Comment s'appellent-ils (elles)? *What are their names?*
Il (elle) s'appelle ... *His (her) name is ...*
Ils (elles) s'appellent ... *Their names are ...*
il y a *there is (are)*
Je suis né(e) *I was born*
Je vous présente ... *Let me introduce you to ...*
Qu'est-ce qu'il y a ... ? *What is there ... ?*
Qu'est-ce qu'il y a? *What's the matter?*
Quel âge avez-vous? (a-t-il?, etc.) *How old are you? (is he?, etc.)*
sans doute *probably*
Si! *Yes!*
sur la photo *in the picture*
voici *here is; here are*
vous dites *you say*

La France et la francophonie

L'importance du français dans le monde

La revue *Language Today* propose un classement des langues les plus importantes. Ce classement est basé sur les critères suivants: le nombre de personnes qui parlent la langue, l'usage de la langue dans les domaines scientifiques et diplomatiques, la puissance économique des nations où on parle la langue, et le prestige social et littéraire de la langue.

LES LANGUES LES PLUS IMPORTANTES	
1. l'anglais	6. le chinois
2. le français	7. l'allemand
3. l'espagnol	8. le japonais
4. le russe	9. le portugais
5. l'arabe	10. l'hindi / l'urdu

L'anglicisme: un grand souci. Les Français utilisent un nombre considérable d'expressions d'origine anglo-américaine: **le drugstore, le jogging, le fast food, le footing, le chewing-gum, le jean,** etc. La proportion de ces anglicismes a fait l'objet de mesures législatives en France. En 1993, Jacques Toubon, à l'époque ministre de la Culture de la Francophonie, a proposé un projet de loi sur l'emploi du français car, disait-il, la valeur et le prestige de la langue française, «un élément fondamental de la personnalité et du patrimoine de la France», sont menacés par la domination et la globalisation de l'anglais et par ce que l'écrivain et journaliste René Étiemble a baptisé le «franglais.» Les défenseurs de la loi Toubon (votée le 4 août 1994) pensent qu'il faut défendre le français contre les assauts de l'anglo-américain. Les détracteurs leur opposent que l'anglais ne menace en rien l'intégrité et l'avenir de la langue française, et ils nous rappellent que l'anglais utilise lui-même des

mots et des expressions d'origine française comme *à la carte, coup d'état, cul de sac, R.S.V.P., fait accompli, soupe du jour, laissez-faire* et *déjà vu.*

À vous!

1. **Pour quelles raisons est-ce que l'anglais est la langue la plus importante?**
2. **Pourquoi le français est-il numéro deux dans le classement par ordre d'importance?**
3. **Cherchez d'autres exemples d'expressions françaises utilisées en anglais.**

Les origines

Les explorateurs français des XVIe et XVIIe siècles ont étendu l'hégémonie de la France à l'Amérique du Nord (voir Escale 2). Au XIXe siècle, la recherche d'espaces nouveaux, de matière première et de nouveaux marchés commerciaux a incité la France à coloniser plusieurs pays africains et certaines régions de la Caraïbe et de l'Indochine. Après une occupation d'un siècle, la langue française est devenue la langue véhiculaire, voire même la langue officielle, dans la majorité des anciennes colonies.

La francophonie est le terme inventé en 1880 par le géographe Onésime Reclus pour définir l'ensemble des pays où le français est parlé. Parmi les pays francophones il faut citer en Europe la Belgique, le Luxembourg et la Suisse. L'influence et la langue françaises se sont aussi étendues à la Bulgarie, à la Roumanie et, plus loin, à l'Égypte, au Liban et à Madagascar.

La négritude

Quoique l'universalité de la langue française soit perçue comme un avantage par de nombreux Africains des régimes coloniaux, d'autres trouvent que ce «décombre du régime colonial» est source de malaise (*discomfort*). Dans les années 30, de jeunes Antillais et Africains se rencontrent en France où ils font des études et contestent le colonialisme de l'époque. Trois étudiants en particulier, Aimé Césaire de la Martinique, Léon Gontron Damas de Guyane et Léopold Senghor du Sénégal, s'unissent pour publier à Paris en 1932 une petite revue, *Légitime défense*. Ils y lancent un appel à la dignité humaine et invitent leur peuple à être fiers de leurs origines africaines. Le gouvernement français n'a pas été lent à réagir. Les bourses de ces trois étudiants ont été supprimées pendant plusieurs mois, et *Légitime défense* n'a donc eu qu'un seul numéro. Mais la graine était semée, et ces trois mêmes jeunes, à l'esprit indomptable, sont revenus deux ans plus tard et ont fondé avec de nouveaux adeptes le journal *L'Étudiant noir*.

En 1939, Aimé Césaire publie le *Cahier d'un retour au pays natal*. C'est ici que le terme «négritude» apparaît pour la première fois et décrit les objectifs de ce mouvement. Selon Césaire, la négritude est «la simple reconnaissance du fait d'être noir, et l'acceptation de ce fait, de notre destin de noir, de notre histoire et de notre culture». C'est donc ainsi que le mouvement de la négritude est né et que l'âme africaine a commencé à faire entendre sa voix.

Histoire récente

En 1970, l'ensemble des pays francophones, sous l'impulsion des chefs d'État africains Léopold Senghor du Sénégal, Habib Bourguiba de Tunisie et Hanani Diori du Niger, ont souhaité utiliser leur lien linguistique au service de la paix, de la coopération et du développement culturel et économique. Ils ont ainsi créé l'**Agence de la Francophonie.** Cette agence est l'organisation principale des programmes décidés par les pays membres. Elle regroupe 50 États et gouvernements. Elle siège à Lomé (Togo), à Libreville (Gabon) et à Hanoï (Vietnam). Le **Secrétaire général de la Francophonie** et son administration veillent à l'harmonisation des programmes. C'est ainsi que l'Agence de la Francophonie est responsable de la TV5, une chaîne de télévision en langue française, et de l'Université Senghor d'Alexandrie qui a pour vocation d'assurer le perfectionnement des cadres supérieurs des pays francophones de l'Afrique. Parmi ses priorités sont la promotion du français dans le monde, la jeunesse et les technologies nouvelles, et le renforcement de la démocratie et des droits de l'homme.

La France et l'Union européenne

La francophonie n'est pas la seule communauté internationale dont fait partie la France. Depuis 1957, la France forme avec l'Allemagne, l'Italie, la Belgique, les Pays-Bas et le Luxembourg la **Communauté économique européenne.** Dans les années qui suivent, les pouvoirs en commun et les liens économiques et culturels ont augmenté ainsi que le nombre de pays participants. En 1995 l'union inclut quinze pays, et onze d'entre eux ont voté de faire l'unité monétaire en janvier 2002. L'euro est la nouvelle monnaie pour ces pays.

La France et ses partenaires ont lancé une politique ambitieuse pour défendre les intérêts européens, pour renforcer la puissance économique et la croissance de l'emploi et de la formation, pour fortifier les capacités militaires européennes, pour protéger l'environnement, et pour lutter contre le trafic de la drogue. La France a assuré la présidence de l'Union européenne en l'an 2000 et joue un rôle très important dans la promotion d'une Europe forte.

Le bâtiment de l'Union européenne à Strasbourg

L'Hexagone

Benjamin Franklin a écrit: «Tout homme a deux pays: le sien et la France.»

Quelques statistiques

D'après *La Fédération internationale des professeurs de français* (FIPF), cent douze millions de personnes parlent régulièrement le français, une progression de 7,7%. Soixante millions de personnes parlent occasionnellement le français, une progression de 11,8%. Trente-deux millions de personnes apprennent le français dans les pays non-francophones et un million de personnes enseignent le français dans le monde. (*AATF National Bulletin, Vol. 26, No. 4*)

Voir Paris et mourir!

Paris, la «ville lumière», tient son rayonnement universel à ses deux mille ans d'histoire, à sa mode, à son prestige au point de vue art, science et pensée. L'une des plus grandes métropoles mondiales, Paris est devenu, et depuis longtemps, un carrefour et un lieu d'échanges, un grand centre financier, la destination touristique par excellence en France.

La tour Eiffel: emblème de Paris. Par l'audace et l'immensité de sa taille, la tour Eiffel, dès le début de sa construction en 1887, a été l'objet de controverses parmi les Parisiens. De nombreux artistes, hommes de lettres et hommes politiques ont exprimé leur indignation, voire même leur colère. Mais aujourd'hui des millions de personnes visitent cet emblème somptueux de Paris pour admirer la finesse de sa ligne et célébrer le génie de sa construction.

Construite par Gustave Eiffel pour célébrer le centenaire de la Révolution à l'occasion de l'Exposition universelle de 1889

Paris l'ancien et Paris le nouveau. La ville rassemble en contrastes frappants (*striking*) l'architecture ancienne et nouvelle, comme en témoigne le Louvre.

Le Louvre

L'immigration

Il y a toujours eu en France de nombreuses personnes nées à l'étranger qui ont décidé de vivre dans ce pays. Depuis la Seconde Guerre mondiale, la pauvreté des anciennes colonies ainsi que les besoins de main-d'œuvre (*labor*) en France ont causé d'importants flux migratoires. Bientôt le nombre de ces «invités» a fait l'objet de tensions politiques. Aujourd'hui, la question de l'immigration met en conflit la gauche et la droite politiques. Les uns voient dans l'immigration un péril à l'identité nationale. La présence sur le territoire national de communautés étrangères importantes

Le onze tricolore. L'équipe multiethnique de France championne du monde de foot en 1998 est surnommée «Black, Blanc, Beur». Cette équipe, source de fierté nationale, sert aujourd'hui de modèle de la diversité et de l'unité.

risque, selon les slogans du Front national, «de signifier la fin de la France». Les autres pensent que sous ce masque se cachent du racisme, de la xénophobie et de la discrimination. Pour ces derniers l'immigration et la diversité contribuent à la richesse économique et culturelle du pays.

Parmi les immigrés, les nationalités les plus représentées sont les Portugais, les Algériens, les Marocains, les Italiens, les Espagnols, les Turcs et les Tunisiens. Il faut ajouter à cette liste les ressortissants de l'Afrique noire. La présence des Maghrébins et des Africains, qui travaillent pour la plupart comme ouvriers (56%), employés (21%) ou personnel domestique (53% des femmes) et qui occupent souvent des logements défavorisés, suscite beaucoup de polémique.

La France et la technologie

Le train à grande vitesse (TGV), qui circule à 300 km/h (186 *mph*), est un des symboles de la place que la France occupe dans le monde. La technologie du TGV a été exportée aux États-Unis, en Corée du Sud et en Chine. En France, le nouveau TGV Méditerranée a été mis en service en 2001. Marseille et Paris ne sont plus qu'à trois heures de distance.

En aéronautique, malgré (*in spite of*) l'accident tragique qui a eu lieu à Paris en juillet 2000, le Concorde demeure toujours un grand succès de la technologie française. Cet avion supersonique franco-britannique traverse les 5.600 km entre Paris et New York en 3h30. Le nouveau modèle d'Airbus qui sera mis en service en 2005 aura une capacité énorme. Mis à part ces domaines où elle prend la première place en technologie, la France rivalise avec d'autres pays dans d'autres sphères (appareils digitalisés, communications, recherche médicale, par exemple).

Le Tour de France

L'histoire du vélo est très attachée à la France. L'invention de la bicyclette est souvent attribuée à un forgeron (*blacksmith*) écossais, Kirkpatrick Macmillan, mais la popularisation de ce véhicule est due à deux Français, Pierre Michaux et son fils, Ernest. Cette équipe de père et fils construit à Paris en 1861 le premier «vélocipède», un engin avec deux roues (*wheels*) et deux manivelles (*cranks*) attachées à une grande roue. Un an plus tard la famille Michaux fabrique 142 vélos; et, depuis, la production annuelle a considérablement augmenté.

La France est aussi le premier pays à organiser une course cycliste. En 1869, la revue *Vélocipède illustre* sponsorise une course de 80 km entre Rouen et Paris; et en 1903, le Tour de France, ou la Grande Boucle comme on dit aujourd'hui, fait son début. Cette course par étapes est aujourd'hui la plus longue et la plus prestigieuse. Des millions de personnes s'alignent le long des routes pour voir passer les cyclistes pédalant à une vitesse de 40 km à l'heure. Le Tour de France n'est pas seulement une course cycliste mais un symbole de la France et un des plus grands événements sportifs annuels.

L'arrivée du Tour à Paris

Buts communicatifs
Describing personal attributes
Describing clothing
Describing people and things
Describing what you do at home
Identifying someone's profession

Structures utiles
Quelques groupes d'adjectifs
Ne ... jamais
Les adjectifs de couleur
L'adjectif démonstratif
La place de l'adjectif
Le verbe **faire**
Les mots interrogatifs **qui, que** et **quel**

Culture
Au pair
Le franglais
Les McDo et l'influence américaine
Les cartes postales

Coup d'envoi

Prise de contact

Qu'est-ce que c'est?
(Quel est ce vêtement?°)

What is this article of clothing?

C'est ...

Ce sont°...

These are

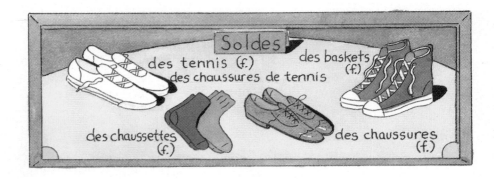

Et vous? Qu'est-ce que vous portez aujourd'hui?° *What are you wearing today?*
Moi, je porte ...

| Lettre | ## Une carte postale au professeur |

Lori Becker adresse une carte postale à son professeur américain, Madame Walter.

> Chère Madame,   Angers, le 2 octobre
> Me voilà au pair chez[1] les Martin.
> J'aime bien cette[2] famille! Je
> garde[3] deux des enfants et je fais
> quelquefois le ménage[4]. Ça me donne[5]
> beaucoup de travail mais c'est
> Mme Martin qui fait la cuisine[6]. Et
> puis les enfants font la vaisselle[7]
> le soir.
>   Quelle belle ville[9]! Et les gens[10] sont
> charmants! Je me sens chez moi[11].
> Tout le monde[12] porte un jean et
> un tee-shirt. Et il y a deux McDo à
> Angers! Avec mon meilleur souvenir,
>   Lori

1. *at (the house of)*   2. *this*   3. *look after*   4. *do housework sometimes*   5. *That gives me*
6. *who does the cooking*   7. *then*   8. *do the dishes*   9. *city*   10. *people*   11. *I feel at home*
12. *Everybody*

▶ Compréhension. Taking turns, read the following statements with your partner. Decide whether they are true (**C'est vrai**) or false (**C'est faux**). If a sentence is false, correct it.

1. Lori Becker habite à Angers.
2. Elle habite chez ses parents.
3. Elle travaille pour les Martin.
4. Elle fait la cuisine et la vaisselle.
5. Elle est contente d'être en France.
6. Les vêtements des jeunes Français sont très différents des vêtements des jeunes Américains.

Il y a un geste

Bravo!   The "thumbs up" gesture is used in French to signify approval.

Pourquoi est-ce que Lori fait le ménage et garde les enfants de Madame Martin?

a. Elle est masochiste.

b. Elle est très gentille et désire aider *(help)* la famille Martin.

c. Il y a souvent des jeunes filles qui habitent avec une famille française et qui travaillent pour payer leur chambre et leurs repas *(meals).*

Au pair

Many young women from foreign countries work as **jeunes filles au pair** *(nannies)* in France. They are able to spend a year abroad by agreeing to work in a French home. In exchange for room and board, but only a token salary, they do some light housework and help to take care of the children. Lori is **au pair chez les Martin.**

Le franglais

Borrowing inevitably takes place when languages come in contact. The Norman conquest in 1066 introduced thousands of French words into English and many English words have been borrowed by the French. While some of these French cognates are obvious in meaning (**le chewing-gum, un tee-shirt, un sweat-shirt**), others may surprise you: **un smoking,** for instance, means a *tuxedo.* Official measures have been adopted in France to try to stem the flow of English expressions into the French language. Currently, for example, the term **le logiciel** is being encouraged rather than the English cognate **le software.**

Les McDo et l'influence américaine

Lori is, of course, exaggerating when she says **Tout le monde porte un jean.** There has been, however, a change in French cities with respect to clothing style and the use of fast-food restaurants, and many of the French claim this is due to the influence of American culture. Decried by some and praised by others, these changes also reflect the fast-paced life of modern France.

Les cartes postales

When sending postcards, most French people will insert the card in an envelope and put stamp and address on the envelope. This perhaps speeds delivery and ensures privacy.

À vous. Describe to your partner what your classmates are wearing.

> MODÈLE: VOTRE PARTENAIRE: **Qu'est-ce que Sean porte aujourd'hui?**
> VOUS: **Il porte ...**

Entre amis

J'aime beaucoup vos chaussures. Elles sont très belles.

1. Compliment your partner on some article of clothing s/he is wearing.
2. S/he should respond in a culturally appropriate manner.
3. Point to two other articles of clothing and ask what they are.
4. If s/he doesn't know, s/he should say **Je ne sais pas.**
5. If s/he *is* able to name the articles, be sure to say that s/he speaks French well.

Prononciation

Les voyelles nasales: [ɛ̃], [ɑ̃] et [ɔ̃]

- Note the pronunciation of the following words:

[ɛ̃]
- **im**possible, **im**probable, **in**telligent, c**in**quante, v**in**, v**in**gt, m**in**ce
- s**ym**pathique, s**ym**phonie, s**yn**thèse
- f**aim**, améric**ain**, maroc**ain**, mexic**ain**, tr**ain**
- h**ein**
- canadi**en**, itali**en**, bi**en**, je vi**en**s, chi**en**, combi**en**, ti**en**s

[ɑ̃]
- ch**am**bre, **an**, fr**an**çais, ch**an**ter, m**an**ger, gr**an**d, pend**an**t, étudi**an**te, t**an**te, dem**an**dent
- **en**sem**ble**, m**em**bre, par ex**em**ple, **en**, **en**core, comm**en**t, souv**en**t

Exception exam**en** [ɛgzamɛ̃]

[ɔ̃]
- t**om**ber, c**om**bien, n**om**, prén**om**, **on**, **on**t, c**on**versati**on**, n**on**, **on**cle, **on**ze

- Now go back and look at how these sounds are spelled and in what kinds of letter combinations they appear. What patterns do you notice?

- When **-m-** or **-n-** is followed by a consonant or is at the end of a word, it is usually not pronounced. It serves instead to indicate that the preceding vowel is nasal.

  c**in**quante   **en**sem**ble**   c**om**bien   **im**possible

- When **-m-** or **-n-** is followed by a written vowel (pronounced or not pronounced), the preceding vowel is *not* nasal.

  ca**n**adien   crè**m**e   téléph**on**e
  bru**n**e   i**n**évitable   i**m**aginaire

Note The vowel preceding a written **-mm-** or **-nn-** is also not nasal.

i**nn**ocent i**mm**obile co**mm**e perso**nn**e

 Practice saying the following words after your instructor, paying particular attention to the highlighted vowel sound. In these words, the highlighted vowel sound is *not* nasal.

américain	m**ê**me	lim**o**nade	c**o**mme	**u**ne
Mad**a**me	**ai**me	cous**i**ne	c**o**mment	l**u**nettes
ex**a**men	améric**ai**ne	**i**nactif	pers**o**nne	f**u**me

 In each of the following pairs of words, one of the words contains a nasal vowel and one does not. Pronounce each word correctly.

1. impossible / immobile
2. minuit / mince
3. faim / aime
4. marocain / marocaine
5. canadienne / canadien
6. une / un
7. ambulance / ami
8. anglaise / année
9. crème / membre
10. dentiste / Denise
11. combien / comment
12. bonne / bon

Buts
communicatifs

1 Describing Personal Attributes

Comment est votre meilleur(e) ami(e)? Est-il (elle) ...

calme	ou	nerveux (nerveuse)?
charmant(e)	ou	désagréable?
compréhensif (compréhensive)°	ou	intolérant(e)°	*understanding / intolerant*
discret (discrète)	ou	bavard(e)°?	*talkative*
généreux (généreuse)	ou	avare°?	*miserly*
gentil(le)	ou	méchant(e)°?	*mean*
heureux (heureuse)	ou	triste°?	*sad*
intelligent(e)	ou	stupide?
intéressant(e)	ou	ennuyeux (ennuyeuse)°?	*boring*
optimiste	ou	pessimiste?
patient(e)	ou	impatient(e)?
travailleur (travailleuse)°	ou	paresseux (paresseuse)°?	*hard-working / lazy*

 Et vous? Comment êtes-vous? Comment sont vos professeurs?

Les étudiants sont très
bavards et le garçon
est un peu impatient.

1 **La famille de Sandrine.** Correct the following false impressions, beginning with **Mais pas du tout!** Make sure each adjective agrees with the noun it modifies.

MODÈLE: Le frère de Sandrine est désagréable.
Mais pas du tout! Il est charmant.

1. Sandrine est paresseuse.
2. Ses parents sont ennuyeux.
3. Leurs enfants sont très stupides.
4. La mère de Sandrine est triste et pessimiste.
5. Ses frères sont désagréables.
6. La sœur de Sandrine est méchante.
7. Son père est impatient.
8. Sa famille est bavarde.

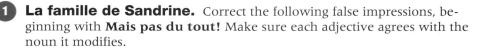

Il y a
un geste

Paresseux.   The thumb and index finger of one hand "caress" an imaginary hair in the palm of the other hand. This gesture signifies that someone is so lazy that a hair could grow in his/her palm.

Ennuyeux.   The gesture for ennuyeux is made by rubbing the knuckles back and forth on the side of the jaw. This rubbing of the "beard" is used to indicate that something is so boring that one could grow a beard while it is happening.

A. Quelques groupes d'adjectifs

féminin	masculin
discrète(s)	discret(s)
ennuyeuse(s)	ennuyeux
généreuse(s)	généreux
heureuse(s)	heureux
nerveuse(s)	nerveux
paresseuse(s)	paresseux
travailleuse(s)	travailleur(s)
gentille(s)	gentil(s)
intellectuelle(s)	intellectuel(s)
active(s)	actif(s)
compréhensive(s)	compréhensif(s)
sportive(s)	sportif(s)
naïve(s)	naïf(s)
veuve(s)	veuf(s)

■ The **-l** in the masculine form **gentil** is not pronounced. The final consonant sound of the feminine form **gentille** is [j], like the English **y** in *yes*.

gentil   [3ᾶti]   gentille   [3ᾶtij]

■ In written French, some feminine adjectives (ending in **-e-** + consonant + **-e**) are distinguishable from their masculine forms not only by a final **-e,** but also by a grave accent on the **-e-** before the consonant.

ch**è**re   cher   discr**è**te   discret

■ Some French adjectives are invariable. There is no change to indicate gender or number.

deux femmes **snob**   des chaussures **chic**

2 **Qui est comme ça?** Answer the following questions. Make sure each adjective agrees with the subject.

MODÈLE: Qui est patient dans votre famille?
   Ma mère est patiente.
   Mes sœurs sont patientes aussi.

1. Qui est travailleur dans votre famille?
2. Qui est bavard dans votre cours de français?
3. Qui est quelquefois triste?
4. Qui est généreux et optimiste?
5. Qui est sportif?
6. Qui est discret?
7. Qui est snob?
8. Comment sont vos parents?
9. Avez-vous des amis qui sont naïfs?
10. Et-vous? Comment êtes vous?

B. *Ne ... jamais*

Review the formation of the negative in Ch. 1, p. 20.

Mon amie **n'**est **jamais** méchante.   *My friend is never mean.*
Mon petit ami **ne** porte **jamais**   *My boyfriend never wears socks.*
  de chaussettes.

■ **Ne ... jamais** *(never)* is placed around the conjugated verb just like **ne ... pas.** It is one of the possible answers to the question **Quand?** *(When?).*

Quand est-ce que tu étudies?
Je **n'**étudie **jamais!**

Note **Jamais** can be used alone to answer a question.

Quand est-ce que tu pleures?
Jamais!

VOCABULAIRE

Adverbes de fréquence

toujours	*always*	quelquefois	*sometimes*
d'habitude	*usually*	rarement	*rarely*
généralement	*generally*	(ne ...) jamais	*never*
souvent	*often*		

3 **Comment sont-ils?** Describe the following people with as many true sentences as you can create. Use items from the lists below (or their opposites). Make all necessary changes, paying special attention to the form of the adjectives.

MODÈLE: **Mes parents ne sont jamais impatients.**
          Ils sont toujours patients.

mes parents		intolérant
je		méchant
mon petit ami	ne ... jamais	triste
ma petite amie	rarement	paresseux
mes amis	quelquefois	bavard
mon professeur	souvent	impatient
nous (les étudiants)	d'habitude	pessimiste
le (la) président(e) de l'université	toujours	ennuyeux
		désagréable
		avare

4 **Un test de votre personnalité.** Complete the questionnaire by answering **oui** or **non**. Then read the analysis that follows and write a paragraph to describe yourself.

	oui	*non*
1. Vous parlez beaucoup avec certaines personnes, mais vous refusez de parler avec tout le monde.	___	___
2. Vous aimez beaucoup les sports, mais vous détestez étudier et travailler.	___	___
3. Vous détestez jouer, danser ou chanter avec les autres, mais vous aimez bien étudier.	___	___
4. Vous avez beaucoup d'argent *(money)*, mais vous donnez rarement de l'argent à vos amis.	___	___
5. Vous n'avez pas d'argent, mais vous n'êtes jamais triste.	___	___
6. Votre conversation est toujours agréable et vous parlez avec tout le monde.	___	___
7. Vous étudiez beaucoup, vous aimez parler français et vous êtes certain(e) que votre professeur de français est charmant.	___	___

Une analyse de vos réponses

1. Si vous répondez **oui** au numéro 1, vous êtes extroverti(e) et bavard(e), mais vous êtes aussi un peu snob.
2. Si vous répondez **oui** au numéro 2, vous êtes sportif (sportive), mais aussi paresseux (paresseuse). Vous n'avez probablement pas de bonnes notes *(good grades)*.
3. Un **oui** au numéro 3, et vous êtes introverti(e), mais aussi travailleur (travailleuse). Vous avez probablement des notes excellentes.
4. Un **oui** au numéro 4, et vous êtes avare et pessimiste. Vous n'avez probablement pas beaucoup d'amis.
5. Si vous répondez **oui** au numéro 5, vous êtes d'habitude optimiste et heureux (heureuse), mais peut-être aussi un peu naïf (naïve).
6. Si vous répondez **oui** au numéro 6, vous n'êtes pas du tout ennuyeux (ennuyeuse). Vos amis sont contents d'être avec vous.
7. Enfin *(finally)*, si votre réponse est **oui** au numéro 7, vous êtes certainement très intelligent(e), charmant(e) et intéressant(e). Les professeurs de français adorent les étudiant(e)s comme vous.

5 **Cinq personnes que j'aime.** Write a description of five people you like. How much can you tell about each one?

MODÈLE: **Charles Thomas est mon ami.**
Charles est petit et un peu gros.
Il est très gentil et intelligent.
Mais il est aussi un peu paresseux.
Voilà pourquoi il n'est pas du tout sportif.

Entre amis

Qui est la personne sur la photo?

1. Show your partner a picture (real or imaginary) of someone.
2. Identify that person (name, age, address).
3. Describe his/her personality.
4. Give a physical description as well.
5. Tell what the person is wearing in the picture.

2 Describing Clothing

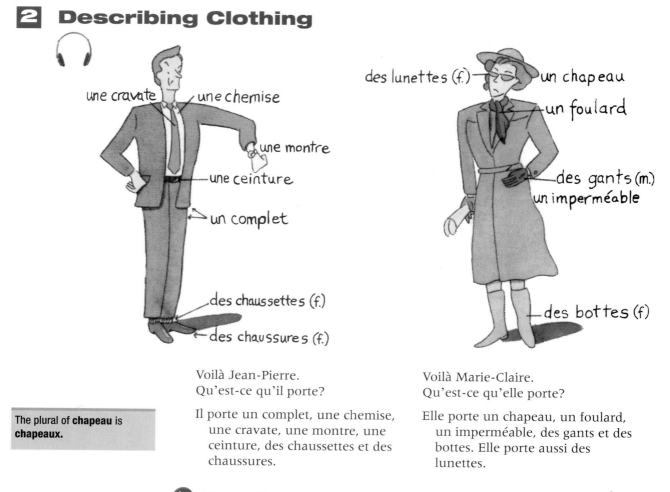

The plural of **chapeau** is **chapeaux.**

Voilà Jean-Pierre.
Qu'est-ce qu'il porte?

Il porte un complet, une chemise, une cravate, une montre, une ceinture, des chaussettes et des chaussures.

Voilà Marie-Claire.
Qu'est-ce qu'elle porte?

Elle porte un chapeau, un foulard, un imperméable, des gants et des bottes. Elle porte aussi des lunettes.

▶ **Et vous?** Qu'est-ce que vous portez aujourd'hui?

6 **Qu'est-ce que c'est?** Identify the following items.

MODÈLES:

—Qu'est-ce que c'est?   —Qu'est-ce que c'est?
—C'est une ceinture.   —Ce sont des chaussures.

1.

2.

3.

4.

5.

6.

7.

8.

9.

7 **Qu'est-ce qu'ils portent?** Describe the clothing tastes of several people you know. What items of clothing do they wear often, rarely, never?

MODÈLES: **Mon professeur de français ne porte jamais de jean.**
Je porte souvent un tee-shirt mais je porte rarement un chapeau.

1. mon professeur de français
2. les étudiants de mon cours de français
3. une actrice/un acteur de Hollywood
4. mon/ma meilleur(e) ami(e)
5. les musiciens d'un groupe rock
6. les membres de ma famille
7. moi

C. Les adjectifs de couleur

De quelle couleur est le pantalon de Jean-Pierre?
Il est **gris**. C'est un pantalon **gris**.

De quelle couleur est sa chemise?
Elle est **bleue**. C'est une chemise **bleue**.

De quelle couleur sont ses chaussures?
Elles sont **noires**. Ce sont des chaussures **noires**.

▶ **Et vous?** De quelle couleur sont vos vêtements?

VOCABULAIRE

Quelques couleurs

	Féminin	*Masculin*		*Féminin*	*Masculin*
	blanche	blanc		marron	marron
	grise	gris		jaune	jaune
	verte	vert		orange	orange
	violette	violet		rose	rose
	bleue	bleu		rouge	rouge
	noire	noir		beige	beige

Note Plurals of colors are formed by adding **-s.** Exceptions in this list are **gris,** which already ends in **-s, marron,** and **orange,** which are invariable: **des éléphants** *gris,* **des cheveux** *orange,* **des chemises** *marron.*

8 **De quelle couleur sont leurs vêtements?** Ask your partner about the color of the following articles of clothing.

MODÈLES: les chaussures de Jérôme (noir)
VOUS: **De quelle couleur sont ses chaussures?**
VOTRE PARTENAIRE: **Elles sont noires. Ce sont des chaussures noires.**

le pull de Martine (bleu)
VOUS: **De quelle couleur est son pull?**
VOTRE PARTENAIRE: **Il est bleu. C'est un pull bleu.**

1. la cravate de Denis (jaune et bleu)
2. la robe de Françoise (vert)
3. la veste de Jean (gris)
4. l'imperméable d'Annette (blanc)
5. les chaussettes d'un(e) autre étudiant(e)
6. la chemise d'une autre personne
7. les chaussures de votre partenaire
8. les vêtements du professeur

Il y a un geste

VOCABULAIRE

Pour décrire *(to describe)* les vêtements

bon marché	*inexpensive*	ou	cher (chère)	*expensive*
chic	*stylish*	ou	confortable	*comfortable*
élégant(e)	*elegant*	ou	ordinaire	*ordinary, everyday*
propre	*clean*	ou	sale	*dirty*
simple	*simple, plain*	ou	bizarre	*weird, funny-looking*

Cher! Similar to its English equivalent, the gesture for **cher!** is made by rubbing the thumb, index, and middle fingers together.

Confortable is not used to describe how a person feels. It is used to describe a thing: **une chemise confortable, une vie confortable.**

Note **Chic** and **bon marché** are invariable. They do not change in the feminine or in the plural: **Ce sont des chaussures** *chic,* **mais elles sont** *bon marché.*

Synthèse: Les adjectifs invariables

bon marché	chic	marron	orange	snob

9 **Au contraire!** Your partner will make a series of statements with which you will disagree. Provide the corrections by following the model.

MODÈLE: la robe de Simone (cher)
VOTRE PARTENAIRE: **La robe de Simone est chère.**
VOUS: **Non, elle n'est pas chère. C'est une robe bon marché.**

1. la veste de Martin (élégant)
2. le sweat-shirt de Monsieur Dupont (propre)
3. la robe de Pascale (chic)
4. les chaussettes du professeur (?)
5. l'imperméable de l'inspecteur Colombo (?)
6. les vêtements de deux autres étudiants (?)

Supply the adjectives for 4–6.

10 **À vous.** Answer the following questions.

1. Qu'est-ce que vous portez aujourd'hui?
2. De quelle couleur sont vos vêtements?
3. Décrivez les vêtements que vous portez.
4. Décrivez les vêtements d'un(e) autre étudiant(e).
5. Qu'est-ce que le professeur porte d'habitude?
6. De quelle couleur sont ses vêtements?
7. Qui ne porte jamais de jean dans votre classe de français?
8. Qui porte rarement des chaussures bon marché?
9. Qu'est-ce qu'on porte pour skier ou pour patiner?

Aimez-vous les défilés de mode *(fashion shows)*? Ce mannequin est chic, n'est-ce pas?

11 **Qui est-ce?** Describe as completely as possible the clothing of a fellow classmate.

MODÈLE: **Cette personne porte un pull jaune et un pantalon vert. Elle porte des chaussures marron. Elle ne porte pas de chaussettes. Ses vêtements ne sont peut-être pas très élégants mais ils sont confortables.**

Entre amis

Au téléphone

You are meeting a friend for dinner in twenty minutes.

1. Call to find out what s/he is wearing.
2. Find out the colors of his/her clothing.
3. Describe what you are wearing as completely as possible.

The French answer the phone by saying **«Allô!»**.

D. L'adjectif démonstratif

Cette femme est très intelligente.   *That (this) woman is very intelligent.*
Ce vin est excellent!   *This (that) wine is excellent.*
Vous aimez **cet** appartement?   *Do you like this (that) apartment?*
Qui sont **ces** deux personnes?   *Who are those (these) two people?*

	singulier	pluriel
masculin:	**ce (cet)**	**ces**
féminin:	**cette**	**ces**

■ The demonstrative adjectives are the equivalent of the English adjectives *this (that)* and *these (those).*

ce garçon   *this boy*   or   *that boy*
cet ami   *this (male) friend*   or   *that (male) friend*
cette amie   *this (female) friend*   or   *that (female) friend*
ces amis   *these friends*   or   *those friends*
ces amies   *these (female) friends*   or   *those (female) friends*

■ **Cet** is used before masculine singular words that begin with a vowel sound. It is pronounced exactly like **cette.**

cet homme   *this man*   or   *that man*
cet autre professeur   *this other teacher*   or   *that other teacher*

■ If the context does not distinguish between the meanings *this* and *that* or *these* and *those,* it is possible to make the distinction by adding **-ci** (for *this/these*) or **-là** (for *that/those*) to the noun.

J'aime beaucoup cette chemise**-ci.**   *I like this shirt a lot.*
Ces femmes**-là** sont françaises.   *Those women are French.*

12 **Au grand magasin** *(At the department store).* While shopping, you overhear a number of comments but are unable to make out all the words. Try to complete the following sentences using one of the demonstrative adjectives **ce, cet, cette,** or **ces,** as appropriate.

1. Vous aimez _____ chaussures? Oui, mais je déteste _____ chemise.
2. _____ pantalon est beau. Mais _____ jupes sont très chères.
3. _____ jean est trop petit pour _____ homme-là.
4. Je ne sais pas comment s'appelle _____ vêtement-là.
5. _____ robes sont jolies, mais _____ sweat-shirt est laid.
6. J'aime beaucoup _____ pull-là, mais je trouve _____ veste trop longue.

13 **Non, je n'aime pas ça.** Your shopping has made you tired and grouchy. Respond to your friend's questions or comments by saying that you dislike the item(s) in question. Use a demonstrative adjective in each response and invent a reason for your disapproval.

MODÈLE: Voilà une robe rouge.
Je n'aime pas beaucoup cette robe; elle est bizarre.

1. Voilà une belle cravate.
2. Voilà un ordinateur!
3. Oh! la petite calculatrice!
4. C'est un beau chapeau!
5. Tu aimes les chaussures vertes?
6. Voilà des chaussettes blanches intéressantes.
7. J'adore le chemisier bleu.
8. Tu aimes la veste de ce monsieur?

Entre amis

Cette robe est très élégante!

1. Pay your partner at least three compliments on his/her clothing.
2. S/he should respond in a culturally appropriate manner to each compliment.
3. Together, comment on the clothing of one of your neighbors.

3 Describing People and Things

De quelle couleur sont les yeux° et les cheveux°   *eyes / hair*
   de Michèle?
Elle a les yeux bleus.
Elle a les cheveux blonds.

De quelle couleur sont les yeux et les cheveux de
   Thierry?
Il a les yeux verts et les cheveux roux°.   *red*

De quelle couleur sont les yeux et les cheveux de
   Monsieur Monot?
Il a les yeux noirs, mais il n'a pas de cheveux.
Il est chauve°.   *bald*

▶ **Et vous?** De quelle couleur sont vos yeux et vos cheveux?

Remarques

1. Use the definite article **les** with the verb **avoir** to describe the color of a person's hair and eyes.

    Thierry **a les** yeux verts et **les** cheveux roux.

2. The word **cheveu** is almost always used in the plural, which is formed by adding **-x.**

    Michèle a **les cheveux** blonds.

3. Note that the adjective used to describe red hair is **roux** (**rousse**), never **rouge.**

    Il a les cheveux **roux.**   Notre petite-fille est **rousse.**

4. Use the adjective **brun**(**e**) to describe brown hair, never **marron.**

    Alissa a les cheveux **bruns.**   Elle est **brune.**

> Remember that the masculine plural adjective is used with the words **yeux** and **cheveux:** **les yeux bleus, les cheveux noirs.**

14 **Leurs yeux et leurs cheveux.** Complete the following sentences with a form of the verb **être** or **avoir,** as appropriate.

1. Mon père _____ les yeux bleus. Il _____ chauve.
2. Brigitte et Virginie _____ les cheveux roux.
3. Vous _____ les yeux noirs.
4. De quelle couleur _____ les yeux de votre mère?
5. Elle _____ les yeux verts.
6. Mes oncles _____ les cheveux blonds, mais ils _____ aussi un peu chauves.

15 **De quelle couleur ... ?** Ask and answer questions with a partner based on the list below. If you don't know the answer, guess.

MODÈLES: vos yeux
> **VOUS:** **De quelle couleur sont vos yeux?**
> **VOTRE PARTENAIRE:** **J'ai les yeux verts.**

> les cheveux de votre oncle
> **VOUS:** **De quelle couleur sont les cheveux de votre oncle?**
> **VOTRE PARTENAIRE:** **Il n'a pas de cheveux. Il est chauve.**

1. vos yeux
2. vos cheveux
3. les yeux de votre meilleur(e) ami(e)
4. les cheveux de votre meilleur(e) ami(e)
5. les yeux et les cheveux d'un(e) autre étudiant(e)
6. les cheveux de vos grands-parents
7. les yeux et les cheveux de vos frères et sœurs (ou de vos amis)

Entre amis

Dans ma famille

1. Find out how many people there are in your partner's family.
2. Find out their names and ages.
3. Find out the color of their hair.
4. Find out their eye color.

E. La place de l'adjectif

un livre **intéressant**	*an interesting book*
une femme **charmante**	*a charming woman*
un **bon** livre	*a good book*
l'**autre** professeur	*the other teacher*

■ Most adjectives (including colors and nationalities) follow the noun they modify.

un homme **charmant**	un garçon **bavard**
une femme **intelligente**	une fille **sportive**
une robe **bleue**	une voiture **française**

■ Certain very common adjectives, however, normally precede the noun.

1. Some that you already know are:

autre	grand	joli
beau	gros	petit
bon	jeune	vieux

2. Two others that usually precede the noun are:

masculin singulier	féminin singulier	masculin pluriel	féminin pluriel	équivalent anglais
mauvais	**mauvaise**	**mauvais**	**mauvaises**	*bad*
nouveau	**nouvelle**	**nouveaux**	**nouvelles**	*new*

Remember that **nouveau**, like **beau** and **chapeau**, forms the plural by adding **-x**.

3. **Beau, vieux,** and **nouveau** each have a special masculine singular form (**bel, vieil, nouvel**) for use when they precede a noun beginning with a vowel sound. These special forms are pronounced exactly like the feminine forms.

un **bel** homme   un **vieil** ami   un **nouvel** appartement

4. Adjectives ending in a silent consonant are linked by liaison to words beginning with a vowel sound. When linked, a final **-s** or **-x** is pronounced [z] and a final **-d** is pronounced [t].

un mauvais [z]hôtel   deux vieux [z]amis   un grand [t]hôtel

FOR RECOGNITION ONLY:

- In formal spoken and written French, **des** is replaced by **de** if a plural adjective comes *before* the noun.

    des professeurs intelligents   **des** voitures françaises

    Mais: **de** bons professeurs intelligents   **d'**autres voitures françaises

- A few adjectives can be used either before or after the noun. Their position determines the exact meaning of the adjective.

un **ancien** professeur	*a former teacher*
un château **ancien**	*an ancient castle*
le **pauvre** garçon	*the unfortunate boy*
le garçon **pauvre**	*the boy who has no money*

16 **C'est vrai.** Restate the following sentence.

MODÈLES: Les chaussures de Monsieur Masselot sont sales.
C'est vrai. Il a des chaussures sales.

L'appartement de Monsieur Masselot est vieux.
C'est vrai. Il a un vieil appartement.

1. L'appartement de Monsieur Masselot est beau.
2. Les enfants de Monsieur Masselot sont jeunes.
3. La femme de Monsieur Masselot est intelligente.
4. Les parents de Monsieur Masselot sont charmants.
5. Le chat de Monsieur Masselot est gros.
6. Le chien de Monsieur Masselot est méchant.
7. La voiture de Monsieur Masselot est mauvaise.
8. L'ordinateur de Monsieur Masselot est nouveau.
9. L'appartement de Monsieur Masselot est grand.
10. Le réfrigérateur de Monsieur Masselot est petit.
11. La cravate de Monsieur Masselot est bleue.
12. Les chaussettes de Monsieur Masselot sont bizarres.

17 **Quelques compliments.** Select items from each of the lists to pay a few compliments. How many compliments can you create? Make all necessary changes.

MODÈLES: **C'est une jolie robe.**
Tu as des chaussures chic.

		robe	joli
		maison	élégant
		appartement	bon
tu as	un	vêtements	magnifique
c'est	une	chemise	intéressant
ce sont	des	chemisier	superbe
		chaussettes	beau
		chaussures	chic
		jean	

Review pp. 22, 93, and 104.

18 Une identité secrète. Choose the name of someone famous that everyone will recognize. The other students will attempt to guess the identity of this person by asking questions. Answer only **oui** or **non**.

MODÈLE: **C'est une femme?**
Est-ce qu'elle est belle?
A-t-elle les cheveux roux?
Est-ce qu'elle porte souvent des vêtements élégants?
etc.

Entre amis

Mon ami(e)

Interview your partner to find out as much as you can about his/her best friend's personality and physical appearance. Inquire also about the clothing that the friend usually wears.

4 Describing What You Do at Home

Que fais°-tu chez toi°, Catherine? *do / at home*
   Je regarde la télé ou j'écoute la radio.
   J'étudie et je fais mes devoirs°. *homework*
   Je fais souvent la cuisine°. *the cooking*
   Je parle avec mes parents.
   Je fais quelquefois la vaisselle°. *the dishes*
   Je fais rarement le ménage°. *housework*

Et vous? Que faites-vous chez vous?

F. Le verbe *faire*

<table>
<tr><td>

VOCABULAIRE À RETENIR

courses *shopping*
provisions *grocery shopping*
lessive *wash*
</td></tr>
</table>

Je déteste **faire** les courses, mais j'aime **faire** la liste. *I hate doing the shopping, but I like making the list.*
Ma mère **fait** les provisions. *My mother does the grocery shopping.*
Mes sœurs **font** la cuisine. *My sisters do the cooking.*
Et c'est moi qui **fais** la vaisselle. *And I'm the one who does the dishes.*
Nous **faisons** tous la lessive. *We all do the wash.*

faire *(to do; to make)*			
je	**fais**	nous	**faisons**
tu	**fais**	vous	**faites**
il/elle/on	**fait**	ils/elles	**font**

En France, on aime
faire ses provisions
au marché.

■ The **-ai-** in **nous faisons** is pronounced [ə] as in **le, de,** etc.

■ The plural **les devoirs** means *homework*. The singular **la vaisselle** means *the dishes*. The plural **les courses** means *the shopping*.

Je fais **mes devoirs.**	*I do my homework.*
Qui aime faire **la vaisselle?**	*Who likes to do the dishes?*
Nous faisons **nos courses** ensemble.	*We do our shopping together.*

■ There are a number of idiomatic uses of the verb **faire.**

Je ne **fais** jamais **la sieste.**	*I never take a nap.*
Veux-tu **faire une promenade?**	*Would you like to take a walk?*
Quel temps fait-il?	*What is the weather like?*
Il fait chaud.	*It's hot out.*
Faites attention!	*Pay attention!* or *Watch out!*

■ A question using **faire** does not necessarily require the verb **faire** in the response.

Que **faites**-vous?
Je *patine*, je *chante*, je *regarde* la télé, j'*écoute* la radio, etc.

19 **Nous faisons beaucoup de choses.** Use the list below to create as many factual sentences as you can.

MODÈLES: **Mon petit ami ne fait jamais de promenade.**
Ma mère ne fait jamais la sieste.
Nous faisons souvent les courses.

mes amis
mon petit ami
ma petite amie
ma mère   faire
mon père
nous (ma famille)
je

toujours
d'habitude
souvent
quelquefois
rarement
ne ... jamais

la lessive — *laundry*
la vaisselle *dishes*
la sieste
les courses
la cuisine
une promenade
le ménage
les provisions
attention

20 **À vous.** Answer the following questions.

1. Faites-vous toujours vos devoirs pour le cours de français?
2. Quand faites-vous la sieste?
3. Faites-vous une promenade après le dîner?
4. Aux USA, est-ce le mari ou la femme qui fait le ménage d'habitude?
5. Qui aime faire les courses dans votre famille?
6. Aimez-vous faire la cuisine? Si non, qu'est-ce que vous aimez faire?
7. Aimez-vous la cuisine italienne?
8. Qui fait les provisions pour votre famille d'habitude?
9. Qui fait la lessive d'habitude?

Entre amis

Chez toi

1. Find out where your partner lives.
2. Find out who does the grocery shopping and who does the cooking at his/her house.
3. Ask if s/he likes French cooking.
4. Find out what s/he does or doesn't like to do.

5 Identifying Someone's Profession

—Chantal, qu'est-ce que tu veux faire dans la vie?°   *what do you want to do in life?*
—Je voudrais être journaliste. Et toi?
—Je ne sais pas encore.°   *I don't know yet.*

▶ **Et vous?** Qu'est-ce que vous voulez faire dans la vie?

VOCABULAIRE

Quelques professions

architecte		infirmier (infirmière)	*nurse*
artiste		*ingénieur	*engineer*
assistant(e) social(e)	*social worker*	interprète	
athlète		journaliste	
avocat(e)	*lawyer*	*médecin	*doctor*
*cadre	*executive*	ouvrier (ouvrière)	*laborer*
comptable	*accountant*	patron(ne)	*boss*
cuisinier (cuisinière)	*cook*	pharmacien(ne)	
*écrivain	*writer*	*professeur	
employé(e)		programmeur	
fermier (fermière)	*farmer*	(programmeuse)	
fonctionnaire	*civil servant*	secrétaire	
homme (femme) d'affaires	*businessman (-woman)*	vendeur (vendeuse)	*salesperson*
homme (femme) politique	*politician*		

*Certain professions are used only with masculine articles and adjectives **(un, mon, ce)** for a woman, as well as a man: **Elle est médecin. C'est un médecin.***

A more extensive list of professions can be found in Appendix B at the end of this book.

Nouns of profession, nationality, and religion all act like adjectives when used this way.

Remarques

1. There are two ways to identify someone's profession:

   • One can use a name or a subject pronoun + **être** + profession, without any article.

Céline **est artiste.**	*Céline is an artist.*
Je **suis pharmacienne.**	*I am a pharmacist.*
Il **est ouvrier.**	*He is a factory worker.*

   • For *he, she,* and *they,* one can also say **c'est** (**ce sont**) + indefinite article + profession.

C'est un professeur.	*He (she) is a teacher.*
Ce n'est pas un employé; c'est le patron.	*He isn't an employee; he's the boss.*
Ce sont des fonctionnaires.	*They are civil servants.*

2. To give more detail, one can use a possessive adjective or an article with an adjective. **C'est** (**ce sont**), not **il/elle est** (**ils/elles sont**), is used.

C'est ton secrétaire?	*Is he your secretary?*
Monique est une athlète **excellente.**	*Monique is an excellent athlete.*
Ce sont des cuisiniers **français.**	*They are French cooks.*

 Que voulez-vous faire? Use the list above to select professions that you would like and professions that you would not like.

Modèle: **Je voudrais être journaliste mais je ne voudrais pas être écrivain.**

22 **Qu'est-ce qu'il faut faire?** *(What do you have to do?)* The following sentences tell what preparation is needed for different careers. Complete the sentences with the name of the appropriate career(s).

MODÈLE: Il faut étudier la biologie pour être **médecin, dentiste** ou **infirmier.**

1. Il faut étudier la pédagogie pour être ...
2. Il faut étudier la comptabilité pour être ...
3. Il faut étudier le commerce pour être ...
4. Il faut étudier le journalisme pour être ...
5. Il faut étudier l'agriculture pour être ...
6. Il faut parler deux ou trois langues pour être ...
7. Il faut désirer aider les autres pour être ...
8. Il faut avoir une personnalité agréable pour être ...
9. Il faut faire très bien la cuisine pour être ...

23 **Cinq personnes que je connais** *(Five people I know).* Give a description of five people you know. How much can you tell about each one? Be sure to include information about what they do and what they want to do.

MODÈLE: **Anne Smith est étudiante. C'est une jeune fille travailleuse et très gentille. Elle a les cheveux roux et les yeux verts. Elle étudie le français et elle désire être femme d'affaires. Elle fait bien la cuisine et elle adore la cuisine française.**

G. Les mots interrogatifs *qui, que* et *quel*

Qui fait la cuisine dans votre famille?	*Who does the cooking in your family?*
Que faites-vous après le dîner?	*What do you do after dinner?*
À **quelle** heure dînez-vous?	*At what time do you eat dinner?*

■ **Qui** *(who, whom)* is a pronoun. Use it in questions as the subject of a verb or as the object of a verb or preposition.

Qui est-ce?	*Who is it?*
Qui regardez-vous?	*At whom are you looking?*
Avec **qui** parlez-vous?	*With whom are you talking?*

■ **Que** *(what)* is also a pronoun. Use it in questions as the object of a verb. It will be followed either by inversion of the verb and subject or by **est-ce que.** There are therefore two forms of this question: **Que ... ?** and **Qu'est-ce que ... ?**

Que font-ils?	*What do they do?*
Qu'est-ce qu'ils font?	

■ Don't confuse **Est-ce que ... ?** (simple question) and **Qu'est-ce que ... ?** *(What?).*

Est-ce que vous voulez danser?	*Do you want to dance?*
Qu'est-ce que vous voulez faire?	*What do you want to do?*
Qu'est-ce qu'il y a?	*What is it? What's the matter?*

■ **Quel** *(which, what)* is an adjective. It is always used with a noun and agrees with the noun.

Quel temps fait-il?   *What is the weather like?*
Quelles actrices aimez-vous?   *Which actresses do you like?*

	singulier	pluriel
masculin	**quel**	**quels**
féminin	**quelle**	**quelles**

Note   The noun may either follow **quel** or be separated from it by the verb **être.**

Quels vêtements portez-vous?   *Which clothes are you wearing?*
Quelle est votre **adresse?**   *What is your address?*

 Quelles questions! Ask questions using the appropriate form of **quel** with the words provided below.

> **Modèle:**   votre profession
> **Quelle est votre profession?**

1. heure/il est
2. à/heure/vous mangez
3. temps/il fait
4. votre nationalité
5. âge/vous avez
6. vêtements/vous portez/quand il fait chaud
7. votre numéro *(m.)*/de téléphone
8. de/couleur/vos yeux

 Qui, que ou quel? Complete the following sentences.

1. _____ fait le ménage chez toi?
2. _____ font tes parents?
3. _____ âge ont tes amis?
4. De _____ couleur sont les cheveux du professeur?
5. Avec _____ parles-tu français?
6. À _____ heure dînes-tu d'habitude?
7. _____ désires-tu faire dans la vie?
8. _____ fais-tu après le dîner?

À vous. Answer the following questions.

1. Avez-vous des frères ou des sœurs? Si oui, que font-ils à la maison? Qu'est-ce qu'ils désirent faire dans la vie?
2. Que voulez-vous faire dans la vie?
3. Qu'est-ce que vous étudiez ce semestre?
4. Qu'est-ce que votre meilleur(e) ami(e) désire faire dans la vie?
5. Qui fait la cuisine chez vous?
6. À quelle heure faites-vous vos devoirs d'habitude?
7. Que font vos amis après le dîner?
8. Qui ne fait jamais la vaisselle?

27 **Une nouvelle identité.** Give yourself a new identity and give the information requested in the form below as completely as possible.

Consult the list of professions p. 111 and Appendix B when filling this out.

AIR FRANCE economique

Pour mieux vous servir, aidez-nous à vous mieux connaître.

Nom du passager _____

Adresse personnelle _____

_____ Pays _____

Ville _____ N° Tél. _____

Entreprise _____

_____ N° Tél. _____

Adresse professionnelle _____

Pays _____ Ville _____

Profession _____

Vol Air France N° _____ du _____
(jour et mois)

Entre amis

Dans un avion (In an airplane)

1. Greet the person sitting next to you on the plane.
2. Find out his/her name and address.
3. Find out what s/he does.
4. What can you find out about his/her family?
5. Find out what the family members do.

Révision

A **Portraits personnels.** Provide the information requested below.

1. Décrivez les membres de votre famille.
2. Décrivez votre meilleur(e) ami(e).
3. Décrivez une personne dans la salle de classe. Demandez à votre partenaire de deviner *(guess)* l'identité de cette personne.

B **Trouvez quelqu'un qui ...** Interview your classmates in French to find someone who ...

MODÈLE: wants to be a doctor
> **VOUS: Est-ce que tu désires être médecin?**
> **UN(E) AUTRE ÉTUDIANT(E): Oui, je désire être médecin.** ou
> **Non, je ne désire pas être médecin.**

1. likes to wear jeans and a sweatshirt
2. is wearing white socks
3. never wears a hat
4. has green eyes
5. likes to cook
6. likes French food
7. hates to do housework
8. wants to be a teacher
9. takes a nap in the afternoon

C **À vous.** Answer the following questions.

1. De quelle couleur sont les vêtements que vous portez aujourd'hui?
2. Qu'est-ce que vos amis portent en classe d'habitude?
3. Quels vêtements aimez-vous porter quand il fait chaud?
4. De quelle couleur sont les yeux et les cheveux de votre meilleur(e) ami(e)?
5. Qui a les yeux bleus et les cheveux bruns?
6. Que faites-vous à la maison?
7. Que font les autres membres de votre famille chez vous?
8. Que voulez-vous faire dans la vie?
9. Qu'est-ce que votre meilleur(e) ami(e) désire faire?

Pas de problème!

Preparation for the video:
1. Video worksheets in the *Cahier d'activités*
2. CD-ROM, *Module 2*

Complete the following exercise if you have watched the video, *Module 2*. Choose the most appropriate answer.

1. Marie-Christine habite dans la rue *(street)* _____. (Bonaparte, Saint-Sulpice, de Tournon)
2. Elle habite _____. (dans une maison, dans un appartement)
3. Il faut _____ pour ouvrir la porte. (la clé, le code, la télécarte)
4. Jean-François est assez _____. (nerveux, calme)
5. _____ est nécessaire pour téléphoner dans une cabine téléphonique. (l'argent, le code, la télécarte)

Lecture I

A **Parcourez les petites annonces.** Glance at the classified ads below to find out what kind of job each one is advertising. Guess which one would pay the most. Which ones require a car? Which ones do not require experience? Which ones are for summer employment only?

Offres d'emploi

1 _____
Bébé, un an et demi, cherche fille au pair de nationalité américaine ou canadienne, expérience avec enfants. Appelez Cunin en fin de matinée 02.43.07.47.26.

2 _____
Nous recherchons des secrétaires bilingues. Appelez l'Agence bilingue Paul Grassin au 02.42.76.10.14.

3 _____
Professeurs anglophones pour enseigner l'anglais aux lycéens étrangers en France, école internationale, château. Deux sessions: du 30 juin au 21 juillet; du 25 juillet au 14 août. Tél. 02.41.93.21.62.

4 _____
Famille offre logement et repas en échange de baby-sitting le soir et certains week-ends. Les journées sont libres. Écrivez BP 749, 49000 Angers.

5 _____
Opportunité de carrière. Compagnie internationale, établie depuis 71 ans, est à la recherche de jeunes personnes ambitieuses pour compléter son équipe commerciale. Si vous avez une apparence soignée, si vous êtes positif(ve), si vous possédez une voiture, appelez-nous au 02.41.43.00.22.

6 _____
Vous cherchez un job d'été (juillet et août) bien rémunéré, vous aimez discuter et vous possédez une voiture: venez rejoindre notre équipe de commerciaux. Formation assurée. Débutants acceptés. Tél. 02.41.43.15.80.

B **Cela vous intéresse?** *(Does this interest you?)* Reorder the classified ads above according to how much they appeal to you (which ones you would apply for and in what order). Be prepared to explain your reasons.

C **Votre petite annonce.** Write a classified ad to say you are looking for work in France. Mention your personal description and experience and include the fact that you speak French. Be sure to tell how you can be contacted.

Lecture II

A **Que savez-vous déjà?** Previous knowledge of a topic is a definite asset in understanding a text. Answer the following before reading the poem.

1. Qui est Hamlet et quelle est son expression préférée?
2. Quelle est la nationalité du Hamlet de Shakespeare?
3. Faites une liste de quatre mots qui ont un accent grave.
4. Quelle différence y a-t-il entre **ou** et **où?** Que veulent dire ces deux mots?

B **Étude du vocabulaire.** Study the following sentences and choose the English words that correspond to the French words in bold print: *Do you understand?, so much, pupils, everyone, serious, you can answer, unhappy, What?, day dreaming.*

1. Quand on est étudiant, il y a **tant** de travail à faire!
2. Si vous n'êtes pas absent, **vous pouvez répondre** «présent».
3. Un étudiant qui ne fait pas attention est quelquefois **dans les nuages.**
4. **Hein** ou **quoi** sont souvent des synonymes de «Comment?».
5. À l'université il y a des étudiants; les **élèves** sont généralement à l'école secondaire.
6. Si un professeur désire vérifier si un étudiant ou un élève comprend, il demande: **«Vous y êtes?».**
7. Si un étudiant ne fait pas attention, son professeur risque d'être **mécontent.**
8. La situation est **grave.** Il faut faire très attention.
9. Est-ce que **tout le monde** parle français en France?

L'ACCENT GRAVE

Le professeur
Élève Hamlet!

L'élève Hamlet *(sursautant[1])*
... Hein ... Quoi ... Pardon ... Qu'est-ce qui se passe ... Qu'est-ce qu'il y a ... Qu'est-ce que c'est?

Le professeur *(mécontent)*
Vous ne pouvez pas répondre «présent» comme tout le monde? Pas possible, vous êtes encore dans les nuages.

L'élève Hamlet
Être ou ne pas être dans les nuages!

Le professeur
Suffit. Pas tant de manières. Et conjuguez-moi le verbe être, comme tout le monde, c'est tout ce que je vous demande.

L'élève Hamlet
To be ...

Le professeur
En français, s'il vous plaît, comme tout le monde.

L'élève Hamlet
Bien, monsieur. (Il conjugue:)
Je suis ou je ne suis pas
Tu es ou tu n'es pas
Il est ou il n'est pas
Nous sommes ou nous ne sommes pas ...

Review the meaning of **pauvre** on p. 107.

Le professeur (*excessivement mécontent*)
Mais c'est vous qui n'y êtes pas, mon pauvre ami!

L'élève Hamlet
C'est exact, monsieur le professeur,
Je suis «où» je ne suis pas
Et, dans le fond², hein, à la réflexion,
Être «où» ne pas être
C'est peut-être aussi la question.

Jacques Prévert, Éditions Gallimard

1. *startled*   2. *after all*

C **Questions.** Répondez.

1. Quelle réponse est-ce qu'on donne d'habitude en classe pour indiquer qu'on n'est pas absent?
2. Dans le poème, est-ce que l'élève Hamlet est en cours de français ou en cours d'anglais? Expliquez votre réponse.
3. Qui est impatient? Justifiez votre réponse.
4. Quel verbe est-ce que Hamlet conjugue?
5. Quelle est l'expression préférée du professeur?
6. Êtes-vous quelquefois comme cet élève Hamlet? Expliquez votre réponse.

D **Discussion.**

1. Why does Prévert call this poem **l'accent grave**?
2. Describe the personality of each of the characters in this poem.

VOCABULAIRE ACTIF

Quelques professions
un(e) assistant(e) social(e) *social worker*
un(e) avocat(e) *lawyer*
un cadre *executive*
un(e) comptable *accountant*
un cuisinier/une cuisinière *cook*
un écrivain *writer*
un(e) employé(e) *employee*
un fermier/une fermière *farmer*
un(e) fonctionnaire *civil servant*
un homme d'affaires/une femme d'affaires *businessman/business-woman*
un homme politique/une femme politique *politician*
un infirmier/une infirmière *nurse*
un ingénieur *engineer*

un médecin *doctor*
un ouvrier/une ouvrière *laborer*
un(e) patron(ne) *boss*
un vendeur/une vendeuse *salesman/saleswoman*

Description personnelle
avare *miserly*
bavard(e) *talkative*
calme *calm*
chauve *bald*
compréhensif (compréhensive) *understanding*
discret (discrète) *discreet; reserved*
ennuyeux (ennuyeuse) *boring*
extroverti(e) *outgoing*
généreux (généreuse) *generous*
gentil (gentille) *nice*

heureux (heureuse) *happy*
impatient(e) *impatient*
intellectuel (intellectuelle) *intellectual*
intelligent(e) *intelligent*
intéressant(e) *interesting*
intolérant(e) *intolerant*
naïf (naïve) *naive*
sportif (sportive) *athletic*
travailleur (travailleuse) *hard-working*
méchant(e) *nasty; mean*
nerveux (nerveuse) *nervous*
paresseux (paresseuse) *lazy*
patient(e) *patient*
triste *sad*

Activités qu'on fait

les courses (f. pl.) errands, shopping
la cuisine cooking; food
les devoirs (m. pl.) homework
la lessive wash; laundry
le ménage housework
une promenade walk; ride
les provisions (f. pl.) groceries
la sieste nap
la vaisselle dishes

D'autres noms

une adresse address
une carte postale postcard
les cheveux (m. pl.) hair
une chose thing
une couleur color
le dîner dinner
les gens people
un magasin store
une note note; grade, mark
un numéro de téléphone
    telephone number
le temps weather
la vie life
une ville city
les yeux (m. pl.) eyes

Adjectifs de couleur

beige beige
blanc (blanche) white
bleu(e) blue
blond(e) blond
brun(e) brown(-haired)
gris(e) grey
jaune yellow
marron brown
noir(e) black
orange orange
rose pink
rouge red
roux (rousse) red(-haired)
vert(e) green
violet(te) purple

Pour décrire les vêtements

bizarre weird, funny-looking
bon marché inexpensive
cher (chère) dear; expensive
chic chic; stylish
confortable comfortable
élégant(e) elegant
ordinaire ordinary, everyday
propre clean
sale dirty
simple simple, plain

Vêtements

des baskets (f.) high-top sneakers
un blouson windbreaker, jacket
des bottes (f.) boots
une ceinture belt
un chapeau hat
des chaussettes (f.) socks
des chaussures (f.) shoes
une chemise shirt
un chemisier blouse
un complet suit
une cravate tie
un foulard scarf
des gants (m.) gloves
un imperméable raincoat
un jean (pair of) jeans
une jupe skirt
des lunettes (f. pl.) eyeglasses
un manteau coat
une montre watch
un pantalon (pair of) pants
un pull-over (un pull) sweater
une robe dress
un short (pair of) shorts
un sweat-shirt sweatshirt
un tee-shirt tee-shirt
des tennis (f.) tennis shoes
une veste sportcoat
un vêtement an article of
    clothing

D'autres adjectifs

ce/cet (cette) this; that
ces these; those
mauvais(e) bad
nouveau/nouvel (nouvelle) new

Pronoms

cela (ça) that
toi you
tout le monde everybody

Verbes

dîner to eat dinner
donner to give
faire to do; to make
garder to keep; to look after
porter to wear; to carry

Adverbes qui répondent à Quand?

aujourd'hui today
d'habitude usually
généralement generally
jamais (ne ... jamais) never
quand when
quelquefois sometimes
rarement rarely
toujours always

Mots invariables

chez at the home of
puis then; next

Mots interrogatifs

que ... ? what ... ?
qu'est-ce que ... ? what ... ?
quel(le) ... ? which ... ?

Expressions utiles

Au contraire! On the contrary!
avec mon meilleur souvenir with
    my best regards
Comment est (sont) ... ? What is
    (are) ... like?
De quelle couleur est (sont) ... ?
    What color is (are) ... ?
en classe in class; to class
faire attention to pay attention
Il fait chaud. It's hot out.
Il faut ... It is necessary ...
Quel temps fait-il? What is the
    weather like?
Qu'est-ce que c'est? What is this?

5 Quoi de neuf?

Buts communicatifs
Expressing future time
Telling time
Explaining your
 schedule
Telling where to find
 places

Structures utiles
À + article défini
Le verbe **aller**
L'heure
Les jours de la semaine
Le verbe **devoir**
Quelques prépositions
 de lieu
L'impératif
Les prépositions de lieu
 avec une ville ou un
 pays
Les mots interrogatifs
 où et **quand**

Culture
Quelques malentendus
 culturels
Pour dire *au revoir*

Coup d'envoi

Qu'est-ce que vous allez faire?

Qu'est-ce que tu vas faire° le week-end prochain°, Sylvie?	*What are you going to do / next weekend*
Je vais sortir vendredi° soir.	*I'm going to go out on Friday*
Je vais danser parce que j'adore danser.	
Je vais déjeuner dimanche° avec mes amis.	*I'm going to have lunch on Sunday / I'm going to go to the library.*
Je vais aller à la bibliothèque.°	
Je vais étudier et faire mes devoirs.	
Mais je ne vais pas rester° dans ma chambre tout le week-end°.	*to stay* *the whole weekend*

 Et vous? Qu'est-ce que vous allez faire le week-end prochain? Où allez-vous étudier?

Conversation

Une sortie

C'est vendredi après-midi. Lori rencontre° son amie Denise — meets
après° son cours de littérature française. — after

LORI: Salut, Denise. Comment vas-tu?

DENISE: Bien, Lori. Quoi de neuf?° — *What's new?*
(Elles s'embrassent° trois fois°.) — *kiss / times*

LORI: Pas grand-chose°, mais c'est vendredi et je n'ai — *Not much*
pas l'habitude de passer° tout le week-end — *I'm not used to spending*
dans ma chambre.
Tu as envie d'aller au cinéma?° — *Do you feel like going to the movies?*

DENISE: Quand ça?

LORI: Ce soir ou demain° soir? — *tomorrow*

DENISE: Ce soir je ne suis pas libre°. Mais demain — *free*
peut-être. Tu vas voir° quel film? — *to see*

LORI: Ça m'est égal.° Il y a toujours un bon film au — *I don't care.*
cinéma Variétés.

DENISE: D'accord°, très bien. À quelle heure? — *Okay*

LORI: Vers 7 heures et demie°. Ça va?° Rendez-vous — *Around 7:30 / Okay?*
devant° le cinéma? — *in front of*

DENISE: C'est parfait°. — *perfect*

LORI: Bonne soirée, Denise, et à demain soir.

▶ **Jouez ces rôles.** Répétez la conversation avec votre partenaire. Utilisez vos noms et le nom d'un cinéma près de chez vous.

Il y a un geste

Au revoir/Salut. When waving good-bye, the open palm, held at about ear level, is normally turned toward the person to whom one is waving. It is often moved toward the other person.

La bise. The French kiss their friends and relatives on both cheeks. This is referred to as **faire la bise.** The number of times that their cheeks touch varies, however, from one region to another: twice in Besançon, three or four times in Angers, and four times in Quimper! In Paris, the number varies from two to four, most likely because people have moved to the capital from different regions.

Pourquoi est-ce que Lori et Denise s'embrassent trois fois?

a. Elles sont superstitieuses.
b. Denise habite à Angers et elle a l'habitude d'embrasser ses amis trois fois.
c. En France on embrasse tout le monde.

Quelques malentendus culturels

A possible misunderstanding may result from the use of expressions that seem to be equivalent in two languages. In the United States, for example, the expression *see you later* is often used as an alternate to *good-bye,* without necessarily implying any real meeting in the near future. This has proven to be frustrating for French visitors, for whom *see you later* is interpreted as meaning *see you soon.* Likewise, any North American who uses the French expression **À tout à l'heure** should realize that this implies that the people in question will be meeting again very soon.

This example is perhaps a useful springboard to understanding one of the basic differences between North Americans and the French: while typically more hesitant to extend an invitation to their home and certainly more reluctant to chat with strangers, once an invitation is extended or a conversation begun, the French take it seriously. North Americans may complain about not being invited to French homes right away, but they themselves have readily and casually extended invitations to "come and see us" and have then been surprised when French acquaintances write to say they are actually coming.

Another source of error for English speakers is the attempt to translate expressions such as *good morning* and *good afternoon* literally when greeting someone. **Bon après-midi** is used only when taking leave of someone. When saying hello, the only common expressions in French are **bonjour, bonsoir,** and **salut.** When saying good-bye, however, the range of possible expressions is much more extensive as can be seen in the list to the right.

Pour dire *au revoir*

à bientôt	*see you soon*
à demain	*see you tomorrow*
à la prochaine	*until next time, be seeing you*
à tout à l'heure	*see you in a little while*
au plaisir (de vous revoir)	*(I hope to) see you again*
au revoir	*good-bye, see you again*
bon après-midi	*have a good afternoon*
bonne journée	*have a good day*
bonne nuit	*pleasant dreams* (lit. *good night*)
bonne soirée	*have a good evening*
bonsoir	*good evening, good night*
salut	*bye(-bye)* (fam.)
tchao	*bye* (fam.)

123

 **À vous.** Répondez.

1. Comment allez-vous?
2. Allez-vous rester dans votre chambre ce soir?
3. À quelle heure allez-vous faire vos devoirs?
4. Qu'est-ce que vous allez faire demain soir?
5. Avez-vous envie d'aller au cinéma?

Entre amis

Le week-end prochain

1. Greet your partner.
2. Find out how s/he is doing.
3. Find out what s/he is going to do this weekend.
4. Find out if s/he wants to go to a movie.
5. If so, agree on a time.
6. Be sure to vary the way you say good-bye.

Prononciation

Les syllabes ouvertes

■ There is a strong tendency in French to end spoken syllables with a vowel sound. It is therefore important to learn to link a pronounced consonant to the vowel that follows it.

| il a | [i la] | votre ami | [vɔ tʀa mi] |
| elle a | [ɛ la] | femme américaine | [fa ma me ʀi kɛn] |

■ The above is also true in the case of liaison. Liaison must occur in the following situations.

Synthèse: Les liaisons obligatoires

	Alone	With liaison
1. when a pronoun is followed by a verb	nous	nous [z]a vons
	vous	vous [z]êtes
2. when a verb and pronoun are inverted	est	est-[t]elle
	ont	ont-[t]ils
	sont	sont-[t]ils
3. when an article or adjective is followed by a noun	un	un [n]homme
	des	des [z]en fants
	deux	deux [z]heures
	trois	trois [z]ans
	mon	mon [n]a mi
	petit	petit [t]a mi
4. after one-syllable adverbs or prepositions	très	très [z]im por tant
	en	en [n]A mé rique
	dans	dans [z]une fa mille

Buts communicatifs

1 Expressing Future Time

Qu'est-ce que tu vas faire samedi° prochain, Julien?   *Saturday*
     D'abord° je vais jouer au tennis avec mes   *First (of all)*
       amis.
     Ensuite° nous allons étudier° à la   *Next / we're going to study*
       bibliothèque.
     Je n'aime pas manger seul°, alors après°,   *alone / so after(wards)*
       nous allons dîner ensemble au
       restaurant universitaire.
     Enfin°, nous allons regarder la télé.   *Finally*

▶ **Et vous?** Qu'est-ce que vous allez faire?

NOTE CULTURELLE
Le restaurant universitaire, qu'on appelle d'habitude **le Resto U,** est très bon marché. C'est parce qu'en France on subventionne *(subsidizes)* en partie les repas *(meals)* des étudiants. Si on a une carte d'étudiant, on bénéficie d'une réduction du prix des repas.

Remember to consult Appendix C, the Glossary of Grammatical Terms, at the end of the book to review any terms with which you are not familiar.

A. À + article défini

Céline ne travaille pas **à la** bibliothèque.   *Céline doesn't work at the library.*
Elle travaille **au** restaurant universitaire.   *She works in the dining hall.*

■ The preposition **à** can mean *to, at,* or *in,* depending on the context. When used with the articles **la** and **l'**, it does not change, but when used with the articles **le** and **les,** it is contracted to **au** and **aux.**

à	+	le	**au**	au restaurant
à	+	les	**aux**	aux toilettes
à	+	la	**à la**	à la maison
à	+	l'	**à l'**	à l'hôtel

■ Liaison occurs when **aux** precedes a vowel sound.
aux [z]États-Unis

VOCABULAIRE

Quelques endroits *(A few places)*

A. Sur le campus

un bâtiment	*building*	une librairie	*bookstore*
une bibliothèque	*library*	un parking	*parking lot, garage*
une cafétéria	*cafeteria*	une piscine	*swimming pool*
un campus	*campus*	une résidence	
un couloir	*hall, corridor*	(universitaire)	*dormitory*
un cours	*course, class*	une salle de classe	*classroom*
un gymnase	*gymnasium*	les toilettes *(f. pl.)*	*restroom*

[suite]

VOCABULAIRE [suite]

Quelques endroits *(A few places)*

B. En ville

un aéroport	*airport*	une école	*school*
une banque	*bank*	une église	*church*
un bistro	*bar and café*	une épicerie	*grocery store*
une boulangerie	*bakery*	une gare	*railroad station*
un bureau de poste	*post office*	un hôtel	*hotel*
un bureau de tabac	*tobacco shop*	un musée	*museum*
un centre	*shopping center,*	une pharmacie	*pharmacy*
commercial	* mall*	un restaurant	*restaurant*
un cinéma	*movie theater*	une ville	*city*
un château	*chateau, castle*		

1 **Qu'est-ce que c'est?** Identifiez les endroits suivants.

MODÈLE: **C'est une église.**

1.

2.

3.

4.
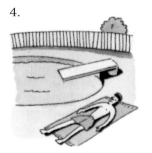

5.

6.

Où vas-tu? Posez la question. Votre partenaire va répondre d'après le modèle *(according to the model)*.

MODÈLE: restaurant (bibliothèque)
—**Tu vas au restaurant?**
—**Non, je ne vais pas au restaurant; je vais à la bibliothèque.**

1. bureau de poste (pharmacie)
2. église (centre commercial)
3. restaurant (cinéma)
4. librairie (bibliothèque)
5. hôtel (appartement de ma sœur)
6. gare (aéroport)

 Qu'est-ce que vous allez faire? Indiquez vos projets avec **Je vais à** + article défini et les mots donnés *(given)*. Utilisez aussi les mots **d'abord, ensuite** et **après**.

MODÈLE: banque, centre commercial, épicerie
D'abord je vais à la banque, ensuite je vais au centre commercial et après je vais à l'épicerie.

1. école, bibliothèque, librairie
2. banque, restaurant, aéroport
3. bureau de poste, pharmacie, cinéma
4. église, campus, résidence

Entre amis

D'abord, ensuite, après

1. Tell your partner that you are going to go out.
2. S/he will try to guess three places where you are going.
3. S/he will try to guess in what order you are going to the three places.

B. Le verbe *aller*

Je vais en classe à 8 heures.	*I go to class at eight o'clock.*
Allez-vous en ville ce soir?	*Are you going into town this evening?*
Où **allons-nous** dîner?	*Where are we going to eat dinner?*
Les petits Français ne **vont** pas à l'école le mercredi.	*French children don't go to school on Wednesday.*

aller *(to go)*			
je	**vais**	nous	**allons**
tu	**vas**	vous	**allez**
il/elle/on	**va**	ils/elles	**vont**

■   The fundamental meaning of **aller** is *to go*.
Où **vas-tu?**   *Where are you going?*

■ The verb **aller** is also used to discuss health and well-being.

Comment allez-vous?	*How are you?*
Je vais bien, merci.	*I'm fine, thanks.*
Ça va, merci.	*Fine, thanks.*

■ The verb **aller** is also very often used with an infinitive to indicate the future, especially the near future.

Qu'est-ce que **tu vas faire** ce soir?	*What are you going to do this evening?*
Je vais étudier, comme d'habitude.	*I'm going to study, as usual.*
Nous allons passer un test demain.	*We are going to take a test tomorrow.*

Note In the negative of this construction, **ne ... pas** is placed around the verb **aller,** not around the infinitive.

Thierry **ne va pas déjeuner** demain. *Thierry won't eat lunch tomorrow.*

4 **Comment vont-ils?** Utilisez le verbe **aller** pour poser des questions. Votre partenaire va répondre.

> **MODÈLE:** ton frère
>
> **VOUS:** **Comment va ton frère?**
> **VOTRE PARTENAIRE:** **Il va très bien, merci.**   ou
>   **Quel frère? Je n'ai pas de frère.**

1. tes amis du cours de français
2. tu
3. ton professeur de français
4. ta sœur
5. ton ami(e) qui s'appelle _____
6. tes grands-parents
7. ta nièce
8. tes neveux

VOCABULAIRE

Quelques expressions de temps (futur)

Several of these expressions can be preceded by **à** to mean *"See you ..."* or *"Until ...,"* e.g., **à ce soir, au week-end prochain.**

tout à l'heure	*in a little while*
dans une heure	*one hour from now*
ce soir	*tonight*
avant (après) le dîner	*before (after) dinner*
demain (matin, soir)	*tomorrow (morning, evening)*
dans trois jours	*three days from now*
le week-end prochain	*next weekend*
la semaine prochaine	*next week*

5 **Que vont-ils faire ce soir?** Qu'est-ce qu'ils vont faire et qu'est-ce qu'ils ne vont pas faire? Si vous ne savez pas, devinez *(If you don't know, guess.)*

MODÈLE: mes parents / jouer au tennis ou regarder la télévision
Ce soir, ils vont regarder la télévision; ils ne vont pas jouer au tennis.

1. je / sortir ou rester dans ma chambre
2. le professeur / dîner au restaurant ou dîner à la maison
3. mes amis / étudier à la bibliothèque ou étudier dans leur chambre
4. je / regarder la télévision ou faire mes devoirs
5. mon ami(e) _____ / travailler sur ordinateur ou aller au centre commercial
6. les étudiants / rester sur le campus ou aller au bistro

6 **À vous.** Répondez.

1. Quand allez-vous regarder la télévision?
2. Quand allez-vous sortir avec vos amis?
3. Quand allez-vous passer un test?
4. Quand est-ce que vous allez manger?
5. Où allez-vous déjeuner demain midi?
6. Où et à quelle heure allez-vous dîner demain soir?
7. Allez-vous dîner seul(e) ou avec une autre personne?
8. Quand allez-vous étudier? Avec qui?
9. Qu'est-ce que vous allez faire samedi prochain?
10. Qu'est-ce que vous allez faire dimanche après-midi?

Entre amis

Est-ce que tu vas jouer au tennis?

1. Tell your partner that you are not going to stay in your room this weekend.
2. S/he will try to guess three things you are going to do.
3. S/he will try to guess in what order you will do them.

2 Telling Time

Quelle heure est-il maintenant?°   *What time is it now?*
Il est 10 heures et demie.°   *It's half past ten.*
Je vais au cours de français à 11 heures.
Je déjeune à midi.°   *I eat lunch at noon.*
Je vais à la bibliothèque à une heure.
Je vais au gymnase à 4 heures.
J'étudie de 7 heures à 10 heures du soir.

> -- cours de français 11 h
> -- déjeuner 12 h avec Étienne
> -- bibliothèque 13 h
> -- gymnase 16 h

▶ Et vous? À quelle heure déjeunez-vous?
À quelle heure allez-vous à la bibliothèque?
À quelle heure allez-vous au gymnase?
À quelle heure allez-vous au cours de français?
Quelle heure est-il maintenant?

Remarque   The word **heure** has more than one meaning.

J'étudie trois **heures** par jour.   *I study three hours a day.*
De quelle **heure** à quelle **heure**?   *From what time to what time?*
De 15 **heures** à 18 **heures**.   *From three until six o'clock.*

C. L'heure

■ You have already learned to tell time in a general way. Now that you know how to count to 60, you can be more precise. There are two methods of telling time. The first is an official 24-hour system, which can be thought of as a digital watch on which the hour is always followed by the minutes. The other is an informal 12-hour system that includes the expressions **et quart** *(quarter past, quarter after),* **et demi(e)** *(half past),* **moins le quart** *(quarter to, quarter till),* **midi,** and **minuit** *(midnight).*

**VOCABULAIRE
À RETENIR**

quart   *quarter*
demi(e)   *half*
minuit   *midnight*
midi   *noon*

Review *Understanding Basic Expressions of Time,* p. 3, and numbers, pp. 3, 63.

The word **heure(s)** is usually represented as **h** (without a period) on schedules, e.g., **5 h 30.**

Système officiel	**Système ordinaire**
neuf heures une	neuf heures une
neuf heures quinze	neuf heures et quart
neuf heures trente	neuf heures et demie
neuf heures quarante-cinq	dix heures moins le quart
douze heures trente	midi et demi
treize heures trente	une heure et demie
dix-huit heures cinquante et une	sept heures moins neuf
vingt-trois heures quarante-cinq	minuit moins le quart

■ In both systems, the feminine number **une** is used to refer to hours and minutes because both **heure** and **minute** are feminine.

1 h 21 **une** heure vingt et **une**

■ In the 12-hour system, **moins** is used to give the time from 1 to 29 minutes *before* the hour. For 15 minutes *before* or *after* the hour, the expressions **moins le quart** and **et quart,** respectively, are used. For 30 minutes past the hour, one says **et demie.**

9 h 40	dix heures **moins** vingt
9 h 45	dix heures **moins le quart** ✓
10 h 15	dix heures **et quart** ✓
10 h 30	dix heures **et demie**

Note After **midi** and **minuit,** which are both masculine, **et demi** is spelled without a final **-e**: midi **et demi.**

■ The phrases **du matin, de l'après-midi,** and **du soir** are commonly used in the 12-hour system to specify A.M. or P.M. when it is not otherwise clear from the context.

trois heures **du matin** (3 h)	dix heures **du matin** (10 h)
trois heures **de l'après-midi** (15 h)	dix heures **du soir** (22 h)

7 **Quelle heure est-il?** Donnez les heures suivantes. Indiquez l'heure officielle et l'heure ordinaire s'il y a une différence.

MODÈLE: 13 h 35
système officiel: **Il est treize heures trente-cinq.**
système ordinaire: **Il est deux heures moins vingt-cinq de l'après-midi.**

1. 2 h 20	4. 1 h 17	7. 22 h 05	9. 11 h 15
2. 4 h 10	5. 6 h 55	8. 3 h 45	10. 10 h 30
3. 15 h 41	6. 1 h 33		

Remember that these numbers are based on a 24-hour system.

Quelle heure est-il?

8 **Décalages horaires** *(Differences in time).* Vous êtes à Paris et vous voulez téléphoner à des amis. Mais quelle heure est-il chez vos amis? Demandez à votre partenaire.

> Use the maps on the inside covers of this book to locate as many of these places as possible.

Décalages horaires
(calculés par rapport à l'heure de Paris)

Anchorage (USA)	− 10	Montréal (CDN)		− 6
Athènes (Grèce)	+ 1	Mexico (MEX)		− 7
Bangkok (Thaïlande)	+ 6	Nouméa		
Casablanca (MA)	− 1	(Nouvelle-Calédonie)		+ 10
Chicago (USA)	− 7	New York (USA)		− 6
Dakar (SN)	− 1	Papeete (Polynésie)		− 11
Denver (USA)	− 8	Saint-Denis (Réunion)		+ 3
Fort-de-France		San Francisco (USA)		− 9
(Martinique)	− 5	Sydney (Australie)		+ 9
Halifax (CDN)	− 5	Tokyo (J)		+ 8
Le Caire (Égypte)	+ 1	Tunis (Tunisie)		0
Londres (GB)	− 1			

MODÈLE: 3 h à Paris/Bangkok?

> VOUS: **S'il est trois heures à Paris, quelle heure est-il à Bangkok?**
>
> VOTRE PARTENAIRE: **Il est neuf heures à Bangkok.**

1. 23 h à Paris/Anchorage?
2. 6 h à Paris/Montréal?
3. 14 h à Paris/Londres?
4. 18 h 30 à Paris/Fort-de-France?
5. 12 h à Paris/Mexico?
6. 3 h 20 à Paris/Chicago?
7. 15 h 45 à Paris/Saint-Denis?
8. 11 h à Paris/Tokyo?

9 **À vous.** Répondez.

1. Quelle heure est-il maintenant?
2. À quelle heure déjeunez-vous d'habitude?
3. Allez-vous faire vos devoirs ce soir? Si oui, de quelle heure à quelle heure?
4. Combien d'heures étudiez-vous par jour?
5. À quelle heure allez-vous dîner ce soir?
6. Allez-vous sortir ce soir? Si oui, à quelle heure? Avec qui?
7. Allez-vous regarder la télévision ce soir? Si oui, de quelle heure à quelle heure? Qu'est-ce que vous allez regarder?

Entre amis

À l'aéroport

1. Ask your partner what time it is.
2. Ask if s/he is going to Paris. (S/he is.)
3. Ask what time it is in Paris now.
4. Ask at what time s/he is going to arrive in Paris.
5. Find out what s/he is going to do in Paris.

3 Explaining Your Schedule

Quel jour est-ce aujourd'hui?
C'est ...

lundi°	*Monday*
mardi°	*Tuesday*
mercredi	
jeudi°	*Thursday*
vendredi	
samedi	
dimanche	

Quel jour est-ce demain?

D. Les jours de la semaine

■ Days of the week are not capitalized in French.

■ The calendar week begins on Monday and ends on Sunday.

	janvier					
lundi	mardi	mercredi	jeudi	vendredi	samedi	dimanche
		1	2	3	4	5
6	7	8	9	10	11	12
13	14	15	16	17	18	19
20	21	22	23	24	25	26
27	28	29	30	31		

> Review the verb **avoir**, p. 60. It is used with **envie**, **l'intention**, and **l'habitude**. Remember to use **de** + infinitive after these expressions.

■ When referring to a specific day, neither an article nor a preposition is used.

Demain, c'est **vendredi.**	*Tomorrow is Friday.*
C'est **vendredi** demain.	*Tomorrow is Friday.*
J'ai envie de sortir **vendredi** soir.	*I feel like going out Friday evening.*
J'ai l'intention d'étudier **samedi.**	*I plan to study Saturday.*

■ To express the meaning *Saturdays, every Saturday, on Saturdays,* etc., the article **le** is used with the name of the day.

Je n'ai pas de cours **le samedi.**	*I don't have class on Saturdays.*
Le mardi, mon premier cours est à 10 heures.	*On Tuesdays, my first class is at ten o'clock.*
Le vendredi soir, j'ai l'habitude de sortir avec mes amis.	*On Friday nights, I usually go out with my friends.*

■ Similarly, to express the meaning *mornings, every morning, in the morning,* etc., with parts of the day, **le** or **la** is used before the noun.

Le matin, je vais au cours de français.	*Every morning, I go to French class.*
L'après-midi, je vais à la bibliothèque.	*Afternoons, I go to the library.*
Le soir, je fais mes devoirs.	*In the evening, I do my homework.*
La nuit, je suis au lit.	*At night, I'm in bed.*

⑩ Le samedi soir. Utilisez l'expression **avoir envie de** ou **avoir l'habitude de,** d'après les modèles.

MODÈLES: les étudiants / envie / sortir ou rester dans leur chambre
Le samedi soir, ils ont envie de sortir; ils n'ont pas envie de rester dans leur chambre.

Ma sœur / l'habitude / aller au cinéma ou faire des devoirs
Le samedi soir, elle a l'habitude d'aller au cinéma; elle n'a pas l'habitude de faire ses devoirs.

1. les étudiants / envie / rester sur le campus ou aller au cinéma
2. je / l'habitude / voir un film ou faire mes devoirs
3. le professeur / l'habitude / préparer ses cours ou regarder la télévision
4. mes amis et moi, nous / envie / dîner entre amis ou dîner seuls
5. mon ami(e) _____ / l'habitude / sortir avec moi ou rester dans sa chambre

11 **À vous.** Répondez.

1. Quels sont les jours où vous allez au cours de français?
2. À quelle heure est votre cours?
3. Quels sont les jours où vous n'avez pas de cours?
4. Qu'est-ce que vous avez l'intention de faire le week-end prochain?
5. Avez-vous l'habitude d'aller au gymnase? Si oui, quels jours et à quelle heure?
6. À quelle heure avez-vous votre premier cours le mardi?
7. Quand est-ce que vous allez à la bibliothèque?
8. Quand écoutez-vous la radio?
9. Quand avez-vous envie de regarder la télévision?

VOCABULAIRE

Quelques cours

l'art *(m.)*	*art*	les mathématiques *(f. pl.)*	*math*
la chimie	*chemistry*	la musique	*music*
le commerce	*business*	la pédagogie	*education, teacher*
la comptabilité	*accounting*		*preparation*
la gestion	*management*	la philosophie	*philosophy*
la gymnastique	*gymnastics*	la psychologie	*psychology*
l'histoire *(f.)*	*history*	les sciences *(f. pl.)*	*science*
l'informatique *(f.)*	*computer science*	les sciences économiques *(f. pl.)*	*economics*
la littérature	*literature*	les sciences politiques *(f. pl.)*	*political science*

12 **Mon emploi du temps** *(My schedule).* Indiquez votre emploi du temps pour ce semestre. Indiquez le jour, l'heure et le cours.

MODÈLE: **Le lundi à dix heures, j'ai un cours de français.**
Le lundi à onze heures, j'ai un cours de mathématiques.
Le lundi à une heure, j'ai un cours d'histoire.

13 **As-tu un cours de commerce?** Essayez de deviner *(try to guess)* deux des cours de votre partenaire. Demandez ensuite quels jours et à quelle heure votre partenaire va à ces cours. Votre partenaire va répondre à vos questions.

MODÈLE: **As-tu un cours d'histoire?**
Quels jours vas-tu à ce cours?
À quelle heure vas-tu à ce cours?

E. Le verbe *devoir*

Les étudiants doivent beaucoup travailler.   *Students have to work a lot.*

Vous devez être fatigués.   *You must be tired.*

devoir *(to have to, must; to owe)*			
je	**dois**	nous	**devons**
tu	**dois**	vous	**devez**
il/elle/on	**doit**	ils/elles	**doivent**

- **Devoir** is often used with the infinitive to express an obligation or a probability.

  Vous **devez faire** attention! *(obligation)*   *You must pay attention!*

  Lori **doit avoir** vingt ans. *(probability)*   *Lori must be twenty.*

- **Devoir** plus a noun means *to owe*.

  Je dois vingt dollars à mes parents.   *I owe my parents twenty dollars.*

Synthèse:	**Révision des verbes**					
	parler	être	avoir	faire	aller	devoir
je	**parle**	**suis**	**ai**	**fais**	**vais**	**dois**
tu	**parles**	**es**	**as**	**fais**	**vas**	**dois**
il/elle/on	**parle**	**est**	**a**	**fait**	**va**	**doit**
nous	**parlons**	**sommes**	**avons**	**faisons**	**allons**	**devons**
vous	**parlez**	**êtes**	**avez**	**faites**	**allez**	**devez**
ils/elles	**parlent**	**sont**	**ont**	**font**	**vont**	**doivent**

(handwritten annotations: to speak, to be, to have, to do, to go, to have to / must / to owe)

14 **Mais qu'est-ce qu'on doit faire?** Utilisez l'expression entre parenthèses pour indiquer ce que chaque personne doit faire.

> **MODÈLE:** Gérard a envie d'aller au cinéma. (étudier)
> **Gérard a envie d'aller au cinéma mais il doit étudier.**

1. Nous avons envie de sortir ce soir. (préparer un examen)
2. Les étudiants ont envie de regarder la télévision. (étudier)
3. Tu as envie de danser ce soir. (faire tes devoirs)
4. J'ai envie de rester au lit. (aller aux cours)
5. Le professeur a envie de faire un voyage. (enseigner)
6. Tes amis ont envie d'aller en ville. (faire la lessive)

15 **Je dois faire ça cette semaine.** Faites une liste de sept choses que vous devez faire cette semaine (une chose pour chaque jour).

> **MODÈLE:** **Samedi, je dois faire le ménage.**

16 **Et alors?** Pour chaque phrase, inventez une ou deux conclusions logiques.

> **MODÈLE:** Lori n'a pas envie de passer le week-end dans sa chambre. Qu'est-ce qu'elle va faire?
> **Elle va sortir.** ou **Elle a l'intention d'aller au cinéma.**

1. Lori a envie de sortir ce soir. Où va-t-elle? Que fait-elle?
2. Mais son amie Denise n'est pas libre. Qu'est-ce qu'elle doit faire?
3. Lori et Denise font souvent les courses ensemble. Où vont-elles?
4. Aujourd'hui Denise reste dans sa chambre. Pourquoi? Comment va-t-elle?
5. Lori téléphone à Denise. Pourquoi? De quoi parle-t-elle?

Entre amis

Ton emploi du temps

1. Find out what time it is.
2. Find out what day it is today.
3. Find out what classes your partner has today.
4. Find out when your partner goes to the library.
5. Find out if your partner has to work and, if so, on what days.
6. Find out if your partner feels like going to the movies tonight.

4 Telling Where to Find Places

Où se trouve° la souris?   *is located*

La souris est loin
du fromage.

La souris est près
du fromage.

La souris est devant
le fromage.

La souris est derrière
le fromage.

La souris est sur
le fromage.

La souris est sous
le fromage.

La souris est dans
le fromage.

Où se trouve le
fromage? Le fromage
est dans la souris.

F. Quelques prépositions de lieu

Les toilettes se trouvent **dans** le couloir.

Les toilettes sont **à côté de** la salle
de classe.

Le cinéma se trouve **au** centre
commercial.

La banque est **à droite** ou **à gauche**
du parking?

Allez **tout droit** et ensuite tournez
à droite.

The restroom is in the hall.

*The restroom is next to the
classroom.*

*The movie theater is at
the mall.*

*Is the bank on the right or on the
left of the parking lot?*

*Go straight ahead and then
turn to the right.*

à	*at; in; to*		**dans**	*in*
à côté de	*beside*		**entre**	*between; among*
à droite de	*on the right of*	≠	**à gauche de**	*on the left of*
derrière	*behind*	≠	**devant**	*in front of*
loin de	*far from*	≠	**près de**	*near*
sous	*under*	≠	**sur**	*on*

■ **À côté, à droite, à gauche, loin,** and **près** can all drop the **de** and stand alone.

<blockquote>
Nous habitons **à côté d'**une église.   *We live next to a church.*
But: **L'église est à côté.**   *The church is next door.*
</blockquote>

Note   **À droite** means *to (on) the right*, while **tout droit** means *straight ahead*.

17   **Où se trouvent ces endroits?**   Répondez à la question posée par *(asked by)* votre partenaire.

> **MODÈLE:**   La bibliothèque (près / bâtiment des sciences)
> > **VOTRE PARTENAIRE: Où se trouve la bibliothèque?**
> > **VOUS: Elle est près du bâtiment des sciences.**

1. le bâtiment administratif (près / bibliothèque)
2. la pharmacie (à côté / église)
3. les résidences universitaires (sur / campus)
4. le restaurant universitaire (dans / résidence)
5. le cinéma (à / centre commercial)
6. le bureau de poste (derrière / pharmacie)
7. le centre commercial (loin / campus)
8. les toilettes (devant / salle de classe)
9. le parking (à gauche / banque)

18   **Votre campus.**   Faites rapidement le plan *(Draw a map)* de votre campus. Expliquez où se trouvent cinq endroits différents.

> **MODÈLE:**   **Voilà la résidence qui s'appelle Brown Hall. Elle est près de la bibliothèque.**

<aside>Review contractions with **de**, p. 74.</aside>

G. L'impératif

Regarde!	*Look!*
Regardez!	*Look!*
Regardons!	*Let's look!*
Tourne à gauche!	*Turn to the left!*
Tournez à gauche!	*Turn to the left!*
Tournons à gauche!	*Let's turn to the left!*

<aside>You already learned a number of imperatives in the preliminary chapter, p. 2.</aside>

■ The imperative is used to give commands and to make suggestions. The forms are usually the same as the present tense for **tu, vous,** and **nous.**

Note   If the infinitive ends in **-er,** the final **-s** is omitted from the form that corresponds to **tu.**

parler français	tu parle**s** français	But: **Parle** français!
aller aux cours	tu va**s** aux cours	But: **Va** aux cours!

■ For negative commands, **ne** precedes the verb and **pas** follows it.

Ne regardez **pas** la télévision!
Ne fais **pas** attention à Papa!

19 **En ville.** Regardez le plan (*map*) de la ville. Demandez où se trouvent les endroits suivants. Votre partenaire va expliquer où ils se trouvent.

MODÈLE: cinéma

> VOUS: **Où se trouve le cinéma, s'il vous plaît?**
>
> VOTRE PARTENAIRE: **Il est à côté du café. Allez tout droit et tournez à gauche. Il est à droite.**

1. café	6. bureau de tabac
2. épicerie	7. banque
3. église	8. cinéma
4. boulangerie	9. pharmacie
5. bureau de poste	10. hôtel

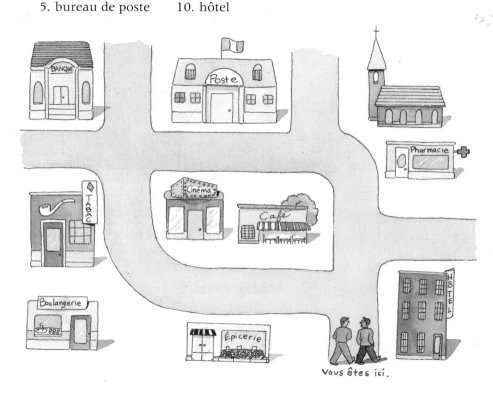

Vous êtes ici.

20 **Qu'est-ce que les bons étudiants doivent faire?** Utilisez l'impératif pour répondre à la question. Décidez ce qu'un bon étudiant doit ou ne doit pas faire.

MODÈLE: Est-ce que je dois passer tout le week-end dans ma chambre?
> **Ne passez pas tout le week-end dans votre chambre!** ou
> **Oui, passez tout le week-end dans votre chambre!**

1. Est-ce que je dois habiter dans une résidence universitaire?
2. Est-ce que je dois manger à la cafétéria?
3. Est-ce que je dois faire mes devoirs dans ma chambre?
4. Est-ce que je dois étudier à la bibliothèque?
5. Est-ce que je ne dois pas aller au bistro?
6. Est-ce que je ne dois pas parler anglais au cours de français?

Entre amis

Vous êtes un(e) nouvel(le) étudiant(e)

1. Find out where a shopping center is.
2. Find out where the cafeteria is.
3. Find out where the library is.
4. Ask where the restroom is.

H. Les prépositions de lieu avec une ville ou un pays

Review the contractions in this chapter on p. 125.

■ Use **à** to say that you are in a city or are going to a city.

Note In cases where the name of a city contains the definite article **(Le Mans, Le Caire, La Nouvelle-Orléans),** the article is retained and the normal contractions occur where necessary.

Emmanuelle habite **à La Nouvelle-Orléans.** Nous allons **au Mans.**
Je suis **à Paris.** Je vais **à New York.**

■ Most countries, states, and provinces ending in **-e** are feminine. An exception is **le Mexique.**

la Belgiqu**e**	**la** Colombi**e** Britannique
la Virgini**e**	**la** Californi**e**

But: **le Mexique**

■ To say you are in or going to a *country,* the preposition varies. Use **en** before feminine countries or those that begin with a vowel sound. Use **au** before masculine countries which begin with a consonant and use **aux** when the name of the country is plural.

en France	**au** Canada	**aux** États-Unis
en Israël	**au** Mexique	**aux** Pays-Bas

■ To say you are in or going to an American *state* or a Canadian *province,* **en** is normally used before those that are feminine or that begin with a vowel sound. The preposition **au** is often used with masculine provinces that begin with a consonant and with the states of Texas and New Mexico.

en Virginie	**en** Ontario	**au** Manitoba
en Nouvelle-Écosse	**en** Ohio	**au** Nouveau-Mexique

Note You may also use **dans l'état de** or **dans la province de.**

J'habite **dans l'état de** New York.
Je voyage **dans la province d'**Alberta.

Review the adjectives of nationality in Ch. 1, p. 18.

See how many of the countries listed you can find on the maps on the inside covers of your text.

Quelques langues et quelques pays

On parle ...	allemand	**en** ...	Allemagne
	anglais		Angleterre
	français et flamand		Belgique
	chinois		Chine
	espagnol		Espagne
	français		France
	anglais et irlandais		Irlande
	italien		Italie
	russe		Russie
	suédois		Suède
	français, allemand et italien		Suisse
On parle ...	français et anglais	**au** ...	Canada
	japonais		Japon
	français et arabe		Maroc
	espagnol		Mexique
	portugais		Portugal
	français et wolof		Sénégal
On parle ...	anglais, espagnol et français	**aux** ...	États-Unis
	hollandais		Pays-Bas

■ When talking about more than one country, use a preposition before each one.

On parle français **en** France, **en** Belgique, **au** Canada, **au** Maroc, **au** Sénégal, etc.

■ When there is no preposition with a country, state, or province, the definite article must be used.

La France est un beau pays.
J'adore **le Canada**.

Note **Israël** is an exception.

Israël est à côté de la Syrie.

21 **Où habitent-ils?** Dans quel pays les personnes suivantes habitent-elles?

MODÈLE: Vous êtes français.
Vous habitez en France.

1. Lucie est canadienne.
2. Les Dewonck sont belges.
3. Phoebe est anglaise.
4. Pepe et María sont mexicains.
5. Yuko est japonaise.
6. Yolande est sénégalaise.
7. Sean et Deirdre sont irlandais.
8. Caterina est italienne.
9. Hassan est marocain.
10. Nous sommes américains.

Qui sont ces personnes? Où habitent-elles? Vous êtes à l'aéroport d'Orly et vous écoutez des touristes de divers pays. Devinez leur nationalité et où ils vont.

> **MODÈLE:** Il y a deux hommes qui parlent espagnol.
> **Ils doivent être espagnols ou mexicains.**
> **Ils vont probablement en Espagne ou au Mexique.**

1. Il y a un homme et une femme qui parlent français.
2. Il y a deux enfants qui parlent anglais.
3. Il y a une jeune fille qui parle russe.
4. Il y a trois garçons qui parlent arabe.
5. Il y a une personne qui parle suédois.
6. Il y a un homme qui parle allemand.
7. Il y a deux couples qui parlent flamand.
8. Il y a deux jeunes filles qui parlent italien.
9. Il y a un homme et une femme qui parlent japonais.

I. Les mots interrogatifs *où* et *quand*

■ A question using **quand** or **où** is formed like any other question, using inversion or **est-ce que.**

> Où habitent-ils? Quand arrive-t-elle?
> Où est-ce qu'ils habitent? Quand est-ce qu'elle arrive?

Review interrogative forms, pp. 45–46.

Note In **Quand est-ce que,** the **-d** is pronounced [t]. When **quand** is followed by inversion, there is no liaison.

■ With a *noun* subject, the inversion order is *noun + verb + subject pronoun.*

> Où **tes parents habitent-ils?** Quand **ta sœur arrive-t-elle?**

■ In addition, if there is only one verb and no object, the noun subject and the verb may be inverted.

> Où **habitent tes parents?** Quand **arrive ta sœur?**

 Où et quand? Pour chaque phrase, posez une question avec **où.** Votre partenaire va inventer une réponse. Ensuite, posez une question avec **quand.** Votre partenaire va inventer une réponse à cette question aussi.

> **MODÈLE:** Mon frère fait un voyage.
> **VOUS: Où est-ce qu'il fait un voyage?**
> **VOTRE PARTENAIRE: Il fait un voyage en France.**
> **VOUS: Quand est-ce qu'il fait ce voyage?**
> **VOTRE PARTENAIRE: Il fait ce voyage la semaine prochaine.**

1. Mon amie a envie de faire des courses.
2. Nous avons l'intention de déjeuner ensemble.
3. Je vais au cinéma.
4. Mon cousin travaille.
5. Mes amis étudient.

24 **À vous.** Répondez.

1. Où les étudiants de votre université habitent-ils?
2. Où se trouve la bibliothèque sur votre campus?
3. Quels bâtiments se trouvent près de la bibliothèque?
4. Où se trouve la salle de classe pour le cours de français?
5. Quand avez-vous votre cours de français?
6. Où les étudiants dînent-ils d'habitude le dimanche soir?
7. Où allez-vous vendredi prochain? Pourquoi?

Entre amis

Un pays où on ne parle pas anglais

1. Tell your partner you are going to a country where English is not spoken.
2. S/he will try to guess where.
3. S/he will try to guess the language(s) spoken there.
4. S/he will ask when you are going to that country.

Intégration

Révision

A **Au revoir.** Quels sont cinq synonymes de l'expression **au revoir?**

B **Les pays.** Répondez.

1. Quels sont cinq pays où on parle français?
2. Nommez deux pays en Europe, deux pays en Asie et deux pays en Afrique.
3. Dans quels pays se trouvent ces villes: Dakar? Genève? Trois-Rivières? Lyon? Montréal? Prairie du Chien? Rabat? Bruxelles? Des Moines? Bâton Rouge?

C **À vous.** Répondez.

1. Qu'est-ce que vous avez envie de faire ce week-end? (trois choses)
2. Qu'est-ce que vous devez faire?
3. Qu'est-ce que vos amis aiment faire le samedi soir?
4. Qu'est-ce que vous faites le lundi? (trois choses)
5. Quels sont les jours où vous allez à votre cours de français?
6. À quelle heure allez-vous à ce cours?
7. Dans quel bâtiment avez-vous ce cours? Où se trouve ce bâtiment?
8. Quel est votre jour préféré? Pourquoi?

D **Trouvez quelqu'un qui ...** Interviewez les autres.

1. Find someone who is studying computer science.
2. Find someone who rarely goes to the library.
3. Find someone who speaks another language.
4. Find someone who plans to go to France or Quebec.
5. Find someone who has to work next weekend.
6. Find someone who is going to go out on Friday evening.
7. Find someone who usually does homework on Friday evening.

Pas de problème!

Cette activité est basée sur la vidéo *Pas de problème (Module 2)*. Répondez.

Preparation for the video:
1. Video worksheet in the *Cahier d'activités*
2. CD-ROM, *Module 2*

1. Qu'est-ce que Jean-François et Marie-Christine vont faire aujourd'hui?
2. Est-ce que Marie-Christine habite Rive *(bank)* gauche ou Rive droite?
3. Quelle est son adresse?
4. Pourquoi est-ce que Jean-François ne téléphone pas tout de suite *(right away)* à Marie-Christine?
5. Où est-ce qu'on va pour trouver des télécartes?
6. Quel est le code pour la porte de chez Marie-Christine?

Lecture I

A **Étude du vocabulaire.** Étudiez les phrases suivantes et choisissez *(choose)* les mots anglais qui correspondent aux mots français en caractères gras *(bold print): river, friendly, winter, foreign, summer, holiday, king, team, schedule.*

1. Le 14 juillet est un **jour férié** parce que c'est la fête nationale française.
2. Il faut consulter l'**horaire** des trains avant d'aller à la gare.
3. La Loire est le **fleuve** le plus long de France.
4. Les Angevins sont très **accueillants.** Ils vous invitent souvent.
5. L'**équipe** canadienne a gagné le match de hockey.
6. Un **roi** est le monarque d'un pays.
7. En **hiver** il fait d'habitude froid et en **été** il fait souvent très chaud.
8. À Paris on rencontre toujours beaucoup d'**étrangers:** des touristes allemands, américains, anglais et des immigrés aussi.

B **Parcourez la publicité.** Lisez rapidement la lecture pour trouver l'adresse et le numéro de téléphone de l'Office de Tourisme.

Vos vacances à Angers

Douces vacances à Angers
Capitale de l'Anjou
Au cœur d'une province accueillante,
Angers vous offre
mille et une promenades.

Angers
Capitale de l'Anjou

Il y a en France, le long d'un fleuve majestueux qu'on appelle la Loire, une vallée célèbre par ses richesses, son climat et sa beauté. C'était dans cette région que les seigneurs, les princes et les rois de France ont fait construire les plus beaux châteaux, les plus belles maisons. C'est dans cette vallée de la Loire que se trouve l'Anjou et la capitale de l'Anjou s'appelle Angers.

VISITES GUIDÉES
Visites panoramiques
Visites à thèmes
Visites «scolaires»

RÉCEPTIF
Forfaits
Séjours à la carte
Événementiel

ACCUEIL
Information
Documentation
Billetterie
Change

ANGERS
TOURISME

Une équipe compétente qui vous simplifie la ville
Place du Président Kennedy - BP 5157 - 49 051 ANGERS Cédex 02
Tél. FRANCE : 02 41 23 51 11 - Fax. FRANCE : 02 41 23 51 10
Tél. FRANCE : 332 41 23 51 11 - Fax. ETRANGER : 332 41 223 51 10
Horaires d'hiver : du lundi au samedi : 9h30 à 18h30 - dimanche : 10h à 13h
Horaires d'été : du lundi au samedi : 9h à 19h - dimanches et jours fériés : 10h à 13h - 14h à 18h

Questions. Relisez toute la lecture et ensuite répondez aux questions suivantes.

1. Où se trouve la ville d'Angers?
2. Qu'est-ce que c'est que la Loire?
3. Pourquoi la vallée de la Loire est-elle célèbre?
4. À quelle heure l'Office de Tourisme ouvre-t-il le dimanche?
5. À quelle heure l'Office de Tourisme ferme-t-il le samedi en été?
6. À quelle heure ferme-t-il le 14 juillet? Pourquoi?

 Familles de mots. Essayez de deviner le sens *(try to guess the meaning)* des mots suivants.

1. accueillir, un accueil, accueillant(e)
2. célébrer, une célébrité, célèbre
3. construire, la construction, constructif, constructive
4. offrir, une offre, offert(e)
5. simplifier, la simplification, simple

Lecture II

 Trouvez le Cameroun. Cherchez le Cameroun sur la carte à l'intérieur de la couverture de ce livre. Sur quel continent se trouve ce pays? Quelle est la capitale du Cameroun? Quels sont les pays qui se trouvent près du Cameroun?

Étude du vocabulaire. Étudiez les phrases suivantes et choisissez les mots anglais qui correspondent aux mots français en caractères gras: *birds, against, a cooking utensil, I see, each one, I hear, people, a popular African food, peace, bark, roof.*

1. **J'entends** quelquefois des chiens qui **aboient** quand une voiture passe.
2. Il y a des **oiseaux** sur le **toit** de la maison.
3. **Je vois** des **gens** qui portent des vêtements africains.
4. **Chacun** porte des sandales.
5. Dans leur village on mange du **taro.**
6. On prépare la cuisine avec un **pilon.**
7. Êtes-vous pour ou **contre** la **paix** dans ce pauvre pays?

Village Natal

Ici je suis chez moi,
Je suis vraiment chez moi.
Les hommes que je vois,
Les femmes que je croise[1]
M'appellent leur fils
Et les enfants leur frère.
Le patois qu'on parle est le mien,
Les chants que j'entends expriment[2]
Des joies et des peines qui sont miennes.
L'herbe que je foule reconnaît mes pas[3].
Les chiens n'aboient pas contre moi,
Mais ils remuent la queue[4]
En signe de reconnaissance.
Les oiseaux me saluent au passage
Par des chants affectueux.
Des coups de pilon m'invitent

À me régaler de[5] taro
Si mon ventre est creux[6].
Sous chacun de ces toits qui fument
Lentement dans la paix du soir
On voudra m'accueillir[7].
Bientôt c'est la fête, la fête de chaque soir:
Chants et danses autour du feu[8],
Au rythme du tam-tam, du tambour, du balafon[9].
Nos gens sont pauvres
Mais très simples, très heureux;
Je suis simple comme eux[10]
Content comme eux,
Heureux comme eux.
Ici je suis chez moi,
Je suis vraiment chez moi.

Jean-Louis Dongmo,
Neuf poètes camerounais, Éditions Clé

1. *that I meet*   2. *express*   3. *the grass I walk on recognizes my steps*   4. *wag their tails*   5. *have a delicious meal of*
6. *stomach is empty*   7. *people will welcome me*   8. *around the fire*   9. *musical instruments*   10. *them*

C **Discussion.** Répondez en anglais ou en français.

1. Cherchez les exemples dans le poème qui prouvent que le poète est heureux d'être dans son village.
2. Quelles ressemblances et quelles différences y a-t-il entre le poète et vous?

VOCABULAIRE ACTIF

Adverbes
après *after*
avant *before*
d'abord *at first*
demain *tomorrow*
enfin *finally*
ensuite *next, then*
maintenant *now*

Jours de la semaine
lundi *(m.) Monday*
mardi *(m.) Tuesday*
mercredi *(m.) Wednesday*
jeudi *(m.) Thursday*
vendredi *(m.) Friday*
samedi *(m.) Saturday*
dimanche *(m.) Sunday*

Adjectifs
libre *free*
parfait(e) *perfect*
premier (première) *first*
prochain(e) *next*
seul(e) *alone; only*

Expressions de lieu
à côté *next door; to the side*
à côté de *next to, beside*
derrière *behind*
devant *in front of*
à droite *on (to) the right*
à gauche *on (to) the left*
entre *between, among*
loin *far*
sous *under*
tout droit *straight ahead*

Pays
l'Allemagne *(f.) Germany*
l'Angleterre *(f.) England*
la Belgique *Belgium*
le Canada *Canada*
la Chine *China*
l'Espagne *(f.) Spain*
les États-Unis *(m. pl.) United States*
la France *France*
l'Irlande *(f.) Ireland*
Israël *(m.) Israel*

l'Italie *(f.) Italy*
le Japon *Japan*
le Maroc *Morocco*
le Mexique *Mexico*
les Pays-Bas *(m. pl.) Netherlands*
le Portugal *Portugal*
la Russie *Russia*
le Sénégal *Senegal*
la Suède *Sweden*
la Suisse *Switzerland*

Verbes
aller *to go*
aller en ville *to go into town*
avoir envie de *to want to; to feel like*
avoir l'habitude de *to usually; to be in the habit of*
avoir l'intention de *to plan to*
déjeuner *to have lunch*
devoir *to have to, must; to owe*
faire un voyage *to take a trip*
passer un test *to take a test*
rester *to stay*
tourner *to turn*

Cours
la chimie *chemistry*
le commerce *business*
la comptabilité *accounting*
la gestion *management*
la gymnastique *gymnastics*
l'informatique *(f.) computer science*
la littérature *literature*
la pédagogie *education, teacher preparation*
les sciences *(f.) science*
les sciences économiques *(f.) economics*

Autre préposition
vers (8 heures) *approximately, around (8 o'clock)*

Expressions de temps
Quelle heure est-il? *What time is it?*
Quel jour est-ce? *What day is it?*

Il est ... heure(s). *It is ... o'clock.*
Il est midi (minuit). *It is noon (midnight).*
et demi(e) *half past*
et quart *quarter past, quarter after*
moins le quart *quarter to, quarter till*
ce soir *tonight*
dans une heure (trois jours, etc.) *one hour (three days, etc.) from now*
une minute *minute*
une semaine *week*
tout à l'heure *in a little while*
tout le week-end *all weekend (long)*

D'autres expressions utiles
Cela (ça) m'est égal. *I don't care.*
D'accord. *Okay.*
Je vais sortir. *I'm going to go out.*
Où se trouve (se trouvent) ... ? *Where is (are) ... ?*
pas grand-chose *not much*
Quoi de neuf? *What's new?*
Ça va? *Okay?*
Tu vas voir. *You are going to see.*

D'autres noms
une bise *kiss*
un emploi du temps *schedule*
un film *film, movie*
le fromage *cheese*
un rendez-vous *appointment; date*
une souris *mouse*
un voyage *trip, voyage*
l'arabe *Arabic*
le flamand *Flemish*
le portugais *Portuguese*
le wolof *Wolof*

Endroits
un aéroport *airport*
une banque *bank*
un bâtiment *building*
une bibliothèque *library*
un bistro *bar and café; bistro*
une boulangerie *bakery*

un bureau de poste *post office*
un bureau de tabac *tobacco shop*
une cafétéria *cafeteria*
un campus *campus*
un centre commercial *shopping center, mall*
un château *chateau; castle*
un cinéma *movie theater*
un couloir *hall; corridor*
un cours *course; class*
une école *school*
une église *church*
un endroit *place*
une épicerie *grocery store*
un état *state*

un gymnase *gymnasium*
une librairie *bookstore*
un musée *museum*
un parking *parking lot, garage*
un pays *country*
une pharmacie *pharmacy*
une piscine *swimming pool*
une province *province*
une résidence (universitaire) *dormitory*
un restaurant *restaurant*
une salle de classe *classroom*
les toilettes *(f. pl.) restroom*
une ville *city*

6 Vos activités

Buts communicatifs
Relating past events
Describing your study habits
Describing your weekend activities

Structures utiles
Le passé composé avec **avoir**
Les verbes **écrire** et **lire**
Ne ... rien
Temps, heure et **fois**
Les verbes pronominaux
Jouer de et **jouer à**
Les pronoms accentués
Les verbes **dormir, partir** et **sortir**
Les verbes **nettoyer** et **envoyer**

Culture
La maison
Relativité culturelle: La maison

Coup d'envoi

Qu'est-ce que tu as fait hier?

Sébastien, qu'est-ce que tu as fait hier?°	*What did you do yesterday?*
J'ai téléphoné à deux amis.	
J'ai envoyé des messages électroniques°.	*sent e-mail*
J'ai fait mes devoirs.	
J'ai étudié pendant° trois heures.	*for*
J'ai déjeuné à midi et j'ai dîné à 7 heures du soir.	
J'ai regardé un peu la télévision.	
Mais je n'ai pas fait le ménage.	
Et je n'ai pas passé d'examen°.	*test*

▶ **Et vous?** Qu'est-ce que vous avez fait?

Lettre

This letter is recorded on the Student Audio included with your text.

Une lettre à des amis

Lori a écrit une lettre à deux de ses camarades du cours de français aux États-Unis.

Angers, le 15 décembre

Chers John et Cathy,

Merci beaucoup de vos lettres. Que le temps passe vite![1] Je suis en France depuis déjà trois mois[2]. Vous avez demandé si j'ai le temps de voyager. Oui, mais je suis très active et très occupée parce qu[3]'il y a toujours tant de[4] choses à faire. C'est la vie, n'est-ce pas?

Dimanche dernier[5], j'ai accompagné ma famille française au Mans chez les parents de Mme Martin. Nous avons passé trois heures à table! Cette semaine, j'ai lu une pièce[6] de Molière pour mon cours de littérature et j'ai écrit une dissertation[7]. J'ai aussi fait le ménage et j'ai gardé[8] les enfants pour Mme Martin. Heureusement, je ne me lève pas tôt[9] le samedi.

Vous avez demandé si j'ai remarqué[10] des différences entre la France et les États-Unis. Eh bien, oui. Chez les Martin, par exemple, les portes à l'intérieur de la maison sont toujours fermées[11], les toilettes ne sont pas dans la salle de bain et les robinets[12] sont marqués «C» et «F». J'ai déjà oublié[13] deux fois[14] que «C» ne veut pas dire «cold». Aïe![15]

Dites bonjour[16] pour moi à Madame Walter, s.v.p. Écrivez-moi à lbecker@wanadoo.fr

Bonnes vacances!

Votre amie «française»,

Lori

1. *How time flies!* 2. *I've already been in France for three months* 3. *because* 4. *so many* 5. *last* 6. *I read a play* 7. *I wrote a (term) paper* 8. *watched, looked after* 9. *Fortunately, I don't get up early* 10. *I noticed* 11. *closed* 12. *faucets* 13. *I already forgot* 14. *times* 15. *Ouch!* 16. *Say hello*

Compréhension. Décidez si les phrases suivantes sont vraies ou fausses. Si une phrase est fausse, corrigez-la.

1. Lori a déjà passé trois mois en France.
2. En France on passe beaucoup de temps à table.
3. Lori a beaucoup de temps libre.
4. On ferme les portes dans une maison française.
5. «C» sur un robinet veut dire «chaud».
6. «F» sur un robinet veut dire «français».

À PROPOS

Pourquoi est-ce que les portes sont fermées à l'intérieur d'une maison française?

a. Les Français désirent être différents des autres.

b. Les Français préfèrent l'ordre et l'intimité *(privacy)*.

c. Les Français ont peur des voleurs *(are afraid of thieves)*.

La maison

Living in France has meant more to Lori than just learning the French language. She has also had the opportunity to become part of a French family and has had to learn to cope with a number of cultural differences. There is no need in French for a separate word to distinguish between *house* and *home.* Both are **la maison,** and **la maison** is seen as a refuge from the storm of the world outside, a place to find comfort and solace and to put order into one's existence. Given the French attitude about **la maison,** it is not surprising to find social and architectural indications of that need for order. There is a set time for meals, and family members are expected to be there. There is an order to a French meal that is quite different from the everything-on-one-plate-at-one-time eating style prevalent in English-speaking North America. The walls around French houses, the shutters on the windows, and the closing of the doors inside the home

are other examples of the French desire for order and clearly established boundaries.

Relativité culturelle: La maison

The home is undoubtedly the scene of the greatest number of cultural contrasts. There are, therefore, some potentially troublesome adjustments.

In France	In North America
Doors are closed, especially the bathroom door, even when no one is in the room.	Doors inside a house are often left open.
Since the toilet is often not in the bathroom, one has to be more specific about whether one is looking for **la salle de bain** or **les toilettes.**	Since the toilet, tub, and shower are all in the bathroom, one person may inconvenience the rest of the family.
Hands can be scalded trying to test "cold" water from a faucet marked "C."	Turning on a faucet marked "C" will not make the water get hot (**chaud**) no matter how long one waits.
There are no screens on windows to keep out insects.	Screens on windows don't allow the wide-open feeling one gets from French windows.
There are almost always walls or a hedge to ensure privacy and clearly mark the limits of one's property.	In many neighborhoods there are no walls to separate houses.
See, for example, p. 80	

Il y a un geste

C'est la vie.   A gesture often accompanies the expression **C'est la vie:** the shoulders are shrugged, and the head is slightly tilted to one side. Sometimes the lips are pursed as well, and the palms are upturned. The idea is *That's life and I can't do anything about it.*

J'ai oublié!   The palm of the hand is raised against the temple. This gesture conveys the meaning that you have forgotten something or have made a mistake.

▶ **À vous.**   Donnez une réponse personnelle.

1. Où avez-vous dîné hier soir?
2. Combien de temps avez-vous passé à table?
3. Qu'est-ce que vous avez fait après le dîner?

Entre amis

Hier

1. Ask what your partner did yesterday.
2. S/he will tell you at least two things.
3. Choose one of the things s/he did and find out as much as you can about it (at what time, where, etc.).

Prononciation

Les sons [u] et [y]

■   Because of differences in meaning in words such as **tout** and **tu,** it is very important to distinguish between the vowel sounds [u] and [y]. The following words contain these two important vowel sounds. Practice saying these words after your teacher, paying particular attention to the highlighted vowel sound.

[u]   • bonj**ou**r, r**ou**ge, c**ou**rs, éc**ou**ter, j**ou**er, tr**ou**ver, v**ou**lez, je v**ou**drais, t**ou**j**ou**rs, beac**ou**p, p**ou**rquoi, s**ou**vent, c**ou**sin, d**ou**te, **ou**vrier, bl**ou**son, c**ou**leur, c**ou**rse, n**ou**veau, auj**ou**rd'hui, c**ou**loir, s**ou**s, t**ou**t, **ou**blié

       • **où**

[y]   • j**u**s, **u**ne, ét**u**dier, ét**u**diants, t**u,** b**u**reau, çalc**u**latrice, voit**u**re, s**u**r, j**u**pe, l**u**nettes, p**u**ll-over, n**u**méro, diffic**u**lté, br**u**ne, st**u**pide, camp**u**s, **u**niversitaire, m**u**sique, R**u**ssie, min**u**te, d**u,** occ**u**pé, j'ai l**u,** littérat**u**re

■ The [**u**] sound, represented by written **ou** or **où,** is close to the sound in the English word *tooth*.

n**ou**s r**ou**ge **où**

■ The [**y**] sound is represented by a single written **-u-**. There is, however, no English "equivalent" for this French sound. To produce it, round your lips as if drinking through a straw; then, without moving your lips, pronounce the vowel in the word **ici.**

d**u** **u**ne sal**u**t v**u**e

Use the Student Audio to help practice pronunciation.

▶ In each of the following pairs of words, one of the words contains the [u] sound, the other the [y] sound. Pronounce each word correctly.

1. sur / sous
2. jour / jupe
3. vous / vu
4. pure / pour
5. cours / cure
6. russe / rousse
7. roux / rue
8. ou / eu
9. tout / tu

Buts communicatifs

1 Relating Past Events

Avez-vous déjà[1] nettoyé[2] votre chambre ce semestre?

Oui, j'ai déjà nettoyé ma chambre.
Non, je n'ai pas encore nettoyé ma chambre.

	oui	non
Avez-vous déjà chanté en français?	____	____
Avez-vous déjà dansé la valse?	____	____
Avez-vous déjà mangé des crêpes?	____	____
Avez-vous déjà joué au tennis?	____	____
Avez-vous déjà travaillé dans un restaurant?	____	____
Avez-vous déjà fumé[3] un cigare?	____	____
Avez-vous déjà été absent(e) ce semestre?	____	____
Avez-vous déjà eu un accident?	____	____
Avez-vous déjà fait vos devoirs pour demain?	____	____

1. *already* 2. *cleaned* 3. *smoked*

A. Le passé composé avec *avoir*

Remember to consult Appendix C at the end of the book to review any grammatical terms with which you are not familiar.

Hier soir, **Michel a regardé** la télévision. — *Last night, Michel watched television.*
Et puis **il a fait** ses devoirs. — *And then he did his homework.*
Pendant combien de temps **a-t-il étudié?** — *How long did he study?*
Il a étudié pendant deux heures. — *He studied for two hours.*

■ The passé composé *(compound past)* is used to tell about or narrate specific events that have already taken place. Depending on the context, its English translation may be any one of several possibilities.

J'ai mangé une pomme.
{ *I ate an apple.*
I did eat an apple.
I have eaten an apple. }

■ The passé composé is formed with the present tense of an auxiliary verb (normally **avoir**) and a past participle.

manger *(au passé composé)*			
j'ai	**mangé**	nous avons	**mangé**
tu as	**mangé**	vous avez	**mangé**
il/elle/on a	**mangé**	ils/elles ont	**mangé**

■ The past participles of all **-er** verbs are pronounced the same as the infinitive. They are spelled by replacing the **-er** ending of the infinitive with **-é.**

étudier	+	-é	⟶	**étudié**
manger	+	-é	⟶	**mangé**
jouer	+	-é	⟶	**joué**

■ The past participles of many verbs that *don't* end in **-er** must be memorized.

In the expression **j'ai eu** *(I had)* the word **eu** is pronounced [y].

eu (avoir)   **été** (être)   **fait** (faire)   **dû** (devoir)

J'**ai eu** la grippe pendant trois jours! — *I had the flu for three days!*
Anne et Guy **ont fait** la cuisine ensemble. — *Anne and Guy did the cooking together.*
Ils ont **dû** dîner à la maison. — *They must have eaten at home. / They had to eat at home.*

■ In the negative, **ne ... pas (ne ... jamais)** is placed around the auxiliary verb.

ne (n') + auxiliary verb + **pas (jamais)** + past participle

Il **n'a pas** écouté la radio. — *He didn't listen to the radio.*
Nous **n'avons pas** fait de promenade. — *We didn't take a walk.*
La plupart des étudiants **n'ont jamais** fumé de cigare. — *Most students have never smoked a cigar.*

Review the formation of questions in Ch. 2, pp. 45–46.

■ Questions in the passé composé are formed the way they are in the present tense. Note, however, that in all cases of inversion, only the auxiliary verb and the subject pronoun are involved. The past participle follows the inverted pronoun.

Il a fait ses devoirs?
Est-ce qu'il a fait ses devoirs?
A-t-il fait ses devoirs?
Marc a-t-il fait ses devoirs?

} *Has he (Marc) done his homework?*

① **Mais il a fait ça hier.** Demandez si David fait les choses suivantes aujourd'hui. Votre partenaire va répondre que David a fait ces choses hier.

> MODÈLE: parler à ses parents
> VOUS: **Est-ce que David travaille aujourd'hui?**
> VOTRE PARTENAIRE: **Non, mais il a travaillé hier.**

1. jouer au tennis
2. être absent
3. avoir une lettre de ses grands-parents
4. dîner avec Véronique
5. manger une pizza
6. faire la vaisselle
7. regarder la télé

② **Véronique.** Pierre aime Véronique et il vous pose des questions parce qu'elle a dîné avec David hier soir. Répondez à ses questions d'après le modèle.

> MODÈLE: Véronique a-t-elle dîné seule? (avec David)
> **Non, elle n'a pas dîné seule; elle a dîné avec David.**

1. Ont-ils dîné au restaurant? (chez David)
2. David a-t-il fait la cuisine? (la vaisselle)
3. Ont-ils mangé un sandwich? (une pizza)
4. Véronique a-t-elle détesté la pizza? (aimé)
5. Ont-ils dansé après le dîner? (regardé la télévision)

③ **La plupart des étudiants.** Qu'est-ce que la plupart des étudiants ont fait hier? Décidez.

Be sure to use plural verb forms with **la plupart des**.

> MODÈLE: fumer une cigarette
> VOTRE PARTENAIRE: **Est-ce que la plupart des étudiants ont fumé une cigarette hier?**
> VOUS: **Non, la plupart des étudiants n'ont pas fumé de cigarette.**

1. étudier à la bibliothèque
2. faire leurs devoirs
3. passer un test
4. avoir une bonne note
5. déjeuner avec leurs professeurs
6. travailler après les cours

VOCABULAIRE

Expressions de temps (passé)

tout à l'heure	*a little while ago*
ce matin	*this morning*
hier soir	*last night*
hier	*yesterday*
hier matin	*yesterday morning*
lundi dernier	*last Monday*
le week-end dernier	*last weekend*
la semaine dernière	*last week*
le mois dernier	*last month*
l'année dernière	*last year*
il y a deux (trois, etc.) ans	*two (three, etc.) years ago*
il y a longtemps	*a long time ago*
la dernière fois	*the last time*
pendant les vacances	*during vacation*

Remember that **tout à l'heure** can also refer to the future: *in a little while.* The expression à **tout à l'heure** means *see you soon.*

Notes

1. **Il y a,** used with an expression of time, means *ago*: **il y a deux mois** *(two months ago)*; **il y a trois ans** *(three years ago).*
2. In general, the word **an** is used when counting the number of years: **un an,** **deux ans,** etc. The word **année** is normally used when referring to a specific year: **cette année, l'année dernière,** etc. The same distinction is made between **jour** and **journée: Il y a trois jours; une belle journée.**

4 Il y a combien de temps? Qu'avons-nous fait? Que n'avons-nous pas fait? Utilisez un élément de chaque colonne pour composer des phrases affirmatives ou négatives.

**MODÈLES: Mes parents ont fait un voyage il y a deux ans.
Mes parents n'ont jamais parlé français.**

	faire un voyage	ne ... jamais
je	avoir des vacances	il y a ...
mes parents	dîner au restaurant	... dernier (dernière)
mon meilleur ami	avoir une lettre	pendant les vacances
ma meilleure amie	être absent(e)(s)	hier (...)
nous	faire la vaisselle	ce matin
	parler français	tout à l'heure
	étudier pendant trois heures	

5 **La dernière fois.** Demandez à votre partenaire quand il (elle) a fait ces choses pour la dernière fois. Il (elle) va répondre.

MODÈLE: être absent(e)

> VOUS: **Quelle est la dernière fois que vous avez été absent(e) ce semestre?**
>
> VOTRE PARTENAIRE: **J'ai été absent(e) la semaine dernière.** ou **Je n'ai jamais été absent(e).**

1. étudier seul(e)
2. fumer
3. devoir passer un examen
4. être malade
5. téléphoner à un ami
6. avoir «A» à l'examen
7. passer trois heures à table
8. nager à la piscine
9. manger une pizza

6 **À vous.** Répondez.

1. Pendant combien de temps avez-vous étudié hier soir?
2. Pendant combien de temps avez-vous regardé la télévision?
3. Quelle est la dernière fois que vous avez téléphoné à un(e) ami(e)? Pendant combien de temps avez-vous parlé au téléphone?
4. Quelle est la dernière fois que vous avez eu la grippe? Pendant combien de temps avez-vous été malade?
5. Quelle est la dernière fois que vous avez été absent(e)?
6. Pendant combien de jours avez-vous été absent(e) ce semestre?

Entre amis

Hier soir

1. Find out where your partner ate last night.
2. Find out if s/he watched TV or listened to the radio.
3. If so, find out what s/he watched or listened to.
4. Find out if s/he did his/her homework.
5. If so, find out where.
6. If so, find out how long s/he studied.

Les étudiants font quelquefois leurs devoirs au café.

2 Describing Your Study Habits

	vrai	*faux*
J'aime étudier seul(e).	_____	_____
Je fais mes devoirs à la bibliothèque.	_____	_____
J'écris[1] souvent des dissertations.	_____	_____
Je ne passe pas beaucoup de temps à faire mes devoirs.	_____	_____
Je passe au moins[2] trois heures à étudier par jour.	_____	_____
Je lis[3] au moins un livre par semaine.	_____	_____
J'écoute la radio pendant que[4] j'étudie.	_____	_____
Je regarde la télé pendant que j'étudie.	_____	_____

1. *write*   2. *at least*   3. *read*   4. *while*

Remarque   Use **passer** + unit(s) of time + **à** + infinitive to express how long you spend doing something.

Nous **avons passé deux heures à manger.**	*We spent two hours eating.*
D'habitude, Marc **passe quatre heures à faire** ses devoirs.	*Marc usually spends four hours doing his homework.*

B. Les verbes *écrire* et *lire*

J'aime **lire** des romans policiers.	*I like to read detective stories.*
J'ai passé trois heures à **lire** hier soir.	*I spent three hours reading last night.*
Quelles langues **lisez-vous?**	*What languages do you read?*
Éric lit le journal pendant qu'il mange.	*Éric reads the newspaper while he eats.*
Mes parents n'**écrivent** pas souvent.	*My parents don't write often.*
À qui **écrivez-vous** régulièrement?	*To whom do you write regularly?*
Comment est-ce qu'**on écrit** le mot «lisent»?	*How do you spell the word "lisent"?*

écrire *(to write)*		**lire** *(to read)*	
j'	**écris**	je	**lis**
tu	**écris**	tu	**lis**
il/elle/on	**écrit**	il/elle/on	**lit**
nous	**écrivons**	nous	**lisons**
vous	**écrivez**	vous	**lisez**
ils/elles	**écrivent**	ils/elles	**lisent**
passé composé: j'**ai écrit**		*passé composé:* j'**ai lu**	

■ Note the pronunciation distinction between the third person singular and plural forms.

il écrit [ekRi]   elle lit [li]
ils [z]écrivent [ekRiv]   elles lisent [liz]

■ The verb **décrire** *(to describe)* is conjugated like **écrire**.

Nous **décrivons** nos familles au professeur.

See p. 22. The plural of **journal** is **journaux**.

VOCABULAIRE

Des choses à lire ou à écrire

une bande dessinée	*comic strip*	un magazine	*magazine*
une carte postale	*postcard*	une pièce	*play*
une dissertation	*(term) paper*	un poème	*poem*
un journal	*newspaper*	un roman	*novel*
une lettre	*letter*	un roman policier	*detective story*
un livre	*book*		

7 **Qu'est-ce qu'ils lisent? Qu'est-ce qu'ils écrivent?** Répondez aux questions. Si vous ne savez pas la réponse, devinez.

1. Combien de livres lisez-vous par semestre?
2. Vos parents écrivent-ils beaucoup de lettres?
3. À qui écrivez-vous des messages électroniques?
4. Qui, dans votre famille, lit des bandes dessinées?
5. Combien de dissertations un étudiant écrit-il par an?
6. Avez-vous déjà écrit une dissertation ce semestre? Si oui, pour quel(s) cours?
7. Avez-vous lu un journal ou un magazine cette semaine? Si non, pourquoi pas?

C. *Ne ... rien*

■ The opposite of **quelque chose** is **ne ... rien** *(nothing, not anything)*.

Mangez-vous **quelque chose?**   *Are you eating something?*
Non, je **ne** mange **rien.**   *No, I am not eating anything.*

■ **Ne ... rien** works like **ne ... pas** and **ne ... jamais;** that is, **ne** and **rien** are placed around the conjugated verb. This means that in the passé composé, **ne** and **rien** surround the auxiliary verb and the past participle follows **rien.**

Je **ne** vais **rien** écrire.   *I'm not going to write anything.*
Je **n'**ai **rien** écrit hier soir.   *I didn't write anything last night.*

■ **Rien** can follow a preposition.

Je **n'**ai pensé **à rien.**   *I didn't think about anything.*
Je **ne** pense **à rien.**   *I'm not thinking about anything.*

Review the use of **ne ... jamais,** p. 96.

■ Unlike English, French allows the use of more than one negative word in a sentence.

Il **ne** fait **jamais rien!**   *He never does anything!*

■ Like **jamais, rien** can be used alone to answer a question.

Qu'est-ce que tu as lu? **Rien.**

FOR RECOGNITION ONLY:

- **Quelque chose** and **rien** can be made slightly more specific by the addition of **de** + *masculine adjective* or of **à** + *infinitive*. The two constructions can even be combined.

Jean lit **quelque chose** *d'intéressant.*	Éric **ne** lit **rien** *d'intéressant.*
Il a **quelque chose** *à lire.*	Il **n'**a **rien** *à lire.*
Il a **quelque chose** *d'intéressant à lire.*	Il **n'**a **rien** *d'intéressant à lire.*

8 **Une personne paresseuse.** Éric ne fait rien. Répondez aux questions suivantes avec le mot **rien**.

MODÈLES: Qu'est-ce qu'il fait le vendredi soir? **Il ne fait rien.**
Qu'est-ce qu'il a fait vendredi dernier? **Il n'a rien fait.**
Qu'est-ce qu'il va faire vendredi prochain? **Il ne va rien faire.**

1. Qu'est-ce qu'il étudie à la bibliothèque?
2. Qu'est-ce qu'il lit pendant le week-end?
3. Qu'est-ce qu'il va faire cet après-midi?
4. Qu'est-ce qu'il va lire pour ses cours?
5. Qu'est-ce qu'il a écrit pendant les vacances?
6. Qu'est-ce qu'il a lu l'année dernière?

9 **Ces travailleurs.** Sylvie et David sont très travailleurs et la semaine dernière, ils n'ont pas eu le temps de faire des choses amusantes. Posez une question à leur sujet au passé composé. Votre partenaire va utiliser **rien** dans sa réponse.

MODÈLE: regarder quelque chose à la télé
VOUS: **Est-ce qu'ils ont regardé quelque chose à la télé?**
VOTRE PARTENAIRE: **Non, ils n'ont rien regardé.**

1. écouter quelque chose à la radio
2. écrire des poèmes
3. chanter quelque chose ensemble
4. lire un roman policier
5. faire quelque chose en ville

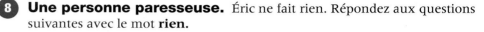

10 **À vous.** Répondez.

1. D'habitude qu'est-ce que vous lisez le matin?
2. À qui avez-vous écrit la semaine dernière?
3. Qu'avez-vous lu hier soir?
4. Avez-vous écouté la radio ce matin? Si oui, qu'est-ce que vous avez écouté?
5. Avez-vous des amis qui regardent la télé pendant qu'ils étudient?
6. Qu'est-ce que vous regardez à la télévision pendant que vous étudiez?
7. Combien de temps passez-vous d'habitude à préparer vos cours?
8. Lisez-vous souvent des magazines? Si oui, quels magazines?
9. Combien de dissertations écrivez-vous par semestre?

D. *Temps, heure et fois*

■ Depending on the context, the French use different words to express what, in English, could always be expressed by the word *time*.

- **L'heure,** as you already know, means *clock time.*

Quelle **heure** est-il?   *What time is it?*

Reminder **Heure** can also mean *hour* or *o'clock.*

J'ai étudié pendant trois **heures.**   *I studied for three hours.*
Il est deux **heures.**   *It is two o'clock.*

- **La fois** means *time* in a countable or repeated sense.

Combien de **fois** par an?   *How many times per year?*
la dernière **fois**   *the last time*

- **Le temps** means *time* in a general sense.

Je n'ai pas **le temps** d'étudier.   *I don't have time to study.*
Avez-vous **le temps** de voyager?   *Do you have time to travel?*
Combien de **temps** avez-vous?   *How much time do you have?*

> Remember that **temps** can also mean *weather:* **Quel temps fait-il aujourd'hui?**

11 **Hier soir.** Utilisez **temps, heure** ou **fois** pour compléter ce dialogue.

1. J'ai passé quatre _____ à faire mes devoirs.
2. Avez-vous eu assez de _____ pour regarder la télévision?
3. Non, parce que mes parents ont téléphoné trois _____.
4. À quelle _____ ont-ils téléphoné la première _____?
5. À six _____.
6. Combien de _____ par mois allez-vous chez vos parents?
7. Trois ou quatre _____.
8. Quand avez-vous dîné hier soir? À sept _____.
9. Combien de _____ avez-vous passé à table?
10. Une _____.

12 **À vous.** Répondez.

1. D'habitude combien de temps passez-vous à faire vos devoirs?
2. Pendant combien d'heures avez-vous étudié hier soir? Combien de temps avez-vous passé à faire vos devoirs pour le cours de français?
3. À quelle heure avez-vous dîné? Combien de temps avez-vous passé à table?
4. Combien de temps par semaine passez-vous avec votre meilleur(e) ami(e)?
5. Combien de fois par mois allez-vous au cinéma?
6. Combien de temps avez-vous passé à la bibliothèque la semaine dernière?

Entre amis

Es-tu un(e) bon(ne) étudiant(e)?

1. Find out if your partner spends a lot of time studying.
2. Ask if s/he watches TV while s/he studies.
3. Find out how long s/he studied last night.
4. Ask what s/he read for your French course.
5. Ask your partner how to spell some word in French.
6. Compliment your partner on his/her French.

3 Describing Your Weekend Activities

Qu'est-ce que vous faites pendant le week-end?

	oui	non
Je pars[1] du campus.	——	——
Je sors[2] avec mes amis.	——	——
Je m'amuse[3] bien.	——	——
Je vais au cinéma.	——	——
Je joue du piano.	——	——
Je joue au golf.	——	——
Je fais beaucoup de sport.	——	——
Je dors[4] beaucoup.	——	——
Je me lève tard[5].	——	——
Je ne me couche[6] pas tôt.	——	——
Je nettoie[7] ma chambre.	——	——

1. *leave*   2. *go out*   3. *have fun*   4. *sleep*   5. *late*   6. *go to bed*   7. *clean*

E. Les verbes pronominaux

■ Reflexive verbs **(les verbes pronominaux)** are those whose subject and object are the same. English examples of reflexive verbs are *he cut himself* or *she bought herself a dress.*

■ You have already learned a number of expressions that use reflexive verbs in French.

Comment vous appelez-vous?	*What is your name?*
Je m'appelle ...	*My name is ...*
Comment s'appellent vos amis?	*What are your friends' names?*
Asseyez-vous là!	*Sit there!*

■ Reflexive verbs use an object pronoun **(me, te, se, nous, vous)** in addition to the subject. With the exception of affirmative commands, this pronoun is always placed directly in front of the verb.

	s'amuser				se lever		
je	**m'**amuse	nous	**nous** amusons	je	**me** lève	nous	**nous** levons
tu	**t'**amuses	vous	**vous** amusez	tu	**te** lèves	vous	**vous** levez
il/elle/on	**s'**amuse	ils/elles	**s'**amusent	il/elle/on	**se** lève	ils/elles	**se** lèvent

■ Use **est-ce que** or a rising intonation to ask a yes/no question.

Est-ce que tu te lèves tôt le matin?   *Do you get up early in the morning?*
Tu t'amuses au cours de français?   *Do you have fun in French class?*

■ In the negative, **ne** is placed before the object pronoun and **pas** after the verb.

Je **ne** me lève **pas** tôt.   *I don't get up early.*
Mes professeurs **ne** s'amusent **pas.**   *My teachers don't have fun.*
Vous **ne** vous couchez **pas** avant   *Don't you go to bed before midnight?*
  minuit?

■ When the reflexive verb is used in the infinitive form after another verb, the reflexive pronoun agrees with the subject of the sentence.

À quelle heure vas-**tu te** coucher?   *At what time are you going to go to bed?*
Je n'aime pas **me** lever tôt.   *I don't like to get up early.*
Les étudiants ont l'habitude de   *Students are used to having fun on*
  s'amuser le samedi soir.   *Saturday night.*

13 **Identifications.** Identifiez, si possible, des personnes qui correspondent aux descriptions suivantes.

MODÈLE: une personne qui se lève très tôt le dimanche matin
           Mon père se lève très tôt le dimanche matin.

1. une personne qui se couche tôt le dimanche soir
2. une personne qui ne se couche pas s'il y a quelque chose d'intéressant à la télévision
3. deux étudiants qui se couchent tard s'ils ont un examen
4. deux personnes qui s'amusent beaucoup au cours de français
5. deux de vos amis qui ne se lèvent pas tôt le samedi matin
6. une personne qui ne va pas s'amuser pendant les vacances
7. une personne qui se lève quelquefois trop tard pour le cours de français

14 **À vous.** Répondez.

1. Comment vous appelez-vous et comment s'appelle votre meilleur(e) ami(e)?
2. Quel jour est-ce que vous vous couchez tard?
3. Est-ce que vous vous levez tôt ou tard le samedi matin? Expliquez votre réponse.
4. Avez-vous des amis qui ne s'amusent pas beaucoup? Si oui, comment s'appellent-ils?
5. Est-ce que vos professeurs aiment s'amuser en classe?
6. Est-ce que vous vous amusez au cours de français? Pourquoi ou pourquoi pas?
7. À quelle heure est-ce que vous vous levez le lundi matin? Pourquoi?
8. À quelle heure est-ce que vous allez vous coucher ce soir? Expliquez votre réponse.

F. *Jouer de et jouer à*

■ *To play a musical instrument* is expressed by **jouer de** + definite article + musical instrument. The definite article is retained in the negative before the name of the instrument.

Mon frère **joue du** saxophone, mais il ne **joue** pas **de la** guitare.   *My brother plays the saxophone but he doesn't play the guitar.*

De quoi **jouez**-vous?   *What (instrument) do you play?*

Moi, je ne **joue de** rien.   *I don't play any (instrument).*

VOCABULAIRE

Review **de** + article, p. 74, and **à** + article, p. 125.

Quelques instruments de musique

un accordéon	*accordion*	un piano	*piano*
une batterie	*drums*	un saxophone	*saxophone*
une flûte	*flute*	une trompette	*trumpet*
une guitare	*guitar*	un violon	*violin*

■ *To play a game* is expressed by **jouer à** + definite article + game.

—Mon amie **joue au** golf le lundi, elle **joue à la** pétanque le mercredi et elle **joue aux** cartes le vendredi soir. Mais elle ne **joue** jamais **aux** échecs.
—**À** quoi **jouez**-vous?
—Moi, je ne **joue à** rien.

VOCABULAIRE

Quelques jeux *(Several games)*

le basket-ball (le basket)	*basketball*
le bridge	*bridge*
les cartes *(f. pl.)*	*cards*
les dames *(f. pl.)*	*checkers*
les échecs *(m. pl.)*	*chess*
le football (le foot)	*soccer*
le football américain	*football*
le golf	*golf*
le hockey	*hockey*
la pétanque	*lawn bowling (bocce)*
le rugby	*rugby*
le tennis	*tennis*

NOTE CULTURELLE
La pétanque est un jeu de boules très populaire en France. On joue à la pétanque à l'extérieur, par exemple près des cafés. Pour marquer des points, il faut placer les boules le plus près possible du cochonnet *(small wooden ball).*

15 **Tout le monde joue.** À quoi jouent-ils? De quoi jouent-ils? Faites des phrases complètes avec les éléments donnés.

MODÈLES: **Les Canadiens jouent au hockey.**
Ma sœur ne joue pas de l'accordéon.

les Français			la pétanque
Tiger Woods			l'accordéon
Shaquille O'Neal			le piano
ma sœur			les cartes
mon frère		de	le saxophone
les violonistes	(ne ... pas) jouer	à	le basket-ball
les Américains			la guitare
les Canadiens			les échecs
Martina Hingis			le violon
je			le golf
mon ami(e) ...			le hockey
...			le tennis

16 **À vous.** Répondez.

1. Quel est votre instrument de musique préféré?
2. Quel est votre sport préféré?
3. Jouez-vous d'un instrument de musique? Si oui, de quoi jouez-vous?
4. Êtes-vous sportif (sportive)? Si oui, à quoi jouez-vous?
5. Avez-vous des amis qui jouent aux cartes? Si oui, à quel jeu de cartes jouent-ils?
6. Avez-vous des amis qui jouent d'un instrument de musique? Si oui, de quoi jouent-ils?

G. Les pronoms accentués

■ *Stress pronouns* (**les pronoms accentués**) are used in certain circumstances where a subject pronoun cannot be used. Each stress pronoun has a corresponding subject pronoun.

je	→	**moi**	nous	→	**nous**
tu	→	**toi**	vous	→	**vous**
il	→	**lui**	ils	→	**eux**
elle	→	**elle**	elles	→	**elles**

■ Stress pronouns are used in the following circumstances:

• to stress the subject of a sentence

Moi, je n'aime pas le café.   *I don't like coffee.*
Ils aiment le thé, **eux.**   ***They** like tea.*

• in a compound subject

Mes parents et **moi,** nous habitons ici.   *My parents and I live here.*
Monsieur Martin a des enfants?
Oui, sa femme et **lui** ont six enfants.   *Yes, his wife and he have six children.*

• after a preposition

chez **moi**   *at my house*   pour **lui**   *for him*
entre **nous**   *between us*   sans **elles**   *without them*

Note   A stress pronoun after the expression **être à** indicates possession.

Ce livre est **à moi.**   *This book belongs to me.*
Il est **à toi,** ce pull?   *Is this sweater yours?*

• after **c'est** and **ce sont**   Est-ce une photo de Lori?

C'est **moi.**   *It is I (me).*   Ce n'est pas **elle.**   *It is not she (her).*

Note   **C'est** is used with **nous** and **vous. Ce sont** is used only with **eux** and **elles.**

C'est nous.   *It is we (us).*   **Ce sont** eux.   *It is they (them).*

• alone or in phrases without a verb

Lui!   *Him!*
Et **toi?**   *And you?*
Elle aussi.   *So does she. So has she. So is she. She too.*
Moi non plus.   *Me neither. Nor I.*

• with the suffix **-même(s)**

toi-même   *yourself*   **eux**-mêmes   *themselves*

17   **Eux aussi.** La famille de Paul fait exactement ce qu'il fait *(what he does).* Utilisez un pronom accentué pour répondre à la question. Si la première phrase est affirmative, répondez affirmativement. Si la première phrase est négative, répondez négativement.

Modèles: Paul a fait le ménage. Et sa sœur?
        Elle aussi.

        Paul n'a pas regardé la télévision. Et son frère?
        Lui non plus.

1. Paul n'a pas lu le journal ce matin. Et ses sœurs? — *Elles non plus*
2. Paul écrit des lettres. Et ses parents? — *Eux aussi*
3. Paul ne se lève jamais tard. Et sa sœur?
4. Il a déjà mangé. Et son frère? — *Lui aussi*
5. Paul n'aime pas les cigares. Et ses parents? *Eux non plus*
6. Il va souvent au cinéma le vendredi soir. Et sa sœur? *Elle aussi*

18 **À vous.** Répondez aux questions suivantes. Utilisez un pronom accentué dans chaque réponse.

1. Faites-vous la cuisine vous-même?
2. Déjeunez-vous d'habitude avec votre meilleur(e) ami(e)?
3. Avez-vous dîné chez cet(te) ami(e) hier soir?
4. Avez-vous passé les dernières vacances chez vos parents?
5. Vos amis et vous, allez-vous souvent au cinéma?
6. Faites-vous vos devoirs avec vos amis?

H. Les verbes *dormir, partir* et *sortir*

Je ne **dors** pas bien.	*I don't sleep well.*
Quand **partez-vous** en vacances?	*When are you leaving on vacation?*
Avec qui Annie **sort-elle** vendredi?	*With whom is Annie going out on Friday?*

dormir *(to sleep)*		**partir** *(to leave)*		**sortir** *(to go out)*	
je	**dors**	je	**pars**	je	**sors**
tu	**dors**	tu	**pars**	tu	**sors**
il/elle/on	**dort**	il/elle/on	**part**	il/elle/on	**sort**
nous	**dormons**	nous	**partons**	nous	**sortons**
vous	**dormez**	vous	**partez**	vous	**sortez**
ils/elles	**dorment**	ils/elles	**partent**	ils/elles	**sortent**

■ Note the pronunciation distinction between the third person singular and plural forms.

elle dort [dɔR]	il part [paR]	elle sort [sɔR]
elles dorment [dɔRm]	ils partent [paRt]	elles sortent [sɔRt]

> **Partir** and **sortir** use **être** as the auxiliary in the passé composé and will be studied in the past tense in Ch. 7.

■ The past participle of **dormir** is **dormi**.

J'ai **dormi** pendant huit heures.

19 **Notre vie à l'université.** Utilisez les phrases suivantes pour poser des questions à votre partenaire.

MODÈLE: tu/sortir souvent
> VOUS: **Est-ce que tes amis et toi, vous sortez souvent?**
> VOTRE PARTENAIRE: **Oui, nous sortons souvent.**   ou
> **Non, nous ne sortons pas souvent.**

1. tu / dormir quelquefois pendant les cours
2. tes amis et toi / dormir mal pendant la semaine des examens
3. tu / sortir le vendredi soir avec tes amis
4. tes amis et toi / partir le week-end
5. les étudiants / sortir tous les soirs *(every night)*
6. le professeur de français / partir souvent en vacances

20 **La vie des étudiants.** Répondez aux questions suivantes.

1. Combien d'heures dormez-vous d'habitude par nuit?
2. Pendant combien de temps avez-vous dormi la nuit dernière?
3. Y a-t-il des étudiants qui ne dorment pas le samedi matin? Si oui, pourquoi?
4. Qui dort mal avant un examen important? Pourquoi?
5. Les étudiants sortent-ils quelquefois pendant la semaine? Si oui, où vont-ils? Si non, pourquoi pas?
6. Est-ce que la plupart des étudiants partent le week-end ou est-ce qu'ils restent sur le campus?
7. Quand allez-vous partir en vacances cette année?

I. Les verbes *nettoyer* et *envoyer*

Tu nettoies ta chambre ce matin? | *Are you cleaning your room this morning?*

Oui, mais d'abord **j'envoie** un message électronique. | *Yes, but first I'm sending an e-mail message.*

nettoyer *(to clean)*		**envoyer** *(to send)*	
je	**nettoie**	j'	**envoie**
tu	**nettoies**	tu	**envoies**
il/elle/on	**nettoie**	il/elle/on	**envoie**
nous	**nettoyons**	nous	**envoyons**
vous	**nettoyez**	vous	**envoyez**
ils/elles	**nettoient**	ils/elles	**envoient**
passé composé: **j'ai nettoyé**		**j'ai envoyé**	

■ In the present tense, these verbs are conjugated like **parler,** except that **i** is used in place of **y** in the singular and the third-person plural.

21 **Vrai ou faux?** Faites d'abord des phrases. Ensuite décidez si ces phrases sont vraies ou fausses pour vous. Attention au présent et au passé composé.

Modèles: ma sœur / nettoyer ma chambre / le week-end dernier
Elle a nettoyé ma chambre le week-end dernier. (C'est faux!)

ma sœur / nettoyer souvent sa chambre
Elle nettoie souvent sa chambre. (C'est vrai!)

1. les étudiants / nettoyer leur chambre / pendant le week-end
2. je / nettoyer ma chambre / hier
3. nous / envoyer souvent des messages à nos parents
4. nos parents / envoyer des lettres une fois par semaine
5. je / envoyer un message au professeur / il y a trois jours

Entre amis

Le week-end

1. Ask your partner what s/he usually does on weekends.
2. Find out if s/he has fun.
3. Ask if s/he goes out with friends.
4. If so, find out where s/he goes.
5. Find out if s/he gets up early or late on Sunday morning.
6. Find out when s/he cleans her room.
7. What else can you find out?

Intégration

Révision

A **Mon week-end.** Que faites-vous d'habitude le week-end? Avez-vous beaucoup de temps libre?

B **Notre vie à l'université.** Posez des questions. Votre partenaire va répondre. Attention au présent et au passé composé.

> **MODÈLE:** parler français avec tes amis pendant le cours de français
>
> **VOUS:** **Est-ce que tu parles français avec tes amis pendant le cours de français?**
>
> **VOTRE PARTENAIRE:** **Oui, je parle français avec eux.** ou
> **Non, je ne parle pas français avec eux.**

1. dormir bien quand il y a un examen
2. aller souvent à la bibliothèque après le dîner
3. écouter la radio quelquefois pendant que tu étudies
4. être absent(e) le mois dernier
5. jouer aux cartes avec tes amis le week-end dernier
6. faire la vaisselle d'habitude après le dîner
7. sortir avec tes amis ce soir

Emmanuel s'amuse bien au-dessus des Alpes.

Trouvez quelqu'un qui ... Interviewez les autres étudiants pour trouver quelqu'un qui ...

1. écoute la radio pendant qu'il étudie
2. joue de la guitare
3. a eu le temps de lire un livre la semaine dernière
4. a déjà écrit une dissertation ce semestre
5. n'a rien mangé ce matin
6. a eu la grippe l'année dernière
7. a nettoyé sa chambre le week-end dernier
8. ne sort jamais le dimanche soir
9. envoie souvent des messages électroniques à ses professeurs

 À vous. Répondez.

1. Que fait-on pour s'amuser le week-end sur votre campus?
2. Qu'est-ce que la plupart des étudiants font le dimanche soir?
3. Avez-vous regardé la télévision hier soir? Si oui, combien de temps avez-vous passé devant la télévision?
4. Quelle est la dernière fois que vous avez dîné au restaurant? Combien de temps avez-vous passé à table?
5. Combien de fois avez-vous été malade cette année?
6. Jouez-vous d'un instrument de musique? Si oui, de quel instrument jouez-vous?
7. À quoi joue-t-on au Canada et aux États-Unis? Jouez-vous aussi à ce(s) sport(s)?
8. Quelle est la dernière fois que vous avez nettoyé votre chambre?

Pas de problème!

Cette activité est basée sur la vidéo, *Module 3*. Choisissez la bonne réponse *(Choose the right answer)* pour compléter les phrases suivantes.

Preparation for the video:
1. Video worksheet in the *Cahier d'activités*
2. CD-ROM, *Module 3*

1. Marie-Christine admire _____ dans la vitrine *(store window)*.
(un foulard, une carte, un pull)
2. Jean-François et Marie-Christine traversent la ville de Paris pour
_____.
(jouer au tennis, aller au magasin, prendre *(take)* un autobus)
3. Ils ont pris *(took)* _____ ensemble.
(un autobus, le métro, un taxi)
4. Le métro ferme à _____.
(minuit, une heure de l'après-midi, une heure du matin)
5. Jean-François a mis *(put)* _____ dans la petite machine.
(son ticket, sa carte orange)

Lecture I

A **Étude du vocabulaire.** Étudiez les phrases suivantes et choisissez *(choose)* les mots anglais qui correspondent aux mots français en caractères gras *(bold print)*: *saw, to move, the south of France, meals, knife, trees, fingers, all.*

1. Je ne comprends pas **tous** les mots français.
2. Un homme attaque deux jeunes filles au **couteau.**
3. Quand on est paralysé, on n'est pas capable de **bouger.**
4. Les enfants comptent souvent sur les **doigts** pour faire l'addition.
5. Marseille est dans le **Midi** de la France.
6. Nous avons **vu** un film intéressant le week-end dernier.
7. Il y a beaucoup d'**arbres** dans une forêt.
8. Le déjeuner et le dîner sont des **repas.**

B **Parcourez les deux articles.** Skim each of the following selections to find: (1) an example of personal charity and (2) the reward that was given.

UN HOMME COURAGEUX

PARIS: Aziz Soubhane a 17 ans. Il est marocain, mais il habite en France depuis sept ans et fait ses études au Lycée d'enseignement professionnel privé de Notre-Dame, à la Loupe, en Eure-et-Loir.

Aziz a désarmé un homme qui attaquait au couteau deux jeunes filles anglaises dans le métro. Aziz a été le seul à bouger; les autres passagers n'ont pas levé le petit doigt.

Pour son courage, Aziz a reçu le «Prix servir» du Rotary-club de Paris et un chèque de 10.000 francs. C'est l'adjoint au maire de Paris qui a donné le prix à Aziz.

Ce jeune homme est un très bon exemple pour nous.

Les Soldats ont Planté des Arbres

TOULON: L'été dernier, des feux ont détruit une grande partie de la forêt dans le Midi de la France. Le 29 décembre, on a vu des soldats américains aider tous les volontaires de la région à nettoyer la forêt et à replanter des arbres. En une journée, ils ont replanté 5.000 arbres près de la ville d'Hyères, dans la région du Var.

Le 2 janvier, le maire de la ville a donné un grand méchoui à tous les volontaires. Les 165 soldats américains sont en escale à Toulon en ce moment. Ils ont profité de leur temps libre pour aider les Français.

Adjoint au maire = *deputy mayor;* **feux** = *fires;* **méchoui** = *a North African specialty in which a whole lamb is roasted over an open pit of live coals for several hours.*

C **Vrai ou faux?** Si une phrase est fausse, corrigez-la.

1. Aziz n'est pas français.
2. Il étudie dans une école publique.
3. Les soldats américains ont aidé les Français.
4. Les soldats ont été obligés d'aider les Français.
5. Les soldats ont travaillé une semaine.

D **Questions.** Répondez.

1. Qui sont les «bons Samaritains» dans ces deux articles?
2. Qu'est-ce qu'Aziz a fait? Et les soldats américains?
3. Est-ce que les autres personnes dans le métro ont aidé Aziz?
4. Qui a travaillé avec les soldats américains?
5. Qu'est-ce qu'on a donné à Aziz après son acte de courage?
6. Qu'est-ce qu'on a donné aux soldats après leur travail?

E **Familles de mots.** Essayez de deviner le sens des mots suivants.

1. détruire, la destruction
2. donner, un don, un donneur, une donneuse
3. enseigner, l'enseignement *(m.)*, un enseignant, une enseignante
4. voir, vu, la vue, une vision

F **Discussion.**

1. Identify three aspects of French culture mentioned in these newspaper articles that are similar to or different from American culture.
2. Are North African people and their cultures viewed favorably or unfavorably in these articles? Explain your answer.

A **Étude du vocabulaire.** Étudiez les phrases suivantes et choisissez les mots anglais qui correspondent aux mots français en caractères gras: *therefore, head, let go, voice, told.*

1. Le professeur nous a **raconté** une anecdote amusante.
2. Les aviateurs ont **lâché** des bombes sur la ville.
3. Cette chanteuse a une jolie **voix**.
4. As-tu des cachets d'aspirine? J'ai mal à la **tête**.
5. Marc habite à Paris. **Donc** il doit bien parler le français.

Moi

—Comment t'appelles-tu?

Le petit homme lève la tête sans répondre.

Voilà une plaisante question!

—Comment t'appelles-tu?

Il lâche d'une voix triomphante:

—Moi!

—Allons, allons! Tu t'appelles Jean.

—Oui! Jean Moi!

Cette réponse me plaît beaucoup. J'ai formé le projet de la rapporter à un philosophe de mes amis qui étudie ce qu'il appelle «la mentalité des enfants». J'appelle donc mon philosophe au téléphone et je demande: «Qui est à l'appareil[1]?» Une voix grêle et dénaturée[2] me répond: «Moi!» Impossible de raconter mon histoire au philosophe.

Georges Duhamel, *Les Plaisirs et les jeux*

---

1. *on the phone*   2. *shrill and distorted*

B **Questions.** Choisissez *(Choose)* la meilleure réponse.

1. Le «petit homme» est ...
   a. un garçon   b. un homme qui est petit
2. La question du narrateur est ...
   a. sérieuse   b. juste pour parler avec l'enfant
3. Le narrateur ...
   a. aime la réponse   b. trouve la réponse ridicule
4. Le philosophe trouve la question «Qui est à l'appareil?» ...
   a. sérieuse   b. bizarre

VOCABULAIRE ACTIF

Instruments de musique
un accordéon *accordion*
une batterie *drums*
une flûte *flute*
une guitare *guitar*
un piano *piano*
un saxophone *saxophone*
une trompette *trumpet*
un violon *violin*

D'autres noms
un examen *test, exam*
un exercice *exercise*
un cigare *cigar*
une cigarette *cigarette*
la grippe *flu*
un robinet *faucet*
la valse *waltz*
une crêpe *crepe (pancake)*

Pronoms accentués
moi *I, me*
toi *you*
lui *he, him*
elle *she, her*
nous *we, us*
vous *you*
eux *they, them*
elles *they, them (female)*

Jeux
le basket-ball (le basket) *basketball*
le bridge *bridge*
les cartes *(f. pl.) cards*
les dames *(f. pl.) checkers*
les échecs *(m. pl.) chess*

le football (le foot) *soccer*
le football américain *football*
le golf *golf*
le hockey *hockey*
un jeu *game*
la pétanque *lawn bowling*
le rugby *rugby*
le tennis *tennis*

Choses à lire ou à écrire
une bande dessinée *comic strip*
une carte postale *postcard*
une dissertation *(term) paper*
un journal *newspaper*
une lettre *letter*
un magazine *magazine*
un message électronique *e-mail*
un mot *word*
une pièce *play*
un poème *poem*
un roman *novel*
un roman policier *detective story*

Divisions du temps
une année *year*
une fois *one time*
une journée *day*
un mois *month*
un semestre *semester*
le temps *time; weather*
les vacances *(f. pl.) vacation*

Prépositions
par *per; by; through*
pendant *for; during*
sans *without*

Verbes
accompagner *to accompany*
s'amuser *to have fun*
se coucher *to go to bed*
décrire *to describe*
demander *to ask*
dormir *to sleep*
écrire *to write*
envoyer *to send*
être à *to belong to*
fermer *to close*
fumer *to smoke*
se lever *to get up*
lire *to read*
nettoyer *to clean*
oublier *to forget*
partir *to leave*
préparer (un cours) *to prepare (a lesson)*
remarquer *to notice*
sortir *to go out*
téléphoner (à qqn) *to telephone (someone)*

Expressions de temps
il y a ... ans (mois, etc.) ... *years (months, etc.) ago*
Je suis ici depuis ... mois (heures, etc.). *I've been here for ... months (hours, etc.).*
Pendant combien de temps ... ? *How long ... ?*
tous les soirs *every night*
tout à l'heure *a little while ago; in a little while*

Adverbes de temps

déjà *already*
hier *yesterday*
hier soir *last night*
longtemps *a long time*
récemment *recently*
tard *late*
tôt *early*

D'autres adverbes

au moins *at least*
heureusement *fortunately*
rien (ne ... rien) *nothing, not anything*
tant *so much; so many*

D'autres expressions utiles

À quoi jouez-vous? *What (game, sport) do you play?*
Aïe! *Ouch!*
à l'intérieur de *inside of*
à table *at dinner, at the table*
Bonnes vacances! *Have a good vacation!*
C'est la vie! *That's life!*
De quoi jouez-vous? *What (instrument) do you play?*
Eh bien *Well*
en vacances *on vacation*
faire du sport *to play sports*
la plupart (de) *most (of)*

parce que *because*
par exemple *for example*
Pourquoi pas? *Why not?*
... veut dire ... *... means ...*

escale 2
L'Amérique du Nord

LE FRANÇAIS DANS L'AMÉRIQUE DU NORD: APERÇU HISTORIQUE

1534 Jacques Cartier prend possession de la «Nouvelle-France», territoire des Amérindiens et des Inuits.

1608 Samuel de Champlain fonde la ville de Québec.

1682 Robert Cavelier de La Salle descend le Mississippi. Il nomme le bassin du Mississippi «Louisiane» en l'honneur du roi Louis XIV.

1755 Les Anglais déportent les Acadiens de Nouvelle-Écosse (le «Grand Dérangement»). De nombreux Acadiens s'installent en Louisiane. Le mot «cajun» est une déformation du mot «acadien».

1756–1763 Guerre de Sept Ans: Par le traité de Paris, la France cède (*yields*) son territoire de la Nouvelle-France à la Grande-Bretagne. Création de la province de Québec.

1803 Napoléon vend la Louisiane aux États-Unis pour 15 millions de dollars.

1848 La Grande-Bretagne forme le Canada-Uni. La langue anglaise devient langue officielle.

1921 Suite à la vive réaction des Canadiens français, Londres reconnaît et accepte l'usage de la langue française au Québec.

1966–1970 Développement du mouvement indépendantiste.

1977 La loi 101, la Charte de la langue française, rétablit le français comme seule langue officielle du Québec.

1982 Échec du référendum sur l'indépendance et la souveraineté du Québec désirée par le Parti québécois.

1998 Au référendum sur la souveraineté du Québec, les partisans du maintien de la province dans la confédération canadienne obtiennent une très faible victoire.

Le Québec

Que savez-vous?

Répondez aux questions suivantes. Les réponses se trouvent dans cette escale.

1. Le Québec est-il plus grand que le Texas?
2. Qui a fondé la ville de Québec?
3. Quel pourcentage de la population parle français?
4. Quelle est la plus grande ville du Québec?
5. Quelle est la capitale du Québec?
6. Quelle est la réaction des Québécois face à la suprématie de l'anglais?

REPÈRES: LE QUÉBEC

Population: 6.895.963 habitants; 83% d'origine française, 10% britannique, 7% Inuits ou immigrés francophones

Capitale: Québec

Administration: Province du Canada

Climats: continental, humide et arctique

Religion: 86% de catholiques

Ressources: industrie (forestière, pêcheries, métallurgique, hydroélectrique, minière); agriculture; tourisme

Langue officielle: français; 60% parlent seulement français, 35% parlent français et anglais

Territoire: la plus vaste des dix provinces; aussi grande que l'Alaska

ÉTUDE DU VOCABULAIRE

Quels mots en caractères gras correspondent aux mots suivants: *more, king, century, city, approximately, French-speaking world, most*?

1. La ville de New-York est **plus** grande que Montréal.
2. C'est la **plus** grande ville des États-Unis.
3. La France est une république. Elle n'a pas de **roi**.
4. Il y a **environ** 60 millions de Français en France.
5. Dans les pays de la **francophonie** on parle français.
6. **Un siècle** est une période de 100 ans.

Le port de Montréal

Les Canadiens de Montréal en action

Le hockey: une passion sportive

Le hockey sur glace fait partie de la culture nationale du Canada, où ce sport est immensément populaire. Plus de cinq millions de Canadiens—un sur cinq—ont la passion de ce sport et y participent soit en tant que joueurs professionnels ou amateurs, soit en tant qu'entraîneurs, membres de comités, arbitres ou spectateurs de tous âges. Le Canada a plusieurs *(several)* équipes professionnelles de hockey sur glace. Le hockey sur glace est tellement populaire que la saison de ce sport d'hiver se prolonge jusqu'au mois de juin! L'origine précise du hockey est inconnue. Cependant, c'est à Montréal, la plus grande ville du Québec, que le premier match officiel de hockey a eu lieu au Victoria Rink durant l'hiver de 1875. Aujourd'hui, les habitants de Montréal et du Québec tout entier suivent avec intérêt les matchs de leur équipe favorite, les Canadiens de Montréal. Cette célèbre équipe a gagné la coupe Stanley 24 fois depuis 1916 et a compté plusieurs super-vedettes telles que Maurice «Rocket» Richard, Jean Béliveau et Guy Lafleur.

Le vélo est écolo

Le vélo devient un des moyens les plus populaires d'aller à la découverte du Québec! La géographie du Québec présente des reliefs et des paysages qui offrent aux cyclotouristes des promenades très variées et accessibles. La plaine fluviale du Saint-Laurent se prête très bien aux randonnées cyclistes et même les circuits en pays plus montagneux ne découragent pas les amateurs. Le Québec offre un réseau «vert» de plus de 3.000 km d'itinéraires cyclables sillonnant le territoire même dans les régions urbaines. Montréal, avec plus de 300 km de voies cyclables, possède un des réseaux les plus importants en Amérique du Nord. Plusieurs autres villes comme Québec, Laval et Sherbrooke possèdent aussi d'importantes pistes cyclables.

Et vous?

- **Aimez-vous le hockey sur glace? Jouez-vous à ce sport ou regardez-vous quelquefois des matchs de hockey à la télévision?**
- **Faites-vous du vélo? Si oui, préférez-vous le vélo tout terrain (VTT) ou le vélo de course (*speed bike*)?**
- **Quelles expressions venant de l'anglais sont utilisées en québécois?**

LE FRANÇAIS «QUÉBÉCOIS»

Au Québec, on dit ...	En France, on dit ...
un char	*une voiture*
le gaz	*l'essence*
un chien chaud	*un hot-dog*
jaser	*bavarder*
un melon d'eau	*une pastèque*
les lumières	*les feux (de circulation)*
avoir du fun	*s'amuser*
la poudrerie	*une tempête de neige*
ça mouille	*il pleut*
il fait méchant	*il fait mauvais*
la noirceur	*l'obscurité*
la fin de semaine	*le week-end*
magasiner	*faire des achats*
faire du pouce	*faire de l'autostop*

Le Québec: une province menacée

Au début des années 70, les Canadiens français se considéraient moins comme une minorité de la confédération canadienne, que comme la majorité francophone de la province du Québec. Par leurs efforts, la Charte de la langue française en 1977 a donné au français le statut de seule langue officielle dans la province de Québec, dans le but «d'assurer la qualité et le rayonnement de la langue française» dans la civilisation nord-américaine. Malgré la Charte, le Québec est encore menacé par l'invasion anglophone et l'idée d'un Québec indépendant et souverain tente toujours de nombreux citoyens québécois.

La question de séparation fait l'objet d'une guerre continue entre les fédéralistes, représentés par le Parti libéral du Québec (PL), qui veulent rester membres de la Confédération, et les séparatistes ou «souverainistes», représentés par le Parti québécois (PQ), qui veulent préserver leur identité linguistique et culturelle en Amérique du Nord. Lors d'un référendum en 1998, les Québécois s'exprimaient ainsi vis-à-vis de la séparation:

ui 49.42% **NON** 50.58%

Le canadien-français

C'est une langue de France
Aux accents d'Amérique
Elle déjoue[1] le silence
À grands coups de musique
C'est la langue de mon cœur
Et le cœur de ma vie
Que jamais elle ne meure[2]
Que jamais on ne l'oublie

(Michel Rivard, «Le Cœur de ma vie» Les Éditions Sauvages)
1. *thwarts* 2. *May it never die*

Et vous?

Êtes-vous pour ou contre la séparation du Québec du reste du Canada? Expliquez votre réponse.

Dans les villes où ils sont nombreux, les Franco-Américains habitent souvent dans des quartiers séparés, groupés autour d'une église catholique. (Soldier Pond, dans le nord du Maine)

Le Maine

REPÈRES: LE MAINE
Population: 1.253.000 habitants
Population franco-américaine: 348.900 habitants (28% de la population du Maine)
Population qui parle français à la maison: 81.000 (23% de la population franco-américaine)
Villes industrielles «franco-américaines»: Lewiston, Biddeford, Waterville, Augusta

Les Français de la Nouvelle-Angleterre

À partir de 1830 et pendant le siècle suivant, plus d'un million de Canadiens français ont traversé la frontière canado-américaine à la recherche d'une meilleure vie dans les villes industrielles des États-Unis. C'est surtout dans les grandes villes textiles des six états de la Nouvelle-Angleterre que ces immigrés du nord ont transporté leur langue et leur culture. Les francophones de la Nouvelle-Angleterre sont appelés encore aujourd'hui les Franco-Américains.

Le français qu'ils parlent ressemble au français des Québécois. Cette langue française n'est pas un français classique ou littéraire, mais plutôt *(rather)* un français populaire et rural qui a ses origines dans le parler des premiers colons, venus de France au XVIIe siècle. Petit à petit, les Canadiens français ont adapté leur langue aux besoins et aux circonstances de leur situation. Aujourd'hui, le français que parlent les Franco-Américains de la Nouvelle-Angleterre a beaucoup de mots empruntés à l'anglais.

Vrai ou faux?

1. **Les Canadiens français sont venus aux États-Unis pour faire de l'agriculture.**
2. **Le français canadien ressemble au français des anciens colons.**
3. **Dans le Maine, la majorité des familles d'origine canadienne parlent français à la maison.**

La Louisiane

REPÈRES: LA LOUISIANE

Superficie: 125.674 km^2

Population: 4.372.035 habitants

Langues: anglais, français, créole

Capitale: Baton Rouge

Ville principale: La Nouvelle-Orléans

Ressources: pétrole, gaz naturel

Population dont la langue au foyer est le français: 572.262 (15% de la population)

Des paroisses «cajun»: Lafayette, Lafourche, Acadia, Vermilion, St. Martin

Que savez-vous?

Répondez aux questions suivantes. Les réponses se trouvent dans cette escale.

1. Qui a découvert la Louisiane?
2. D'où sont les habitants de la Louisiane?
3. Quelle est l'origine du mot cajun?
4. Quelle est la capitale de la Louisiane?
5. Quelles langues parlent-ils?

LE FRANÇAIS «CAJUN»

En Louisiane,

- on prononce le son «h» dans les mots *haut* et *hache*;

- on prononce les consonnes finales et muettes des mots *debout* et *lit*;

- on ne prononce pas le *ne* dans la négation (*e[elle] peut pas aller* pour *elle ne peut pas aller*);

- on crée des combinaisons grammaticales innovatrices (*reparment* pour *réparation* et *jolisit* pour *beauté*);

- on ajoute parfois l'article à la racine du mot (*deleau* pour *de l'eau* et *zoiseau* pour *oiseau*).

- on régularise des conjugaisons (*server* pour *servir*).

En Louisiane, on dit ...	En France, on dit ...
bois	*arbre*
fréquenter	*faire l'amour*
dame	*femme*
naviguer	*voyager*
un chrétien	*une personne*
une blonde	*une petite amie*
chariot	*voiture*
baler	*danser*

> ## Laissez les bons temps rouler!

Le Cadien/Cajun*

Dans son poème, *Le Cadien/Cajun*, Christy Dugas Maraist, présidente du Conseil de la Fondation du Monument Acadien, donne plusieurs exemples de différences entre le cadien/cajun et le français standard, comme l'illustre l'extrait suivant:

> *... Écoute, c'est:*
> *"Attendre," pas "espérer,"*
> *"Pleurer," pas "brailler,"*
> *"Penser," pas "jongler."*
> *Je pense que t'as jamais jonglé de ça.*
> *Apprends:*
> *"Lentement," au lieu de*
> *"doucement,"*
> *"Gentil," au lieu de "vaillant,"*
> *"Beaucoup," au lieu de "joliment."*
> *L'essence ce n'est pas du parfum,*
> *tu vois.*
> *Étudie cette liste:*
> *"Une piastre," c'est "un dollar,"*
> *C'est une "voiture," pas un "char,"*
> *Une "fête," c'est un "anniversaire,"*
> *C'est "pourquoi," pas "quo'faire."*
> *L'essence va dans ta voiture,*
> *rappelle-toi!*
> *Tu me demandes quo'faire*
> *Tout ça, c'est nécessaire.*
> *Juste jongle comment vaillant ça*
> *serait,*
> *Si tu rencontrais un vrai Français.*

Christy Dugas Maraist

* *Cajun* is the english translation of the French *Cadien*.

www

Buts communicatifs
Relating past events (continued)
Describing your background
Stating what you just did

Structures utiles
Le passé composé avec **être**
Le pronom **y**
Le verbe **venir**
Les prépositions de lieu avec une ville ou un pays (suite)
Les mois de l'année, les saisons, le temps
Venir de + infinitif

Culture
L'amabilité
Une technologie de pointe
La télécarte
Le TGV

Coup d'envoi

J'ai fait un voyage

 Où es-tu allée l'été° dernier, Stéphanie?   *summer*
    Je suis allée en Europe.

Parle-moi de ce voyage, s'il te plaît.
    Eh bien! Je suis arrivée à Londres le 15
        juin°.   *June*
    J'ai passé quinze jours à voyager en
        Angleterre.
    Puis je suis partie pour Paris le premier
        juillet°.   *July first*
    Je suis restée chez des amis de mes
        parents qui habitent à Paris.
    Je me suis très, très bien amusée.
    Enfin je suis revenue° le 10 août°.   *I came back / August*
    Voilà!

▶ **Et vous?**   Qu'est-ce que vous avez fait pendant les vacances? Êtes-vous
parti(e) en voyage ou êtes-vous resté(e) chez vous?

Monsieur et Madame Smith sont arrivés à Angers

Monsieur et Madame Smith, amis de la famille de Lori Becker, sont partis pour Angers. Là, ils sont descendus du TGV° à la gare Saint-Laud. Monsieur Smith est entré dans une cabine télé-phonique, a utilisé sa télécarte et a formé le numéro des Martin.   got off the high-speed train

MME MARTIN:	Allô.
M. SMITH:	Madame Martin?
MME MARTIN:	Oui, qui est à l'appareil°?
M. SMITH:	Bonjour, Madame. C'est Joseph Smith.
MME MARTIN:	Ah! les amis de Lori. Vous êtes arrivés?
M. SMITH:	Oui, nous sommes un peu en avance°. Nous venons de descendre° du train.
MME MARTIN:	Mon mari et Lori sont déjà partis vous chercher. Restez là; ils arrivent.
M. SMITH:	D'accord. Merci, Madame. À tout à l'heure.
MME MARTIN:	À tout de suite°, Monsieur. Au revoir. *(Une demi-heure plus tard, chez les Martin)*
LORI:	Madame Martin, je vous présente Monsieur et Madame Smith.
MME MARTIN:	Bonjour, Madame. Bonjour, Monsieur. Vous devez être fatigués après votre voyage.
MME SMITH:	Bonjour, Madame. Non, pas trop.
M. MARTIN:	C'est la première fois que vous venez° en France?
MME SMITH:	Non, nous sommes déjà venus° il y a deux ans.
M. SMITH:	Mais la dernière fois, nous n'avons pas beaucoup voyagé.
MME SMITH:	C'est gentil de vous occuper° de nous. Ça ne vous dérange pas trop?
MME MARTIN:	Mais non! Je vous en prie.°

on the phone · *early* · *we just got off* · *See you very soon* · *come* · *came* · *take care of* · *Don't mention it.*

▶ **Jouez ces rôles.** Répétez la conversation avec votre partenaire. Une personne joue le rôle des Smith et de Lori et l'autre joue le rôle des Martin. Utilisez vos propres *(own)* noms.

Je vous en prie. With palm open and fingers spread, one hand (or both hands) is held at the waist level and the shoulders are shrugged. The lips are often rounded. This gesture indicates that you are pleased to be of service and that it is not worth mentioning.

Il y a un geste

Pourquoi est-ce que Monsieur Smith utilise une télécarte?

a. Il n'a pas d'argent *(money)* français.
b. Il faut une carte pour utiliser les cabines téléphoniques à la gare Saint-Laud.
c. On peut utiliser des pièces de monnaie ou une carte pour téléphoner dans les cabines téléphoniques.

L'amabilité (Kindness)

The Martins go out of their way to be helpful to Lori's friends. A warm welcome is the norm rather than the exception in Angers. Many *Angevins* serve as host families to foreign students who are enrolled at the *Centre international d'études françaises* or in one of the institutes organized on the campus of the *Université Catholique de l'Ouest*. Others, such as the Martins, employ a **jeune fille au pair** who often becomes a "member" of the family. The tourist who stays only a few days in Paris may not get to appreciate the generosity and the friendliness of the French.

Une technologie de pointe

France is known worldwide for its leadership in art, fashion, perfume, food, and drink. France is also the world's fifth largest economy and fourth largest exporter. It is a leader in transportation (the TGV bullet train), aerospace (Airbus and the Ariane rocket), telecommunications (mobile phones and wireless technology), and civil engineering (the Normandy bridge and the Channel tunnel).

La télécarte

The **télécarte** is an electronic smart card used throughout France for both local and long distance phone calls. It can be purchased in post offices, railroad stations, and tobacco shops in France. Tourists are often caught off guard believing that they will be able to use French coins to make a telephone call. Coin operated phones are becoming increasingly rare in France. In Angers, for example, none of the phone booths at the railroad station accept coins.

Le TGV

France is also a world leader in public transportation *(les transports en commun)*. Buses, subways, and trains run well, are on time, and are widely used. Among the latter, the **TGV, Train à Grande Vitesse,** is a spectacular technological achievement and a commercial success! The **TGV Atlantique** is a "bullet train" that serves the western part of France and transports over 40,000 customers per day. With a top speed of over 300 kilometers (200 miles) per hour, it offers exceptional comfort and service. **TGV Atlantique** passengers can even phone to all parts of the world. The **télécarte** is sold in the **TGV** lounge.

Pour utiliser la télécarte:	
Décrochez le téléphone.	*Pick up the phone.*
Introduisez votre télécarte.	*Put your telecarte in the slot.*
Composez le numéro.	*Dial the number.*
Attendez que quelqu'un réponde.	*Wait until someone answers.*
Quand vous avez fini, raccrochez le téléphone.	*When you've finished, hang up the phone.*
Reprenez votre télécarte.	*Take your telecarte.*

À vous.   Vous téléphonez à un(e) ami(e). Répondez.

VOTRE AMI(E):	Allô.
VOUS:	_____
VOTRE AMI(E):	Tu es arrivé(e)?
VOUS:	_____
VOTRE AMI(E):	Où es-tu?
VOUS:	_____
VOTRE AMI(E):	Reste là. J'arrive.
VOUS:	_____

Entre amis

Vous êtes arrivé(e) à la gare

You are a foreign student at a French university and will be staying with a host family.

1. Call your host family and identify yourself.
2. Say that you are at the train station.
3. Reassure them that you are not too tired after your trip.
4. Express your thanks and say "See you very soon."

Prononciation

Les sons [ɔ] et [o]

■ French has an open [ɔ] sound and a closed [o] sound. The following words contain these sounds. Practice saying the words after your instructor, paying particular attention to the highlighted sound.

[ɔ] • orange, bonne, comme, alors, sommes, connaissez, encore, poste, personnes, accordéon, hockey, postale, dormir, sortir, notre, note, jogging

[o] • radio, piano, mot, vos, gros

  • chose, quelque chose, rose

  • hôtel, à la vôtre, drôle

  • chaud, faux, au fait, d'autres, au moins, à gauche, il faut, faux, fausse, jaune

  • eau, beaucoup, beau, chapeau

▶ Now go back and look at how these sounds are spelled and in what kinds of letter combinations they appear. What patterns do you notice?

■ The sound [ɔ] is always followed by a pronounced consonant.

téléph**o**ne   ad**o**re   p**o**stale   n**o**te   d**o**rment   m**o**de   **o**ctobre

■ The sound [o] is used in several circumstances.

o as the word's final sound	pian**o,** m**o**t
o + [z]	ch**o**se, r**o**se
ô	h**ô**tel, v**ô**tre
au	**au** fait, il f**au**t
eau	l'**eau,** b**eau**coup

■ Say the following pairs of words, making sure to pronounce the [ɔ] and [o] sounds correctly.

1. n**o**s / n**o**tre
2. r**o**binet / r**o**se
3. v**o**tre / v**ô**tre
4. ch**au**d / ch**o**colat
5. b**eau** / b**o**nne

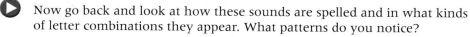

Buts communicatifs

1 Relating Past Events *(continued)*

Tu es sortie vendredi dernier, Nathalie?
      Oui, je suis sortie.
Où es-tu allée?
      Je suis allée au restaurant et chez des
        amis.
À quelle heure es-tu rentrée° chez toi?   *did you get back*
      Je suis rentrée à minuit.

▶ **Et vous?**   Vous êtes sorti(e) le week-end dernier?
           Si oui, où êtes-vous allé(e)?
           À quelle heure êtes-vous rentré(e)?

A. Le passé composé avec *être*

Review the formation of the **passé composé** with **avoir,** p. 157.

Remember to consult Appendix C at the end of the book to review any terms with which you are not familiar.

Êtes-vous **arrivée** en train? — *Did you arrive by train?*
Non, je **suis venue** en voiture. — *No, I came by car.*

Paul et Karine **sont sortis** hier soir? — *Did Paul and Karine go out last night?*
Oui, mais ils **sont rentrés** à neuf heures. — *Yes, but they came home at nine o'clock.*

Mon père **est né** à Paris en 1935. — *My father was born in Paris in 1935.*
Mais sa famille **est partie** aux États-Unis avant la guerre. — *But his family left for the United States before the war.*
En 1985 il **est tombé** malade. — *He got sick in 1985.*
Il **est mort** en 1986. — *He died in 1986.*

■ While most verbs use **avoir** to form the passé composé (see Ch. 6), there are a limited number that use **être**. These verbs are intransitive; that is, they do not take a direct object. The most common are listed on the opposite page.

Ils sont arrivés à la gare.

VOCABULAIRE

Quelques verbes qui forment le passé composé avec *être*

Infinitif		Participe passé
aller	*to go*	**allé**
venir	*to come*	**venu**
devenir	*to become*	**devenu**
revenir (ici)	*to come back (here)*	**revenu**
retourner (là)	*to go back; to return (there)*	**retourné**
rentrer (à la maison)	*to go (come) back;* *to go (come) home*	**rentré**
arriver	*to arrive; to happen*	**arrivé**
rester (à la maison)	*to stay, remain (at home)*	**resté**
partir	*to leave*	**parti**
monter (dans une voiture)	*to go up; to get into* *(a car)*	**monté**
descendre (d'une voiture)	*to go down; to get out (of* *a car)*	**descendu**
tomber	*to fall*	**tombé**
entrer (dans la classe)	*to enter (the classroom)*	**entré**
sortir (de la classe)	*to go out (of the classroom)*	**sorti**
naître	*to be born*	**né**
mourir	*to die*	**mort**

DR
Mrs
VANDERTRAMP

> Remember that if a plural subject is of mixed gender, the masculine plural form of the participle will be used.

■ Past participles used with **être** agree in gender and number with the subject, just as if they were adjectives. To show agreement, add **-e** (feminine singular), **-s** (masculine plural), or **-es** (feminine plural).

Masculin	**Féminin**
Je suis **né** à Paris.	Je suis **née** à Paris.
Tu es **né** à New York.	Tu es **née** à New York.
Il est **né** à Montréal.	Elle est **née** à Montréal.
Nous sommes **nés** à Boston.	Nous sommes **nées** à Boston.
Vous êtes **né(s)** à Angers.	Vous êtes **née(s)** à Angers.
Ils sont **nés** à Halifax.	Elles sont **nées** à Halifax.

VOCABULAIRE À RETENIR

à l'heure *on time*
en avance *early*
en retard *late*

■ Most of these verbs are followed by a preposition when they precede the name of a place.

Sandrine est entrée **dans** la salle de classe.	*Sandrine went into the classroom.*
Moi, je suis arrivé **au** cours de français à l'heure.	*I arrived at the French class on time.*
Mais Nicolas est retourné **chez** lui pour chercher son livre. Alors, il est arrivé en retard.	*But Nicolas went back home for his book. So, he came late.*

■ Reflexive verbs also use **être** to form the passé composé.

Review reflexive verbs, p. 165.

There is no accent on the first -e- of the past participle **levé(e)**.

Les étudiants **se sont amusés** à la soirée.	*Students had fun at the party.*
Ils ne **se sont** pas **couchés** tôt.	*They did not get to bed early.*
Est-ce que Mélanie **s'est levée** tard le jour suivant?	*Did Mélanie get up late the following day?*
Elle et sa sœur ne **se sont** pas **levées** avant midi.	*She and her sister didn't get up before noon.*

Remember to choose the appropriate object pronoun.

se coucher *(to go to bed)*			
je	**me** suis couché(e)	nous	**nous** sommes couché(e)s
tu	**t'es** couché(e)	vous	**vous** êtes couché(e)(s)
il	**s'est** couché	ils	**se** sont couchés
elle	**s'est** couchée	elles	**se** sont couchées

1 **Thierry ne fait jamais rien comme les autres.** Expliquez d'après le modèle.

MODÈLE: Les autres (partir pour le Canada) / Et Thierry?
Les autres sont partis pour le Canada, mais Thierry n'est pas parti pour le Canada.

1. vous (aller au concert) / Et Thierry?
2. nous (sortir hier soir) / Et Thierry?
3. Marie et Monique (arriver à l'heure) / Et Thierry?
4. ses amis (tomber malades) / Et Thierry?
5. Madame Dubuque (monter dans un taxi) / Et Thierry?
6. les étudiants (rester sur le campus) / Et Thierry?
7. les étudiants (s'amuser) / Et Thierry?

Remember that the past participles of **descendre** and **sortir** are **descendu** and **sorti**.

2 **Le voyage.** Racontez la journée *(Tell about the day)* de Monsieur et Madame Smith. Attention à l'emploi des verbes **avoir** et **être**.

MODÈLES: se lever à 7 heures
Ils se sont levés à 7 heures.

chercher un taxi
Ils ont cherché un taxi.

1. voyager en train
2. arriver à Angers
3. descendre du train à la gare Saint-Laud
4. téléphoner aux Martin
5. monter dans la voiture de Monsieur Martin
6. parler avec Lori Becker
7. aller chez les Martin
8. déjeuner chez les Martin
9. s'amuser

3 **Qu'est-ce que tu as fait la semaine dernière?** Utilisez **tu** et les expressions suivantes pour interviewer votre partenaire.

> **MODÈLE:** manger une pizza
>
> > **VOUS:** **Est-ce que tu as mangé une pizza la semaine dernière?**
> >
> > **VOTRE PARTENAIRE:** **Oui, j'ai mangé une pizza.** ou
> > **Non, je n'ai pas mangé de pizza.**

1. aller au cinéma
2. étudier à la bibliothèque
3. regarder la télévision
4. passer un examen
5. tomber malade
6. entrer dans un bistro
7. descendre en ville
8. lire un journal
9. se lever à 5 heures du matin

4 **La plupart des étudiants.** Qu'est-ce que la plupart des étudiants ont fait la semaine dernière? Utilisez les expressions suivantes pour la question et pour la réponse.

> **MODÈLE:** manger une pizza —**Est-ce que la plupart des étudiants ont mangé une pizza la semaine dernière?**
> —**Oui, ils ont mangé une pizza.** ou
> **Non, ils n'ont pas mangé de pizza.**

1. aller aux cours
2. faire leurs devoirs
3. nettoyer leur chambre
4. sortir avec leurs amis
5. se coucher tard
6. se lever tôt
7. tomber malades

5 **À vous.** Répondez.

1. Êtes-vous resté(e) sur le campus le week-end dernier?
2. Qu'est-ce que vous avez fait le week-end dernier?
3. Quelle est la dernière fois que vous êtes sorti(e) avec vos amis? Où êtes-vous allés? Qu'est-ce que vous avez fait? À quelle heure êtes-vous rentrés?
4. Vos parents ont-ils déjà visité votre campus? Si oui, quand sont-ils venus?
5. Est-ce que vous arrivez d'habitude à l'heure au cours?
6. Quelle est la dernière fois que vous êtes arrivé(e) en retard au cours?
7. Est-ce que quelqu'un aime arriver en avance au cours de français? Qui est-ce?

6 **Le voyage des Smith.** Racontez l'histoire suivante au passé composé.

Monsieur et Madame Smith passent la nuit à Paris. Ils se lèvent tôt. D'abord ils sortent de leur hôtel. Ensuite ils montent dans un taxi pour aller à la gare Montparnasse. Quand ils arrivent à la gare, ils trouvent leur train et ils cherchent leurs places. Enfin le train part. Ils ne mangent rien pendant le voyage. Après une heure et demie, leur train arrive à la gare Saint-Laud. Monsieur Smith s'occupe de leurs bagages et ils descendent du train.

Entre amis

La dernière fois

1. Find out when the last time was that your partner went out.
2. Ask where s/he went.
3. Find out what s/he did.
4. Find out when s/he got back home.
5. Find out at what time s/he went to bed.

B. Le pronom *y*

Ta sœur est **en France?**	Oui, elle **y** est.
Va-t-elle souvent **à Paris?**	Non, elle n'**y** va pas souvent.
Quand pars-tu **en France?**	J'**y** pars dans un mois.
Ton frère est resté **chez lui?**	Non, il n'**y** est pas resté.
Est-il allé **au cinéma?**	Oui, il **y** est allé.
Tu vas rester **dans ta chambre?**	Non, je ne vais pas **y** rester.

■ **Y** *(There)* is very often used in place of expressions that tell where something is located (**à l'université, dans la voiture,** etc.). The pronoun **y** replaces both the preposition (**à, chez, dans, en, sur,** etc.) and the name of the place.

Nous allons **au cinéma.**   Nous **y** allons.

■ **Y** is placed directly before the conjugated verb. This means that in the passé composé, it goes in front of the auxiliary.

Nous **y** allons la semaine prochaine.	*We are going there next week.*
Nous n'**y** allons pas demain.	*We are not going there tomorrow.*
J'**y** suis allé.	*I went there.*
Ma mère n'**y** est jamais allée.	*My mother has never gone there.*

■ When there is more than one verb, **y** is placed directly in front of the verb to which it is related (usually the infinitive).

Je vais **y** aller.	*I am going to go there.*
Je ne vais pas **y** rester.	*I am not going to stay there.*
J'ai envie d'**y** passer un mois.	*I feel like spending a month there.*
Je n'ai pas l'intention d'**y** habiter.	*I don't plan to live there.*

Review **Quelques endroits,** pp. 125–126.

7 **Non, je n'y vais pas.** Un(e) étudiant(e) demande **Vas-tu à la pharmacie?** Un(e) autre répond **Non, je n'y vais pas; je vais ... (au centre commercial, à l'église,** etc.). Inventez au moins 10 questions.

8 **Tu y vas souvent?** Demandez si votre partenaire fait souvent les choses suivantes. Votre partenaire va utiliser **y** dans chaque *(each)* réponse.

MODÈLE: aller au cinéma

> VOUS: **Tu vas souvent au cinéma?**
>
> VOTRE PARTENAIRE: **Oui, j'y vais souvent.** ou
> **Non, je n'y vais pas souvent.**

1. aller chez le médecin
2. étudier à la bibliothèque
3. dîner au restaurant
4. arriver au cours en retard

5. monter dans ta voiture
6. retourner chez tes parents
7. aller à la poste

9 **Tu y es allé(e) hier?** Refaites l'exercice 8, mais posez les questions au passé composé. Votre partenaire va utiliser **y** dans chaque réponse.

MODÈLE: aller au cinéma

> VOUS: **Es-tu allé(e) au cinéma hier?**
>
> VOTRE PARTENAIRE: **Oui, j'y suis allé(e).** ou
> **Non, je n'y suis pas allé(e).**

Paris patchwork *édition révolutionnaire*

COMMENT S'Y PERDRE, COMMENT S'Y RETROUVER

ALLEZ-Y EN MÉTRO

10 **À vous.** Répondez. Utilisez **y** dans chaque réponse.

1. Êtes-vous sur le campus maintenant?
2. Êtes-vous allé(e) à la bibliothèque hier soir? Si oui, à quelle heure y êtes-vous entré(e)? Combien de temps y êtes-vous resté(e)?
3. Combien de fois par semaine allez-vous au cours de français? Y allez-vous demain?
4. Êtes-vous resté(e) chez vous pendant les dernières vacances?
5. La plupart des étudiants ont-ils dîné au restaurant hier soir?
6. Avez-vous envie d'aller un jour en France? Y êtes-vous déjà allé(e)? Si oui, combien de temps y avez-vous passé?
7. Allez-vous au cinéma ce soir? Si oui, avec qui y allez-vous?

Entre amis

Au campus et à la maison

Use **y,** if possible, in your answers.

1. Ask if your partner went to the library last night.
2. Find out if s/he is going there this evening.
3. Find out the same information with respect to the gymnasium, the post office, and the grocery store.
4. Find out if your partner is going home next weekend.
5. Find out when s/he went home last.
6. Find out what s/he did when s/he went home.

Review the vocabulary on pp. 125–126.

2 Describing Your Background

D'où viennent ces personnes?

Alain et Sylvie viennent de Nantes.
Tom vient d'Angleterre. Il vient de Londres.
Mike vient des États-Unis et Rose vient du Canada.
Il vient de l'état d'Iowa et elle vient de la province d'Ontario.

Et vous?   D'où venez-vous?

C. Le verbe *venir*

Est-ce que **Monique vient** de France?	*Does Monique come from France?*
Non, **elle vient** du Canada.	*No, she comes from Canada.*
Elle est devenue médecin.	*She became a doctor.*
Elle n'est pas ici mais **elle revient** à 6 heures.	*She isn't here but she's coming back at six o'clock.*

venir *(to come)*			
je	**viens**	nous	**venons**
tu	**viens**	vous	**venez**
il/elle/on	**vient**	ils/elles	**viennent**

passé composé: je **suis venu(e)**

This is similar to the distinction between **américain** and **américaine**, pp. 92–93.

■ Note the pronunciation distinction between the third person singular and plural forms.

vient   [vjɛ̃]   viennent   [vjɛn]

■ The verbs **revenir** *(to come back)* and **devenir** *(to become)* are conjugated like **venir.**

11 **Les gens partent.** Demandez quand ils reviennent. Votre partenaire va répondre.

> **MODÈLE:** Marie-Dominique (à 15 h 30)
> **VOUS: Quand est-ce qu'elle revient?**
> **VOTRE PARTENAIRE: Elle revient à quinze heures trente.**

1. Stéphanie (à 12 h 45)
2. Colette et Karine (à midi)
3. nous (la semaine prochaine)
4. tu (ce soir)
5. le patron (demain matin)
6. vos amis (mercredi)
7. vous (dans une heure)
8. ta sœur et toi (tout de suite)

D. Les prépositions de lieu avec une ville ou un pays (suite)

You have already learned to use prepositions to express *to* or *at* with a city, state, province, or country (see Ch. 5).

D'où viennent vos parents?	*Where do your parents come from?*
Mon père est originaire **du** Canada.	*My father is a native of Canada.*
Ma mère vient **des** États-Unis.	*My mother comes from the United States.*
Je viens **de** Bruxelles.	*I come from Brussels.*
Monsieur et Madame Luc viennent **de** France.	*Monsieur and Madame Luc come from France.*

■ To tell where a person is *from,* some form of **de** is used.

• **de** with cities:
    de Paris, **d'**Angers

• **de** with feminine countries or countries that begin with a vowel sound:
    de France, **d'**Iran

• **du** with masculine countries:
    du Mexique, **du** Canada

• **des** with plural countries:
    des États-Unis

■ To say that someone is from a U.S. state or Canadian province, **de** is normally used before those that are feminine or that begin with a vowel sound. The preposition **du** is often used with masculine states and provinces that begin with a consonant.

de Géorgie	**d'**Iowa	**du** Kansas
de Terre-Neuve	**d'**Alberta	**du** Québec

Note   You may also use **de l'état de** or **de la province de** to say which U.S. state or Canadian province someone is from.

> Mon meilleur ami vient **de l'état d'**Arizona.
> Je viens **de la province d'**Ontario.

See Ch. 5 for a list of countries already studied, p. 142.

■ Use the expression **d'où** with **venir** to inquire where someone comes from.

D'où vient Guy—du Canada ou de France?

Review prepositions of place, p. 138.

	Je viens ...	J'habite ... / Je vais ...
Synthèse: Les prépositions de lieu		
ville	**de**	**à**
pays féminin ou pays qui commence par une voyelle	**de**	**en**
pays masculin	**du**	**au**
pays pluriel	**des**	**aux**

One can also say **la Hollande** for **les Pays-Bas.**

Je viens **d'**Atlanta. Je vais **à** New York.
María vient **d'**Espagne. Elle habite **en** France.
Emilio téléphone **du** Mexique **au** Canada.
Nous venons **des** États-Unis. Nous allons **aux** Pays-Bas en vacances.
John vient **de l'état de** Nebraska mais il habite **dans l'état d'**Arizona.
Denise vient **de la province d'**Ontario, mais elle habite **dans la province de** Québec.

12 **André va voyager.** Il a l'intention de donner de ses nouvelles *(keep in touch)* à ses parents et à ses amis. Qu'est-ce qu'il va faire?

> **MODÈLE:** écrire / Italie
> **Il va écrire d'Italie.**

1. téléphoner / Allemagne
2. poster une lettre / Moscou
3. écrire une carte postale / Japon
4. téléphoner / Mexique
5. écrire / état de New York
6. écrire un message / province d'Ontario
7. poster une cassette / Liverpool

13 **André est retourné chez lui.** Il a contacté ses parents et ses amis pendant son voyage. Qu'est-ce qu'il a fait?

> **MODÈLE:** écrire / Rome
> **Il a écrit de Rome.**

1. téléphoner / Berlin
2. poster une lettre / Russie
3. écrire une carte postale / Tokyo
4. téléphoner / Mexico
5. écrire / États-Unis
6. écrire un message / Canada
7. poster une cassette / Angleterre

D'où viennent-ils? La liste des passagers du vol *(flight)* Air France n° 0748 inclut des personnes de différents pays. Expliquez d'où viennent ces personnes et où elles habitent maintenant.

> **MODÈLE:** Sandrine (Paris / New York)
> **Sandrine vient de Paris, mais elle habite à New York maintenant.**

1. Ralph (Canada / États-Unis)
2. Alice (Belgique / France)
3. Helmut et Ingrid (Allemagne / Italie)
4. William (Angleterre / Irlande)
5. José et María (Mexique / États-Unis)
6. Gertrude (Ontario / Manitoba)
7. Judy et Bill (Michigan / Allemagne)

15 **À vous.** Répondez.

1. De quelle ville venez-vous?
2. De quelle(s) ville(s) viennent vos parents?
3. D'où vient votre meilleur(e) ami(e)?
4. D'où viennent vos grands-parents?
5. D'où vient votre professeur de français? (Devinez.)
6. D'où viennent deux autres étudiants du cours de français?

VOCABULAIRE

Les mois de l'année, les saisons, le temps

Les mois de l'année	Les saisons	Le temps
janvier	l'hiver	Il fait froid.
février		Il neige.
mars		Il fait du vent.
avril	le printemps	Il pleut.
mai		Il fait frais.
juin		
juillet	l'été	Il fait beau.
août		Il fait du soleil.
septembre		Il fait chaud.
octobre	l'automne	Il fait encore beau.
novembre		Il commence à faire froid.
décembre		Il fait mauvais.

The opposite of **Il fait beau** is **Il fait mauvais.**

Note The negation of **il fait du vent** is **il ne fait pas** *de* **vent.**

E. Les mois de l'année, les saisons, le temps

■ Names of months begin with lowercase letters in French. Use the preposition **en** before the months to mean *in.*

en février   **en** août   **en** septembre

■ Use **en** also with all seasons except **le printemps.**

      en été   **en** automne   **en** hiver
But: **au** printemps

■ The French represent the date by giving the day first, then the month.

Amy est née **le premier mai.**	*Amy was born on the first of May.*
Mon anniversaire est **le dix février.**	*My birthday is the tenth of February.*
Le bébé est né **le vingt-cinq avril.**	*The baby was born on April twenty-fifth.*

Note   Use **le premier** (*... first, the first of ...*), but then **le deux, le trois,** etc.

     La fête nationale suisse est **le premier** août.

VOCABULAIRE

Quelques dates

le premier janvier	le Jour de l'An
le premier juillet	la fête nationale canadienne
le quatre juillet	la fête nationale américaine
le quatorze juillet	la fête nationale française
le premier novembre	la Toussaint
le vingt-cinq décembre	Noël

 En quelle saison sont-ils nés? Expliquez quand et en quelle saison les personnes suivantes sont nées.

Modèle: Monique (15/4)
     Elle est née le quinze avril. Elle est née au printemps.

     1. Martin Luther King, fils (15/1)
     2. Maureen (10/2) et Michel (23/9)
     3. Anne (25/8) et Stéphanie (13/7)
     4. George Washington (22/2)
     5. vous

Quelle est la date? Votre partenaire va poser une question. Donnez la réponse.

> **MODÈLE:** Noël
>> **VOTRE PARTENAIRE:** **Quelle est la date du jour de Noël?**
>> **VOUS:** **C'est le vingt-cinq décembre.**

1. ton anniversaire
2. l'anniversaire de ton (ta) meilleur(e) ami(e)
3. le Jour de l'An
4. le commencement du printemps
5. le commencement de l'été
6. le commencement de l'automne
7. le commencement de l'hiver
8. le commencement des vacances d'été à ton université
9. la fête nationale américaine
10. la fête nationale canadienne
11. la fête nationale française

c'est le quatre juillet

 Quel temps fait-il? Posez des questions. Si votre partenaire ne sait pas la réponse, il (elle) va deviner.

> **MODÈLE:** février / chez toi
>> **VOUS:** **Quel temps fait-il en février chez toi?**
>> **VOTRE PARTENAIRE:** **Il fait froid et il neige.**

1. été / chez toi
2. hiver / Montréal
3. automne / Chicago
4. printemps / Washington, D.C.
5. août / Maroc
6. avril / Paris
7. décembre / Acapulco

DÉCEMBRE   25°   −3°   17°   11°   18°   11°

 À vous. Répondez.

1. En quelle saison êtes-vous né(e)?
2. En quel mois êtes-vous né(e)?
3. En quel(s) mois les membres de votre famille sont-ils nés?
4. En quelle saison est-ce qu'il pleut chez vous?
5. En quelle saison est-ce qu'il commence à faire froid chez vous?
6. Quelle est votre saison préférée? Pourquoi?
7. Qu'est-ce que vous avez fait l'été dernier?

Entre amis

D'où viennent-ils?

1. Find out where your partner comes from.
2. Find out if that is where s/he was born.
3. Find out where your partner lives now.
4. Find out his/her birthdate.
5. Find out if your partner has ever gone to France, Canada, or some other French-speaking country.

3 Stating What You Just Did

Tu as déjà mangé, Thierry?

    Oui, il y a une demi-heure. Je viens de manger.°   *I just ate.*

Tes amis ont téléphoné?

    Oui, il y a dix minutes. Ils viennent de téléphoner.°   *They just called.*

 Et vous? Qu'est-ce que vous venez de faire?
Est-ce que vous venez de parler français?

F. *Venir de* + infinitif

■ **Venir de** followed by an infinitive means *to have just.*

Je **viens d'arriver.**	*I have just arrived.*
Ils **viennent de manger.**	*They just ate.*
Mon frère **vient de se coucher.**	*My brother just went to bed.*
Qu'est-ce que tu **viens de faire?**	*What did you just do?*

20 **Qu'est-ce qu'ils ont fait?** Chaque phrase est assez vague. Posez une question qui commence par **Qu'est-ce que** pour demander une précision. Ensuite votre partenaire va suggérer *(suggest)* une réponse à la question.

Modèle: Mes amis viennent de manger quelque chose.
          vous: **Qu'est-ce qu'ils ont mangé?**
   votre partenaire: **Ils ont mangé une pizza.**

1. Pierre vient de lire quelque chose.
2. Nous venons de regarder quelque chose.
3. Je viens d'étudier quelque chose.
4. Mon frère et ma sœur viennent de trouver quelque chose.
5. Je viens d'écrire quelque chose.
6. Nous venons de faire quelque chose.

21 **Elle vient de téléphoner.** Votre camarade de chambre vient de rentrer chez vous. Répondez **oui** à ses questions et utilisez **venir de** dans chaque réponse.

MODÈLE: Martine a téléphoné?
Oui, elle vient de téléphoner.

1. Est-elle rentrée chez elle?
2. Est-ce qu'elle a déjà dîné?
3. Vous avez parlé de moi?
4. A-t-elle trouvé ma lettre?
5. Est-ce qu'elle a lu ma lettre?
6. Tu as expliqué pourquoi je n'ai pas téléphoné?

22 **La naissance (birth) de Vianney.** Vous êtes le frère de Brigitte et vos parents vous téléphonent de la maternité (maternity hospital). Vous posez des questions au passé composé. Votre partenaire joue le rôle des parents et utilise **venir de** pour répondre.

MODÈLE: Vous / monter à la salle d'attente (waiting room)
LE FRÈRE: Est-ce que vous êtes montés à la salle d'attente?
LES PARENTS: Oui, nous venons de monter à la salle d'attente.

1. Brigitte / avoir son bébé
2. Vianney / naître
3. le médecin / partir
4. vous / entrer dans la chambre de Brigitte
5. Matthieu, Antoine et Julien / parler avec leurs parents
6. Chantal / téléphoner

Matthieu Monnier est né le 17 mai 1989. Ses frères s'appellent Antoine, Julien et Vianney. Antoine est né le 4 avril 1991, Julien le 29 mars 1993 et Vianney le 18 mai 1997. Ils habitent à Angers avec leurs parents, Brigitte et Jean-Philippe.

Bonjour ! Ça y est !! Bébé est né !!!

Matthieu   ANTOINE   JULIEN

Nous sommes heureux de vous annoncer la naissance de

VIANNEY

le dimanche 18 mai 1997

Intégration

Révision

A Les mois et les saisons

1. Nommez les mois de l'année.
2. Nommez les saisons de l'année.
3. Parlez du temps qu'il fait pendant chaque *(each)* saison.
4. Pour chaque saison, mentionnez une activité qu'on fait.

B Le week-end dernier. Faites une liste de vos activités du week-end dernier. Essayez ensuite de deviner ce que votre partenaire a écrit.

C À vous. Répondez.

1. Quelle est la date de votre anniversaire?
2. De quel pays venez-vous?
3. Dans quelle ville êtes-vous né(e)?
4. D'où viennent vos parents?
5. Quand les membres de votre famille sont-ils nés?
6. À quelle heure êtes-vous arrivé(e) au cours de français la dernière fois? Y êtes-vous arrivé(e) en retard, à l'heure ou en avance?
7. Êtes-vous déjà allé(e) dans un pays où on parle français? Si oui, où, et avec qui?
8. Qu'est-ce que vous venez d'étudier au cours de français?
9. Avez-vous déjà voyagé en train ou en avion? Où êtes-vous allé(e)?

D Trouvez quelqu'un qui ... Interviewez les autres étudiants.

1. Find someone who was born in another state or province.
2. Find someone who comes from a large city.
3. Find someone who has been to a French-speaking country.
4. Find someone who spent last summer on campus.
5. Find someone who did not go out last Friday evening.
6. Find someone who stayed in his/her room last night.
7. Find someone who went to the library last night.
8. Find someone who did not watch television last night.
9. Find someone who has just eaten.

Pas de problème!

Preparation for the video:
1. Video worksheet in the *Cahier d'activités*
2. CD-ROM, *Module 4*

Cette activité est basée sur la vidéo, *Module 4*. Choisissez la bonne réponse pour compléter les phrases suivantes.

1. Jean-François a l'intention d'acheter *(buy)* _____.
   (du pain, des croissants, des pâtisseries)
2. Il est _____ quand Jean-François parle avec l'artiste pour la première fois.
   (9 h 15, 9 h 45, 8 h 45)
3. L'artiste se trouve _____.
   (à Montparnasse, au Quartier Latin, à Montmartre)
4. L'artiste dessine *(is drawing)* _____.
   (Notre-Dame, le Sacré-Cœur, la Sainte-Chapelle)
5. Jean-François parle _____ fois avec lui.
   (deux, trois, quatre)
6. C'est _____.
   (mercredi, vendredi, dimanche)
7. L'homme qui entre dans la boulangerie avant Jean-François veut _____ croissants.
   (deux, trois, quatre)

Lecture I

 Étude du vocabulaire. Étudiez les phrases suivantes et choisissez les mots anglais qui correspondent aux mots français en caractères gras: *second, according to, in fact, only, understand, such as, remember, following.*

1. D'abord, nous faisons cet exercice. Ensuite nous allons faire l'exercice **suivant.**
2. Il est important de **se rappeler** que cinq et demi s'écrit 5,5 en France mais 5.5 aux États-Unis.
3. Il est souvent difficile de **comprendre** ces différences culturelles.
4. **D'après** les experts, il fait plus chaud au mois d'août qu'au mois de juillet.
5. Y a-t-il **seulement** vingt-huit jours au mois de février?
6. **En effet** il y a d'habitude 28 jours dans le **deuxième** mois de l'année.
7. Dans certaines villes, **telles que** Paris, Lyon et Montréal, il y a un métro.

B **Identifiez les pays.** Combien de pays y a-t-il dans l'Union européenne? Combien de ces pays se trouvent sur la carte au début du livre?

Les femmes parlementaires européennes

Les femmes représentent cinquante-deux pour cent de la population française mais, d'après des statistiques récemment publiées dans le magazine *L'Express,* les femmes françaises constituent seulement 5,5 pour cent des parlementaires en France. C'est en effet le plus petit pourcentage de femmes parlementaires des quinze pays de l'Union européenne.

Tableau I.	À l'Assemblée nationale		
	pays	femmes députés	pourcentage de l'Assemblée
1	la Suède	151	43
2	le Danemark	59	34
3	la Finlande	67	33,5
4	les Pays-Bas	43	28,5
5	l'Allemagne	176	26,5
6	l'Autriche	47	25,7
7	l'Espagne	76	22
8	le Luxembourg	11	18
9	le Portugal	31	13,5
10	la Belgique	18	12
11	l'Irlande	20	12
12	la Grande-Bretagne	63	10
13	l'Italie	60	9,5
14	la Grèce	17	5,6
15	la France	32	5,5

NOTE CULTURELLE
En France, en octobre 2000, le pourcentage de femmes parlementaires avait un peu changé. Il y avait (*there were*) cinquante-sept femmes députées à l'Assemblée nationale et vingt femmes au Sénat. Consultez les activités WWW pour le Chapitre 7 pour trouver combien il y a de femmes parlementaires aujourd'hui en France.

Tableau II.	Au Sénat ou dans les Chambres hautes		
	pays	femmes sénateurs	pourcentage du Sénat
1	les Pays-Bas	43	22,5
2	l'Autriche	13	20,3
3	la Belgique	13	18,3
4	l'Allemagne	12	17,4
5	l'Espagne	31	15
6	l'Irlande	8	13
7	l'Italie	26	8
8	la Grande-Bretagne	82	6
9	la France	18	5,6

Née au Sénégal de père militaire avant l'indépendance, Ségolène Royal fait ses études en France en sciences politiques, économiques et administratives. Elle est députée socialiste depuis 1988.

Pour bien comprendre ces statistiques, il faut d'abord se rappeler que, dans certains pays y compris la France, il y a deux chambres parlementaires; dans d'autres, telles que la Suède et le Danemark, il y en a seulement une. Donc il y a quinze pays qui ont représentation à l'Assemblée nationale (tableau I), mais seulement neuf qui ont un Sénat (tableau II). En France, il y a 577 députés à l'Assemblée nationale et 303 sénateurs.

L'Express, juin 1996

 Vrai ou faux? Décidez si les phrases suivantes sont vraies ou fausses. Si une phrase est fausse, corrigez-la.

1. Il y a plus de cinquante pour cent de femmes dans la population française.
2. Il y a neuf pays qui n'ont pas de chambre correspondant à l'Assemblée nationale.
3. Il y a 545 députés hommes en France.
4. Les Suédois ont le plus grand pourcentage de sénateurs féminins.
5. La Hollande est un des pays de l'Union européenne.
6. L'Irlande a le plus petit nombre de femmes sénateurs.
7. La France a le plus petit nombre de députées.

D **Discussion.**

1. Y a-t-il beaucoup, assez ou trop peu de femmes parlementaires dans votre pays? Expliquez votre réponse.
2. Comparez votre pays aux différents pays de l'Union européenne.

Lecture II

A **Parlons du genre** *(gender).* Identifiez les mots suivants qui sont masculins, féminins ou peuvent *(can)* être les deux.

	M	F	M/F
1. personne	_____	_____	_____
2. enfant	_____	_____	_____
3. professeur	_____	_____	_____
4. artiste	_____	_____	_____
5. victime	_____	_____	_____
6. médecin	_____	_____	_____
7. ingénieur	_____	_____	_____

B **Faites une liste.** Faites une liste de toutes les expressions que vous connaissez *(that you know)* qui commencent par «Il».

IL

Il pleut Il pleut
Il fait beau
Il fait du soleil
Il est tôt
Il se fait[1] tard
Il
Il
Il
toujours Il
Toujours Il qui pleut et qui neige
Toujours Il qui fait du soleil
Toujours Il
Pourquoi pas Elle
Jamais Elle
Pourtant[2] Elle aussi
Souvent se fait[3] belle!

Jacques Prévert, Éditions Gallimard

1. *is getting*   2. *However*   3. *makes herself*

C **Discussion.** Quel est le point de vue du poète? Êtes-vous d'accord avec lui? Pourquoi ou pourquoi pas?

VOCABULAIRE ACTIF

Les mois de l'année
janvier *(m.) January*
février *(m.) February*
mars *(m.) March*
avril *(m.) April*
mai *(m.) May*
juin *(m.) June*
juillet *(m.) July*
août *(m.) August*
septembre *(m.) September*
octobre *(m.) October*
novembre *(m.) November*
décembre *(m.) December*

Les saisons de l'année
le printemps *spring*
l'été *(m.) summer*
l'automne *(m.) fall*
l'hiver *(m.) winter*
une saison *season*

Expressions météorologiques
Il fait froid. *It's cold.*
Il fait chaud. *It's hot (warm).*
Il fait frais. *It's cool.*
It fait beau. *It's nice out.*
Il fait mauvais. *The weather is bad.*
Il fait du soleil. *It's sunny out.*
Il fait du vent. *It's windy.*
Il pleut. *It's raining.*
Il neige. *It's snowing.*

Il commence à faire froid. *It's starting to get cold.*

Expressions de temps
à l'heure *on time*
en avance *early*
en retard *late*
une demi-heure *half an hour*
puis *then; next*
tout de suite *immediately; right away*
À tout de suite. *See you very soon.*

D'autres noms
un anniversaire *birthday*
un avion *airplane*
un bébé *baby*
la fête nationale *national holiday*
une guerre *war*
le monde *world*
une place *seat*
un problème *problem*
une victime *victim (male or female)*

Expressions utiles
Ça ne vous dérange pas? *That doesn't bother you?*
D'où venez-vous? *Where do you come from?*
en voiture *by car*
être originaire de *to be a native of*

Je vous en prie. *Don't mention it; You're welcome; Please do.*
Parlez-moi de ce voyage. *Tell me about this trip.*
Qui est à l'appareil? *Who is speaking (on the phone)?*
suivant(e) *following; next*
y *there*

Verbes
arriver *to arrive; to happen*
commencer *to begin*
descendre *to go down; to get out of*
devenir *to become*
entrer *to enter*
monter *to go up; to get into*
mourir *to die*
naître *to be born*
poster *to mail*
rentrer *to go (come) back; to go (come) home*
retourner *to go back; to return*
revenir *to come back*
tourner *to turn*
venir *to come*
venir de ... *to have just ...*

Quelques fêtes
la Toussaint *All Saints Day*
le Jour de l'An *New Year's Day*
Noël *Christmas*

On mange bien en France

Buts communicatifs
Ordering a French meal
Discussing quantities
Expressing an opinion
Expressing a preference

Structures utiles
L'article partitif
Ne ... plus
Le verbe **prendre**
Les expressions de quantité
Le verbe **boire**
Les pronoms objets directs **le, la, les**
Quelques expressions avec **avoir**
Les verbes comme **préférer**

Culture
L'apéritif
L'art d'apprécier le vin
Tout se fait autour d'une table
Un repas français
Sans façon
Relativité culturelle: Les repas

Quelque chose à manger?

Tu as faim°, Bruno?   *You are hungry*
    Qu'est-ce qu'il y a?
Il y a ...
    du pain° .   *bread*
    des hors-d'œuvre°.   *appetizers*
    de la soupe.
    du poisson.
    de la viande°.   *meat*
    des légumes°.   *vegetables*
    de la salade.
    du fromage.
Qu'est-ce que tu vas prendre?°   *What are you going to have?*

 Et vous?   Qu'est-ce que vous allez prendre?
                Je voudrais ...
                Merci, je n'ai pas faim.
                Je regrette° mais j'ai déjà mangé.   *I'm sorry*

Conversation

L'apéritif chez les Aspel

James Davidson est invité à prendre l'apéritif° chez Monsieur   have a before-dinner drink
et Madame Aspel, les parents de Karine. Monsieur Aspel lui
offre quelque chose à boire.

M. ASPEL: Que voulez-vous boire, James? J'ai du vin,
de la limonade, du jus de pomme°, de la   *apple*
bière ...

JAMES: Quel choix!° Comment s'appelle ce vin?   *What a choice!*

M. ASPEL: C'est du beaujolais. Et voilà une bouteille°   *bottle*
de bordeaux.

JAMES: Alors, un peu de beaujolais, s'il vous plaît.

M. ASPEL: Bien sûr°, voilà.   *Of course*
(James lève° son verre et Monsieur Aspel verse°   *lifts/pours*
du vin.)

JAMES: Merci beaucoup.

M. ASPEL: Je vous en prie.
(Un peu plus tard)

M. ASPEL: Alors, que pensez-vous° de ce petit vin?   *what do you think*

JAMES: Il est délicieux.

M. ASPEL: Encore à boire?°   *More to drink?*

JAMES: Non, merci.

M. ASPEL: C'est vrai?

JAMES: Oui, vraiment. Sans façon.°   *Honestly.*

M. ASPEL: Alors, je n'insiste pas.°   *I won't insist.*

▶ **Jouez ces rôles.** Répétez la conversation avec votre partenaire.
Utilisez vos noms.

L'apéritif

A before-dinner drink is often offered. This might be **un kir, un porto** *(port wine)*, **un jus de pomme,** etc.

L'art d'apprécier le vin

Wine is an integral part of French social life and there are a number of polite gestures, such as lifting one's glass when wine is to be poured, that are associated with wine appreciation.

Tout se fait autour d'une table (Everything takes place around a table)

It does not take long in France to realize how much time is spent sitting around a table. Not only is a table the place to enjoy a meal or share a drink, it is also a primary spot for business deals, serious discussion, pleasant companionship, courtship, and child rearing! It is not surprising, therefore, to find that the table has a place of honor in France, whether it is in **la cuisine, la salle à manger, le restaurant, le café, le bistro,** or **la cafétéria.**

Un repas français (A French meal)

A good example of the presence of structure in French lives is the order of a French meal. There

are as many as five separate courses at both lunch and dinner, although these are not necessarily heavy meals. After the **hors-d'œuvre,** the **plat principal** is served. There may be more than one **plat principal** (e.g., fish *and* meat). **La salade** normally comes next, followed by **le fromage** and **le dessert.** In a light meal, either the cheese or the dessert may be omitted.

Any variation in the order of the French meal is almost always minor. In some regions, such as **Angers,** the salad is often eaten with the main course. The number of courses in a French meal reflects not only the French feeling for structure, but also the French appreciation of savoring each taste individually.

Sans façon

Refusing additional servings is often quite difficult in France. The French are gracious hosts and are anxious that their guests have enough to eat and drink. There is therefore a need to find ways to convey politely that you are full. Do not, incidentally, say **Je suis plein(e)** (literally, *I am full*), since this would convey that you were either drunk or pregnant. When all else fails (e.g., **Merci; Non, merci; Vraiment; Je n'ai plus faim/soif; J'ai très bien mangé/bu,** etc.), the expression **Sans façon** *(Honestly; No kidding)* will usually work. Of course, if you feel like having a second serving, you may say **Volontiers!** or **Je veux bien.**

In France	In North America
Eating several courses, even light ones, means that you have to stop after each course and wait for the next. Much more time is spent at the table.	Everything may be served at once and, therefore, much less time is spent at the table.
A green salad is served *after* (occasionally with) the **plat principal.** It is not eaten as a first course.	If there is a salad, it is eaten at the start of the meal.
There is only one type of dressing (oil and vinegar) served with a salad.	There is a variety of salad dressings available. What is referred to as *French dressing* is nothing like what is served with a salad in France.
Bread is always served with the meal, usually without butter, and is bought fresh every day.	Bread is not always served with the meal.
Coffee is not served during lunch or dinner. It is served, without cream, at the end of these meals.	Coffee is occasionally served right away at the start of the meal.
Café au lait is served only at breakfast. This mixture of 1/2 coffee and 1/2 warm milk is often served in a bowl.	Many people put milk in their coffee at every meal.

En France, on boit beaucoup d'eau minérale.

Il y a un geste

Encore à boire?   A fist is made with the thumb extended to somewhat resemble a bottle. Then the thumb is pointed toward a glass as an invitation or a request to have more to drink.

 **À vous.** Répondez.

1. Que voulez-vous? J'ai de la limonade, du jus de pomme, ...
2. Bien sûr, voilà.
3. Aimez-vous la limonade, le jus de pomme, ... ?
4. Encore à boire?

Entre amis

Tu as faim?

1. Find out if your partner is hungry. (S/he is.)
2. Ask if s/he wants something to eat.
3. S/he will ask what there is.
4. Tell what there is.
5. Find out what s/he is going to have.

Prononciation

Les sons [k], [s], [z], [ʃ], [ʒ] et [ɲ]

■ The following words contain some related French consonant sounds. Practice saying the words after your instructor, paying particular attention to the highlighted sound. As you pronounce the words for one sound, look at how that sound is spelled and in what kinds of letter combinations it appears. What patterns do you notice?

[k]
- **c**afé, en**c**ore, bicy**c**lette, chi**c**
- cin**q**, **qu**el**qu**efois
- **k**ir, vod**k**a

[s]
- **s**a, **s**ur, di**s**cret, **s**kier, conver**s**ation, val**s**e, fil**s**, mar**s**
- pre**ss**é, poi**ss**on
- **c**itron, exer**c**ice, bi**c**yclette
- **ç**a, fran**ç**ais, gar**ç**on
- si**x**, di**x**, soi**x**ante

[z]
- mai**s**on, va**s**e, poi**s**on, maga**s**in
- **z**éro, sei**z**e, maga**z**ine

[ʃ]
- **ch**aud, blan**ch**e, mé**ch**ant
- **sh**ort, sweat-**sh**irt

[ʒ]
- **j**ouer, tou**j**ours, dé**j**euner, dé**j**à
- oran**g**e, **g**énéral, gara**g**e, refri**g**érateur

[ɲ]
- espa**gn**ol, Allema**gn**e, rensei**gn**ement

■ In most situations, **-s-** is pronounced [s]. But when it appears between two vowels, it is pronounced as [z].

soir **s**alade **s**eul cla**ss**e con**s**idération
But: va**s**e pré**s**ente rai**s**on cho**s**e mu**s**ée

■ As in English, **-c-** is usually pronounced [k], but becomes [s] when it precedes the letters **-e, -i,** or **-y.** To create the [s] sound of **-c-** in some words where it is not followed by **e, i,** or **y,** it is written as **ç.**

en**c**ore **c**assis **c**omment Maro**c** **c**rème
But: Fran**c**e voi**c**i bi**c**yclette fran**ç**ais Fran**ç**ois

■ Finally, as in English, the letter **-g-** is usually pronounced [g], but becomes [ʒ] when it precedes the letters **-e, -i,** or **-y.** To create the [ʒ] sound of **-g-** in some words where it is not followed by **e, i,** or **y,** an **-e** is added after it.

re**g**arder **g**olf **g**uitare **g**rippe é**g**lise
But: **g**entil oran**g**ina **g**ymnase man**g**eons voya**g**eons

▶ Pronounce the following words correctly.

1. chocolat, commerce, chaussures, citron, bicyclette, ça, garçon, chercher, chance, avec
2. cinq, cinquante, quelques, pourquoi, Belgique, quart, chaque, question, banque
3. kir, vodka, skier, baskets, hockey
4. excellent, saxophone, examen, exercice, six, dix, soixante
5. Sénégal, orange, mangeons, voyageur, garage, gauche, âge, ménage, agent, gymnastique
6. surprise, Suisse, sous, semestre, saison, sieste, poisson, plaisir, ensuite
7. conversation, télévision, fonctionnaire, attention, provisions, dissertation
8. zéro, onze, magazine, douze
9. jupe, jeune, je, janvier, aujourd'hui, déjeuner, déjà
10. espagnol, Allemagne, accompagner, renseignement

En été, on commence souvent le repas par un demi-melon bien froid. C'est délicieux.

Buts communicatifs

1 Ordering a French Meal

Client(e)	Serveur/Serveuse°	waiter / waitress
Qu'est-ce que vous avez comme ...	Il y a ...	
hors-d'œuvre?	des crudités°.	raw vegetables
	du pâté°.	pâté (meat spread)
	de la salade de tomates.	
soupes?	de la soupe aux légumes.	
	de la soupe à l'oignon°.	onion
plats principaux?	de la truite°.	trout
	du saumon°.	salmon
	du bœuf°.	beef
	du porc.	
	du poulet°.	chicken
légumes?	des haricots verts°.	green beans
	des petits pois°.	peas
	des épinards°.	spinach
	des frites°.	French fries
	du riz°.	rice
fromages?	de l'emmental°.	Swiss cheese
	du camembert.	
	du chèvre°.	goat cheese
	du brie.	
desserts?	des fruits.	
	de la glace°.	ice cream
	des pâtisseries°.	pastries
	de la tarte°.	pie
	du gâteau°.	cake

> **Garçon** is the traditional way of referring to a waiter; however, the word **serveur** is increasingly used.

▶ **Et vous?** Avez-vous décidé? Qu'est-ce que vous allez commander? Je vais prendre ...

Remarques

1. The words **hors-d'œuvre** and **haricot** begin with the letter **h-** but are treated as if they began with a pronounced consonant. Liaison does not take place after words like **les** and **des,** nor is the letter **-e** dropped in words like **le** and **de.**

   Nous aimons **les/hors-d'œuvre.**   Il n'y a pas **de haricots.**

2. **Hors-d'œuvre** is invariable in the plural.

   un **hors-d'œuvre**   des **hors-d'œuvre**

A. L'article partitif

Apportez-moi **du** pain, s'il vous plaît.	*Bring me some bread, please.*
Vous voulez **de la** glace?	*Do you want (some) ice cream?*
Vous avez **de l'**eau minérale?	*Do you have (any) mineral water?*
Je vais manger **des** frites.	*I'm going to eat (some) French fries.*

■ You have already learned about definite articles and indefinite articles in French. There is a third type of article in French called **l'article partitif** *(the partitive article)* that is used when a noun represents a certain quantity, or a part, of a larger whole. In English, we sometimes use the words *some* or *any* to represent this idea, but sometimes we use no article at all.

Je voudrais **du** gâteau.	*I would like cake (but just some of it).*
Le professeur a **de la** patience.	*The professor has patience (not all the patience in the world, just a portion of it).*
Jean a **des** livres.	*Jean has books (but not all the books in the whole world).*

partitive article	when to use	examples
du	before a masculine singular noun	**du** pain
de la	before a feminine singular noun	**de la** salade
de l'	before a masculine or feminine singular noun that begins with a vowel sound	**de l'**eau
des	before all plural nouns, masculine or feminine	**des** frites

■ Like the indefinite article, the partitive article usually becomes **de** after a negation.

Est-ce qu'il y a **de l'**eau minérale?	*Is there any mineral water?*
Non, il n'y a **pas d'**eau minérale.	*No, there isn't any mineral water.*
Il y a **des** légumes?	*Are there any vegetables?*
Non, il n'y a **pas de** légumes.	*No, there aren't any vegetables.*

Note　This rule does not apply after **être**.

Ce n'est pas **du** vin, ce n'est pas **de la** limonade, ce n'est pas **de l'**eau. C'est **du** lait.

■ In a series, the article must be repeated before each noun.

Vous voulez **de la** glace, **de la** tarte ou **du** gâteau?

Be sure to use the contractions **l', de l',** and **d'** before a vowel.

Review the definite article, p. 41, and the indefinite article, p. 59.

Synthèse: Les articles

	définis	indéfinis	partitifs
masculin singulier	le	un	du
féminin singulier	la	une	de la
pluriel	les	des	des
dans une phrase négative	le/la/les	de	de

Voici un des desserts préférés des Français. Ces gâteaux font venir l'eau à la bouche, n'est-ce pas?

1 **Qu'est-ce que c'est?** Identifiez les choses suivantes.

MODÈLES:

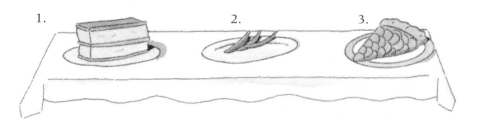

C'est du pain. Ce sont des petits pois.

1. 2. 3.

4. 5. 6.

2 **Qu'est-ce que vous commandez?** Dites au garçon ou à la serveuse que vous aimez la catégorie indiquée. Ensuite demandez quels sont les choix. Il (elle) va mentionner deux choix. Décidez.

MODÈLE: vegetables
> VOUS: **J'aime beaucoup les légumes. Qu'est-ce que vous avez comme légumes?**
> SERVEUR/SERVEUSE: **Nous avons des petits pois et des épinards.**
> VOUS: **Je voudrais des petits pois, s'il vous plaît.**

1. appetizers
2. meat
3. fish
4. vegetables
5. wine
6. cheese
7. desserts

3 **Ils viennent de pique-niquer.** Qu'est-ce qu'ils ont apporté *(brought)*? Qu'est-ce qu'ils n'ont pas apporté?

MODÈLE: Les Delille (pain, salade)
> **Les Delille ont apporté du pain, mais ils n'ont pas apporté de salade.**

1. Séverine (salade, fromage)
2. Roland (haricots verts, petits pois)
3. Serge et Christelle (fromage, vin rouge)
4. Patricia (poisson, viande)
5. Vous (... , ...)

4 **Un(e) touriste va au restaurant.** Jouez la scène suivante avec votre partenaire en complétant les phrases avec **du, de la, de l', des, de** ou **d'.**

—Vous avez décidé?
—Oui, je voudrais _____ pâté _____ truite, _____ frites et _____ épinards.
—Et comme boisson?
—Apportez-moi _____ café, s'il vous plaît.
—Mais c'est impossible! Il n'y a jamais _____ café avec le plat principal.
—Qu'est-ce qu'il y a?
—Nous avons _____ vin ou _____ eau minérale.
—Vous n'avez pas _____ orangina?
—Si, si vous insistez. Et comme dessert?
—Je crois que je voudrais _____ gâteau.
—Nous n'avons pas _____ gâteau. Il y a _____ glace et _____ fruits.
—Merci, je ne vais pas prendre _____ dessert.

B. *Ne ... plus*

■ The opposite of **encore** is **ne ... plus** *(no more, not any more, no longer).*

Avez-vous **encore** soif?
Non, je **n'**ai **plus** soif et je **n'**ai **plus** faim.

Are you still thirsty?
No, I'm not thirsty any more and I'm no longer hungry.

■ **Ne ... plus** works like the other negations you have learned; that is, **ne** and **plus** are placed around the conjugated verb. This means that in the passé composé, **ne** and **plus** surround the auxiliary verb and the past participle follows **plus**.

<table>
<tr><td>Je regrette; nous **n'avons plus** de glace.</td><td>*I'm sorry; we have no more ice cream.*</td></tr>
<tr><td>Je **ne** vais **plus** manger de dessert.</td><td>*I am not going to eat <u>any more</u> dessert.*</td></tr>
<tr><td>Delphine **n'a plus** dîné dans ce restaurant-là.</td><td>*Delphine did not eat in that restaurant again.*</td></tr>
</table>

Remember that the partitive article becomes **de** after a negation: **plus** *de* glace, **plus** *de* dessert.

5 **Encore à manger ou à boire?** Offrez encore à manger ou à boire. Votre partenaire va refuser poliment.

MODÈLES: bière   glace
    —**Encore de la bière?**   —**Encore de la glace?**
    —**Sans façon, je n'ai plus soif.**   —**Merci, je n'ai plus faim.**

1. café   5. viande   9. légumes
2. eau   6. frites   10. beaujolais
3. limonade   7. tarte   11. salade
4. pâté   8. poisson   12. fromage

6 **Le restaurant impossible.** Il n'y a plus beaucoup à manger ou à boire. Le serveur (la serveuse) répond toujours **Je regrette** et suggère autre chose. Insistez! Expliquez que vous n'aimez pas ce qu'il (elle) propose.

MODÈLE: poisson (viande)
    VOUS: **Avez-vous du poisson?**
    SERVEUR/SERVEUSE: **Je regrette, nous n'avons plus de poisson; mais nous avons de la viande.**
    VOUS: **Mais je voudrais du poisson! Je n'aime pas la viande.**

1. coca (vin)   6. pâtisseries (glace)
2. soupe (hors-d'œuvre)   7. chocolat chaud (café)
3. épinards (frites)   8. haricots verts (petits pois)
4. truite (saumon)   9. orangina (limonade)
5. pâté (crudités)

Il y a un geste

L'addition, s'il vous plaît *(Check, please).* When the French want to signal to a waiter or waitress that they want the check, they pretend to be writing on the open palm of one hand. This is discreetly held up for the waiter to see.

Entre amis

L'addition, s'il vous plaît

You have just finished your meal in a French restaurant. You signal the waiter/waitress.

1. Ask the waiter/waitress for your bill.
2. S/he will verify the items you ordered.
3. Confirm or <u>correct</u> what s/he says.

C. Le verbe *prendre*

Nous prenons souvent un repas ensemble.	*We often have a meal together.*
Je prends un café.	*I'm having a cup of coffee.*
Mes amis ne **prennent** pas le petit déjeuner.	*My friends don't eat breakfast.*
Qui a pris mon dessert?	*Who took my dessert?*

prendre *(to take; to eat, drink)*			
je	**prends**	nous	**prenons**
tu	**prends**	vous	**prenez**
il/elle/on	**prend**	ils/elles	**prennent**

passé composé: j'**ai pris**

■ Note the pronunciation distinction between the third person singular and plural forms.

il prend   [prɑ̃]   ils pren**n**ent   [prɛn]

■ The verbs **apprendre** *(to learn)* and **comprendre** *(to understand; to include)* are conjugated like **prendre.**

Quelle langue **apprenez-vous?**	*What language are you learning?*
J'apprends le français.	*I'm learning French.*
Peggy comprend bien le français.	*Peggy understands French well.*
Comprennent-ils toujours le professeur?	*Do they always understand the teacher?*
Pardon, **je** n'**ai** pas **compris.**	*Excuse me, I didn't understand.*
Le service est **compris.**	*The service (tip) is included.*

Note   *To learn to do something* is **apprendre à** + infinitive.

Nous **apprenons à parler** français.   *We are learning to speak French.*

7 **Les voyageurs.** Les personnes suivantes vont voyager. Expliquez quelle langue elles apprennent.

MODÈLE: Je vais en France.
Alors j'apprends à parler français.

Review **langues et pays,** in Ch. 5.

1. Mes parents vont en Italie.
2. Mon cousin va en Allemagne.
3. Ma sœur va au Mexique.
4. Mon oncle et ma tante vont en Russie.
5. Mes amis et moi allons en Belgique.
6. Vous allez en Chine.
7. Je vais au Maroc.

8 **La plupart des étudiants.** Interviewez votre partenaire à propos des étudiants de votre cours de français. Attention au présent et au passé composé.

MODÈLES: apprendre le français
—Est-ce que la plupart des étudiants apprennent le français?
—Bien sûr, ils apprennent le français.

apprendre le français à l'âge de quinze ans
—Est-ce que la plupart des étudiants ont appris le français à l'âge de quinze ans?
—Non, ils n'ont pas appris le français à l'âge de quinze ans.

1. prendre quelquefois un verre de vin au petit déjeuner
2. prendre le petit déjeuner ce matin
3. comprendre toujours le professeur de français
4. apprendre l'espagnol à l'âge de cinq ans
5. prendre souvent un taxi
6. prendre un taxi hier
7. comprendre cet exercice

9 **À vous.** Répondez.

1. Vos amis prennent-ils le petit déjeuner d'habitude? Si oui, qu'est-ce qu'ils prennent comme boisson?
2. D'habitude, qu'est-ce que vous prenez comme boisson au petit déjeuner? au déjeuner? au dîner?
3. Qu'est-ce que vous avez pris comme boisson ce matin?
4. Qu'est-ce que la plupart des Français prennent comme boisson au dîner?
5. Qu'est-ce que vous allez prendre si vous dînez dans un restaurant français?
6. Si vous commandez un dessert, que prenez-vous d'habitude?
7. Comprenez-vous toujours les menus qui sont en français?
8. Avez-vous appris à faire la cuisine?

Entre amis

Tu comprends les serveurs de restaurant?

1. Ask if your partner is learning French.
2. Find out if s/he understands French waiters.
3. Ask if s/he is hungry. (S/he is.)
4. Invite your partner to go to a French restaurant.
5. Discuss what you are going to have.

2 Discussing Quantities

Qu'est-ce que tu manges, Solange?
Je mange ...
    beaucoup de frites.
    un peu de gâteau.
    peu d'épinards.
    très peu de moutarde°.   *mustard*
Je mange ...
    un morceau° de pizza.   *piece*
    une tranche de jambon°.   *slice of ham*
    une assiette° de crudités.   *plate*
    une boîte de bonbons°.   *box of candy*

Et vous?   Qu'est-ce que vous mangez?
                Je mange ...
                Qu'est-ce que vous buvez°?   *you drink*
                Je bois° ...   *I drink*

Remarque   The plural of **un morceau** is **des morceaux**.

Thomas a mangé cinq **morceaux** de pizza.

D. Les expressions de quantité

■ You have already been using expressions of quantity throughout this course. There are two kinds of expressions of quantity: specific measures (**une tasse, un verre,** etc.) and indefinite expressions of quantity (**assez, beaucoup,** etc.).

■ To use these expressions of quantity with nouns, insert **de** (but no article) before the noun.

Une bouteille de vin, s'il vous plaît.	*A bottle of wine, please.*
Une douzaine d'œufs, s'il vous plaît.	*A dozen eggs, please.*
Il faut **un kilo de porc.**	*We need a kilo of pork.*
Trois kilos de pommes de terre aussi.	*Three kilos of potatoes also.*
Je voudrais **un morceau de pain.**	*I'd like a piece of bread.*
Ils n'ont pas **beaucoup d'amis.**	*They don't have a lot of friends.*
Combien de frères ou **de sœurs** avez-vous?	*How many brothers or sisters do you have?*

VOCABULAIRE À RETENIR

un œuf *egg*
une pomme de terre
    potato
le brocoli *broccoli*

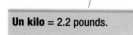

Un kilo = 2.2 pounds.

■ **Trop, beaucoup, assez,** and **peu** can be used with either singular or plural nouns. *Un* **peu** can only be used with singular nouns, those that cannot be counted. To express the idea of a small amount with a plural noun (which *can* be counted), use **quelques** *(a few, some)* without **de.**

	Voulez-vous **un peu de** fromage?	*Would you like a little cheese?*
But:	Voulez-vous **quelques** frites?	*Would you like a few French fries?*

■ The indefinite expressions of quantity can also be used with verbs, without the addition of **de.**

Je chante **beaucoup.**	*I sing a lot.*
Rip van Winkle a **trop** dormi.	*Rip van Winkle slept too much.*
Nous avons **assez** travaillé!	*We have worked enough!*

■ To express how much you like or dislike a thing, the definite article (not **de**) is used before the noun.

Je n'aime pas **beaucoup le** lait.	*I don't much like milk.*
Mon frère aime **trop la** glace.	*My brother likes ice cream too much.*

■ **Peu de** can be introduced by the word **très** to make it more emphatic. **Très** cannot be used with the other expressions of quantity.

L'ex-président mange **très peu de** brocoli.

E. Le verbe *boire*

Quel vin **boit-on** avec du poisson?
Nous buvons un peu de thé.
Nos amis mangent de la salade et **ils boivent** de l'eau.
Hélène a trop **bu!**

boire *(to drink)*			
je	**bois**	nous	**buvons**
tu	**bois**	vous	**buvez**
il/elle/on	**boit**		
ils/elles	**boivent**		
passé composé: j'**ai bu**			

■ Note the pronunciation distinction between the third person singular and plural forms.

elle boit   [bwa]   elles boivent   [bwav]

10 **Les goûts et les couleurs** *(Tastes and colors).* Donnez des précisions en utilisant *(by using)* les expressions de quantité entre parenthèses.

MODÈLES: Nous buvons du vin. (peu)   Nous aimons les fruits. (beaucoup)
Nous buvons peu de vin.   **Nous aimons beaucoup les fruits.**

1. Ma sœur boit de l'orangina. (trop)
2. Elle aime l'orangina. (beaucoup)
3. Nos parents prennent du café. (un peu)
4. Vous avez de la salade? (assez)
5. Jean n'aime pas le vin. (beaucoup)
6. Il boit de l'eau. (peu)
7. J'aime le poisson. (assez bien)
8. Du vin blanc, s'il vous plaît. (un verre)
9. Marie désire des hors-d'œuvre. (quelques)
10. Je voudrais de la viande et du vin. (quatre tranches / une bouteille)

 beaucoup le vin / assez bien le poisson / quelques hors-d'œuvre (varioptms)

11 **Dans ma famille.** Décrivez les habitudes de votre famille.

MODÈLES: **Nous mangeons beaucoup de glace.**
Ma sœur boit très peu de lait.

			épinards
			fruits
		trop *too much*	limonade
mes parents		beaucoup *a lot*	lait
ma sœur	manger	assez *sort of*	glace
mon frère	boire	peu *a little*	salade
je		très peu *very little*	poisson
nous		jamais *ever / never*	eau
			chocolat chaud
			pommes de terre

12 **Sur le campus.** Utilisez une expression de quantité pour répondre à chaque question.

MODÈLE: Les étudiants ont-ils du temps libre?
Ils ont très peu de temps libre.

1. Avez-vous des amis à l'université?
2. Est-ce que les étudiants de votre université boivent de la bière?
3. Aiment-ils le coca light?
4. Est-ce que vos amis boivent du thé?
5. Vos amis mangent-ils du fromage?
6. Les étudiants mangent de la pizza, n'est-ce pas?
7. Les étudiants ont-ils des devoirs?

13 **L'appétit vient en mangeant** *(Eating whets the appetite).* Complétez les paragraphes avec **le, la, l', les, du, de la, de l', des, de** et **d'**.

Before doing this activity, review the use of the definite article in Ch. 2 (p. 42) and also the use of **de** after a negation.

Review

1. Françoise est au restaurant. Elle va manger *des* hors-d'œuvre, *du* poisson, *de la* viande, *de la* salade, un peu *de* fromage et beaucoup *de* glace. Elle va boire *du* vin blanc avec *le* poisson et *du* vin rouge avec *la* viande et *du* fromage. Mais elle ne va pas manger *de* soupe parce qu'elle n'aime pas *la* soupe.

le = la going to order.

2. Monsieur et Madame Blanc ne boivent jamais *de* café. Ils détestent *le* café mais ils aiment beaucoup *le* thé. Quelquefois ils boivent *du* vin, mais jamais beaucoup. Leurs enfants adorent *l'* orangina et *le* coca-cola classique. Mais il n'y a jamais *d'* orangina ou *de* coca chez eux. Les parents pensent que *le* coca et *l'* orangina ne sont pas bons pour les jeunes enfants. Alors leurs enfants boivent *du* lait ou *de l'* eau.

not a gen. statement about quality

NOTE CULTURELLE
Les Québécois disent «déjeuner» pour **petit déjeuner,** «dîner» pour **déjeuner** et «souper» pour **dîner.**

Le petit déjeuner à Paris

du pain
un croissant
du beurre
de la confiture
du café au lait
du thé
du chocolat chaud

Le petit déjeuner à Québec

du jus de fruits (orange, pomme, canneberge)
des céréales (froides ou chaudes)
un œuf
du jambon ou du bacon
du pain grillé
des crêpes
du beurre
de la confiture
du sirop d'érable *= maple syrup*
du café
du thé
du lait
du chocolat chaud

Entre amis

Tu prends le petit déjeuner d'habitude?

Use the breakfast menu on the previous page, if possible.

1. Find out if your partner usually has breakfast.
2. Find out if s/he had breakfast this morning.
3. If so, find out what s/he ate.
4. Ask what s/he drank.

Qu'est-ce que vous prenez le petit déjeuner?
Qu'est-ce que vous Avez pris le petit déjeuner ce matin?

Qu'est-ce que vous avez bu?

3 Expressing an Opinion

NOTE CULTURELLE
Le croque-monsieur *(open-faced toasted ham and cheese sandwich):* Un des choix les plus populaires dans les cafés et les bistros de France. C'est une tranche de pain au jambon et au fromage qu'on fait griller.

Miam°, je trouve ce croque-monsieur délicieux! — *Yum*
Qu'en penses-tu°, René? — *What's your opinion?*
    Je suis d'accord avec toi. Je le trouve très bon.° — *I think it's very good.*

Comment trouves-tu ces épinards?
    Ils sont bons. Je les aime bien.

Que penses-tu de la pizza aux anchois°? — *anchovies*
    Berk°, je la trouve affreuse°. — *Yuck / awful*

▶ **Et vous?**   Que pensez-vous du thé au citron? Est-il ... délicieux? bon? affreux?

Que pensez-vous des croissants français? Sont-ils ... délicieux? bons? affreux?

Que pensez-vous de la glace au chocolat? Est-elle ... délicieuse? bonne? affreuse?

Que pensez-vous des soupes froides? Sont-elles ... délicieuses? bonnes? affreuses?

F. Les pronoms objets directs *le, la, les*

J'aime beaucoup mes amis. — *I like my friends a lot.*
Je **les** aime beaucoup. — *I like them a lot.*

Mes amis étudient le français. — *My friends study French.*
Ils **l'**étudient. — *They study it.*

Ils ne regardent pas souvent la télé. — *They don't watch TV often.*
Ils ne **la** regardent pas souvent. — *They don't watch it often.*

■ A direct object pronoun replaces a noun that is the direct object of a verb (where no preposition precedes the noun). Object pronouns are placed directly in front of the verb.

Direct object pronouns	examples of nouns	examples of pronouns
le	Je déteste **le fromage**.	Je **le** déteste.
la	Je trouve **cette pâtisserie** affreuse.	Je **la** trouve affreuse.
l'	Je n'aime pas **la bière**.	Je ne **l'**aime pas.
les	J'adore **les croque-monsieur**.	Je **les** adore.

NB: Use **l'** in place of **le** or **la** if the following word begins with a vowel sound.

 Qu'en penses-tu? *(What do you think of it/of them?)* Vous êtes à une soirée avec un(e) ami(e). Donnez votre opinion des choix indiqués et demandez l'opinion de votre ami(e). Suivez les modèles.

Modèles: hors-d'œuvre

> **vous:** **Que penses-tu de ces hors-d'œuvre?**
> **votre ami(e):** **Je les trouve très bons. Qu'en penses-tu?**
> **vous:** **Je suis d'accord. Ils sont délicieux.**

pâtisserie

> **vous:** **Que penses-tu de cette pâtisserie?**
> **votre ami(e):** **Je la trouve affreuse. Qu'en penses-tu?**
> **vous:** **Je ne suis pas d'accord. Elle est excellente.**

1. fromage	3. café	5. fruits *(m.)*	7. légumes *(m.)*	9. viande
2. bière	4. glace	6. poisson	8. croque-monsieur	10. salade

Entre amis

Que penses-tu de ... ?

1. Give your partner something to eat and drink.
2. Toast your partner.
3. Ask what s/he thinks of the food you offered.
4. Find out what s/he thinks of the drink.
5. Offer some more.

Review the verb **avoir**, p. 60.

Use **très** with **faim, soif,** etc. to express the meaning *very*.

VOCABULAIRE À RETENIR

The expressions with **avoir** in this section

G. Quelques expressions avec *avoir*

■ A number of idiomatic expressions in French use **avoir** with a noun where English would use *to be* with an adjective.

Feelings		*Opinions/Judgments*	
j'ai faim	*I am hungry*	j'ai raison	*I am right*
j'ai soif	*I am thirsty*		*I am wise*
j'ai froid	*I am cold*	j'ai tort	*I am wrong*
j'ai chaud	*I am hot*		*I am unwise*
j'ai sommeil	*I am sleepy*		
j'ai peur	*I am afraid*		

■ **Peur, raison,** and **tort** can be used alone, but are often followed by **de** and an infinitive. **Peur** can also be followed by **de** and a noun.

Paul **a tort de** fumer.	*Paul is wrong to smoke.*
Tu **as raison d'**étudier souvent.	*You are wise to study often.*
Nous **avons peur d'**avoir une mauvaise note.	*We are afraid of getting a bad grade.*
Je **n'ai pas peur des** examens.	*I am not afraid of tests.*

■ When an infinitive is negative, both **ne** and **pas** precede it.

Il a eu tort de **ne pas étudier.** *He was wrong not to study.*

15 **Explications.** Donnez une explication ou exprimez votre opinion. Complétez les phrases suivantes avec une des expressions idiomatiques qui emploient le verbe **avoir.**

MODÈLE: Olivier ne porte pas de manteau en novembre. Il …
Il a froid. ou **Il a tort.**

1. Je suis fatigué. J' …
2. Ah! Quand nous pensons à une bonne pizza au fromage, nous …
3. Christelle pense qu'on parle espagnol au Portugal. Elle …
4. Mon frère … des gros chiens.
5. Vous pensez que notre professeur est charmant? Ah! Vous …
6. Nous allons boire quelque chose parce que nous …
7. Cet après-midi je voudrais aller à la piscine. J' …
8. C'est le mois de décembre et nous …

16 **Si c'est comme ça** *(If that's the way it is).* Utilisez une ou deux expressions avec **avoir** pour compléter les phrases suivantes.

MODÈLE: Si on travaille beaucoup, on …
Si on travaille beaucoup, on a faim et soif.

1. On a envie de manger quelque chose si on …
2. Si on ne va pas aux cours, on …
3. Si on ne porte pas de manteau en décembre, on …
4. Si on pense que deux fois quatre font quarante-quatre, on …
5. S'ils font leurs devoirs, les étudiants …
6. Si on porte beaucoup de vêtements en été …
7. Si on ne boit pas d'eau, on …
8. Si on pense que les professeurs sont méchants, on …

17 **À vous.** Répondez.

1. À quel(s) moment(s) de la journée avez-vous faim? Que faites-vous quand vous avez faim?
2. À quel(s) moment(s) de la journée avez-vous soif? Que faites-vous?
3. Où vont les étudiants de votre université quand ils ont soif?
4. À quel(s) moment(s) de la journée avez-vous sommeil? Que faites-vous?
5. Pendant quels cours avez-vous envie de dormir?
6. Quels vêtements portez-vous si vous avez froid?
7. Que faites-vous si vous avez chaud?
8. Avez-vous peur d'avoir une mauvaise note?
9. Avez-vous peur avant un examen? Si oui, de quels examens avez-vous peur?
10. Vos professeurs ont-ils toujours raison?

Entre amis

Un examen

1. Tell your partner that there is a test next week.
2. Find out if s/he is afraid.
3. Find out if s/he is going to study this weekend.
4. Depending on the answer, say whether you think s/he is wise or unwise.

4 Expressing a Preference

Quelle sorte° de sandwichs préfères-tu, Valérie? *type*
　　Je préfère les sandwichs au fromage.

Quelle sorte de pizzas préfères-tu?
　　Je préfère les pizzas aux champignons°. *mushrooms*

Quelle sorte de glace préfères-tu?
　　Je préfère la glace à la fraise°. *strawberry*

▶ Et vous?　Que préférez-vous?
　　Moi, je préfère les sandwichs ...

　　　　au beurre°　*with butter*
　　　　au beurre d'arachide°　*with peanut butter*
　　　　à la confiture°　*with jam*
　　　　au fromage
　　　　au jambon
　　　　à la mayonnaise
　　　　à la moutarde
　　　　au pâté

Et je préfère les pizzas ...

　　　　au fromage
　　　　aux champignons
　　　　aux oignons
　　　　aux anchois
　　　　à l'ail°　*with garlic*

la laitue = lettuce

Et je préfère la glace ...

　　　　au chocolat
　　　　à la vanille
　　　　à la fraise
　　　　au café

tout sortes de glace (all kinds of ...)

Remarque　Use **à** and the definite article to specify ingredients.　✗

Review the use of **à** with the definite article, p. 125.

une omelette **au fromage**　*a cheese omelet*
une crêpe **à la confiture**　*a crepe with jam*
une pizza **aux champignons**　*a mushroom pizza*
un croissant **au beurre**　*a croissant made with butter*

Quel choix! Vous êtes dans une pizzeria à Paris. Demandez à la serveuse ou au serveur le choix qu'elle (il) offre. Elle (il) va répondre. Ensuite commandez quelque chose.

> **MODÈLE:** pizzas
>
> **VOUS:** Quelles sortes de pizzas avez-vous?
>
> **SERVEUSE/SERVEUR:** Nous avons des pizzas au jambon, aux champignons et au fromage.
>
> **VOUS:** Je voudrais une pizza au fromage et au jambon, s'il vous plaît.

1. sandwichs
2. omelettes
3. pizzas
4. glaces
5. crêpes
6. croissants

19 **Mes préférences.** Écrivez trois petits paragraphes pour décrire ...

1. les choses que vous aimez beaucoup.
2. les choses que vous mangez si vous avez très faim.
3. les choses que vous ne mangez jamais.

H. Les verbes comme *préférer*

Vous préférez la glace ou la pâtisserie?
Je préfère la glace.

Do you prefer ice cream or pastry?
I prefer ice cream.

Espérez-vous aller en France un jour?

Do you hope to go to France sometime?

Oui, et **j'espère** aller au Canada aussi.

Yes, and I hope to go to Canada also.

Répétez, s'il vous plaît.
Les étudiants **répètent** après leur professeur.

Repeat, please.
The students repeat after their teacher.

■ The verbs **préférer** *(to prefer)*, **espérer** *(to hope)*, **répéter** *(to repeat; to practice)*, and **exagérer** *(to exaggerate)* are all conjugated as regular **-er** verbs except that before a silent ending (as in the present tense of the **je, tu, il/elle/on,** and **ils/elles** forms), the **-é-** before the ending becomes **-è-.**

Préférer usually is followed by **le, la, les,** when used with a noun.

préférer *(to prefer)*			
silent endings		pronounced endings	
je	**préfère**	nous	**préférons**
tu	**préfères**	vous	**préférez**
il/elle/on	**préfère**		
ils/elles	**préfèrent**		
passé composé: j'**ai préféré**			

20 **Vos amis et vous.** Interviewez une autre personne d'après le modèle.

MODÈLE: la truite ou les anchois

> **VOUS:** **Est-ce que vos amis préfèrent la truite ou les anchois?**
> **VOTRE PARTENAIRE:** **Ils préfèrent la truite.**
> **VOUS:** **Et vous, qu'est-ce que vous préférez?**
> **VOTRE PARTENAIRE:** **Moi, je préfère les anchois.**
> **VOUS:** **Berk!**

1. le samedi soir ou le lundi matin
2. faire la vaisselle ou faire la cuisine
3. New York ou Los Angeles
4. la politique ou les mathématiques
5. partir en vacances ou travailler
6. étudier ou jouer au tennis
7. le cinéma ou le théâtre
8. le petit déjeuner ou le dîner
9. voyager ou rester à la maison
10. les sandwichs ou les omelettes
11. le coca ou le coca light
12. apprendre les mathématiques ou apprendre le français
13. regarder la télévision ou écouter la radio

21 **Microconversation: Vous déjeunez au restaurant.** Qu'est-ce qu'il y a à manger et à boire? Il y a toujours un choix. Vous préférez autre chose, mais il faut choisir *(you have to choose)*. Suivez *(follow)* le modèle.

Review the choices on p. 215.

MODÈLE: le fromage

> **VOUS:** **Qu'est-ce que vous avez comme fromage?**
> **SERVEUR:** **Nous avons du brie et du camembert.**
> **VOUS:** **Je préfère le chèvre. Vous n'avez pas de chèvre?**
> **SERVEUR:** **Je regrette, mais le brie et le camembert sont très bons.**
> **VOUS:** **Très bien, je vais prendre du brie, s'il vous plaît.**
>
> *(Un peu plus tard)*
> **SERVEUR:** **Comment trouvez-vous le brie?**
> **VOUS:** **Je pense qu'il est excellent!**

1. les hors-d'œuvre   2. la viande   3. les légumes
4. le fromage   5. les desserts

Entre amis

Au snack-bar

1. Find out if your partner is hungry. (S/he is.)
2. Find out if s/he likes sandwiches, pizza, ice cream, etc.
3. Find out what kind of sandwich, etc., s/he prefers.
4. Tell your partner what you are going to order.

Intégration www

Révision

A À la carte

1. Nommez trois sortes de pizzas.
2. Nommez trois sortes de sandwichs.
3. Nommez trois sortes de légumes.
4. Nommez trois sortes de plats principaux.

B À vous. Répondez.

1. Où allez-vous si vous avez faim ou soif?
2. Aimez-vous les sandwichs? Si oui, quelle sorte de sandwich préférez-vous?
3. Qu'est-ce que vous préférez comme pizza? Qu'est-ce que vos amis préfèrent?
4. Si vous allez au restaurant, qu'est-ce que vous commandez d'habitude? Qu'est-ce que vous refusez de manger?
5. Avez-vous pris le petit déjeuner ce matin? Si oui, qu'est-ce que vous avez mangé? Qu'est-ce que vous avez bu?
6. Qu'est-ce que vous buvez le soir d'habitude? Qu'est-ce que vos amis boivent?
7. Qu'est-ce que vous pensez du vin de Californie? du vin de New York? du vin français?
8. Qu'est-ce que vous pensez du fromage américain? du fromage français?
9. Que pensez-vous des repas au restaurant universitaire?
10. À quel moment avez-vous sommeil? Pourquoi?
11. Qu'est-ce que vous espérez faire dans la vie?

On trouve en France beaucoup de restaurants vietnamiens ou marocains. Les propriétaires sont généralement immigrés de ces pays francophones.

Chez Jacques

Menu à 20 euros

assiette de crudités
soupe à l'oignon
pâté du chef
tarte à l'oignon
salade de tomates

bœuf bourguignon
truite aux amandes
canard à l'orange
steak-frites
poulet frites

salade

fromage

omelette norvégienne
mousse au chocolat
tarte maison
glace

Boisson non comprise; service compris

Entre amis

Le menu, s'il vous plaît

You are a waiter (waitress). Use the menu provided and wait on two customers. When you have finished taking their order, tell the chef (the teacher) what they are having.

Pas de problème!

Preparation for the video:
1. Video worksheet in the *Cahier d'activités*
2. CD-ROM, *Module 5*

NOTE CULTURELLE
«Faire le pont» *(bridge):* Si, par exemple, on a un jour de congé *(holiday)* le mardi, on ne travaille pas le lundi. Comme cela, on a quatre jours de suite *(in a row)* sans travail: le week-end plus lundi et mardi.

Cette activité est basée sur la vidéo, *Module 5*. Répondez.

1. Quelle est la nationalité de Bruno?
2. Qu'est-ce que les quatre jeunes personnes commandent au café?
3. Quel temps fait-il?
4. Quels sont les quatre jours mentionnés par Marie-Christine pour expliquer le mot «pont»?
5. Qui a un ami qui s'appelle Noël?
6. Pourquoi est-ce qu'ils ne partent pas en voiture?
7. Comment vont-ils voyager?
8. Qui ne va pas voyager? Pourquoi pas?

Lecture I

A **Imaginez la scène.** Deux personnes prennent le petit déjeuner ensemble. Imaginez cette scène. Répondez aux questions suivantes.

1. Qu'est-ce qu'il y a sur la table?
2. Qui sont les deux personnes?
3. Que font-elles?

4. Que boivent-elles?
5. De quoi est-ce qu'elles parlent?
6. Quel temps fait-il?

Déjeuner du Matin

Il a mis[1] le café
Dans la tasse
Il a mis le lait
Dans la tasse de café
Il a mis le sucre
Dans le café au lait
Avec la petite cuiller[2]
Il a tourné
Il a bu le café au lait
Et il a reposé[3] la tasse
Sans me parler

Il a allumé[4]
Une cigarette
Il a fait des ronds[5]
Avec la fumée
Il a mis les cendres[6]
Dans le cendrier[7]
Sans me parler
Sans me regarder

Il s'est levé
Il a mis
Son chapeau sur sa tête[8]
Il a mis
Son manteau de pluie[9]
Parce qu'il pleuvait[10]
Et il est parti
Sous la pluie
Sans une parole[11]
Sans me regarder
Et moi j'ai pris
Ma tête dans ma main[12]
Et j'ai pleuré.

Jacques Prévert

1. *He put* 2. *spoon* 3. *he set down* 4. *He lit* 5. *rings* 6. *ashes* 7. *ashtray* 8. *head*
9. *rain* 10. *it was raining* 11. *a word* 12. *hand*

B **Questions.** Répondez.

1. Où sont ces personnes?
2. Qui sont les deux personnes? (Imaginez)
3. Quels problèmes y a-t-il? (Imaginez)
4. Est-ce que ce poème est triste? Expliquez votre réponse.

C **Jouez cette scène.** Faites tous les gestes nécessaires et présentez le poème *Déjeuner du Matin* sans parler.

Lecture II

A **Étude du vocabulaire.** Étudiez les phrases suivantes et choisissez les mots anglais qui correspondent aux mots français en caractères gras: *not including, in force, until, way, leisure activities, valid.*

1. Cette carte visa est **valable?** Oui, **jusqu'au** mois de juillet.
2. Les **loisirs** comprennent les promenades, les jeux de cartes, etc.
3. Jean-François joue au tennis d'une **façon** bizarre.
4. C'est le prix **hors**-taxe ou est-ce que les taxes sont comprises?
5. La nouvelle loi entre **en vigueur** le premier janvier.

B **Un coup d'œil sur la lecture.** Lisez rapidement la publicité et faites une liste des avantages du Week-end Privilège.

C **Vrai ou faux?** Décidez si les phrases suivantes sont vraies ou fausses d'après la lecture. Si une phrase est fausse, corrigez-la.

1. Cette offre comprend une nuit à l'hôtel et deux repas.
2. Il faut payer le double si deux personnes restent dans une chambre.
3. L'hôtel Royal est un hôtel de luxe.
4. Si on est seul, cette offre n'est pas valable.
5. Le Week-end Privilège comprend deux nuits à l'hôtel.
6. En novembre le prix change.
7. Au dîner, le vin est compris dans le repas.

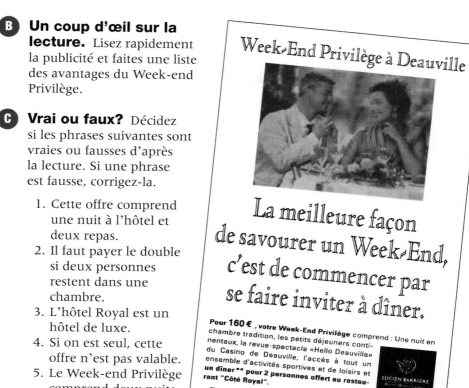

Week-End Privilège à Deauville

La meilleure façon de savourer un Week-End, c'est de commencer par se faire inviter à dîner.

Pour **160 €** , votre **Week-End Privilège** comprend : Une nuit en chambre tradition, les petits déjeuners continentaux, la revue-spectacle «Hello Deauville» du Casino de Deauville, l'accès à tout un ensemble d'activités sportives et de loisirs et **un dîner** ** **pour 2 personnes offert au restaurant "Côté Royal".**

LUCIEN BARRIÈRE

Hôtel Royal ★ ★ ★ ★

Réservations au 02 31 98 66 93
*Prix par personne en chambre double.
Offre exceptionnelle valable jusqu'au 31 octobre, non cumulable avec d'autres offres en vigueur.
** Dîner offert sur la base du menu "Côté Royal" hors boissons.

D **Discussion.** Répondez.

1. En quoi consiste un petit déjeuner continental? Faites une liste.
2. Cherchez Deauville dans une encyclopédie. Expliquez son intérêt touristique.
3. Est-ce que cette offre est vraiment exceptionnelle? Expliquez votre réponse.

VOCABULAIRE ACTIF

Boissons
un apéritif *before-dinner drink*
du beaujolais *Beaujolais*
du bordeaux *Bordeaux*

Hors-d'œuvre ou soupe
des crudités *(f. pl.) raw vegetables*
un hors-d'œuvre *appetizer*
du pâté *pâté (meat spread)*

de la salade de tomates *tomato salad*
de la soupe *soup*
de la soupe aux légumes *vegetable soup*

Viandes
du bœuf *beef*
du jambon *ham*

du poulet *chicken*
du porc *pork*
de la viande *meat*

Poissons
des anchois *(m. pl.) anchovies*
du saumon *salmon*
de la truite *trout*

Légumes
de l'ail (m.) garlic
du brocoli broccoli
des épinards (m. pl.) spinach
des frites (f. pl.) French fries
des haricots verts (m. pl.) green beans
un légume vegetable
un oignon onion
des petits pois (m. pl.) peas
une pomme de terre potato
du riz rice

Fromages
du brie Brie
du camembert Camembert
du chèvre goat cheese
de l'emmental (m.) Swiss cheese

D'autres choses à manger
du beurre butter
du beurre d'arachide peanut butter
des céréales (f. pl.) cereal
des champignons (m.) mushrooms
de la confiture jam
un croissant croissant
un croque-monsieur open-faced toasted ham and cheese sandwich
de la mayonnaise mayonnaise
de la moutarde mustard
un œuf egg
une omelette omelet
du pain bread
du pain grillé toast
de la salade salad
un sandwich sandwich
une tomate tomato

Desserts
un bonbon candy
une crêpe crepe, French pancake
un dessert dessert
des fraises (f.) strawberries

un fruit fruit
du gâteau cake
de la glace (à la vanille) (vanilla) ice cream
des pâtisseries (f.) pastries
une pomme apple
de la tarte pie

Quantités et mesures
une assiette plate
une boîte box; can
une bouteille bottle
une douzaine dozen
un kilo kilogram
un morceau piece
une tranche slice

D'autres noms
l'addition (f.) (restaurant) bill, check
un choix choice
le déjeuner lunch
un garçon waiter; boy
le petit déjeuner breakfast
le plat principal main course, main dish
un repas meal
un serveur waiter
une serveuse waitress
le théâtre theater

Adjectifs
affreux (affreuse) horrible
délicieux (délicieuse) delicious
quelques a few; some

Verbes
apporter to bring
apprendre to learn; to teach
avoir chaud to be hot
avoir faim to be hungry
avoir froid to be cold
avoir peur to be afraid

avoir raison to be right; to be wise
avoir soif to be thirsty
avoir sommeil to be sleepy
avoir tort to be wrong; to be unwise
boire to drink
commander to order
comprendre to understand
espérer to hope
penser to think
préférer to prefer
prendre to take; to eat, to drink
répéter to repeat; to practice

Adverbes
naturellement naturally
peu (de) little; few
plus (ne ... plus) no more; no longer

Expressions utiles
à propos de regarding, on the subject of
au contraire on the contrary
Berk! Yuck! Awful!
bien sûr of course
Encore à boire (manger)? More to drink (eat)?
Encore de ... ? More ... ?
Je n'insiste pas. I won't insist.
je regrette I'm sorry
Le service est compris. The tip is included.
Miam! Yum!
Quelle(s) sorte(s) de ... ? What kind(s) of ... ?
Qu'en penses-tu? What do you think of it (of them)?
Qu'est-ce que vous avez comme ... ? What do you have for (in the way of) ... ?
sans façon honestly; no kidding
si vous insistez if you insist

9

Où est-ce qu'on l'achète?

Buts communicatifs
Finding out where things are sold
Describing an illness or injury
Making a purchase

Structures utiles
Les verbes en **-re**
Depuis
Le verbe **acheter**
Le pronom relatif

Culture
La pharmacie
Le tabac
Les petits magasins
On achète des fleurs.

Coup d'envoi

Les achats

Où est-ce qu'on achète° des journaux?	*buy*
On peut° aller ...	*you can*
au bureau de tabac.	
à la gare.	
au kiosque°.	*newsstand*
Où est-ce qu'on achète des cadeaux°?	*gifts*
On peut aller ...	
chez un fleuriste°.	*florist's shop*
dans une boutique.	
dans un grand magasin°.	*department store*
au marché aux puces°.	*flea market*
Où est-ce qu'on achète quelque chose à manger?	
On peut aller ...	
au marché°.	*(open-air) market*
au supermarché.	
à l'épicerie.	

un hypermarché

▶ **Et vous?**   Qu'est-ce que vous voulez acheter?
Où allez-vous faire cet achat°?   *purchase*

GALERIES Lafayette

THE DEPARTMENT STORE CAPITAL OF FASHION.
LE GRAND MAGASIN CAPITALE DE LA MODE

DEPUIS 1893
LES BOUTIQUES
DU CHÂTEAU

À la pharmacie

Joseph Smith est un touriste. Il désire acheter un journal américain et il pense qu'on achète les journaux à la pharmacie. Mais en France on n'y vend pas de journaux.

JOSEPH SMITH:	Bonjour, Monsieur. Vous avez le *Herald Tribune?*
PHARMACIEN:	Comment? Qu'est-ce que vous dites?°
JOSEPH SMITH:	Je voudrais acheter le *Herald Tribune*.
PHARMACIEN:	Qu'est-ce que c'est?
JOSEPH SMITH:	C'est un journal.
PHARMACIEN:	Mais on ne vend° pas de journaux ici, Monsieur.
JOSEPH SMITH:	Vous n'en° avez pas?
PHARMACIEN:	Non, Monsieur. C'est une pharmacie. Nous vendons seulement des médicaments°.
JOSEPH SMITH:	Mais aux États-Unis on achète des journaux à la pharmacie.
PHARMACIEN:	Désolé°, Monsieur, mais nous sommes en France.
JOSEPH SMITH:	Pouvez-vous me dire° où on peut trouver des journaux, s'il vous plaît?
PHARMACIEN:	Ça dépend°. Si vous cherchez un journal d'un autre pays, il faut aller au bureau de tabac qui est dans la rue° de la Gare.
JOSEPH SMITH:	Merci, Monsieur. Vous êtes très aimable°.

What are you saying?

sell

any

medicine

Sorry

Can you tell me

depends

street

kind

▶ **Jouez ces rôles.** Répétez la conversation avec votre partenaire. Utilisez le nom de votre journal préféré.

Il y a un geste

Désolé(e). When saying **désolé(e),** the shoulders are hunched and the upturned palms are often raised. Sarcasm is added to the gesture by also pursing one's lips and raising one's eyebrows.

Pourquoi le pharmacien ne vend-il pas de journal à Monsieur Smith?

a. Parce que Monsieur Smith est américain.
b. Parce que le pharmacien ne comprend pas Monsieur Smith quand il parle français.
c. Parce qu'on vend les journaux dans un magasin différent.

Quel est le meilleur cadeau si on est invité à dîner dans une famille française?

a. une boîte de bonbons
b. une bouteille de vin
c. un bouquet de fleurs

La pharmacie

Pharmacists in France don't sell magazines, newspapers, candy, drinks, or greeting cards. They will fill a prescription and are much less reticent than North American pharmacists to suggest treatments for non-serious illnesses, including a cold, a sore throat, and a headache. In this respect French pharmacies are a convenient and helpful solution for travelers who become ill.

Le tabac

One can buy magazines, newspapers, and postcards at the tobacco shop. Among the most popular English language publications available in France are the *International Herald Tribune* and the international edition of *Time* magazine. Since **le bureau de tabac** is under state license, one can also purchase stamps and cigarettes. Smoking is more widespread in France than in North America. While there have been some efforts to suggest that smoking is bad for your health, the state monopoly on the sale of tobacco has meant that, until recently, little was done to restrict the purchase or the use of cigarettes. However, for several years smoking has been confined to specific areas in public places. Fines can be levied on those who refuse to obey.

Les petits magasins

Although supermarkets (**supermarchés**) and even larger, all-in-one **hypermarchés** are found in every French city, the tourist in France will readily discover a variety of shops that specialize in one type of food. **La boulangerie** *(bakery),* **la pâtisserie** *(pastry shop),* **la boucherie** *(butcher),* **la charcuterie** *(pork butcher, delicatessen),* and **l'épicerie** *(grocery store)* are found in most neighborhoods. Not only, for example, do the French buy fresh bread daily, they will also go out of their way and pay a bit more, if necessary, to get bread that they consider more tasty. The French often use the possessive adjective to refer to **mon boulanger** *(my baker),* a phenomenon that is very rare or nonexistent in North America.

On achète des fleurs

Flower shops play an important role in French culture. More than any other gift, flowers are the number one choice when one is invited to dinner. Unless you plan on giving a dozen, choose an uneven **(impair)** number of flowers. Various reasons are given for the custom of offering three, five, or seven flowers rather than an even number. These include the implication that the donor has carefully selected them or that they may be more attractively arranged.

*Une réponse homéopathique
...à la décalcification.*

OSTÉOCYNÉSINE
DÉCALCIFICATION

Ceci est un médicament.   LHF: 4 rue Rabelais - 92600 Asnières

Laboratoires Homéopathiques de France

L H F

▶ **À vous.** Entrez dans une pharmacie et essayez d'acheter *(try to buy)* un magazine—*Time, Paris Match, Elle,* etc. Répondez au pharmacien.

PHARMACIEN: Bonjour, Monsieur (Madame/Mademoiselle).
VOUS: _____

PHARMACIEN: Comment? Qu'est-ce que vous dites?
VOUS: _____

PHARMACIEN: Mais on ne vend pas de magazines ici.
VOUS: _____

Entre amis

Au tabac

Your partner will take the role of the proprietor of a tobacco shop.

1. Ask if s/he has a certain newspaper or magazine.
2. S/he will say s/he doesn't.
3. Ask if s/he has bread, milk, wine, etc.
4. S/he will say s/he is sorry, but s/he doesn't.
5. Find out where you can find the things you are looking for.
6. Get directions.

Le son [R]

■ The most common consonant sound in French is [R]. While there are acceptable variations of this sound, [R] is normally a friction-like sound made in roughly the same area of the mouth as [g] and [k]. Keeping the tongue tip behind the lower teeth, the friction sound is made when the back of the tongue comes close to the back part of the mouth (pharynx). Use the word **berk!** to practice several times. It might also be helpful to use the following process: (1) say "ahhh ... ," (2) change "ahhh ... " to "ahrrr ... " by beginning to gargle as you say "ahhh ... ," (3) add [g] at the beginning and say **gare** several times, (4) say **garçon.** Then practice the following words.

- pou**r**, su**r**, bonjou**r**, bonsoi**r**

- ga**r**çon, me**r**ci, pa**r**lez

- **r**usse, **r**ien, **R**obert, **r**ouge

- t**r**ès, t**r**ois, c**r**ois, d**r**oit, f**r**ère, éc**r**i**r**e

- vot**r**e, quat**r**e, not**r**e, p**r**op**r**e, septemb**r**e

Buts
communicatifs

1 Finding Out Where Things Are Sold

🎧 Qu'est-ce qu'on vend à la pharmacie?
    On y vend ...
        des médicaments.
        des cachets d'aspirine°.   *aspirin tablets*
        des pastilles°.   *lozenges*
        du dentifrice°   *toothpaste*
        des pilules°.   *pills*
        du savon°.   *soap*
Qu'est-ce qu'on vend au bureau de tabac?
    On y vend ...
        du tabac°.   *tobacco*
        un paquet° de cigarettes.   *pack*
        des timbres°.   *stamps*
        des télécartes.
        des journaux.
        des magazines.
        des cartes postales.

Contrary to the general rule requiring a pronounced final **-c** (**avec, chic, Luc, Marc,** etc.), **tabac** has a silent final **-c.**

A. Les verbes en -re

J'**attends** mon amie avec impatience.	*I'm anxiously waiting for my friend.*
Entendez-vous son train?	*Do you hear her train?*
Elle **a répondu** «oui» à mon invitation.	*She responded "yes" to my invitation.*
Elle aime **rendre visite** à ses amis.	*She likes to visit her friends.*
La voilà. Elle **descend** du train.	*There she is. She's getting off the train.*
J'espère qu'elle n'**a** pas **perdu** sa valise.	*I hope she hasn't lost her suitcase.*

> Be careful to distinguish between the endings for **-re** verbs and those of **-er** verbs, p. 36.

vendre *(to sell)*					
je	**vend**	**s**	nous	**vend**	**ons**
tu	**vend**	**s**	vous	**vend**	**ez**
il/elle/on	**vend**		ils/elles	**vend**	**ent**

passé composé: j'**ai vendu**

conj

■ A number of frequently used verbs are conjugated like **vendre**.

VOCABULAIRE

> Be careful to avoid confusing **attendre** and **entendre**. Review the nasal vowels on p. 92. **Entendre** begins with a nasal vowel.

> The verb **visiter** is normally reserved for use with *places*. **Rendre visite à** is used with *persons*.

Quelques verbes réguliers en -re

conj

attendre (un ami)	*to wait (for a friend)*
descendre	*to go down; to get out of*
entendre (un bruit)	*to hear (a noise)*
perdre (une valise)	*to lose (a suitcase)*
rendre (les devoirs)	*to give back (homework)*
rendre visite à quelqu'un	*to visit someone*
répondre (à une question)	*to answer (a question)*

■ The singular (**je, tu, il/elle/on**) forms of each of these verbs are pronounced alike.

je perds	tu perds	il perd	[pɛR]
je rends	tu rends	elle rend	[Rɑ̃]

■ There is no ending added to the stem in the **il/elle/on** forms of regular **-re** verbs. In inversion of the **il/elle/on** form, the **-d** is pronounced [t].

	ven**d**ons	[vɑ̃dɔ̃]	ven**d**ent	[vɑ̃d]
But:	ven**d**-on	[vɑ̃tɔ̃]	ven**d**-elle	[vɑ̃tɛl]

■ Past participles of regular **-re** verbs are formed by adding **-u** to the present tense verb stem.

ven**du**   per**du**   répon**du**

■ **Rendre visite** and **répondre** are used with the preposition **à** before an object.

J'**ai rendu visite à** mon frère.   *I visited my brother.*
Anne **répond** toujours **aux**   *Anne always answers the teacher's*
questions du professeur.   *questions.*

■ **Attendre** does not use a preposition before an object.

J'**attends** mes amis.   *I am waiting for my friends.*

■ In the expressions **perdre patience** and **perdre courage** the article or possessive adjective is omitted.

Le professeur a **perdu patience** avec moi.
But: J'ai **perdu *mes*** devoirs.

1 **Mes professeurs et moi.** Indiquez si *oui* ou *non* vos professeurs font les choses suivantes. Et vous, est-ce que vous les faites?

MODÈLE: perdre des livres
Mes professeurs ne perdent jamais de livres, mais moi, je perds quelquefois des livres.

1. perdre patience
2. attendre les vacances avec impatience
3. répondre à beaucoup de questions
4. rendre visite à des amis
5. vendre des livres

2 **Un petit sketch: Au bureau de tabac.** Lisez ou jouez le sketch suivant et répondez ensuite aux questions.

M. SMITH: Madame, est-ce que vous avez le *Herald Tribune?*
LA MARCHANDE: Non, Monsieur. Je n'ai plus de journaux américains.
M. SMITH: Où est-ce que je peux acheter un journal américain, s'il vous plaît?
LA MARCHANDE: Il faut aller à la gare.
M. SMITH: Pourquoi à la gare?
LA MARCHANDE: Parce qu'on vend des journaux d'autres pays à la gare.
M. SMITH: Merci, Madame.
LA MARCHANDE: Je vous en prie, Monsieur.

Questions

1. Quelle sorte de journal Joseph cherche-t-il?
2. La marchande vend-elle des journaux?
3. A-t-elle le *Herald Tribune?* Expliquez.
4. Où Joseph va-t-il aller? Pourquoi?
5. Où vend-on des journaux dans votre ville?
6. Quel journal préférez-vous?

3 **À vous.** Répondez.

1. Où vend-on des cigarettes dans votre pays?
2. Qu'est-ce que les pharmaciens vendent dans votre pays?
3. À qui rendez-vous visite pendant les vacances?
4. Attendez-vous les vacances avec impatience? Pourquoi (pas)?
5. Dans quelles circonstances perdez-vous patience?
6. Est-ce que vous répondez rapidement aux lettres de vos amis?
7. À qui avez-vous répondu récemment?

Entre amis

Des achats

Your partner will take the role of a pharmacist.

1. Find out if s/he has postcards, stamps, cigarettes, bread, meats, gifts, etc. (S/he doesn't.)
2. Find out where these items are sold.
3. Ask directions to one of the stores.

2 Describing an Illness or Injury

le dos
les cheveux (m.pl.)
un œil (les yeux)
une oreille
le nez
la tête
une épaule
un bras
les dents (f.pl.)
l'estomac (m.)
un genou
une jambe
la bouche
la gorge
une main
un pied

Jacques, qu'est-ce que tu as?° Tu as l'air° malade.
  J'ai mal au dos° depuis° hier. J'ai trop fait
  de gymnastique.
Oh là là! Moi aussi, mais j'ai mal aux jambes, moi!

what's the matter with you? / You look / My back hurts / since

 Et vous? Avez-vous eu la grippe cette année? Avez-vous souvent mal à la tête?
Et les étudiants? S'ils étudient trop, ont-ils mal aux yeux?

Remarques

1. Like the word **tabac, estomac** has a silent final **-c.**
2. **Si** *(if)* becomes **s'** only before the words **il** and **ils.** Before other words beginning with vowels, it does not elide.

> **Si on** a mal à la tête, on prend des cachets d'aspirine.
> **Si elle** est malade, elle doit rester au lit.
> *But:* **S'il** est malade, il doit rester au lit.

Review the contractions on p. 125.

3. **Avoir mal à** is used with the definite article and a part of the body to express that one has a sore hand, arm, etc.

> Mon fils **a mal au bras.**   *My son's arm hurts.*
> J'**ai mal à la gorge.**   *I have a sore throat.*
> **Avez**-vous **mal aux dents?**   *Do you have a toothache?*

4. **Avoir l'air** *(to seem, appear, look)* is often followed by an adjective.

> Hélène **a l'air sportive.**   Jean-Yves **a l'air fatigué.**

VOCABULAIRE

Qu'est-ce que vous avez?

Je suis malade.	*I'm sick.*
J'ai de la fièvre.	*I have a fever.*
J'ai un rhume.	*I have a cold.*
J'ai la grippe.	*I have the flu.*
J'ai le nez qui coule.	*I have a runny nose.*
Je tousse.	*I am coughing.*
J'ai mal ...	
à l'estomac.	*I have a stomachache. My stomach hurts.*
aux oreilles.	*My ears hurt.*
au pied.	*I have a sore foot. My foot hurts.*
Je suis ...	
déçu(e).	*I'm disappointed.*
déprimé(e).	*I'm depressed.*
triste.	*I'm sad.*

éternuer = to sneeze

4 **Ça ne va pas.** Complétez les phrases suivantes.

> **MODÈLE:** Si on a de la fièvre, ...   **Si on a de la fièvre, on est malade.** ou
> **Si on a de la fièvre, on a peut-être la grippe.**

1. Si on regarde trop la télévision, ...
2. Si on danse trop souvent, ...
3. Si on boit trop, ...
4. Si on a le nez qui coule, ...
5. Si on tousse beaucoup, ...
6. Si on mange trop, ...
7. Si on fume trop, ...
8. Si on écrit trop, ...
9. Si on étudie trop, ...
10. Si on fait une trop longue promenade, ...
11. Si on entend trop de bruit, ...
12. Si on mange trop de bonbons, ...
13. Si on skie mal, ...
14. Si on passe trop d'examens, ...

5 **Pauvres étudiants!** Répondez aux questions suivantes.

1. Que prenez-vous si vous avez la grippe?
2. Est-ce que vous restez au lit si vous êtes malade?
3. Qu'est-ce que vous faites si vous avez un rhume?
4. Quand les étudiants ont-ils mal à la tête?
5. Quand les étudiants ont-ils mal aux pieds?
6. Quand les étudiants ont-ils mal à l'estomac?
7. Fumez-vous des cigarettes? Pourquoi ou pourquoi pas?

6 **Aïe!** Utilisez les expressions suivantes pour faire des phrases, mais ajoutez une explication *(add an explanation)* avec **si** ou **parce que.**

MODÈLES: **Les étudiants ont mal aux yeux s'ils étudient trop.**
J'ai mal à la tête parce que je passe trop d'examens.

les étudiants je un(e) de mes ami(e)s	avoir mal	la tête le dos les bras les yeux la main les jambes les pieds les dents la gorge l'estomac le nez l'épaule le genou	si ... parce que ...

B. *Depuis*

Depuis combien de temps habites-tu ici?	*How long (for how much time) have you been living here?*
J'habite ici **depuis un an.**	*I've been living here for a year.*
Depuis quand étudies-tu le français?	*How long (since when) have you been studying French?*
J'étudie le français **depuis septembre.**	*I've been studying French since September.*

■ Use **depuis combien de temps** or **depuis quand** with the present tense to ask about something that has already begun but is *still continuing.* **Depuis combien de temps** asks for the length of time so far and **depuis quand** asks for the starting date.

> verb (present tense) + **depuis** + { length of time / starting date

Depuis combien de temps ... ?	*For how much time ... ?*
Depuis quand ... ?	*Since when ... ?*

Review expressions of time in Ch. 6, p. 159.

■ In the affirmative, the English translation of the present tense verb and **depuis** is usually *has (have) been ... ing for* a certain length of time or *since* a certain date.

Chantal **habite** à Chicago **depuis un an.**

Chantal has been living in Chicago for a year.

Chantal **habite** à Chicago **depuis février dernier.**

Chantal has been living in Chicago since last February.

■ To state that something has *not* happened for a period of time, however, the negative of the passé composé is used with **depuis.**

Je **n'ai pas été** malade **depuis** six mois.

I haven't been sick for six months.

Mes parents **n'ont pas écrit depuis** deux semaines.

My parents haven't written for two weeks.

Attention   **Depuis** is used to talk about situations that are still going on. To ask or state how much time was spent doing something that has already been *completed,* use **pendant** with the passé composé.

J'étudie depuis deux heures.   *I've been studying for two hours (and I haven't finished yet).*

But: **J'ai étudié pendant** deux heures.   *I studied for two hours (and now I'm finished).*

7 **Ils sont tous malades. Qu'est-ce qu'ils doivent faire?** D'abord utilisez les expressions entre parenthèses pour indiquer depuis combien de temps chaque personne est malade. Ensuite répondez aux questions qui suivent.

MODÈLE: Virginie (pieds / deux jours)
Virginie a mal aux pieds depuis deux jours.
Qui doit changer de chaussures?
Virginie doit changer de chaussures.

1. Michel (gorge / deux heures).
2. Madame Matté (dents / une semaine).
3. Anne (yeux / un mois).
4. Monsieur Monneau (fièvre / ce matin).
5. Guy (genou / trois mois).

Questions

1. Qui doit changer de lunettes?
2. Qui doit se coucher et doit rester au lit?
3. Qui ne doit plus jouer au tennis?
4. Qui ne doit plus fumer et doit prendre des pastilles?
5. Qui doit aller chez le dentiste?

Comment allez-vous? Utilisez les expressions suivantes pour faire des phrases.

> **Modèles:** **Mon frère est malade depuis trois mois.**
> **Je n'ai pas été malade depuis cinq ans.**
> **Je n'ai pas eu mal à la tête depuis cinq ans.**

je		malade
ma sœur	(ne ... pas) avoir	rhume
mon frère	(ne ... pas) être	fièvre depuis ...
un(e) des mes ami(e)s		déprimé(e)
		mal ...
		fatigué(e)

9 **Une interview.** Posez des questions logiques avec **depuis** ou **pendant**. Votre partenaire va répondre.

> **Modèles:** parler français
>
> > **vous:** **Depuis combien de temps parles-tu français?**
> >
> > **votre partenaire:** **Je parle français depuis six mois.**
>
> regarder la télé hier soir
>
> > **vous:** **Pendant combien de temps as-tu regardé la télé hier soir?**
> >
> > **votre partenaire:** **J'ai regardé la télé pendant une heure.**

1. étudier le français
2. étudier hier soir
3. habiter à l'adresse que tu as maintenant
4. écouter la radio ce matin
5. être étudiant(e) à cette université
6. faire cet exercice

Entre amis

Tu es malade depuis longtemps?

1. Greet your partner and inquire about his/her health. (S/he is sick.)
2. Find out what the matter is.
3. Find out how long s/he has been sick.
4. Suggest a remedy.

3 Making a Purchase

NOTE CULTURELLE
À la boucherie, on vend de la viande de bœuf et on vend aussi du mouton. On y trouve des steaks, des rôtis *(roasts)*, etc. À la charcuterie, on vend de la viande de porc et on vend aussi du poulet et du lapin *(rabbit).* On y trouve du jambon, des pâtés variés, du bacon, des saucisses, du saucisson *(salami)*, etc.

Où vas-tu Alain?
 Je vais faire des achats.
De quoi as-tu besoin?°   *What do you need?*
 J'ai besoin de toutes sortes de choses.°   *I need all kinds of things.*
 J'ai besoin de pain, de bœuf, de saucisses°,   *sausages*
  de légumes et de fruits.
 J'ai besoin d'un livre et de fleurs° aussi.   *flowers*
 Je vais acheter° ...   *to buy*
  du pain à la boulangerie,
  du bœuf à la boucherie,
  des saucisses à la charcuterie°,   *delicatessen*
  des légumes et des fruits à l'épicerie,
  des fleurs chez un fleuriste
  et un livre à la librairie.
 Alors, j'ai besoin d'argent° pour payer   *money*
  tout cela.

▶ **Et vous?** De quoi avez-vous besoin?

Boucherie *Charcuterie*

Traiteur

Les trésors gourmands

Dominique CHAMEAU

Brissac-Quincé   02 41 54 22 33

Remarques

1. **Avoir besoin** *(to need)* works much like **avoir envie.** It is used with **de** and an infinitive or a noun. If **avoir besoin** is used with a noun, the definite article is usually omitted.

   J'**ai besoin d'**étudier.   *I need to study.*
   Nous **avons besoin de** légumes et   *We need vegetables and mineral*
    d'eau minérale.   *water.*

2. Use **un (une)** with **avoir besoin d'** to say that *one* item is needed.

   Vous **avez besoin d'une** feuille   *You need a sheet of paper.*
    de papier.

Tu as besoin
d'autre chose?

10 **Où faut-il aller?** Où est-ce qu'on trouve les produits suivants? Suivez
(follow) le modèle.

MODÈLE: pâté   **Si on a besoin de pâté, il faut aller à la charcuterie.**

1. épinards
2. médicaments
3. un kilo d'oranges

4. un rôti de bœuf
5. croissants
6. fleurs

7. jambon
8. un livre
9. cigarettes

Entre amis

Je viens d'arriver

You are new in town and need some information. Your partner will play the role
of a neighbor.

1. Tell your neighbor that you are going shopping.
2. Tell him/her what you need.
3. Ask where to buy it.
4. Be sure to express your gratitude for your neighbor's help.

C. Le verbe *acheter*

Mon père va **acheter** une autre voiture.
Nous **achetons** nos livres à la librairie.
On **achète** un journal au bureau de tabac.
J'**ai acheté** cinq kilos de pommes de terre.

Review the formation of
préférer, p. 230.

■ As you have already learned with **préférer,** certain verbs change their
spelling of the verb stem of the present tense depending on whether or not
the ending is pronounced.

Vous préf**é**rez le blanc ou le rouge?   Je préf**è**re le rouge.

■ The verb **acheter** also contains a spelling change in the verb stem of the present tense. When the ending is not pronounced, the **-e-** before the **-t-** becomes **-è.**

acheter *(to buy)*			
silent endings		**pronounced endings**	
j'	**achète**	nous	**achetons**
tu	**achètes**	vous	**achetez**
il/elle/on	**achète**		
ils/elles	**achètent**		
passé composé: j'**ai acheté**			

11 **Nous achetons tout ça.** On fait des achats. Utilisez les expressions suivantes pour faire des phrases. Utilisez la forme négative, si vous voulez.

MODÈLES: **J'achète de la glace pour mes amis.**
Nous n'achetons jamais de cigarettes pour nos amis.

Review the possessive adjectives on p. 76.

	glace		
je	cigarettes		amis
nous	cachets d'aspirine		classe *(f.)*
le professeur	magazines		parents
mes amis	acheter	pommes	pour	professeur
ma mère	timbres		famille
mon père	pain		moi
les étudiants	bonbons		nous
	médicaments		
	fleurs		

12 **Pourquoi y vont-ils?** Demandez ce que ces personnes achètent. Votre partenaire va répondre.

MODÈLE: Je vais au bureau de tabac.
>**VOUS:** **Qu'est-ce que tu achètes au bureau de tabac?**
>**VOTRE PARTENAIRE:** **J'achète des timbres.**

Both **un** and **une** may be used with fleuriste.

1. Je vais à la boucherie.
2. Nous allons à la pharmacie.
3. Mon père va au supermarché.
4. Nous allons dans un grand magasin.
5. Les étudiants vont à la boulangerie.
6. Paul va à l'épicerie.
7. Ces deux femmes vont au bureau de tabac.
8. Marie va à la librairie près de l'université.
9. Je vais chez un fleuriste.

VOCABULAIRE

NOTE CULTURELLE
Depuis 2002, **l'euro** est la seule monnaie officielle de la France et de la plupart des pays de l'Union européenne. Il existe huit pièces de monnaie et sept billets, d'une pièce de 1 cent jusqu'à un billet de 500 euros.

Pour payer les achats

de l'argent *(m.)*	*money*
un billet	*bill (paper money)*
la monnaie	*change; currency*
une pièce (de monnaie)	*coin*
un euro	*euro*
un dollar	*dollar*
une carte de crédit	*credit card*
un chèque	*check*
un chèque de voyage	*traveler's check*
coûter	*to cost*
payer	*to pay*

Note **Payer** is often found with a spelling change. Before silent endings, the **-y-** becomes **-i-: je paie, tu paies,** etc. *But:* **nous payons, vous payez.**

13 **Un petit sketch: Au bureau de tabac de la gare.** Lisez ou jouez le sketch. Ensuite répondez aux questions.

Joseph Smith parle avec un marchand de journaux au bureau de tabac de la gare.

M. SMITH:	Vous vendez des journaux américains?
LE MARCHAND:	Ça dépend du journal.
M. SMITH:	Avez-vous le *Herald Tribune?*
LE MARCHAND:	Oui, nous l'avons.
M. SMITH:	Bien. Je vous dois combien?
LE MARCHAND:	Un euro dix.
M. SMITH:	Voilà, Monsieur.
LE MARCHAND:	C'est parfait, Monsieur. Merci.
M. SMITH:	Au revoir, Monsieur. Bonne journée.
LE MARCHAND:	Merci. Vous aussi, Monsieur.

Questions

1. Où Joseph achète-t-il son journal?
2. Quel journal demande-t-il?
3. Est-ce que le marchand a ce journal?
4. Combien coûte le journal?
5. Est-ce que Joseph l'achète?

VOCABULAIRE

Mots utiles pour faire des achats

une barquette	*small box; mini crate*
une boîte	*box; can*
un bouquet	*bouquet*
une bouteille	*bottle*
un kilo	*kilogram (2.2 pounds)*
un litre	*liter*
une livre	*pound*
un paquet	*package*

14 **Ça coûte combien?** Demandez combien coûte l'objet. Votre partenaire va donner la réponse en euros.

MODÈLE: bonbons (3€ le paquet)
> **VOUS:** **Combien coûte un paquet de bonbons?**
> **VOTRE PARTENAIRE:** **Les bonbons coûtent trois euros le paquet.**

1. bordeaux (7€ le litre)
2. fromage Pont l'Évêque (3€ la livre)
3. fraises d'Espagne (1€ la barquette)
4. orangina (2€ la bouteille)
5. jambon de Bayonne (10€ le kilo)
6. cigarettes (3€ le paquet)
7. œufs (2€ la douzaine)
8. fleurs (8€ le bouquet)

Notice the use of the *indefinite* article in the question and the *definite* article in the answer.

En ville. Vous avez besoin de plusieurs *(several)* choses. Utilisez les deux listes suivantes pour trouver l'adresse et le numéro de téléphone des magasins nécessaires.

MODÈLE: pour acheter des médicaments
Pour acheter des médicaments, l'adresse est un, place de la Laiterie. Téléphonez au zéro deux/quarante et un/quatre-vingt-sept/cinquante-huit/trente-neuf.

Review numbers on pp. 3 and 63.

Place de la Laiterie		Rue de la Gare	
1 PHARMACIE GODARD	02.41.87.58.39	1 PHOTO PLUS	02.41.87.67.31
4 CHEVALIER, Yves		2 MOD COIFFURE	02.41.88.00.03
bureau de tabac	02.41.87.48.37	3 CRÉDIT AGRICOLE	02.41.88.12.56
5 BANQUE NATIONALE DE PARIS	02.41.88.00.23	4 CATFISH	
7 ARMORIC POISSONNERIE	02.41.88.39.84	restaurant grill	02.41.87.14.87
9 BOUCHERIE DU RONCERAY	02.41.87.57.28	5 PHARMACIE DE LA GARE	02.41.87.66.67
11 FAÏENCERIE DU RONCERAY	02.41.87.40.29	6 LE FLORENTIN	
15 SALOUD, Gérard		fleuriste	02.41.87.41.72
assurances	02.41.87.50.27	7 LE RELAIS	
18 COLIN, Jean		hôtel	02.41.88.42.51
boulangerie-pâtisserie	02.41.88.01.62	8 CINÉMA LE FRANÇAIS	02.41.87.66.66
19 VERNAUDON, Michel		9 LE PEN DUICK	
vêtements	02.41.87.01.96	restaurant	02.41.87.46.59
21 DACTYL BURO ANJOU		10 BAR BRASSERIE LE SIGNAL	02.41.87.49.41
machines bureaux	02.41.88.59.52		

1. pour acheter un kilo de bœuf
2. pour acheter un paquet de cigarettes
3. pour acheter du pain
4. pour demander à quelle heure le film va commencer
5. pour acheter un bouquet de fleurs
6. pour réserver une table pour dîner
7. pour acheter un pull ou un pantalon
8. pour acheter du saumon
9. pour acheter des euros si on a des dollars

Le restaurant Catfish se trouve dans la rue de la Gare.

16 **Une révision des nombres.** Répondez.

1. Quelle est votre adresse?
2. Quel est votre code postal?
3. Quel est votre numéro de téléphone?
4. Quel est le numéro de téléphone de votre meilleur(e) ami(e)?
5. En quelle année êtes-vous né(e)?
6. Combien de jours y a-t-il dans une année?
7. Combien de pages y a-t-il dans ce livre de français?
8. Combien de minutes y a-t-il dans une journée?
9. En quelle année Christophe Colomb est-il arrivé au Nouveau Monde?
10. Combien d'étudiants y a-t-il sur ce campus?

D. Le pronom relatif

■ Relative pronouns like *who, whom, which,* and *that* relate or tie two clauses together. They refer to a word in the first clause.

Le cadeau est sur la table. Il est pour ma sœur.	
La cadeau **qui** est sur la table est pour ma sœur	*The gift (that is) on the table is for my sister.*
Le cadeau est pour ma sœur. Je l'ai acheté ce matin.	
Le cadeau **que** j'ai acheté ce matin est pour ma sœur.	*The gift (that) I bought this morning is for my sister.*

■ The choice of the relative pronoun **qui** or **que** depends on its function as subject or object.

■ **Qui** *(who, that, which)* replaces a person or a thing that is the *subject* of a relative clause.

Une boulangerie est un magasin **qui** vend du pain.

■ **Que/qu'** *(whom, that, which)* replaces a person or a thing that is the *object* of a relative clause.

Le Monde est un journal **que** je lis avec intérêt.
Le Monde est un journal **qu'**on achète souvent.
Voilà un professeur **que** les étudiants aiment beaucoup.

■ Although the relative pronoun may be omitted in English, it is never omitted in French.

C'est le magasin **que** je préfère.   *It's the store (that) I prefer.*

FOR RECOGNITION ONLY:

The relative pronoun **dont** *(whose, of which, about which)* is normally used when the French expression would require the preposition **de.** In the following example, one needs to remember that **besoin** is used with **de.**

C'est le livre **dont** j'ai besoin.   *It's the book (that) I need.*

Identifications. Identifiez la personne ou la chose qui correspond à la description.

> **MODÈLE:** quelqu'un qui parle français depuis longtemps
> **Le professeur de français est quelqu'un qui parle français depuis longtemps.**

1. un magasin qui vend des médicaments
2. quelque chose qu'on vend à l'épicerie
3. un restaurant que vous recommandez pour sa cuisine italienne
4. un livre que vous avez déjà lu et que vous recommandez
5. quelque chose que vous mangez souvent
6. quelque chose dont on a besoin pour payer ses achats au centre commercial
7. quelqu'un qui parle français avec vous
8. une personne qui vend des fleurs
9. quelque chose qu'on achète à la librairie
10. quelque chose dont les étudiants ont besoin pour être heureux

 Définitions. Décrivez les personnes ou les choses suivantes.

> **MODÈLES:** un McDo   **C'est un restaurant qui vend des Big Macs.**
> un professeur   **C'est une personne qui enseigne.**
> ma mère   **C'est une personne que j'aime.**

1. un bureau de tabac
2. une pizza aux anchois
3. une pharmacienne
4. la France
5. mon professeur de français
6. un francophone
7. un supermarché

Entre amis

Vous entrez dans un bureau de tabac

Your partner takes the role of a merchant.

1. Ask if s/he has a specific English-language magazine (name it).
2. Your partner will inquire what it is.
3. Identify it. How much can you say?
4. Your partner will say s/he is sorry but that s/he doesn't have it.
5. Find out the name of the French magazines s/he has.
6. Select one and find out how much it costs.
7. Pay for it.

Intégration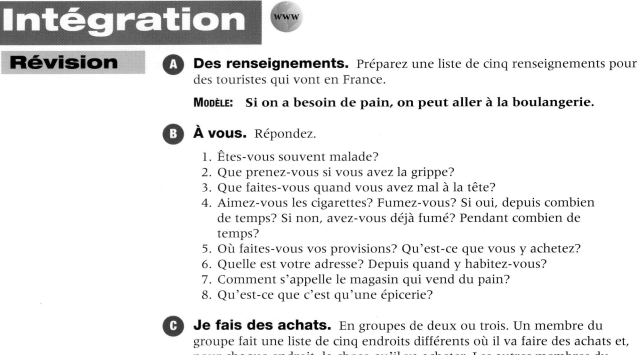

www

Révision

A **Des renseignements.** Préparez une liste de cinq renseignements pour des touristes qui vont en France.

MODÈLE: **Si on a besoin de pain, on peut aller à la boulangerie.**

B **À vous.** Répondez.

1. Êtes-vous souvent malade?
2. Que prenez-vous si vous avez la grippe?
3. Que faites-vous quand vous avez mal à la tête?
4. Aimez-vous les cigarettes? Fumez-vous? Si oui, depuis combien de temps? Si non, avez-vous déjà fumé? Pendant combien de temps?
5. Où faites-vous vos provisions? Qu'est-ce que vous y achetez?
6. Quelle est votre adresse? Depuis quand y habitez-vous?
7. Comment s'appelle le magasin qui vend du pain?
8. Qu'est-ce que c'est qu'une épicerie?

C **Je fais des achats.** En groupes de deux ou trois. Un membre du groupe fait une liste de cinq endroits différents où il va faire des achats et, pour chaque endroit, la chose qu'il va acheter. Les autres membres du groupe vont deviner *(guess)* 1. où il va faire ses achats, et 2. ce qu'il achète. Il répond seulement par oui ou par non.

MODÈLE: **Est-ce que tu achètes quelque chose à la librairie?**
    Est-ce que tu achètes un livre?

Pas de problème!

Preparation for the video:
1. Video worksheet in the *Cahier d'activités*
2. CD-ROM, *Module 6*

Cette activité est basée sur la vidéo, *Module 6.* Choisissez la bonne réponse pour compléter les phrases suivantes.

1. Bruno rend visite à _____.
   (Alissa, Nogent, Noël)
2. Avec ses amis, il visite le château _____.
   (Sainte-Jeanne, Saint-Jean, Nogent)
3. Le château se trouve en _____.
   (Normandie, Picardie, Alsace)
4. Dans la salle des gardes, ils admirent _____.
   (la fenêtre, la forêt, la cheminée)
5. La maison de Noël se trouve _____
   derrière la forêt.
   (à droite, à gauche, tout droit)

Lecture I

A **Étude du vocabulaire.** Étudiez les phrases suivantes et choisissez les mots anglais qui correspondent aux mots français en caractères gras: *grief, love, hate, rain, roofs, gentle, ground, heart.*

1. J'aime le son de la **pluie** qui tombe sur les **toits** des maisons.
2. L'**amour** et la **haine** sont deux émotions opposées. Quand on aime, c'est l'**amour** et quand on déteste, c'est la **haine.**
3. Le **cœur** fait circuler le sang dans les veines et les artères.
4. La **terre** noire de l'Iowa est très fertile.
5. La mort du président nous a plongés dans le **deuil.**
6. Une voix **douce** est agréable à entendre.

B **Anticipez le contenu.** Avant de lire le poème, répondez aux questions suivantes.

1. Aimez-vous la pluie?
2. Pleut-il souvent là où vous habitez?
3. Quand il pleut, êtes-vous content(e), triste ou indifférent(e)? Expliquez.

Il pleure dans mon cœur

Il pleure dans mon cœur
Comme il pleut sur la ville,
Quelle est cette langueur
Qui pénètre mon cœur?

Ô bruit doux de la pluie
Par terre et sur les toits!
Pour un cœur qui s'ennuie[1]
Ô le chant de la pluie!

Il pleure sans raison
Dans ce cœur qui s'écœure[2].
Quoi! nulle trahison[3]?
Ce deuil est sans raison.

C'est bien la pire peine[4]
De ne savoir[5] pourquoi,
Sans amour et sans haine,
Mon cœur a tant de peine.

Paul Verlaine

---

1. *is saddened* 2. *is depressed* 3. *no treason* 4. *the worst suffering* 5. *not to know*

C **Discussion.** Répondez.

1. Quelle est la réaction du poète à la pluie? Quelles expressions utilise-t-il pour exprimer cette émotion?
2. Est-ce que le poète sait pourquoi il a cette réaction à la pluie? Expliquez.

D **Familles de mots.** Essayez de deviner le sens des mots suivants.

1. pleuvoir, la pluie, pluvieux (pluvieuse)
2. aimer, l'amour, aimable, amoureux (amoureuse)
3. s'ennuyer, l'ennui, ennuyeux (ennuyeuse)
4. peiner, la peine, pénible

Lecture II

A **Étude du vocabulaire.** Étudiez les phrases suivantes et choisissez les mots anglais qui correspondent aux mots français en caractères gras: *flight, sponsoring, places, beat, billboard, sidewalks, samples, building.*

1. Nos joueurs de basket-ball espèrent **battre** leurs adversaires.
2. Un **vol** est un voyage en avion.
3. Un **immeuble** est un grand bâtiment où les gens travaillent ou habitent.
4. Les gens restent sur les **trottoirs** parce que les rues sont dangereuses.
5. Le mot **lieux** est souvent un synonyme pour le mot *endroits.*
6. Les représentants commerciaux donnent des **échantillons** pour encourager les gens à acheter leurs produits.
7. Sur le **panneau d'affichage** de la bande dessinée, on peut lire: «Le tabac tue».
8. Le **parrainage** d'une équipe de football coûte quelquefois très cher à une entreprise.

Devinez de quoi il s'agit. Lisez rapidement le titre et la première phrase de chaque article pour identifier le sujet des articles et les deux pays qu'il concerne.

Hystérie Anti-Tabac

Le Canada est en train de battre les États-Unis en matière d'hystérie anti-tabac. Le conseil municipal de Toronto—la capitale économique et financière du pays—a adopté un règlement draconien contre les fumeurs: depuis le 1er janvier 1997, le Torontois a seulement sa maison, sa voiture ou la rue pour prendre sa bouffée[1] de nicotine. La croisade contre[2] la cigarette ne date pas d'hier. La compagnie aérienne nationale Air Canada a été la première à l'interdire[3] sur les vols transatlantiques. Dans les hôtels, le principe des chambres fumeurs et non fumeurs est en vigueur. Les immeubles du gouvernement fédéral sont des zones strictement non-fumeurs. On voit, sur les trottoirs des grandes villes, les fumeurs irréductibles faire la pause cigarette avant de regagner leur bureau[4].

Les mesures du président

Principales mesures annoncées par la Maison-Blanche, pour limiter l'accès des adolescents au tabac:
- les distributeurs automatiques sont interdits dans certains lieux fréquentés par les jeunes;
- les échantillons et paquets de moins de 20 cigarettes sont interdits;
- les publicités pour le tabac sont interdites dans un rayon[5] de 500 mètres autour des établissements scolaires et des terrains de jeux;
- sauf[6] dans les lieux interdits aux moins de 18 ans, et à condition qu'elles ne soient[7] pas visibles de l'extérieur, les publicités sur les panneaux d'affichage et les lieux de vente doivent se limiter à des textes en noir et blanc;
- la publicité dans les publications dont les lecteurs sont constitués en grande partie d'adolescents (plus de 15%) doit se limiter à des textes en noir et blanc;
- le parrainage d'événements sportifs est interdit.

d'après Le Point

---

1. *puff*   2. *crusade against*   3. *to forbid it*   4. *go back to their office*   5. *in a radius*   6. *except*
7. *provided that they are*

C **Dans quel article?** Relisez les deux articles et décidez si les idées suivantes se trouvent dans l'article sur le Canada ou dans l'article sur les États-Unis.

1. On n'accepte pas d'annonces publicitaires pour les cigarettes près des écoles.
2. Certains fumeurs continuent à fumer avant d'entrer dans le bâtiment où ils travaillent.
3. Il n'y a plus de publicité en couleur pour les cigarettes dans les magazines lus par les jeunes.
4. Cette mesure stricte a été appliquée juste après Noël.
5. On ne permet plus que les entreprises qui vendent du tabac sponsorisent les matchs de tennis, de base-ball, etc.
6. Dans les endroits où vont les jeunes, on ne vend plus de cigarettes dans des machines.
7. On n'accepte plus depuis longtemps que les gens fument dans les avions s'ils font un voyage dans un autre pays.
8. Il n'est plus permis de donner des cigarettes gratuites pour encourager les individus à fumer.

D **Familles de mots.** Essayez de deviner le sens des mots suivants.

1. interdire, interdit(e), une interdiction
2. vendre, la vente, un vendeur, une vendeuse
3. fumer, un fumeur, une fumeuse, la fumée
4. conseiller, le conseil, un conseiller, une conseillère
5. distribuer, un distributeur, la distribution

VOCABULAIRE ACTIF

Argent
l'argent *(m.) money*
un billet *bill (paper money)*
une carte de crédit *credit card*
un chèque *check*
un chèque de voyage *traveler's check*
un centime *centime*
un dollar *dollar*
un euro *euro*
la monnaie *change*
une pièce (de monnaie) *coin*

Adjectifs
aimable *kind; nice*
déçu(e) *disappointed*
déprimé(e) *depressed*
désolé(e) *sorry*
long (longue) *long*

Magasins
une boucherie *butcher shop*
une boutique *(gift, clothing, etc.) shop*
une charcuterie *pork butcher's; delicatessen*
un grand magasin *department store*
un kiosque *newsstand*
un marché *(open-air) market*
un marché aux puces *flea market*
une pâtisserie *pastry shop; pastry*
un supermarché *supermarket*

À la pharmacie
un cachet d'aspirine *aspirin tablet*
un dentifrice *toothpaste*
un médicament *medicine*
une pastille *lozenge*
une pilule *pill*
un savon *bar of soap*

Parties du corps
la bouche *mouth*
un bras *arm*
une dent *tooth*
le dos *back*
une épaule *shoulder*
l'estomac *(m.) stomach*
un genou *knee*
la gorge *throat*
une jambe *leg*
une main *hand*
le nez *nose*
un œil *eye*
une oreille *ear*
un pied *foot*
la tête *head*

D'autres noms

un achat *purchase*
une barquette *small box*
un billet *ticket*
un bouquet *bouquet*
un bruit *noise*
un cadeau *gift*
un code postal *zip code*
un coin *corner*
une feuille *leaf; sheet (of paper)*
une fièvre *fever*
une fleur *flower*
un(e) fleuriste *florist*
l'impatience (f.) *impatience*
un litre *liter*
une livre *pound*
un(e) marchand(e) *merchant*
le papier *paper*
un paquet *package; pack*
un rhume *a cold*
une rue *street*
une sardine *sardine*
une saucisse *sausage*
le tabac *tobacco; tobacconist's shop*
un timbre *stamp*
une valise *suitcase*

Verbes

acheter *to buy*
attendre *to wait (for)*
avoir besoin de *to need*
avoir l'air *to seem, appear, look*
avoir mal (à) *to be sore, to have a pain (in)*
coûter *to cost*
dépendre *to depend*
entendre *to hear*
payer *to pay (for)*
perdre *to lose*
perdre patience *to lose (one's) patience*
rendre *to give back*
rendre visite à quelqu'un *to visit someone*
répondre (à) *to answer*
réserver *to reserve*
tousser *to cough*
vendre *to sell*

Préposition

depuis *for; since*

Expressions utiles

avec intérêt *with interest*
Ça dépend. *That depends.*
C'est bien simple. *It's quite simple.*
De quoi avez-vous besoin? *What do you need?*
Depuis combien de temps? *For how much time?*
Depuis quand? *Since when?*
je peux *I can*
le nez qui coule *runny nose*
Oh là là! *Oh dear!*
on peut *one can*
Pouvez-vous me dire ... ? *Can you tell me ... ?*
Qu'est-ce que tu as? *What's the matter (with you)?*
Qu'est-ce que vous dites? *What are you saying?*
Vous n'en avez pas? *Don't you have any?*

LE SAVEZ-VOUS?
Dans quels pays de l'Afrique noire parle-t-on français? Pourquoi?

Formée en majeure partie d'anciennes *(former)* colonies françaises, l'Afrique noire francophone consiste en deux grandes régions: l'Afrique occidentale, qui va de la Mauritanie au golfe de Guinée, et l'Afrique équatoriale, qui regroupe les pays du Tchad au Congo et l'ancien Congo belge (voir la carte de l'Afrique à la fin du livre). Le climat est tropical dans le nord de cette vaste région, désertique dans le centre, plus humide près de l'océan. Vers le sud, le désert fait place à la savanne, puis à la forêt équatoriale.

Sanctuaire Yoruba

CHRONOLOGIE

Préhistoire L'Afrique, berceau *(cradle)* de l'humanité, riche en souvenirs préhistoriques.

Ier–Xe siècles Civilisations Nok au Nigéria, Ifé au Bénin.

XIe–XIVe siècles Dans la région des fleuves Sénégal et Niger, s'établissent les empires du Ghana, du Mali, du Songhaï. L'Islam, introduit par des caravanes arabes, devient la religion dominante.

XIVe–XVe siècles Civilisations yoruba au Bénin et bantoue au royaume du Kongo.

XVe–XVIIIe siècles Explorateurs et marchands d'Europe établissent des centres de commerce le long des côtes africaines. La traite des esclaves se développe.

1659 La France fonde la ville de Saint-Louis au nord de Dakar.

1858–1958 La France s'établit en Afrique occidentale et équatoriale.

1908 La Belgique acquiert le Congo belge.

1960 Indépendance de la plupart des colonies africaines.

Léopold Sédar Senghor

La négritude dans l'Afrique indépendante

Vers 1960, au lendemain de l'indépendance, le mouvement de la négritude prend un caractère nouveau. Ce n'est plus une protestation contre le racisme, mais la défense des anciennes traditions dans un monde qui non seulement se modernise à une vitesse vertigineuse, mais qui devient aussi de plus en plus uniforme. Le but du mouvement devient d'intégrer l'Afrique dans le monde moderne avec son commerce et son industrie sans perdre les légendes, les valeurs, la perspective unique de l'univers de l'Afrique ancienne.

Les problèmes et les contradictions engendrés par le régime colonial et l'influence européenne font place aujourd'hui en Afrique à de nouveaux défis. Comment rester africain tout en adoptant un style de vie urbain et moderne? Les femmes, silencieuses par le passé, prennent la plume et revendiquent leurs droits. Parmi celles-ci, Mariama Bâ adresse le problème que pose le concubinage pour la femme moderne; Calixthe Beyala (Grand Prix du Roman de l'Académie française en 1996 pour son roman *Les honneurs perdus*) décrit le monde cruel et insensé des bidonvilles (*shantytowns*) des grandes agglomérations africaines et l'exploitation entre Africains où la femme est plus que jamais victime de l'homme. Dans cette littérature nouvelle, un thème constant se retrouve: celui d'une lutte pour une identité qui ne se soumet à aucun pouvoir opprimant.

Poème de la négritude

Le mouvement de la négritude inspire beaucoup d'auteurs noirs. Ici Bernard Dadié, de la Côte d'Ivoire, exprime sa fierté (*pride*) d'être noir.

> Je vous remercie mon Dieu de m'avoir créé noir,
> D'avoir fait de moi
> la somme de toutes les douleurs,
> mis sur ma tête,
> Le Monde.
> J'ai la livrée du Centaure
> Et je porte le Monde depuis le premier matin.
>
> Le blanc est une couleur de circonstance
> Le Noir, la couleur de tous les jours
> Et je porte le Monde depuis le premier soir.
>
> Je suis content
> de la forme de ma tête
> faite pour porter le Monde,
> satisfait de la forme de mon nez
> Qui doit humer tout le vent du Monde,
> heureux
> de la forme de mes jambes
> prêtes à courir toutes les étapes du Monde.

Calixthe Beyala

Le français en Afrique

La colonisation a formé des liens contradictoires entre la France et l'Afrique. Dans la majorité des anciennes colonies d'Afrique, le français est la langue officielle ou la langue véhiculaire. Pour plusieurs intellectuels et hommes politiques africains, ce «décombre du régime colonial» est une source de malaise. Il faudrait, pensent-ils, s'exprimer dans la langue maternelle. Pour d'autres, comme le président du Sénégal, Abdoulaye Wade, la présence et l'universalité de la langue française, perpétuée et célébrée par l'institution de la francophonie, est un avantage commercial et politique. Le français représente un outil de modernité et une solution pratique à la communication dans les pays plurilingues de l'Afrique noire. «Je suis», écrivait Abdoulaye Wade dans *L'Express* du 13 juillet 2000, «de la génération des Africains qui ont appris l'histoire de France dans des manuels qui com-

mençaient par le fameux 'Nos ancêtres, les Gaulois'. Toutefois, la signification qui en a été donnée a été biaisée par la doctrine anticolonialiste. En effet, aucun d'entre nous, élèves, n'a un seul moment pensé qu'il descendait des Gaulois. Nous savions parfaitement que l'on nous prêtait ou donnait des manuels écrits pour les petits Français. Nous trouvions ces Gaulois, avec leurs longues barbes, laids et probablement très sales. Nos professeurs, français ou sénégalais, le savaient tout aussi bien. Ce que nous avons malgré tout apprécié, dans ces manuels contestés, c'était que la France ne faisait pas de discrimination dans la qualité de l'enseignement qu'elle nous dispensait. »

À vous!

À votre avis, la langue française représente-t-elle un avantage ou un inconvénient pour les pays de l'Afrique noire francophone?

Quelques Pays où le français est la langue officielle

REPÈRES:	**LE BÉNIN**		**LE BURKINA**		**LE CONGO-BRAZZAVILLE**
Nom officiel:	République du Bénin		Burkina Faso		République du Congo
Capitale:	Porto-Novo		Ouagadougou		Brazzaville
Superficie:	112.622 km²		274.200 km²		341.821 km²
Population:	4,5 millions		10,1 millions		2,8 millions

	LE CONGO-KINSHASA		**LA CÔTE D'IVOIRE**		**LE MALI**
Nom officiel:	République démocratique du Congo		République de Côte d'Ivoire		République du Mali
Capitale:	Kinshasa		Yamoussoukro		Bamako
Superficie:	2.344.885 km²		322.462 km²		1.241.231 km²
Population:	51,9 millions		20 millions		8,8 millions

La femme africaine, mythe ou réalité?

L'Afrique, continent de contrastes frappants et de diversités bouleversantes, regroupe des pays où l'on parle des milliers de langues indigènes et où on adopte des langues européennes comme langues officielles, le résultat de plusieurs années de colonisation. Étant donné la diversité qui marque ce continent, peut-on parler à juste titre de *la* femme africaine? Allons en Afrique *la* chercher.

Notre avion vient d'atterrir à l'aéroport de Dakar. Après avoir passé par la douane, je retrouve mon amie sénégalaise, Aminata. Nous étions copines de chambre quand j'étais étudiante à Paris. Aminata avait souvent le mal du pays; sa famille lui manquait beaucoup. Le soir, elle me parlait de sa famille; une grande famille qui se composait non seulement de la mère, du père, des frères et des sœurs mais aussi des grands-parents, tantes, oncles, nièces, neveux, cousins et cousines. Sa famille avait une grande importance dans sa vie, j'en étais persuadée.

Deux semaines après avoir reçu son diplôme, Aminata a regagné le Sénégal et s'est vite mariée avec son petit ami, Samba. En trois ans elle a eu deux garçons. Je n'étais pas surprise parce que je savais qu'Aminata était obsédée par une seule idée, devenir maman. Mais Aminata est aussi devenue directrice d'une banque. Et son mari, Samba, est professeur de chimie à l'Université Cheikh Anta Diop. Ils ont acheté une grande maison près de la plage où ils mènent une vie tranquille avec leurs enfants et la mère d'Aminata, qui a soixante-douze ans. Samba et Aminata ne veulent plus d'enfants; leurs deux fils, Michel et Antoine, leur suffisent. Samba et Aminata s'entendent bien; ils font le ménage ensemble. Samba adore faire la cuisine et j'ai pris du poids à cause de ses plats appétissants. La mère d'Aminata est veuve. Elle habite chez sa fille depuis six ans et y restera pour le reste de sa vie.

Trois jours après mon arrivée à Dakar, Aminata et moi allons rendre visite à son oncle qui habite dans un village à soixante-dix kilomètres de Dakar. Au grand

portail de la concession, Aïssatou nous accueille chaleureusement. Aminata me la présente comme la première femme de son oncle. «Première femme? Ton oncle est-il divorcé?» lui dis-je. «Non, il ne l'est pas. Tu sais, plus de 80 pour cent des Sénégalais sont musulmans et pas mal parmi eux sont polygames», dit-elle. Me voyant étonnée, elle me dit: «Oui, mon oncle, Modou, est polygame; il a quatre femmes—Aïssatou, Ndèye, Fatou and Nabou.»

Modou et ses deux frères, Ousseynou et Mawdo, vivent ensemble avec leurs familles dans une concession d'une dizaine de maisons qui entourent une grande cour. Au milieu se trouve un grand arbre à l'ombre duquel des femmes font la lessive en bavardant et des enfants écoutent attentivement des contes. Dans la concession, il n'y a que les femmes et les filles qui font le ménage. Mais toutes les femmes de Modou travaillent pour s'assurer l'indépendance financière. Ndèye est fermière, et le jour où nous visitons leur petit village, elle travaille dans sa ferme à cinq kilomètres du village. Fatou est commerçante et va souvent au marché vendre du poisson. Pendant qu'elles travaillent, Ndèye et Fatou ne s'inquiétent pas de leurs enfants (il y en a treize) parce que leurs coépouses, Aïssatou et Nabou, s'occupent d'eux. «Eh bien, ma poulette, tu vois que la polygamie a ses avantages», me dit Aminata d'un ton moqueur.

Au bout de deux semaines de séjour au Sénégal, je fais connaissance de plusieurs femmes africaines dans des situations différentes—il y en a qui ont des coépouses mais Aminata a un mariage monogame; il y en a qui habitent dans les grandes villes mais d'autres vivent dans des petits villages qui facilitent la coexistence de la tradition et la modernité. Malgré toutes ces différences, il y a des ressemblances—les femmes travaillent et, par conséquent, ont une indépendance économique appréciable; elles ont un grand respect pour la maternité et les personnes âgées. Finalement, la question se pose: Avons-nous découvert *la* femme africaine? À vous la parole!

Obioma Nnaemeka

10 Dans la rue et sur la route

Buts communicatifs
Giving reasons; making excuses
Expressing familiarity and judgment
Giving orders and advice
Describing ways of doing things

Structures utiles
Les verbes **vouloir** et **pouvoir**
Le verbe **connaître**
Les pronoms objets directs (suite)
L'impératif (suite)
Le subjonctif (*an overview*)
Les pronoms à l'impératif
Les nombres ordinaux
Le verbe **conduire**
Les adverbes

Culture
Conduire en France
Les expressions de tendresse

Coup d'envoi

un rond

Prise de contact   Les indications

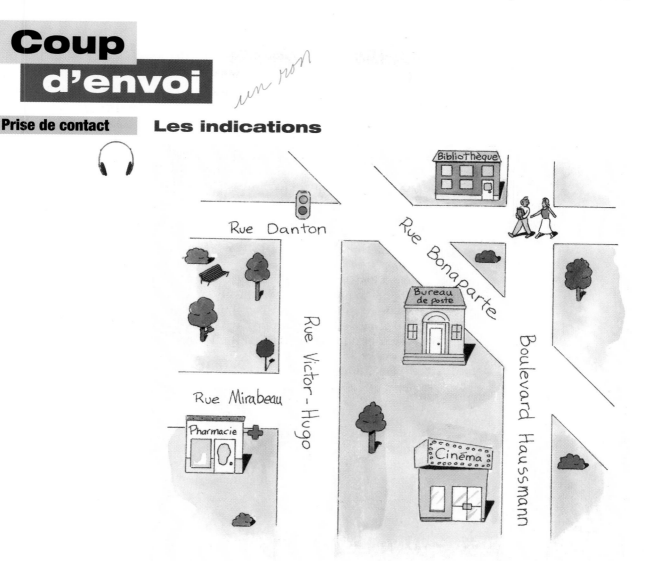

Pardon, pouvez-vous me dire où se trouve la pharmacie?

Oui, c'est dans la rue Mirabeau.
Prenez la rue Danton.
Continuez jusqu'au feu°.   *until the traffic light*
Puis, tournez à gauche. C'est la rue Victor-Hugo.
Ensuite, la rue Mirabeau est la première rue à
  droite après le stop°.   *stop sign*

▶ **Et vous?**   Pouvez-vous me dire où se trouve la poste?
                  Où se trouve le cinéma, s'il vous plaît?
                  Pour la bibliothèque, s'il vous plaît?

Review the directions in Ch. 5, p. 138.

VOCABULAIRE À RETENIR

dans la rue *on the street*
sur l'avenue *on the avenue*
sur le boulevard *on the boulevard*
sur la route *on the highway*

Conversation

Un père très nerveux

Michel Avoine est très nerveux parce que sa fille apprend à conduire°.   *to drive*

CATHERINE: Papa, est-ce que je peux conduire?	
MICHEL: Tu veux° conduire, ma chérie°?	*You want/honey*
Eh bien, attache ta ceinture de sécurité° et	*seat belt*
prends le volant°. Mais fais attention!	*steering wheel*
CATHERINE: Chut!° Pas de commentaires, s'il te plaît.	*Shh!*
Laisse-moi tranquille.°	*Leave me alone.*
MICHEL: D'accord, démarre°. Regarde à gauche, à	*start*
droite et dans ton rétroviseur°.	*rearview mirror*
Avance lentement°, ma fille.	*slowly*
Change de vitesse.° Continue tout droit.	*Shift; change speed.*
Ne conduis pas si vite°.	*so fast*
(un peu plus tard)	
Ne prends pas le sens interdit°.	*one-way street*
Prends la première rue à gauche.	
Et ne regarde pas les garçons qui passent.	
CATHERINE: Mais, tais-toi!° Tu n'arrêtes° pas de parler!	*keep quiet!/stop*
MICHEL: Excuse-moi, ma puce°. Je suis un peu	*(lit.) flea*
nerveux.	
C'est promis, plus un mot°.	*not one more word*
CATHERINE: Plus un mot, mon œil!° Je te connais° trop	*my eye!/I know you*
bien.	

▶ **Jouez ces rôles.**   Répétez la conversation avec votre partenaire. Changez ensuite de rôle: c'est un fils qui demande à sa maman s'il peut conduire. Faites les changements nécessaires: par exemple, la mère appelle son fils «mon chéri» et «mon grand».

Il y a un geste

Chut!   The index finger is raised to the lips to indicate that silence is in order.

Tais-toi!   The thumb and fingers are alternately opened and closed to tell someone to "shut up."

Mon œil!   There is a gesture meaning that one does not believe what was said. The index finger is placed under an eyelid and pulls down slightly on the skin.

Pourquoi est-ce que Michel est nerveux?

a. Sa fille conduit très mal.
b. Tous les pères sont nerveux.
c. On conduit vite en France et il est important d'être prudent.

Michel appelle sa fille «ma puce». Pourquoi?

a. C'est une expression de tendresse (term of endearment).
b. Il est sexiste. Les puces sont petites et il pense que sa fille est inférieure.
c. Les Français aiment beaucoup les insectes.

Conduire en France

One of the most unsettling discoveries one makes on a trip to France is the speed at which most people drive. Much has already been written about the French **appétit de la vitesse.** For example, Daninos's Major Thompson (see the **Lecture,** page 292) complains about the "peaceful citizen" who "can change in front of your eyes into a demonic pilot." That this can be the case, in spite of a very demanding driver's license test, a very elaborate and expensive training period in **l'auto-école,** the fact that one must be eighteen to get a license, and the fact that one must be at least sixteen years old to have a learner's permit and be accompanied by someone who is at least twenty-eight years old while learning to drive, may justify Major Thompson's comment that **Les Français conduisent plutôt bien, mais follement** (The French drive rather well, but wildly).

Les expressions de tendresse

Ma chérie, ma puce, mon chéri, and **mon grand** are common terms of endearment, but there are many others. Among couples, **mon chou** (honey, literally *my cabbage*) is very frequent. It is most likely a shortened form of **chou à la crème** (cream puff). In French families such expressions seem to be more frequently used than is the case among members of North American families. Terms of endearment are perhaps the verbal equivalent of the greater amount of physical contact found in France.

Quelques expressions de tendresse		
femme	*homme*	*femme ou homme*
ma chérie	mon chéri	mon chou
ma puce (flea)	mon grand	mon cœur (heart)
ma biche (deer)	mon lapin (rabbit)	mon ange (angel)
		mon bijou (jewel)

VATEL AUTO-ECOLE

PRÈS DE LA FACULTÉ DES LETTRES

5, RUE CONSTANTINE - TOURS

COURS DE CODE PAR AUDIOSCOPE

**FORMATION TRADITIONNELLE
OU ACCÉLÉRÉE SUR DEMANDE
FORFAIT SUR 2 SEMAINES**   *SUR FORD FIESTA*

▶ **À vous.**   Votre ami(e) apprend à conduire. Répondez à ses questions.

1. Est-ce que je peux conduire?
2. Tu vas attacher ta ceinture de sécurité?
3. Où allons-nous?
4. Où se trouve cet endroit?

Entre amis

Votre partenaire conduit

1. Ask if your partner wants to drive. (S/he does)
2. Tell your partner to take the wheel.
3. Tell him/her to start the car.
4. Tell him/her to look left and right.
5. Tell him/her to move ahead slowly.
6. Tell him/her to take the first street on the right.
7. Ask if s/he is nervous.

La lettre *h*

■ The letter **h** is never pronounced in French. There are, however, two categories of **h-** words:

1. Some **h-** words act *as if they began with a vowel:* These words are said to begin with **h muet** *(mute h)*. Elision (dropping a final vowel and replacing it with an apostrophe) and liaison (pronouncing a normally silent final consonant and linking it to the next word) both occur before **h muet,** just as they would with a word beginning with a vowel.

d'habitude	**l'**heure	**j'**habite
un [n]homme	elle est [t]heureuse	deux [z]heures

2. Some **h-** words act *as if they began with a consonant:* These words are said to begin with **h aspiré** *(aspirate h)*. Elision and liaison do not occur before **h aspiré.**

pas **de** haricots	**le** huit décembre	**le** hockey
un/hamburger	les/haricots	des/hors-d'œuvre

■ In addition, note that the combination **-th-** is pronounced [t].

thé   **Th**omas   a**th**lète   biblio**th**èque   ma**th**s

Buts
communicatifs

1 Giving Reasons; Making Excuses

Tu vas à la boum°, Brigitte?   *to the party*
　　Oui, j'ai envie de danser.
　　Oui, je veux m'amuser.
　　Oui, je veux être avec mes amis.
　　Je regrette. Je ne peux pas° sortir ce soir.   *I am unable to, I can't*

 Et vous? Voulez-vous aller danser?
　　　　　　　　Je veux bien! J'adore danser.
　　　　　　　　Je regrette. Je ne sais pas danser.
　　　　　　　　Non, je suis trop fatigué(e).
　　　　　　　　Je voudrais bien, mais j'ai besoin d'étudier.
　　　　Voulez-vous sortir ce soir? Pourquoi ou pourquoi pas?

Il y a un geste

Invitation à danser. When inviting someone to dance, the index finger is pointed toward the floor and makes a small circular motion.

A. Les verbes *vouloir* et *pouvoir*

Mes amis veulent sortir tous les soirs.	*My friends want to go out every night.*
Mais **ils ne peuvent pas.**	*But they can't.*
As-tu pu parler avec Paul?	*Were you able to talk to Paul?*
J'ai voulu mais **je n'ai pas pu.**	*I wanted to (I tried to) but I wasn't able to.*

Veux and **peux** are pronounced like **deux.**

vouloir *(to want; to wish)*		**pouvoir** *(to be able; to be allowed)*	
je	**veux**	je	**peux**
tu	**veux**	tu	**peux**
il/elle/on	**veut**	il/elle/on	**peut**
nous	**voulons**	nous	**pouvons**
vous	**voulez**	vous	**pouvez**
ils/elles	**veulent**	ils/elles	**peuvent**
passé composé: j'**ai voulu**		*passé composé:* j'**ai pu**	

VOCABULAIRE À RETENIR

J'ai voulu *I tried*
J'ai pu *I succeeded*
Je n'ai pas pu *I failed*

■ **Vouloir** and **pouvoir** are frequently followed by an infinitive.

Qui **veut sortir** ce soir?	*Who wants to go out tonight?*
Je **ne peux pas sortir** ce soir.	*I can't go out tonight.*

■ The passé composé of **vouloir, j'ai voulu,** means *I tried.* The passé composé of **pouvoir, j'ai pu,** means *I succeeded,* and the negative **je n'ai pas pu** means *I failed.*

■ **Vouloir** can also be used with a noun or pronoun, often to offer something or to make a request.

> **Voulez**-vous **quelque chose** à boire?   *Do you want something to drink?*

Note   When making requests, it is more polite to use **je voudrais** instead of **je veux.**

> **Je voudrais** un verre d'eau.   *I'd like a glass of water.*

❶ Pourquoi y vont-ils? Expliquez où vont les personnes suivantes et pourquoi. Utilisez le verbe **aller** et le verbe **vouloir** dans chaque phrase.

> **Modèle:**   Les étudiants vont à la boum parce qu'ils veulent danser.

		à la résidence		étudier
		à la bibliothèque		acheter quelque chose
		à la boum		danser
		au restaurant		écouter un sermon
on		aux cours		dormir
je		à l'église		parler avec des amis
nous	aller	au bistro	vouloir	manger
tu		à la piscine		boire
vous		à la patinoire		prendre un avion
les étudiants		au cinéma		patiner
		au centre com-mercial		nager
		en France		voir un film
		à l'aéroport		visiter des monuments
				apprendre quelque chose

❷ Un petit sketch. Lisez ou jouez le sketch suivant. Répondez ensuite aux questions.

Deux étudiants parlent de leurs activités.

JACQUES: Je peux porter ta veste grise?
CHRISTOPHE: Oui, si tu veux. Pourquoi?
JACQUES: Ce soir je sors.
CHRISTOPHE: Je vais être indiscret. Et tu vas où?
JACQUES: Les étudiants organisent une boum.
CHRISTOPHE: Tu y vas avec qui?
JACQUES: J'y vais seul, mais je crois que Sandrine a l'intention d'y aller aussi.
CHRISTOPHE: Et tu vas pouvoir l'inviter à danser, bien sûr?
JACQUES: Je voudrais bien danser avec elle. Mais elle a beaucoup d'admirateurs.
CHRISTOPHE: Tu as pu danser avec elle la dernière fois?
JACQUES: Non, elle n'a pas voulu. Mais cette fois, ça va être différent.

Questions

1. Qui va à la boum?
2. Avec qui y va-t-il?
3. Quels vêtements veut-il porter?
4. Avec qui Jacques veut-il danser?
5. Pourquoi est-ce qu'il n'a pas pu danser avec Sandrine la dernière fois?

3 **Pourquoi pas?** Utilisez le verbe **pouvoir** à la forme négative et l'expression **parce que** pour expliquer pourquoi quelque chose n'est pas possible.

MODÈLE: **Tu ne peux pas sortir parce que tu es trop fatigué(e).**

		aller à un concert	avoir la grippe
tu		sortir	avoir un rhume
vous		dîner	être malade(s)
mes amis	ne pas	voyager	être trop fatigué(e)(s)
mon ami(e)	pouvoir	jouer aux cartes	ne pas avoir d'argent
je		étudier	avoir sommeil
nous		venir au cours	avoir besoin d'étudier
les étudiants		danser	être occupé(e)(s)
		regarder la télévision	ne pas avoir le temps
		skier	avoir mal aux yeux
			avoir mal aux pieds
			ne pas être libre(s)

4 **Qu'est-ce qu'il a?** Raymond répond toujours «non». Utilisez les expressions suivantes avec **vouloir** ou **pouvoir** pour expliquer quelle excuse il peut avoir.

MODÈLE: Si nous l'invitons à manger quelque chose, ...
Si nous l'invitons à manger quelque chose, Raymond va répondre qu'il ne veut pas manger parce qu'il n'a pas faim.

1. Si nous l'invitons à boire quelque chose, ...
2. Si nous l'invitons à chanter une chanson, ...
3. Si nous l'invitons à danser la valse, ...
4. Si nous l'invitons à nager à la piscine, ...
5. Si nous l'invitons à aller à un match de football, ...
6. Si nous l'invitons à faire du ski, ...
7. Si nous l'invitons à dîner chez nous, ...
8. Si nous l'invitons à étudier avec nous, ...

Entre amis

Pourquoi pas?

1. Ask if your partner can go to a movie with you. (S/he can't.)
2. Find out why not.
3. Suggest other activities. How many excuses can s/he find?

2 Expressing Familiarity and Judgment

Tu connais Éric, Céline?
Oui, je le connais.
Tu connais ses parents?
Je les connais mais pas très bien.
Tu connais la ville de Boston?
Non, je ne la connais pas.

Le Québec refers to the province of Quebec. *Quebec City* is referred to simply as **Québec.**

▶ **Et vous?**   Vous connaissez la ville de Paris?
Vous connaissez le Québec?

B. Le verbe *connaître*

Est-ce que **vous connaissez** Paris?   *Do you know Paris?*
Anne ne **connaît** pas cette ville.   *Anne doesn't know that city.*
Je connais cet homme.   *I know that man.*
J'ai connu cet homme à Paris.   *I met that man in Paris.*

connaître		
(to know, be acquainted with, be familiar with)		
je **connais**	nous **connaissons**	
tu **connais**	vous **connaissez**	
il/elle/on **connaît**	ils/elles **connaissent**	

passé composé: j'**ai connu** = I met

imparfait = I knew

■ There is a circumflex accent on the **-i-** only in the verb stem of the **il/elle/on** form and in the infinitive.

Je **connais** bien la mentalité américaine.
But: Il ne **connaît** pas l'histoire de France.

■ **Connaître** denotes familiarity and means *to know, be acquainted with (a person, a place, a concept, a thing).* It is always accompanied by a direct object and cannot stand alone.

Connaissez-vous **les parents de Thomas?**   *Do you know Thomas's parents?*
Non, mais je connais **leur maison.**   *No, but I'm familiar with their house.*

Note   In the passé composé, **connaître** denotes a first meeting.

J'**ai connu** Robert en janvier.   *I met Robert in January.*

Review the direct object pronouns on p. 226.

C. Les pronoms objets directs (suite)

Connais-tu Christelle?	*Do you know Christelle?*
Non, je ne **la** connais pas personnellement.	*No, I don't know her personally.*
Est-ce qu'elle **te** connaît?	*Does she know you?*
Non, elle ne **me** connaît pas.	*No, she doesn't know me.*
Tu **nous** invites chez toi?	*Are you inviting us to your house?*
Non, ce soir je ne peux pas **vous** inviter.	*No, tonight I can't invite you.*
As-tu acheté ton livre?	*Did you buy your book?*
Je **l'**ai acheté mais je ne **l'**ai pas encore lu.	*I bought it but I haven't read it yet.*

See Appendix C for grammatical terms.

Pronoms objets directs			
singulier		pluriel	
me (m')	*me*	**nous**	*us*
te (t')	*you*	**vous**	*you*
le (l')	*him; it*	**les**	*them*
la (l')	*her; it*		

■ Remember that object pronouns are placed directly in front of the verb.

Aimes-tu *les sandwichs?*	Oui, je **les** aime.
Connais-tu *ma mère?*	Non, je ne **la** connais pas.

■ When used with a verb followed by an infinitive, direct object pronouns are put directly in front of the verb to which they are related (usually the infinitive).

Pascale veut **me** connaître?	Oui, elle veut **vous** connaître.
Je vais demander *l'addition.*	Je vais **la** demander.
Nous ne pouvons pas regarder *la télévision.*	Nous ne pouvons pas **la** regarder.
J'ai envie d'écouter *la radio.*	J'ai envie de **l'**écouter.

■ Direct object pronouns can be used with **voici** and **voilà.**

Où est Robert? **Le** voilà!	*Where is Robert? There he is!*
Vous venez? **Nous** voilà!	*Are you coming? Here we are.*

■ In the passé composé, object pronouns are placed directly in front of the auxiliary verb.

Marc a acheté *son livre?*	Oui, il **l'**a acheté.
As-tu aimé *le film?*	Non, je ne **l'**ai pas aimé.

FOR RECOGNITION ONLY:

The past participle agrees in gender and number with a *preceding* direct object.

Tu n'as pas **écouté** *la radio*.   *But:* Tu ne *l*'as pas écouté**e**.

Nous avons **attendu** nos amis.   *But:* Nous *les* avons attendu**s**.

5 **C'est vrai?** D'abord utilisez le verbe **connaître** pour faire des phrases à la forme affirmative. Ensuite utilisez un pronom objet dans une deuxième phrase pour dire si c'est vrai ou faux.

MODÈLE: je / la Côte-d'Ivoire
Je connais la Côte-d'Ivoire.
C'est faux. Je ne la connais pas.   ou
C'est vrai. Je la connais.

1. nos parents / notre professeur de français
2. notre professeur de français / nos parents
3. nous / l'avenue des Champs-Élysées
4. je / les amis de mes parents
5. mon ami(e) ... / le musée du Louvre
6. les étudiants / le (la) président(e) de l'université

6 **Qui les connaît?** Interviewez un(e) partenaire. Utilisez le verbe **connaître**. Employez un pronom objet dans votre réponse.

MODÈLES: tu / mes amis
VOUS: **Est-ce que tu connais mes amis?**
VOTRE PARTENAIRE: **Oui, je les connais.**   ou
Non, je ne les connais pas.

tes amis / me
VOUS: **Est-ce que tes amis me connaissent?**
VOTRE PARTENAIRE: **Oui, ils te connaissent.**   ou
Non, ils ne te connaissent pas.

1. tu / mes parents
2. tes parents / me
3. tes amis / le professeur de français
4. le professeur de français / tes amis
5. tu / les autres étudiants de notre cours de français
6. les autres étudiants de notre cours de français / te
7. le (la) président(e) de notre université / nous
8. nous / le (la) président(e) de notre université

Pourquoi ou pourquoi pas? Répondez en utilisant un pronom objet direct. Ensuite expliquez votre réponse.

MODÈLES: Aimez-vous étudier le français?
Oui, j'aime l'étudier parce que j'ai envie de le parler.

Voulez-vous faire la vaisselle?
Non, je ne veux pas la faire parce que c'est ennuyeux.

1. Aimez-vous faire les courses?
2. Allez-vous regarder la télévision ce soir?
3. Voulez-vous connaître la ville de Paris?
4. Pouvez-vous chanter *la Marseillaise*?
5. Préférez-vous faire vos devoirs à la bibliothèque?
6. Comprenez-vous l'espagnol?
7. Me comprenez-vous?

 Une devinette *(A riddle).* À quoi correspond le pronom? Devinez!

MODÈLE: On le trouve dans la classe de français.
On trouve le livre de français dans la classe de français. ou
On trouve Mike dans la classe de français.

1. On le prend le matin.
2. On la regarde quelquefois.
3. On l'écoute souvent.
4. On peut les faire à la bibliothèque.
5. On le lit pour préparer ce cours.
6. On aime le parler avec le professeur.
7. Les étudiants l'adorent.
8. On la fait après le dîner.
9. On les achète à la librairie.

Entre amis

Une enquête: vous êtes journaliste

Find out the following information. Your partner should use an object pronoun whenever possible.

1. Find out if your partner knows a specific radio program (choose one).
2. If so, find out if s/he listens to it often.
3. Find out if your partner knows a TV program (choose one from tonight's schedule.)
4. Ask if s/he is going to watch it this evening.
5. Find out why or why not.
6. Find out if s/he listens to the radio while s/he studies.
7. Find out if s/he watches TV while s/he studies. If not, inquire why not.

3 Giving Orders and Advice

Quelqu'un parle au chauffeur°:   *driver*
       Démarrez!
       Changez de vitesse!
       Continuez tout droit!
       Prenez à droite!
       Arrêtez au stop!
       Reculez!°   *Back up!*
       Faites attention aux voitures!

Le chauffeur répond
       Taisez-vous!°   *Keep quiet!*

> **Et vous?** Parlez au chauffeur!

See also p. 139

> **Taisez-vous** is the **vous** form of the imperative **tais-toi**, used on p. 270.

D. L'impératif (suite)

Fais attention!	*Pay attention!*
Faites attention!	*Pay attention!*
Faisons attention!	*Let's pay attention!*

Ne sors pas!	*Don't go out!*
Ne sortez pas!	*Don't go out!*
Ne sortons pas!	*Let's not go out!*

> Review the imperative on p. 139.

■ The imperative is used to give commands and to make suggestions. The forms are usually the same as the present tense for **tu, vous,** and **nous.**

■ **Être** and **avoir** have irregular imperatives:

être	avoir
sois	aie
soyez	ayez
soyons	ayons

Sois gentil!	*Be nice!*
Soyons sérieux!	*Let's be serious!*
Ayez pitié de nous!	*Have pity on us!*
N'**aie** pas peur!	*Don't be afraid!*

9 **Le pauvre professeur.** Les étudiants refusent de faire ce qu'il veut. Utilisez **Mais je ne veux pas ...** et répondez.

MODÈLE: Écoutez!
      Mais je ne veux pas écouter.

1. Allez en classe!
2. Prenez ce livre!
3. Écrivez votre dissertation!
4. Lisez ce roman!
5. Parlez à votre professeur!
6. Soyez raisonnable!
7. Arrêtez de parler!
8. Ayez pitié de vos professeurs!
9. Faites attention!
10. Sortez de cette classe!

> Remember that the final **-s** is omitted from the **tu** form of the imperative if the infinitive ends in **-er.**

⑩ Un père exaspéré. Michel trouve que sa fille n'est pas raisonnable. Il décide que sa fille peut faire ce qu'elle veut.

MODÈLE: Je veux aller au cinéma.
            Alors, va au cinéma!

1. Je ne peux rien manger.
2. Je ne veux pas faire la vaisselle.
3. Je veux regarder la télévision.
4. Je ne veux pas étudier.
5. Je ne peux pas écrire de rédaction.
6. Je ne veux pas avoir de bonnes notes en français.
7. Je ne veux pas être raisonnable.

⑪ Des touristes. Vous aidez des touristes francophones près de votre campus. Répondez et expliquez aux touristes où il faut aller.

MODÈLE: Où est le centre commercial, s'il vous plaît?
            Prenez la rue Main. Ensuite tournez à gauche dans la rue Madison.

1. Pouvez-vous me dire où je peux trouver un supermarché?
2. Je voudrais trouver une pharmacie, s'il vous plaît.
3. Y a-t-il un bureau de poste dans cette ville?
4. Y a-t-il un arrêt d'autobus près d'ici?
5. Où sont les toilettes, s'il vous plaît?
6. Connaissez-vous un restaurant près d'ici?

E. Le subjonctif: un bref aperçu *(an overview)*

■ You have learned to use the infinitive after a number of verbal expressions. This happens when both verbs have the same subject or when the first verb is an impersonal expression with no specific subject.

Je veux parler français.   *I want to speak French.*
Il faut étudier.   *One (You, We, etc.) must study.*

■ Expressions that are used to give advice to someone, however, are frequently followed by **que** plus the subject and its verb in a form called the subjunctive.

Je veux **que vous parliez** français.   *I want you to speak French.*
Il faut **qu'on étudie.**   *One (You, We, etc.) must study.*

■ The stem of the subjunctive is usually the same as the stem of the **ils/elles** form of the present tense. Except for **avoir** and **être,** the endings of the subjunctive are the same for all verbs.

-e	-ions
-es	-iez
-e	-ent

■ Here are the subjunctive forms of regular **-er** and **-re** verbs.

-er verbs (parlent)		
que je	parl	**e**
que tu	parl	**es**
qu'il/elle/on	parl	**e**
que nous	parl	**ions**
que vous	parl	**iez**
qu'ils/elles	parl	**ent**

-re verbs (vendent)		
que je	vend	**e**
que tu	vend	**es**
qu'il/elle/on	vend	**e**
que nous	vend	**ions**
que vous	vend	**iez**
qu'ils/elles	vend	**ent**

■ Note that the subjunctive forms for **je, tu, il/elle/on,** and **ils/elles** of regular **-er** verbs look and sound the same as the present tense.

Il faut que tu **changes** de vitesse.   *You must change gears.*
Je veux qu'elle **invite** sa cousine.   *I want her to invite her cousin.*

■ The **nous** and **vous** forms of the subjunctive look and sound different from the present tense because of the **-i-** in their endings.

Le prof veut **que nous parlions** français.   *The teacher wants us to speak French.*

Il faut **que vous étudiiez.**   *It is necessary that you study. (You have to study.)*

> Note the double **-i-** in the **nous** and **vous** forms of **étudier.**

■ The subjunctive forms of **avoir** and **être** are very similar to their imperative forms.

Il ne faut pas que vous **ayez** peur.   *You must not be afraid.*
Il est important qu'ils ne **soient** pas en retard.   *It is important that they not be late.*
Il vaut mieux que vous **soyez** à l'heure.   *It's better that you be on time.*

VOCABULAIRE

Ordres et Conseils
To order, to counsel

il est essentiel que	*it is essential that*
il est important que	*it is important that*
il est indispensable que	*it is essential that*
il est nécessaire que	*it is necessary that*
il faut que	*it is necessary that; (someone) must*
il ne faut pas que	*(someone) must not*
il vaut mieux que	*it is preferable that; it is better that*
je préfère que	*I prefer that*
je veux que	*I want*
je voudrais que	*I would like*

■ With the above expressions, it is important to remember that, if there is no change of subjects, the infinitive is used. The preposition **de** is, however, required after **il est nécessaire/important/essentiel/indispensable.**

| Je ne veux pas **perdre** mon temps. | *I don't want to waste my time.* |
| Il est important d'**étudier** beaucoup. | *It's important to study a lot.* |

■ When the above expressions are followed by **que** and a change of subjects, the subjunctive must be used.

| Ma mère ne veut pas **que je perde** mon temps. | *My mother doesn't want me to waste my time.* |
| Il est important **que j'étudie** beaucoup. | *It's important that I study a lot.* |

⑫ Ils veulent que je fasse tout ça? Tout le monde vous demande de faire quelque chose. Décidez si vous êtes d'accord.

> **MODÈLE:** Votre père veut que vous étudiiez beaucoup.
> **Très bien, je vais étudier beaucoup.**   ou
> **Mais je ne veux pas étudier beaucoup.**

1. Vos parents veulent que vous restiez à la maison.
2. Votre mère veut que vous rendiez visite à vos grands-parents.
3. Vos parents ne veulent pas que vous vendiez vos livres.
4. Vos parents ne veulent pas que vous sortiez tous les soirs.
5. Votre professeur veut que vous ayez «A» à votre examen de français.
6. Vos parents ne veulent pas que vous fumiez.
7. Vos professeurs ne veulent pas que vous perdiez vos devoirs.
8. Vos parents veulent que vous attachiez votre ceinture de sécurité.

⑬ Conseils aux étudiants de première année. Ces recommandations de l'administration et des professeurs sont-elles pertinentes? Quelle est votre opinion? Utilisez l'impératif dans chaque réponse et faites tous les changements nécessaires.

> **MODÈLE:** Il ne faut pas que les étudiants sortent souvent.
> **C'est un bon conseil. Ne sortez pas souvent!**   ou
> **C'est un mauvais conseil. Sortez souvent, si vous voulez.**

1. Il est important que les étudiants étudient le français.
2. Il ne faut pas qu'ils soient absents.
3. Il est essentiel qu'ils dorment huit heures par jour.
4. Il faut qu'ils mangent au restaurant universitaire.
5. L'administration veut que les étudiants habitent dans une résidence universitaire.
6. Il vaut mieux qu'ils prennent le petit déjeuner.
7. Il est important qu'ils aient de bonnes notes.
8. Il est absolument indispensable qu'ils écoutent leurs professeurs.

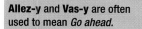

See p. 139

F. Les pronoms à l'impératif

Allez-y and **Vas-y** are often used to mean *Go ahead*.

■ In an affirmative sentence, an object pronoun follows the imperative.

Je peux prendre la voiture?	**Prends-la!**	**Prenez-la!**
Je veux acheter ce livre.	**Achète-le!**	**Achetez-le!**
Je vais porter ces chaussures.	**Porte-les!**	**Portez-les!**
Je vais au cinéma.	**Vas-y!***	**Allez-y!**
Je m'amuse bien.	**Amuse-toi!**	**Amusez-vous!**
Je me lève.	**Lève-toi!**	**Levez-vous!**

Note   Used after a verb, **me** and **te** become **moi** and **toi**.

Regardez-**moi!**   *Look at me!*   Écoute-**moi!**   *Listen to me!*

*While the final **-s** of the **tu** form of verbs that end in **-er** is dropped in the imperative (see p. 139), it is retained when it is followed by a pronoun beginning with a vowel.

■ If the sentence is negative, the object pronoun precedes the verb.

Je ne veux pas acheter ce livre.	**Ne l'achète pas!**	**Ne l'achetez pas!**
Je ne veux pas porter ces chaussures.	**Ne les porte pas!**	**Ne les portez pas!**
Vous me regardez tout le temps.	**Ne me regarde pas!**	**Ne me regardez pas!**
Je ne veux pas aller au cinéma.	**N'y va pas!**	**N'y allez pas!**
Je ne me lève pas.	**Ne te lève pas!**	**Ne vous levez pas!**

pronoun/vowel

14 **La voix de ma conscience** *(The voice of my conscience).* Qu'est-ce que votre conscience vous dit de faire ou de ne pas faire? Utilisez un pronom objet avec l'impératif.

Votre conscience est une bonne amie. Alors, quand elle vous parle, elle utilise **tu**.

Modèle: Je vais manger ces bonbons.   **Mange-les!** ou
                                            Ne les mange pas!

1. Je ne vais pas faire mes devoirs.
2. Je veux prendre la voiture de mon ami(e).
3. Je ne veux pas attacher ma ceinture de sécurité.
4. Je vais boire cette bouteille de vin.
5. Je veux acheter ces vêtements.
6. Je veux faire la sieste.
7. Je ne veux pas me lever pour aller au cours.
8. Je vais regarder la télévision.
9. Je peux aller au cinéma?
10. Je vais m'amuser ce soir.

G. Les nombres ordinaux

Prends la **première** rue à gauche.
C'est la **deuxième** fois que je viens en France.
Elle habite dans la **quatrième** maison.
Victor Hugo est né au **dix-neuvième** siècle *(century)*.

■ To form most ordinal numbers, one simply adds **-ième** to the cardinal number. The abbreviated form is a numeral followed by a raised **e**.

deux	⟶ **deuxième**	**2e**
trois	⟶ **troisième**	**3e**

For cardinal numbers such as **vingt et un,** the ordinal number is formed according to the normal rule: **vingt et un → vingt et unième (21ᵉ).**

■ There are a few exceptions.

1. The ordinal number for **un (une)** is **premier (première).** It is the only ordinal number whose ending is altered to show gender agreement with the noun it modifies.

un (une) ⟶ **premier (première)**   1ᵉʳ (1ʳᵉ)

2. **Cinq** and numbers built on **cinq** add a **-u-** before the ending.

cinq ⟶ **cinq*u*ième**   5ᵉ

3. **Neuf** and numbers built on **neuf** change the **-f-** to **-v-** before the ending.

neuf ⟶ **neu*v*ième**   9ᵉ

4. Cardinal numbers ending in **-e** drop the **-e** before the ending.

quatre ⟶	**quatrième**	4ᵉ
onze ⟶	**onzième**	11ᵉ
douze ⟶	**douzième**	12ᵉ

■ In dates, **le premier** is used, as in English, to express the meaning *the first,* but the cardinal numbers are used for the rest of the days in the month.

le **premier** mai   *But:* le **deux** mai, le **trois** mai

Remember that **Premier** agrees in the feminine: Elizabeth **Première.**

■ This is also true when talking about monarchs. **Premier (Première)** is used for *the First,* but the cardinal numbers are used thereafter. Note that the definite article is not used in French.

François **Premier**   *But:* Henri **Quatre**

15 **Prononcez et écrivez.** Lisez ces expressions et écrivez en toutes lettres.

MODÈLE: le 21ᵉ siècle
le vingt et unième siècle

1. Henri Iᵉʳ
2. la 2ᵉ année consécutive
3. la 3ᵉ fois
4. le 1ᵉʳ mois de l'année
5. Louis XV
6. la 6ᵉ fois
7. le 20ᵉ siècle
8. la 1ʳᵉ rue à droite
9. le 25 décembre

16 **Le calendrier.** Répondez.

MODÈLE: Quelle est la date de Noël?
C'est le vingt-cinq décembre.

Review days, p. 133, and months, p. 197.

1. Quelle est la date d'aujourd'hui?
2. Quelle est la date du Jour de l'An?
3. Quelles sont les dates de votre fête nationale et de la fête nationale française?
4. Quelle est la date de votre anniversaire?
5. Quelle est la date de l'anniversaire de mariage de vos parents?
6. Quel est le troisième mois de l'année?
7. Quel est le dernier jour de l'année?
8. Quel est le cinquième jour de la semaine en France?
9. Quel est le cinquième jour de la semaine pour vous?

Entre amis

Excusez-moi de vous déranger

You are visiting a French-speaking city.

1. Stop a native and explain that you don't know the city.
2. Ask for directions to a good restaurant, a good hotel, and a post office.
3. Be sure to thank the native properly.

4 Describing Ways of Doing Things

À quelle vitesse conduisez-vous?
  Moi, je conduis ...
        comme un escargot°.   *like a snail*
        lentement.
        tranquillement°.   *calmly*
        prudemment°.   *prudently*
        vite.
        à toute vitesse°.   *at top speed*
        comme un fou (une folle)°.   *like a crazy person*

Comment vos amis conduisent-ils?

Il y a un geste

À toute vitesse. A closed fist is held at chest level and moved horizontally away from the body and back in a few rapid motions. This suggests a rapid speed. It may also be used to describe someone who has a "hard-driving" personality.

H. Le verbe *conduire*

Est-ce que tu as peur de **conduire**?
Je conduis très souvent.
Hier, **nous avons conduit** une voiture de sport.

conduire *(to drive)*			
je	**conduis**	nous	**conduisons**
tu	**conduis**	vous	**conduisez**
il/elle/on	**conduit**	ils/elles	**conduisent**
passé composé: j'**ai conduit**			

■ The verb **conduire** is not used to tell that you drive to a destination. It is used alone or with adverbs or direct objects. To tell *where* you are driving, use **aller en voiture**.

> Il **conduit** une Renault. *He drives a Renault.*
> *But:* Il **va** à Monte-Carlo **en voiture.** *He is driving to Monte Carlo.*

(17) Comment ces gens conduisent-ils? Votre partenaire va vous poser des questions. Répondez. Si vous ne savez pas, inventez une réponse.

> **MODÈLE:** votre tante
> **VOTRE PARTENAIRE:** Comment votre tante conduit-elle?
> **VOUS:** Ma tante conduit à toute vitesse.

1. les étudiants de cette université
2. le professeur de français
3. les professeurs (en général)
4. les femmes
5. les hommes
6. les Français
7. les Américains
8. votre meilleur(e) ami(e)
9. vous

Entre amis

Vous donnez des conseils au chauffeur

1. Be a back-seat driver. Tell your partner that s/he is driving too fast.
2. Tell him/her to go slowly.
3. Tell him/her to pay attention.
4. Tell him/her to shift.
5. Tell him/her where to go and how to drive.

I. Les adverbes

> If necessary, consult Appendix C at the end of the book to review the distinction between an adjective and an adverb.

■ While there are exceptions, most French adverbs end in **-ment.**

> Avance **lentement!**   Tu vas trop **rapidement.**

■ If the masculine singular form of the adjective ends in a consonant, **-ment** is added to the feminine form.

premier (première)	⟶ **premièrement**	*first*
sérieux (sérieuse)	⟶ **sérieusement**	*seriously*
attentif (attentive)	⟶ **attentivement**	*attentively*
personnel (personnelle)	⟶ **personnellement**	*personally*

■ The suffix **-ment** is added to the masculine singular form of an adjective if it ends in a vowel.

vrai	⟶ **vraiment**	*truly*
facile	⟶ **facilement**	*easily*
absolu	⟶ **absolument**	*absolutely*

Exception   fou (folle) ⟶ **follement**   *crazily*

■ For masculine adjectives ending in **-ant** or **-ent**, the adverbs will end in **-amment** or **-emment** respectively. The first vowel in both spellings is pronounced [a].

constant	⟶ **constamment**	*constantly*
patient	⟶ **patiemment**	*patiently*
prudent	⟶ **prudemment**	*prudently*

■ Several of the most common adverbs are completely different from their corresponding adjectives.

bon	⟶ **bien**	*well*	Loïc danse **bien.**
mauvais	⟶ **mal**	*poorly*	Il chante **mal.**
petit	⟶ **peu**	*little*	Et il mange très **peu.**

Note **Rapide** has two corresponding adverbs: **rapidement** and **vite.**

 18 **Tout le monde est chauffeur.** Décrivez les chauffeurs suivants. Pour chaque adjectif, faites une phrase avec le verbe **être** et un adjectif, et puis une autre phrase, avec le verbe **conduire** et un adverbe.

MODÈLE: ma tante/lent   **Ma tante est lente. Elle conduit lentement.**

	rapide
	sérieux
nous (les étudiants)	bon
mon oncle	prudent
ma tante	patient
mon père	nerveux
ma mère	admirable
je	raisonnable
le professeur	parfait
les hommes	tranquille
les femmes	attentif
	fou

 19 **Identification.** Identifiez des personnes qui correspondent aux questions suivantes.

MODÈLE: Qui conduit lentement?
Mes parents conduisent lentement.   ou
Mon oncle conduit lentement.

1. Qui conduit nerveusement?
2. Qui parle rapidement le français?
3. Qui fait bien la cuisine?
4. Qui parle constamment?
5. Qui apprend facilement les maths?
6. Qui travaille sérieusement?
7. Qui écoute patiemment?
8. Qui étudie attentivement?
9. Qui chante mal?
10. Qui écrit peu?

Entre amis

Vous êtes journaliste

1. Find out if your partner speaks French.
2. Explain that you are a reporter for a newspaper called *L'Équipe (The Team)*.
3. Get permission to ask a few questions.
4. Find out if s/he plays tennis, swims, skates, or skis.
5. If so, find out how well and how often.
6. Double-check the answers by reporting back what your partner has told you.

Intégration

Révision

Ⓐ Des indications. Aidez un(e) touriste francophone qui cherche ...

   1. un restaurant   2. un bureau de poste   3. une pharmacie

Ⓑ Jacques a dit *(Simon says)*. Faites l'action ou le geste indiqué par le professeur, s'il commence par «Jacques a dit». Si le professeur n'utilise pas l'expression «Jacques a dit», ne faites pas l'action ou le geste décrit.

Frappez à la porte!	Mon œil!	Reculez!
Taisez-vous!	Comme ci, comme ça.	Prenez le volant!
Dites bonjour!	Comptez sur une main!	Conduisez!
Mangez!	Regardez à gauche!	Changez de vitesse!
Buvez!	Regardez à droite!	Asseyez-vous!
Invitez-moi à danser!	Avancez!	

Ⓒ Les étudiants sérieux. Décidez si les étudiants sérieux font ou ne font pas les choses suivantes. Utilisez un pronom objet direct dans chaque réponse.

Modèle: regarder la télé pendant des heures
Ils ne la regardent pas pendant des heures.

   1. oublier leurs livres dans leur chambre
   2. conduire follement la voiture de leurs parents
   3. pouvoir facilement apprendre le subjonctif
   4. vouloir étudier le français
   5. faire toujours leurs devoirs
   6. passer la nuit à regarder la télévision

D **La voiture de votre professeur de français.** Répondez.

1. Comment? Vous voulez conduire ma voiture?
2. Avez-vous votre permis de conduire?
3. Depuis combien de temps l'avez-vous?
4. Conduisez-vous souvent les voitures des autres?
5. Vous allez attacher votre ceinture de sécurité?
6. Prenez le volant.
7. Faites bien attention aux autres voitures, n'est-ce pas?
8. Soyez prudent(e), s'il vous plaît.

Pas de problème!

Preparation for the video:
1. Video worksheet in the *Cahier d'activités*
2. CD-ROM, *Module 7*

Cette activité est basée sur la vidéo, *Module 7*. Choisissez la bonne réponse pour compléter les phrases suivantes.

1. Quand Alicia dit que les cartes sont jolies, Bruno répond ＿＿＿.
   (Merci, Tu trouves?, Tu as raison)
2. Bruno veut envoyer ＿＿＿ à sa mère.
   (un cadeau, une carte postale, une lettre)
3. Une femme explique à Bruno que la poste se trouve à ＿＿＿ mètres.
   (100, 500, 50)
4. On vend de la porcelaine ＿＿＿.
   (dans les boutiques, dans les petits magasins, à la pharmacie)
5. Bruno a acheté ＿＿＿ carte(s) postale(s).
   (une, deux, douze)
6. Pour poster ses cartes postales et son colis, Bruno doit payer ＿＿＿ francs.
   (59, 69, 79)

Lecture I

A **Étude du vocabulaire.** Étudiez les phrases suivantes et choisissez les mots anglais qui correspondent aux mots français en caractères gras: *more, convinced, rather, hates, approximately, those, latecomer, less, thus, bother.*

1. Un avion est **plus** rapide qu'un train.
2. L'état de Rhode Island est **moins** grand que le Texas.
3. Notre professeur **exècre** le tabac. Les cigarettes le rendent malade.
4. Pourquoi est-ce que vous me parlez **ainsi**? Qu'est-ce que je vous ai fait?
5. Mon frère est toujours **retardataire**. Il n'arrive jamais à l'heure.
6. Est-ce que cela vous **dérange** si je fume?
7. **Ceux** qui étudient sont **ceux** qui ont les meilleures notes.
8. Christian chante **plutôt** mal, mais il aime chanter quand même.
9. Il y a **à peu près** trente personnes au restaurant.
10. Je suis **convaincu** que le professeur veut que j'étudie beaucoup.

Qu'en pensez-vous? Quelle est la réputation des Français au volant? Quelle est la réputation des chauffeurs californiens? des chauffeurs new-yorkais? Et vous, comment conduisez-vous?

Vous voulez prendre le volant?

La France au volant

Il faut se méfier des[1] Français en général, mais sur la route en particulier. Pour un Anglais qui arrive en France, il est indispensable de savoir d'abord qu'il existe deux sortes de Français: les à-pied et les en-voiture. Les à-pied exècrent les en-voiture, et les en-voiture terrorisent les à-pied, les premiers passant instantanément dans le camp des seconds si on leur met un volant entre les mains. (Il en est ainsi au théâtre avec les retardataires qui, après avoir dérangé douze personnes pour s'asseoir, sont les premiers à protester contre ceux qui ont le toupet[2] d'arriver plus tard.)

Les Anglais conduisent plutôt mal, mais prudemment. Les Français conduisent plutôt bien, mais follement. La proportion des accidents est à peu près la même dans les deux pays. Mais je me sens[3] plus tranquille avec des gens qui font mal des choses bien[4] qu'avec ceux qui font bien de mauvaises choses.

Les Anglais (et les Américains) sont depuis longtemps convaincus que la voiture va moins vite que l'avion. Les Français (et la plupart des Latins) semblent encore vouloir prouver le contraire.

Pierre Daninos, *Les Carnets du Major Thompson*

---

1. *watch out for*   2. *nerve*   3. *feel*   4. *do good things poorly*

 Vrai ou faux? Décidez si les phrases suivantes sont vraies ou fausses d'après la lecture. Si une phrase est fausse, corrigez-la.

1. Les Français sont dangereux quand ils conduisent.
2. Les Anglais sont de bons conducteurs (*drivers*) mais ils conduisent plutôt vite.
3. En France, ceux qui marchent n'apprécient pas beaucoup ceux qui sont au volant.
4. Ceux qui conduisent adorent les à-pied.
5. Les Anglais ont moins d'accidents que les Français.
6. L'avion va plus vite que la voiture mais les Américains ne le comprennent pas encore.

Questions. Répondez.

1. Pourquoi dit-on qu'il y a deux sortes de Français?
2. Quelle transformation y a-t-il quand un Français prend le volant?
3. Les retardataires sont-ils hypocrites? Expliquez votre réponse.
4. Quelles différences y a-t-il entre les Anglais et les Français?
5. Qui sont les Latins?
6. Qui sont ceux qui font mal des choses qui sont bonnes?

 Familles de mots. Essayez de deviner le sens des mots suivants.

1. conduire, un conducteur, une conductrice, la conduite
2. exister, l'existence, l'existentialisme
3. retarder, un(e) retardataire, un retard
4. terroriser, un(e) terroriste, le terrorisme, la terreur

Lecture II

A **Les voitures françaises.** Lisez la lecture suivante et identifiez deux marques *(makes)* de voitures françaises.

AUTOMOBILES	
Vends Renault Espace RN 21 Turbo D, mod 96, 8.000 kms, bleue, climatisée, airbag, radio. Tél. 02.43.81.75.79 ap. 18h.	Vends Laguna ii TD 2.2 RXE 7 cv, janvier 1999, 25.000 km, ABS, climatisation automatique, airbags, direction assistée, vitres électriques avant. Pare-brise athermique. Radio commande au volant. Etat neuf. 20.000€. Tél. 02.41.58.87.18 le soir.
Vends Renault 9 GTL, 68.000 kms, 5 vitesses, vitres teintées électriques, gris métallique, direction assistée, toit ouvrant. Tél. 02.41.34.63.23 après 20h.	
Vds Mercedes C 250 D Élégance 95, 1ᵉ main, 44.000 kms, état neuf, clim, radio (Sony), alarme, radiocommandée, vert métal. Tél. 02.41.64.35.70.	Xantia turbo D VSX Export, année modèle 1996, gris Quartz, 97.500 km, suspension hydractive, direction assistée, climatisation régulée, radio commande volant, 4 vitres électriques, ABS, pastille verte, verrouillage et anti-démarrage par plip HF. Non fumeur. Parfait état, entretien Citroën, contrôle technique ok. Disponible 15 avril. Tél. 02.41.62.53.58.
VDS R5 pour pièces détachées, roulante mais accidentée, petit prix. Tél. 02.41.32.51.61.	
Vds Renault Twingo, 6 mois, noire, toit ouvrant, bag, 3.200 kms, 10.000€. Tél. 02.43.75.64.98.	

B **Pouvez-vous décider?**

1. Quelle est probablement la plus vieille voiture?
2. Quelle voiture est probablement la plus chère?
3. Quelle voiture est probablement la moins chère?
4. Quelle voiture n'est pas française?
5. Quelles voitures ne sont certainement pas rouges?
6. Quelles voitures sont confortables quand il fait chaud?
7. Quels propriétaires ne sont pas chez eux pendant la journée?

 Une voiture à vendre. Écrivez une petite annonce pour une voiture que vous voulez vendre.

VOCABULAIRE ACTIF

Sur la route

un arrêt (d'autobus) *(bus) stop*
arrêter *to stop*
à toute vitesse *at top speed*
attacher *to attach; to put on*
avancer *to advance*
une ceinture de sécurité *safety belt, seat belt*
changer (de) *to change*
un chauffeur *driver*
comme un fou *like a crazy person*
conduire *to drive*
démarrer *to start a car*
un feu *traffic light*
jusqu'au feu *until the traffic light*
un permis de conduire *driver's license*
reculer *to back up*
une route *highway*
un rétroviseur *rearview mirror*
le sens interdit *one-way street*
un stop *stop sign*
la vitesse *speed*
un volant *steering wheel*

D'autres noms

l'année scolaire *(f.) school year*
un anniversaire de mariage *wedding anniversary*
une boum *party*
un commentaire *commentary*
un conseil *(piece of) advice*
un escargot *snail*
un fou (une folle) *fool; crazy person*
un match *game*
une patinoire *skating rink*
un(e) propriétaire *owner*
un siècle *century*

Adjectifs

attentif (attentive) *attentive*
constant(e) *constant*
fou (folle) *crazy; mad*
lent(e) *slow*
neuf (neuve) *brand-new*
prudent(e) *cautious*
raisonnable *reasonable*
rapide *rapid; fast*
sérieux (sérieuse) *serious*
tranquille *calm*

Verbes

avoir pitié (de qqn.) *to have pity (on s.o.); to feel sorry (for s.o.)*
connaître *to know; be acquainted with; be familiar with*
inviter *to invite*
laisser *to leave; to let*
pouvoir *to be able; to be allowed*
vouloir *to want; to wish*

Adverbes

absolument *absolutely*
constamment *constantly*
follement *in a crazy manner*
lentement *slowly*
patiemment *patiently*
personnellement *personally*
prudemment *prudently*
rapidement *rapidly*
sérieusement *seriously*
si *so*
vite *quickly; fast*

Pronoms objets directs

me *me*
te *you*
le *him; it*
la *her; it*
nous *us*
vous *you*
les *them*

Des ordres et des conseils

il est essentiel que *it is essential that*
il est important que *it is important that*
il est indispensable que *it is essential that*
il est nécessaire que *it is necessary that*
il faut que *it is necessary that; (someone) must*
il ne faut pas que *(someone) must not*
il vaut mieux que *it is preferable that; it is better that*
je préfère que *I prefer that*
je veux que *I want*
je voudrais que *I would like*

Expressions utiles

C'est promis. *It's a promise.*
Chut! *Shh!*
je veux m'amuser *I want to have fun*
Laisse-moi (Laissez-moi) tranquille! *Leave me alone!*
(mon/ma) chéri(e) *(my) dear, honey*
Mon œil! *My eye!*
ma puce *honey (lit. my flea)*
Plus un mot. *Not one more word.*
Tais-toi! (Taisez-vous!) *Keep quiet!*

un rond-point / roundabout
un carrefour / intersection
le stop

11

Comme si c'était hier

Buts communicatifs
Describing conditions and feelings in the past
Setting the scene in the past
Making comparisons

Structures utiles
L'imparfait
Ne ... que
L'imparfait et le passé composé
Le comparatif
Le comparatif de **bon** et de **bien**
Le superlatif

Culture
La famille
Les jeunes
Le mariage en France

Coup d'envoi

Prise de contact ## Quand vous étiez jeune

Qu'est-ce que tu faisais° quand tu avais seize ans°,   *used to do / were sixteen*
    Caroline?
       J'allais au lycée°.   *high school*
       J'étudiais l'anglais et les mathématiques.
       J'habitais une petite maison.
       Je sortais quelquefois avec mes amis.
       Nous allions au cinéma ensemble.
       Mais je n'avais pas encore mon permis de
         conduire.

 Et vous?   Qu'est-ce que vous faisiez quand vous aviez seize ans?

Conversation

This and all Conversations are recorded for your convenience on the Student Audio.

L'album de photos

Lori et son amie Denise sont en train de° regarder un album de photos.   *in the process of*

LORI: C'est une photo de toi?

DENISE: Oui, c'était° au mariage de ma sœur.   *it was*

LORI: Elle est plus âgée que° toi?   *older than*

DENISE: Oui, de deux ans.

LORI: Ah! La voilà en robe de mariée°, n'est-ce pas?   *wedding dress*
Comme elle était belle!°   *How beautiful she was!*

DENISE: Tu vois° la photo de ce jeune homme en   *You see*
smoking°? C'est mon beau-frère.   *in a tuxedo*

LORI: Il avait l'air jeune.

DENISE: Il n'avait que vingt ans.°   *He was only twenty.*
À mon avis°, il en avait assez de° porter son   *In my opinion / he was fed up*
smoking.   *with*

LORI: Il faisait chaud?

DENISE: Très! Et il avait déjà porté° son smoking pour le   *had already worn*
mariage à la mairie°.   *town hall*

LORI: Quand est-ce que ce mariage a eu lieu°?   *took place*

DENISE: Il y a deux ans.

LORI: Alors, c'est ton tour°. Quand est-ce que tu vas   *turn*
épouser° ton petit ami?   *marry*
(Elles rient.°)   *They laugh.*

DENISE: Lori, occupe-toi de tes oignons!°   *mind your own business!*

 Jouez ces rôles. Répétez la conversation avec votre partenaire. Remplacez «mariage de ma sœur» par «mariage de mon frère». Faites tous les changements nécessaires.

Il y a un geste

J'en ai assez. The right hand is raised near the left temple. The hand is open but bent at a right angle to the wrist. The gesture is made by twisting the wrist so that the hand passes over your forehead, implying that you are "fed up to here."

À PROPOS

Pourquoi le beau-frère avait-il déjà porté son smoking à la mairie?

a. Il aimait beaucoup porter un smoking.
b. C'est normal. On porte toujours des vêtements élégants à la mairie.
c. Il y a eu deux cérémonies de mariage: à la mairie et à l'église.

La famille

Quite attached to home, family, and friends, the French are usually very fond of weddings, family re-unions, picnics, social gatherings, etc., which provide an opportunity to nurture the close relationships found within the circle of their social and emotional ties. In general, these family and friendship bonds seem stronger and longer-lasting than those typically found in English-speaking North America. The French are often equally attached to the region in which they live. It is therefore rather common, for example, to find homes that have been lived in by successive genera-tions of the same family.

Les jeunes

High unemployment (over 12% in 1997) and the in-creasing length of their studies have meant that few young adults are able to become financially indepen-dent of their families. At age twenty-two, 60% of the men and 45% of the women are still living with their parents. Very few students, for example, are able to have a part-time job or purchase a car. Fortunately public transportation is widely available and universi-ties are inexpensive.

Le mariage en France

In order to be legally married in France, all couples are wed in a civil ceremony at the town hall. The mayor (**le maire**), or the mayor's representative, performs the ceremony and the couples express their consent by saying **oui**. Many couples choose to have a religious ceremony as well. This takes place at the church, temple, or mosque, after the civil ceremony.

Currently the average age for marriage is approx-imately 30 (men) and 28 (women). (See **Lecture II, "La famille",** p. 81.) Since after marriage two women out of three continue to work and the birth rate has fallen to 1.8 children per family, attempts have been made by the government to help couples who have children. There are paid maternity (or paternity) leaves, public day care centers, and subsidies to families with more than two children. Nursery schools accept children as young as two years of age and, if parents wish, will supervise the children, at school, from 7:30 AM until 7 PM.

 À vous.   Répondez.

1. Où habitiez-vous quand vous aviez seize ans?
2. Comment s'appelaient vos amis?
3. À quelle école alliez-vous?
4. Qu'est-ce que vous étudiiez?

Entre amis

Une vieille photo

1. Show your partner an old photo of a group of people.
2. Tell who the people are.
3. Tell how old each one was in the photo.
4. Describe what they were wearing.
5. Tell where they lived.

Prononciation

🎧 Use the Student Audio to help practice pronunciation.

Les sons [i] et [j]

■ Two related sounds in French are the pure vowel sound [i] (as in the English word *teeth*), and the semi-consonant/semi-vowel [j] (as in the English word *yes*). Practice saying the following words after your instructor, paying particular attention to the highlighted sound. As you pronounce the words for one sound, look at how that sound is spelled and in what kinds of letter combinations it appears. What patterns do you notice?

[i]
- **il, ici,** r**i**z, p**i**zza, pol**i**tique, asp**i**rine
- su**i**s, fru**i**t, depu**i**s, tru**i**te, condu**i**re, ju**i**llet
- br**i**e, am**i**e, Soph**i**e
- S**y**lv**i**e, bic**y**clette, **y**

[j]
- mar**i**é, jan**vi**er, h**i**er, m**i**am, k**i**osque, nat**i**onal, mons**i**eur, b**i**en
- déta**il**, somme**il**, œ**il**, trava**ill**e, Marse**ill**e, feu**ill**e
- gent**ill**e, f**ill**e, past**ill**e, van**ill**e, ju**ill**et
- **y**eux, essa**y**er, pa**y**er

■ The [i] sound is represented by written -i- or -y- in the following situations:

1. **i** not in combination with another vowel: merc**i**, avr**i**l, f**i**lle
2. **i** following a **u**: pu**i**s, bru**i**t, tru**i**te
3. final **-ie**: br**ie**, étud**ie**
4. **-y-** between two consonants: il **y** va, S**y**lvie

■ The [j] sound is required in the following circumstances:

1. **i-** before a pronounced vowel in the same syllable: p**i**ed, v**i**ande, mar**i**age
2. **-il, -ill** after a pronounced vowel in the same syllable: trava**il**, conse**ill**er, œ**il**
3. **-ll** after [i]: fi**ll**e, jui**ll**et

Exceptions   mi**ll**ion, mi**ll**iard, mi**ll**e, vi**ll**e, vi**ll**age, tranqui**ll**e

4. initial **y-** before a vowel, **-y-** between two vowels: **y**eux, essa**y**er.

Note   Between the sound [i] at the end of one syllable and another vowel at the beginning of the next syllable, [j] is pronounced even though there is no letter representing the sound.

quatrième [ka tRi jɛm]

▶ **Practice the following words.**

1. Sylvie, yeux, bicyclette, y, payer
2. télévision, brioche, nuit, addition, cuisine, principal, délicieux, insister, feuille
3. pitié, amie, papier, pièce, prier, pâtisserie, client, habitiez, impatient, oublier
4. milliard, juillet, ville, fille, bouteille, travail, travaille, conseil, allions, vanille, mille, œil, oreille, tranquille, gentil, gentille, million

Buts
communicatifs

1 Describing Conditions and Feelings in the Past

Quand vous étiez jeune, ...

	oui	non
aviez-vous un chien ou un chat?	——	——
étiez-vous souvent malade?	——	——
habitiez-vous une grande ville?	——	——
aviez-vous beaucoup d'amis?	——	——
regardiez-vous beaucoup la télé?	——	——

Que faisiez-vous après l'école?
Comment s'appelaient vos voisins°?   *neighbors*
À votre avis, quelle était la meilleure émission°   *best program*
    de télé?

Faisiez is pronounced [fəzje]; see also p. 109.

A. L'imparfait

■ You have already been using one past tense, the passé composé, to relate what happened in the past. The imperfect (**l'imparfait**) is a past tense used to describe conditions and feelings and to express habitual actions.

1. Describing conditions *[handwritten: Physical app; color; health; weather; time {dress {home]*

Ma sœur **était** belle.	My sister was beautiful.
Mon beau-frère **avait** l'air jeune.	My brother-in-law seemed young.
Léa **portait** une jolie robe.	Léa was wearing a pretty dress.
Anne **était** malade.	Anne was sick.
Il **pleuvait.**	It was raining.
Il y **avait** trois chambres dans notre maison.	There were three bedrooms in our house.

2. Describing feelings *[handwritten: — verbs + adjectives]*

Ma sœur **était** nerveuse.	My sister was nervous.
Mon beau-frère en **avait** assez.	My brother-in-law was fed up.
Je **détestais** les épinards.	I used to hate spinach.
Tout le monde **était** heureux.	Everybody was happy.

3. Expressing habitual past actions

Nous **regardions** des dessins animés le samedi.	We used to watch cartoons on Saturday.
À cette époque, Marie **sortait** avec Paul.	Back then, Marie used to go out with Paul.

But: Nous **avons regardé** des dessins animés samedi.	We watched cartoons (last) Saturday. (once, not a repeated event)
Marie **est sortie** avec Paul vendredi dernier.	Marie went out with Paul last Friday. (one day, not habitually)

> Review uses of the passé composé, pp. 157–158.

■ To form the imperfect tense, take the **nous** form of the present tense, drop the **-ons** ending, and add the endings **-ais, -ais, -ait, -ions, -iez, -aient.**

jouer (jouons)		
je	**jou**	ais
tu	**jou**	ais
il/elle/on	**jou**	ait
nous	**jou**	ions
vous	**jou**	iez
ils/elles	**jou**	aient

avoir (avons)		
j'	**av**	ais
tu	**av**	ais
il/elle/on	**av**	ait
nous	**av**	ions
vous	**av**	iez
ils/elles	**av**	aient

aller (allons)		
j'	**all**	ais
tu	**all**	ais
il/elle/on	**all**	ait
nous	**all**	ions
vous	**all**	iez
ils/elles	**all**	aient

■ Impersonal expressions also have imperfect tense forms.

infinitive	present	imperfect	
neiger	il neige	**il neigeait**	*it was snowing*
pleuvoir	il pleut	**il pleuvait**	*it was raining*
falloir	il faut	**il fallait**	*it was necessary*
valoir mieux	il vaut mieux	**il valait mieux**	*it was better*

■ **Être** is the only verb that has an irregular stem: **ét-.** The endings are regular.

J'**étais** malade.
Nous **étions** désolés.

■ The **je, tu, il/elle/on,** and **ils/elles** forms of the imperfect all sound alike because the endings are all pronounced the same.

je **jouais**　　tu **jouais**　　il **jouait**　　elles **jouaient**

■ The **-ions** and **-iez** endings are pronounced as one syllable, with the letter **-i-** pronounced [j].

> Note that the **nous** and **vous** forms of the imperfect of most verbs are identical to the subjunctive forms. See Ch. 10, p. 283.

vous habit**iez**　　[a bi tje]
nous all**ions**　　[a ljɔ̃]

■ You have already learned that if the present tense stem of a verb ends in **-g,** an **-e-** is added before endings beginning with **-o-.** This is also true in other tenses before endings beginning with **-a-** or **-u-.**

present:　nous mang**e**ons
imperfect:　je mang**e**ais　　tu mang**e**ais　　il mang**e**ait　　ils mang**e**aient
(*But:* nous mangions, vous mangiez)

■ Similarly, if the stem of a verb ends in **-c,** a **-ç-** is used instead before endings beginning with **-a-, -o-,** or **-u-.**

present:　nous commen**ç**ons
imperfect:　je commen**ç**ais　　tu commen**ç**ais　　il commen**ç**ait
(*But:* nous commencions, vous commenciez)

Les petits Français commencent l'école plus tôt que les petits Américains. Ils peuvent entrer à l'école maternelle à l'âge de deux ans.

Quand ils étaient jeunes. Qu'est-ce que ces personnes faisaient ou ne faisaient pas quand elles étaient jeunes? Si vous ne savez pas, devinez. Utilisez **et** ou **mais** et la forme négative pour les décrire.

> **MODÈLE:** mes amis / aller à l'école / conduire
> **Quand mes amis étaient jeunes, ils allaient à l'école mais ils ne conduisaient pas.**

1. mes amis / regarder souvent des dessins animés / lire beaucoup
2. nous / aller à l'école / faire toujours nos devoirs
3. je / manger beaucoup de bonbons / avoir souvent mal aux dents
4. je / me coucher tôt / être toujours raisonnable
5. mes parents / se connaître depuis longtemps / sortir ensemble
6. le professeur de français / avoir de bonnes notes / aller souvent à la bibliothèque

2 Ma grand-mère. Transformez le paragraphe suivant à l'imparfait.

Ma grand-mère habite dans une petite maison qui est très jolie et qui a deux chambres. Dans cette région, il pleut souvent et en hiver, quand il neige, on reste à la maison. Ma grand-mère est fragile et elle travaille très peu. Elle est petite et assez vieille. Elle a soixante-quinze ans et elle est seule à la maison depuis la mort de mon grand-père. Mais quand je vais chez elle, nous parlons de beaucoup de choses et quelquefois nous chantons. Elle veut toujours nous préparer quelque chose à manger, mais je fais la cuisine moi-même. Ensuite nous mangeons ensemble. Je l'aime beaucoup et elle m'aime beaucoup aussi.

3 Quand vous aviez quatorze ans. Répondez.

1. Qui était président des États-Unis quand vous aviez quatorze ans?
2. Quelles émissions regardiez-vous à la télé?
3. Quels acteurs et quelles actrices étaient populaires?
4. Quel âge avaient les autres membres de votre famille quand vous aviez quatorze ans?
5. Qu'est-ce que vous faisiez le vendredi soir?
6. Qu'est-ce que vous aimiez manger? Qu'est-ce que vous détestiez?
7. Qui faisait la cuisine pour vous?
8. À quelle école alliez-vous?
9. Comment s'appelaient vos voisins?

B. *Ne ... que*

Sylvie **n**'a **que** dix-huit ans.	*Sylvie is only eighteen.*
Ses parents **n**'ont **qu**'une fille.	*Her parents have only one daughter.*
Il **n**'y a **que** trois personnes dans la famille.	*There are only three people in the family.*

■ **Ne ... que,** a synonym of **seulement,** is used to express a limitation. **Ne** comes before the verb and **que** is placed directly before the expression that it limits.

Il **ne** sort **qu**'avec Renée.	*He goes out only with Renée.*
Il **ne** sort avec Renée **que** le vendredi soir.	*He goes out with Renée on Friday nights only.*

Review **il y a** + expressions of time, p. 159.

(4) **Quel âge avaient-ils il y a cinq ans?** Décidez quel âge tout le monde avait il y a cinq ans. Si vous ne savez pas *(If you don't know),* devinez. Utilisez **ne ... que.**

MODÈLE: votre frère **Il y a cinq ans, mon frère n'avait que seize ans.**

1. vous
2. votre meilleur(e) ami(e)
3. votre mère ou votre père
4. les étudiants de cette classe
5. votre acteur préféré
6. votre actrice préférée
7. le professeur de français (Imaginez.)

Entre amis

Quand tu étais enfant

1. Find out where your partner lived ten years ago.
2. Ask how old s/he was.
3. Ask what s/he did on Saturdays.
4. Find out what her/his school's name was.
5. Ask if s/he had a dog or a cat. If so, find out its name.
6. Find out who his/her neighbors were.

2 Setting the Scene in the Past

Quand vous êtes arrivé(e) sur ce campus pour la première fois ...

c'était en quelle saison?
c'était en quel mois?
quel âge aviez-vous?
étiez-vous seul(e) ou avec des amis?
quel temps faisait-il?
quels vêtements portiez-vous?

C. L'imparfait et le passé composé

Review the passé composé, pp. 157 and 188–189.

■ The **imparfait** is often used to give background information that "sets the scene" for some other verb in the past. This scene-setting information describes what was going on. It describes the conditions surrounding some other action. If the other verb specifies what *happened,* it is in the **passé composé.**

J'étais en train de faire mes devoirs quand **Alain a téléphoné.**	*I was (busy) doing my homework when Alain telephoned.*
Il était huit heures quand **Renée est arrivée.**	*It was eight o'clock when Renée arrived.*
Jeanne avait quinze ans quand **elle a commencé** à fréquenter les garçons.	*Jeanne was fifteen when she started dating boys.*

■ For weather expressions:

• Use the **imperfect** when the weather sets the scene for another past action.

Il faisait beau quand **nous sommes sortis.**   *It was nice outside when we went out.*

Il pleuvait quand **nous sommes rentrés.**   *It was raining when we got home.*

Il neigeait. Alors **Karine a décidé** de porter ses bottes.   *It was snowing. So Karine decided to wear her boots.*

• Use the **passé composé** when you simply state what the weather was like at a specific time.

Hier, **il a plu** à Paris, mais **il a neigé** dans les montagnes. **Il a fait beau** à Nice.

5 **Qu'est-ce qu'elle faisait?** Utilisez les expressions suivantes pour créer des phrases logiques.

MODÈLE: **Léa faisait du ski quand elle est tombée.**

	être en train d'étudier		entrer
	regarder la télévision		partir
	être en train de lire	son fiancé	arriver
	conduire	ses parents	tomber
Léa	manger	je	avoir un accident
	boire	quand elle	perdre patience
	faire la sieste	nous	téléphoner
	écrire une lettre	ses amis	
	prendre le petit déjeuner		
	descendre d'une voiture		

6 **Les Lauprête ont fait un voyage.** Quel temps faisait-il? Complétez les phrases suivantes.

MODÈLE: faire du vent / sortir de chez eux
Il faisait du vent quand les Lauprête sont sortis de chez eux.

1. pleuvoir / prendre le taxi
2. faire beau / arriver à l'aéroport
3. faire chaud / monter dans l'avion
4. faire froid / descendre de l'avion
5. neiger / commencer à faire du ski

7 **Dernière sortie au restaurant.** Décrivez la dernière fois que vous êtes allé(e) au restaurant.

1. Quel jour est-ce que c'était?
2. Quel temps faisait-il?
3. Quels vêtements portiez-vous?
4. Quelle heure était-il quand vous êtes arrivé(e)?
5. Étiez-vous seul(e)? Si non, qui était avec vous?
6. Environ combien de personnes y avait-il au restaurant?
7. Quelle était la spécialité du restaurant?
8. Comment était le serveur (la serveuse)?
9. Aviez-vous très faim?
10. Qu'est-ce que vous avez commandé?
11. Comment était le repas?

UN SIECLE DE MOULES ET DE FRITES, ÇA SE FÊTE !

Léon de Bruxelles a 100 ans ! En famille ou entre amis, profitez de ce centenaire pour découvrir nos savoureuses spécialités de moules, nos plats gourmands typiquement belges ... sans oublier nos inimitables frites ! Chez Léon de Bruxelles, on fait la fête tous les jours !

Léon de Bruxelles 1893

La Brasserie Belge

8 **Renseignements.** Écrivez un petit paragraphe pour chaque numéro. Expliquez les conditions et ce qui est arrivé.

MODÈLE: Quand je suis tombé(e), ...
(Qu'est-ce que vous faisiez? Avec qui étiez-vous? Qu'est-ce que vous avez dit?)
Quand je suis tombé(e), je faisais du ski. J'étais seul(e) et j'ai dit «Aïe!».

1. Quand j'ai trouvé mon ami, ...
(Qu'est-ce qu'il portait? Où allait-il? Avec qui était-il? Qu'est-ce que vous avez fait?)
2. Quand ma mère a téléphoné, ...
(Quelle heure était-il? Que faisiez-vous? Qu'est-ce qu'elle voulait? Qu'est-ce que vous avez répondu?)
3. Quand mon cousin (mon ami(e), mon frère, etc.) a eu son accident, ...
(Où était-il? Qu'est-ce qu'il faisait? Quel âge avait-il? Quel temps faisait-il? Qu'est-ce qu'il a fait après?)
4. Quand je suis entré(e) dans la classe, ...
(Quelles personnes étaient là? Qu'est-ce qu'elles portaient? Quelle heure était-il? Avec qui avez-vous parlé?)

Entre amis

Tu t'es bien amusé(e)?

1. Find out when the last time was that your partner went out.
2. Ask where s/he went and what s/he did.
3. Find out what s/he was wearing.
4. Find out what the weather was like.
5. Ask if s/he had fun.
6. Ask at what time s/he got home.
7. Find out if s/he was tired when s/he got home.

Que faisiez-vous
à cet âge-là?

3 Making Comparisons

Est-ce que ta vie était différente quand tu avais
seize ans, Christine?

Pas vraiment. À cette époque°, je
travaillais autant° que maintenant.
Et j'étudiais aussi° souvent que
maintenant.
Mais j'étais moins° active.
Et j'avais plus° de soucis°.

Back then
as much
as

less
more / worries

▶ Et vous?

Quand vous n'aviez que seize ans, ...
est-ce que vous étudiiez moins que maintenant?
faisiez-vous autant de sport?
aviez-vous plus de temps libre que maintenant?
est-ce que vous aviez moins de soucis?
étiez-vous plus heureux (heureuse) que maintenant?
étiez-vous aussi grand(e)?
sortiez-vous plus souvent que maintenant?
est-ce que vous parliez aussi couramment° le   *fluently*
   français?

D. Le comparatif

■ To make comparisons, the French use the words **plus** *(more)* and **moins** *(fewer; less)*. They also use **autant** *(as much; as many)* for comparing verbs and nouns and **aussi** *(as)* for comparing adjectives and adverbs. All comparatives may be followed by **que** *(than, as)* and a second term of comparison.

Donald a plus d'argent (**que** d'amis).	*Donald has more money (than friends).*
Je travaille autant (**que** lui).	*I work as much (as he).*
Guy parle moins souvent avec moi (**qu'**avec Anne).	*Guy talks less often with me (than with Anne).*
Éric est aussi pauvre (**qu'**avant).	*Éric is as poor (as before).*

> **Review the forms of stressed pronouns, Ch. 6, p.168.**

Note   When a personal pronoun is required after **que,** a stress pronoun is used.

Tu bois plus de café **que moi.**	*You drink more coffee than I.*
Nous avons moins d'enfants **qu'eux.**	*We have fewer children than they.*

■ To compare how much of a particular action people do, the words **plus, moins,** and **autant** are used *after a verb.*

René **parle plus** que son père.	*René talks more than his father.*
Il **parle moins** que sa mère.	*He talks less than his mother.*
Il **parle autant** que moi.	*He talks as much as I.*

> **Review the use of expressions of quantity, Ch. 8, p. 222.**

■ To compare how much of something one has, eats, drinks, etc., the expressions of quantity **plus de, moins de,** and **autant de** are used *before a noun.*

Je mangeais **plus de pommes** que d'oranges.	*I used to eat more apples than oranges.*
André a **moins de soucis** qu'il y a trois ans.	*André has fewer worries than three years ago.*
J'ai **autant de responsabilités** que vous.	*I have as many responsibilities as you.*

■ To compare descriptions of people, things, or actions, the words **plus, moins,** and **aussi** are used *before an adjective or an adverb.*

Je suis **plus âgé** que mon frère.	*I am older than my brother.*
Ma mère est **moins grande** que mon père.	*My mother is not as tall as my father.*
Lisa parle **aussi couramment** que Pierre.	*Lisa speaks as fluently as Pierre.*

Monique a quinze jours de vacances. Décidez si Monique a plus, moins ou autant de vacances que les autres.

> **MODÈLE:** Ses parents ont un mois de vacances.
> **Monique a moins de vacances qu'eux.**

1. Alice a huit jours de vacances.
2. Nous avons deux mois de vacances.
3. Tu as un jour de vacances.
4. Son frère a deux semaines de vacances.
5. Vous avez trente jours de vacances.
6. Je n'ai pas de vacances.
7. Michel et Jean ont trois mois de vacances.
8. Philippe a une semaine de vacances.
9. Ses amies ont quinze jours de vacances.

🔟 **À mon avis.** Utilisez un élément de chaque colonne pour faire des phrases logiques.

> **MODÈLES:** **À mon avis, les étudiants ont autant de soucis que les professeurs.**
> **À mon avis, ma mère conduit aussi rapidement que mon père.**

les étudiants / les professeurs			responsabilités
ma mère / mon père		plus (de)	soucis
le président des États-Unis / moi	avoir	moins (de)	argent
mes amis / moi		autant (de)	travail
les femmes / les hommes			temps libre
un patron / un employé			
un pilote / une hôtesse de l'air	conduire	plus	rapidement
les parents / les enfants		moins	prudemment
nous / notre professeur		aussi	attentivement
			nerveusement
			follement

⓫ **À mon avis et de l'avis du professeur.** Donnez votre opinion et devinez l'opinion du professeur. Attention aux adjectifs!

> **MODÈLE:** la musique classique / la musique pop / beau
> **À mon avis, la musique pop est aussi belle que la musique classique.**
> **De l'avis du professeur, la musique classique est plus belle que la musique pop.**

1. la statue de la Liberté / la tour Eiffel / beau
2. les jeunes filles / les garçons / travailleur
3. cette université / l'université de Paris / important
4. une moto / un vélo / dangereux
5. un chien / un chat / intelligent
6. un examen / un médicament / affreux
7. un restaurant français / un restaurant mexicain / chic
8. la télévision / un livre / ennuyeux

Entre amis

Il y a dix ans

1. Find out where your partner lived ten years ago.
2. Find out if s/he had more free time than now.
3. Find out if s/he had fewer worries.
4. Find out if s/he had more friends.
5. Find out if s/he had as much homework.
6. Find out if s/he spoke French as fluently.

E. Le comparatif de *bon* et de *bien*

Danielle est une **meilleure** étudiante que sa sœur.	*Danielle is a better student than her sister.*
Elle conduit **mieux** que sa sœur.	*She drives better than her sister.*

■ The comparative forms of the *adjective* **bon(ne)** are **moins bon(ne), aussi bon(ne),** and **meilleur(e).** Like all adjectives, these agree with the noun they modify.

Est-ce que sa sœur est **aussi bonne** que Danièle?	*Is her sister as good as Danièle?*
Non, comme étudiante, elle est **moins bonne.**	*No, as a student, she's worse.*
Danièle est **meilleure.**	*Danièle is better.*

■ The comparative forms of the adverb **bien** are **moins bien, aussi bien,** and **mieux.** Like all adverbs, these are invariable.

Review the distinction between adjectives and adverbs in Appendix C at the end of the book.

Marc travaille **moins bien** que Paul.	*Marc doesn't work as well as Paul.*
Monique travaille **aussi bien** que Paul.	*Monique works as well as Paul.*
Marc travaille bien. Paul travaille **mieux.**	*Marc works well. Paul works better.*
Chantal chante **mieux** que son frère.	*Chantal sings better than her brother.*

Attention

1. Both French and English have two separate words to distinguish between an adjective and an adverb when indicating quality.

Pascal est un **bon** étudiant.	Pascal parle **bien** le français.
*Pascal is a **good** student.*	*Pascal speaks French **well.***

2. In English, however, the comparative form of both *good* and *well* is the same word: *better.* In French, there is still a separate word for each.

Tom est un **meilleur** étudiant.	Tom parle **mieux** le français.
*Tom is a **better** student.*	*Tom speaks French **better.***

12 **Deux frères.** Pauvre François! Son frère David fait toujours mieux que lui. Comparez-les.

> **Modèle:** François est bon en anglais.
> **Oui, mais son frère David est meilleur en anglais que lui.**

1. François parle bien l'anglais.
2. François a une bonne voiture.
3. François a une bonne note en anglais.
4. François joue bien au tennis.
5. François conduit attentivement.
6. François est un bon étudiant.
7. François chante bien.
8. François est intelligent.

13 **Nos meilleurs amis et nous.** D'abord faites une comparaison entre vous et votre meilleur(e) ami(e). Ensuite encouragez votre partenaire à faire la même chose.

> **Modèle:** chanter bien
>
> **VOUS:** Moi, je chante mieux que mon meilleur ami (ma meilleure amie). Et toi?
> **VOTRE PARTENAIRE:** Moi, je chante moins bien que lui (qu'elle).

1. être bon(ne) en maths
2. parler bien le français
3. être patient(e)
4. conduire bien
5. être un(e) bon(ne) étudiant(e)
6. être grand(e)
7. danser bien
8. être bavard(e)

F. Le superlatif

Mathusalem est **la personne la plus âgée** de la Bible.
Job est **la personne la moins impatiente** de la Bible.
Le Rhode Island est **le plus petit état** des États-Unis.
Les Canadiens sont **les meilleurs joueurs** de hockey du monde.

■ Superlatives are preceded by a definite article and may be used with an expression including **de** *(in, of)* plus a noun to make the extent of the superlative clear.

C'est **la meilleure** chanson (**de** l'année).	*It's the best song (of the year).*
De tous les étudiants, c'est lui qui étudie **le plus attentivement.**	*Of all the students, he's the one who studies the most attentively.*
Elle voyage **le moins** (**de** sa famille).	*She travels the least (in her family).*
De tous les enfants, c'est Joël qui a demandé **le plus** de cadeaux.	*Of all the children, it's Joël who asked for the most gifts.*

■ With the superlative of an adverb, a verb, or an expression of quantity, **le** is always used.

De tous les membres de ma famille, c'est mon frère qui fait *le* **plus de voyages.**	*Of all my family members, it's my brother who takes the most trips.*
Ma sœur voyage *le* **moins.**	*My sister travels the least.*
Elle voyage *le* **moins fréquemment.**	*She travels the least frequently.*

■ With a superlative *adjective,* the definite article agrees with the adjective.

le plus petit   la plus petite
le moins grand   la moins grande

les plus petits   les plus petites
les moins grands   les moins grandes

Review the adjectives that normally precede a noun, Ch. 4, pp. 106–107.

Note   Superlative adjectives are placed either before or after the noun according to where they would be placed normally.

1. If the adjective follows the noun, the definite article must be repeated.

La Tour d'Argent est *le restaurant le plus chic* de Paris.
Les romans policiers sont *les romans les plus intéressants.*
Sandrine est *l'étudiante la moins paresseuse.*

2. If the adjective precedes the noun, only one definite article is used.

Paris et Lyon sont *les plus grandes villes* de France.
Le français est *la plus belle langue* du monde.
C'est *le moins bon restaurant* de la ville.

14 **Quelle exagération!** Aimez-vous votre cours de français? Exagérez un peu. Utilisez le superlatif dans les phrases suivantes.

MODÈLE: C'est un cours important.
            C'est le cours le plus important du monde!

Try to use other endings besides **du monde.** For instance, **de l'université, des États-Unis,** etc.

1. C'est un cours intéressant.
2. C'est un bon cours.
3. C'est un professeur intelligent.
4. Ce sont des étudiants travailleurs.
5. Ce sont de bons étudiants.
6. Ce sont de belles étudiantes.
7. Ce sont de beaux étudiants.
8. C'est un livre bizarre.

15 **Quel est le plus … ?** Répondez à ces questions. Si vous ne savez pas, devinez.

MODÈLE: Quel est le plus grand état des États-Unis?
            L'Alaska est le plus grand état des États-Unis.

1. Quelle est la plus grande ville des États-Unis? du Canada?
2. Quelle est la plus grande ville francophone du monde après Paris?
3. Qui est la meilleure actrice de votre pays?
4. Quel est le film le plus ennuyeux de cette année?
5. Qui est la femme politique la plus célèbre du monde?
6. Qui est la personne la moins âgée de cette classe?
7. Quelle est l'émission de télévision la plus intéressante le jeudi soir?

16 **Rien que des superlatifs!** Donnez votre opinion personnelle. Faites des phrases au superlatif.

> MODÈLES: un bon restaurant (de la ville)
> **Joe's Diner est le meilleur restaurant de la ville.**
>
> un sport intéressant (du monde)
> **Le golf est le sport le plus intéressant du monde.**

1. une bonne actrice (de mon pays)
2. un professeur charmant (de cette université)
3. un film ennuyeux (de cette année)
4. un bel acteur (de mon pays)
5. une mauvaise chanson (de cette année)
6. une personne amusante (de ma famille)

17 **Microconversation: Tu n'es jamais d'accord** (in agreement) **avec moi.** Utilisez les expressions suivantes pour compléter la conversation.

Review the gesture for **non**, Ch. 2, p. 30.

> MODÈLE: le meilleur restaurant
> VOTRE PARTENAIRE: **Quel est le meilleur restaurant de la ville?**
> VOUS: **C'est le restaurant qui s'appelle** *Chez Tony.*
> VOTRE PARTENAIRE: **Mais non! C'est le plus mauvais restaurant.**
> VOUS: **Tu n'es jamais d'accord avec moi!**

Tu as raison

1. le meilleur bistro de la ville
2. le cours le plus intéressant de cette université
3. le bâtiment le plus laid de cette université
4. la plus belle ville du pays
5. le meilleur supermarché de la ville
6. le professeur le plus charmant de cette université

18 **À vous.** Répondez.

1. Quel est le mois que vous aimez le mieux? Pourquoi?
2. Quel est le mois que vous aimez le moins? Pourquoi?
3. Quelle est l'émission de radio que vous écoutez le plus? Pourquoi l'écoutez-vous?
4. Quelle est l'émission de télévision que vous regardez le plus?
5. Quelle est la meilleure équipe de football de votre pays?
6. Qui fait le mieux la cuisine de votre famille?
7. Qui est la personne la plus gentille de votre famille?
8. Quelle personne conduit le plus rapidement de votre famille?

A useful structure is ... **que j'aime le mieux (le plus, le moins).**
Le printemps est la saison **que j'aime le mieux.**
L'hiver est la saison **que j'aime le moins.**

Entre amis

Description d'une famille

1. Find out how many people there are in your partner's family.
2. Find out who is the oldest, tallest, shortest, youngest.
3. Find out who sings the best, who dances the best.
4. Find out who is the most generous and who is the most stingy.
5. Find out who gives the most presents and who gives the least.

Intégration

Révision

A Quelles différences!

1. Nommez trois choses que vous faisiez quand vous étiez à l'école secondaire et que vous ne faites plus maintenant.
2. Nommez trois différences entre vous et un autre membre de votre famille.
3. Quelles différences y a-t-il entre un chien et un chat?
4. Quelles différences y a-t-il entre un avion et un train?

B Un sondage. Complétez le formulaire suivant.

1. Le plus bel homme du monde: _____
2. La plus belle femme du monde: _____
3. Le meilleur groupe rock: _____
4. Le meilleur chanteur: _____
5. La meilleure chanteuse: _____
6. La meilleure émission de télévision: _____
7. L'émission la moins intéressante: _____
8. Le meilleur film: _____
9. Le livre le plus intéressant: _____
10. Le sport que vous aimez le mieux: _____
11. La personne que vous admirez le plus: _____
12. Le moment le plus ennuyeux de votre journée: _____

C À vous. Répondez.

1. Quel âge aviez-vous quand vous avez commencé vos études au lycée?
2. Où habitiez-vous à cette époque?
3. Avez-vous changé d'adresse depuis?
4. Combien de personnes y avait-il dans votre famille?
5. Quelle était votre émission de télévision préférée?
6. Comment s'appelait votre meilleur(e) ami(e)?
7. Quelle était la chanson la plus populaire quand vous étiez au lycée?
8. Quels cours aimiez-vous le mieux quand vous étiez au lycée? Pourquoi?
9. Écoutiez-vous la radio aussi souvent que maintenant?

Pas de problème!

Preparation for the video:
1. Video worksheet in the *Cahier d'activités*
2. CD-ROM, *Module 8*

Cette activité est basée sur la vidéo, *Module 8*. Choisissez la bonne réponse pour compléter les phrases suivantes.

1. Noël doit payer _____ francs pour faire le plein d'essence *(gas)*.
   (105, 115, 150)
2. Noël vient d'acheter _____.
   (une nouvelle voiture, une nouvelle batterie, un nouveau système électrique)
3. Émile va regarder. Il faut qu'il ouvre _____.
   (le capot *(hood)*, le système électrique, la batterie)
4. La voiture ne démarre pas parce que _____ ne marche *(work)* pas.
   (le capot, le système électrique, la batterie)
5. Émile peut la réparer _____.
   (tout de suite, ce soir, demain)
6. Sur l'autoroute, la vitesse est limitée à _____ kilomètres à l'heure.
   (300, 130, 103)
7. Sur les routes nationales, la vitesse est limitée à _____ kilomètres à l'heure.
   (70, 80, 90)

Lecture I

A Étude du vocabulaire. Étudiez les phrases suivantes et choisissez les mots anglais qui correspondent aux mots français en caractères gras: *especially, earth, to send, when, rather, beyond, around, full, happiness.*

1. Quel **bonheur lorsque** les étudiants sont en vacances!
2. Elle était fatiguée **au-delà** des limites de ses forces.
3. Les tasses étaient **remplies** de café.
4. Il faisait froid? Non, il faisait **plutôt** chaud.
5. La **terre** de l'Iowa est fertile, **surtout** quand elle est noire.
6. Marie va **envoyer** une lettre à sa mère.
7. Marc a regardé **autour** de lui pour voir s'il connaissait des gens.

B Parcourez cette sélection. Lisez rapidement la lecture suivante pour trouver un ou deux exemples de l'amour et du courage d'Aïda.

La Grand-mère Aïda

Marie-Célie Agnant est née à Port-au-Prince, en Haïti, mais habite actuellement à Montréal. Dans **La Dot de Sara** *(Sara's Dowry) elle raconte l'histoire de quatre générations de femmes haïtiennes.*

Grand-mère Aïda c'était comme la bonne terre. Amoureuse de la vie, généreuse et intelligente. Elle donnait, donnait, la femme Aïda, pour le plaisir de donner, pour l'amour de l'amour, l'amour de la tendresse, pour l'amour sans raison d'aimer, au-delà de la raison et de l'amour, cet amour de la vie pour ce qu'elle est véritablement: trésor, mystère, beauté, bonheur simple dans le tourbillon[1] de l'existence, au milieu des siens[2]: enfants, petits-enfants, nièces et neveux. Aïda, les jupes toujours remplies d'enfants. Et lorsque j'y pense, au fait, qu'avait-elle d'autre, qu'avions-nous d'autre? ...

Grand-mère Aïda m'avait élevée au doigt et à la baguette[3], comme cela se faisait dans ce temps-là. Ma mère à moi, Man Clarisse, n'avait pas survécu à ma naissance[4]. Elle avait été emportée par une septicémie[5], dit-on, quelque temps après que je sois née et n'avait jamais voulu révéler le nom de celui qui l'avait mise en mal d'enfant[6]. Elle avait alors vingt ans. Comme tant d'autres, elle avait dû se dire que les enfants, c'est plutôt l'affaire des femmes. Il y avait autour de nous et avec nous cette communauté de commères, matantes et marraines[7], qui étaient pour moi comme autant de mamans. Elle avait tenu[8], grand-mère, à m'envoyer à l'école. À l'époque, c'était un grand pas[9], comme on dit, car les petites filles—et croyez-moi, cela n'a pas beaucoup changé—on les gardait surtout pour aider à la maison, ou à faire marcher le commerce. L'école, lorsqu'on le pouvait, on y envoyait plutôt les futurs messieurs. S'il y avait quelque argent à investir, mieux valait l'employer à garnir la caboche[10] des petits hommes, ceux qui, pensait-on, devaient par la suite sauver la famille de la faim en devenant agronomes[11], avocats, ingénieurs, et peut-être même médecins.

Envoyer les enfants à l'école, c'était, disait-on, comme mettre de l'argent en banque. J'y suis allée, moi, jusqu'à la deuxième année du secondaire, puis à l'école d'économie domestique du bourg, chez madame Souffrant. C'était énorme.

Marie-Célie Agnant, *La Dot de Sara*

---

1. *whirlwind*   2. *surrounded by her family*   3. *had raised me strictly*   4. *hadn't survived my birth*
5. *blood poisoning*   6. *the one who had made her pregnant*   7. *neighbors, aunts and godmothers*
8. *had insisted on*   9. *step*   10. *head*   11. *by becoming agricultural specialists*

 Vrai ou faux? Décidez si les phrases suivantes sont vraies ou fausses. Si une phrase est fausse, corrigez-la.

1. La narratrice est la fille d'Aïda.
2. On sait le nom du père de la narratrice.
3. Elle a sans doute appris à faire la cuisine dans une école spécialisée.
4. Sa mère était assez âgée quand elle est morte.
5. Les garçons devaient, plus tard, gagner de l'argent pour la famille.
6. Il était normal que les filles fassent des études.
7. Aïda s'occupait de beaucoup d'enfants.

Discussions. Relisez la lecture et cherchez des exemples ...

1. pour comparer Aïda et les grands-mères que vous avez connues.
2. de généralisations/stéréotypes en ce qui concerne les hommes et les femmes.
3. de ressemblances ou de différences entre la culture haïtienne et la culture de votre pays.

E **Familles de mots.** Essayez de deviner le sens des mots suivants.

1. aimer, l'amour, aimable, amoureux (amoureuse)
2. naître, la naissance, né(e)
3. raisonner, la raison, raisonnable
4. la vérité, véritable, véritablement, vrai(e)

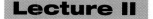

Lecture II

A **Parcourez les annonces personnelles.** Lisez rapidement la lecture pour identifier 1. la personne la plus âgée et 2. la personne la plus égoïste.

ANNONCES PERSONNELLES	
Jeune homme, 20 ans, bien physiquement et moralement, bonne situation[1], cherche en vue mariage jeune fille 18–22 ans, réponse assurée, joindre photo qui sera retournée. Ecr. Réf. 5093	Jeune fille, 27 ans, désire rencontrer jeune homme, âge en rapport[2], joindre photo si possible. Ecr. Réf. 5095
Dame agréable, élégante, sans enfants, jeune de cœur[3], désire rencontrer, pour sorties amicales, Monsieur, cinquante–soixante ans, bien[4] sous tous rapports[5], libre, optimiste, aimant[6] la nature, joindre photo qui sera retournée, discrétion absolue, mariage exclu. Ecr. Réf. 5094	Homme, 37 ans, propriétaire appartement, voiture, passé irréprochable, intelligent, éducation, très gentil cœur, très sympathique[7], se marierait[8] av. J.F., même[9] secrétaire, ouvrière, mais affectueuse, douce[10], très sincère, réponse assurée dans l'immédiat, discrétion. Ecr. Réf. 5096

1. *job* 2. *similar* 3. *heart* 4. *nice* 5. *in every respect* 6. *who likes* 7. *likeable* 8. *would marry* 9. *even* 10. *sweet*

B **Vrai ou faux?** Relisez les annonces personnelles et ensuite décidez si les phrases suivantes sont vraies ou fausses. Si une phrase est fausse, corrigez-la.

1. Tous les auteurs des annonces parlent de mariage.
2. Ils demandent tous qu'une photo accompagne la réponse.
3. La plus jeune personne travaille.
4. Les deux femmes sont moins discrètes que les deux hommes.
5. La personne la plus riche est une femme.
6. La personne la plus matérialiste est un homme.

 Inventez une annonce personnelle. Inventez une annonce pour vous ou pour un(e) ami(e). Utilisez la lecture comme modèle.

VOCABULAIRE ACTIF

Noms

un chanteur/une chanteuse *singer*
un dessin animé *cartoon*
une émission (de télé) *(TV) program*
une équipe *team*
une hôtesse de l'air *(female) flight attendant*
un lycée *senior high school*
le maire *mayor*
la mairie *town hall*
le mariage *marriage; wedding*
un pilote *pilot*
une responsabilité *responsibility*
une robe de mariée *wedding dress*
un smoking *tuxedo*
un souci *worry; care*
une statue *statue*
un tour *turn, tour*
une tour *tower*
un voisin/une voisine *neighbor*

Pour faire une comparaison

aussi ... *as ...*
autant *as much*
mieux *better*
moins *less*
plus *more*

Adjectifs

âgé(e) *old*
amusant(e) *amusing, funny; fun*
dangereux (dangereuse) *dangerous*
meilleur(e) *better*
pauvre *poor*
populaire *popular*
préféré(e) *favorite*
sincère *sincere*

Verbes

avoir lieu *to take place*
en avoir assez *to be fed up*
épouser (quelqu'un) *to marry (someone)*
être en train de *to be in the process of*
fréquenter (quelqu'un) *to date (someone)*
neiger *to snow*
pleuvoir *to rain*

Expressions utiles

à cette époque *at that time; back then*
à mon (ton, etc.) avis *in my (your, etc.) opinion*
Comme il (elle) était ... ! *How ... he (she) was!*
huit jours *one week*
il neigeait *it was snowing*
il pleuvait *it was raining*
j'aime le mieux (le plus) *I like best*
j'aime le moins *I like least*
ne ... que *only*
Occupe-toi de tes oignons! *Mind your own business!*
parler couramment *to speak fluently*
quinze jours *two weeks*
toute la famille *the whole family*
tu vois *you see*

Buts communicatifs
Making a request
Making a restaurant or
  hotel reservation
Making a transportation
  reservation

Structures utiles
Le verbe **savoir**
Les verbes réguliers en
  -ir (-iss-)
L'adjectif **tout**
Le futur
Le futur avec **si** et
  quand

Culture
Pour répondre au
  téléphone
La politesse (rappel)
À l'hôtel
Mince!

Coup d'envoi

Prise de contact
Au restaurant ou à l'hôtel

Puis-je° réserver une table?   *May I*
    Pour combien de personnes?
    Pour quel jour?
    Et pour quelle heure?
    À quel nom°, s'il vous plaît?   *In what name*

Puis-je réserver une chambre?
    Pour combien de personnes?
    Pour quelle(s) nuit(s)?
    À quel nom, s'il vous plaît?

Faites de votre prochain voyage d'affaires une vraie partie de plaisir.

Appelez gratuitement le 0800 905 999 et nous vous enverrons tous les détails concernant Executive Extravaganza.

Holiday Inn®

8 MOIS DE DEFI ET D'INCROYABLES PRIX

en association avec *Hertz*   AMERICAN EXPRESS Cards

Conversation

Une réservation par téléphone

Joseph Smith téléphone pour réserver une table pour demain soir dans un restaurant à Angers. Mais le restaurant sera° fermé demain.

will be

Mme Dupont: Allô! Ici le restaurant La Pyramide. J'écoute.

Joseph Smith: Bonjour, Madame. Je voudrais réserver une table pour demain soir.

Mme Dupont: Je regrette, Monsieur. Nous serons fermés demain.

Joseph Smith: Mince!° Je ne savais pas° que vous fermiez le mardi. Qu'est-ce que je vais faire? Vous serez ouvert après-demain?°

Darn it! / I didn't know

You will be open the day after tomorrow?

Mme Dupont: Mais oui, Monsieur.

Joseph Smith: Bien, alors puis-je réserver une table pour après-demain?

Mme Dupont: Oui, c'est pour combien de personnes?

Joseph Smith: Cinq. Une table pour cinq personnes.

Mme Dupont: À quel nom, s'il vous plaît?

Joseph Smith: Au nom de Smith.

Mme Dupont: Pouvez-vous épeler° le nom, s'il vous plaît?

spell

Joseph Smith: S-M-I-T-H.

Mme Dupont: Et pour quelle heure?

Joseph Smith: Pour huit heures, si possible.

Mme Dupont: Très bien, Monsieur. C'est entendu°. Une table pour cinq pour vingt heures.

agreed

Joseph Smith: Je vous remercie° beaucoup. Au revoir, Madame.

thank

Mme Dupont: Au revoir, Monsieur. À mercredi soir.

Review the French alphabet on p. 4.

▶ **Jouez ces rôles.** Répétez la conversation avec votre partenaire. Utilisez vos propres *(own)* noms et demandez une réservation pour neuf heures. Faites tous les changements nécessaires.

Il y a un geste

Qu'est-ce que je vais faire? The mouth is open, with a look of exasperation. An alternate gesture is to expel air through slightly pursed lips.

Comment dit-on «second floor» en français?

a. le premier étage
b. le deuxième étage
c. le troisième étage

Pourquoi est-ce que Joseph dit «Mince!»?

a. Il n'est pas gros.
b. Il mange trop et doit maigrir *(lose weight).*
c. Il regrette que le restaurant ferme le mardi.

Pour répondre au téléphone

Allô is only used, in French, when responding to the phone. Likewise, **J'écoute** *(lit. I'm listening)* and **Qui est à l'appareil?** *(Who is on the phone?)* are appropriate in this context. See p. 175 for an example of the latter.

La politesse (rappel)

Remember to use **je voudrais,** and not **je veux,** when making a polite request. Respect and politeness will not fail to make a good impression in France. Conversely, impatience and lack of courtesy will be met with similar treatment. Review the polite expressions on p. 9.

À l'hôtel

Most French hotels have private bathrooms, but there are exceptions. It is still possible to find hotels in which the toilet and the showers are located down the hall from the room. However, every room will have a sink of its own.

The first floor of any French building is called **le rez-de-chaussée** and the second floor is **le premier étage.** If your room is **au deuxième étage,** you will need to climb two flights of stairs, not one. In an elevator, you must remember to press **RC** and not **1** if you wish to get to the ground floor.

In order to conserve electricity, many French hotels have installed **minuteries.** These are hall lights that stay lit for only one minute. Unsuspecting tourists are occasionally surprised to have the hall light go off before they can get their door key in the lock.

Mince!

This is one of a number of euphemisms used to avoid another "five-letter word." Other inoffensive expressions used to express disappointment are **zut!** and **flûte!** *(darn, shucks).*

À vous. Vous avez téléphoné à l'hôtel de Champagne pour réserver une chambre. Parlez avec la réceptionniste.

RÉCEPTIONNISTE: Allô! Ici l'hôtel de Champagne.
VOUS: _____
RÉCEPTIONNISTE: Ce soir?
VOUS: _____
RÉCEPTIONNISTE: Pour combien de personnes?
VOUS: _____
RÉCEPTIONNISTE: Et à quel nom?
VOUS: _____
RÉCEPTIONNISTE: Épelez le nom, s'il vous plaît.
VOUS: _____
RÉCEPTIONNISTE: Très bien. C'est entendu.
VOUS: _____

Entre amis

Vous êtes hôte/hôtesse au restaurant

You are speaking on the telephone to a customer. Your partner will take the role of the customer.

1. Ask if s/he wants to reserve a table.
2. Find out how many there are in the party.
3. Find out at what time s/he wishes to dine.
4. Find out his/her name.
5. Find out how to spell the name.
6. Repeat back the information you received.

Prononciation

Les sons [l] et [j]

■ You learned in Chapter 11 that the letter **l** in certain situations is pronounced [j], as in the English word *yes*. However, in many cases it is pronounced [l], as in the French word **la.**

■ While the [l] sound is somewhat close to the sound of **l** in the English word *like,* it is far from that in the English word *bull.* Special attention is therefore necessary when pronouncing [l], especially at the end of a word. To produce the [l] sound, the tongue must be in a curved, convex position. Practice saying the following words:

la   pilote   bleu   quel   elle

■ Now practice saying the following words after your instructor, paying particular attention to the highlighted sound. As you pronounce the words for one sound, look at how that sound is spelled and in what kinds of letter combinations it appears. What patterns do you notice?

Use the Student Audio to help practice pronunciation.

[j] • déta**il**, somme**il**, œ**il**, sole**il**, trava**ille**, ore**ille**, feu**ille**, me**ill**eur
     • genti**lle**, fi**lle**, pasti**lle**, vani**lle**, fami**lle**, cédi**lle**, jui**ll**et, bi**ll**et

[l] • **l**e, **l**a, **l**es, **l**'air, **l**à, **l**ycée, **l**aisser, **l**ent, **l**entement, **l**ongue
     • pi**l**ote, déso**l**é, faci**l**e, popu**l**aire, fidè**l**e, fo**l**ie, vo**l**ant, épau**l**e, pi**l**u**l**e
     • i**l**, ba**l**, posta**l**, que**l**
     • p**l**eut, p**l**us, b**l**eu, c**l**ient
     • do**ll**ar, inte**ll**igent, a**ll**emand, appe**ll**e, e**ll**e, fo**ll**e, mademoise**ll**e

■ Remember that the [j] sound is required for the letter **l** in the following circumstances:

1. **-il** or **-ill** after a pronounced vowel in the same syllable: trav**ail,** conse**iller**
2. **-ll** after [i]: fi**lle,** jui**ll**et

> Be sure to distinguish between **gentil** [ʒɑ̃ti] and **gentille** [ʒɑ̃tij].

Exceptions   million, milliard, mille, ville, tranquille, village

■ In a few words, the letter **l** is silent: genti**l,** fi**l**s

■ In all other cases, the letter **l** or the combination **ll** is pronounced as [l]—that is, at the beginning or end of a word, between two vowels, or following a consonant.

le   il   pilule   inutile   pleut   dollar

■ Pronounce the following sentences correctly.

1. Les lilas sont merveilleux.
2. Il habite dans un village près de Marseille.
3. Le soleil m'a fait mal aux yeux.
4. Aïe! J'ai mal à l'oreille!
5. Ma fille Hélène travaille au lycée.

Buts communicatifs

1 Making a Request

—C'est ici le bureau des renseignements°?   *information*
—Oui.
—Puis-je vous demander quelques renseignements?
—Mais certainement. Allez-y.
—Pourriez-vous me dire° où sont les toilettes?   *Could you tell me*
—Elles sont dans le couloir.
—Pouvez-vous m'indiquer où se trouve la gare?
—Oui, elle est tout près°. Quand vous sortirez,   *very near*
tournez à gauche dans la rue.
—Savez-vous° si le bureau de poste est ouvert toute   *Do you know*
la journée°?   *all day long*
—Oui, il reste ouvert. Il ne ferme pas à midi.
—Je voudrais savoir à quelle heure les banques
ferment.
—Elles ferment à 17 heures.
—La pharmacie est ouverte jusqu'à quelle heure?
—Jusqu'à 19 heures.
—Merci, vous êtes très aimable.
—De rien.° Je suis là pour ça.   *You're welcome.*

The final **-e** in **Puis-je ...** is silent: [pɥiʒ]. When inverted, **je** does not change before a vowel.

Remarque   When asking permission to do something, you may use **Est-ce que je peux ... ?** or **Puis-je ... ?**

Est-ce que je peux conduire?   *May I drive?*
Puis-je avoir un verre d'eau?   *May I have a glass of water?*

V O C A B U L A I R E

Pour demander un service

faire une demande	*to make a request*
poser une question	*to ask a question*
demander un renseignement	*to ask for information*
réserver une place	*to reserve a seat*
louer une voiture	*to rent a car*
recommander un bon restaurant	*to recommend a good restaurant*
commander un repas	*to order a meal*
confirmer un départ	*to confirm a departure*

❶ Allez-y! Utilisez la liste suivante pour faire une demande. Votre partenaire va vous donner la permission.

Modèle: ask you for information
    vous: **Est-ce que je peux vous demander un renseignement, s'il vous plaît?**
    votre partenaire: **Mais certainement.**   ou   **Allez-y!**

Bien sûr
Oui
Volontiers

1. speak with you
2. ask a question
3. ask something
4. read your newspaper
5. have a glass of water — *avoir*
6. order something
7. watch television

❷ Il n'y en a plus *(There are no more).* Utilisez les listes suivantes pour faire des demandes. Ensuite votre partenaire va expliquer qu'il n'y en a plus.

Modèle: **vous:** **Puis-je réserver une table?**
    votre partenaire: **Je regrette. Il n'y a plus de tables.**

	réserver	un journal
	louer	un verre d'eau
	commander	une chambre
puis-je	avoir	un vélo
	acheter	une tasse de café
	demander	une voiture
	boire	une place

The word **carte** has various meanings depending on the context: **carte postale** *(postcard)*, **jouer aux cartes** *(cards)*, **carte** *(map)* **de France**. In Ch. 13, it will be used in a restaurant setting: **à la carte**.

3 **Microconversation: Pour aller au château de Rigny.** Utilisez la carte *(map)* suivante pour expliquer quelles routes il faut prendre pour aller des villes indiquées au château de Rigny.

MODÈLE: la route de Paris au château de Rigny

> **TOURISTE:** **Puis-je vous demander un renseignement?**
> **GUIDE:** **Certainement. Allez-y.**
> **TOURISTE:** **Pouvez-vous m'indiquer la route de Paris au château de Rigny?**
> **GUIDE:** **Oui, regardez la carte. Prenez l'autoroute 6 et l'autoroute 38 jusqu'à Dijon et ensuite prenez la départementale 70 jusqu'au château de Rigny.**
> **TOURISTE:** **Je vous remercie. Vous êtes bien aimable.**

NOTE CULTURELLE
Les routes de France sont marquées **A** pour autoroute, **N** pour route nationale et **D** pour route départementale. On dit, par exemple, **l'autoroute A six, la nationale cinquante-sept** ou **la départementale quatre cent soixante-quinze**. Il faut payer pour utiliser l'autoroute.

[Map: routes including Reims, Nancy, Epinal, Langres, Combeaufontaine, Vesoul, Belfort, Troyes, Château de Rigny, Gray, Mulhouse, Belfort, Paris, Dijon, Beaune/Lyon, Genève/Dôle, Besançon, Lausanne/Suisse, with routes A.26, A.31, N.74, N.19, N.57, D.70, D.67, D.2, N.71, A.36, D.475, A.6, A.38, 376/190]

1. la route de Besançon au château de Rigny
2. la route de Langres au château de Rigny
3. la route de Vesoul au château de Rigny
4. la route de Troyes au château de Rigny
5. la route de Belfort au château de Rigny
6. la route de Nancy au château de Rigny

Entre amis

Quelques renseignements

You are a French-speaking tourist in your partner's hometown.

1. Find out if s/he speaks French.
2. Get permission to ask a question.
3. Find out if there is a hotel nearby.
4. Get directions to the hotel.
5. Ask if s/he can recommend a good restaurant.
6. Ask directions on how to get there.
7. Express your gratitude for her/his help.

A. Le verbe *savoir*

Cette femme **sait** bien **danser**. *That woman really knows how to dance.*

Savez-vous **comment** elle s'appelle? *Do you know her name?*
Je **sais que** son prénom est Sophie. *I know her first name is Sophie.*
Je ne **sais** pas **si** elle est célibataire. *I don't know if she is single.*

savoir *(to know)*			
je	**sais**	nous	**savons**
tu	**sais**	vous	**savez**
il/elle/on	**sait**	ils/elles	**savent**

passé composé: j'**ai su** *(I found out, I learned)*

- The verb **savoir** *(to know)* is used to express a skill or knowledge of a fact. It is used alone (**Je sais / Je ne sais pas**), or is followed by an infinitive, by the words **que** *(that)* or **si** *(if, whether)*, or by question words such as **où, comment, combien, pourquoi, quand, quel.**

Je ne **savais** pas **que** tu venais. *I didn't know that you were coming.*
Je ne **savais** pas **si** tu venais. *I didn't know whether you were coming.*
Je ne **savais** pas **quand** tu venais. *I didn't know when you were coming.*

Note   Followed by an infinitive, **savoir** means *to know how (to do something).*

Savez-vous parler espagnol? *Do you know how to speak Spanish?*

Review the use of **connaître**, Ch. 10, p. 277.

- The verbs **connaître** and **savoir** are used in different circumstances. Both are used with direct objects, but **connaître** (which means *to know* in the sense of *to be acquainted with, to be familiar with*) is used in general with people and places, while **savoir** is used with facts.

Vous **connaissez** ma sœur? *Do you know my sister?*
Je ne **sais** pas son nom. *I don't know her name.*

- The passé composé of **savoir** means *found out, learned.*

Je l'**ai su** hier. *I found it out yesterday.*

4 **C'est inutile** *(It's useless).* On suggère que vous demandiez quelques renseignements. Répondez que c'est inutile. Ensuite utilisez le verbe **savoir** pour expliquer pourquoi c'est inutile.

Modèle: Demandons à Jacques comment s'appelle cette jeune fille.
C'est inutile! Jacques ne sait pas comment elle s'appelle.

1. Demandons à Jacques si Jeanne va à la boum.
2. Demandons à nos amis où habite le professeur.
3. Demandons au professeur le nom de cette voiture.
4. Demandons à ces personnes quand le film va commencer.
5. Demandons à Jean-Michel où sont les toilettes.
6. Demandons à Françoise la date du concert.
7. Demandons à nos amis pourquoi ils sont déprimés.

5 **Une interview.** Interviewez votre partenaire. Attention aux verbes **savoir** et **connaître**.

MODÈLES: où j'habite

> VOUS: **Sais-tu où j'habite?**
>
> VOTRE PARTENAIRE: **Non, je ne sais pas où tu habites.** ou
> **Oui, je sais où tu habites.**

mes parents

> VOUS: **Connais-tu mes parents?**
>
> VOTRE PARTENAIRE: **Non, je ne les connais pas.** ou
> **Oui, je les connais.**

1. danser le tango
2. quelle heure il est
3. la famille du professeur
4. parler espagnol
5. la ville de Québec
6. mon adresse
7. pourquoi tu étudies le français
8. la différence entre **savoir** et **connaître**

MOI, JE SAIS OÙ JE VAIS.

ECOLE SUPERIEURE D'INFORMATIQUE DE COMMERCE ET DE GESTION

ESIG

6 **Un petit sketch: À la boum.** Lisez ou jouez le sketch suivant et ensuite répondez aux questions.

Georges parle avec son ami Thomas à la boum. Ils regardent une jeune fille.

GEORGES: Est-ce que tu connais cette jeune fille?

THOMAS: Oui, je la connais, mais je ne sais pas comment elle s'appelle.

GEORGES: Elle est jolie, n'est-ce pas?

THOMAS: Oui. Sais-tu si elle danse bien?

GEORGES: Je ne sais pas mais je vais l'inviter.

THOMAS: Bonne chance!

Questions (Répondez à l'imparfait):

1. Qui connaissait la jeune fille?
2. Savait-il comment elle s'appelait?
3. Qu'est-ce que Thomas voulait savoir?
4. Qu'est-ce que Georges allait faire?

7 **Vous connaissez ce restaurant?** Complétez les phrases suivantes avec la forme convenable de **savoir** ou de **connaître**.

1. _____-vous s'il y a un bon restaurant près d'ici?
2. Oui, je _____ un restaurant qui est excellent, mais je ne _____ pas s'il est ouvert le mardi.
3. Je vais téléphoner à mon frère. Il _____ bien la ville et il va certaine-ment _____ quel jour le restaurant est fermé. Est-ce que vous _____ mon frère?
4. Je le _____ un peu, mais je ne _____ pas comment il s'appelle.
5. Il s'appelle Paul. Vous _____ où nous habitons, n'est-ce pas?
6. Non, mais je _____ que ce n'est pas loin d'ici.

8 **À vous.** Répondez.

1. Connaissez-vous le président (la présidente) de votre université?
2. Savez-vous comment il (elle) s'appelle?
3. Vos parents savent-ils que vous étudiez le français?
4. Savent-ils à quelle heure vous allez au cours de français?
5. Connaissent-ils vos amis?
6. Vos amis savent-ils faire du ski?
7. Savez-vous s'ils étudient le français?
8. Connaissiez-vous ces amis quand vous étiez au lycée?
9. Est-ce qu'ils savent la date de votre anniversaire?
10. Saviez-vous parler français quand vous étiez au lycée?

Entre amis

Connais-tu X? Sais-tu si ... ?

1. Find out if your partner knows some person (name someone). Keep asking until you find someone s/he knows.
2. Ask if your partner knows if that person speaks French.
3. Ask if your partner knows that person's family.
4. Find out if your partner knows the person's age, address, whether s/he likes pizza, etc.

2 Making a Restaurant or Hotel Reservation

Il vous reste° des chambres, s'il vous plaît?   *Do you still have*
    Oui, pour combien de personnes?
    Non, je regrette. Nous sommes complets°.   *full*
Quel est le prix° d'une chambre avec salle de bain?   *price*
    ... euros par nuit.
Est-ce que le petit déjeuner est compris dans le
  prix de la chambre?
    Oui, tout est compris.
    Non, il y a un supplément° de 3 euros.   *extra charge*
Puis-je demander d'autres serviettes°?   *towels*
    Mais certainement.
    Je regrette. Il n'y en a plus.°   *There are no more.*

VOCABULAIRE

Review the distinction between **les toilettes** and **la salle de bain**, p. 154.

À l'hôtel

une clé	*key*	une serviette	*towel*
un couloir	*hallway*	un supplément	*extra charge*
une douche	*shower*	les toilettes	*restroom, toilet*
le premier étage	*second floor*	complet (complète)	*full*
le rez-de-chaussée	*first floor*	compris(e)	*included*
une salle de bain	*bathroom*		

 Microconversation: Il vous reste des chambres? Complétez la conversation avec les détails suivants. Décidez ensuite combien de chambres il vous faut.

MODÈLE: trois personnes / une nuit / 50€ (60€) / p.déj. (4€)

> **TOURISTE:** **Il vous reste des chambres?**
> **HÔTELIER:** **Oui, pour combien de personnes?**
> **TOURISTE:** **Pour trois personnes.**
> **HÔTELIER:** **Très bien. Pour combien de nuits?**
> **TOURISTE:** **Pour une seule nuit. Quel est le prix des chambres, s'il vous plaît?**
> **HÔTELIER:** **Cinquante euros pour une chambre pour une personne ou soixante euros pour une chambre pour deux personnes.**
> **TOURISTE:** **Est-ce que le petit déjeuner est compris?**
> **HÔTELIER:** **Non, il y a un supplément de quatre euros.**
> **TOURISTE:** **Très bien. Je vais prendre une chambre pour une personne et une chambre pour deux personnes.**

1. une personne / deux nuits / 40€ / p.déj. 5€
2. quatre personnes / une semaine / 45€ (60€) / tout compris
3. deux personnes / une nuit / 40€ (50€) / p.déj. 4€
4. vingt-cinq étudiants / un mois / 25€ (30€) / tout compris

 Si vous alliez à l'hôtel. Posez des questions. Votre partenaire va donner une réponse appropriée.

MODÈLE: You want to know if there are any rooms left.

> **VOUS:** **Est-ce qu'il vous reste des chambres?** ou **Avez-vous encore des chambres?**
> **VOTRE PARTENAIRE:** **Oui, certainement.**

You want to know ...

1. where the toilet is.
2. if there is a bathroom in the room.
3. if there is a shower in the bathroom.
4. if you can have extra towels.
5. how much the room costs.
6. if breakfast is included in the price.
7. at what time you can have breakfast.
8. if there is a television set in the room.

Entre amis

À l'hôtel Ibis

Your partner will take the role of a hotel clerk.

1. Find out if there are still rooms available.
2. Find out the price.
3. Find out if breakfast is included.
4. Ask if the toilet and shower are in the room.
5. Ask if you can have extra towels.

B. Les verbes réguliers en *-ir (-iss-)*

Qu'est-ce que vous **choisissez?**	*What do you choose?*
J'**ai** déjà **choisi** une pâtisserie.	*I have already chosen a pastry.*
Nous **finissons** à cinq heures.	*We finish at five o'clock.*
Obéis à ta mère!	*Obey your mother!*
Ralentissez, s'il vous plaît.	*Please slow down.*
Avez-vous **réussi** à votre examen?	*Did you pass your test?*

■ You have already learned several French verbs whose infinitives end in **-ir.**

sortir	je sors	nous sortons	ils sortent
partir	je pars	nous partons	ils partent
dormir	je dors	nous dormons	ils dorment

■ There is a larger group of French verbs that also have infinitives ending in **-ir** but that are conjugated differently.

choisir *(to choose)*					
je	**chois**	**is**	nous	**chois**	**issons**
tu	**chois**	**is**	vous	**chois**	**issez**
il/elle/on	**chois**	**it**	ils/elles	**chois**	**issent**

passé composé: j'**ai choisi**

■ Because there are a number of verbs formed in this way, these **-ir** verbs are said to be *regular*. The following verbs are conjugated like **choisir.**

VOCABULAIRE

Quelques verbes réguliers en *-ir (-iss-)*

finir	*to finish*
grossir	*to put on weight*
maigrir	*to take off weight*
obéir (à quelqu'un)	*to obey (someone)*
ralentir	*to slow down*
réussir (à un examen)	*to succeed; to pass (an exam)*

- When used with an infinitive, **finir** and **choisir** are followed by **de,** and **réussir** is followed by **à.**

  Nous **avons fini de** manger.   *We finished eating.*

  Karine **a choisi d'**aller au centre commercial.   *Karine decided to go to the mall.*

  Elle **a réussi à** trouver des desserts délicieux.   *She succeeded in finding delicious desserts.*

- The past participle of regular **-ir (-iss-)** verbs is formed by adding **-i** to the present tense verb stem.

  choisi   fini   obéi

Choisissez une orientation pour votre épargne.
Nos spécialistes feront le reste.

SOCIÉTÉ GÉNÉRALE

---

11   **Qu'est-ce qu'ils choisissent d'habitude?**   Posez la question et votre partenaire va répondre.

> **MODÈLE:**   tu / pâté ou soupe à l'oignon?
>
> **VOUS:**   **Est-ce que d'habitude tu choisis du pâté ou de la soupe à l'oignon?**
>
> **VOTRE PARTENAIRE:**   **D'habitude je choisis du pâté.**

Review the partitive article, p. 216.

1. tu / crudités, soupe ou pâté?
2. les végétariens / viande ou poisson?
3. les enfants / épinards ou frites?
4. le professeur de français / camembert ou fromage américain?
5. tes amis / glace, fruits, tarte ou gâteau?
6. tu / café ou thé?

12   **À vous.**   Répondez.

1. Est-ce que vous choisissez un dessert d'habitude?
2. Qu'est-ce que vous avez choisi comme dessert la dernière fois que vous avez dîné au restaurant?
3. Qu'est-ce que vos amis choisissent comme dessert?
4. Est-ce que vous avez tendance à grossir?
5. Réussissez-vous à maigrir quand vous voulez?
6. Que peut-on choisir au restaurant si on veut grossir?
7. Que peut-on choisir au restaurant si on veut maigrir?
8. Finissez-vous toujours votre repas?
9. Finissiez-vous toujours votre repas quand vous étiez jeune?

Entre amis

À la fin du repas

1. Tell your partner s/he has lost weight.
2. Find out whether s/he is going to finish his/her cheese.
3. Encourage him/her to choose a dessert.
4. Say that s/he is not going to get fat.

C. L'adjectif *tout*

Il y a des toilettes dans **toutes** les chambres.	*There are toilets in all the rooms.*
Je parle avec mes amis **tous** les jours.	*I speak with my friends every day.*
Nous regardons la télévision **tous** les soirs.	*We watch television every evening.*
J'ai passé **toute** la journée à la bibliothèque.	*I spent the whole day at the library.*
Tout le monde aime dîner au restaurant.	*Everybody likes to dine out.*

■ **Tout** *(all, every, each, the whole)* is often used as an adjective. In those cases it is usually followed by one of the determiners: **le, un, ce,** or **mon, ton, son, notre, votre, leur.** Both **tout** and the determiner agree with the noun they modify.

	masculin	féminin
singulier	**tout**	**toute**
pluriel	**tous**	**toutes**

■ In the singular, the meaning of **tout** is usually *the whole* or *all ... (long).*

toute la journée	*all day (long)*
toute l'année	*all year*
toute la classe	*the whole class*
tout le temps	*all the time*
tout le monde	*everybody* (literally, *the whole world*)

■ In the plural, the meaning of **tout** is usually *all* or *every.*

tous mes amis	*all my friends*
tous les hommes et **toutes** les femmes	*all (the) men and all (the) women*
tous les deux	*both (masc.)*
toutes les deux	*both (fem.)*
toutes ces personnes	*all these people*
toutes sortes de choses	*all sorts of things*
tous les jours	*every day*
toutes les semaines	*every week*
tous les ans	*every year*

■ Only when **tous** is used as a pronoun is the final **-s** pronounced.

Mes amis sont **tous** ici.   [tus]   *My friends are all here.*

13 **Toute la famille Jeantet.** Complétez les phrases avec la forme convenable de l'adjectif **tout**.

1. Monsieur et Madame Jeantet parlent anglais, _____ les deux.
2. _____ le monde dit qu'ils sont très gentils.
3. _____ leurs filles ont les yeux bleus.
4. Elles passent _____ leur temps à regarder la télévision.
5. _____ la famille va en Angleterre _____ les ans.
6. Ils achètent _____ sortes de choses.
7. Les filles Jeantet écrivent une carte postale à _____ leurs amis.
8. Elles sont contentes de voyager, _____ les trois.

14 **À votre avis.** Ajoutez **tout** et posez une question. Votre partenaire va décider ensuite si la généralisation est vraie ou fausse.

MODÈLE: Les hommes sont beaux.
          VOUS: **Est-ce que tous les hommes sont beaux?**
VOTRE PARTENAIRE: **Oui, à mon avis tous les hommes sont beaux.**   ou
          Non, à mon avis tous les hommes ne sont pas beaux.

1. Les femmes sont belles.
2. Les repas au restaurant universitaire sont délicieux.
3. Les professeurs sont gentils.
4. Le campus est très beau.
5. Tes amis adorent parler français.
6. Ta famille chante bien.
7. Tes cours sont intéressants.

Entre amis

La Pyramide

Call the restaurant La Pyramide and ask if the restaurant is open every day. Then make a reservation.

Restaurant LA PYRAMIDE

Cuisine française traditionnelle
Recommandé par les meilleurs guides

Réservation: 02-41-83-15-15

Restaurant non fumeur
Ouvert tous les jours

3 Making a Transportation Reservation

Bonjour, Madame.
    Bonjour, Monsieur. Puis-je avoir un billet°   *ticket*
      pour Strasbourg, s'il vous plaît?
Un aller simple°?   *one way*
    Oui, un aller simple.
    Non, un aller-retour°.   *round trip*
En quelle classe?
    En première.
    En seconde.
Quand partirez-vous?°   *When will you leave?*
    Tout de suite.°   *Right away.*
    Bientôt.
    Dans quelques jours.
Très bien. N'oubliez pas de composter° votre billet.   *punch, stamp*

Remarque   **Second(e)** is normally used in place of **deuxième** when there are only two in a series. Note that the **c** is pronounced [g].

    Un billet en **seconde** classe, s'il vous plaît.

NOTE CULTURELLE
Les billets de train peuvent être utilisés pendant quelques mois. Il est donc nécessaire de composter le billet le jour où on prend le train. Si on oublie de le composter, on peut être obligé de payer une amende *(fine)*.

Bonjour, Madame. Puis-je avoir un billet?

15 **Microconversation: Nous prenons le train.** Réservez des places dans le train. Complétez la conversation avec les catégories suivantes.

MODÈLE: 1 / Paris 17 h / ven. / 1re / vous ne fumez pas
          VOUS: Puis-je réserver une place?
    EMPLOYÉ(E): Dans quel train, s'il vous plaît?
          VOUS: Le train pour Paris qui part à 17 heures.
    EMPLOYÉ(E): Quel jour, s'il vous plaît?
          VOUS: Vendredi.
    EMPLOYÉ(E): Et en quelle classe?
          VOUS: En première.
    EMPLOYÉ(E): Fumeur ou non fumeur?
          VOUS: Non fumeur.
    EMPLOYÉ(E): Très bien, une place en première classe non fumeur dans le train pour Paris qui part à 17 heures vendredi.

1. 1 / Marseille 11 h / lun. / 2e / vous ne fumez pas
2. 4 / Dijon 18 h / dim. / 2e / vous fumez
3. 15 / Biarritz 8 h / sam. / 2e / vous ne fumez pas
4. 2 / Madrid 23 h / merc. / 1re / vous ne fumez pas

16 **Un petit sketch: On confirme un départ.** Lisez ou jouez le sketch et ensuite répondez aux questions.

Un touriste téléphone à la compagnie Air France.

L'EMPLOYÉ: Allô, Air France. J'écoute.
LE TOURISTE: Bonjour, Monsieur. Je voudrais confirmer un départ, s'il vous plaît.
L'EMPLOYÉ: Très bien, Monsieur. Votre nom, s'il vous plaît?
LE TOURISTE: Paul Schmitdz.
L'EMPLOYÉ: Comment? Pouvez-vous épeler votre nom, s'il vous plaît?
LE TOURISTE: S-C-H-M-I-T-D-Z.
L'EMPLOYÉ: Très bien. Votre jour de départ et le numéro de votre vol?
LE TOURISTE: Mardi prochain, et c'est le vol 307.
L'EMPLOYÉ: Très bien, Monsieur Schmitdz. Votre départ est confirmé.
LE TOURISTE: Merci beaucoup.
L'EMPLOYÉ: À votre service, Monsieur.

Questions (Répondez au passé)

1. Pour quelle compagnie l'employé travaillait-il?
2. Quelle était la première question de l'employé?
3. Quand le vol partait-il?
4. Quel était le numéro du vol?

VOCABULAIRE À RETENIR

un vol *flight*

Entre amis

Confirmez votre départ

1. Call Air Canada.
2. State that you wish to confirm your departure.
3. Identify yourself and your flight number.
4. Verify the time of departure.
5. Find out at what time you need to arrive at the airport.
6. End the conversation appropriately.

D. Le futur

Nous **aurons** notre diplôme en juin.	*We will get our diplomas in June.*
Nous **irons** en France l'été prochain.	*We will go to France next summer.*
Nous **prendrons** l'avion pour Paris.	*We will take the plane to Paris.*
J'espère qu'il ne **pleuvra** pas.	*I hope it won't rain.*
Nous **passerons** une nuit à l'hôtel Ibis.	*We will spend a night at the Ibis Hotel.*

Review the formation of the near future, Ch. 5, p. 128.

■ You have already learned to express future time by using **aller** plus an infinitive.

Ils **vont sortir** ensemble.   *They are going to go out together.*

■ Another way to express what will take place is by using the future tense.

Ils **sortiront** ensemble.   *They will go out together.*

■ To form the future tense for most verbs, take the infinitive and add the endings **-ai, -as, -a, -ons, -ez, -ont.** For infinitives ending in **-e,** drop the **-e** before adding the endings. Note that the future endings are similar to the present tense of the verb **avoir.**

> The future has only three different pronounced endings: [e] **-ai, -ez;** [a] **-as, -a;** and [ɔ̃] **-ons, -ont.**

finir					
je	**finir**	**ai**	nous	**finir**	**ons**
tu	**finir**	**as**	vous	**finir**	**ez**
il/elle/on	**finir**	**a**	ils/elles	**finir**	**ont**

vendre					
je	**vendr**	**ai**	nous	**vendr**	**ons**
tu	**vendr**	**as**	vous	**vendr**	**ez**
il/elle/on	**vendr**	**a**	ils/elles	**vendr**	**ont**

> Review the formation of **acheter,** Ch. 9, p. 252.

■ Verbs like **acheter** keep their spelling change in the future, even for the **nous** and **vous** forms.

J'achèterai une voiture l'année prochaine.
Nous achèterons une Renault.
Les étudiants **se lèveront** tard pendant les vacances.

■ All future stems end in **-r** and the future endings are always the same. There are, however, a number of verbs with irregular stems.

infinitive	stem	future
être	**ser-**	je **serai**
avoir	**aur-**	j'**aurai**
faire	**fer-**	je **ferai**
aller	**ir-**	j'**irai**
venir (devenir)	**viendr- (deviendr-)**	je **viendrai** (je **deviendrai**)
pouvoir	**pourr-**	je **pourrai**
savoir	**saur-**	je **saurai**
vouloir	**voudr-**	je **voudrai**

■ Here are the future forms of two impersonal expressions.

infinitive	present	future
pleuvoir	il pleut	**il pleuvra**
falloir	il faut	**il faudra**

 Pendant les vacances. Qu'est-ce que tout le monde fera? Utilisez le futur au lieu *(in place)* du verbe **aller** plus l'infinitif.

Modèle: Nous n'allons pas étudier.　　　**Nous n'étudierons pas.**

1. Joe va voyager avec ses parents.
2. Ils vont faire un voyage en France.
3. Ils vont visiter Paris.
4. Je vais les accompagner.
5. Nous allons prendre un avion.
6. Nous allons partir bientôt.
7. Une semaine à l'hôtel à Paris va coûter cher.
8. Je vais acheter des souvenirs.
9. Il va falloir que j'achète une autre valise.
10. Il ne va pas pleuvoir.

18 **À vous.** Répondez.

1. Est-ce que vous resterez sur le campus l'été prochain?
2. Est-ce que vous travaillerez? Si oui, où? Si non, pourquoi pas?
3. Est-ce que vous ferez un voyage? Si oui, où?
4. Qu'est-ce que vous lirez?
5. Qu'est-ce que vous regarderez à la télévision?
6. À qui rendrez-vous visite?
7. Sortirez-vous avec des amis? Si oui, où irez-vous probablement?
8. Serez-vous fatigué(e) à la fin des vacances?
9. J'espère qu'il fera beau pendant les vacances.

E. Le futur avec *si* et *quand*

> The **si**-clause may either precede or follow the main clause.

■ When a main clause containing a *future* tense verb is combined with a clause introduced by **si** *(if)*, the verb in the **si**-clause is in the *present* tense. English works the same way.

Nous ferons un pique-nique demain **s'il fait beau.**	*We will have a picnic tomorrow if it is nice out.*
Si tu veux, nous sortirons vendredi soir.	*If you want, we will go out on Friday night.*
Si tu travailles cet été, est-ce que tu gagneras beaucoup d'argent?	*If you work this summer, will you earn a lot of money?*

■ However, when a main clause with a future tense verb is combined with a clause introduced by **quand,** the verb in the **quand** clause is in the *future*. Be careful not to allow English to influence your choice of verb tense. English uses the present in this case.

> **VOCABULAIRE À RETENIR**
>
> **gagner** de l'argent
> *to earn money*
> **gagner** à la loterie
> *to win the lottery*

Quand il fera beau, nous ferons un pique-nique.	*When it is nice out, we will have a picnic.*
Aurez-vous beaucoup d'enfants **quand vous serez marié(e)?**	*Will you have a lot of children when you are married?*
Quand j'aurai le temps, j'écrirai.	*When I have time, I will write.*
Quand je gagnerai à la loterie, je ferai un long voyage.	*When I win the lottery, I will take a long trip.*

Beaucoup d'étudiants feront les vendanges *(grape harvest)* en automne. Ils veulent gagner de l'argent.

19 **Si nous gagnons beaucoup d'argent.** Utilisez **si** avec l'expression **gagner beaucoup d'argent** et complétez les phrases suivantes.

> MODÈLE: moi / acheter des vêtements
> **Si je gagne beaucoup d'argent, j'achèterai des vêtements.**

1. mes amis / être très contents
2. le professeur de français / habiter dans un château
3. les étudiants du cours de français / aller en France
4. nous / dîner dans les meilleurs restaurants
5. moi / arrêter de travailler
6. ma meilleure amie / faire un long voyage

20 **Quand ferons-nous tout cela?** Combien de phrases logiques pouvez-vous faire? Chaque phrase commence par **quand**.

> MODÈLE: **Quand j'aurai faim, j'irai au restaurant.**

| quand | mes amis
je
mon ami(e)
nous
les étudiants | réussir aux examens
avoir faim
avoir un diplôme
être riche(s)
parler bien le français
avoir soif
finir d'étudier
gagner de l'argent | avoir ... ans
boire ...
acheter ...
(ne ... pas) travailler
aller ...
chanter
être fatigué(e)(s)
manger ...
faire un voyage ... |

21 **Qu'est-ce que tu feras?** Utilisez les expressions suivantes pour interviewer votre partenaire.

> MODÈLE: quand / avoir le temps / écrire à tes parents
> VOUS: **Quand tu auras le temps, écriras-tu à tes parents?**
> VOTRE PARTENAIRE: **Oui, quand j'aurai le temps, j'écrirai à mes parents.**

1. si / être libre / écrire à tes parents
2. quand / finir tes études / avoir quel âge
3. quand / travailler / gagner beaucoup d'argent
4. si / être marié(e) / faire la cuisine
5. quand / faire la cuisine / préparer des spécialités françaises
6. si / avoir des enfants / être très content(e)
7. quand / parler français / penser à cette classe

Entre amis

Quand auras-tu ton diplôme?

1. Find out when your partner will graduate.
2. Find out what s/he will do afterwards.
3. Ask if s/he will travel. If so, ask where s/he will go.
4. Ask what s/he will buy, if s/he has enough money.

Intégration www

Révision

A **Au téléphone.** «Téléphonez» à votre partenaire et jouez les rôles suivants.

1. Réservez une table au restaurant.
2. Réservez une place dans un train.
3. Confirmez un départ en avion.
4. Réservez une chambre d'hôtel.

B **Diseur (diseuse) de bonne aventure (fortuneteller).** Écrivez cinq phrases pour prédire l'avenir (predict the future) d'un(e) de vos camarades de classe.

Modèle: **Tu parleras français comme un Français.**

C **À vous.** Répondez.

1. En quelle année avez-vous fini vos études au lycée?
2. Saviez-vous déjà parler français?
3. Est-ce que vous réussissiez toujours à vos examens quand vous étiez au lycée?
4. Quand finirez-vous vos études universitaires?
5. Qu'est-ce que vous ferez quand vous aurez votre diplôme?
6. Où irez-vous si vous faites un voyage?
7. Quelles villes visiterez-vous si vous avez le temps?
8. Qui fera le ménage quand vous serez marié(e)?

Pas de problème!

Preparation for the video:
1. Video worksheet in the *Cahier d'activités*
2. CD-ROM, *Module 9*

Cette activité est basée sur la vidéo, *Module 9*. Choisissez la bonne réponse pour compléter les phrases suivantes.

1. D'abord, Yves et Moustafa faisaient des recherches _____.
   (au musée, à la librairie, à la bibliothèque)
2. Moustafa faisait une étude sur _____.
   (la lecture, l'agriculture, l'architecture)
3. Le Louvre est aujourd'hui _____.
   (un musée, un château, une pyramide)
4. La Pyramide du Louvre est fermée _____.
   (le lundi, le mardi, le mercredi)
5. Moustafa a décidé de faire une description de _____ de la Pyramide.
   (l'intérieur, l'extérieur)
6. Le passant a expliqué à Yves et à Moustafa que l'entrée du musée était _____.
   (à côté d'eux, devant eux, derrière eux)

Lecture I

A **Étude du vocabulaire.** Étudiez les phrases suivantes et choisissez les mots anglais qui correspondent aux mots français en caractères gras: *holiday, until, schedule, except, beginning on, run.*

1. J'ai téléphoné à l'aéroport pour savoir **l'horaire** des vols.
2. Nous serons en France **à partir du** 10 juin.
3. Certains trains ne **circulent** pas le week-end.
4. Tout le monde est venu **sauf** Christian. Pourquoi est-ce qu'il n'est pas venu?
5. Le magasin est ouvert **jusqu'à** dix-huit heures.
6. Le quatorze juillet est la **fête** nationale en France.

B **Parcourez l'horaire.** Lisez rapidement pour trouver le nom de la gare d'Angers et le nombre de trains qui vont de Montparnasse à Angers.

L'horaire des trains (Paris-Nantes)

Numéro de train	3741	3741	8849	8955	8957	13557	86743	6816/7	8859	86745	86745	86745	3789	8863	8967	8869	8975	8879	566/7
Notes à consulter	1	2	3	4	5	6	7	8	9	10	11	12	13	4	14	9	15	16	9
	TGV	TGV		TGV	TGV			TGV						TGV	TGV	TGV	TGV	TGV	TGV
Paris-Montparnasse 1-2 D	16.43	16.43	16.50	17.25	17.30			17.50						18.10	18.25	18.40	**18.45**	19.25	19.50
Massy D																			21.02
Versailles-Chantiers D																			
Chartres D	17.30	17.30																	
Le Mans A	18.27	18.27	17.44					18.44					19.55			19.39			
Le Mans D		17.46			17.53	18.27		18.46	18.54	18.54	19.21	19.57				19.41			
Sablé A					18.16	19.00			19.29	19.29	19.56	20.21				20.00			
Angers-St-Laud A			18.24					19.02	**19.23**		20.02	20.46				20.21			22.28
Ancenis A												21.20				20.45			
Nantes A			19.01	19.27	19.29			19.43	20.01			21.39	20.27	20.39	**21.03**	21.27	21.49	23.04	

Notes :

1. Circule : jusqu'au 3 juil   : les ven;les 4, 11, 18 et 25 sept   - Départ de Paris Montp 3 Vaug.- ♦ ⚫ assuré certains jours.

2. Circule : du 10 juil au 28 août   : les ven- ♦.

3. Circule : tous les jours sauf les sam, dim et fêtes et sauf le 13 juil   - ♦- &.

4. Circule : les ven- ♦- &.

5. Circulation périodique- ♦- &.

6. Circule : les lun, mar, mer, jeu sauf les 8 juin, 13 et 14 juil   - ⚫.

7. Circule : tous les jours sauf les sam, dim et fêtes- ⚫.

8. Circule : jusqu'au 3 juil   : les ven, dim et fêtes sauf le 7 juin   ;Circule du 4 juil au 6 sept   : tous les jours;à partir du 11 sept   : les ven et dim- ♦- &.

9. ♦- &.

10. Circule : tous les jours sauf les ven, dim et fêtes- ⚫.

11. Circule : les dim et fêtes- ⚫.

12. Circule : les ven- ⚫.

13. Circule : les ven- ♦.

14. Circule : tous les jours sauf les ven, dim et fêtes;Circule les 7 juin, 12 juil et 15 août   - ⚫1reCL assuré certains jours-♦- &.

15. Circule : les ven- ⚫1reCL- ♦- &.

16. Circulation périodique- ⚫1reCL assuré certains jours-♦- &.

C **Questions.** Répondez.

1. Quel est le train le plus rapide entre Paris-Montparnasse et Angers?
2. Quel est le train le moins rapide entre Paris-Montparnasse et Angers? Pourquoi?
3. Combien d'arrêts y a-t-il pour ce train?
4. Combien de temps le TGV prend-il entre Massy et Angers?
5. Quels sont les trains qui offrent des facilités aux handicapés?
6. Quels trains ne circulent pas le samedi?
7. Si on est au Mans, quels trains peut-on prendre pour Angers?
8. Si on part de Paris-Montparnasse, quels trains peut-on prendre si on veut arriver pour dîner à Angers à vingt heures?

Lecture II

A **Étude du vocabulaire.** Étudiez les phrases suivantes et choisissez les mots anglais qui correspondent aux mots français en caractères gras: *full board, huts, dugout canoe, housing, mattress, bush country, river, water skiing, wind surfing, beach.*

1. Les Sénégalais circulent beaucoup en **pirogue** le long de leurs rivières.
2. Un **fleuve** est une grande rivière qui rejoint la mer.
3. La **brousse** est une région qui se trouve loin des villes.
4. Les habitants des villages africains vivent dans des **cases.**
5. Sur le lac, les plus sportifs peuvent faire du **ski nautique** ou, quand il y a du vent, de la **planche à voile.**
6. L'**hébergement** pendant le séjour peut se faire dans un hôtel ou dans des bungalows près de l'hôtel.
7. À l'hôtel, on peut choisir la **pension complète** ou prendre ses repas dans les restaurants de la ville.
8. En vacances, de nombreux touristes aiment passer leur temps au bord de la mer à la **plage.**
9. Si on ne veut pas avoir mal au dos, il vaut mieux avoir un **matelas** sur son lit.

B **Parcourez la lecture.** Lisez rapidement la lecture pour trouver ...

1. quatre types de transport.
2. cinq endroits à visiter qui se trouvent sur la carte.

Séjours organisés au Sénégal

Brousse et plage

Une semaine: 3 nuits en brousse en pension complète à l'hôtel Le Pélican/4 nuits à l'hôtel Village Club Les Filaos.

L'hôtel **Le Pélican** à 2 h 30 de Dakar au bord du fleuve Saloum joint le confort aux charmes de la vie africaine. Un site géographique exceptionnel, la province du Siné Saloum est réputée pour la richesse de sa faune et de sa flore.

L'hôtel **Village Club Les Filaos** se trouve à 73 kilomètres au sud de Dakar, en bordure de plage. Ses bungalows sont entièrement équipés, notamment avec salle de bain et toilettes privées. Restaurants, piscines. Sports et loisirs gratuits: tennis, planches à voile, volley-ball, pétanque. Sports et loisirs payants: ski nautique, excursions.

Le Circuit Cap Vert

Deux semaines. Ce circuit traverse une très belle région du Sénégal, sauvage et peu fréquentée par les touristes: le pays Bassari. Le déplacement se fait en minibus. Ce type de voyage vous fera côtoyer en permanence les habitants du pays et favorisera les contacts avec une population toujours accueillante. Il procure un confort limité. Les voyageurs sont hébergés dans des cases, des écoles ou en bivouac. Un sac de couchage et un petit matelas de mousse sont indispensables. Une réunion de préparation avec votre accompagnateur aura lieu deux à trois semaines avant le départ.

Itinéraire type: Visite de Dakar et de l'île de Gorée, descente en taxi-brousse sur Thiès (visite du marché), Saint-Louis (marché), Mlomp (cases à étages), Elinkine (promenade en pirogue), île de Karabane (baignade), parc de Basse Casamance, Gambie, région du Siné Saloum (promenade en pirogue), Toubakouta, Koalack, M'Bour-Dakar.

Le prix comprend:

- l'assistance à l'aéroport
- les transports au Sénégal, la nourriture et l'hébergement (petits hôtels, chez l'habitant)
- un accompagnateur
- l'assurance

Le prix ne comprend pas:

- le transport aérien
- les boissons

Vrai ou faux? Décidez si les phrases suivantes sont vraies ou fausses. Si une phrase n'est pas vraie, corrigez-la.

1. L'hôtel Le Pélican se trouve à Dakar.
2. Il y a beaucoup d'animaux et de plantes dans la région de Siné Saloum.
3. Il ne sera pas nécessaire de payer pour faire usage de la planche à voile.
4. Les participants seront hébergés dans des hôtels de luxe pour toute la durée du circuit Cap Vert.
5. Beaucoup de touristes ont déjà fait ce voyage et connaissent le pays Bassari.
6. Il est peu probable qu'on doive passer la nuit dans des cases pendant le circuit.
7. Le voyage en avion est compris dans le prix du circuit.
8. Les repas sont compris dans le prix du circuit, mais pour les boissons il faudra payer un supplément.

 Discussion. Lequel des deux séjours préférez-vous? Expliquez votre réponse.

VOCABULAIRE ACTIF

Les voyages
un aller-retour *round-trip ticket*
un aller simple *one-way ticket*
l'autoroute (f.) *turnpike, throughway, highway*
un billet *ticket*
une carte *map*
composter (un billet) *to punch (a ticket)*
confirmer (un départ) *to confirm (a departure)*
le départ *departure*
en première *in first class*
en seconde *in second class*
fumeur *smoking (car)*
non fumeur *non-smoking (car)*
ralentir *to slow down*
un renseignement *item of information*
la route *route, way, road*
le vol *flight*

Adjectifs
complet (complète) *full; complete*
inutile *useless*
ouvert(e) *open*
riche *rich*
tout (toute/tous/toutes) *all; every; the whole*

D'autres noms
une demande *request*
un diplôme *diploma*
un pique-nique *picnic*

Expressions utiles
Allez-y. *Go ahead.*
Allô! *Hello! (on the phone)*
après-demain *day after tomorrow*
À quel nom ... ? *In whose name ... ?*
avoir tendance à *to tend to*
Bonne chance! *Good luck!*
Comment je vais faire? *What am I going to do?*
De rien *You're welcome*
entendu *agreed; understood; O.K.*
Il n'y en a plus. *There is (are) no more.*
Il vous reste ... ? *Do you still have ... ?*
Mince! *Darn it!*
Pourriez-vous me dire ... ? *Could you tell me ... ?*
Puis-je ... ? *May I ... ?*
tous (toutes) les deux *both*
tout de suite *right away*
tout près *very near*

À l'hôtel
une clé *key*
une douche *shower*
un étage *floor*
le prix *price*
le rez-de-chaussée *ground floor*
une serviette *towel*
un supplément *extra charge; supplement*

Verbes
choisir *to choose*
épeler *to spell*
faire une demande *to make a request*
finir *to finish*
gagner (à la loterie) *to win (the lottery)*
gagner (de l'argent) *to earn (money)*
grossir *to put on weight*
indiquer *to tell; to indicate; to point out*
louer *to rent*
maigrir *to lose weight*
obéir *to obey*
poser une question *to ask a question*
recommander *to recommend*
remercier *to thank*
réussir *to succeed; to pass*
savoir *to know*

escale 4
Le Maghreb

Que savez-vous?

Répondez aux questions suivantes. Les réponses se trouvent dans cette escale.

1. Quels sont les trois pays du Maghreb?
2. Quelles civilisations se sont établies au Maghreb dans l'antiquité?
3. Quels événements historiques ont le plus marqué les pays du Maghreb?

CHRONOLOGIE

- Premiers habitants de la région: les Berbères
- 814 avant J.-C. Empire carthaginois; site ancien de Carthage près de Tunis.
- 264–146 avant J.-C. Guerres puniques entre Carthage et Rome; destruction de Carthage.
- Colonie romaine jusqu'à l'invasion des Vandales en 439.
- Conquête arabe à la fin du VIIᵉ siècle; islamisation.
- Formation d'empires berbères s'étendant à l'Andalousie (Espagne).
- Au XVIᵉ siècle, domination turque. Le Maghreb fait partie de l'Empire ottoman.
- Retour au nomadisme. Rivalités des pays européens pour contrôler la région.
- Période coloniale: En 1830, l'Algérie est, en fait, un département français.
- Protectorat français en Tunisie en 1881 et au Maroc en 1912.
- 1954–1962: Guerre d'indépendance en Algérie.
- 1956: Indépendance de la Tunisie et du Maroc.

Vrai ou faux?

1. Le Maroc est le plus grand pays du Maghreb.
2. Le Maroc est très proche de l'Espagne.
3. Il y a de nombreux Berbères en Tunisie.
4. L'Algérie et le Maroc ont approximativement la même population.

Avenue Bourguiba à Tunis

REPÈRES:	LE MAROC	L'ALGÉRIE	LA TUNISIE
Superficie:	710.850 km², comparable à celle du Texas	environ 2.381.740 km², plus de trois fois le Texas	163.610 km²; un peu plus grand que la Géorgie
Population:	environ 30 millions	environ 29 millions	près de 9 millions
Ethnicité:	99% Arabes et Berbères; quelques Harratins (noirs) dans le sud	83% Arabes, 16% Berbères surtout dans les montagnes de l'Atlas, 1% Européens	98% Arabes, 2% Européens
Capitale:	Rabat	Alger	Tunis
Langues:	arabe, français, berbère, un peu d'espagnol	arabe, français, berbère	arabe, français

On mange le couscous assis par terre autour du grand plat et on se sert avec la main droite seulement.

ÉTUDE DU VOCABULAIRE

Identifiez dans les phrases suivantes les mots en caractères gras qui correspondent aux mots suivants: *mix, baste, hollow, cooked, wash, layer, spicy, dough.*

1. Pour éviter les microbes, on recommande de manger la viande bien **cuite**.
2. Quand un plat a beaucoup de sauce liquide, on le sert dans un plat **creux**.
3. En Inde on aime la cuisine **épicée**.
4. Il faut **laver** les légumes avant de les préparer.
5. Pour faire un gâteau, on **mélange** la farine, le beurre, le lait avec les œufs pour faire une **pâte**.
6. Un gâteau d'anniversaire a souvent une **couche** de sucre glacé et des décorations.
7. Quand la viande est rôtie au feu ouvert, il faut bien **l'arroser** pour qu'elle ne sèche pas.

La cuisine maghrébine
«Bismillah!»[1]

Voici la description de quelques plats traditionnels de la cuisine maghrébine.

- **Le couscous:** Semoule cuite à la vapeur et servie dans un grand plat creux avec carottes, navets (*turnips*), aubergines (*eggplants*), courgettes (*zucchinis*) et une viande bien cuite, généralement du mouton ou du bœuf; le tout arrosé d'un bouillon épicé pour donner un plat exotique. Après le couscous, on sert un thé à la menthe (*mint*) bien chaud et très sucré. On mange ce plat le vendredi midi (jour de la grande prière de la semaine) ainsi que les jours de fête.

- **Le tagine:** plat savoureux fait avec du foie de veau (*calf's liver*) avec petits pois et raisins secs ou du foie de poulet aux amandes et aux prunes (*plums*). Son goût sucré en fait un plat délicieux.

- **La harira:** soupe, probablement d'origine berbère, qui est le repas favori des musulmans durant le mois du Ramadan[2].

- **Le méchoui[3]:** mouton couvert d'un mélange de paprika, cumin, beurre et sel et rôti tout entier à feu vif pendant deux heures pour obtenir une viande tendre. On le sert aux fêtes religieuses et aux grandes occasions.

- **La bastela:** Entre de fines couches d'une pâte presque transparente appelée «warka», on place des amandes et du poulet ou parfois du pigeon. On le sert aussi aux réunions importantes dans une large assiette avec une couche de sucre glacé et de la cannelle (*cinnamon*) en poudre.

- **Desserts:** Pâtisseries au miel (*honey*), noix (*nuts*) et amandes, qui se servent avec du thé à la menthe.

---

1. Bismillah! *Praise be to God!* 2. Ramadan: Holy month during which Muslims do not eat or drink from sunrise to sunset. 3. Méchoui: Review the reading in Ch. 6, p. 174.

La littérature maghrébine d'expression française

Que savez-vous?

1. Pourquoi les auteurs maghrébins publient-ils leurs œuvres en français?
2. Parmi les écrivains suivants, lesquels sont du Maghreb? Ousmane Sembène, Tahar Ben Jelloun, Pham duy Khiêm, Assia Djebar, Aimé Césaire?
3. Que signifie «littérature maghrébine»?

La littérature francophone des Maghrébins s'est développée après la Seconde Guerre mondiale[1]. Elle attire[2] l'attention sur la misère et les désillusions de l'après-guerre, l'espoir et l'identité nationale des pays récemment émancipés, le conflit entre les valeurs et le style de vie occidentaux et la culture et les traditions orientales. Depuis l'indépendance de l'Algérie, de la Tunisie et du Maroc, les écrivains et les intellectuels de ces pays ont animé à travers leurs écrits des discussions passionnantes sur l'effet du colonialisme, la coexistence du moderne et du traditionnel, et la situation souvent marginalisée de la femme. Cette littérature s'est rarement contentée d'être un témoignage[3] sociologique; elle a souvent été une revendication personnelle à caractère autobiographique, en même temps qu'une critique sociale audacieuse.

Ces auteurs publient leurs œuvres en arabe et en français et s'adressent ainsi au monde occidental aussi bien qu'à leurs compatriotes. Il faut se rappeler que la majorité d'entre eux ont reçu leur formation dans des écoles françaises. Élèves doués[4], ils ont souvent bénéficié de bourses[5] pour faire leurs études universitaires en France. Plusieurs des écrivains maghrébins d'expression française témoignent de la présence en France d'une immigration nombreuse d'origine maghrébine; cette littérature «beure»[6] révèle l'identité incertaine des jeunes gens, enfants de deux cultures, souvent exilés dans des HLM[7] de banlieue.

---

1. *world* 2. *attracts* 3. *testimony* 4. *talented* 5. *scholarships*
6. Beur: *first generation born of North African immigrants*
7. HLM (habitation à loyer modéré): *inexpensive housing*

À vous!

1. **Selon l'article, quels sont les trois thèmes principaux trouvés dans la littérature maghrébine?**
2. **Pourquoi le thème de «l'identité» est-il important?**
3. **Expliquez comment les écrits sociologiques dans la littérature maghrébine ont souvent un caractère autobiographique et de critique sociale.**

Tahar Ben Jelloun et la migration linguistique

Né à Fès en 1944, Tahar Ben Jelloun a fait des études de philosophie et de psychiatrie sociale, d'abord à Rabat au Maroc et ensuite à Paris, où il vit actuellement. Mais la littérature est sa vocation principale. Il a

Tahar Ben Jelloun

publié plusieurs romans et recueils de poésie et d'essais. En 1987, il a reçu le prix Goncourt, le plus prestigieux prix littéraire français, pour son roman *La Nuit sacrée.*

Ben Jelloun essaye de rattacher sa culture d'origine et son expression en langue française. Ainsi, il a libéré ses écrits de contraintes politiques. Ben Jelloun refuse d'être catégorisé comme écrivain marocain, francophone ou français. Cette question n'a pas de sens, explique-t-il. «Les intellectuels n'étant pas des douaniers, ils n'ont pas à nous demander sans arrêt d'exhiber un passeport.»

Ses romans traitent en effet de thèmes interlinguistiques et interculturels: l'homme dépaysé, l'homme dépossédé de ses racines et de son identité, les difficultés de la vie d'émigré et les problèmes de ceux qui vivent en dehors de leur culture maternelle. C'est ainsi que Ben Jelloun explique la schizophrénie culturelle de l'émigré: «Ne me dites pas pourquoi j'écris en français, mais comment j'habite cette langue. Certes, c'est encore une histoire d'amour, une histoire où les conflits sont violents et fréquents. Rien n'est acquis. La séduction est un travail quotidien, une exigence plus qu'une esthétique.»

À vous!

1. **Quelle est la source d'inspiration créatrice de Tahar Ben Jelloun?**
2. **Où habite-t-il actuellement?**
3. **Pourquoi les émigrés se sentent-ils parfois schizophrènes?**
4. **Pourquoi est-ce que des intellectuels comme Ben Jelloun n'ont pas besoin de s'attacher à une nationalité particulière?**

Assia Djebar: romancière et cinéaste algérienne

Née en 1936 et éduquée en Algérie, d'abord à l'école coranique puis au lycée français, Assia obtient une bourse d'étude et part en France à 19 ans. Elle interrompt ses études pour participer à la grève (*strike*) des étudiants en Algérie en 1956. En 1958, elle fait des études supérieures d'histoire en Tunisie et poursuit des enquêtes (*surveys*) dans les camps de réfugiés à la frontière algéro-tunisienne pendant la guerre d'indépendance. L'expérience des réfugiés se retrouve dans plusieurs de ses romans.

Dans *Femmes d'Alger dans leur appartement*, Assia Djebar rassemble plusieurs nouvelles, où elle se met «à l'écoute» de ses sœurs algériennes, femmes de tout âge, de toutes conditions, «dont les corps sont prisonniers, mais les âmes (*souls*) plus que jamais mouvantes.» Ces femmes sont cloîtrées dans le silence. Pour sortir des siècles d'ombre (*shadows*), il faut:

> Parler, parler sans cesse d'hier et d'aujourd'hui,
> parler entre nous [...] et regarder [...] hors des murs
> et des prisons.

Ces récits de femmes, elle les traduit d'un «arabe féminin» autant dire d'un «arabe souterrain».

Comme pour beaucoup d'autres auteurs maghrébins, écrire en français, la langue des colonisateurs, a pour Assia une signification très particulière. Au début de son roman, *L'Amour, la fantasia* (1985), elle décrit «la fillette arabe allant pour la première fois à l'école [française], mais dans la main du père.» C'est donc le père qui l'a introduite à cette langue et à cette culture[1]. Elle explique qu'en étudiant le français, «son corps s'occidentalisait à sa manière». Pour elle, s'exprimer en français, langue de l'ancien conquérant, représente un dévoilement, une mise à nu, mais aussi un exil de l'enfance. Ce n'est pas du nom de son père qu'elle signe ses œuvres mais d'un pseudonyme. Parler d'elle-même, hors de la tradition, n'est possible qu'en français, cette langue qui est pour elle à la fois libération et dissimulation.

---

1. Jean Déjeux, *La littérature féminine de langue française au Maghreb*, p. 199.

À vous!

1. Dans quels pays est-ce qu'Assia Djebar a fait ses études?
2. Qui sont les personnages principaux dans les œuvres d'Assia Djebar?
3. Pourquoi est-ce qu'Assia Djebar fait référence à la langue arabe comme «arabe souterrain»?

Fatima Bellahcène

Cette libération du silence est évoquée dans le poème d'une autre jeune Algérienne, qui se voit traitée en étrangère par sa famille parce qu'elle est écrivain.

L'Étrangère

Vous dites j'ai changé
Comme tous les autres
Je me suis trahie[1].
Non, je n'ai pas changé
J'ai seulement appris à parler.
Vous avez cru que j'étais un livre ouvert,
Un livre aux feuilles blanches[2],
Parce que je me taisais,
Parce que derrière mon silence, je me terrais[3].
[...]

Actualités de l'émigration, no. 80

---

1. *betrayed*   2. *blank pages*   3. *I kept hidden*

À vous!

1. Expliquez la métaphore d'un «livre aux feuilles blanches».
2. Avez-vous remarqué des ressemblances entre les œuvres de Djebar et de Bellahcène?
3. Pouvez-vous expliquer comment la culture traditionnelle du Maghreb a contribué au silence des femmes?
4. À votre avis, est-ce que la situation des femmes maghrébines ressemble à celle des femmes de votre pays?

www

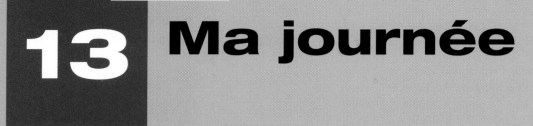

Chapitre
13 Ma journée

Buts communicatifs
Describing a table setting
Describing one's day
Describing past activities
Expressing one's will

Structures utiles
Le verbe **mettre**
Les verbes pronominaux (suite)
Les verbes **se promener, s'inquiéter, s'appeler** et **s'asseoir**
Le passé des verbes pronominaux
Le subjonctif (suite)

Culture
L'étiquette à table
Au menu ou à la carte?

Coup d'envoi

Prise de contact

Bon appétit!

une assiette creuse - boul

cuiller à soupe

petite cuiller

Avant de manger

Mettez° une nappe° sur la table. — *Put / tablecloth*
Mettez des assiettes sur la nappe.
Mettez un verre et une cuiller° devant chaque assiette. — *spoon*
Mettez une fourchette° à gauche de l'assiette. — *fork*
Mettez un couteau° à droite de l'assiette. — *knife*

À table

Asseyez-vous.
Mettez une serviette° sur vos genoux°. — *napkin / lap*
Coupez° le pain. — *Cut*
Mettez un morceau de pain sur la nappe à côté de l'assiette.
Versez° du vin dans le verre. — *Pour*
Levez° votre verre et admirez la couleur du vin. — *Lift*
Humez° le vin. — *Smell*
Goûtez-le.° — *Taste it.*
Bon appétit!

> You learned in Ch. 9 that **genou** means *knee*. In the plural, it can refer to either *lap* or *knees*.

Conversation

Nous nous mettons à table

Monsieur et Madame Smith et Monsieur et Madame Martin
sont arrivés au restaurant, mais Lori n'est pas encore là.

MAÎTRE D'HÔTEL:	Bonsoir, Messieurs, Bonsoir, Mesdames. Vous avez réservé?
M. SMITH:	Oui, Monsieur, au nom de Smith.
MAÎTRE D'HÔTEL:	Très bien, un instant, s'il vous plaît. *(Il vérifie sa liste.)* C'est pour cinq personnes, n'est-ce pas?
MME SMITH:	C'est exact.°
MAÎTRE D'HÔTEL:	Vous voulez vous asseoir°?
M. SMITH:	Volontiers, notre amie ne va pas tarder°.
MAÎTRE D'HÔTEL:	Par ici°, s'il vous plaît. *(ensuite)* Voici votre table. *(Ils s'asseyent.°)*
M. SMITH:	Merci beaucoup, Monsieur. *(Le maître d'hôtel sourit° mais ne répond pas. Il s'en va°.)*
MME MARTIN:	C'est très gentil à vous de nous inviter.
MME SMITH:	Mais c'est un plaisir pour nous.
M. MARTIN:	Voilà Lori qui arrive. Bonsoir, Lori. *(Lori serre la main à Monsieur et Madame Martin et fait la bise à Monsieur et Madame Smith.)*
LORI BECKER:	Excusez-moi d'être en retard.
MME MARTIN:	Ne vous inquiétez pas°, Lori. Nous venons d'arriver.

That's right.

to sit down

won't be long

This way

They sit down.

smiles
leaves

Don't worry

▶ **Jouez ces rôles.**   Répétez la conversation avec vos partenaires. Ensuite imaginez une excuse pour Lori. Pourquoi est-elle arrivée en retard?

Il y a un geste

Il n'y a pas de quoi.   Although the French have numerous spoken formulae that convey the idea of *You're welcome* (**Il n'y a pas de quoi, De rien, Je vous en prie,** etc.), they frequently respond with only a discreet smile. This smile is often unnoticed by North Americans, who may interpret the lack of a verbal response to their "thank you" as less than polite.

Pourquoi Monsieur Smith n'avance-t-il pas la chaise de sa femme quand elle va s'asseoir?

a. Ce n'est pas l'habitude en France.
b. Il a oublié de le faire.
c. Il est marié depuis longtemps.

Quelle est la différence entre un menu et une carte dans un restaurant?

a. C'est la même chose, mais un menu est plus élégant qu'une carte.
b. C'est la même chose, mais une carte est plus élégante qu'un menu.
c. Un menu propose deux ou trois repas à prix fixe. Une carte donne la liste de tous les plats.

Pourquoi le maître d'hôtel ne répond-il pas quand Monsieur Smith dit merci?

a. Il est impoli.
b. Il ne dit rien mais il répond par un sourire (smile).
c. Parce que Monsieur Smith n'est pas français.

L'étiquette à table

When Mrs. Smith is about to be seated, it is very likely that the gentlemen will not pull out her chair as a courtesy as might be the case in a North American setting. This is simply not done in France.

While the table is set, as in North America, with the forks to the left and the knives to the right, there are differences: forks are often turned tines down; glasses are above the plate rather than to one side; teaspoons are placed between the glass and the plate. If soup is served, the soup spoon is not held sideways but rather placed, tip first, in the mouth.

The French do not pick up a slice of bread and bite off a piece. Rather, they break off a small bite-sized piece and may even use this as a utensil to guide food onto the fork. From time to time, this piece is eaten and another piece broken off. Review page 211 for additional information.

Au menu ou à la carte?

La carte lists all of the dishes that the restaurant prepares. Customers can choose any combination of items they wish (**à la carte**). **Le menu** has one or more set (complete) lunches or dinners at a set price. There might, for example, be **le menu à 15€** and **le menu à 20€**. Each **menu** will include three or more courses, with or without beverage. Menus are usually by far the less expensive way to order food in France.

In France

Ice cubes are not readily available at restaurants.

Dinner is often at 8:00 P.M. or later.

Meals may last two hours or more.

Bread is placed on the tablecloth instead of on a plate.

People keep both hands above the table while eating.

The service charge, or tip, is already included in the bill (**le service est compris**).

In North America

Ice water is often served automatically with meals. Cold drinks are very common.

Dinner is often at 6:00 P.M. or earlier.

Meals may last only 20 or 25 minutes.

Bread is not always served with a meal. When it is served, it is always kept on the plate.

People put one hand in their lap while eating.

The tip is often not included in the bill.

 **À vous.** Répondez au maître d'hôtel.

1. Bonsoir, Monsieur (Madame / Mademoiselle). Vous avez réservé?
2. Pour deux personnes?
3. Vous voulez vous asseoir?
4. Par ici, s'il vous plaît. Voici votre table.

Entre amis

Au restaurant

You are the maître d'hôtel at a restaurant. Your partner is a customer.

1. Ask if s/he has made a reservation. (S/he has.)
2. Find out for how many people.
3. Ask if the others have already arrived.
4. Ask him/her if s/he wants to sit down.
5. Tell him/her "This way, please."

Prononciation

Les voyelles arrondies [ø] et [œ]

- Lip rounding plays a much greater role in the accurate pronunciation of French than it does in English. French has rounded vowels that are produced in the front part of the mouth, a combination that does not exist in English. Use the word **euh** to practice. This word is prevalent and is very characteristic of the normal position for French pronunciation: the lips are rounded and the tongue is behind the lower teeth.

- For the [ø] sound in **euh,** round your lips and then try to say **et.** For the [œ] sound in **neuf,** the lips are more open than for **euh.** There is, moreover, always a pronounced consonant after the vowel sound in words like **neuf, sœur,** etc.

[ø] • **eu**h, d**eu**x, v**eu**t, p**eu**t, bl**eu,** ennuy**eu**x, pl**eu**t

[œ] • n**eu**f, s**œu**r, b**eu**rre, profess**eu**r, h**eu**re, v**eu**lent, p**eu**vent, pl**eu**re

▶ **Listen and repeat.**

1. Est-ce que je peux vous aider?
2. La sœur du professeur arrive à neuf heures.
3. Ils veulent du beurre sur leur pain.
4. Les deux portent un pull bleu.
5. «Il pleure dans mon cœur comme il pleut sur la ville.» *(Verlaine)*

Buts communicatifs

1 Describing a Table Setting

Où est-ce qu'on met la nappe?   On la met sur la table.
Où est-ce qu'on met l'assiette?   On la met sur la nappe.
Où est-ce qu'on met le couteau?   On le met à droite de l'assiette.
Où est-ce qu'on met la cuiller?   On la met entre l'assiette et le verre.
Où est-ce qu'on met la serviette?   On la met sur ses genoux.
Où est-ce qu'on met les mains?   On les met sur la table.
Où est-ce qu'on met le pain?   On le met sur la nappe, à côté
                                      de l'assiette.

Et vous?   Qu'est-ce qu'on met à gauche de l'assiette?
                  Où est-ce qu'on met les verres?

A. Le verbe *mettre*

Je vais **mettre** mon pyjama.	*I'm going to put on my pajamas.*
Nous **mettons** un maillot de bain pour aller à la piscine.	*We put on a bathing suit to go to the pool.*
J'**ai mis** le sel, le poivre et le sucre sur la table.	*I put the salt, pepper, and sugar on the table.*

> **mettre** *(to put, place, lay; to put on)*
>
> | | | | | |
> |---|---|---|---|---|
> | je | **mets** | | nous | **mettons** |
> | tu | **mets** | | vous | **mettez** |
> | il/elle/on | **met** | | ils/elles | **mettent** |
>
> *passé composé:* j'**ai mis**

> Notice that, like the **-re** verbs, p. 243, the endings for **mettre** are **-s, -s, –, -ons, -ez, -ent.** The plural stem, however, has **-tt-.**

■ **Mettre** can also mean *to turn on* (the radio, the heat, etc.) and is used in the expression **mettre la table** to mean *to set the table.*

Qui **a mis** la table ce soir?	*Who set the table this evening?*
Mets le chauffage; j'ai froid.	*Turn on the heat; I'm cold.*
Mais je viens de **mettre** la climatisation.	*But I just turned on the air conditioning.*

> **VOCABULAIRE À RETENIR**
>
> **le chauffage** *heat*
> **la climatisation** *air conditioning*

1 **Qu'est-ce qu'ils mettent?** Indiquez les vêtements que mettent les personnes suivantes.

MODÈLES: Qu'est-ce que vos amis mettent pour nager?
Ils mettent un maillot de bain.

Review articles of clothing on pp. 89 and 98.

1. Qu'est-ce que les étudiants mettent pour aller à leurs cours?
2. Qu'est-ce que le professeur de français met pour aller au cours de français?
3. Qu'est-ce que vous mettez s'il neige?
4. Qu'est-ce que vous mettez s'il fait chaud?
5. Qu'est-ce qu'on met pour faire du jogging?
6. Qu'est-ce que vos amis mettent s'ils vont à une boum?
7. Que mettez-vous si vous allez dîner dans un restaurant très chic?

2 **Un petit test de votre savoir-vivre.** Choisissez une réponse pour chaque question et ensuite lisez l'analyse de vos réponses.

1. Que mettez-vous quand vous allez dîner au restaurant?
   a. des vêtements chic
   b. un jean et des baskets
   c. un bikini
   d. rien

2. Que buvez-vous pendant le repas?
   a. du vin ou de l'eau
   b. du lait ou du café
   c. du whisky
   d. de l'eau dans un bol

3. Où mettez-vous le pain pendant le repas?
   a. sur la nappe à côté de l'assiette
   b. dans mon assiette
   c. dans l'assiette de mon (ma) voisin(e)
   d. sous la table

4. Où est votre main gauche pendant que vous mangez?
   a. sur la table
   b. sur mes genoux
   c. sur le genou de mon (ma) voisin(e)
   d. sous la table

5. Combien de temps passez-vous à table?
   a. entre une et deux heures
   b. entre 25 et 45 minutes
   c. Ça dépend du charme de mon (ma) voisin(e).
   d. cinq minutes

Remember that you learned in Ch. 8 *not* to say **Je suis plein(e),** literally *I am full,* because in French it can mean either *I am drunk* or *I am pregnant.*

6. Que dites-vous à la fin du repas?
   a. C'était très bon.
   b. Je suis plein(e).
   c. Veux-tu faire une promenade, chéri(e)?
   d. Oua! oua! *(bow-wow!)*

Résultats

a. Si vous avez répondu **a** à toutes les questions, vous êtes peut-être français(e) ou vous méritez de l'être.
b. Si vous avez répondu **b,** vous êtes probablement américain(e), comme la personne qui a écrit ce questionnaire.
c. Si votre réponse est **c,** vous êtes trop entreprenant(e) *(forward, bold)* et vous dérangez beaucoup votre voisin(e).
d. Si votre réponse est **d,** vous vous identifiez beaucoup aux chiens.

3 **À vous.** Répondez.

1. Mettez-vous du sucre ou de la crème dans votre café?
2. Que mettez-vous dans une tasse de thé?
3. Où met-on le pain quand on mange à la française?
4. Que faut-il faire pour mettre la table?
5. À quel moment de l'année met-on le chauffage dans la région où vous habitez? À quel moment de l'année met-on la climatisation?
6. En quelle saison met-on un gros manteau?
7. Quels vêtements les étudiants mettent-ils d'habitude sur votre campus?
8. Quels vêtements avez-vous mis hier? Pourquoi avez-vous décidé de porter ces vêtements-là?

Entre amis

L'éducation d'un(e) enfant

You are a French parent instructing your child (your partner) on table manners. Remember to use **tu**.

1. Tell your child to put the napkin on his/her lap.
2. Tell him/her to put a piece of bread on the table.
3. Tell him/her not to play with the bread.
4. Tell him/her to put water in his/her glass.
5. Find out what s/he did at school today.

2 Describing One's Day

Le matin

7 h	Je me réveille tôt et je me lève.
7 h 10	Je me lave ou je prends une douche.
7 h 25	Je m'habille.
7 h 35	Je me brosse les cheveux.
7 h 50	Après avoir mangé°, je me brosse les dents.

After eating

L'après-midi

3 h	Je me repose.
5 h	Je m'amuse avec mon chien.

Le soir

11 h	Je me couche assez tard et je m'endors.

Et vous? À quelle heure vous réveillez-vous?
Que faites-vous le matin? l'après-midi? le soir?

Review pp. 165 and 189.

Remarque **Tôt** and **tard** mean *early* and *late* in the day. They should not be confused with **en avance** and **en retard,** which mean *early* and *late* for a specific meeting, class, etc.

Il se lève **tard!** (à midi)
Il est **en retard.** (pour son cours de français)

Review **Les verbes pronominaux**, Ch. 6, p. 165.

VOCABULAIRE

Quelques verbes pronominaux

se réveiller	*to wake up*
se laver	*to get washed*
se brosser (les dents, les cheveux)	*to brush (one's teeth, one's hair)*
s'habiller	*to get dressed*
s'amuser	*to have fun*
se souvenir (de)	*to remember*
s'inquiéter	*to worry*
s'asseoir	*to sit down*
se promener	*to take a walk, ride*
se dépêcher	*to hurry*
s'appeler	*to be named*
s'endormir	*to fall asleep*
se reposer	*to rest*

B. Les verbes pronominaux (suite)

■ Remember that the reflexive pronouns are **me, te, se, nous, vous,** and **se.**

se laver *(to get washed, to wash oneself)*

je	**me** lave	nous	**nous** lavons
tu	**te** laves	vous	**vous** lavez
il/elle/on	**se** lave	ils/elles	**se** lavent

s'endormir *(to fall asleep)*

je	**m'**endors	nous	**nous** endormons
tu	**t'**endors	vous	**vous** endormez
il/elle/on	**s'**endort	ils/elles	**s'**endorment

Note The reflexive pronoun always changes form as necessary to agree with the subject of the verb, even when it is part of an infinitive construction.

Je vais **m'**amuser.   **Tu** vas **t'**amuser aussi.   **Nous** allons **nous** amuser!

■ Many verbs can be used reflexively or nonreflexively, depending on whether the object of the verb is the same as the subject or not.

Jean **se lave** avant de manger. (*Jean* is the subject *and* the object.)
Mais: Jean **lave sa voiture.** (*Jean* is the subject but *sa voiture* is the object.)

Noëlle adore **se promener.** (*Noëlle* is the subject *and* the object.)
Mais: Noëlle refuse de **promener le chien.** (*Noëlle* is the subject but *le chien* is the object.)

■ Like all other object pronouns, the reflexive pronoun is always placed immediately before the verb (except in an affirmative command). This rule is true, no matter whether the verb is in an affirmative, interrogative, negative, or infinitive form.

Comment **vous** appelez-vous?	*What is your name?*
Tu veux **t'**asseoir?	*Do you want to sit down?*
Ne **s'**amusent-ils pas en classe?	*Don't they have fun in class?*
Je ne **m'**appelle pas Aude.	*My name is not Aude.*
Roman ne **se** réveille jamais très tôt.	*Roman never wakes up very early.*
Nous allons **nous** promener.	*We are going to take a walk.*
J'ai décidé de ne pas **me** lever.	*I decided not to get up.*

> Review the imperative with pronouns, Ch. 10, p. 285. Remember that when **me** and **te** follow the verb they become **moi** and **toi.**

■ As you have already seen (see Ch. 10), when the imperative is affirmative, the object pronoun is placed after the verb. This is true even when the object pronoun is a reflexive pronoun.

Dépêche-**toi**!	*Hurry (up)!*
Dépêchez-**vous**!	*Hurry (up)!*
Dépêchons-**nous**!	*Let's hurry!*

■ You also know that if the imperative is negative, normal word order is followed and the object pronoun precedes the verb.

Ne **te** dépêche pas.	*Don't hurry.*
Ne **vous** dépêchez pas.	*Don't hurry.*
Ne **nous** dépêchons pas.	*Let's not hurry.*

4 **Vrai ou faux?** Décidez si les phrases suivantes sont vraies. Si elles ne sont pas vraies, corrigez-les.

MODÈLE: Vous vous réveillez toujours tôt le matin.
   C'est faux. Je ne me réveille pas toujours tôt le matin.

1. Vous vous brossez les dents avant le petit déjeuner.
2. On se lave normalement avec de l'eau froide.
3. Les étudiants de votre université se douchent une fois par semaine.
4. Ils s'habillent avant la douche.
5. Vous vous endormez quelquefois en classe.
6. Vous vous reposez toujours après les repas.
7. D'habitude, on se brosse les cheveux avec une brosse à dents.
8. Les professeurs se souviennent toujours des noms de leurs étudiants.

5 **Nos activités de chaque jour.** Faites des phrases logiques. Vous pouvez utiliser la forme négative.

> MODÈLE: **Ma sœur se brosse les cheveux trois fois par jour.**

	se laver	tôt
	s'amuser	tard
	se dépêcher	le matin
nous	se coucher	le soir
les étudiants	prendre une douche	dans un fauteuil
mon père	s'habiller	dans la salle de bain
ma mère	s'endormir	avec de l'eau chaude
je	se réveiller	avec de l'eau froide
ma sœur	se brosser les cheveux	une (deux, etc.) fois par jour
mon frère	se brosser les dents	avec une brosse à cheveux
	se mettre à table	avec une brosse à dents
	se reposer	

6 **Fais ce que tu veux.** Utilisez l'impératif et l'expression **Eh bien, ...** pour encourager les autres à faire ce qu'ils veulent.

> MODÈLES: Je voudrais m'asseoir.   Je ne voudrais pas me lever.
> **Eh bien, assieds-toi.**   **Eh bien, ne te lève pas.**

1. Je voudrais me coucher.
2. Je ne voudrais pas me dépêcher.
3. Je ne voudrais pas me brosser les dents.
4. Je voudrais m'amuser.
5. Je ne voudrais pas me lever à 7 heures.
6. Je ne voudrais pas étudier.
7. Je voudrais sortir avec mes amis.
8. Je voudrais m'endormir en classe.

C. Les verbes *se promener, s'inquiéter, s'appeler* et *s'asseoir*

■ Some reflexive verbs contain spelling changes in the verb stem of the present tense.

Review **se lever,** p. 165, **préférer,** p. 230, and **acheter,** p. 252.

■ Like **se lever** and **acheter, se promener** changes **-e-** to **-è-** before silent endings.

se promener *(to take a walk, ride)*			
je	me prom**è**ne	nous	nous promenons
tu	te prom**è**nes	vous	vous promenez
il/elle/on	se prom**è**ne		
ils/elles	se prom**è**nent		

■ Like **préférer, s'inquiéter** changes **-é-** to **-è-** before silent endings.

s'inquiéter *(to worry)*			
je	m'inqui**è**te	nous	nous inquiétons
tu	t'inqui**è**tes	vous	vous inquiétez
il/elle/on	s'inqui**è**te		
ils/elles	s'inqui**è**tent		

■ **S'appeler** changes **-l-** to **-ll-** before silent endings.

s'appeler *(to be named)*			
je	m'appe**ll**e	nous	nous appelons
tu	t'appe**ll**es	vous	vous appelez
il/elle/on	s'appe**ll**e		
ils/elles	s'appe**ll**ent		

Note **S'asseoir** is irregular and is conjugated as follows:

s'asseoir *(to sit down)*			
je	m'**assieds**	nous	nous **asseyons**
tu	t'**assieds**	vous	vous **asseyez**
il/elle/on	s'**assied**	ils/elles	s'**asseyent**

La journée des étudiants. Utilisez des verbes pronominaux pour compléter les phrases suivantes.

> **MODÈLE:** Nous _____ à nos places.
> **Nous nous asseyons à nos places.**

1. Le soir, les étudiants ne _____ pas avant minuit parce qu'ils ont beaucoup de travail.
2. S'ils sont en retard pour un cours, ils _____.
3. Ils _____ s'il y a un examen.
4. Le week-end, les étudiants _____.
5. Le samedi matin, ils font la grasse matinée; ils ne _____ pas avant 10 heures.
6. Ils _____ très tard et ils _____ tout de suite.
7. Ils _____ en jean normalement parce que les jeans sont confortables.

 Pour avoir du succès à l'université. Vous êtes très docile et vous répondez systématiquement que vous êtes d'accord. Utilisez le futur.

> **MODÈLE:** Ne vous couchez pas trop tard.
> **D'accord, je ne me coucherai pas trop tard.**

Review the future on p. 336.

1. Ne vous endormez pas pendant le cours de français.
2. Ne vous lavez pas avec de l'eau froide.
3. Amusez-vous bien pendant le week-end.
4. Dépêchez-vous pour ne pas être en retard.
5. Levez-vous avant 8 heures.
6. Ne vous inquiétez pas quand vous avez un examen.
7. Ne vous promenez pas après 22 heures.

9 Un petit sondage *(A small poll).* Vous êtes journaliste. Interviewez une autre personne (votre partenaire). Demandez ...

> **MODÈLE:** s'il (si elle) se lève tôt
> **VOUS: Est-ce que vous vous levez tôt le samedi matin?**
> **VOTRE PARTENAIRE: Non, je me lève assez tard.**

1. s'il (si elle) parle français
2. comment il (elle) s'appelle
3. comment il (elle) va
4. s'il (si elle) est fatigué(e)
5. à quelle heure il (elle) se lève en semaine
6. à quelle heure il (elle) se couche
7. s'il (si elle) se lève tôt ou tard le samedi matin
8. s'il (si elle) s'endort à la bibliothèque
9. avec quel dentifrice il (elle) se brosse les dents
10. s'il (si elle) s'inquiète quand il y a un examen
11. depuis quand il (elle) étudie le français

Entre amis

Et ta journée?

Interview your partner about his/her typical day.

1. Find out at what time your partner wakes up.
2. Find out what s/he does during the day.
3. Find out at what time your partner goes to bed.

3 Describing Past Activities

La dernière fois que j'ai dîné au restaurant avec des amis ...

	oui	non
ils y sont arrivés avant moi.	____	____
je me suis dépêché(e) pour arriver à l'heure.	____	____
mes amis s'inquiétaient parce que j'étais en retard.	____	____
nous nous sommes mis à table à huit heures.	____	____
je me suis bien amusé(e).	____	____
nous nous sommes promenés après le repas.	____	____
je me suis couché(e) assez tôt.	____	____

[handwritten note: We put/started at 8:00?]

D. Le passé des verbes pronominaux

- The imperfect tense of reflexive verbs is formed in the same way as that of simple verbs. The reflexive pronoun precedes the verb.

> There are no spelling changes in the imperfect for stem changing verbs; **s'appeler: Il s'appelait Pierre; se lever: Je me levais tôt.**

s'inquiéter *(inquiétons)*			
je	**m'inquiétais**	nous	**nous inquiétions**
tu	**t'inquiétais**	vous	**vous inquiétiez**
il/elle/on	**s'inquiétait**	ils/elles	**s'inquiétaient**

> Review the passé composé of **se coucher** in Ch. 7, p. 190.

- All reflexive verbs use the auxiliary **être** to form the passé composé. The past participle agrees in gender and number with the preceding direct object (usually the reflexive pronoun).

se reposer			
je	**me**	**suis**	**reposé(e)**
tu	**t'**	**es**	**reposé(e)**
il/on	**s'**	**est**	**reposé**
elle	**s'**	**est**	**reposée**
nous	**nous**	**sommes**	**reposé(e)s**
vous	**vous**	**êtes**	**reposé(e)(s)**
ils	**se**	**sont**	**reposés**
elles	**se**	**sont**	**reposées**

> The past participle of stem changing verbs is not affected by spelling changes; it is based on the infinitive: **promené, inquiété, appelé.**

Delphine **s'est couchée** tôt parce qu'elle était fatiguée.

Nous **nous sommes** bien **amusé(e)s** le week-end dernier.

Note Except for **s'asseoir,** the past participles of reflexive verbs are formed by the normal rules. The past participle of **s'asseoir** is **assis.**

Les deux femmes se sont **assises** à côté de moi.

■ In the negative, **ne ... pas** (**jamais,** etc.) are placed around the reflexive pronoun and the auxiliary verb.

Les enfants **ne** se sont **pas** couchés.
Je **ne** me suis **jamais** endormi(e) en classe.

■ In questions with inversion, as in all cases of inversion, the *subject* pronoun is placed after the auxiliary verb. The *reflexive* pronoun always directly precedes the auxiliary verb.

À quelle heure **t'es-tu** couchée, Christelle?
Vos amies **se** sont-**elles** reposées?

> Reflexive pronouns are object pronouns, just like **le, la, les.** They follow the same general placement rules. See Ch. 10, p. 278.

FOR RECOGNITION ONLY:

• The past participle of a reflexive verb agrees with a preceding direct object. In most cases, the direct object is the reflexive pronoun, which precedes the past participle.

Claire **s'**est lavée.   *Claire washed **herself.***
Nous **nous** sommes amusés.   *We had a good time. (We amused **ourselves.**)*

• However, with some reflexive verbs (such as **se laver** and **se brosser**), the direct object often follows the verb and the reflexive pronoun is not the direct object. The past participle *does not agree* with a reflexive pronoun that is not a direct object.

Claire s'est lavé **les cheveux.**   *Claire washed **her hair.***
Elle s'est brossé **les dents.**   *She brushed **her teeth.***

 Mais oui, Maman. Madame Cousineau pose beaucoup de questions à sa fille. Utilisez l'expression entre parenthèses pour répondre à ces questions.

Modèle: Tu t'es réveillée à 7 heures? (mais oui)
     Mais oui, je me suis réveillée à 7 heures.

1. Est-ce que tu t'es lavée ce matin? (mais oui)
2. Tu ne t'es pas dépêchée? (mais si!)
3. As-tu pris le petit déjeuner? (mais oui)
4. À quelle heure es-tu partie pour l'école? (à 7 heures 45)
5. Est-ce que tu t'es amusée à l'école? (non)
6. Tu ne t'es pas endormie en classe? (mais non)
7. À quelle heure es-tu rentrée de l'école? (à 5 heures)
8. Est-ce que tu as fait tes devoirs? (euh ... non)

Le professeur et ses étudiants s'amusent après le cours.

 Vous aussi? Décidez si les phrases suivantes sont vraies pour vous. Utilisez **Moi aussi, Moi non plus** ou **Pas moi** pour répondre. Si vous choisissez **Pas moi,** ajoutez une explication.

MODÈLE: Les professeurs se sont bien amusés le week-end dernier.
Pas moi, je ne me suis pas amusé(e). J'ai étudié pendant tout le week-end.

1. Les professeurs se sont couchés avant minuit hier.
2. Ils se sont réveillés à 8 heures ce matin.
3. Ils ont pris le petit déjeuner.
4. Ils ont pris une douche ensuite.
5. Ils sont allés à leur premier cours à 9 heures.
6. Ils ne se sont pas assis pendant leurs cours.
7. Ils se sont bien amusés en classe.
8. Ils ont bu du café après le cours.

 Votre vie sur le campus. Vous êtes journaliste. Interviewez un(e) étudiant(e). Demandez ...

MODÈLES: s'il (si elle) s'est levé(e) tôt ce matin.
Vous êtes-vous levé(e) tôt ce matin?

ce qu'il (elle) a mangé.
Qu'est-ce que vous avez mangé?

1. s'il (si elle) arrive quelque-fois en retard en classe.
2. s'il (si elle) s'est dépêché(e) ce matin.
3. où il (elle) va pour s'amuser.
4. ce qu'il (elle) a fait hier soir.
5. s'il (si elle) s'est amusé(e) hier soir.
6. à quelle heure il (elle) s'est couché(e).
7. s'il (si elle) s'est endormi(e) tout de suite.
8. combien d'heures il (elle) a dormi.
9. s'il (si elle) se repose d'habitude l'après-midi.
10. s'il (si elle) s'inquiète avant un examen.

Entre amis

Hier

1. Find out at what time your partner got up yesterday.
2. Find out what clothing s/he put on.
3. Ask if s/he took a walk.
4. Find out what else s/he did.
5. Ask if s/he had fun.
6. Find out at what time s/he went to bed.

4 Expressing One's Will

Que veux-tu que je fasse°, Emmanuelle?   *What do you want me to do*

Je voudrais ...
 que tu ailles° au marché.   *go*
 que tu achètes des fruits et des légumes.
 que tu fasses la cuisine.
 que tu mettes la table.

▶ **Et vous?** Que voulez-vous que vos amis fassent?

E. Le subjonctif (suite)

Review Ch. 10, pp. 282–284.

Je voudrais **que mes amis fassent** la cuisine pour moi.
Je voudrais **que mon ami** me **téléphone.**
Je voudrais **que vous veniez** au centre commercial avec moi.

■ You have already learned that the subjunctive is used after the word **que** in
 the second clause of a sentence in situations in which you are advising others. It is also used in other situations, such as when you are telling others
 what you want them to do.

VOCABULAIRE

La volonté *(will)*

exiger que	*to demand that*	souhaiter que	*to wish, hope that*
vouloir que	*to want*	préférer que	*to prefer that*
désirer que	*to want*		

Review   With the exception of **être** and **avoir**, the subjunctive endings are always **-e, -es, -e, -ions, -iez, -ent**. The stem is usually formed by taking the present tense **ils/elles** form and dropping the **-ent** ending.

chanter (ils chantent)		
que je	chant	**e**
que tu	chant	**es**
qu'il/elle/on	chant	**e**
que nous	chant	**ions**
que vous	chant	**iez**
qu'ils/elles	chant	**ent**

vendre (ils vendent)		
que je	vend	**e**
que tu	vend	**es**
qu'il/elle/on	vend	**e**
que nous	vend	**ions**
que vous	vend	**iez**
qu'ils/elles	vend	**ent**

choisir (ils choisissent)		
que je	choisiss	**e**
que tu	choisiss	**es**
qu'il/elle/on	choisiss	**e**
que nous	choisiss	**ions**
que vous	choisiss	**iez**
qu'ils/elles	choisiss	**ent**

Note   Even many irregular verbs follow this basic rule.

écrire	(ils écrivent)	que j'**écrive**, que nous **écrivions**
lire	(ils lisent)	que je **lise**, que nous **lisions**
partir	(ils partent)	que je **parte**, que nous **partions**
connaître	(ils connaissent)	que je **connaisse**, que nous **connaissions**
conduire	(ils conduisent)	que je **conduise**, que nous **conduisions**
mettre	(ils mettent)	que je **mette**, que nous **mettions**

■   Some verbs have one stem for **je, tu, il/elle/on,** and **ils/elles** forms and another stem for **nous** and **vous.** Many of these are the same verbs that have two stems in the present tense. Some verbs of this type that you have already learned are **venir, prendre, boire, préférer, acheter,** and **se lever.**

venir					
	(ils	viennent)		(nous	venons)
que je		vienn	**e**	que nous	ven	**ions**
que tu		vienn	**es**	que vous	ven	**iez**
qu'il/elle/on		vienn	**e**		
qu'ils/elles		vienn	**ent**		

Note   **Aller** also has two stems (**aill-,** which is irregular, and **all-**).

Aille, ailles, aille, and aillent are pronounced like **aïe!** (ouch!) and **ail** (garlic): [aj].

aller					
	(aill-)			(nous	allons)
que j'	aill	**e**	que nous	all	**ions**
que tu	aill	**es**	que vous	all	**iez**
qu'il/elle/on	aill	**e**		
qu'ils/elles	aill	**ent**		

■ Some verbs have totally irregular stems. Their endings, however, are regular.

faire *(fass-)*		
que je	**fass**	**e**
que tu	**fass**	**es**
qu'il/elle/on	**fass**	**e**
que nous	**fass**	**ions**
que vous	**fass**	**iez**
qu'ils/elles	**fass**	**ent**

savoir *(sach-)*		
que je	**sach**	**e**
que tu	**sach**	**es**
qu'il/elle/on	**sach**	**e**
que nous	**sach**	**ions**
que vous	**sach**	**iez**
qu'ils/elles	**sach**	**ent**

Aie, aies, ait, and **aient** are pronounced like **est** *(is).*

■ Only **être** and **avoir** have irregular stems *and* endings.

être	
que je	**sois**
que tu	**sois**
qu'il/elle/on	**soit**
que nous	**soyons**
que vous	**soyez**
qu'ils/elles	**soient**

avoir	
que j'	**aie**
que tu	**aies**
qu'il/elle/on	**ait**
que nous	**ayons**
que vous	**ayez**
qu'ils/elles	**aient**

Review the use of the infinitive and the use of the subjunctive on p. 284.

Attention   If there is not a change of subjects, the infinitive must be used.

Je voudrais **téléphoner** à mon ami.	*I would like to call my friend.*
Je voudrais **parler** avec lui.	*I would like to speak with him.*
Mais: Je voudrais que mon ami fasse la cuisine.	*I would like my friend to cook.*

⓭ Nos professeurs sont si exigeants! *(Our teachers are so demanding!)* Utilisez les expressions suivantes pour faire des phrases.

Modèle: les professeurs / vouloir / les étudiants / venir aux cours
Les professeurs veulent que les étudiants viennent aux cours.

1. les professeurs / désirer / les étudiants / faire leurs devoirs
2. les professeurs / vouloir / les étudiants / avoir de bonnes notes
3. les professeurs / exiger / les étudiants / être à l'heure
4. notre professeur / vouloir absolument / nous / parler français en classe
5. notre professeur / désirer / nous / réussir
6. notre professeur / souhaiter / nous / aller en France
7. notre professeur / préférer / nous / habiter chez une famille française
8. notre professeur / souhaiter / nous / savoir parler comme les Français

14 **Que veulent-ils que je fasse?** Tout le monde veut que vous fassiez quelque chose. Faites des phrases pour expliquer ce qu'ils veulent. Vous pouvez utiliser la forme négative si vous voulez.

MODÈLES: **Mes amis désirent que je sorte tous les soirs.**
Ma mère ne veut pas que je conduise vite.
Mon père préfère que je n'aie pas de voiture.

mes amis mon père ma mère	exiger vouloir désirer souhaiter préférer	que je	étudier beaucoup sortir tous les soirs aller au bistro tomber malade être heureux/heureuse avoir une voiture conduire vite faire la cuisine partir en vacances m'amuser beaucoup m'inquiéter quand il y a un examen acheter moins de vêtements

Il faut qu'elles se dépêchent parce qu'elles vont bientôt se mettre à table.

Un petit sketch: Une fille au pair. Lisez ou jouez le sketch suivant et répondez ensuite aux questions.

MME MARTIN: Je serai absente toute la journée.

LORI: Très bien, Madame. Que voulez-vous que je fasse aujourd'hui?

MME MARTIN: Je préparerai le dîner, mais je voudrais que vous alliez au marché.

LORI: D'accord.

MME MARTIN: Vous pouvez aussi y envoyer les enfants. J'ai laissé ma liste sur la table de la cuisine.
(Elle regarde sa montre.)
Aïe! Il faut que je parte. Au revoir, Lori. Au revoir, les enfants.
(après le départ de Mme Martin)

LORI: David! Sylvie! Dépêchez-vous! Votre mère veut que vous achetiez six tomates et un kilo de pommes de terre. Et n'oubliez pas de dire «s'il vous plaît» et «merci» à la dame au marché.

DAVID ET SYLVIE: Mais Lori!

LORI: Dépêchez-vous! Et mettez vos manteaux! Il pleut.

DAVID ET SYLVIE: Où est l'argent?

LORI: Attendez, le voilà. *(Elle donne l'argent aux enfants.)* Allez-y! Il ne faut pas que vous oubliiez la monnaie.

Questions

1. Que faut-il que Lori fasse?
2. Est-il nécessaire qu'elle aille au marché elle-même?
3. Pourquoi veut-elle que les enfants mettent leurs manteaux?
4. Pourquoi les enfants ne partent-ils pas tout de suite?

 Fais comme il faut. Votre mère vous donne des conseils. Utilisez un verbe de volonté avec **que** et le subjonctif. Qu'est-ce qu'elle dit?

MODÈLES: ne pas t'endormir en classe
Je souhaite que tu ne t'endormes pas en classe.

conduire lentement
J'exige que tu conduises lentement.

1. prendre le petit déjeuner
2. ne pas boire de bière
3. mettre un chapeau s'il fait froid
4. aller aux cours tous les jours
5. savoir l'importance d'une bonne éducation
6. ne sortir avec tes ami(e)s que le week-end
7. être prudent(e)
8. rentrer tôt
9. ne pas te lever tard

17 **À vous.** Répondez.

1. Que voulez-vous que vos parents fassent pour vous?
2. Qu'est-ce qu'ils veulent que vous fassiez pour eux?
3. Où voulez-vous que vos amis aillent avec vous?
4. Que voulez-vous que vos amis vous donnent pour votre anniversaire?
5. Quels vêtements préférez-vous mettre pour aller à vos cours?
6. Quels vêtements préférez-vous que le professeur mette?
7. Qu'est-ce que le professeur veut que vous fassiez?

Entre amis

Des projets pour visiter la ville de Québec

1. Tell your partner that your teacher wants you to go to Québec.
2. Tell your partner that you want him/her to come with you.
3. Explain that you have to speak French there.
4. Tell your partner that your teacher wants you to leave next week.

Intégration

Révision

A **Pour mettre la table.** Que faut-il qu'on fasse pour mettre la table à la française? Donnez une description complète.

MODÈLE: **Il faut qu'on mette une nappe sur la table.**

B **Ma journée.** D'abord décrivez votre journée habituelle. Ensuite décrivez votre journée d'hier.

C **Catégories.** Interviewez les étudiants de votre cours de français. Pouvez-vous trouver une personne pour chaque catégorie? *Attention:* Certains verbes ne sont pas des verbes pronominaux.

MODÈLE: quelqu'un qui se lève avant 7 heures du matin

VOUS: **Te lèves-tu avant 7 heures du matin?**
UN(E) AUTRE ÉTUDIANT(E): **Oui, je me lève avant 7 heures du matin.**
ou
Non, je ne me lève pas avant 7 heures du matin.

1. quelqu'un qui se lève avant 7 heures du matin
2. quelqu'un qui se couche après minuit
3. quelqu'un qui s'endort quelquefois en classe
4. quelqu'un qui lave sa voiture une fois par mois
5. quelqu'un qui se brosse les dents avant le petit déjeuner
6. quelqu'un qui se réveille quelquefois pendant la nuit

7. quelqu'un qui se promène après le dîner
8. quelqu'un qui promène souvent son chien
9. quelqu'un qui s'amuse au cours de français
10. quelqu'un qui s'inquiète s'il (si elle) est en retard
11. quelqu'un qui s'assied toujours à la même place au cours de français

D **À vous.** Répondez.

1. Que font les étudiants de votre université pour s'amuser?
2. Qu'est-ce que les professeurs veulent que leurs étudiants fassent?
3. Qu'est-ce que vos parents ne veulent pas que vous fassiez?
4. Dans quelles circonstances vous dépêchez-vous?
5. À quel(s) moment(s) de la journée vous brossez-vous les dents?
6. Avez-vous quelquefois envie de vous endormir en classe? Pourquoi ou pourquoi pas?

Pas de problème!

Preparation for the video:
1. Video worksheet in the *Cahier d'activités*
2. CD-ROM, *Module 10*

Cette activité est basée sur la vidéo, *Module 10*. Écoutez attentivement pour savoir si les choses suivantes sont mentionnées. Cochez *(check)* les expressions que vous entendez.

— les anchois
— les champignons
— les desserts
— le fromage
— les légumes
— le pâté
— les pommes de terre
— la salade
— les croissants
— les concombres
— le fromage de brebis

— les artichauts
— la charcuterie
— les épinards
— les fruits
— les melons
— la pâtisserie
— le porc
— les sardines
— le thon
— les tomates
— les saucisses

— les bananes
— les cornichons
— les fraises
— le gâteau
— les œufs
— les petits pois
— le poulet
— le saumon
— la truite
— les framboises
— le fromage de chèvre

— le bifteck
— la tarte
— les frites
— la glace
— le pain
— le poisson
— le riz
— la soupe
— la viande
— les radis
— le fromage de vache

Lecture I

A **Étude du vocabulaire.** Étudiez les phrases suivantes et choisissez les mots qui correspondent aux mots français en caractères gras: *sand, those, burning, gently, shovel, lived, erased, pick up, sea.*

1. Le professeur a écrit une phrase au tableau et ensuite il a **effacé** la phrase.
2. Marie, regarde ta chambre! Tu as laissé tes vêtements sur ton lit. **Ramasse**-les tout de suite!
3. **Ceux** qui habitent près de la **mer** peuvent souvent s'amuser dans l'eau.
4. Quand nous étions jeunes, nous **vivions** heureux avec notre famille.
5. En été, les enfants aimaient bien nager dans la **mer** ou jouer avec une **pelle** dans le **sable**.
6. Quand il faisait très chaud, le **sable** était **brûlant**. On ne pouvait pas marcher sans chaussures.
7. Parlez **doucement**! Les enfants dorment.

B **Pensez à la saison.** À quelle saison pensez-vous quand vous entendez les expressions suivantes?

1. la mer et le sable
2. le soleil brûlant
3. les feuilles mortes
4. le vent du nord

5. la belle vie
6. la nuit froide
7. les jours heureux

Les Feuilles mortes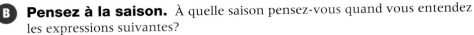

Oh! Je voudrais tant que tu te souviennes
Des jours heureux où nous étions amis.
En ce temps-là la vie était plus belle
Et le soleil plus brûlant qu'aujourd'hui.
Les feuilles mortes se ramassent à la pelle,
Tu vois, je n'ai pas oublié.
Les feuilles mortes se ramassent à la pelle,
Les souvenirs et les regrets aussi
Et le vent du nord les emporte[1]
Dans la nuit froide de l'oubli.
Tu vois, je n'ai pas oublié
La chanson que tu me chantais.

C'est une chanson qui nous ressemble,
Toi, tu m'aimais, et je t'aimais.
Nous vivions tous les deux ensemble,
Toi, qui m'aimais; moi, qui t'aimais.
Mais la vie sépare ceux qui s'aiment
Tout doucement, sans faire de bruit
Et la mer efface sur le sable
Les pas des amants désunis.[2]

Jacques Prévert

---

1. *carries away*   2. *the footprints of separated lovers*

C **À votre avis.** Relisez le poème et faites deux listes: (1) des expressions qui vous semblent tristes ou nostalgiques et (2) des expressions qui vous semblent plus heureuses.

Lecture II

A **Étude du vocabulaire.** Étudiez les phrases suivantes et choisissez les mots qui correspondent aux mots français en caractères gras: *corn, dry, dust, maid, rooms, harvest.*

1. C'était une maison avec quatre **pièces**: deux chambres, une cuisine et une salle de séjour.
2. Il y a longtemps que j'ai nettoyé cette chambre. Les meubles sont couverts de **poussière**.
3. Sans pluie, toute la région était **sèche**.
4. L'automne est la saison de la **récolte** du **maïs** dans l'Iowa.
5. Quelquefois les familles ont une **bonne** pour les aider au ménage.

B **Situez ces expressions.** Étudiez les expressions suivantes qui sont utilisées dans la lettre que Madame Nabi a envoyée du Burkina Faso. Ensuite cherchez-les dans sa lettre.

barrage *dam*, bouillie de mil *millet porridge*, dolo *a type of punch*, ignames *yams*, marmite *large pot*, occasions de rencontre *chances to meet others*, oseille *sorrel*, pagne *(grass) skirt*, Pâques *Easter*, prière *prayer*, tamarin *tamarind fruit*, tarissent *dry up*, tuteurs, *legal guardians*, volaille *poultry*

Une lettre du Burkina Faso

Madame Nabi adresse une lettre à son amie américaine où elle lui parle de sa vie au Burkina Faso. Madame Nabi et son mari s'occupent d'un CSPS, Centre de santé et promotion sociale, pour procurer à leurs compatriotes aide et conseils au point de vue santé.

Zitenga, le 3 avril 1997

À Madame Baer

Je suis ravie de vous écrire cette lettre. Vous avez le bonjour de mon mari, M. Nabi, et de mon bébé, Wen Danga Benaja (puissance de Dieu, en mooré), qui a quatre mois. Mon bonjour également à toute votre famille et à tous ceux et celles qui vous sont chers. Nous vous ferons découvrir le Burkina par notre correspondance.

Les notables du village habillés pour la fête

Nous habitons à Zitenga, qui est à 53 km au nord de la ville d'Ouagadougou, capitale du Burkina Faso. Ce village se trouve dans la province d'Oubritenga, une des 45 provinces du pays. Nous avons un climat sahélien : il pleut de juin à octobre, il fait froid de novembre à janvier et chaud de février à mai. Pendant la saison froide, le vent, qu'on appelle le Harmattan et qui vient du désert, couvre tout de poussière. Les villageois sont des cultivateurs, surtout de mil, d'arachides et de riz, et des éleveurs de moutons, de bœufs et de volailles. En saison sèche, on fait du jardinage et du commerce.

Le village respecte la hiérarchie traditionnelle. Le chef est généralement le plus vieux de la tribu et c'est lui qui est gardien de la tradition. Parmi les principales religions, l'animisme, la plus ancienne, est en voie de disparaître. Les gens qui la pratiquent adorent des idoles et placent leur confiance dans les ancêtres. Il y a aussi des catholiques, des protestants et des musulmans; ces derniers sont les plus nombreux. Les ethnies existantes sont les Mossis, qui sont en majorité, et les Peuhls qui sont nomades. On parle le mooré, le foulfouldé (peuhl) et le français.

Les occasions de rencontre sont surtout les fêtes traditionnelles mossis, dont le Basga, fête des récoltes où les vieux animistes préparent des boissons comme le dolo fait à base de sorgho rouge. Il y a aussi la fête musulmane du Ramadan et la Tabaski, fête des moutons. Les Chrétiens fêtent Noël et Pâques. Après un décès dans le village, on se réunit pour fêter le mort et demander à Dieu de l'accepter dans sa maison. On prépare un repas avec poulet et mouton, on boit le dolo, et on assiste à la danse des masques, exécutée au rythme des tams-tams. Ces masques sont des objets sacrés qui ne sortent que pour les funérailles et certaines fêtes mossis. Les jours de grands marchés, tous les 21 jours, le vendredi, les jeunes organisent des fêtes, les Damandassés, qui sont l'occasion pour eux de montrer leurs beaux habits, leurs belles robes et pagnes. C'est l'occasion aussi pour garçons et filles de se lier d'une amitié qui peut souvent aller jusqu'au mariage. Les Damandassés commencent après les récoltes à quatre heures de l'après-midi et durent jusqu'au petit matin.

Les maisons sont construites en "banco" ou terre séchée au soleil. Notre maison a deux pièces et un salon. J'y habite avec mon mari, mon bébé, ainsi que la femme d'un grand frère de mon mari, trois élèves (ma petite sœur qui fait la sixième, et une fille et un garçon qui font la cinquième, dont nous sommes les tuteurs), deux garçons qui nous aident pour les travaux domestiques et la construction, une bonne et un homme de 45 ans qui est chez nous depuis trois mois. En tout nous sommes onze dans la famille.

Nous commençons chaque journée par une prière protestante de 6h à 6h30. Puis, mon mari et moi, nous allons au Centre de santé et de promotion sociale[2], où nous sommes agents de santé. À 12h30 c'est le déjeuner, et de 15h à 17h nous repartons au CSPS. Vers 19h c'est le dîner. Nous nous couchons chaque soir vers 22h, si nous n'avons pas de malade à surveiller au dispensaire. Quand on a un peu de temps, on lit un bon roman.

Le repas du matin, c'est la bouillie de mil préparée avec le jus de tamarin, cuite avec du sucre. Très rarement, on prend du café, du lait ou du pain. À midi, on prépare du riz avec sauce ou haricots; ou bien des ignames avec sauce tomate ou simplement salées, avec de l'huile d'arachide. Le soir, on mange du tô. Le tô est fait avec de la farine de maïs ou de mil, de l'eau et du jus de tamarin. On y ajoute une sauce faite avec des légumes tels que de l'oseille, des oignons, des tomates, ou de la viande ou du poisson fumé. On utilise aussi l'huile ou la pâte d'arachide. On mange assis par terre autour de la marmite et on prend la nourriture avec la main droite. Les femmes et les hommes mangent séparément.

Nous cherchons l'eau de boisson à un forage (une pompe) assez loin de chez nous, parce que le forage du dispensaire est en panne et nous n'avons pas les moyens suffisants pour le réparer. En plus des forages, les habitants puisent l'eau des puits, des mares ou des marigots[3]. Malheureusement ces sources d'eau tarissent très vite. Les femmes portent l'eau sur leur tête. Ceux qui ont les moyens vont à

Mme Nabi et sa petite sœur dans les champs

l'eau avec des charrettes. Les légumes frais, qu'on achète au marché, viennent des villages environnants où il y a des barrages et donc des terres irriguées. Le problème de l'eau est crucial à Zitenga.

Je remercie Madame Baer des cadeaux qu'elle a offerts à mon bébé. Si vous voulez d'autres détails, vous pouvez nous écrire. Nous vous souhaitons courage dans votre travail et surtout bonne réception de cette lettre.

Madame Nabi, née Ouedraogo Abzèta, Zitenga

---

1. *climate of transition between the desert and damper regions* 2. *M. Nabi is head of the Center, but not a doctor. His wife has nursing skills. Two midwives do pre-natal and post-natal counseling, including family planning. A second man does vaccination tours, and a third is a fix-it person and also gives shots and does circumcisions.* 3. *dead branch of a river bed*

C **Vrai ou faux?** Décidez si les phrases suivantes sont vraies ou fausses d'après la lecture. Si une phrase est fausse, corrigez-la.

1. Madame Nabi habite une grande maison.
2. Il y a plus de protestants que de membres d'autres religions.
3. On ne parle que le français au Burkina Faso.
4. La famille se met à table pour manger.
5. On utilise une fourchette, un couteau et une cuiller et on mange «à la française».
6. Les légumes frais viennent du jardin des Nabi.
7. Madame Nabi et son mari travaillent dans une sorte de clinique.
8. Ils se lèvent avant six heures du matin.
9. Pour avoir de l'eau, on doit simplement ouvrir le robinet dans la cuisine.

D **Questions.** Répondez.

1. Combien d'hommes et combien de femmes habitent la maison de Madame Nabi?
2. D'après cette lettre, combien de langues est-ce qu'on parle au Burkina Faso?
3. Quelles sont les quatre religions dont parle Madame Nabi?
4. Quelles sont les différentes sortes de viande mentionnées dans cette lettre?
5. Quels sont les besoins essentiels pour les gens du village?

E **Cherchez des exemples.** Relisez la lettre et cherchez des exemples ...

1. qui indiquent que le Burkina Faso se trouve en Afrique.
2. qui prouvent que le Burkina Faso est un pays pauvre.
3. qui montrent l'influence de l'Islam au Burkina Faso.
4. qui révèlent la foi *(faith)* et la charité des Nabi.

VOCABULAIRE ACTIF

À table

un bol *bowl*
un couteau *knife*
une cuiller *spoon*
une fourchette *fork*
une nappe *tablecloth*
le poivre *pepper*
le sel *salt*
une serviette *napkin*
le sucre *sugar*

Au restaurant

une carte *(à la carte) menu*
un menu *(fixed price) menu*

D'autres noms

une brosse à cheveux (à dents)
   hairbrush (toothbrush)
le chauffage *heat*
la climatisation *air conditioning*
une dame *lady*
les genoux *(m. pl.) lap; knees*
un maillot de bain *bathing suit*
un pyjama *(pair of) pajamas*
des skis *(m.) skis*
une soirée *evening party*
un sourire *smile*

La routine quotidienne

se brosser (les dents) *to brush
   (one's teeth)*
se coucher *to go to bed*
s'endormir *to fall asleep*
s'habiller *to get dressed*
se laver *to get washed; to wash up*
se lever *to get up; to stand up*
se mettre à table *to sit down to eat*
se promener *to take a walk, ride*
se reposer *to rest*
se réveiller *to wake up*

Expressions utiles

à la française *in the French style*
Bon appétit! *Have a good meal.*
C'est exact. *That's right.*
de rien *you're welcome; don't mention it; not at all*
Excusez-moi (nous, etc.) d'être
   en retard. *Excuse me (us, etc.) for
   being late.*
Il n'y a pas de quoi. *Don't mention
   it.; Not at all.*
il sourit *he smiles*
Par ici. *(Come) this way.; Follow me.*

Verbes

s'appeler *to be named; to be called*
s'asseoir *to sit down*
couper *to cut*
se dépêcher *to hurry*
exiger (que) *to demand (that)*
goûter *to taste*
s'inquiéter *to worry*
laver *to wash*
lever *to lift; to raise*
mettre *to put; to place; to lay*
mettre la table *to set the table*
mettre le chauffage *to turn on the
   heat*
souhaiter (que) *to wish; to hope
   (that)*
se souvenir (de) *to remember*
tarder *to be a long time coming*
verser *to pour*

14 Les hommes et les femmes

Buts communicatifs
Describing interpersonal relationships
Describing television programs
Expressing emotion

Structures utiles
Le verbe **dire**
Les pronoms objets indirects
Les verbes **voir** et **croire**
Les interrogatifs **quel** et **lequel**
Le pronom relatif (suite)
Le subjonctif (suite)
Le pronom **en**

Culture
La télévision française
Qu'est-ce que les Français regardent à la télé?
Les faux amis

Coup d'envoi

Prise de contact   ## Une histoire d'amour

David et Marie sortent ensemble.
Ils s'entendent° très bien.   *get along*
Ils s'embrassent°.   *kiss*
Ils s'aiment.
Il lui° a demandé si elle voulait l'épouser.   *her*
Elle lui° a répondu que oui.   *him*
Il lui a acheté une très belle bague de   *engagement ring*
    fiançailles°.
Ils vont se marier.

Et vous?   Connaissez-vous des couples
                célèbres° qui sont fiancés?   *famous*
                Connaissez-vous des couples
                célèbres qui sont mariés?
                Connaissez-vous des couples
                célèbres qui sont divorcés?

M. et Mme Jean-Pierre Delataille   M. et Mme Émile Baron

ont l'honneur de vous annoncer le mariage de leurs enfants

Marie et David

et vous prient d'assister ou de vous unir d'intention à la Messe de Mariage

qui sera célébrée le samedi 13 juillet 2002 à 17 heures, en l'Église St-Gervais.

27, rue Mahler—75004 Paris   27, rue des Tournelles—75004 Paris

Conversation

Quelle histoire!

Lori et son amie Denise sont assises à la terrasse d'un café.
Denise lui demande si elle a regardé le feuilleton° d'hier soir. — soap opera, series

DENISE: Encore à boire, Lori?

LORI: Non, vraiment, sans façon.

DENISE: Au fait, tu as regardé le feuilleton hier à la télé?

LORI: Lequel?° — *Which one?*

DENISE: *Nos chers enfants.*

LORI: Non. Qu'est-ce qui est arrivé?° — *What happened?*

DENISE: David et Marie ne s'aiment plus. Marie a un petit ami maintenant.

LORI: Eh! ça devient sérieux.

DENISE: Tu ne sais pas tout. Ils vont divorcer. David lui a dit qu'il allait partir.

LORI: Il est sans doute très malheureux°, n'est-ce pas? — *unhappy*

DENISE: Bien sûr. Il dit que le mariage est une loterie. Pour se consoler le plus vite possible, il a mis une annonce° dans le journal local. — *advertisement*

LORI: Ça, c'est original°. Et il y a des candidates? — *a novel idea*

DENISE: Oui, trois femmes lui ont répondu et veulent le rencontrer°. — *meet*

LORI: Sans blague?° — *No kidding?*

DENISE: Je te le jure.° C'est passionnant! — *I swear.*

LORI: Quelle histoire!

▶ **Jouez ces rôles.** Répétez la conversation avec votre partenaire. Remplacez ensuite *David* par *Marie* et *Marie* par *David*, par exemple: **Elle lui a dit qu'elle allait partir.** Faites tous les changements nécessaires.

Il y a un geste

Je te le jure. An outstretched hand, palm down, means *I swear,* perhaps originally meaning "I would put my hand in the fire (if it were not true)."

Quelle histoire! To indicate that something is amazing, exaggerated, or far-fetched, the French hold the hand open with fingers pointing down and shake the wrist several times. Other expressions used with this gesture are **Oh là là!** *(Wow!, Oh dear!)* and **Mon Dieu!** *(My goodness!).*

Comment dit-on «passionnant» en anglais?

a. passionate   b. amazing   c. exciting

Que veut dire «sans doute»?

a. certainement   b. probablement   c. peut-être

En France il y a cinq chaînes (channels) de télévision nationales. Sur ces cinq, _____ sont des chaînes publiques.

a. Deux   b. Trois   c. Quatre

La télévision française

Until recently, commercials **(la publicité),** if allowed at all, were grouped into relatively lengthy segments and shown between programs. Today, however, commercials often interrupt programs, especially on the private channels. As in North America, many viewers cope by channel "surfing" **(zapper).**

Of the five major channels available to all, only two **(TF1** and **M6)** are private. The others **(France 2, France 3,** and **Arte/La 5)** are public. In addition to commercials and government subsidies, public television is financed in France (and in most European countries) by a user tax. Everyone who has a color TV set, currently 96% of French households, must pay 700 francs per year.

France 2 programming, especially the evening news **(le Journal de vingt heures),** is made available throughout the francophone world and in most other countries. It may be found on the French-language channels in Canada and on SCOLA and the International channel in the United States.

Recently cable TV watching and Internet use have increased considerably in France. French has become, after English, the second language of the World Wide Web.

Les faux amis (False cognates)

It is estimated that as much as 50% of our English-language vocabulary comes from French. Most of these words are true cognates and facilitate comprehension. There are, however, a number of false cognates whose meaning *in a given context* is quite different from what we might expect. Some examples are given on page 381.

Qu'est-ce que les Français regardent à la télé?

Si on ne considère que les chaînes nationales TF1, France 2, France 3, Arte/La Cinquième et M6, les Français regardent, en moyenne *(on the average),* 1.051 heures de programmes par an, dont 272 h. de fiction (feuilletons, etc.); 152 h. de magazines, de documentaires et de débats; 151 h. de journaux télévisés (informations); 99 h. de publicité; 88 h. de films; 86 h. de jeux; 71 h. de sport; 54 h. de variétés; 31 h. d'émissions pour enfants; 2 h. de théâtre et de musique classique; 45 h. d'autres programmes. *(d'après le Quid)*

épouser
marier
se marier

VOCABULARIE

Quelques faux amis

maintenant oui

actuellement	*now*
une annonce	*advertisement*
arriver	*to happen*
assister (à)	*to attend*
attendre	*to wait for*
un avertissement	*warning*
compréhensif (-ve)	*understanding*
confus(e)	*ashamed, embarrassed*
demander	*to ask*
une émission	*program*
formidable	*wonderful*
une histoire	*story*
un journal	*newspaper*
original(e)	*novel, odd; different*
passionnant(e)	*exciting, fascinating*
passer un examen	*to take a test*
rester	*to stay*
sans doute	*probably*

Review *cognate*, p. 25 and *false cognate*, p. 49.

impair(e)   *uneven*

 **À vous.** Répondez.

1. Avez-vous un feuilleton préféré? Si oui, lequel?
2. Que pensez-vous des feuilletons en général?
3. Quel feuilleton aimez-vous le moins?

Entre amis

Mon émission préférée

1. Ask your partner what his/her favorite TV show is.
2. Find out why s/he likes it.
3. Find out if s/he watched it this week.
4. If so, find out what happened. If not, ask what happened the last time s/he watched it.

Prononciation

La tension

■ There is much more tension in the facial muscles when speaking French than when speaking English. Two important phenomena result from this greater tension.

1. *There are no diphthongs (glides from one vowel sound to another) in French.* French vowels are said to be "pure." The positions of mouth and tongue remain stable during the pronunciation of a vowel, and therefore one vowel sound does not "glide" into another as often happens in English.

▶ **Contrast:**

English	French
d**ay**	d**es**
aut**o**	aut**o**

■ Notice that in the English word *day*, the **a** glides into an **ee** sound at the end, and that in the English word *auto*, the **o** glides to **oo**.

▶ Now practice "holding steady" the sound of each of the vowels in the following French words.

étudiant, am**é**ricain, sant**é**, soir**ée**, dans**er**, parl**ez**, l**es**, j'**ai** ch**o**se, styl**o**, tr**o**p, zér**o**, **au**ssi, ch**au**d, b**eau**, mant**eau**

2. *Final consonants are completely released.* The pronunciation of final French consonants is much more "complete" than is the case for those of American English.

■ Note that in American English, the final consonants are often neither dropped nor firmly enunciated. In similar French words, the final consonants are all clearly pronounced.

▶ **Contrast:**

English	French	English	French
ro**b**	ro**be**	home	ho**mm**e
gran**d**	gran**de**	American	américai**ne**
ba**g**	ba**gue**	gri**p**	gri**ppe**
be**ll**	be**lle**	intelligen**t**	intelligen**te**

▶ Now practice "releasing" the highlighted final consonant sounds below so that you can hear them clearly.

1. u**ne** gran**de** fi**lle**
2. E**lle** s'appe**lle** Michè**le**.
3. un pi**que**-ni**que**
4. une ba**gue** de fiançailles
5. un ho**mme** et une fe**mme**
6. sa ju**pe** ver**te**

Buts communicatifs

1 Describing Interpersonal Relationships

L'histoire d'un divorce

David et Marie ne s'entendent plus très bien.
Ils se fâchent°.   *get angry*
Ils se disputent°.   *argue; fight*
Il ne lui envoie plus de fleurs.
Elle ne lui parle plus.
Il lui a dit° qu'il ne l'aime plus.   *He told her*
Ils vont se séparer.
Ils ont même° l'intention de divorcer.   *even*

Review also p. 378

▶ **Et vous?** Choisissez un couple (de Hollywood, de Washington, de vos amis, etc.) que vous connaissez. Comment s'appellent-ils? Est-ce qu'ils s'entendent bien? Est-ce qu'ils se disputent quelquefois? Décrivez ce couple.

A. Le verbe *dire*

David **dit** qu'il va partir.   *David says (that) he's going to leave.*
Dites à Marie de faire attention.   *Tell Marie to watch out.*

dire *(to say; to tell)*			
je	**dis**	nous	**disons**
tu	**dis**	vous	**dites**
il/elle/on	**dit**	ils/elles	**disent**
passé composé: j'**ai dit**			

■ The verb **dire** should not be confused with the verb **parler**. Both can mean *to tell*, but they are used differently.

- **Dire** can be followed by a quote or by an item of information (sometimes contained in another clause introduced by **que**).

Bruno **dit bonjour** à Alissa.	*Bruno **says hello** to Alissa.*
Il **lui dit un secret.**	*He **tells her a secret.***
Il **dit qu'il l'aime.**	*He **says that he loves her.***
Il **dit** toujours **la vérité.**	*He always **tells the truth.***

- **Parler** can stand alone or can be followed by an adverb, by **à** (or **avec**) and the person spoken to, or by **de** and the topic of conversation.

Bruno **parle** (lentement).	*Bruno **is speaking** (slowly).*
Il **parle à** Alissa.	*He **is talking to** Alissa.*
Il **parle de** lui-même.	*He **is telling about** himself.*

Note When the meaning is *to tell (a story)*, the verb **raconter** is used.

Raconte-nous une histoire.   *Tell us a story.*

1 **Qu'est-ce qu'ils disent?** Quelles sont les opinions de chaque personne? Utilisez le verbe **dire** et le verbe **être** dans chaque phrase.

Modèle: Ma grand-mère / le rap / facile ou difficile à comprendre
Ma grand-mère dit que le rap est difficile à comprendre.

1. je / la publicité à la télé / très bonne ou très mauvaise
2. nos grands-parents / nous / charmants ou désagréables
3. nous / le cours de français / formidable ou ennuyeux
4. le professeur de français / nous / travailleurs ou paresseux
5. mes professeurs / je / intelligent(e) ou stupide
6. mes amis / le football à la télé / passionnant ou affreux

2 **À vous.** Répondez.

1. Que dites-vous quand vous avez une bonne note à un examen?
2. Que dit votre professeur de français quand vous entrez en classe?
3. Que dites-vous quand vous êtes en retard à un cours?
4. Que dites-vous à un(e) ami(e) qui vous téléphone à 6 heures du matin?
5. De quoi parlez-vous avec vos amis?
6. Vos professeurs racontent-ils quelquefois des histoires en classe? Si oui, quelle sorte d'histoires?
7. Comment dit-on «Oh dear!» en français?
8. Dites-vous toujours la vérité?

3 **Le perroquet et la fourmi** *(the parrot and the ant).* **Quelle histoire!** Utilisez les verbes **dire, parler** et **raconter** pour compléter le paragraphe suivant.

Mon frère _____ qu'il adore les histoires drôles. Hier soir, par exemple, *dit* il m'a _____ l'histoire d'une femme anglaise qui achète un perroquet qui *raconté* ne _____ que le français. Mais la pauvre dame ne peut rien _____ en *parle,* français et ne peut pas _____ avec lui. Un jour, la dame va boire un verre *dir* de lait mais dans le verre il y a une fourmi. Le perroquet veut _____ à la *parler* dame de ne pas boire le lait; il _____ FOURMI!! parce qu'il ne _____ pas *ditte* anglais. La dame pense que le perroquet a _____ «For me!» et elle part *dit* chercher un verre de lait pour son perroquet. J'ai _____ à mon frère que je *Pare* n'apprécie pas beaucoup les histoires qu'il _____.   *dit*

raconte   *dit*

B. Les pronoms objets indirects *raconte*

David parle *à Marie.*	*David is speaking to Marie.*
Il **lui** dit qu'il l'aime.	*He tells **her** that he loves her.*
Il **lui** demande l'épouser.	*He asks **her** to marry him.*
Il **lui** achète une bague de fiançailles.	*He buys **her** an engagement ring.*
Ils écrivent *à leurs parents.*	*They write to their parents.*
Ils **leur** disent qu'ils vont se marier.	*They tell **them** that they are going to get married.*

Il lui a demandé si elle voulait se promener.

■ Indirect object nouns in French are preceded by the preposition **à.** Many verbs take indirect objects, either in addition to a direct object or with no direct object.

VOCABULAIRE

Quelques verbes qui prennent un objet indirect

acheter		to buy
demander		to ask
dire		to say; to tell
donner		to give
écrire		to write
emprunter	quelque chose **à quelqu'un**	to borrow
envoyer		to send
montrer		to show
prêter		to lend
raconter		to tell
rendre		to give back
vendre		to sell
obéir		to obey
parler	**à quelqu'un**	to speak, talk
répondre		to respond, answer
téléphoner		to telephone

Two additional expressions that you have already learned take a specific direct object plus an indirect object: **poser une question à quelqu'un; rendre visite à quelqu'un.** J'ai posé une question **au professeur.** *(I asked the teacher a question.)* Vas-tu rendre visite **à tes parents?** *(Are you going to visit your parents?)*

Note   Do not be confused by verbs that take an indirect object in French but a direct object in English.

Paul obéit **à ses parents.**	*Paul obeys his parents.*
Je téléphone **à Brigitte.**	*I call Brigitte.*
Marc rend visite **à ses amis.**	*Marc visits his friends.*

■ Indirect object nouns can be replaced in sentences by indirect object pronouns.

Review the direct object pronouns on pp. 226 and 278.

me (m')	*(to) me*	**nous**	*(to) us*
te (t')	*(to) you*	**vous**	*(to) you*
lui	*(to) him; (to) her*	**leur**	*(to) them*

Note   The indirect object pronouns **me, te, nous,** and **vous** are identical to the direct object pronouns. But unlike direct objects, **lui** is used for both *(to) him* and *(to) her,* and **leur** is used for *(to) them.*

Alain a-t-il téléphoné **à Pierre?**	Oui, il **lui** a téléphoné.
A-t-il téléphoné aussi **à Anne?**	Oui, il **lui** a téléphoné aussi.
A-t-il téléphoné **à Guy et à Ariel?**	Oui, il **leur** a téléphoné après.
Vous a-t-il parlé de tout ça?	Non, il ne **m'**a pas parlé de ça.
	Ariel **m'**a dit ça.

Note Often in English, the preposition *to* is omitted. Also, in some contexts indirect object pronouns may mean *for someone, from someone,* etc.

Est-ce que je **t'**ai donné de l'argent? | *Did I give* **you** *some money? (= to you)*
Mais non, tu **m'**as emprunté 5 dollars! | *No, you borrowed 5 dollars* **from me!**
Alors, je **t'**achèterai quelque chose. | *Then I'll buy* **you** *something. (= for you)*

■ Like a direct object pronoun, an indirect object pronoun is almost always placed directly *before* the verb.

Nous **lui** répondons tout de suite. | *We answer him (her) right away.*
Ils ne **nous** ont pas téléphoné. | *They didn't telephone us.*
Vous dit-elle la vérité? | *Is she telling you the truth?*
Elle va **leur** rendre visite. | *She is going to visit them.*
Ne **m'**écris pas. | *Don't write to me.*

Review the use of pronouns with the imperative, Ch. 10, p. 285.

Note Also like direct object pronouns, indirect object pronouns follow the verb *only* in affirmative commands, and in that case **me** and **te** become **moi** and **toi.**

Écris-**lui** immédiatement! | *Write to him immediately!*
Donne-**moi** de l'eau, s'il te plaît. | *Give me some water, please.*

Synthèse: Object pronouns						
direct:	me	te	le/la	nous	vous	les
indirect:	me	te	lui	nous	vous	leur
reflexive:	me	te	se	nous	vous	se

Carrefour
vous simplifie la vie!
Tout en faisant vos courses, vous pouvez aussi...

4 **Le professeur et les étudiants.** Utilisez les expressions suivantes pour faire des phrases. Utilisez un pronom objet indirect dans chaque phrase et utilisez la forme négative si vous voulez.

MODÈLES: **Le professeur leur parle toujours en français.**
Les étudiants ne lui rendent jamais visite.

In this activity **lui** refers to **le professeur,** and **leur** refers to **les étudiants.**

		dire bonjour	
		parler en français	
		écrire des lettres	toujours
		téléphoner	d'habitude
le professeur	leur	rendre visite	souvent
les étudiants	lui	poser des questions	quelquefois
		demander un conseil	rarement
		raconter des histoires	jamais
		obéir	
		donner des tests faciles	

5 **Vrai ou faux?** Décidez si les phrases suivantes sont vraies ou fausses. Ensuite répondez chaque fois avec un pronom objet indirect. Si une phrase est fausse, corrigez-la.

MODÈLES: Le professeur dit toujours bonjour aux étudiants.
C'est vrai. Il leur dit toujours bonjour.

Le président vous a téléphoné.
C'est faux. Il ne m'a pas téléphoné.

1. Le professeur de français ne donne pas beaucoup de devoirs aux étudiants.
2. Le professeur vous pose beaucoup de questions.
3. Les étudiants répondent toujours correctement au professeur.
4. Vous écrivez quelquefois des lettres à vos amis.
5. Vos amis vous répondent chaque fois.
6. Vous téléphonez souvent à votre meilleur(e) ami(e).
7. Vous ne rendez jamais visite à vos cousins.
8. Vous montrez toujours vos notes à vos parents.
9. Vos parents vous prêtent souvent leur voiture.

6 **Faites-le donc!** *(Then do it!)* Encouragez la personne d'après les modèles. Utilisez des pronoms objets indirects.

MODÈLES: Je vais rendre visite à Jean.
Eh bien, rendez-lui donc visite!

Je voudrais poser une question au professeur.
Eh bien, posez-lui donc une question!

1. Je vais parler à Claire.
2. Je voudrais répondre au professeur.
3. Je vais rendre visite à mes grands-parents.
4. Je vais prêter ma voiture à mon amie.
5. J'ai envie de vous poser une question.
6. Je voudrais dire bonjour à Thierry.
7. J'ai envie de téléphoner à mes parents.

7 **Non, ne le faites pas!** Employez encore les phrases de l'activité 6 pour dire à la personne de *ne pas* faire ce qu'elle veut faire. Utilisez des pronoms objets indirects.

MODÈLES: Je vais rendre visite à Jean.
Mais non, ne lui rendez pas visite!

Je voudrais poser une question au professeur.
Mais non, ne lui posez pas de question!

La voiture de Paul. Remplacez chaque expression en italique par un des pronoms suivants: **le, la, les, lui** ou **leur.**

MODÈLES: Les parents de Paul ont acheté une voiture *à leur fils.*
Les parents de Paul lui ont acheté une voiture.

Ils aiment beaucoup *leur fils.*
Ils l'aiment beaucoup.

1. Il a dit merci *à ses parents.*
2. Georges a demandé *à Paul* s'il pouvait conduire *la voiture.*
3. Paul a prêté sa voiture *à Georges.*
4. Georges rend visite *à sa petite amie.*
5. Elle aime beaucoup *la voiture.*
6. Elle demande *à Georges* si elle peut conduire *la voiture.*
7. Il prête la voiture *à sa petite amie.* Elle dit merci *à Georges.*
8. Il dit *à son amie* de prendre *le volant.*
9. Elle va rendre la voiture *à Georges* la semaine prochaine.

9 **Je vais le faire.** Répondez affirmativement à chaque ordre par l'expression **Je vais** + un infinitif. Remplacez les expressions en italique par un pronom objet direct ou indirect.

MODÈLES: Il faut que vous téléphoniez *à Léa!*   Il faut que vous écriviez
D'accord, je vais lui téléphoner.   *votre nom.*
D'accord, je vais l'écrire.

1. Il faut que vous obéissiez *à vos parents!*
2. Il faut que vous prêtiez votre livre *à votre voisine!*
3. Il faut que vous regardiez *cette émission!*
4. Il faut que vous écriviez une lettre *à vos grands-parents!*
5. Il faut que vous disiez *la vérité!*
6. Il ne faut pas que vous demandiez *à Agnès* quel âge elle a!
7. Il ne faut pas que vous buviez *ce verre de vin!*
8. Il faut que vous posiez une question *au professeur!*
9. Il faut que vous *me* répondiez!

10 **À vous.** Répondez.

1. Téléphonez-vous souvent à vos amis?
2. À qui avez-vous parlé récemment?
3. Qu'est-ce que vous lui avez dit?
4. Qu'est-ce que vous lui avez demandé?
5. Qu'est-ce qu'il vous a répondu?
6. Allez-vous rendre visite à des amis bientôt?
7. Si oui, quand est-ce que vous leur rendrez visite? Si non, comment les contacterez-vous?
8. Que prêtez-vous à vos amis?
9. Qu'est-ce que vous empruntez à vos parents?

Entre amis

Votre meilleur(e) ami(e)

Talk to your partner about his/her best friend. Use indirect object pronouns where appropriate.

1. Find out the name of your partner's best friend.
2. Ask if your partner wrote to him/her this week.
3. Ask if your partner visited him/her this week.
4. Ask if your partner called him/her this week.
5. If so, try to find out what your partner said to his/her friend.

2 Describing Television Programs

Quelles émissions y a-t-il à la télévision?

Il y a ...

les informations, par exemple, *le Journal du soir*.
la météorologie, par exemple, *le Bulletin météo*.
les sports, par exemple, *le Tour de France*.
les films, par exemple, *Tous les matins du monde*.
les pièces, par exemple, *L'Avare* de Molière.
les feuilletons, par exemple, *Le Fond du problème*.
les dessins animés, par exemple, *Popeye*.
les jeux, par exemple, *la Roue de la fortune*.
la publicité, par exemple, les spots publicitaires pour Perrier, Coca-Cola.

Et vous? Qu'est-ce que vous regardez à la télévision?

11 À vous. Répondez.

1. Combien de temps par jour passez-vous à regarder la télévision?
2. Que regardez-vous à la télévision?
3. Quelles sont les émissions que vous ne regardez presque *(almost)* jamais?
4. Quelle émission trouvez-vous la plus drôle?
5. Quelle émission trouvez-vous la plus ennuyeuse?
6. Regardez-vous quelquefois des feuilletons? Si oui, quel feuilleton préférez-vous?
7. Que pensez-vous de la publicité à la télévision?
8. Voudriez-vous qu'il y ait plus, autant ou moins de sports à la télévision? Pourquoi?

C. Les verbes *voir* et *croire*

Je **crois** qu'il va neiger. Qu'en pensez-vous?	*I think it's going to snow. What do you think?*
On **verra**.	*We'll see.*
Je **crois** que je **vois** nos amis.	*I think (that) I see our friends.*
Avez-vous déjà **vu** ce film?	*Did you already see this film?*
Je **crois** que oui.	*I believe so.*
Non, je ne **crois** pas.	*No, I don't believe so.*

Note the use of **que** in the expression **Je crois que oui.**

■ The verbs **voir** and **croire** have similar present tense conjugations.

voir *(to see)*		croire *(to believe, think)*	
je	**vois**	je	**crois**
tu	**vois**	tu	**crois**
il/elle/on	**voit**	il/elle/on	**croit**
nous	**voyons**	nous	**croyons**
vous	**voyez**	vous	**croyez**
ils/elles	**voient**	ils/elles	**croient**
passé composé: j'**ai vu**		*passé composé:* j'**ai cru**	

■ The future tense verb stem for **voir** is irregular: **verr-.** The future of **croire** is regular.

Je vous **verrai** demain.	*I will see you tomorrow.*
Mes amis ne me **croiront** pas.	*My friends won't believe me.*

■ The subjunctive forms of **voir** and **croire** have two stems just like other verbs that have two present tense stems.

Il faut que je le **voie**.	Il faut que vous le **voyiez** aussi.
Je veux qu'il me **croie**.	Je veux que vous me **croyiez**.

 Que croient-ils? Tout le monde a son opinion. Utilisez le verbe **croire** et identifiez ce qui, à votre avis, correspond à la description donnée.

> **MODÈLE:** mon père / la meilleure équipe de football
> **Mon père croit que les New York Giants sont la meilleure équipe de football.**

1. je / l'émission la plus intéressante le jeudi soir
2. nous / le cours le plus ennuyeux
3. le professeur de français / les étudiants les plus travailleurs
4. mes parents / la chose la plus importante de ma vie
5. mes amis / le feuilleton le plus passionnant
6. je / le plus mauvais film de cette année

13 **Que croyez-vous?** Est-ce que la phrase est vraie pour la plupart des étudiants de votre cours de français? Si oui, répondez **Je crois que oui.** Si non, répondez **Je ne crois pas** et corrigez la phrase.

MODÈLE: La plupart des étudiants croient que le professeur de français est méchant.
Je ne crois pas. Ils croient que le professeur est très gentil.

1. La plupart des étudiants voient leurs parents tous les jours.
2. La plupart des étudiants verront un film le week-end prochain.
3. La plupart des étudiants ont déjà vu un film français.
4. La plupart des étudiants veulent voir un pays où on parle français.
5. La plupart des étudiants verront la tour Eiffel un jour.
6. La plupart des étudiants croient que les femmes conduisent mieux que les hommes.
7. La plupart des étudiants croyaient au Père Noël quand ils étaient petits.
8. La plupart des étudiants croient actuellement au Père Noël.

14 **À vous.** Répondez.

1. Quel film avez-vous vu la dernière fois que vous êtes allé(e) au cinéma?
2. Qui voyez-vous tous les jours?
3. Qui avez-vous vu hier?
4. Quelle note croyez-vous que vous aurez en français?
5. Quand croyez-vous que vous irez en Europe?
6. Qu'est-ce que vous verrez si vous y allez?
7. Qui croit au Père Noël?

D. Les interrogatifs *quel* et *lequel*

Review **quel**, p. 113.

■ You have already learned to use the adjective **quel** (*which? what?*). **Quel** always occurs with a noun and agrees with that noun.

Quel feuilleton avez-vous vu?
De **quelle** actrice parlez-vous?
Quels acteurs préférez-vous?
Quelles sont vos émissions préférées?

■ **Lequel** (*which one*) replaces **quel** and the noun it modifies. Both parts of **lequel** show agreement.

Vous avez vu le feuilleton?	**Lequel?** (Quel feuilleton?)
Que pensez-vous de cette actrice?	**Laquelle?** (Quelle actrice?)
Ces acteurs sont formidables.	**Lesquels?** (Quels acteurs?)
Ce sont vos émissions préférées?	**Lesquelles?** (Quelles émissions?)

	singulier	pluriel
masculin	**lequel**	**lesquels**
féminin	**laquelle**	**lesquelles**

■ Do not use the indefinite article (**un, une, des**) when **quel** is used in an exclamation.

> **Quelle** histoire!   *What a story!*
> **Quel** cours!   *What a course!*
> **Quels** étudiants!   *What students!*

■ **Lequel** is often followed by the preposition **de** to name the group from which the choice is to be made.

> **Laquelle** *de vos amies* s'appelle Mimi?   *Which of your friends is named Mimi?*
>
> **Lesquels** *de vos professeurs* parlent français?   *Which of your teachers speak French?*

FOR RECOGNITION ONLY:

- When **lequel, lesquels,** and **lesquelles** are preceded by the prepositions **à** or **de,** the normal contractions are made. No contraction is made with **laquelle.**

à + lequel	→ **auquel**		de + lequel	→ **duquel**	
à + lesquels	→ **auxquels**		de + lesquels	→ **desquels**	
à + lesquelles	→ **auxquelles**		de + lesquelles	→ **desquelles**	

Alexis parle d'un film, mais **duquel** parle-t-il?
Il parle aussi des émissions de télé, mais **desquelles?**
Auxquelles de ces émissions vous intéressez-vous?

15 **Dans une salle bruyante** *(In a noisy room).* On fait du bruit et vous n'entendez pas bien les réponses de votre partenaire. Demandez-lui de répéter. Utilisez une forme de **quel** dans la première question et une forme de **lequel** dans la deuxième.

> **Modèle:** ville
>
>   **vous:** **Quelle ville préfères-tu?**
> **votre partenaire:** **Je préfère Québec.**
>   **vous:** **Laquelle?**
> **votre partenaire:** **Québec.**

1. émission	5. voiture	9. feuilleton
2. ville	6. acteurs	10. cours
3. dessin animé	7. actrices	11. dessert
4. film	8. chanson	12. sports

16 **Microconversation: Non, je n'ai pas pu.** Interviewez votre partenaire d'après le modèle. Faites tous les changements nécessaires.

MODÈLE: regarder le feuilleton
>VOUS: **As-tu regardé le feuilleton hier?**
>VOTRE PARTENAIRE: **Lequel?**
>VOUS: **«Mes chers enfants».**
>VOTRE PARTENAIRE: **Non, je n'ai pas pu le regarder.**

1. voir le match (de basket-ball, de base-ball, etc.)
2. regarder les informations
3. voir la pièce
4. regarder l'émission
5. regarder les dessins animés
6. voir le film

17 **À vous.** Répondez.

1. Y a-t-il des mois de l'année plus agréables que les autres? Lesquels?
2. Quel est le mois le moins agréable, à votre avis?
3. Lequel des membres de votre famille est le plus jeune?
4. Laquelle des actrices célèbres trouvez-vous la plus belle?
5. Lequel des acteurs célèbres trouvez-vous le plus beau?
6. Lesquels de vos amis voyez-vous tous les jours?
7. Auxquels envoyez-vous des messages électroniques?

E. Le pronom relatif (suite)

■ Relative pronouns like *who, whom,* and *which* relate or tie two clauses together. They refer to a word in the first clause.

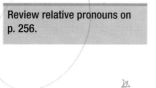

Review relative pronouns on p. 256.

(J'ai des amis. Ils habitent en France.)
J'ai des amis **qui** habitent en France.　　*I have friends who live in France.*
(J'ai des amis. Vous les connaissez bien.)
J'ai des amis **que** vous connaissez bien.　　*I have friends whom you know well.*

■ The choice of the relative pronoun **qui** or **que** depends on its function as subject or object.

• **Qui** *(who, that, which)* replaces a person or a thing that is the *subject* of a relative clause.

«La Roue de la fortune» est une émission **qui** est très populaire.

• **Que** *(whom, that, which)* replaces a person or a thing that is the *object* of a relative clause.

Le film **que** j'ai vu était très intéressant.

■ Past participles conjugated with **avoir** agree with a preceding direct object. Therefore, a past participle will agree with **que** in a relative clause.

Review agreement on p. 279.

la pièce que j'ai vu**e**　　*the play I saw*
la robe qu'elle a mis**e**　　*the dress she put on*
les fleurs que tu as achet**ées**　　*the flowers you bought*

■ Although the relative pronoun may be omitted in English, it is never omitted in French.

C'est l'émission **que** je préfère.   *It's the program (that) I prefer.*

■ Preceded by a preposition, **qui** is normally used with persons and **lequel, laquelle,** etc., is used with things.

la personne **avec qui** j'ai dansé   *the person with whom I danced*
la question **à laquelle** j'ai déjà répondu   *the question I already answered*

■ **Dont** *(whose, of which, about which)* is normally used to replace a relative pronoun and the preposition **de** that precedes it.

(l'émission de laquelle nous avons parlé)
l'émission **dont** nous avons parlé   *the program we spoke about*
(l'annonceur de qui je me souviens bien)
l'annonceur **dont** je me souviens bien   *the announcer I remember well*

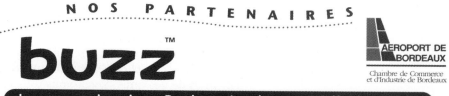

N O S   P A R T E N A I R E S

buzz™

AÉROPORT DE BORDEAUX
Chambre de Commerce
et d'Industrie de Bordeaux

La compagnie qui, sur Bordeaux-Londres, vous offre l'essentiel

18 **Identifiez-les.** Quelles sont les personnes ou les choses suivantes?

Modèle: une personne que vous avez vue à la télé
Jay Leno est une personne que j'ai vue à la télé.

1. une émission qui est très populaire à la télé   CSI
2. une émission que vous refusez de regarder à la télé
3. le dernier film que vous avez vu   LOVE ACTUALLY
4. une personne que vous connaissez qui n'aime pas regarder la télé   VAN
5. la publicité qui est la plus ennuyeuse de la télé
6. le dessin animé que vous croyez le plus drôle
7. l'actrice ou l'acteur que vous préférez
8. une émission de télévision dont vous avez parlé avec vos amis
9. une personne avec qui vous êtes allé(e) au cinéma   BARBARA LYNGS

Entre amis

Un film que j'ai vu

1. Find out the name of the last film that your partner saw.
2. Ask if s/he saw it on TV or at the movies.
3. Ask if s/he liked the film.
4. Find out the names of the actors who were in the film.
5. Find out all you can about this film.

3 Expressing Emotion

Êtes-vous d'accord avec les sentiments exprimés dans les phrases suivantes? Qu'en pensez-vous?[1]

	oui	non
Je suis fâché(e) que les professeurs donnent tant de devoirs!		X
Je regrette que mes notes ne soient pas meilleures.		X
C'est dommage qu'il y ait tant d'émissions sportives à la télévision.		X
C'est ridicule qu'il y ait tant de publicité à la télévision.	X	
Je suis désolé(e) que tant de gens n'aient pas assez à manger.	X	
Le professeur est ravi que je fasse des progrès.	X	

1. *What's your opinion (about them)?*

> Review the forms and uses of the subjunctive in Chs. 10 & 13.

F. Le subjonctif (suite)

■ The subjunctive forms for **vouloir** and **pouvoir** are as follows:

vouloir					
	(veuill-)			(nous voulóns)	
que je	**veuill**	**e**	que nous	**voul**	**ions**
que tu	**veuill**	**es**	que vous	**voul**	**iez**
qu'il/elle/on	**veuill**	**e**			
qu'ils/elles	**veuill**	**ent**			

pouvoir (puiss-)					
que je	**puiss**	e	que nous	**puiss**	ions
que tu	**puiss**	es	que vous	**puiss**	iez
qu'il/elle/on	**puiss**	e	qu'ils/elles	**puiss**	ent

■ In addition to expressing necessity and will, the subjunctive is also used to express emotion.

Je suis content(e) que vous **soyez** ici.   *I am happy (that) you are here.*
Je regrette que Luc ne **puisse** pas venir.   *I am sorry Luc can't come.*

■ If there is no change of subjects, the preposition **de** plus the infinitive is used instead of the subjunctive.

Je suis content(e) **d'être** ici.   *I am happy to be here.*
Luc regrette **de ne pas pouvoir** venir.   *Luc is sorry he can't come.*

VOCABULAIRE

Pour exprimer un sentiment

Je suis ravi(e) que	*I am delighted that*
C'est formidable que	*It's great that*
C'est chouette que	*It's great that*
Je suis content(e) que	*I am happy that*
Ce n'est pas possible que	*It's not possible that*
C'est incroyable que	*It's unbelievable that*
C'est dommage que	*It's too bad that*
C'est ridicule que	*It's ridiculous that*
Je suis triste que	*I am sad that*
Je regrette que	*I am sorry that*
Je suis désolé(e) que	*I am very sorry that*
Je suis fâché(e) que	*I am angry that*

19 **Des réactions différentes.** Décidez si votre professeur est content et si vous êtes content(e) aussi.

MODÈLE: J'ai beaucoup de devoirs.
Mon professeur est content que j'aie beaucoup de devoirs. Mais moi, je ne suis pas content(e) d'avoir beaucoup de devoirs.

1. Je vais souvent à la bibliothèque.
2. Je sais parler français.
3. Je lis *Entre amis* tous les soirs.
4. Je suis un(e) bon(ne) étudiant(e).
5. J'ai «A» à mon examen.
6. Je sors tous les soirs.
7. Je fais régulièrement des rédactions.
8. Je peux aller en France cet été.
9. Je veux étudier le français en France.

20 **Votre réaction, s'il vous plaît.** Choisissez une expression pour réagir *(react)* aux phrases suivantes.

MODÈLE: Véronique va en Floride. Mais il pleut.
C'est formidable qu'elle aille en Floride. Mais c'est dommage qu'il pleuve.

1. Les vacances commencent bientôt. Mais les examens vont avoir lieu avant les vacances.
2. Tous les professeurs sont généreux et charmants. Mais ils donnent beaucoup de devoirs.
3. Les étudiants de cette classe font toujours leurs devoirs. Mais il sont fatigués.

21 **Test psychologique.** Expliquez les causes de vos réactions. Faites deux ou trois phrases chaque fois.

> **MODÈLE:** Je suis triste ...
> **Je suis triste que mon petit ami (ma petite amie) ne m'aime plus.**
> **Je suis triste que tout le monde me déteste.**
> **Je suis triste de ne pas avoir de bons amis.**

1. C'est ridicule ...
2. Nous regrettons ...
3. Je suis ravi(e) ...
4. C'est dommage ...
5. C'est chouette ...

22 **En groupes** *(3 ou 4 étudiants).* Une personne dira une phrase au présent ou au futur (par exemple: **J'ai chaud** ou **Je sortirai ce soir**). Une autre personne réagira (par exemple: **C'est dommage que tu aies chaud** ou **Je suis content(e) que tu sortes ce soir**). Combien de phrases pouvez-vous former?

G. Le pronom *en*

On vend des journaux ici?	*Do you sell newspapers here?*
Non, on n'**en** vend pas. Vous **en** trouverez à la gare.	*No, we don't sell any. You will find some at the station.*
Vous avez du brocoli?	*Do you have any broccoli?*
Oui, j'**en** ai.	*Yes, I have some.*
Il y a beaucoup de fruits cette année?	*Is there a lot of fruit this year?*
Oui, il y **en** a beaucoup.	*Yes, there is a lot (of it).*
Vous avez des oranges?	*Do you have any oranges?*
Oui. Combien **en** voulez-vous?	*Yes. How many (of them) do you want?*
J'**en** voudrais six.	*I would like six (of them).*

■ The pronoun **en** takes the place of a noun that is preceded by some form of **de** (e.g., **de, du, de la, de l', des**) or by a number (e.g., **un, une, deux, trois**), or by an expression of quantity (e.g., **beaucoup de, trop de**).

Vous avez **du** camembert?	Oui, j'**en** ai.
Noël a **une** voiture?	Oui, il **en** a une.
Nous avons **assez de** livres?	Oui, nous **en** avons assez.

■ When a noun is preceded by a number or a quantity word, the number or quantity word must be included in a sentence with **en.**

Vous avez **une** maison?	*Do you have a house?*
Oui, j'**en** ai **une.**	*Yes, I have one.*

Vous avez **deux** valises?	*Do you have two suitcases?*
Non, je n'**en** ai pas **deux.**	*No, I don't have two (of them).*
Je n'**en** ai qu'**une.**	*I have only one.*
Mon père **en** a **beaucoup.**	*My father has a lot (of them).*

Note To say *I don't have any,* use **Je n'en ai pas.**

■ **En** is also used to replace **de** plus an infinitive or **de** plus a noun with expressions of emotion.

Hervé est triste **de partir?**	Oui, il **en** est triste.
Es-tu contente **de tes notes?**	Oui, j'**en** suis ravie.

23 **Sondage** *(Poll).* Utilisez les expressions suivantes pour interviewer votre partenaire. Il (elle) va utiliser **en** dans chaque réponse.

MODÈLE: voitures

VOUS: Combien de voitures as-tu?
VOTRE PARTENAIRE: J'en ai une. ou **Je n'en ai pas.**

1. frères
2. sœurs
3. enfants
4. camarades de chambre

5. professeurs
6. voitures
7. cours
8. cartes de crédit

24 **Quelles réactions!** Composez deux phrases affirmatives ou négatives. La première peut être au présent, à l'imparfait ou au passé composé. Utilisez **en** dans la deuxième.

MODÈLE: **Mes amis n'ont pas gagné à la loterie.**
Ils en sont désolés.

> Remember that **confus** is a false cognate, p. 381.

Reviev

	être fiancé(e)(s)	
	se marier	ravi
je	attendre un bébé	content
mes amis	réussir à un examen	triste
un(e) de mes ami(e)s	avoir une mauvaise note	désolé
	divorcer	fâché
	gagner à la loterie	confus
	arriver en retard	

25 **À vous.** Répondez. Utilisez **en** dans chaque réponse.

1. Combien de tasses de café buvez-vous par jour?
2. Buvez-vous du thé?
3. Voulez-vous du chewing-gum?
4. Êtes-vous content(e) de vos notes?
5. Combien de personnes y a-t-il dans votre famille?
6. Combien de maillots de bain avez-vous?
7. Quelle est votre réaction quand vous avez «A» à l'examen?

Entre amis

Les examens finals

Use **en** whenever possible.

1. Find out how many courses your partner has this semester.
2. Ask if s/he is pleased (happy) with his/her courses.
3. Ask if s/he is pleased (happy) with his/her grades.
4. Find out how many final exams s/he will have.
5. Ask if s/he is afraid of them.

Intégration

Révision

A **Décrivez-les.** Inventez une description pour les couples suivants.

1. un couple qui va se marier.
2. un couple qui divorce.
3. un couple qui habite chez les parents du mari.

B **Un feuilleton.** Choisissez un feuilleton que vous connaissez. Décrivez-le à votre partenaire.

C **Mes réactions.** Quelles sont vos réactions aux circonstances suivantes?

Modèle: Le professeur vous annonce qu'il n'y aura pas de cours demain.
J'en suis ravi(e)! Je lui dis «Merci beaucoup!». C'est chouette qu'il n'y ait pas de cours.

1. Le professeur vous dit qu'il y aura un examen demain.
2. On vous téléphone pour vous annoncer que vous venez de gagner à la loterie.
3. Vous vous êtes disputé(e) avec votre ami(e) et il (elle) vous envoie un message électronique pour vous demander pardon.
4. Vos parents veulent vous parler de vos études et de ce que vous allez faire dans la vie.
5. Une amie vous annonce que son petit ami ne veut plus la voir.
6. Vous dormez et le téléphone sonne à trois heures du matin. Vous y répondez et une personne que vous ne connaissez pas vous demande si vous voulez acheter une encyclopédie.

Pas de problème!

Preparation for the video:
1. Video worksheet in the *Cahier d'activités*
2. CD-ROM, *Module 11*

Cette activité est basée sur la vidéo, *Module 11*. Choisissez la bonne réponse pour compléter les phrases suivantes.

1. Dans ce contexte, le mot «papillon» veut dire _____.
   (une cravate, un insecte, une contravention)
2. Le conducteur doit _____ francs.
   (450, 65, 75)
3. Il dit qu'on lui a donné un papillon pour _____ minutes de stationnement.
   (5, 10, 15)
4. L'homme qui a eu la contravention est de nationalité _____.
   (française, suisse, belge)
5. D'après cette vidéo, il faut que cet homme aille _____ pour acheter un timbre fiscal.
   (à la poste, au tabac, à la gare)

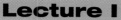 **Lecture I**

A **Que regardez-vous?** Faites une liste des cinq émissions de télé de votre pays qui sont, à votre avis, les plus intéressantes.

B **Parcourez les listes d'émissions.** Lisez rapidement les listes d'émissions pour identifier (1) le jour de la semaine et (2) les différents sports qui sont mentionnés.

La télévision

Les deux colonnes suivantes sont tirées du site web de Yahoo! France.

TF1		**France 2**	
08h10	Disney! (dessin animé)	08h30	Les voix bouddhistes
09h57	Météo	08h45	Connaître l'Islam
10h00	Motocross: Championnat du Monde 250cc	09h15	À bible ouverte
11h00	Téléfoot: Championnat de France	09h30	Orthodoxie
12h15	Le juste prix (jeu)	10h00	Présence protestante
12h50	À vrai dire: Aménager la cuisine	10h30	La Présence du Seigneur
12h55	Météo	11h00	Messe célébrée en la cathédrale St.-Michel
13h00	Le journal	12h00	Cérémonie du Souvenir
13h15	Au nom du sport	13h00	Le journal de treize heures
13h55	Formule 1: Grand Prix d'Italie	13h25	Météo 2
15h40	Dingue de toi (série, comédie)	13h30	Rapport du Loto
17h00	Dawson: La nouvelle Ève (série, comédie)	13h35	Vivement dimanche
17h55	Trente millions d'amis (magazine, animalier)	15h35	Le singe araignée d'Amazonie
18h55	L'euro en poche (magazine, économique)	16h35	Snoops
19h55	Être heureux comme (magazine, culturel)	17h20	Nash Bridges
20h00	Le journal	18h15	Stade 2
20h35	Au nom du sport (magazine, sportif)	19h25	Vivement dimanche prochain
20h40	Le résultat des courses (magazine, sportif)	20h00	Le journal de vingt heures
20h45	Le temps d'un tournage (magazine, cinéma)	20h45	Météo 2
20h50	Météo	20h55	Urgences
20h55	Boomerang (film, comédie)	21h45	Urgences
23h00	Les films dans les salles (magazine, cinéma)	22h35	Urgences
23h05	Le messager de la mort (film, policier)	23h20	Les documents du dimanche

C **À vous de juger.** Lesquelles des émissions intéresseront probablement une personne qui ...

1. pratique sa religion?
2. aime les sports?
3. aime l'émission américaine *ER*?
4. veut gagner de l'argent?
5. veut savoir le temps qu'il fera demain?
6. veut savoir ce qui se passe dans le monde?
7. aime les animaux?
8. est un enfant?

Inférence. Relisez la lecture et cherchez des exemples qui aident à identifier une des chaînes comme privée et l'autre comme publique.

E **Écrivez un téléguide.** Indiquez le(s) jour(s) et l'heure, le nom et une description pour les cinq émissions de télévision que vous avez choisies dans l'activité A.

Lecture II

A **Étude du vocabulaire.** Étudiez les phrases suivantes et choisissez les mots qui correspondent aux mots français en caractères gras: *native, earn, be bored, although, run over, masterpiece.*

1. On **s'ennuie** si on travaille tout le temps sans jamais prendre de vacances.
2. «Hamlet» est un **chef d'œuvre** de Shakespeare.
3. Attention quand vous traversez la rue. Une voiture peut vous **écraser**.
4. J'ai quitté ma ville **natale** il y a quinze ans.
5. Marc veut **gagner** assez d'argent pour pouvoir acheter une voiture.
6. Cet homme est gentil **quoiqu'**un peu bizarre.

 Avant de lire. Réfléchissez aux films que vous avez vus.

1. À votre avis, quel est le meilleur film de cette année?
2. Quel film trouvez-vous le plus bizarre?
3. Quel film trouvez-vous le plus comique?
4. Quel est le film le plus violent?
5. Combien de fois êtes-vous allé(e) au cinéma le mois dernier?
6. Quel est le dernier film que vous avez vu?

C **Parcourez la liste des films.** Lisez rapidement pour identifier les films et les acteurs que vous connaissez.

AU CINÉMA

«LE HUITIÈME JOUR»: Harry est un cadre stressé. Sa vie de routine est troublée par un accident: il écrase un chien et rencontre Georges, un mongolien qui lui redonne goût à la vie. Un regard tendre et plein de fantaisie sur la rencontre de deux univers. Avec Daniel Auteuil, Pascal Duquenne. Gaumont à 12h30, 18h, 21h.

«JANE EYRE»: L'héroïne du chef-d'œuvre de Charlotte Brontë prend les traits de Charlotte Gainsbourg dans ce film néo-romantique où une jeune fille sortie d'un triste orphelinat trouve un emploi de préceptrice chez un homme étrange. De Franco Zeffirelli avec Charlotte Gainsbourg, William Hurt. Montparnasse à 18h30, 21h.

«PRINCESSES»: Apparemment, elles n'avaient rien en commun si ce n'est la jeunesse et la beauté. L'une sage, l'autre rebelle, deux jeunes femmes apprennent qu'elles sont demi-sœurs et que leur père est recherché pour meurtre. Dans l'urgence et la peur d'une issue fatale, elles partent à sa recherche, sur les traces d'un passé encore douloureux. Avec ce film, Sylvie Verheyde joue sur le registre du film noir en imposant le chaos comme moteur de l'action. Avec Emma de Caunes, Jean-Hugues Anglade et Karole Rocher. Cyrano à 14h, 16h, 18h, 20h, 22h.

«LA COUPE D'OR»: L'intrigue: au début du vingtième siècle, un beau prince italien follement amoureux d'une séduisante Américaine se voit dans l'obligation d'épouser la fille d'un richissime collectionneur new-yorkais. Mais la maîtresse, pugnace, parvient, pour ne pas s'éloigner de son amant, à se faire épouser du père de la mariée, compatriote fortuné et ... veuf bien conservé! Le jeu est dangereux et les quatre protagonistes ont beaucoup à perdre. Un drame britannique de James Ivory avec Kate Beckinsale, James Fox, Anjelica Huston et Nick Nolte. Danton à 11h45, 14h15, 16h50, 19h25, 22h.

«APPARENCES»: C'est une belle maison, près d'un lac du Vermont, quoiqu'un peu isolée. C'est un beau couple: lui, brillant et séduisant, mais un peu obsédé par le travail; elle, une belle femme qui-a-tout-pour-être-heureuse. Une porte qui s'ouvre seule, un visage apparu dans l'eau du bain et quelques murmures dans une pièce doivent-ils suffire à vous faire croire que votre nouvelle voisine est morte assassinée? Oui, dans ce film à suspense où le spectateur nage en plein mystère et en fausses déductions ... Un film de Robert Zemeckis avec Harrison Ford, Michelle Pfeiffer, Miranda Otto et James Remar. UGC Maillot à 10h55, 13h30, 16h10, 18h50, 21h25.

«ENDURANCE»: C'est l'histoire incroyable mais authentique d'Haile Gebreselassie, ce jeune Éthiopien, pratiquement inconnu du grand public jusqu'aux Jeux Olympiques d'Atlanta, où il a remporté la course du 10.000 mètres, pulvérisant le précédent record. Derrière cet hommage au champion, interprété par lui-même, il y a un portrait de la vie en Afrique de l'Est. Une comédie dramatique de Leslie Woodhead avec Yonas Zergaw, Shawanness Gebreselassie et Tedesse Haile. L'Arlequin à 18h10 (début 10mn après), 20h10 (début 10mn après), 22h10 (début 10mn après).

«MAUVAISE FILLE»: Film de Régis Franc avec Daniel Gélin et Florence Pernel. Rose, dix-huit ans, s'ennuie dans sa Camargue natale entre un père dépressif, un frère macho et un amoureux ennuyeux. Variétés à 20h15.

«CHIEN ET CHAT»: Film de Philippe Galland. Avec Roland Giraud et André Dussolier. Un officier de la gendarmerie et un commissaire de police unissent leurs forces pour sauver leurs deux enfants compromis dans un trafic de drogue. Les Halles à 19h45, 22h.

«LE BRASIER»: Comme beaucoup de Polonais, Pavlak est venu en France avec son fils Viktor pour travailler à la mine. Pour gagner un peu plus d'argent, il participe à des combats de boxe. Un film d'Éric Barbier avec Jean-Marc Barr, Marushka Detmers et Thierry Fortineau. Vox à 14h30, 21h30.

 Questions. Choisissez parmi *(among)* les films mentionnés dans la lecture.

1. Dans quel film est-ce que le personnage principal est un champion sportif?
2. Dans quel film est-ce que le personnage principal est un handicapé mental?
3. Dans quel film est-ce que le personnage principal est un immigré?
4. Quel films peuvent vous faire peur? Justifiez votre réponse.
5. Quel film a l'air le plus intéressant?
6. Quel film a l'air le plus violent?
7. Quels films est-ce qu'on ne peut voir que le soir?

Familles de mots. Essayez de deviner le sens des mots suivants.

1. débuter, un débutant, une débutante, le début
2. droguer, un drogué, une droguée, la drogue
3. s'ennuyer, ennuyé(e), ennuyeux, ennuyeuse, l'ennui
4. employer, un employé, une employée, un emploi
5. épouser, un époux, une épouse
6. séduire, séduisant(e), un séducteur, une séductrice, la séduction

VOCABULAIRE ACTIF

À propos de la télévision
une annonce *advertisement*
une chaîne (de télé) *(TV) channel*
un feuilleton *soap opera; series*
les informations *(f. pl.) news*
la météo(rologie) *weather forecast*
la publicité *publicity; commercial*

D'autres noms
un avertissement *warning*
un revenant *ghost*
la vérité *truth*

Adjectifs
célèbre *famous*
chouette *great (fam.)*
confus(e) *ashamed; embarrassed*
drôle *funny*
fâché(e) *angry*
formidable *terrific*
incroyable *unbelievable, incredible*
malheureux (malheureuse) *unhappy*
original(e) *different, novel; original*
passionnant(e) *exciting*
ravi(e) *delighted*
ridicule *ridiculous*

Relations personnelles
s'aimer *to love each other*
une bague (de fiançailles) *(engagement) ring*

se disputer *to argue*
un divorce *divorce*
divorcer *to get a divorce*
s'embrasser *to kiss*
s'entendre (avec) *to get along (with)*
se fâcher *to get angry*
se faire des amis *to make friends*
se marier (avec) *to marry*
rencontrer *to meet*
se séparer *to separate (from each other)*

D'autres verbes
assister (à) *to attend*
se consoler *to console oneself*
croire *to believe, think*
dire *to say; to tell*
emprunter *to borrow*
s'intéresser à *to be interested in*
montrer *to show*
prêter *to lend*
raconter (une histoire) *to tell (a story)*
regretter *to be sorry*
voir *to see*

Adverbes
actuellement *now*
même *even*
presque *almost*

Pronoms objets indirects
me *(to) me*
te *(to) you*
lui *(to) him; (to) her*
nous *(to) us*
vous *(to) you*
leur *(to) them*

D'autres pronoms
en *some; of it (them); about it (them)*
dont *whose, of which*
lequel/laquelle/lesquels/lesquelles *which*

Expressions utiles
C'est dommage. *That's (It's) too bad.*
Je crois que oui. *I think so.*
Je ne crois pas. *I don't think so.*
Je te le jure. *I swear (to you).*
Quelle histoire! *What a story!*
Qu'est-ce qui est arrivé? *What happened?*
Sans blague! *No kidding!*

15 Qu'est-ce que je devrais faire?

Buts communicatifs
Seeking and providing information
Making basic hypotheses

Structures utiles
L'imparfait, le passé composé (suite) et le plus-que-parfait
Le verbe **devoir** (suite)
Les pronoms interrogatifs
Ne ... personne et **ne ... rien**
Le conditionnel
Si hypothétique

Culture
Les accidents de la route
Les agents et les gendarmes
Les contraventions

Coup d'envoi

Qu'est-ce qui est arrivé?

Qu'est-ce qui est arrivé, Emmanuelle?
> J'ai eu un accident.
> L'autre conducteur (conductrice)° n'a pas   *driver*
> vu ma voiture.
> Il (elle) a freiné° trop tard.   *braked*
> Sa voiture a dérapé°.   *skidded*
> Il (elle) a heurté° ma voiture.   *struck; hit*

Pourquoi l'accident a-t-il eu lieu?
> Le conducteur (la conductrice) ne faisait pas
> attention.
> Il (elle) croyait que personne° ne venait.   *nobody*
> Il (elle) ne regardait pas à droite.
> Il (elle) roulait° trop vite.   *was going*
> Il (elle) avait trop bu°.   *had had too much to drink*
> Il (elle) était ivre°.   *drunk*

▶ **Et vous.**   Avez-vous déjà eu un accident?
            Avez-vous déjà vu un accident?
            Si oui, qu'est-ce qui est arrivé?

VOTRE SÉCURITÉ

Sur route, sur mer, en montagne, la majorité des accidents sont dûs à des imprudences caractérisées.

Alors soyez attentifs aux conseils que vous rappelleront la Sécurité Routière et la Gendarmerie Nationale.

Sur route

Méfiez-vous de la conduite en plein soleil après un repas, des routes de nuit après une journée d'activité. Bouclez votre ceinture, respectez les limitations de vitesse :
– pas plus de 60 km/h en agglomération,
– pas plus de 90 km/h sur route,
– pas plus de 130 km/h sur autoroute.
Minitel : 36 15 ROUTE.

Conversation

Un accident a eu lieu

James Davidson vient d'avoir un accident de voiture. Il en parle avec son voisin Maurice.

MAURICE: Mais qu'est-ce que tu as? Tu es tout pâle!

JAMES: C'est que j'ai eu très peur ce matin.

MAURICE: Qu'est-ce qui est arrivé?

JAMES: J'ai eu un accident de voiture.

MAURICE: Mon Dieu!

JAMES: J'allais au travail quand l'accident a eu lieu. L'autre ne faisait pas attention. Ce chauffard° avait brûlé un stop° parce qu'il allait trop vite.

bad driver
had run through a stop sign

MAURICE: Quel imbécile!

JAMES: Oui, et nous sommes entrés en collision.

MAURICE: Quel idiot! Et personne n'a vu l'accident?

JAMES: Si! Heureusement il y avait deux témoins° et puis un gendarme qui était juste derrière moi.

witnesses

MAURICE: Quelle chance! Qu'est-ce que le gendarme a fait?

JAMES: Il m'a assuré° qu'il avait tout vu° et que c'était la faute° de l'autre.

assured / had seen everything
fault

MAURICE: J'espère que le gendarme lui a donné une bonne contravention°!

ticket

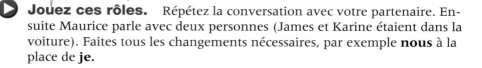

Jouez ces rôles. Répétez la conversation avec votre partenaire. Ensuite Maurice parle avec deux personnes (James et Karine étaient dans la voiture). Faites tous les changements nécessaires, par exemple **nous** à la place de **je.**

Reread **Votre Sécurité** on p. 406 to determine the speed limits in France.

Essayez de classifier les infractions *(violations)* **suivantes d'après leur fréquence.**

3 a. ne pas s'arrêter à un feu rouge ou à un stop
4 b. dépasser le degré légal d'alcool dans le sang *(blood)*
1 c. dépasser la limite de vitesse
2 d. ne pas porter de ceinture de sécurité

Les agents et les gendarmes

The **agent de police** is often found directing traffic at major intersections in French cities. Since the **agents** are normally on foot, they are often stopped by tourists in need of information. The **gendarme,** often found in the countryside and in small towns, is actually part of the French military and is stationed in separate quarters in the **gendarmerie. Gendarmes** are similar to state police in that they are usually on motorcycles or in patrol cars. They would therefore normally be the ones to investigate an accident.

Les contraventions

There are approximately 15 million traffic tickets given in France per year. Of these, 9 million are for illegal parking and 1 million for exceeding the speed limit. The record for a speeding ticket is 243 KPH (over 150 MPH) for which the speeder received a year in prison and a 100.000 franc fine. In addition, approximately 660.000 tickets for not wearing a seat belt and 100.000 for drunken driving are given in an average year. Besides the parking tickets, the following were the most frequent traffic violations in France in a recent year: (1) speeding (43%); (2) not wearing a seat belt while riding in a car, or a helmet when on a motorcycle (24%); (3) failure to give right of way or to stop at a light or a stop sign (13%); (4) failure to pass the alcohol test (7%). Eighty-one percent of those committing a traffic violation were men.

Les accidents de la route

Environ huit mille personnes sont tuées tous les ans dans des accidents de la circulation *(traffic)* en France. Entre 1987 et 1997, ces accidents ont fait plus de 222.000 morts et 5.383.000 blessés, ce qui est très grave. Avec près de 150 décès par million d'habitants, la France a la quatrième place des quinze pays de l'Union européenne, après le Portugal, la Grèce et le Luxembourg. *(d'après Francoscopie)*

J'ai eu très peur. To indicate fear, the open hand is held fingers facing up; the hand is lowered with the fingers "trembling."

Quel imbécile! To indicate that some-one has done something stupid, touch your index finger to your temple. The finger is either tapped on the temple or twisted back and forth.

Ivre. To indicate that someone has had too much to drink, one hand is cupped in a fist, and placed loosely on the nose and rotated.

Il y a un geste

▶ **À vous.** Répondez.

1. Quand avez-vous eu peur?
2. Pour quelle raison avez-vous eu peur?
3. Qu'est-ce que vous avez fait?

Entre amis

C'était la faute du professeur

1. Tell your partner that you had an accident.
2. Explain that you hit the teacher's car.
3. Say that it was the teacher's fault.
4. Explain that s/he was going too slowly.

Prononciation

La voyelle [ə]

■ As you have already learned, the letter **-e-** can stand for any one of the sounds [e], [ɛ], [ɑ̃], and [ɛ̃], depending on the spelling combinations of which it is a part. You have also seen, however, that the letter **-e-** sometimes represents the sound [ə]. The symbol [ə] stands for a vowel called "unstable **e**" or "mute **e.**" It is called unstable because it is sometimes pronounced and sometimes not.

▶ Look at the following pairs of examples and then read them aloud. A highlighted **-e-** represents a pronounced [ə]. An **-e-** with a slash through it represents a silent [ə]. Compare especially changes you find in the same word from one sentence of the pair to the other.

L**e** voilà!	Mais l~~e~~ voilà!
C**e** film est très bon.	Moi, j~~e~~ n'aim~~e~~ pas c~~e~~ film.
D**e**main, vous l~~e~~ trouv~~e~~rez.	Vous l~~e~~ trouv~~e~~rez d~~e~~main.
D**e**nis~~e~~ est américain~~e~~?	Ell~~e~~ est français~~e~~.
R**e**gardez cett~~e~~ femm~~e~~.	Vous r~~e~~gardez cett~~e~~ femm~~e~~?

Nous pr**e**nons l~~e~~ train vendr**e**di.	Nous arriv**e**rons sam**e**di.
Votr**e** pèr~~e~~ est charmant.	Votr~~e~~ ami~~e~~ est charmant~~e~~.
Voilà un~~e~~ tass~~e~~ d**e** café.	Nous n~~e~~ voulons pas d~~e~~ café.
C'est un~~e~~ bagu~~e~~ d**e** fiançaill~~e~~s.	Mais il n'y aura pas d~~e~~ mariag~~e~~.
Qu'est-c~~e~~ qu**e** tu veux?	Elle a dit qu~~e~~ tu voulais m~~e~~ voir.

d**e** rien	Il finit d~~e~~ rir~~e~~.
vous s**e**riez	vous s~~e~~rez

■ In general, [ə] is *silent* in the following circumstances.

1. at the end of a sentence
2. before or after a pronounced vowel
3. when it is preceded by only one pronounced consonant sound

■ In general, [ə] is *pronounced* in the following circumstances.

1. when it is in the first syllable of a sentence
2. when it is preceded by two pronounced consonant sounds (even if there is an intervening silent [ə]) and followed by at least one pronounced consonant
3. when it precedes the combination [Rj]

Note When the letter **-e-** is followed *in the same word* by two consonants or by **-x,** it is normally pronounced [ɛ].

elle	av**e**rtissement	c**e**tte	pr**e**nnent	v**e**rser	m**e**rci
exiger	**e**xcusez-moi	**e**xact	**e**xamen		

▶ **Écoutez et puis répétez.**

1. L'autre conducteur ne faisait pas attention.
2. Qu'est-ce que votre frère a fait?
3. Est-ce que tu regardes des feuilletons le vendredi ou le samedi?
4. De quelle ville venez-vous?
5. Vous venez de Paris, n'est-ce pas?

Buts communicatifs

1 Seeking and Providing Information

Avez-vous entendu parler d'un accident?
Avez-vous vu un accident?

Est-ce que quelqu'un a été blessé°?	*wounded*
Est-ce que quelqu'un a été tué°?	*killed*
Est-ce qu'il y a eu beaucoup de morts°?	*deaths*
Où est-ce que l'accident a eu lieu?	
Quelle heure était-il?	
De quelle couleur étaient les voitures?	
De quelle marque° étaient les voitures?	*make; brand*
De quelle année étaient les voitures?	
Est-ce qu'il avait plu?° *pluparfait?*	*Had it rained?*
La chaussée° devait être glissante°, n'est-ce pas?	*pavement / slippery*
Y avait-il d'autres témoins?	

A. L'imparfait, le passé composé (suite) et le plus-que-parfait

> Review the comparison of the passé composé and imperfect, Ch. 11, p. 304.

■ It is perhaps helpful, when trying to remember whether to use the imperfect or the passé composé, to think of the analogy with a stage play.

- In a play, there is often scenery (trees, birds singing, the sun shining, etc.) and background action (minor characters strolling by, people playing, working, etc.). This scenery and background action are represented by the imperfect.

Il **était** tôt.	*It was early.*
Il **faisait** froid.	*It was cold out.*
James **allait** au travail.	*James was going to work.*
Un autre conducteur ne **faisait** pas attention.	*Another driver wasn't paying attention.*

Que faisaient les acteurs dans la pièce *(play)*?

- Likewise, in a play, there are main actors upon whom the audience focuses, if even for a moment. They speak, move, become aware, act, and react. The narration of these past events requires the passé composé.

Qu'est-ce qui lui **est arrivé?**	*What happened to him?*
Il **a eu** un accident.	*He had an accident.*
Ils **sont entrés** en collision.	*They collided.*
Un gendarme lui **a donné** une contravention.	*A policeman gave him a ticket.*

■ The pluperfect (**le plus-que-parfait**) is used to describe a past event that took place prior to some other past event. This tense normally corresponds to the English *had* plus a past participle.

Il **avait plu** (avant l'accident).	*It had rained (before the accident).*
La dame **était arrivée** (avant moi).	*The lady had arrived (before me).*

■ To form the **plus-que-parfait,** use the **imparfait** of **avoir** or **être** and the past participle.

étudier	arriver	se lever
j'avais étudié	j'étais arrivé(e)	je m'étais levé(e)
tu avais étudié	tu étais arrivé(e)	tu t'étais levé(e)
il/on avait étudié	il/on était arrivé	il/on s'était levé
elle avait étudié	elle était arrivée	elle s'était levée
nous avions étudié	nous étions arrivé(e)s	nous nous étions levé(e)s
vous aviez étudié	vous étiez arrivé(e)(s)	vous vous étiez levé(e)(s)
ils avaient étudié	ils étaient arrivés	ils s'étaient levés
elles avaient étudié	elles étaient arrivées	elles s'étaient levées

1 **Voilà pourquoi.** Répondez aux questions suivantes. Essayez de trouver des raisons logiques.

MODÈLE: Pourquoi Laurent a-t-il téléphoné à Mireille?
Il lui a téléphoné parce qu'il voulait sortir avec elle. ou
Il lui a téléphoné parce qu'il la trouvait gentille.

1. Pourquoi Laurent et Mireille sont-ils sortis samedi soir?
2. Pourquoi ont-ils mis leur manteau?
3. Pourquoi sont-ils allés au restaurant?
4. Pourquoi n'ont-ils pas pris de dessert?
5. Pourquoi ont-ils fait une promenade après?

② **Pourquoi pas, Amélie?** Utilisez la forme négative. Expliquez pourquoi Amélie n'a pas fait les choses suivantes.

> MODÈLE: prendre le petit déjeuner
> **Amélie n'a pas pris le petit déjeuner parce qu'elle n'avait pas faim.** ou
> **Amélie n'a pas pris le petit déjeuner parce qu'elle a oublié.**

1. aller au cinéma
2. étudier dans sa chambre
3. regarder son émission préférée
4. danser avec Gérard
5. nager
6. avoir un accident
7. boire du vin

③ **Quel chauffard!** Utilisez le plus-que-parfait pour indiquer ce que le mauvais chauffeur avait fait avant l'accident.

> MODÈLE: ne pas être prudent
> **Il n'avait pas été prudent.**

1. aller au bistro
2. boire de la bière
3. ne pas attacher sa ceinture
4. oublier de faire attention
5. brûler un stop
6. se regarder dans le rétroviseur

B. Le verbe *devoir* (suite)

Review **devoir,** Ch. 5, p. 136.

Où est Céline?	*Where is Céline?*
Je ne sais pas. Elle **doit** être malade.	*I don't know. She **must** be sick.*
Mais elle **devait** apporter des fleurs pour le prof!	*But she **was supposed to** bring flowers for the teacher!*
Oui, je sais. Puisqu'elle n'est pas venue, j'**ai dû** aller les acheter.	*Yes, I know. Since she didn't come, I **had to** go buy them.*
Maintenant tout le monde me **doit** 5 francs pour le bouquet.	*Now everybody **owes** me 5 francs for the bouquet.*

■ The past participle of **devoir** is **dû.** When it has a feminine agreement, however, it loses the circumflex: **due.** This often occurs when the past participle is used as an adjective.

l'argent **dû** à mon frère   la pollution **due** à l'industrie

■ The future tense verb stem for **devoir** is irregular: **devr-.**

Elle **devra** travailler dur.   *She**'ll have** to work hard.*

■ Like other verbs with two stems in the present tense, **devoir** has two stems in the subjunctive.

que je **doive**   que nous **devions**

■ The passé composé and the imperfect can both mean *had to* or *probably (must have)*. The choice of tense depends, as usual, on whether the verb is a specific action or a description or habitual condition.

Hier j'**ai dû** aller voir ma tante.	*Yesterday, I **had to** go see my aunt.*
En général, je **devais** faire mes devoirs avant de sortir.	*In general, I **had to** do my homework before going out.*
Il **a dû** oublier notre rendez-vous!	*He **probably** forgot our date! (He **must have** forgotten our date!)*
Il **devait** être très occupé.	*He was **probably** very busy. (He **must have** been very busy.)*

Note When **devoir** means *was supposed to*, the imperfect is always used.

Nous **devions** dîner chez les Gilbert.   *We **were supposed to** have dinner at the Gilberts'.*

4 **C'est probable.** Utilisez **devoir** au passé composé d'après le modèle pour modifier les phrases suivantes.

MODÈLE: Delphine n'a probablement pas fait ses devoirs.
Elle n'a pas dû faire ses devoirs.

> Remember that **sans doute** and **probablement** are synonyms.

1. Elle est sans doute sortie avec ses amis.
2. Elle n'a probablement pas étudié.
3. Elle a probablement eu une mauvaise note.
4. Elle a probablement pleuré.
5. Elle a sans doute parlé avec son professeur.
6. Elle a sans doute réussi la semaine d'après.

5 **Toutes ces obligations!** Traduisez *(translate)* la forme verbale anglaise entre parenthèses pour compléter la phrase.

MODÈLE: Chantal _____ étudier pendant le week-end. *(was supposed to)*
Chantal devait étudier pendant le week-end.

devaient 1. Mes parents _____ venir nous chercher il y a 30 minutes. *(were* ~~*devaient*~~ *supposed to)*
~~*doivent*~~ 2. Ils _____ oublier. *(must have)* *ont du*
3. Non, ils _____ être déjà en route. *(must)* *doivent*
4. Nous _____ leur téléphoner, s'ils ne viennent pas bientôt. *(will have to)* *devrons*
5. Il commence à faire froid. Tu _____ mettre ton manteau. *(must)* *dois*
6. Il est onze heures. Je _____ être chez moi avant cette heure-ci. *(was supposed to)* *devais*

C. Les pronoms interrogatifs

> Review **qui, que,** and **quel,** Ch. 4, p. 112.

■ Interrogative pronouns are used to ask questions. You have already learned to use several interrogative pronouns.

Qui est-ce?	*Who is that?*
Qu'est-ce que c'est?	*What is that?*

■ As in English, interrogative pronouns in French change form depending on whether they refer to people or to things.

Qui voyez-vous?   *Whom do you see?*
Que voyez-vous?   *What do you see?*

■ In addition, French interrogative pronouns change form depending on their function in the sentence. For example, the word *what* in English can take three different forms in French depending on whether it is the subject, the direct object, or the object of a preposition.

Qu'est-ce qui est à droite?   *What is on the right?*
Qu'est-ce que tu vois?   *What do you see?*
À **quoi** penses-tu?   *What are you thinking about?*

People		
Subject		
Qui **Qui est-ce qui**	Qui parle? Qui est-ce qui parle?	*Who is speaking?*
Object		
Qui (+ inversion) **Qui est-ce que**	Qui avez-vous vu? Qui est-ce que vous avez vu?	*Whom did you see?*
After a preposition		
... qui (+ inversion) **... qui est-ce que**	À qui écrivez-vous? À qui est-ce que vous écrivez?	*To whom are you writing?*

Things		
Subject		
Qu'est-ce qui	Qu'est-ce qui fait ce bruit?	*What's making that noise?*
Object		
Que (+ inversion) **Qu'est-ce que**	Qu'avez-vous fait? Qu'est-ce que vous avez fait?	*What did you do?*
After a preposition		
... quoi (+ inversion) **... quoi est-ce que**	De quoi avez-vous besoin? De quoi est-ce que vous avez besoin?	*What do you need?*

(handwritten margin notes) Pers. subj
 Pers. d.o.
 obj - subj <br> obj - d.o.

- If the question involves a person, the pronoun will always begin with **qui**. If it is a question about a thing, the pronoun will begin with **que** or **quoi**. There is no elision with **qui** or **quoi,** but **que** becomes **qu'** before a vowel.

  Qui a parlé?   *Who spoke?*
  De **quoi** a-t-il parlé?   *What did he talk about?*
  Qu'est-ce **qu'**il a dit?   *What did he say?*

- As shown in the charts above, there are two forms of each of these interrogative pronouns, except the subject pronoun **qu'est-ce qui**.

- When interrogative pronouns are used as subjects, the verb is normally singular.

  Mes parents ont téléphoné.   Qui **a** téléphoné?

QUOI DE NEUF, DOC?
SAVEZ-VOUS QUE BUGS BUNNY PARLE FRANÇAIS?

 6 Quelqu'un ou quelque chose? Utilisez un pronom interrogatif pour poser une question.

MODÈLES: Quelqu'un m'a téléphoné.   Quelque chose m'intéresse.
Qui vous a téléphoné?   **Qu'est-ce qui vous intéresse?**

J'ai téléphoné à quelqu'un.   J'ai acheté quelque chose.
À qui avez-vous téléphoné?   **Qu'est-ce que vous avez acheté?**

1. J'ai fait quelque chose le week-end dernier.
2. Quelque chose m'est arrivé.
3. J'ai vu quelqu'un.
4. Quelqu'un m'a parlé.
5. J'ai dansé avec quelqu'un.
6. Nous avons bu quelque chose.
7. J'ai dû payer pour quelqu'un.
8. J'ai dit au revoir à quelqu'un.

7 **Comment? Je n'ai pas compris.** Votre partenaire vous a parlé mais vous n'avez pas bien entendu. Demandez qu'il (elle) répète. Remplacez l'expression en italique par un pronom interrogatif.

MODÈLES: *Mon frère* a acheté une voiture.

> VOUS: **Comment? Qui a acheté une voiture?**
> VOTRE PARTENAIRE: **Mon frère.**

J'ai lu *deux livres.*

> VOUS: **Comment? Qu'est-ce que tu as lu?**
> VOTRE PARTENAIRE: **Deux livres.**

1. *Sophie* a écrit une lettre à ses parents.
2. Elle avait besoin *d'argent.*
3. *Ses parents* ont lu la lettre.
4. Ils ont répondu *à Sophie.*
5. Ils lui ont envoyé *l'argent.*
6. Sa mère *lui* a téléphoné hier soir.
7. Elle lui a dit *que son frère était malade.*
8. Sophie aime beaucoup *son frère.*
9. *Sa maladie* lui fait peur.

Entre amis

Ma journée d'hier

1. Find out from your partner what happened yesterday.
2. Ask what s/he did.
3. Find out where s/he went and who was there.
4. Ask with whom s/he spoke.
5. What else can you find out?

D. *Ne ... personne et ne ... rien*

Qui avez-vous rencontré?	Je **n'**ai rencontré **personne.**
Qu'est-ce que vous avez fait?	Je **n'**ai **rien** fait.
Avec qui avez-vous dansé?	Je **n'**ai dansé avec **personne.**
De quoi avez-vous besoin?	Je **n'**ai besoin de **rien.**
Qui est venu?	**Personne n'**est venu.
Qu'est-ce qui est arrivé?	**Rien n'**est arrivé.

Review **ne ... rien,** Ch. 6, p. 162.

■ You have already learned that the opposite of **quelque chose** is **ne ... rien** *(nothing, not anything).* The opposite of **quelqu'un** is **ne ... personne** *(no one, nobody, not anyone).*

■ When used as a *direct object,* **ne ... personne,** like **ne ... rien,** is placed around the conjugated verb.

Entendez-vous quelque chose?	Non, je **n'**entends **rien.**
Voyez-vous quelqu'un?	Non, je **ne** vois **personne.**

Note Unlike **ne ... rien,** however, **ne ... personne** surrounds both the auxiliary verb *and* the past participle in the passé composé.

	Avez-vous entendu quelque chose?	Non, je **n'**ai **rien** entendu.
But:	Avez-vous vu quelqu'un?	Non, je **n'**ai vu **personne.**

■ Both **rien** and **personne** can be used as the *object of a preposition*.

Avez-vous besoin de quelque chose?   Non, je **n'**ai besoin *de* **rien.**
Parlez-vous avec quelqu'un?   Non, je **ne** parle *avec* **personne.**

■ **Personne** and **rien** can also serve as the *subject* of a verb. In this case, **per-sonne** and **rien** come before **ne. Ne** still comes before the conjugated verb.

Personne n'a téléphoné.   *Nobody telephoned.*
Personne ne va à cet endroit.   *No one goes to that place.*
Rien ne m'intéresse.   *Nothing interests me.*

■ Like **jamais** and **rien, personne** can be used alone to answer a question.

Qui est venu?   **Personne.**
Qui avez-vous rencontré? **Personne.**

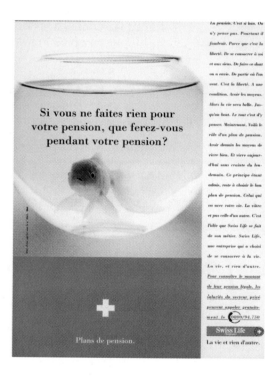

8 **Je n'ai rien fait à personne!** Utilisez **rien** ou **personne** pour répondre aux questions suivantes.

MODÈLES: Qui avez-vous vu?   Qu'avez-vous entendu?
              Je n'ai vu personne.   **Je n'ai rien entendu.**

1. Avec qui êtes-vous sorti(e)?
2. Qu'est-ce que vous avez fait?
3. Qu'est-ce que vous avez bu?
4. Qui est-ce que vous avez vu?
5. De quoi aviez-vous besoin?
6. À qui pensiez-vous?
7. À quoi pensiez-vous?
8. À qui est-ce que vous avez téléphoné?
9. Qu'avez-vous dit?

9 **Personne n'a rien fait.** Utilisez **rien** ou **personne** pour répondre aux questions suivantes.

MODÈLES: Qui a vu l'accident?   Qu'est-ce qui vous intéresse?
          Personne n'a vu l'accident.   **Rien ne m'intéresse.**

1. Qui a pris ma voiture?
2. Qu'est-ce qui est arrivé hier soir?
3. Qui a écrit à Sylvie?
4. Qui lui a téléphoné?
5. Qu'est-ce qui lui est arrivé?
6. Qui est-ce qui est sorti avec elle?
7. Qui va faire ses devoirs ce soir?
8. Qu'est-ce qui va mal?
9. Qui a brûlé un stop?

10 **Ni rien ni personne.** Utilisez **rien** ou **personne** pour répondre aux questions suivantes.

1. Vous avez fait quelque chose le week-end dernier?
2. Quelque chose vous est arrivé?
3. Vous avez rencontré quelqu'un?
4. Quelqu'un vous a invité(e) à danser?
5. Vous avez dansé avec quelqu'un?
6. Après le bal quelqu'un vous a accompagné(e) au café?
7. Vous avez bu quelque chose?
8. Quelqu'un a payé pour vous?
9. Vous avez dit au revoir à quelqu'un?

Entre amis

Je préfère ne pas en parler

Your partner is very secretive and will answer **nothing** or **nobody** to all your questions.

1. Ask your partner who wrote to him/her.
2. Ask who called him/her on the telephone.
3. Find out with whom s/he went out.
4. Ask what happened.
5. Ask what s/he did.
6. Ask whom s/he saw.

PAR TÉLÉPHONE

PAR COURRIER

2 Making Basic Hypotheses

Que feriez-vous[1] ...

	oui	non
... si vous n'aviez pas de devoirs?	____	____
Je resterais dans ma chambre.	____	____
Je sortirais avec mes amis.	____	____
J'irais au cinéma.	____	____
Je m'amuserais.	____	____
... si, par hasard[2], vous gagniez à la loterie?		
J'achèterais une voiture.	____	____
Je paierais mes dettes[3].	____	____
Je donnerais de l'argent aux pauvres.	____	____
Je mettrais de l'argent à la banque.	____	____
... si vous n'étiez pas étudiant(e)?		
Je chercherais du travail.	____	____
Je gagnerais de l'argent.	____	____
Je voyagerais.	____	____
J'irais en France.	____	____

1. *What would you do* 2. *by chance* 3. *debts*

E. Le conditionnel

Je pourrais apporter quelque chose? *Could I bring something?*
J'aimerais inviter les Martin. *I would like to invite the Martins.*
Ils viendraient si tu leur téléphonais *They would come if you called them*
maintenant. *now.*

■ The conditional is used to express hypotheses and also politely stated requests or wishes.

■ The conditional is formed by adding the imperfect endings (**-ais, -ais, -ait, -ions, -iez, -aient**) to the future stem (see Ch. 12).

aimer				vendre		
j'	aimer	ais		je	vendr	ais
tu	aimer	ais		tu	vendr	ais
il/elle/on	aimer	ait		il/elle/on	vendr	ait
nous	aimer	ions		nous	vendr	ions
vous	aimer	iez		vous	vendr	iez
ils/elles	aimer	aient		ils/elles	vendr	aient

■ Remember that a number of verbs have irregular future stems (see Ch. 12). These verbs use the same irregular stem in the conditional. The endings, however, are always regular.

être	**ser-**	je **serais**	*I would be*
avoir	**aur-**	j'**aurais**	*I would have*
faire	**fer-**	je **ferais**	*I would do*
aller	**ir-**	j'**irais**	*I would go*
venir	**viendr-**	je **viendrais**	*I would come*
devenir	**deviendr-**	je **deviendrais**	*I would become*
vouloir	**voudr-**	je **voudrais**	*I would like*
pouvoir	**pourr-**	je **pourrais**	*I could; I would be able*
devoir	**devr-**	je **devrais**	*I should; I ought to*
savoir	**saur-**	je **saurais**	*I would know*

■ Impersonal expressions also have conditional forms.

infinitive	present	conditional
pleuvoir	il pleut	**il pleuvrait**
falloir	il faut	**il faudrait**
valoir mieux	il vaut mieux	**il vaudrait mieux**

■ Since **-e-** is *pronounced* as [ə] before the sound combination [Rj], it is never dropped in the **nous** and **vous** forms of the conditional of **-er** verbs and of irregular verbs such as **vous feriez** and **nous serions**.

Review p. 410.

future	conditional
nous dans**é**rons	nous dans**e**rions
vous chant**é**rez	vous chant**e**riez
nous s**é**rons	nous s**e**rions
vous f**é**rez	vous f**e**riez

■ The conditional is used to make a polite request or suggestion because the present is often considered rather harsh or brusk. **Devoir** is often the verb used to make a polite suggestion.

Je **veux** une tasse de café.	*I **want** a cup of coffee.*
Je **voudrais** une tasse de café.	*I **would like** a cup of coffee.*

Vous **devez** faire attention.	*You **must** pay attention.*
Vous **devriez** faire attention.	*You **should (ought to)** pay attention.*

Tu devrais prendre le métro. C'est plus rapide.

 Quelle audace! *(What nerve!)* Mettez le verbe au conditionnel pour être plus poli(e).

MODÈLE: Vous devez parler plus fort *(loudly)*.
Vous devriez parler plus fort.

1. Je peux vous poser une question?
2. Avez-vous l'heure?
3. Pouvez-vous me dire votre nom?
4. Faites-vous la cuisine ce soir, par hasard?
5. C'est très gentil de m'inviter.
6. Je veux un steak-frites.

⑫ Quel conseil donneriez-vous? Utilisez le verbe **devoir** au conditionnel pour suggérer ce qu'il faudrait faire. Pourriez-vous donner deux suggestions pour chaque phrase?

MODÈLE: Nous n'avons pas de bonnes notes.
Vous devriez étudier.
Vous ne devriez pas sortir tous les soirs.

1. Marc a très faim.
2. Nos amis ont soif.
3. Nous sommes en retard.
4. Robert et Anne sont malades.
5. Gertrude est fatiguée.
6. Je n'ai pas envie de sortir ce soir.
7. Notre professeur donne beaucoup de devoirs.

F. *Si* hypothétique

Review **si** + present, Ch. 12, p. 338.

Si je gagne à la loterie, **j'irai** en Europe et en Asie.
Si je ne gagne pas à la loterie, **je resterai** ici.

Review   Hypothetical statements about the future can be made by using **si** plus the present tense in conjunction with a clause in the future. Such a hypothesis will become a virtual certainty *if* the event described in the **si** clause actually occurs.

Si ma mère me **téléphone** ce soir, je lui **raconterai** cette histoire.
Je n'**irai** pas avec toi si tu **continues** à me parler comme ça.

■ To *suggest* what someone *might* do, **si** can be used with the imperfect as a question.

Si vous veniez à 8 heures?   *How about coming at 8 o'clock?*
Si j'allais au supermarché?   *What if I went to the supermarket?*
Si nous jouions aux cartes?   *How about a game of cards?*

■ Hypothetical statements referring to what would happen if something else were also to take place can be made by using **si** + imperfect with a clause in the conditional. Such hypotheses are not as certain actually to occur as those expressed by **si** + present with a clause in the future.

Si j'étais libre, **je sortirais** avec mes amis.   *If I were free, **I would go out** with my friends.*
Que **feriez-vous si vous étiez** riche?   *What **would you do, if you were** rich?*

Synthèse: *Si* clauses used with the future or the conditional

Si + *le présent,* → *le futur*   **S'il pleut, nous ne sortirons pas.**
Si + *l'imparfait,* → *le conditionnel*   **S'il pleuvait, nous ne sortirions pas.**

 Deux solutions. Pour chaque «problème» vous devez suggérer deux solutions.

MODÈLE: Nous avons faim.
         Si vous mangiez quelque chose?
         Si nous allions au restaurant?

1. Nous avons un examen demain.
2. Je suis malade.
3. Paul a besoin d'argent.
4. Je dois contacter mes amis.
5. J'ai soif.
6. Nous devons faire de l'exercice physique.
7. Nos amis sont tristes.

Que ferais-tu? Lisez ce questionnaire et répondez à chaque question. Interviewez ensuite votre partenaire en mettant les phrases à la forme interrogative avec **tu.** Comparez vos réponses.

> **MODÈLE:**   **VOUS:** **Si tu avais besoin d'argent, est-ce que tu écrirais à tes parents?**
>
> **VOTRE PARTENAIRE:** **Non, je n'écrirais pas à mes parents. Et toi?**

1. Si j'avais besoin d'argent, ...

	oui	*non*
j'écrirais à mes parents.	____	____
je chercherais du travail.	____	____
je vendrais mon livre de français.	____	____
j'irais voir mes amis.	____	____
je pleurerais.	____	____

2. Si j'avais «F» à l'examen, ...

je pleurerais.	____	____
je serais fâché(e).	____	____
je serais très triste.	____	____
je téléphonerais à mes parents.	____	____
je resterais dans ma chambre.	____	____
j'arrêterais mes études.	____	____

3. Si on m'offrait une Mercédès, ...

je l'accepterais.	____	____
je la garderais.	____	____
je la vendrais.	____	____
je la donnerais à mes parents.	____	____

15 **À vous.** Répondez.

1. Si vous étiez professeur, qu'est-ce que vous enseigneriez?
2. Donneriez-vous beaucoup de devoirs à vos étudiants? Pourquoi ou pourquoi pas?
3. Que feriez-vous pendant les vacances?
4. Quelle marque de voiture auriez-vous?
5. Où iriez-vous dans cette voiture?

Entre amis

Des châteaux en Espagne *(Daydreams)*

1. Find out what your partner would do if s/he had a lot of money.
2. Ask where s/he would live.
3. Find out what s/he would buy.
4. Suggest two things your partner could do with the money.

www Intégration

Révision

A **Le témoin.** Un ami francophone a vu un accident. Faites une liste de questions que vous pourriez lui poser.

B **Un remue-méninges *(Brainstorming).*** Faites une liste de choses que vous pourriez faire avec cinquante dollars.

C **Quelques suggestions.**

1. Citez trois choses qu'on pourrait donner à un(e) ami(e) pour son anniversaire.
2. De quoi les étudiants ont-ils besoin pour être heureux sur votre campus? (trois choses)
3. Faites trois suggestions pour les prochaines vacances.
4. Quelles sont trois choses que vous feriez si vous étiez en France?

D **À vous.** Répondez.

1. Quelle sorte de maison aimeriez-vous avoir un jour?
2. Qu'est-ce qu'un étudiant devrait faire pour réussir au cours de français?
3. Que feriez-vous à la place du professeur? Pourquoi?
4. Qu'est-ce que vous apporteriez si vous étiez invité(e) chez une famille française?
5. Si vous alliez faire un long voyage et si vous deviez inviter quelqu'un, qui vous accompagnerait et pourquoi?

Pas de problème!

Preparation for the video:
1. Video worksheet in the *Cahier d'activités*
2. CD-ROM, *Module 12*

Cette activité est basée sur la vidéo, *Module 12.* Choisissez la bonne réponse pour compléter les phrases suivantes.

1. Jean-François invite _____ à la Fête de la musique.
   (Alissa, Betty, Marie-Christine)
2. La Fête de la musique est au mois de _____.
   (mai, juin, juillet)
3. La copine qu'ils vont retrouver à un autre concert s'appelle _____.
   (Alissa, Betty, Marie-Christine)
4. Moustapha a consulté son _____ pour savoir à quelle heure chaque concert devait avoir lieu.
   (livre, programme, ticket)
5. Les jeunes guitaristes vont faire _____.
   (une émission, un disque, une excursion)

Lecture I

A **Étude du vocabulaire.** Étudiez les phrases suivantes et choisissez les mots anglais qui correspondent aux mots français en caractères gras: *unavoidable, when, chase, darted out, stone throwing, was astonished, lived, young girls, imprisoned right away, around, court, cross, district.*

1. Il y avait plusieurs **fillettes** qui jouaient et riaient dans la cour de l'école.
2. Avant son mariage, Mme Dupont **demeurait** chez ses parents dans un **quartier** résidentiel.
3. Paul **s'est étonné** de ne pas voir beaucoup de gens dans les magasins **aux environs de** Noël.
4. Il fallait **traverser** la rue pour rentrer chez nous.
5. Après tous ses accidents, il était **inévitable** que cet homme perde son permis de conduire.
6. Le gendarme **s'est élancé** à la poursuite du criminel.
7. **Lorsque** le **tribunal** a condamné le criminel, on l'a **écroué sur le coup** dans une cellule de la prison.
8. Après une longue **course-poursuite** en voiture, les gendarmes ont réussi à arrêter le criminel.
9. Les **jets de pierre** sont formellement interdits par la police.

Use pp. 406–407 to help you prepare these questions.

B **Une interrogation.** Vous êtes gendarmes et vous devez questionner deux automobilistes. Lisez d'abord les articles qui suivent et ensuite composez huit questions qui commencent par des mots interrogatifs **Qui?, Qu'est-ce qui?,** etc., dont quatre questions pour Mme Walther et quatre pour M. Martin.

Deux accidents

Mulhouse. Sortie d'école tragique, hier, en fin de journée, à Habsheim, près de Mulhouse. Une fillette de onze ans a perdu la vie en rentrant à son domicile. Il était aux environs de 16 h 45. Monique Schoenhoffen se promenait le long de la route, lorqu'elle s'est subitement élancée pour traverser la chaussée, devant la maison où elle demeurait, juste à l'entrée de la commune. Elle n'avait pas vu venir une voiture, qui arrivait de Mulhouse, et qui était pilotée par Mme Georgette Walther, domiciliée dans cette ville. Le choc était inévitable. La fillette a été tuée sur le coup. À l'arrivée des gendarmes, il n'y avait malheureusement plus rien à faire. À 20 h, la gendarmerie n'avait pas encore déterminé les circonstances exactes de ce drame.

Roanne. Un automobiliste de 25 ans, sans permis de conduire, qui avait engagé une course-poursuite avec la police à plus de 110 km/heure dans les rues de Roanne (Loire) et qui avait frappé les policiers après son arrestation, a été condamné mercredi à six mois de prison ferme par le tribunal correctionnel de la ville. M. Djaffar Martin, déjà condamné en mars dernier à quatre mois de prison, avait été reconnu, mardi après-midi, par une patrouille de police qui l'avait aussitôt pris en chasse. Le chauffard avait alors pris une rue du centre en sens interdit, à plus de 110 km/heure, puis brûlé cinq feux rouges, forçant les automobilistes à s'immobiliser, sans cependant provoquer d'accident. Il avait été finalement intercepté par la police dans son quartier. Il a alors violemment attaqué les policiers qui le questionnaient sous les jets de pierre d'une dizaine de jeunes du quartier. Le chauffard a été écroué à la prison de la Talaudière.

C **Une analyse des faits.** Relisez les deux articles et comparez-les. Ensuite choisissez l'accident (Mulhouse ou Roanne) qui correspond mieux aux descriptions suivantes.

1. L'automobiliste n'avait sans doute rien fait de mauvais.
2. L'automobiliste avait déjà été en prison.
3. Une personne est morte dans cet accident.
4. D'autres ont voulu aider l'automobiliste.
5. L'automobiliste allait trop vite.
6. L'automobiliste n'avait pas pu s'arrêter à temps.
7. L'automobiliste habitait la ville où l'accident a eu lieu.

D **À votre avis.** Relisez les deux articles. Ensuite décidez ce que vous feriez si vous étiez le juge (1) au procès *(lawsuit)* de Mme Walther; (2) au procès de M. Martin.

Lecture II

A **Étude du vocabulaire.** Étudiez les phrases suivantes. Essayez de deviner le sens des mots en caractères gras.

1. Est-ce qu'on peut camper ici? Je ne sais pas; demandez au **responsable** du camp.
2. **Je ne suis pas en mesure de** répondre à cette question. Posez-la à un spécialiste.
3. Marc étudie beaucoup et **pourtant** il ne réussit pas.
4. Paul a changé d'emploi. Il espère gagner **davantage** d'argent.
5. J'ai envie de lire; achetez-moi **n'importe quel** journal. Ça m'est égal.
6. Jacques est **nettement** plus grand que sa sœur. Mais il est aussi beaucoup plus âgé qu'elle.
7. Pour construire un grand bâtiment, on utilise du **béton.**
8. Tchernobyl était une **centrale** nucléaire russe.

B **Opinions.** Décidez si vous êtes d'accord avec les phrases suivantes.

1. L'énergie nucléaire est nécessaire pour l'indépendance économique de mon pays.
2. Toutes les centrales nucléaires sont dangereuses.
3. C'est aux États-Unis que les centrales nucléaires produisent le plus grand pourcentage d'électricité.
4. Il y a déjà eu un accident nucléaire aux États-Unis.
5. Il y a déjà eu un accident nucléaire en Russie.

Il existe de nombreuses centrales nucléaires en France. Il semble qu'elles soient mieux acceptées par le public français qu'elles ne le seraient aux États-Unis.

La France nucléaire

«Oui, je crois à la possibilité d'un accident. Ce qui serait dangereux, c'est que je n'y croie pas.» De la part du responsable de la sûreté nucléaire à EDF (Électricité de France), Pierre Tanguy, de tels propos[1] peuvent surprendre. Mais ils illustrent en fait une nouvelle attitude d'EDF après l'accident de Tchernobyl, où l'improbable est arrivé. «C'est en étant[2] sûr que l'accident peut arriver qu'on est le mieux en mesure de l'éviter[3], poursuit[4] Pierre Tanguy. De toute façon[5], je n'arrive pas à imaginer qu'on puisse avoir en France des rejets extérieurs tels[6] qu'une de nos centrales risque de faire des victimes dans la population.»

Pourtant, la France accumule davantage de risques statistiques que n'importe quel autre pays. Au nom de l'indépendance énergétique, elle a la première place pour la part du nucléaire dans l'électricité produite: 70%. Un record, comparé aux Américains, qui en sont à 16%, et aux Soviétiques, à 11%. De plus, la France possède 44 réacteurs électronucléaires qui se trouvent dans un espace[7] nettement plus restreint[8] et plus peuplé. En cas d'incident, pouvons-nous réussir une évacuation de 135.000 personnes, comme à Tchernobyl? Les experts français prévoient[9] l'évacuation des habitants dans un rayon[10] de seulement 5 kilomètres autour de la centrale et le confinement des habitants chez eux jusqu'à 10 kilomètres, mais il n'y a pas de plan de secours à grande échelle[11] plus loin. «Ce n'est pas du laxisme», explique Jean Petit, directeur adjoint de l'Institut de protection et de sûreté nucléaire. La raison de cette assurance? «Des fuites[12] radioactives dans l'atmosphère ne peuvent pas s'échapper[13] des centrales françaises, affirme-t-on à EDF. Car, à la différence de ceux des Soviétiques, nos réacteurs sont enfermés sous un dôme de béton de 90 centimètres d'épaisseur[14].» C'est ainsi que l'accident de Three Mile Island, aux États-Unis, n'a pas fait de victimes, car dans la centrale américaine les poisons radioactifs sont restés enfermés dans le dôme de béton.

Adapté de «Risques: le système France», *Le Point* (n° 761)

---

*1. such words   2. by being   3. avoid   4. continues   5. In any case   6. discharge to the degree   7. space
8. smaller   9. foresee   10. radius   11. large scale   12. leaks   13. escape   14. 90 centimeters thick*

Vrai ou faux? Décidez si les phrases suivantes sont vraies ou fausses d'après la lecture. Si une phrase est fausse, corrigez-la.

1. Les centrales nucléaires françaises sont meilleures que celles des Russes.
2. La centrale nucléaire de Three Mile Island était exactement comme celle de Tchernobyl.
3. Pierre Tanguy est sûr qu'il n'y aura jamais de problème.
4. D'après Tanguy, personne ne sera tué s'il y a un accident nucléaire.
5. L'EDF est sûre qu'il n'y aura jamais de fuite.
6. S'il y a un problème, les Français ont l'intention d'évacuer tous les gens qui habitent très près de la centrale.

D **À votre avis**

1. Êtes-vous pour ou contre l'utilisation de l'énergie nucléaire? Expliquez votre réponse.
2. Que pensez-vous de la sûreté du système nucléaire français?

VOCABULAIRE ACTIF

Noms
un chauffard *bad driver*
un conducteur *driver (male)*
une conductrice *driver (female)*
une dette *debt*
les études *(f. pl.) studies*
une faute *fault; mistake*
un(e) idiot(e) *idiot*
un(e) imbécile *imbecile*
une marque *make, brand*

Adjectifs
pâle *pale*
physique *physical*

Verbes
accepter *to accept*
assurer *to assure; to insure*
entendre parler de *to hear about*

Pronom
personne (ne ... personne) *no one; nobody; not anyone*

Préposition
contre *against; (in exchange) for*

Expressions utiles
juste derrière *right behind*
par hasard *by chance*
parler plus fort *to speak more loudly*
puisque *since*

À propos d'un accident
un accident *accident*
un agent de police *police officer*
un(e) automobiliste *driver*
blessé(e) *wounded*

brûler un stop *to run a stop sign*
la chaussée *pavement*
une contravention *traffic ticket*
déraper *to skid*
entrer en collision *to hit; to collide*
freiner *to brake*
un gendarme *policeman*
glissant(e) *slippery*
heurter *to hit; to run into (something)*
ivre *drunk*
la mort *death*
rouler *to go; to roll*
un témoin *witness*
tuer *to kill*

escale 5
Les Antilles

Haïti

REPÈRES: HAÏTI

Statut politique:	république
Superficie:	27.750 km² (équivalente à celle du Maryland)
Population:	7.320.000 (95% noirs et 5% mulâtres); 72% rurale, 28% urbaine
Langue officielle:	français et créole (depuis 1987); 30% de la population comprend le français
Religion:	catholique, protestant, vaudou
Capitale:	Port-au-Prince
Ressources:	tourisme, agriculture (bananes, canne à sucre, café, mangues), minéraux (bauxite, magnésium)

CHRONOLOGIE

1492 Christophe Colomb découvre l'île où les Arawaks habitent depuis le VIIe siècle. Il l'appelle Hispaniola.

1508 Une cargaison (*cargo*) d'Afrique dépose les premiers esclaves, introduits pour suppléer à la main-d'œuvre indigène, décimée par les maladies et de pénibles conditions de travail.

1697 La France occupe la partie ouest de l'île et en fait une riche colonie agricole.

1750–1801 Rébellions de plus en plus sanglantes contre les colonisateurs. Rivalités entre noirs et mulâtres.

1801 Toussaint Louverture, ancien esclave, devient gouverneur général à vie.

1802 Une armée envoyée par Napoléon reprend l'île. Toussaint est fait prisonnier et envoyé en France.

1803 L'armée haïtienne est victorieuse contre l'armée française, décimée par la maladie.

1804 Déclaration d'indépendance de l'île, qui devient la première république noire autonome moderne.

1825 La France réclame une indemnité de 50 millions de francs avant de reconnaître l'indépendance du pays.

Haïti et ses habitants

La dualité de l'héritage historique des Haïtiens, l'esclavage et la colonisation française, continue à marquer la structure sociale. Une élite riche et peu nombreuse se distingue par la couleur de sa peau, son éducation et l'adoption de la langue et de la culture françaises. La grande majorité du peuple est noire, pauvre, rurale, mais devient de plus en plus urbaine, et parle uniquement créole. Entre ces deux classes s'est créée une classe moyenne, aujourd'hui grandissante, de noirs qui se sont promus par l'éducation ou par une carrière dans l'armée, le gouvernement ou l'industrie. Certains sont très fiers de leurs origines africaines et font un effort pour établir l'usage officiel du créole, alors que les autres souhaitent faire partie de l'élite culturelle française.

Ce pays, qui était la plus riche des colonies françaises au XVIIIe siècle, est devenu l'un des plus pauvres. L'instabilité politique, les rébellions, massacres et dictatures successives ont déchiré le pays. L'érosion, due à la déforestation nécessaire pour la monoculture imposée par le régime colonial, a appauvri la terre. La lourde indemnité exigée par la France comme prix de l'indépendance a contribué à atrophier l'économie du pays.

De même que le français reste la langue officielle et le créole la langue de tous les jours, la religion catholique, adoptée par 90% des habitants, coexiste avec les pratiques vaudoues d'origine africaine, qui influencent les attitudes et la culture de ce peuple. Haïti garde un caractère africain plus marqué que d'autres pays de l'Amérique latine par la majorité de sa population noire, descendant directement des esclaves africains, et par ses croyances vaudoues.

La religion vaudou

Bien que l'église catholique condamne les pratiques vaudou, la plupart des habitants d'Haïti ne perçoivent aucun conflit entre les deux religions. Ils iront souvent à une cérémonie vaudou le samedi soir et à la messe le lendemain matin. Mais qu'est-ce que la religion vaudou? Pour certains, il s'agit avant tout d'un culte des ancêtres; d'autres honorent aussi les esprits qui président aux différents aspects de la vie de tous les jours. Durant leurs cérémonies, les croyants cherchent à entretenir des rapports étroits avec les esprits par des offrandes rituelles. À l'origine, le mot «vaudou» désignait la danse donnée en l'honneur des esprits. Cette danse peut produire un état de trance où le danseur se sent possédé par un esprit. Des prêtres ou prêtresses jouent un rôle d'intermédiaire entre les croyants et les esprits et dirigent les rituels.

Les croyances vaudou apportent au peuple haïtien un certain réconfort dans leurs épreuves. Elles encouragent la joie de vivre et aident à surmonter la violence et les souffrances que ce pays a connues au cours de son histoire. Ce culte sert aussi d'inspiration aux peintres du pays.

La Peinture haïtienne

Venant des milieux les plus simples, souvent sans aucune éducation et sans formation artistique, les peintres haïtiens ne sont pas attachés aux conventions formelles. En 1943, grâce à l'établissement d'un centre d'art à Port-au-Prince, cette peinture devient connue et appréciée d'un public international. Elle représente un réalisme merveilleux. Plus elle se fait connaître, plus la richesse artistique du pays se révèle et se développe.

On distingue deux écoles dans cette tradition primitive. Dans le sud, Hector Hyppolite, le peintre haïtien le plus connu, était prêtre vaudou. Il peignait avec des plumes d'oiseaux et des restes de peinture de bâtiment. Ses tableaux, pleins de mouvement, de lignes audacieuses et de couleurs très vives, expriment une spiritualité et un charme particuliers. Ils intègrent souvent des thèmes ou des symboles vaudou. Au nord, Philomé Obin, employé de bureau, représente des thèmes historiques ou des scènes de la vie de tous les jours de manière plus statique et moins vive mais avec exactitude et minutie. Outre cette peinture dite primitive, qui connaît un grand succès à l'étranger, on trouve une peinture haïtienne moderne et très expressive, émanant de peintres qui ont eu une formation académique. Ainsi, Haïti, un des pays les plus pauvres du monde, est aussi un des plus riches dans le domaine de la peinture contemporaine.

L'œuvre d'un artiste haïtien

Vrai ou Faux?

1. La majorité des Haïtiens parlent français.
2. Les mulâtres sont les premiers habitants d'Haïti.
3. Napoléon voulait qu'Haïti reste française.
4. Les premiers peintres haïtiens n'avaient souvent pas d'éducation formelle.

Les Petites Antilles

CHRONOLOGIE

1493 Christophe Colomb découvre la Guadeloupe et en 1502, la Martinique.

1508 La première cargaison d'esclaves africains arrive.

1635 Occupation française de la Martinique et de la Guadeloupe.

1678 Le nombre d'esclaves aux Antilles françaises atteint 27.000.

1848 La France abolit l'esclavage.

1902 Éruption de la Montagne Pelée à la Martinique, qui détruit l'ancienne capitale, Saint-Pierre, et tue 29.000 personnes.

1946 La Martinique et la Guadeloupe deviennent départements français d'outre-mer, gouvernés par la France. Les habitants sont de nationalité française et ont le droit de vote.

REPÈRES:	LA MARTINIQUE	LA GUADELOUPE
Statut politique:	départements français d'outre-mer	
Superficie:	1.106 km²	1.780 km²
Population:	375.000	426.000
Groupes ethniques:	mulâtres, noirs, créoles, Indiens d'Asie	
Langue officielle:	français	français
Religion:	catholique	catholique
Chef-lieu:	Fort-de-France	Pointe-à-Pitre
Ressources:	subvention de l'État français, tourisme, industrie (rhum, sucre), agriculture (canne à sucre, bananes, ananas)	

Les Petites Antilles françaises: une évasion tropicale

Situées en zone tropicale, les Petites Antilles françaises sont un archipel en forme d'arc où se trouvent la Martinique (mot qui veut dire «île aux fleurs») et la Guadeloupe («île aux belles eaux»). Cette dernière est composée de deux îles principales, qui forment un papillon, Basse-Terre et Grande-Terre.

L'hospitalité des Antillais est célèbre et le touriste appréciera les baignades sous un doux soleil, les promenades dans les forêts tropicales ou les plongées sous-marines parmi des poissons de toutes les couleurs. On peut aussi, à bord d'un voilier, apprécier le calme et la beauté des plages sauvages bordées de palmiers, explorer des villages de pêcheurs ou visiter, à la Martinique, le village des Trois-Îlets où est née en 1763 Marie-Josèphe Rose Tascher de la Pagerie, la future impératrice, femme de Napoléon.

Mais ces îles de rêve ont leur côté sombre. Chaque année, des ouragans violents frappent la région. Ces îles volcaniques sont à la merci d'éruptions, comme celle qui en 1902 a détruit Saint-Pierre à la Martinique. Elles sont aussi menacées de tremblements de terre qui peuvent faire disparaître des portions d'île entières.

Au cours de leur histoire, ces îles ont connu l'exploitation, la violence et la misère. Aujourd'hui encore, le chômage (*unemployment*) est très élevé: 23,5% à la Martinique, plus élevé encore en Guadeloupe. Certains Antillais voudraient se séparer de la France. Aimé Césaire, célèbre poète de la négritude, qui est devenu maire de Fort-de-France, a déclaré que la Martinique «perdait son âme» en restant française et dépendante de la France. Par contre, une séparation de la France serait un désastre économique.

De nombreux Antillais choisissent d'émigrer, surtout en France. Certains vont y faire des études et retrouvent dans les universités françaises des francophones africains dont ils partagent souvent la pensée. Ceux qui restent aux Antilles font face courageusement à une vie très dure, qui s'illumine cependant d'une joie de vivre et d'un amour des fêtes, de la musique et de la danse.

Vrai ou Faux?

1. Il fait assez froid en hiver à la Martinique.
2. La Guadeloupe fait partie de la France.
3. Aimé Césaire a été maire de Fort-de-France.
4. Saint-Pierre avait une population de près de 100.000 habitants.
5. Il y a un volcan sur l'île de la Martinique.

Le carnaval

Dans les Antilles françaises, le carnaval est l'occasion d'une fête de plusieurs jours. À la Martinique, tout commence la dernière semaine avant le carême (*Lent*). Le vendredi soir, on danse jusque très tard dans la nuit. Le lendemain, les Antillais descendent dans les rues «courir le vidé». Les «vidés», immenses personnages habillés de rouge ou de noir, mènent les foules le long des rues en chantant et en dansant, pour qu'elles oublient leurs soucis quotidiens et les conventions sociales. Le dimanche aussi a lieu le défilé de Vaval, roi du carnaval, et l'élection de la reine du carnaval. Le lundi, troisième jour du carnaval, est plus calme. Des femmes déguisées en hommes et vice-versa se promènent dans les rues, figurant, en une parade burlesque, des couples mariés. La journée se termine par des mariages légitimes. Le jour suivant, mardi gras, on célèbre la fête du diable rouge. Vestige de l'influence africaine, ce personnage, habillé de satin rouge et la tête couverte d'un masque rouge et noir surmonté de cornes, danse au son de clochettes en brandissant un trident décoré. Enfin, le mercredi des cendres est jour de deuil. Les participants à la fête s'habillent en noir et blanc pour aller brûler le roi Vaval au milieu des pleurs et des cris, mais avec la certitude de le voir renaître l'année suivante.

Le zouk, musique populaire de la Martinique

Le mot «zouk» vient de la Martinique. Il signifie «danse» en créole. Pendant les années 80, ce mot désignait la danse exécutée au son de la musique du groupe «Kassav». Ce groupe, qui est en grande partie responsable du succès de ce genre de musique, se compose de musiciens et chanteurs de la Martinique et de la Guadeloupe, vivant actuellement en France. Aux Antilles, la popularité du zouk a fait naître de nouveaux groupes de musiciens. Musique composite à l'image du mélange des races antillaises, le zouk combine de nombreux styles, rythmes et mélodies sur synthétiseurs, batteries électroniques et instruments d'origines multiples: tambours, congas, maracas d'influence africaine, banjo et clarinette de La Nouvelle-Orléans, instruments à cordes venant d'Europe. Le zouk se danse sur place avec un mouvement rythmique des hanches (*hips*). Il se rattache au phénomène musical du «world beat» ou «world music». Il résulte de l'union de la musique folklorique et la chanson créole avec la technologie électronique moderne.

Le créole

Le créole est le produit d'une fusion de plusieurs langues. Aux Antilles françaises, il s'est développé au XVIIe siècle avec l'arrivée des esclaves africains. Ces derniers, originaires de communautés linguistiques différentes, devaient communiquer non seulement entre eux mais aussi avec leurs «maîtres». L'apprentissage en masse du français par les Africains ne ressemblait en rien à l'enseignement dans une salle de classe sous la tutelle d'un professeur. Les Africains apprenaient le français dans les champs de canne à sucre en écoutant le langage familier des colons français, qui ressemblait peu au français littéraire. De ces circonstances est née une langue nouvelle, le créole.

Vrai ou Faux?

1. Le carnaval a lieu après la fête de Pâques (*Easter*).
2. Le dernier jour avant le début du carême est un mardi.
3. Le zouk est la langue parlée par les Martiniquais.
4. À leur arrivée aux Antilles, les esclaves parlaient tous la même langue africaine.

Verbes

Infinitif	Présent	Passé Composé	Imparfait
1. parler	je parle	j' ai parlé	je parlais
	tu parles	tu as parlé	tu parlais
	il/elle/on parle	il/elle/on a parlé	il/elle/on parlait
	nous parlons	nous avons parlé	nous parlions
	vous parlez	vous avez parlé	vous parliez
	ils/elles parlent	ils/elles ont parlé	ils/elles parlaient
2. finir	je finis	j' ai fini	je finissais
	tu finis	tu as fini	tu finissais
	il/elle/on finit	il/elle/on a fini	il/elle/on finissait
	nous finissons	nous avons fini	nous finissions
	vous finissez	vous avez fini	vous finissiez
	ils/elles finissent	ils/elles ont fini	ils/elles finissaient
3. attendre	j' attends	j' ai attendu	j' attendais
	tu attends	tu as attendu	tu attendais
	il/elle/on attend	il/elle/on a attendu	il/elle/on attendait
	nous attendons	nous avons attendu	nous attendions
	vous attendez	vous avez attendu	vous attendiez
	ils/elles attendent	ils/elles ont attendu	ils/elles attendaient
4. se laver	je me lave	je me suis lavé(e)	je me lavais
	tu te laves	tu t'es lavé(e)	tu te lavais
	il/on se lave	il/on s'est lavé	il/on se lavait
	elle se lave	elle s'est lavée	elle se lavait
	nous nous lavons	nous nous sommes lavé(e)s	nous nous lavions
	vous vous lavez	vous vous êtes lavé(e)(s)	vous vous laviez
	ils se lavent	ils se sont lavés	ils se lavaient
	elles se lavent	elles se sont lavées	elles se lavaient

Impératif	Futur		Conditionnel		Subjonctif	
parle	je	parlerai	je	parlerais	que je	parle
parlons	tu	parleras	tu	parlerais	que tu	parles
parlez	il/elle/on	parlera	il/elle/on	parlerait	qu'il/elle/on	parle
	nous	parlerons	nous	parlerions	que nous	parlions
	vous	parlerez	vous	parleriez	que vous	parliez
	ils/elles	parleront	ils/elles	parleraient	qu'ils/elles	parlent
finis	je	finirai	je	finirais	que je	finisse
finissons	tu	finiras	tu	finirais	que tu	finisses
finissez	il/elle/on	finira	il/elle/on	finirait	qu'il/elle/on	finisse
	nous	finirons	nous	finirions	que nous	finissions
	vous	finirez	vous	finiriez	que vous	finissiez
	ils/elles	finiront	ils/elles	finiraient	qu'ils/elles	finissent
attends	j'	attendrai	j'	attendrais	que j'	attende
attendons	tu	attendras	tu	attendrais	que tu	attendes
attendez	il/elle/on	attendra	il/elle/on	attendrait	qu'il/elle/on	attende
	nous	attendrons	nous	attendrions	que nous	attendions
	vous	attendrez	vous	attendriez	que vous	attendiez
	ils/elles	attendront	ils/elles	attendraient	qu'ils/elles	attendent
lave-toi	je	me laverai	je	me laverais	que je	me lave
lavons-nous	tu	te laveras	tu	te laverais	que tu	te laves
lavez-vous	il/on	se lavera	il/on	se laverait	qu'il/on	se lave
	elle	se lavera	elle	se laverait	qu'elle	se lave
	nous	nous laverons	nous	nous laverions	que nous	nous lavions
	vous	vous laverez	vous	vous laveriez	que vous	vous laviez
	ils	se laveront	ils	se laveraient	qu'ils	se lavent
	elles	se laveront	elles	se laveraient	qu'elles	se lavent

VERBES RÉGULIERS AVEC CHANGEMENTS ORTHOGRAPHIQUES

Infinitif	Présent		Passé Composé	Imparfait
1. manger	je mange tu manges il/elle/on mange	nous mang**e**ons vous mangez ils/elles mangent	j'ai mangé	je mang**e**ais
2. avancer	j' avance tu avances il/elle/on avance	nous avan**ç**ons vous avancez ils/elles avancent	j'ai avancé	j'avan**ç**ais
3. payer	je pa**i**e tu pa**i**es il/elle/on pa**i**e	nous pa**y**ons vous pa**y**ez ils/elles pa**i**ent	j'ai pa**y**é	je pa**y**ais
4. préférer	je préf**è**re tu préf**è**res il/elle/on préf**è**re	nous préférons vous préférez ils/elles préf**è**rent	j'ai préféré	je préférais
5. acheter	j' ach**è**te tu ach**è**tes il/elle/on ach**è**te	nous achetons vous achetez ils/elles ach**è**tent	j'ai acheté	j'achetais
6. appeler	j' appe**ll**e tu appe**ll**es il/elle/on appe**ll**e	nous appelons vous appelez ils/elles appe**ll**ent	j'ai appelé	j'appelais

Impératif	Futur	Conditionnel	Subjonctif	*Autres verbes*
mange mangeons mangez	je mangerai	je mangerais	que je mange que nous mangions	exiger nager neiger voyager
avance avançons avancez	j'avancerai	j'avancerais	que j'avance que nous avancions	commencer divorcer
paie payons payez	je paierai	je paierais	que je paie que nous payions	essayer
préfère préférons préférez	je préférerai	je préférerais	que je préfère que nous préférions	espérer exagérer répéter s'inquiéter
achète achetons achetez	j'achèterai	j'achèterais	que j'achète que nous achetions	lever se lever se promener
appelle appelons appelez	j'appellerai	j'appellerais	que j'appelle que nous appelions	épeler jeter s'appeler

VERBES IRRÉGULIERS

To conjugate the irregular verbs on the top of the opposite page, consult the verbs conjugated in the same manner, using the number next to the verbs. The verbs preceded by a bullet are conjugated with the auxiliary verb **être**. Of course, when the verbs in this chart are used with a reflexive pronoun (as reflexive verbs), the auxiliary verb **être** must be used in compound tenses.

Infinitif	Présent		Passé Composé	Imparfait
1. aller	je vais tu vas il/elle/on va	nous allons vous allez ils/elles vont	je suis allé(e)	j'allais
2. s'asseoir	je m'assieds tu t'assieds il/elle/on s'assied	nous nous asseyons vous vous asseyez ils/elles s'asseyent	je me suis assis(e)	je m'asseyais
3. avoir	j' ai tu as il/elle/on a	nous avons vous avez ils/elles ont	j'ai eu	j'avais
4. battre	je bats tu bats il/elle/on bat	nous battons vous battez ils/elles battent	j'ai battu	je battais
5. boire	je bois tu bois il/elle/on boit	nous buvons vous buvez ils/elles boivent	j'ai bu	je buvais
6. conduire	je conduis tu conduis il/elle/on conduit	nous conduisons vous conduisez ils/elles conduisent	j'ai conduit	je conduisais
7. connaître	je connais tu connais il/elle/on connaît	nous connaissons vous connaissez ils/elles connaissent	j'ai connu	je connaissais
8. croire	je crois tu crois il/elle/on croit	nous croyons vous croyez ils/elles croient	j'ai cru	je croyais
9. devoir	je dois tu dois il/elle/on doit	nous devons vous devez ils/elles doivent	j'ai dû	je devais

apprendre 25	détruire 6	offrir 21	• repartir 22	• sortir 22
comprendre 25	• devenir 28	permettre 17	• revenir 28	sourire 26
couvrir 21	dormir 22	promettre 17	revoir 29	traduire 6
découvrir 21	élire 16	réduire 6	sentir 22	valoir mieux 15
décrire 11	• s'endormir 22			

Impératif	Futur	Conditionnel	Subjonctif
va allons allez	j'irai	j'irais	que j'aille que nous allions
assieds-toi asseyons-nous asseyez-vous	je m'assiérai	je m'assiérais	que je m'asseye que nous nous asseyions
aie ayons ayez	j'aurai	j'aurais	que j'aie que nous ayons
bats battons battez	je battrai	je battrais	que je batte que nous battions
bois buvons buvez	je boirai	je boirais	que je boive que nous buvions
conduis conduisons conduisez	je conduirai	je conduirais	que je conduise que nous conduisions
connais connaissons connaissez	je connaîtrai	je connaîtrais	que je connaisse que nous connaissions
crois croyons croyez	je croirai	je croirais	que je croie que nous croyions
dois devons devez	je devrai	je devrais	que je doive que nous devions

Infinitif	Présent		Passé Composé	Imparfait
10. dire	je dis tu dis il/elle/on dit	nous disons vous dites ils/elles disent	j'ai dit	je disais
11. écrire	j' écris tu écris il/elle/on écrit	nous écrivons vous écrivez ils/elles écrivent	j'ai écrit	j'écrivais
12. envoyer	j' envoie tu envoies il/elle/on envoie	nous envoyons vous envoyez ils/elles envoient	j'ai envoyé	j'envoyais
13. être	je suis tu es il/elle/on est	nous sommes vous êtes ils/elles sont	j'ai été	j'étais
14. faire	je fais tu fais il/elle/on fait	nous faisons vous faites ils/elles font	j'ai fait	je faisais
15. falloir	il faut		il a fallu	il fallait
16. lire	je lis tu lis il/elle/on lit	nous lisons vous lisez ils/elles lisent	j'ai lu	je lisais
17. mettre	je mets tu mets il/elle/on met	nous mettons vous mettez ils/elles mettent	j'ai mis	je mettais
18. mourir	je meurs tu meurs il/elle/on meurt	nous mourons vous mourez ils/elles meurent	je suis mort(e)	je mourais
19. naître	je nais tu nais il/elle/on naît	nous naissons vous naissez ils/elles naissent	je suis né(e)	je naissais
20. nettoyer	je nettoie tu nettoies il/elle/on nettoie	nous nettoyons vous nettoyez ils/elles nettoient	j'ai nettoyé	je nettoyais
21. ouvrir	j' ouvre tu ouvres il/elle/on ouvre	nous ouvrons vous ouvrez ils/elles ouvrent	j'ai ouvert	j'ouvrais

Impératif	Futur	Conditionnel	Subjonctif
dis disons dites	je dirai	je dirais	que je dise que nous disions
écris écrivons écrivez	j'écrirai	j'écrirais	que j'écrive que nous écrivions
envoie envoyons envoyez	j'enverrai	j'enverrais	que j'envoie que nous envoyions
sois soyons soyez	je serai	je serais	que je sois que nous soyons
fais faisons faites	je ferai	je ferais	que je fasse que nous fassions
—	il faudra	il faudrait	qu'il faille
lis lisons lisez	je lirai	je lirais	que je lise que nous lisions
mets mettons mettez	je mettrai	je mettrais	que je mette que nous mettions
meurs mourons mourez	je mourrai	je mourrais	que je meure que nous mourions
nais naissons naissez	je naîtrai	je naîtrais	que je naisse que nous naissions
nettoie nettoyons nettoyez	je nettoierai	je nettoierais	que je nettoie que nous nettoyions
ouvre ouvrons ouvrez	j'ouvrirai	j'ouvrirais	que j'ouvre que nous ouvrions

Infinitif	Présent		Passé Composé	Imparfait
22. partir*	je pars tu pars il/elle/on part	nous partons vous partez ils/elles partent	je suis parti(e)*	je partais
23. pleuvoir	il pleut		il a plu	il pleuvait
24. pouvoir	je peux** tu peux il/elle/on peut	nous pouvons vous pouvez ils/elles peuvent	j'ai pu	je pouvais
25. prendre	je prends tu prends il/elle/on prend	nous prenons vous prenez ils/elles prennent	j'ai pris	je prenais
26. rire	je ris tu ris il/elle/on rit	nous rions vous riez ils/elles rient	j'ai ri	je riais
27. savoir	je sais tu sais il/elle/on sait	nous savons vous savez ils/elles savent	j'ai su	je savais
28. venir	je viens tu viens il/elle/on vient	nous venons vous venez ils/elles viennent	je suis venu(e)	je venais
29. voir	je vois tu vois il/elle/on voit	nous voyons vous voyez ils/elles voient	j'ai vu	je voyais
30. vouloir	je veux tu veux il/elle/on veut	nous voulons vous voulez ils/elles veulent	j'ai voulu	je voulais

***Servir, dormir,** and **sentir** are conjugated with **avoir** in the passé composé. **Partir, sortir,** and **s'endormir** are conjugated with **être.**

The inverted form of **je peux is **puis-je … ?**

Impératif	Futur	Conditionnel	Subjonctif
pars partons partez	je partirai	je partirais	que je parte que nous partions
—	il pleuvra	il pleuvrait	qu'il pleuve
— — —	je pourrai	je pourrais	que je puisse que nous puissions
prends prenons prenez	je prendrai	je prendrais	que je prenne que nous prenions
ris rions riez	je rirai	je rirais	que je rie que nous riions
sache sachons sachez	je saurai	je saurais	que je sache que nous sachions
viens venons venez	je viendrai	je viendrais	que je vienne que nous venions
vois voyons voyez	je verrai	je verrais	que je voie que nous voyions
veuille veuillons veuillez	je voudrai	je voudrais	que je veuille que nous voulions

Appendices

A list of International Phonetic Alphabet symbols

Voyelles

Son	Exemples	Pages: *Entre amis*
[i]	il, y	93, 299
[e]	et, parlé, aimer, chez	33, 56, 382
[ɛ]	mère, neige, aime, tête, chère, belle	33, 57, 410
[a]	la, femme	57
[wa]	toi, trois, quoi, voyage	57
[ɔ]	folle, bonne	186
[o]	eau, chaud, nos, chose	186, 382
[u]	vous, août	155
[y]	une, rue, eu	155, 157
[ø]	deux, veut, bleu, ennuyeuse	352
[œ]	heure, veulent, sœur	352
[ə]	le, serons, faisons	57, 410
[ɑ̃]	an, lent, chambre, ensemble	92
[ɔ̃]	mon, nom, sont	92
[ɛ̃]	main, faim, examen, important, vin, chien symphonie, brun*, parfum*	92

*Some speakers pronounce written un and um as [œ̃].

Consonnes

[p]	père, jupe	382
[t]	toute, grand ami, quand est-ce que …	106, 143, 382
[k]	comment, qui	213
[b]	robe, bien	382
[d]	deux, rendent	382
[g]	gare, longue, second	335, 382
[f]	fou, pharmacie, neuf	64
[s]	merci, professeur, français, tennis, démocratie	63, 213

[ʃ]	**ch**at, **sh**ort	213
[v]	**v**ous, neu**f** ans	64
[z]	**z**éro, ro**s**e	106, 213
[ʒ]	**j**e, â**g**e, na**ge**ons	37, 213
[l]	**l**ire, vi**ll**e	323
[R]	**r**ue, sœu**r**	242
[m]	**m**es, ai**m**e, co**mm**ent	92
[n]	**n**on, américai**n**e, bo**nn**e	92
[ɲ]	monta**gn**e	213

Semiconsonnes

[j]	f**ill**e, trava**il**, ch**ie**n, vo**y**ez, **y**eux, h**i**er	299, 323
[w]	**ou**i, **w**eek-end	
[ɥ]	h**u**it, t**u**er	

APPENDIX B

Professions

The following professions are in addition to those taught in Ch. 4, p. 111.

agent *m.* **d'assurances** insurance agent
agent *m.* **de police** police officer
agent *m.* **de voyages** travel agent
agent *m.* **immobilier** real-estate agent
artisan *m.* craftsperson
assistant(e) social(e) social worker
avocat(e) lawyer
banquier *m.* banker
boucher/bouchère butcher
boulanger/boulangère baker
caissier/caissière cashier
chanteur/chanteuse singer
charcutier/charcutière pork butcher, delicatessen owner
chauffeur *m.* driver
chercheur/chercheuse researcher
chirurgien(ne) surgeon
commerçant(e) shopkeeper
conférencier/conférencière lecturer
conseiller/conseillère counsellor; advisor
dentiste *m./f.* dentist
douanier/douanière customs officer
électricien(ne) electrician
épicier/épicière grocer
expert-comptable *m.* CPA
facteur/factrice mail deliverer
femme de ménage *f.* cleaning lady
fleuriste *m./f.* florist
garagiste *m./f.* garage owner; mechanic
homme/femme politique politician
hôtelier/hôtelière hotelkeeper
hôtesse de l'air *f.* stewardess
informaticien(ne) data processor

instituteur/institutrice elementary-school teacher
jardinier/jardinière gardener
maire *m.* mayor
mannequin *m.* fashion model
mécanicien(ne) mechanic
ménagère *f.* housewife
militaire *m.* serviceman/servicewoman
moniteur/monitrice (de ski) *(ski) instructor*
musicien(ne) musician
opticien(ne) optician
PDG *m./f.* CEO (chairperson)
pasteur *m.* (Protestant) minister
peintre *m./f.* painter
photographe *m./f.* photographer
pilote *m.* pilot
plombier *m.* plumber
pompier *m.* firefighter
prêtre *m.* priest
psychologue *m./f.* psychologist
rabbin *m.* rabbi
religieuse *f.* nun
reporter *m.* reporter
représentant(e) de commerce traveling salesperson
restaurateur/restauratrice restaurant owner
savant *m.* scientist; scholar
sculpteur *m.* sculptor
serveur/serveuse waiter/waitress
traducteur/traductrice translator
vétérinaire *m./f.* vet

A P P E N D I X   C

Glossary of Grammatical Terms

Term	Definition	Example(s)
accord *(agreement)* 15–16, 22, 68	Articles, adjectives, pronouns, etc. are said to agree with the noun they modify when they "adopt" the gender and number of the noun.	*La voisine de Patrick est allemande. C'est une jeune fille très gentille. Elle est partie en vacances.*
adjectif *(adjective)* 15, 22, 95	A word that describes or modifies a noun or a pronoun, specifying size, color, number, or other qualities.	*Lori Becker n'est pas mariée. Nous sommes américains. Le professeur a une voiture noire. C'est une belle voiture.* (See **adjectif démonstratif, adjectif interrogatif, adjectif possessif.**)
adjectif démonstratif *(demonstrative adjective)* 103	A noun determiner (see **déterminant**) that identifies and *demonstrates* a person or a thing.	*Regarde les couleurs de cette robe et de ce blouson!*
adjectif interrogatif *(interrogative adjective)* 112, 392	An adjective that introduces a question. In French, the word **quel** (*which* or *what*) is used as an interrogative adjective and agrees in gender and number with the noun it modifies.	*Quelle heure est-il? Quels vêtements portez-vous?*
adjectif possessif *(possessive adjective)* 68, 75	A noun determiner that indicates *possession* or *ownership*. Agreement depends on the gender of the noun and not on the sex of the possessor, as in English *(his/her)*.	*Où est mon livre? Comment s'appelle son père?*
adverbe *(adverb)* 96, 288	An invariable word that describes a verb, an adjective, or another adverb. It answers the question *when?* (time), *where?* (place), or *how? how much?* (manner).	*Mon père conduit lentement.* (how?) *On va regarder un match de foot demain.* (when?) *J'habite ici.* (where?)
adverbe interrogatif *(interrogative adverb)* 143	An adverb that introduces a question about time, location, manner, number, or cause.	*Où sont mes lunettes? Comment est-ce que Lori a trouvé le film? Pourquoi est-ce que tu fumes?*

Term	Definition	Example(s)
article *(article)* 41, 59, 216	A word used to signal that a noun follows, and to specify the noun as to its *gender* and *number,* as well as whether it is general, particular, or part of a larger whole. (See **article défini, article indéfini,** and **article partitif.**)	
article défini *(definite article)* 41, 43, 311	The definite articles in French are **le, la, l',** and **les.** They are used to refer to a specific noun, or to things in general, in an abstract sense.	*Le professeur est dans la salle de classe. Le lait est bon pour la santé. J'aime les concerts de jazz.*
article indéfini *(indefinite article)* 59	The indefinite articles in French are **un, une,** and **des.** They are used to designate unspecified nouns.	*Lori Becker a un frère et une sœur. J'ai des amis qui habitent à Paris.*
article partitif *(partitive article)* 216	The partitive articles in French are **du, de la, de l',** and **des.** They are used to refer to *part* of a larger whole, or to things that cannot be counted.	*Je vais acheter du fromage. Tu veux de la soupe?*
comparatif *(comparison)* 308, 310	When comparing people or things, these comparative forms are used: **plus** *(more),* **moins** *(less),* **aussi** *(as … as),* and **autant** *(as much as).*	*Le métro est plus rapide que le bus. Il neige moins souvent en Espagne qu'en France. Ma sœur parle aussi bien le français que moi. Elle gagne autant d'argent que moi.*
conditionnel *(conditional)* 420	A verb form used when stating hypotheses or expressing polite requests.	*Tu devrais faire attention. Je voudrais une tasse de café.*
conjugaison *(conjugation)* 36	An expression used to refer to the various forms of a verb that reflect *person* (1st, 2nd, or 3rd person), *number* (singular or plural), *tense* (present, past, or future), and *mood* (indicative, subjunctive, imperative, conditional). Each conjugated form consists of a *stem* and an *ending.*	Présent: *Nous parlons français en classe.* Passé composé: *Je suis allé à Paris l'année dernière.* Imparfait: *Quand il était jeune, mon frère s'amusait beaucoup.* Futur: *Je ferai le devoir de français ce soir.* Impératif: *Ouvrez vos livres!* Subjonctif: *Il faut qu'on fasse la lessive tout de suite.* Conditionnel: *Je voudrais un verre de coca.*

Term	Definition	Example(s)
contraction *(contraction)* 74, 125, 393	The condensing of two words to form one.	*C'est une photo **du** professeur* [**de + le**]. *Nous allons **au** café* [**à + le**].
déterminant *(determiner)* 333	A word that precedes a noun and *determines* its quality (*definite, indefinite, partitive,* etc.). In French, nouns are usually accompanied by one of these determiners.	Article *(**le** livre)*; demonstrative adjective *(**cette** table)*; possessive adjective *(**sa** voiture)*; interrogative adjective *(**Quelle** voiture?)*; number *(**trois** crayons)*.
élision *(elision)* 14, 20, 41, 246	The process by which some words drop their final vowel and replace it with an apostrophe before words beginning with a vowel sound.	*Je **m'**appelle Martin et **j'**habite près de l'église.*
futur *(future)* 128, 336	A tense used to express what *will* happen. The construction **aller** + *infinitive* often replaces the future tense, especially when making more immediate plans.	*Un jour, nous **irons** en France. Nous **allons partir** cet après-midi.*
genre *(gender)* 4, 14, 41	The term used to designate whether a noun, article, pronoun, or adjective is masculine or feminine. All nouns in French have a grammatical *gender*.	***la** table, **le** livre, **le** garçon, **la** mère*
imparfait *(imperfect)* 301, 411	A past tense used to describe a setting (background information), a condition (physical or emotional), or a habitual action.	*Il **faisait** beau quand je suis parti. Je **prenais** beaucoup de médicaments quand j'**étais** jeune.*
impératif *(imperative)* 139, 281	The verb form used to give commands or to make suggestions.	***Répétez** après moi! **Allons** faire une promenade.*
indicatif *(indicative)* 14, 157, 301	A class of tenses, used to relate facts or supply information. **Le présent, le passé composé, l'imparfait, le futur** all belong to the indicative mood.	*Je ne **prends** pas le petit déjeuner. Le directeur **partira** en vacances le mois prochain. Il **faisait** beau quand je **suis parti**.*
infinitif *(infinitive)* 36, 43	The plain form of the verb, showing the general meaning of the verb without reflecting *tense, person,* or *number.* French verbs are often classified according to the last two letters of their infinitive forms: **-er** verbs, **-ir** verbs, or **-re** verbs.	*étu**dier**, chois**ir**, vend**re***

Term	Definition	Example(s)
inversion *(inversion)* 46, 62, 143, 158	An expression used to refer to the reversal of the subject pronoun-verb order in the formation of questions.	*Parlez-vous français? Chantez-vous bien?*
liaison *(liaison)* 11, 15, 37, 59–61, 124	The term used to describe the spoken linking of the final and usually silent consonant of a word with the beginning vowel sound of the following word.	*Vous [z]êtes américain? Ma sœur a un petit [t]ami.*
mot apparenté *(cognate)* 25, 91, 380	Words from different languages that are related in origin and that are similar are referred to as *cognates*.	**question** [Fr.] = *question* [Eng.]; **semestre** [Fr.] = *semester* [Eng.]
négation *(negation)* 20, 96, 157, 285, 417	The process of transforming a positive sentence into a negative one. In negative sentences the verb is placed between two words, **ne** and another word defining the nature of the negation.	*On **ne** parle **pas** anglais ici. Il **ne** neige **jamais** à Casablanca. Mon grand-père **ne** travaille **plus.** Il **n'**y a **personne** dans la salle de classe. Mon fils **n'**a **rien** dit.*
nombre *(number)* 14, 16, 41	The form of a noun, article, pronoun, adjective, or verb that indicates whether it is *singular* or *plural*. When an adjective is said to agree with the noun it modifies in *number*, it means that the adjective will be singular if the noun is singular, and plural if the noun is plural.	***La** voiture de James **est** très petite. **Les** livres de français ne **sont** pas aussi cher**s** que **les** livre**s** de biologie.*
nom *(noun)* 16	The name of a person, place, thing, idea, etc. All nouns in French have a grammatical gender and are usually preceded by a determiner.	*le **livre**, la **vie**, les **étudiants**, ses **parents**, cette **photo.***
objet direct *(direct object)* 226, 278	A thing or a person bearing directly the action of a verb. (See **pronom objet direct.**)	*Thierry écrit **un poème.** Il aime **Céline.***

Term	Definition	Example(s)
objet indirect *(indirect object)* 385	A person (or persons) to or for whom something is done. The indirect object is often preceded by the preposition **à** because it receives the action of the verb *indirectly.* (See **pronom objet indirect.**)	*Thierry donne une rose à **Céline**.* *Le professeur raconte des histoires drôles **aux étudiants**.*
participe passé *(past participle)* 157, 189, 243	The form of a verb used with an auxiliary to form two-part (compound) past tenses such as **le passé composé.**	*Vous êtes **allés** au cinéma. Moi, j'ai **lu** un roman policier.*
passé composé 157, 188, 417	A past tense used to narrate an event in the past, to tell what happened, etc. It is used to express actions *completed* in the past. The **passé composé** is composed of two parts: an auxiliary **(avoir** or **être)** conjugated in the present tense, and the past participle form of the verb.	*Le président **a parlé** de l'économie. Nous **sommes arrivés** à 5h.*
personne *(person)* 13	The notion *person* indicates whether the subject of the verb is speaking *(1st person)*, spoken to *(2nd person)*, or spoken about *(3rd person)*. Verbs and pronouns are designated as being in the singular or plural of one of the three persons.	First person singular: *Je n'ai rien compris.* Second person plural: *Avez-**vous** de l'argent?* Third person plural: ***Elles** sont toutes les deux sénégalaises.*
plus-que-parfait *(pluperfect)* 412	A past tense used to describe an event that took place prior to some other past event. The **plus-que-parfait** is composed of two parts: an auxiliary **(avoir** or **être)** conjugated in the imperfect tense, and the past participle form of the verb.	*Il était ivre parce qu'il **avait trop bu**.*
préposition *(preposition)* 138, 142, 195	A word (or a small group of words) preceding a noun or a pronoun that shows position, direction, time, etc. relative to another word in the sentence.	*Mon oncle qui habite **à** Boston est allé **en** France. L'hôtel est **en face de** la gare.*
présent *(present)* 14, 36	A tense that expresses an action taking place at the moment of speaking, an action that one does habitually, or an action that began earlier and is still going on.	*Il **fait** très beau aujourd'hui. Je me **lève** à 7h tous les jours.*

Term	Definition	Example(s)
pronom *(pronoun)* 13, 112, 192, 226, 278, 385, 398	A word used in place of a noun or a noun phrase. Its form depends on the *number* (singular or plural), *gender* (masculine or feminine), *person* (1st, 2nd, 3rd), and *function* (subject, object, etc.) of the noun it replaces.	*Tu aimes les fraises? Oui, **je les** adore. Irez-**vous** à Paris cet été? Non, **je** n'**y** vais pas. Prenez-**vous** du sucre? Oui, **j'en** prends. Qui **t'**a dit de partir? **Lui.***
pronom accentué *(stress pronoun)* 168, 302	A pronoun that is separated from the verb and appears in different positions in the sentence.	*Voilà son livre à **elle**. Viens avec **moi!***
pronom interrogatif *(interrogative pronoun)* 112, 392–393, 414–416	Interrogative pronouns are used to ask questions. They change form depending upon whether they refer to people or things and also whether they function as the subject, the direct object, or the object of a preposition of a sentence.	***Qui** est là? **Que** voulez-vous faire dans la vie? **Qu'est-ce que** vous faites? **Qu'est-ce qui** est arrivé?*
pronom objet direct *(direct object pronoun)* 226, 278, 387	A pronoun that replaces a direct object noun.	*Thierry aime Céline et elle **l'**aime aussi.*
pronom objet indirect *(indirect object pronoun)* 385	A pronoun that replaces an indirect object noun.	*Thierry **lui** a donné une rose.*
pronom relatif *(relative pronoun)* 57, 256, 394	A pronoun that refers or "relates" to a preceding noun *(antécédent)* and connects two clauses into a single sentence.	*Le professeur a des amis **qui** habitent à Paris. J'ai lu le livre **que** tu m'as donné.*
pronom sujet *(subject pronoun)* 13	A pronoun that replaces a noun subject.	***Ils** attendent le train. **On** parle français ici.*
sujet *(subject)* 13	The person or thing that performs the action of the verb. (See **pronom sujet**.)	***Les étudiants** font souvent les devoirs à la bibliothèque. **Vous** venez d'où?*
subjonctif *(subjunctive)* 282, 365, 396	A class of tenses, used under specific conditions: (1) the verb is in the second (or subordinate) clause of a sentence; (2) the second clause is introduced by **que**; and (3), the verb of the first clause expresses advice, will, necessity, emotion, etc.	*Mon père préfère que je n'**aie** pas de voiture. Le professeur veut que nous **parlions** français. Ma mère est contente que vous **soyez** ici.*

Term	Definition	Example(s)
superlatif *(superlative)* 311	The superlative is used to express the superior or inferior degree or quality of a person or a thing.	*Le TGV est le train **le plus** rapide du monde. L'eau minérale est la boisson **la moins** chère.*
temps *(tense)* 36, 157, 301, 336	The particular form of a verb that indicates the time frame in which an action occurs: present, past, future, etc.	*La tour Eiffel **est** le monument le plus haut de Paris. Nous **sommes arrivés** à 5h à la gare. Je **ferai** de mon mieux.*
verbe *(verb)* 14, 36, 243	A word expressing action or condition of the subject. The verb consists of a *stem* and an *ending,* the form of which depends on the *subject* (singular, plural, 1st, 2nd, or 3rd person), the *tense* (present, past, future), and the *mood* (indicative, subjunctive, imperative, conditional).	
verbe auxiliaire *(auxiliary verb)* 157, 188	The two auxiliary (or helping) verbs in French are **avoir** and **être.** They are used in combination with a past participle to form **le passé composé.**	*Nous **sommes** allés au cinéma hier. Nous **avons** vu un très bon film.*
verbes pronominaux *(reflexive verbs)* 165, 190, 357	Verbs whose subjects and objects are the same. A reflexive pronoun will precede the verb and act as either the direct or indirect object of the verb. The reflexive pronoun has the same *number, gender,* and *person* as the subject.	*Lori **se réveille.** Elle et James **se sont** bien **amusés** hier soir.*

Vocabulaire

This vocabulary list includes all of the words and phrases included in the *Vocabulaire actif* sections of *Entre amis,* as well as the passive vocabulary used in the text. The definitions given are limited to the context in which the words are used in this book. Entries for active vocabulary are followed by the number of the chapter in which they are introduced for the first time. If a word is formally activated in more than one chapter, a reference is given for each chapter. Some entries are followed by specific examples from the text. Expressions are listed according to their key word. In subentries, the symbol ~ indicates the repetition of the key word.

Regular adjectives are given in the masculine form, with the feminine ending in parentheses. For irregular adjectives, the full feminine form is given in parentheses.

The gender of each noun is indicated after the noun. Irregular feminine or plural forms are also noted beside the singular form.

The following abbreviations are used.

CP   Chapitre préliminaire

adj.	adjective	*m.*	masculine
adv.	adverb	*m.pl.*	masculine plural
art.	article	*n.*	noun
conj.	conjunction	*pl.*	plural
f.	feminine	*prep.*	preposition
f.pl.	feminine plural	*pron.*	pronoun
inv.	invariable	*v.*	verb

à at, in, to   1
  ~ côté next door; to the side   5
  ~ côté de next to, beside   5
  ~ droite (de) to the right (of)   7
  ~ gauche (de) to the left (of)   7
  ~ ... heure(s) at ... o'clock   1
  ~ la vôtre! (here's) to yours!   2
  ~ l'heure on time   7
  ~ l'intérieur de inside   6
  ~ midi at noon   5
  ~ minuit at midnight   5
  ~ toute vitesse at top speed   10
  ~ travers throughout
  être ~ to belong to   6

abord: d' ~ at first   5
absolument absolutely   10
accepter to accept   15
accident *m.* accident   15
accompagner to accompany   6
accord *m.* agreement
  d' ~ okay   5
  être d' ~ (avec) to agree (with)   1, 11
accordéon *m.* accordion   6
accueillant(e) friendly
achat *m.* purchase   9
acheter to buy   9
acteur/actrice *m./f.* actor/actress   1
activité *f.* activity   11
actuellement now   14; nowadays

addition *f.* (restaurant) bill, check   8; addition
adieu *m.* (*pl.* **adieux**) farewell
adjoint au maire *m.* deputy mayor
adorer to adore; to love   2
adresse *f.* address   4
aéroport *m.* airport   5
affaires *f.pl.* business   4
  homme/femme d' ~ *m./f.* businessman/woman   4
affreux (affreuse) horrible   8
âge *m.* age   3
  quel ~ avez-vous? how old are you?   3
âgé(e) old   11
agent (de police) *m.* (police) officer   15

agir: il s'agit de it's (*lit.* it's a matter of)

agrumes *m.pl.* citrus fruits

aider to help 4

aïe! ouch! 6

ail *m.* garlic 8

aimable kind; nice 9

aimer to like; to love 2

 s' ~ to love each other 14

air: avoir l' ~ to seem, to appear, to look 9

album *m.* album 11

alcool *m.* alcohol

Allemagne *f.* Germany 5

allemand(e) German 1

aller to go 5

 ~ en ville to go into town 5

 ~ -retour *m.* round-trip ticket 12

 ~ simple *m.* one-way (ticket) 12

 allez à la porte! go to the door! CP

 allez-y go ahead, let's go 12

 je vais très bien I'm fine 2

allô! hello! *(on the phone)* 12

alors then, therefore; so 2

amener to bring

américain(e) American 1

ami/amie *m./f.* friend 2

amusant(e) amusing, funny; fun 11

s'amuser to have fun; to have a good time 6

 je veux m'amuser I want to have fun 10

an *m.* year 3

 Jour de l' ~ *m.* New Year's Day 7

ananas *m.* pineapple

anchois *m.* anchovy 8

ancien (ancienne) former; old 4

anglais(e) English 1

Angleterre *f.* England 5

année *f.* year 6

 ~ scolaire *f.* school year 10

anniversaire *m.* birthday 7

 ~ de mariage wedding anniversary 10

annonce *f.* advertisement 14

 petites annonces want ads

annuler to cancel

août *m.* August 7

apéritif *m.* before-dinner drink 8

appareil *m.* appliance; phone 7

appartement *m.* apartment 3

s'appeler to be named, be called 13

 comment vous appelez-vous? what is your name? 1

 je m'appelle … my name is … 1

appétit *m.* appetite

 Bon ~! Have a good meal! 13

apporter to bring 8

apprendre to learn; to teach 8

après after 5

après-demain day after tomorrow 12

après-midi *m.* afternoon 1

 de l' ~ in the afternoon 5

 Bon ~. Have a good afternoon.

arabe *m.* Arabic 5; Arab

arachide *f.* peanut

arbre *m.* tree

argent *m.* money 9

armée *f.* army

arrêt (d'autobus) *m.* (bus) stop 10

arrêter to stop 10

arrière- great- 3

arriver to arrive; to happen 7

 qu'est-ce qui est arrivé? what happened? 14

artiste *m./f.* artist 4

aspirine *f.* aspirin 9

s'asseoir to sit down 13

 Asseyez-vous! Sit down! CP

assez sort of, rather, enough 1

 ~ bien fairly well 2

 ~ mal rather poorly 2

 en avoir ~ to be fed up 11

assiette *f.* plate 8

assister (à) to attend 14

assurer to assure; to insure 15

attacher to attach; to put on 10

attendre to wait (for) 9

attentif (attentive) attentive 10

attention: faire ~ to pay attention 4

au contraire to the contrary 4

au revoir good-bye 1

aujourd'hui today 4

aussi also, too 1; as 11

 ~ … que as … as … 11

autant (de) as much 11

autocar *m.* tour bus 12

automne *m.* fall 7

automobiliste *m./f.* driver 15

autoroute *f.* turnpike; throughway, highway 12

autour de around 5

autre other 3

avance *f.* advance

 en ~ early 7

avancer to advance 10

avant before 5

avare miserly 4

avec with 2

avenir *m.* future

avertissement *m.* warning 14

avion *m.* airplane 7

avis *m.* opinion, advice

 à mon (à ton, etc.) ~ in my (your, etc.) opinion 11

avoir to have 3

 ~ besoin de to need 9

 ~ chaud to be hot 8

 ~ envie de to want to; to feel like 5

 ~ faim to be hungry 8

 ~ froid to be cold 8

 ~ l'air to seem, to appear, to look 9

 ~ lieu to take place 11

 ~ l'intention de to plan to 5

 ~ mal (à) to be sore, to have a pain (in) 9

 ~ peur to be afraid 8

 ~ pitié (de) to have pity (on), to feel sorry (for) 10

 ~ raison to be right 8

 ~ rendez-vous to have an appointment, meeting 4

 ~ soif to be thirsty 8

 ~ sommeil to be sleepy 8

 ~ tendance à to tend to 12

 ~ tort to be wrong; to be unwise 8

 en ~ assez to be fed up 11

 qu'est-ce que tu as? what's the matter with you? 9

avril *m.* April 7

bagages *m.pl.* luggage 7

bague *f.* ring 14

bande dessinée *f.* comic strip 6

banque *f.* bank 5

barquette *f.* small box; mini crate 9

basket-ball (basket) *m.* basketball   6

baskets *f.pl.* high-top sneakers   4

bâtiment *m.* building   5

batterie *f.* drums   6

bavard(e) talkative   4

beau/bel/belle/beaux/belles handsome, beautiful   1
   il fait ~ it's nice out   CP, 7

beau-frère *m* brother-in-law   3

beau-père *m.* (*pl.* **beaux-pères**) stepfather (or father-in-law)   3

beaucoup a lot   2; much, many

beaujolais *m.* Beaujolais (*wine*)   8

beaux-parents *m.pl.* stepparents (or in-laws)   3

bébé *m.* baby   7

beige beige   4

belge Belgian   1

Belgique *f.* Belgium   5

belle-mère *f.* (*pl.* **belles-mères**) stepmother (or mother-in-law)   3

belle-sœur *f.* sister-in-law   3

berk! yuck! awful!   8

besoin *m.* need
   avoir ~ de to need   9

beurre *m.* butter   8
   ~ d'arachide *m.* peanut butter   8

bibliothèque *f.* library   5

bien well; fine   2
   ~ que although
   ~ sûr of course   8

bientôt soon
   À bientôt. See you soon.   5

Bienvenue! Welcome!   3

bière *f.* beer   2

billet *m.* bill (*paper money*)   9; ticket   12

bise *f.* kiss   5

bistro *m.* bar and café; bistro   5

bizarre weird; funny looking   4

blague *f.* joke
   sans ~! no kidding!   14

blanc (blanche) white   4

blessé(e) wounded   15

bleu(e) blue   4

bleuet *m.* blueberry (*French-Canadian*)

blond(e) blond   4

blouson *m.* windbreaker, jacket   4

bœuf *m.* beef   8

boire to drink   8
   voulez-vous ~ quelque chose? do you want to drink something?   2

boisson *f.* drink, beverage   2

boîte *f.* box, can   8

bol *m.* bowl   13

bon (bonne) good   2
   bon marché *adj. inv.* inexpensive   4
   bonne journée have a good day   1

bonbon *m.* candy   8

bonjour hello   1

bonsoir good evening   1

bordeaux *m.* Bordeaux (*wine*)   8

bottes *f.pl.* boots   4

bouche *f.* mouth   9

boucherie *f.* butcher shop   9

boulangerie *f.* bakery   5

boum *f.* party   10

bouquet *m.* bouquet   9

bout *m.* end, goal

bouteille *f.* bottle   8

boutique *f.* (gift, clothing) shop   9

bras *m.* arm   9

bridge *m.* bridge (*game*)   6

brie *m.* Brie (*cheese*)   8

brocoli *m.* broccoli   8

brosse *f.* brush
   ~ à cheveux *f.* hairbrush   13
   ~ à dents *f.* toothbrush   13

se brosser (les dents) to brush (one's teeth)   13

bruit *m.* noise   9

brûler to burn; to run through (light)   15

brun(e) brown(-haired)   4

bureau *m.* (*pl.* **bureaux**) desk; office   3
   ~ de poste *m.* post office   5
   ~ de tabac *m.* tobacco shop   5

but *m.* goal

ça (cela) that   4
   ~ dépend It depends   9
   ~ va? How's it going?   2
   ~ va bien (I'm) fine   2
   ~ veut dire … it means …   CP

cachet (d'aspirine) *m.* (aspirin) tablet   9

cadeau *m.* gift   9

cadre *m.* executive   4

café *m.* coffee   2; café   5
   ~ crème *m.* coffee with cream   2

cafétéria *f.* cafeteria   5

calculatrice *f.* calculator   3

calme calm   4

camarade de chambre *m./f.* roommate   3

camembert *m.* Camembert (*cheese*)   8

campagne *f.* country(side)

campus *m.* campus   5

Canada *m.* Canada   5

canadien(ne) Canadian   1

car because

carte *f.* map   12; menu   13
   ~ de crédit *f.* credit card   9
   ~ postale *f.* postcard   4

cartes *f.pl.* cards (*game*)   6

cas: en tout ~ in any case

cassis *m.* blackcurrant

ce/cet/cette/ces this, that, these, those   4

ceinture *f.* belt   4
   ~ de sécurité *f.* safety belt, seat belt   10

cela (ça) that   9

célèbre famous   14

célibataire single, unmarried   1

celui *m.* this (that) one

celle *f.* this (that) one

celles *f.pl.* these; those

cendre *f.* ash   8

cent one hundred   3

centime *m.* centime (*1/100 of a euro*)   3

centre commercial *m.* shopping center, mall   5

cependant however

céréales *f.pl.* cereal; grains   8

certainement surely, of course   1

c'est it is, this is   1
   c'est-à-dire that is to say
   ~ gentil à vous that's nice of you   2
   ~ pour vous it's for you   1

ceux *m.pl.* these; those

CFA (=Communauté financière africaine) African Financial Community

chacun(e) each

chaîne (de télé) *f.* (TV) channel   14

chaise *f.* chair   3

chambre *f.* bedroom   3; room
   camarade de ~ *m./f.* roommate
   3

champignons *m.pl.* mushrooms
   8

chance *f.* luck
   Bonne ~! Good luck!   12

changer (de) to change   10

chanson *f.* song   2

chanter to sing   2

chanteur/chanteuse *m./f.* singer
   11

chapeau *m.* (*pl.* **chapeaux**) hat
   4

chaque each   7

charcuterie *f.* pork butcher's;
   delicatessen   9

charmant(e) charming   3

chat *m.* cat   3

château *m.* castle   5

chaud(e) hot   2
   avoir ~ to be hot   8
   il fait ~ it's hot (warm)   CP, 4,
   7

chauffage *m.* heat   13

chauffard *m.* bad driver   15

chauffeur *m.* driver   10

chaussée *f.* pavement   15

chaussettes *f.pl.* socks   4

chaussures *f.pl.* shoes   4

chauve bald   4

chef *m.* head (*person in charge*);
   boss; chef

chemise *f.* shirt   4

chemisier *m.* blouse   4

chèque *m.* check   9
   ~ de voyage *m.* traveler's check
   9

cher (chère) dear   2; expensive
   4

chercher to look for   2

chéri(e) *m./f.* dear, honey   10

cheveux *m.pl.* hair   4

chèvre *m.* goat cheese   8

chewing-gum *m.* chewing gum
   9

chez at the home of   3
   ~ moi at my house   3
   ~ vous at your house   3

chic *adj. inv.* chic; stylish   4

chien *m.* dog   3

chimie *f.* chemistry   5

Chine *f.* China   5

chinois(e) Chinese   1

chocolat chaud *m.* hot chocolate
   2

choisir to choose   12

choix *m.* choice   8

chose *f.* thing   4
   quelque ~ *m.* something   2
   pas grand- ~ not much   5

chouette great (*fam.*)   14

chut! shh!   10

cigare *m.* cigar   6

cinéma *m.* movie theater   5

cinq five   CP

cinquante fifty   3

circulation *f.* traffic   15

citron pressé *m.* lemonade   2

classe *f.* class
   en ~ in class; to class   4

clé *f.* key   12

climatisation *f.* air conditioning
   13

coca *m.* Coca-Cola   2

code postal *m.* zip code   9

coin *m.* corner

collège *m.* jr. high school

combien (de) how many, how
   much   3

commander to order   8

comme like, as   2; how; since
   ~ ci, ~ ça so-so   2
   ~ il (elle) était …! how … he
   (she) was!   11
   ~ si … as if …

commencer to begin   7
   commencez! begin!   CP

comment how; what   3
   ~ ? what (did you say?)   CP,
   2
   ~ allez-vous? how are you?
   2
   ~ ça va? how is it going?   2
   ~ dit-on …? how do you
   say …?   CP
   ~ est (sont) …? what is (are)
   … like?   4
   ~ est-ce qu'on écrit …? how
   do   you spell …?   2
   ~ je vais faire? what am I going to do?   12
   ~ trouvez-vous …? what do
   you think of …?   2
   ~ vous appelez-vous? what is
   your name?   1

commentaire *m.* commentary
   10

commerce *m.* business   5

communication *f.*
   communication
   votre ~ de … your call from …
   1

complet *m.* suit   4

complet (complète) full; complete   12

composter (un billet) to punch
   (a ticket)   12

compréhensif/compréhensive
   understanding   4
   je ne comprends pas I don't
   understand   CP

comprendre to understand; to
   include   8

compris(e) included; understood
   8

comptabilité *f.* accounting   5

compter to count

condamner: être condamné(e)
   to be sentenced

conducteur/conductrice driver
   15

conduire to drive   10

confirmer to confirm   12

confiture *f.* jam   8

confortable comfortable   4

confus(e) ashamed; embarrassed
   14

connaître to know; to be acquainted with, to be familiar
   with   10

conseil *m.* (piece of) advice   10

se consoler to console oneself
   14

content(e) happy   5

constamment constantly   10

constant(e) constant   10

continuer to continue
   continuez continue   CP

contraire *m.* contrary, opposite
   au ~ on the contrary   4, 8

contravention *f.* traffic ticket   15

contre against; in exchange for
   15
   par ~ on the other hand

corps *m.* body   9

côté *m.* side
   à ~ next door; to the side   5
   à ~ de next to, beside   5

se coucher to go to bed   6

couci-couça so-so

couleur *f.* color   4
   de quelle ~ est (sont) …?
   what color is (are) …?   4

couloir *m.* hall; corridor   5
coup *m.*: ~ **d'envoi** kick-off
couper to cut   13
cour *f.* court
couramment fluently   11
coureur/coureuse runner; cyclist
courir to run
cours *m.* course; class   5
course *f.* race
courses *f.pl.* errands, shopping   4
cousin/cousine *m./f.* cousin   3
couteau *m.* (*pl.* **couteaux**) knife   13
coûter to cost   9
coutume *f.* custom
craie *f.* chalk   CP
cravate *f.* tie   4
crédit: carte de ~ *f.* credit card   9
crème *f.* cream   2
crêpe *f.* crepe; French pancake   8
croire to believe, to think   14
   je crois que oui I think so   14
   je ne crois pas I don't think so   14
croissance *f.* increase, growth
croissant *m.* croissant   8
crudités *f.pl.* raw vegetables   8
cuiller *f.* spoon   13
cuisine *f.* cooking; food   4; kitchen   3
cuisinière *f.* stove   3

d'abord at first   5
d'accord okay   5
   être ~ (avec) to agree (with)   5
dame *f.* lady   13
dames *f.pl.* checkers   6
dangereux (dangereuse) dangerous   11
dans in   2
   ~ une heure one hour from now   5
danser to dance   2
d'après according to
davantage additional, more
de (d') from, of   1
de rien you're welcome   12
décalage horaire *m.* time difference   5
décembre *m.* December   7
décider to decide
décombres *m.pl.* ruins
décrire to describe   6

déçu(e) disappointed   9
dehors outside
déjà already   6
déjeuner *m.* lunch   8
   petit ~ breakfast   8
déjeuner *v.* to have lunch   5
délicieux (délicieuse) delicious   8
demain tomorrow   5
   après- ~ day after tomorrow   12
demande *f.* request   12
   faire une ~ to make a request   12
demander to ask   6
démarrer to start   10
demi(e) half
   et ~ half past (the hour)   5
demi- (frère, sœur) step (brother, sister)   3
demi-heure *f.* half hour   7
dent *f.* tooth   9
dentifrice *m.* toothpaste   9
départ *m.* departure   12
départementale *f.* departmental (local) highway   12
dépasser to pass
se dépêcher to hurry   13
dépendre to depend   9
   ça dépend (de …) it (that) depends (on …)   9
déprimé(e) depressed   9
depuis for   6; since   9
déranger to bother   1
   Excusez-moi de vous ~ Excuse me for bothering you.   1
déraper to skid   15
dernier (dernière) last   6
   la dernière fois the last time   6
derrière behind   5
   juste ~ right behind   15
des some; any   3; of the
descendre to go down, get out of   7
désirer to want   2
désolé(e) sorry   9
dessert *m.* dessert   8
dessin animé *m.* cartoon   11
se détendre to relax   9
détester to hate, to detest   2
détruire to destroy
dette *f.* debt   15
deux two   CP, 1
   tous (toutes) les ~ both   12

devant in front of   5
devenir to become   7
deviner to guess
devoir *m.* obligation
   devoirs *m.pl.* homework   4
devoir *v.* must, to have to, to probably be, to be supposed to; to owe   5
d'habitude usually   4
Dieu *m.* God
   Mon Dieu! My goodness!   2
dimanche *m.* Sunday   5
dîner *m.* dinner   4
dîner *v.* to eat dinner   4
diplôme *m.* diploma   12
dire to say; to tell   14
   … veut ~ … … means …   6
   vous dites you say   3
discret (discrète) discreet, reserved   4
se disputer to argue   14
dissertation *f.* (term) paper   6
divorce *m.* divorce   14
divorcé(e) divorced   1
divorcer to get a divorce   14
dix ten   CP
dix-huit eighteen   CP
dix-neuf nineteen   CP
dix-sept seventeen   CP
doigt *m.* finger
dollar *m.* dollar   9
DOM (=Département d'outre-mer) overseas department (*equivalent of a state*)
dommage *m.* pity, shame
   c'est ~ that's (it's) too bad   14
donc then; therefore
donner to give   4
   donnez-moi … give me …   CP
dont about/of which (whom); whose   14
dormir to sleep   6
dos *m.* back   9
d'où: vous êtes ~? where are you from?   2
douche *f.* shower   12
   prendre une douche to shower
doute *m.* doubt
   sans ~ probably   3
doux (douce) mild
douzaine *f.* dozen   8
douze twelve   CP
droit *m.* right (*entitlement*)

droit(e) *adj.* right
  à ~ (de) to the right (of) 5
  tout ~ straight ahead 5
drôle funny 14
durcir to harden
durée *f.* duration; length

eau *f.* (*pl.* **eaux**) water 2
  ~ minérale mineral water 2
échanger (contre) to trade (for) 15
échecs *m.pl.* chess 6
éclater to burst
école *f.* school 5
écouter to listen (to) 2
  écoutez! listen! CP
écrire to write 6
  comment est-ce qu'on écrit … ? how do you spell … ? 2
  écrivez votre nom! write your name! CP
  … s'écrit … … is spelled … 2
écrivain *m.* writer 4
égal(e) (*m.pl.* **égaux**) equal
  cela (ça) m'est ~ I don't care 5
église *f.* church 5
Eh bien … Well then …
élève *m./f.* pupil 4
élire to elect
elle she, it 1; her 6
elles they 1; them 6
s'éloigner to move away
s'embrasser to kiss 14
émission (de télé) *f.* (TV) show 11
emmenthal *f.* Swiss cheese 8
emploi du temps *m.* schedule 5
employé/employée *m./f.* employee 4
emprunter to borrow 14
en *prep.* in 1; by, through
  ~ avance early 7
  ~ première (seconde) in first (second) class 12
  ~ retard late 7
  ~ tout cas in any case
  ~ voiture by car 7
en *pron.* some, of it (them); about it (them) 14
  je vous ~ prie don't mention it; you're welcome; please do 7

vous n' ~ avez pas? don't you have any? 9
encore again CP; still, more 3
  ~ à boire (manger)? more to drink (eat)? 8
  ~ de …? more …? 8
  pas ~ not yet 2
s'endormir to fall asleep 13
endroit *m.* place 5
enfant *m./f.* child 3
enfin finally 5
ennuyeux (ennuyeuse) boring 4
enseigne *f.* sign
enseigner to teach 2
ensemble together CP, 2
ensoleillé(e) sunny
ensuite next, then 5
entendre to hear 9
  ~ parler de to hear about 15
  s' ~ (avec) to get along (with) 14
  entendu agreed; understood 12
entre between, among 5
  ~ amis between (among) friends 1
entrée *m.* first course, appetizer
entreprise *f.* business
entrer to enter 7
  ~ en collision to hit, collide 15
  entrez! come in! CP
envie: avoir ~ de to want to; to feel like 5
environ approximately
envoyer to send 6
épaule *f.* shoulder 9
épeler to spell 12
épicerie *f.* grocery store 5
épinards *m.pl.* spinach 8
époque *f.* time, period 11
  à cette ~ at that time; back then 11
épouser to marry 11
équilibré(e) stable
équipe *f.* team 11
escale *f.* stop(over)
escargot *m.* snail 10
esclave *m./f.* slave
Espagne *f.* Spain 5
espagnol(e) Spanish 1
espérer to hope 8
essayer to try
essentiel: il est ~ que it is essential that 10

est *m.* east
est-ce que (*question marker*) 2
estomac *m.* stomach 9
et and 1
étage *m.* floor 12
état *m.* state 5
  ~ civil marital status 1
États-Unis *m.pl.* United States 5
été *m.* summer 7
étranger/étrangère *m./f.* foreigner
étranger (étrangère) foreign 12
étroit(e) narrow; close
études *f.pl.* studies 15
étudiant(e) *m./f.* student 3
étudier to study 2
être to be 1
  ~ à to belong to 6
  ~ d'accord (avec) to agree (with) 5
  ~ en train de to be in the process of 11
  ~ originaire de to be a native of 7
  vous êtes d'où? where are you from? 2
eux *m.pl. pron.* they, them 6
exact(e) exact, correct
  c'est ~ that's right 13
exagérer to exaggerate 2
examen *m.* test, exam 6
  à un ~ on an exam 6
excellent(e) excellent 2
excuser to excuse
  excusez-moi excuse me 1
  excusez-moi (nous, etc.) d'être en retard excuse me (us, etc.) for being late 13
exemple *m.* example
  par ~ for example 6
exercice *m.* exercise 6
exiger (que) to demand (that) 13
expédier to send
extroverti(e) outgoing 4

fâché(e) angry 14
se fâcher to get angry 14
facile easy 9
façon *f.* way, manner 8
  sans ~ honestly, no kidding 8
faim *f.* hunger
  avoir ~ to be hungry 8

faculté *f.*: **~ des lettres** College of Liberal Arts
faire to do, to make   4
- **~ attention** to pay attention   4
- **~ du pouce** to hitchhike (*French-Canadian*)
- **~ du sport** to play sports   6
- **~ la cuisine** to cook   4
- **~ la lessive** to do laundry   4
- **~ la sieste** to take a nap   4
- **~ les provisions** to do the grocery shopping   4
- **~ un voyage** to take a trip   5
- **~ une demande** to make a request   12
- **~ une promenade** to take a walk; to take a ride   4
- **il fait chaud** it's hot out   CP, 4, 7
- **se ~ des amis** to make friends   14
fait *m.* fact
- **au ~ ...** by the way ...   2
falloir (il faut) to be necessary   4, 10
famille *f.* family   3
fatigué(e) tired   2
faut: il ~ ... it is necessary ...   4
- **il ~ que** it is necessary that, (someone) must   10
- **il ne ~ pas que** (someone) must not   10
faute *f.* fault; mistake   15
fauteuil *m.* armchair   3
faux (fausse) false; wrong   2
femme *f.* woman   1; wife   3
- **~ d'affaires** businesswoman   4
- **~ politique** (female) politician   4
fermé(e) closed   6
fermer to close   6
- **fermez le livre!** close the book!   CP
- **fermez la porte!** close the door!   CP
fermier/fermière *m./f.* farmer   4
fête *f.* holiday   7
feu *m.* (*pl.* **feux**) traffic light   10; fire
feuille *f.* leaf/sheet (of paper)   9
feuilleton *m.* soap opera; series   14
février *m.* February   7

fiançailles *f.pl.* engagement   14
fiancé(e) engaged   1
fier (fière) proud
fièvre *f.* fever   9
fille *f.* girl   3; daughter   3
film *m.* film, movie   5
fils *m.* son   3
fin *f.* end
finir to finish   12
flamand *m.* Flemish   5
fleur *f.* flower   9
fleuriste *m./f.* florist   9
fleuve *m.* river
flûte *f.* flute   6
- **~ !** darn!; shucks!   12
fois *f.* one time   6; times, multiplied by
- **à la ~** at the same time
- **la dernière ~** the last time   6
- **deux ~** twice
follement in a crazy manner   10
fonctionnaire *m./f.* civil servant   4
football (foot) *m.* soccer   6
- **~ américain** *m.* football   6
formidable great, fantastic   14
fort *adv.* loudly, with strength   15
fou/folle *m./f.* fool; crazy person   10
fou (folle) (*m.pl.* **fous**) crazy   10
foulard *m.* scarf   4
fourchette *f.* fork   13
frais: il fait ~ it's cool   7
fraises *f.pl.* strawberries   8
franc *m.* franc   9
français(e) French   1
- **à la française** in the French style   13
- **en français** in French   CP
France *f.* France   5
francophone French-speaking
frapper to knock
- **Frappez à la porte!** Knock on the door!   CP
freiner to brake   15
fréquenter (quelqu'un) to date (someone)   11
frère *m.* brother   3
frites *f.pl.* French fries   8
- **steak-~** *m.* steak with French fries   15
froid(e) cold   2
- **avoir ~** to be cold   8
- **il fait ~** it's cold   CP, 7

fromage *m.* cheese   5
frontière *f.* border
fruit *m.* a piece of fruit   8
fumer to smoke   6
fumeur/fumeuse *m./f.* smoker
- **non- ~** nonsmoker
fumeur *m.* smoking car   12;
- **non ~** nonsmoking car   12
fumeur/fumeuse *adj.* smoking

gagner to win; to earn
- **~ (à la loterie)** to win (the lottery)   12
gants *m.pl.* gloves   4
garage *m.* garage   3
garçon *m.* boy   3; waiter   8
garder to keep; to look after   4
gare *f.* (train) station   3
gâteau *m.* (*pl.* **gâteaux**) cake   8
- **petit ~** cookie
gauche *adj.* left
- **à ~ (de)** to the left (of)   5
gendarme *m.* (state) policeman   15
général: en ~ in general   2
généralement generally   4
généreux (généreuse) generous
genou *m.* knee   9
- **genoux** *m.pl.* lap, knees   13
gens *m.pl.* people   4
gentil(le) nice   3
- **c'est ~ à vous** that's nice of you   2
gestion *f.* management   5
glace *f.* ice cream   8
glissant(e) slippery   15
golf *m.* golf   6
gorge *f.* throat   9
goudron *m.* tar
goûter to taste   13
grand(e) big, tall   1
- **~ magasin** *m.* department store   9
- **pas grand-chose** not much   5
grand-mère *f.* (*pl.* **grands-mères**) grandmother   3
grand-père *m.* (*pl.* **grands-pères**) grandfather   3
grands-parents *m.pl.* grandparents   3
gras (grasse) fat
- **faire la ~ matinée** to sleep in, to sleep late

gratuit(e) free
grippe *f.* flu   6
gris(e) grey   4
gros(se) fat; large   1
grossir to put on weight   12
guerre *f.* war   7
   en temps de ~ in wartime
guitare *f.* guitar   6
gymnase *m.* gymnasium   5
gymnastique *f.* gymnastics   5

An asterisk indicates that no liaison or elision is made at the beginning of the word.

habile skilful
s'habiller to get dressed   13
habiter to live; to reside   2
   où habitez-vous? where do you live?   1
habitude *f.* habit
   d' ~ usually   4
   avoir l' ~ de to be used to 5
*haricots verts *m.pl.* green beans 8
*hasard *m.* chance, luck
   par ~ by chance   15
heure *f.* hour   CP, 1; (clock) time   5
   à l' ~ on time   7
   dans une ~ one hour from now   5
   il est ... heure(s) it is ... o'clock CP, 5
   tout à l' ~ in a little while   5; a little while ago   6
heureusement fortunately   6
heureux (heureuse) happy   4
*heurter to hit, run into   15
hier yesterday   6
histoire *f.* story   14
   quelle ~! what a story!   14
hiver *m.* winter   7
*hockey *m.* hockey   6
homme *m.* man   1
   ~ d'affaires businessman   4
   ~ politique politician   4
horaire *m.* timetable   12
*hors-d'œuvre *m. inv.* appetizer 8
hôtel *m.* hotel   1
hôtesse de l'air *f.* (female) flight attendant   11
*huit eight   CP

hypermarché *m.* giant super-market   9

ici here   2
   par ~ this way, follow me   13
idiot/idiote *m./f.* idiot   15
il he, it   1
il y a there is (are)   3
   il n'y a pas de quoi you're welcome   13
   il n'y en a plus there is (are) no more   12
   ~ ... jours ... days ago   6
   qu'est-ce qu' ~ ? what's the matter?   3
île *f.* island
ils they   1
imbécile *m./f.* imbecile   15
immeuble *m.* building
impair: nombre ~ *m.* odd number
impatience *f.* impatience   9
impatient(e) impatient   4
imperméable *m.* raincoat   4
important(e) important
   il est ~ que it is important that 10
incroyable *adj.* unbelievable, incredible   14
indications *f.pl.* directions   10
indiquer to tell; to indicate; to point out   12
indispensable indispensable, essential
   il est ~ que it is essential that 10
infirmier/infirmière *m./f.* nurse 4
informations *f.pl.* news   14
informatique *f.* computer science   5
ingénieur *m.* engineer   4
inondation *f.* flood
s'inquiéter to worry   13
insister to insist
   je n'insiste pas I won't insist 8
   si vous insistez if you insist   8
s'installer to move (into)
instrument *m.* instrument   6
intelligent(e) intelligent   4
intellectuel(le) intellectual   4
intention: avoir l' ~ de to plan to   5

interdit(e) forbidden
   sens ~ *m.* one-way street   10
intéressant(e) interesting   4
s'intéresser à to be interested in 14
intérêt *m.* interest   9
intérieur *m.* inside
   à l' ~ de inside of   6
interprète *m./f.* interpreter   4
intolérant(e) intolerant   4
inutile useless   12
inviter to invite   10
Irlande *f.* Ireland   5
Israël *m.* Israel   5
Italie *f.* Italy   5
italien(ne) Italian   1
ivre drunk   15

jamais ever, never
   ne ... ~ never   4
jambe *f.* leg   9
jambon *m.* ham   8
janvier *m.* January   7
Japon *m.* Japan   5
japonais(e) Japanese   1
jaune yellow   4
je I   1
jean *m.* jeans   4
jeu *m.(pl.* **jeux)** game   6
jeudi *m.* Thursday   5
jeune young   1
jogging *m.* jogging   2
joli(e) pretty   1
jouer to play   2
   à quoi jouez-vous? what (game) do you play?   6
   de quoi jouez-vous? what (instrument) do you play?   6
jour *m.* day   1
   ~ de l'An New Year's Day   7
   quinze jours two weeks   11
journal *m.* newspaper   6
journée *f.* day
   bonne ~! have a nice day!   1
juillet *m.* July   7
juin *m.* June   7
jupe *f.* skirt   4
jurer to swear
   je te le jure I swear (to you)   14
jus *m.* juice
   ~ d'orange orange juice   2
jusqu'à *prep.* until   10
   jusqu'au bout right up till the end

juste *adv.* just; right
  ~ **derrière moi** right behind me   15

kilo *m.* kilogram   8
kiosque *m.* newsstand   9
kir *m.* kir   2

la (*see* **le**)
là there   4
laid(e) ugly   1
laisser to leave; to let   10
  laisse-moi (laissez-moi) tranquille! leave me alone!   10
lait *m.* milk   2
langue *f.* language   5
laquelle (*see* **lequel**)
las(se) tired
lave-vaisselle *m.* dishwasher   3
laver to wash   13
  se ~ to get washed; to wash up   13
le/la/l'/les the   2; him, her, it, them   8
légume *m.* vegetable   8
lent(e) slow   10
lentement slowly   10
lequel/laquelle/lesquels/ lesquelles which? which one(s)?   14
les (*see* **le**)
lesquel(le)s (*see* **lequel**)
lessive *f.* wash; laundry   4
lettre *f.* letter   6
leur *pron.* (to) them   14
leur(s) *adj.* their   3
lever to lift; to raise   13
  se ~ to get up; to stand up   6
  Levez-vous! Get up!   CP
librairie *f.* bookstore   5
libre free   5; vacant
lien *m.* tie; bind
lieu *m.* (*pl.* **lieux**) place   5
  avoir ~ to take place   11
limonade *f.* lemon-lime soda   2
lire to read   6
  lisez! read!   CP
lit *m.* bed   3
litre *m.* liter   9
littérature *f.* literature   5
livre *f.* pound   9
livre *m.* book   3
loi *f.* law

loin (de) far (from)   5
loisir *m.* leisure activity
long (longue) long   9
longtemps a long time   6
louer to rent   12
lui he, him   6; (to) him; (to) her   14
lundi *m.* Monday   5
lunettes *f.pl.* eyeglasses   4
lycée *m.* high school

ma (*see* **mon**)
machine à laver *f.* washing machine   3
Madame (Mme) Mrs., ma'am; woman   1
Mademoiselle (Mlle) Miss; young woman   1
magasin *m.* store   4
  grand ~ department store   9
magazine *m.* magazine   6
Maghreb *m.* the three North African countries of Algeria, Morocco, and Tunisia.
mai *m.* May   7
maigrir to lose weight   12
maillot de bain *m.* bathing suit   13
main *f.* hand   9
maintenant now   5
maire *m.* mayor   11
  adjoint au ~ deputy mayor
mairie *f.* town (city) hall   11
mais but   2
maison *f.* house   3
mal *m.:* **avoir ~ (à)** to be sore, to have a pain (in)   9
mal *adv.* poorly   2; badly
malade sick   2
malgré in spite of
manger to eat   2
manquer to miss
manteau *m.* (*pl.* **manteaux**) coat   4
marchand/marchande *m./f.* merchant   9
marché *m.* (open-air) market   9
  ~ aux puces flea market   9
mardi *m.* Tuesday   5
mari *m.* husband   3
mariage *m.* marriage; wedding   11
marié(e) married   1
se marier (avec) to marry   14

marine *f.* navy
Maroc *m.* Morocco   5
marocain(e) Moroccan   1
marque *f.* make, brand   15
marron *adj. inv.* brown   4
mars *m.* March   7
match *m.* game   10
matin *m.* morning   1
matinée: faire la grasse ~ to sleep in late
mauvais(e) bad   4
  il fait ~ the weather is bad   7
mayonnaise *f.* mayonnaise   8
me me   10; (to) me   14
méchant(e) nasty; mean   4
méchoui *m.* roast lamb (*North-African specialty*)
médecin *m.* doctor   4
médicament *m.* medicine   9
se méfier de to watch out for
meilleur(e) better   11
  ~ ami(e) *m./f.* best friend   1
  le/la ~ best   11
  Avec mon ~ souvenir With my best regards   4
membre *m.* member   3
même even   14; same
  -~(s) -self (-selves)   2
ménage *m.* housework   4
menu *m.* (fixed price) menu   13
merci thank you   1; (no) thanks   2
  non, ~ no, thank you   2
mercredi *m.* Wednesday   5
mère *f.* mother   2, 3
mes (*see* **mon**)
mesdames *f.pl.* ladies   13
message *m.* message
  ~ électronique email   6
messieurs *m.pl.* gentlemen   13
mesure *f.* (unit of) measure
météo(rologie) *f.* weather   14
météorologique *adj.* weather
mettre to put; to place; to lay   13
  ~ la table to set the table   13
  ~ le chauffage to turn on the heat   13
  se ~ à table to sit down to eat   13
  Mettez …! Put …!   CP
mexicain(e) Mexican   1
Mexico Mexico City
Mexique *m.* Mexico   5
miam! yum!   8

midi noon 5
le mien/la mienne mine 5
mieux better 11
    il vaut ~ que it is preferable that, it is better that 10
    j'aime le ~ I like best 11
mille *inv.* one thousand 3
milliard *m.* billion 3
million *m.* million 3
mince thin 1
    ~ ! darn it! 12
minuit midnight 5
minute *f.* minute 5
mobylette *f.* moped, motorized bicycle 3
moi me 1; I, me 6
    ~ aussi me too 2
    ~ non plus me neither 2
moins less 11
    au ~ at least 6
    j'aime le ~ I like least 11
    ~ le quart quarter to (the hour) 5
mois *m.* month 6
mon, ma, mes my 3
monde *m.* world 7
    tout le ~ everybody 4
monnaie *f.* change, coins 9
Monsieur (M.) Mr., Sir; man 1
monter to go up; to get into 7
montre *f.* watch 4
montrer to show 14
morceau *m.* (*pl.* **morceaux**) piece 8
mort *f.* death 15
mort(e) dead
mot *m.* word 6
    plus un ~ not one more word 10
moto *f.* motorcycle 3
mourir to die 7
moutarde *f.* mustard 8
musée *m.* museum 5
musique *f.* music 6
myrtille *f.* blueberry

nager to swim 2
naïf (naïve) naive 4
naître to be born 7
    je suis né(e) I was born 3
    né(e) born
nappe *f.* tablecloth 13
nationalité *f.* nationality 1

naturellement naturally 8
navire *m.* ship
ne (n') not 1
    ~ ... jamais never 4
    ~ ... pas not 1
    ~ ... personne no one, nobody, not anyone 15
    ~ ... plus no more, no longer 8
    ~ ... que only 11
    ~ ... rien nothing, not anything 6
    n'est-ce pas? right?; are you?; don't they?; etc. 2
nécessaire: il est ~ que it is necessary that 10
négritude *f.* negritude *(system of black cultural and spiritual values)*
neiger to snow 7
    il neige it's snowing CP, 7
nerveux (nerveuse) nervous 4
nettoyer to clean 6
neuf nine CP
neuf (neuve) brand-new 10
    quoi de neuf? what's new? 5
neveu *m.* (*pl.* **neveux**) nephew 3
nez *m.* nose 9
    le ~ qui coule runny nose 9
nièce *f.* niece 3
Noël *m.* Christmas 7
    le père ~ Santa Claus 1
noir(e) black 4
nom *m.* name CP, 1
    ~ de famille last name 1
    à quel ~ ...? in whose name ...? 12
nombre *m.* number 1
nommer to name
non no 1
non plus neither 6
nord *m.* north
note *f.* note; grade, mark 4
notre, nos our 3
nourrir to feed, to nourish
nous we 1; us 10; (to) us 14
nouveau/nouvel (nouvelle) (*m.pl.* **nouveaux**) new 4
novembre *m.* November 7
nuit *f.* night 1
    Bonne nuit. Pleasant dreams. 5
numéro (de téléphone) *m.* (telephone) number 4

obéir to obey 12
occidental(e) western
occupé(e) busy 6
s'occuper de to be busy with, to take care of 7
    occupe-toi de tes oignons! mind your own business! 11
octobre *m.* October 7
œil *m.* (*pl.* **yeux**) eye 9
    mon ~! my eye!, I don't believe it! 10
œuf *m.* egg 8
œuvre *f.* work
offrir to offer
oh là là! oh dear!, wow! 9
oignon *m.* onion 8
    occupe-toi de tes oignons! mind your own business! 11
oiseau *m.* bird 5
omelette *f.* omelet 8
on one, people, we, they, you 1
oncle *m.* uncle 3
onze eleven CP
or *m.* gold
orange *f.* orange *(fruit)* 4
    jus d' ~ *m.* orange juice 2
orange *adj. inv.* orange 4
orangina *m.* orange soda 2
ordinaire ordinary, everyday 4
ordinateur *m.* computer 3
ordre *m.* order
oreille *f.* ear 9
oriental(e) eastern
original(e) (*m.pl.* **originaux**) different; novel; original 14
ou or 1
où where 1
oublier to forget 6
ouest *m.* west
oui yes 1
ouvert(e) open 12
ouverture *f.* opening
    heures d'~ hours of business
ouvrier/ouvrière *m./f.* laborer 4
ouvrir to open
ouvrez la porte! open the door! CP

pain *m.* bread 8
    ~ grillé toast 8
pâle pale 15

pantalon *m.* (pair of) pants 4
papier *m.* paper 9
paquet *m.* package 9
par by; through 6
~ **contre** on the other hand
~ **exemple** for example 6
~ **ici** (come) this way, follow me 13
~ **jour** per day 5
parce que because 6
pardon: ~? pardon?, what did you say? CP
je vous demande ~ please excuse me; I beg your pardon 9
parents *m.pl.* parents; relatives 3
paresseux (paresseuse) lazy 4
parfait(e) perfect 5
parking *m.* parking lot 5
parler to speak 2
~ **de** to tell about 7
~ **fort** to speak loudly 15
partie *f.* part
partir (de) to leave (from) 6
à partir de from that time on
pas no, not
ne ... ~ not 1
~ **du tout!** not at all! 1
~ **encore** not yet 2
~ **grand-chose** not much 5
~ **trop bien** not too well 2
passer to pass
~ **un an** to spend a year 3
~ **un test** to take a test 5
se passer to happen; to take place
passionnant(e) exciting 14
pastille *f.* lozenge 9
pâte dentifrice *f.* toothpaste 9
pâté *m.* pâté *(meat spread)* 8
patiemment patiently 10
patient(e) patient 4
patiner to skate 2
patinoire *f.* skating rink 10
pâtisserie *f.* pastry shop; pastry 9
patrie *f.* homeland
patron/patronne *m./f.* boss 4
pauvre poor 4, 11
payer to pay (for) 9
pays *m.* country 5
Pays-Bas *m.pl.* Netherlands 5
pêche *f.* fishing
pédagogie *f.* education, teacher preparation 5

pendant for; during 6
~ **que** while 6
~ **combien de temps ...?** how long ...? 6
penser to think 8
qu'en penses-tu? what do you think of it (of them)? 8
perdre to lose 9
~ **patience** to lose (one's) patience 9
père *m.* father 2, 3
père Noël *m.* Santa Claus 1
permettre to allow
permettez-moi de me présenter allow me to introduce myself 1
vous permettez? may I? 1
permis de conduire *m.* driver's license 10
personnage *m.* character; individual
personne *f.* person *(male or female)* 1
ne ... ~ no one, nobody, not anyone 15
personnellement personally 10
pétanque *f.* lawn bowling 6
petit(e) small, short 1
~ **ami(e)** *m./f.* boyfriend/girlfriend 3
petit déjeuner *m.* breakfast 8
petite fille *f.* little girl 3
petits pois *m.pl.* peas 8
petite-fille *f.* (*pl.* **petites-filles**) granddaughter 3
petit-fils *m.* (*pl.* **petits-fils**) grandson 3
petits-enfants *m.pl.* grandchildren 3
peu (de) little, few 8
un ~ a little bit 2
peuple *m.* people
peur *f.* fear
avoir ~ to be afraid 8
peut-être maybe; perhaps 2
pharmacie *f.* pharmacy 5, 9
pharmacien/pharmacienne *m./f.* pharmacist
photo *f.* photograph 3
sur la ~ in the picture 3
physique physical 15
piano *m.* piano 6
pièce *f.* room 3
pièce *f.* play 6

~ **(de monnaie)** coin 9
pied *m.* foot 9
pilote *m.* pilot 11
pilule *f.* pill 9
pique-nique *m.* picnic 12
piscine *f.* swimming pool 5
pitié *f.* pity
avoir ~ **(de)** to have pity, to feel sorry (for) 10
pizza *f.* pizza 2
place *f.* seat; room; place 7
plaire to please
s'il vous plaît please 2
plaisir *m.* pleasure
Au plaisir. See you again. 5
avec ~ with pleasure 2
plan *m.* map (city; house)
plancher *m.* floor 13
plat *m.* course, dish 8
plein(e) full
pleurer to cry 2
pleuvoir to rain 7
il pleut it's raining CP, 7
il pleuvait it was raining 11
plupart *f.* majority
la ~ **(de)** most (of) 6
plus more 11
il n'y en a ~ there is (are) no more 12
le/la/les ~ **...** the most ... 11
moi non ~ nor I, me neither 6
ne ... ~ no more, no longer 8
plusieurs several
poème *m.* poem 6
pois *m.pl.*: **petits** ~ peas 8
poisson *m.* fish 2
poivre *m.* pepper 13
police *f.* police (force)
agent de ~ police officer 15
politique *f.* politics 2; policy
politique: homme/femme ~ *m./f.* politician 4
pomme *f.* apple 8
pomme de terre *f.* potato 8
populaire popular 11
porc *m.* pork 8
porte *f.* door 1
porter to wear; to carry 4
portugais(e) Portuguese 5
poser une question to ask a question 12
possession *f.* possession 3
postale: carte ~ *f.* postcard 4
poste *f.* post office; mail

bureau de ~ *m.* post office 5
poster to mail 7
pouce *m.* thumb
   faire du ~ to hitchhike *(French-Canadian)*
poulet *m.* chicken 8
pour for, in order to 2
   ~ ce qui est de with respect to
pourquoi why 2
   ~ pas? why not? 6
pourvoir to provide
pouvoir *m.* power
pouvoir *v.* to be able; to be allowed 10; can
   je peux I can 9
   on peut one can 9
   pouvez-vous me dire …? can you tell me …? 9
   pourriez-vous …? could you …? 12
   puis-je …? may I …? 12
préciser to specify
préféré(e) favorite 11
préférence *f.*: **de ~** preferably
préférer to prefer 8
   je préfère que I prefer that 10
premier (première) first 5
   en première in first class 12
prendre to take; to eat, to drink 8
   prenez …! take …! CP
prénom *m.* first name 1
préparer (un cours) to prepare (a lesson) 6
près (de) near 1
   tout ~ very near 12
présenter to introduce
   je vous présente … let me introduce you to … 3
presque almost 14
prêter to lend 14
prie: je vous en ~ you're welcome 7
printemps *m.* spring 7
prise de conscience *f.* awareness
prix *m.* price 12
problème *m.* problem
   Pas de problème! No problem!
prochain(e) next 5
   À la prochaine. Until next time. 5
proche near; close
produit *m.* product; article

professeur (prof) *m.* teacher *(male or female)* 1
profession *f.* profession, occupation
promenade *f.* walk; ride 4
   faire une ~ to take a walk; to take a ride 4
se promener to take a walk, ride 13
promettre to promise
   c'est promis it's a promise 10
propos: à ~ de regarding, on the subject of 8
propre clean 4; specific; own
propriétaire *m./f.* owner 10
provisions *f.pl.* groceries 4
   faire les ~ to do the grocery shopping 4
provoquer to cause
prudemment prudently 10
prudent(e) cautious 10
publicité *f.* publicity; commercial 14
puis then; next 4
puis-je …? may I …? 12
puisque since
pull-over (pull) *m.* sweater 4
pyjama *m.* (pair of) pajamas 13

quand when 4
quantité *f.* quantity
quarante forty 3
quart quarter
   et ~ quarter past, quarter after 5
   moins le ~ quarter to, quarter till 5
quatorze fourteen CP
quatre four CP, 1
quatre-vingt-dix ninety 3
quatre-vingt-onze ninety-one 3
quatre-vingt-un eight-one 3
quatre-vingts eighty 3
que that
   ~ …? what …? 4
   ne … ~ only 11
quel(le) …? which …? 4
   quel âge avez-vous? how old are you? 3
   quel jour est-ce? what day is it? 5
   quelle …! what a …! 2

quelle est votre nationalité? what is your nationality? 1
quelle heure est-il? what time is it? 5
quelque chose *m.* something 2
quelquefois sometimes 4
quelques a few; some 8
quelqu'un someone 2
qu'est-ce que/qui what? 4
   qu'est-ce que c'est? what is this? what is it? 4
   qu'est-ce que vous avez comme …? what do you have for (in the way of) …? 8
   qu'est-ce qu'il y a …? what is there …? what's the matter? 3
   qu'est-ce que tu aimes? what do you like? 2
   qu'est-ce que vous voulez? what do you want? 2
qui who 1
   qu'est-ce ~ …? what …? 4
quinze fifteen CP
   ~ jours two weeks 11
quoi what
   il n'y a pas de ~ don't mention it, you're welcome 13
   ~ de neuf? what's new? 5

raconter to tell 14
radio *f.* radio 2
raison *f.* reason
   avoir ~ to be right 8
raisonnable reasonable 10
ralentir to slow down 12
rapide rapid, fast 10
rapidement rapidly 10
rarement rarely 4
ravi(e) delighted 14
récemment recently 6
recette *f.* recipe
recommander to recommend 12
reculer to back up 10
récuser to exclude; to challenge
réduire to reduce
réfrigérateur *m.* refrigerator 3
refuser to refuse
regarder to watch; to look at 2
regretter to be sorry 14
   je regrette I'm sorry 8

relief *m.* relief, hilly area
remarquer to notice   6
remercier to thank   12
remplacer to replace
rencontrer to meet   5, 14
rendez-vous *m.* meeting; date   5
  avoir ~ to have an appoint-ment, meeting
rendre to give back   9
  ~ visite à qqn to visit someone   9
renseignement *m.* item of infor-mation   12
(se) renseigner to inform (one-self); to find out about
rentrer to go (come) back; to go (come) home   7
repas *m.* meal   8
répéter to repeat; to practice   8
  répétez, s'il vous plaît please repeat   CP
répondre (à) to answer   9
  répondez answer   CP
se reposer to rest   13
RER *m.* train to Paris suburbs   2
réserver to reserve   9
résidence (universitaire) *f.* dor-mitory   5
responsabilité *f.* responsibility   11
restaurant *m.* restaurant   5
rester to stay   5; to remain
  il vous reste …? do you still have …?   12
résultat *m.* result; outcome
retard *m.* delay
  en ~ late   7
retour *m.* return
  aller-~ round-trip ticket   12
retourner to go back, to return   7
rétroviseur *m.* rearview mirror   10
réunion *f.* meeting   13
réussir (à) to succeed; to pass (a test)   12
se réveiller to wake up   13
revenant *m.* ghost   14
revenir to come back   7
revoir to see again
  au ~ good-bye   1
rez-de-chaussée *m.* ground floor   12
rhume *m.* cold *(illness)*   9
riche rich   12

ridicule ridiculous   14
rien nothing
  de ~ you're welcome; don't mention it, not at all   12
  ne … ~ nothing, not anything   6
riz *m.* rice   8
robe *f.* dress   4
  ~ de mariée wedding dress   11
robinet *m.* faucet   6
roi *m.* king
roman *m.* novel   6
  ~ policier detective story   6
rose *adj.* pink   4
rôti (de bœuf) *m.* (beef) roast   9
rouge red   4
rouler to roll; to move *(vehicle)*; to go   15
route *f.* route, way, road   10, 12
roux (rousse) red(-haired)   4
rue *f.* street   9
rugby *m.* rugby   6
russe Russian   1
Russie *f.* Russia   5

sa *(see* **son***)*
s'agir to be about
il s'agit de it's a matter of
s'amuser to have a good time; to have fun   6
saison *f.* season   7
salade *f.* salad   8
  ~ (verte) (green) salad   8
sale dirty   4
salle *f.* room
  ~ à manger dining room   3
  ~ de bain(s) bathroom   3
  ~ de classe classroom   P, 5
  ~ de séjour living room; den   3
salon *m.* living room   3
salut! hi!   1; bye (-bye)   5
salutation *f.* greeting
samedi *m.* Saturday   5
sandwich *m.* sandwich   8
sans without   6
  ~ blague! no kidding   14
  ~ doute probably   3
  ~ façon honestly, no kidding   8
santé *f.* health
  à votre ~! (here's) to your health!; cheers!   2

sardine *f.* sardine   9
saucisse *f.* sausage   9
saumon *m.* salmon   8
savoir to know   12
  je ne sais pas I don't know   2
saxophone *m.* saxophone   6
sciences *f.pl.* science   5
  ~ économiques economics   5
scolaire *adj.* school
  année ~ *f.* school year   10
se oneself   6
sec (sèche) dry
second(e) second
  en seconde in (by) second class   12
seize sixteen   CP
séjour *m.* stay
sel *m.* salt   13
semaine *f.* week   5
semestre *m.* semester   6
Sénégal *m.* Senegal   5
sénégalais(e) Senegalese   1
sens interdit *m.* one-way street   10
(se) sentir to feel
se séparar to separate (from each other)   14
sept seven   CP
septembre *m.* September   7
sérieusement seriously   10
sérieux (sérieuse) serious   10
serveur/serveuse *m./f.* waiter/waitress   8
service *m.* service
  à votre ~ at your service
serviette *f.* towel   12; napkin   13
ses *(see* **son***)*
seul(e) alone; only   5
  un ~ a single
seulement only   2
short *m.* (pair of) shorts   4
si *conj.* if   3
  s'il vous plaît please   2
si *adv.* so   10
si! yes!   3
siècle *m.* century   10
sieste *f.* nap   4
  faire la ~ to take a nap   4
simple simple, plain   4
  c'est bien simple it's quite easy
simple: aller ~ one-way ticket   12
sincère sincere   11

se situer to be situated

six six   CP

skier to ski   2

skis *m.pl.* skis   13

smoking *m.* tuxedo   11

SNCF *f.* French railroad system   2

sœur *f.* sister   3

sofa *m.* sofa   3

soif: avoir ~ to be thirsty   8

soir *m.* evening   1

  ce ~ tonight   5

  tous les soirs every night   6

soirée *f.* party   13; evening

soixante sixty   3

soixante et onze seventy-one   3

soixante-dix seventy   3

soixante-douze seventy-two   3

soleil *m.* sun   7

  Il fait du soleil. It's sunny.   CP

son, sa, ses his, her, its   3

sorte *f.* kind   8

  quelle(s) sorte(s) de …? what kind(s) of …?   8

  toutes sortes de choses all kinds of things   9

sortir to go out   6

  je vais ~ I'm going to go out   5

  sortez! leave!   CP

souci *m.* worry; care   11

souffler to blow

souhaiter (que) to wish; to hope (that)   13

soupe *f.* soup   8

sourire *m.* smile   13

sourire *v.* to smile   13

souris *f.* mouse   5

sous under   5

sous-sol *m.* basement   3

se souvenir (de) to remember   13

souvent often   2

sportif (sportive) athletic   4

statue *f.* statue   11

steak *m.* steak

  ~ -frites steak with French fries   15

stéréo *f.* stereo   3

stop *m.* stop sign   10

sucre *m.* sugar   13

sud *m.* south

Suède *f.* Sweden   5

suédois(e) Swedish   1

Suisse *f.* Switzerland   5

suisse *adj.* Swiss   1

suite: tout de ~ right away   1

suivant(e) following, next   7

superficie *f.* area

supermarché *m.* supermarket   9

supplément *m.* extra charge; supplement   12

sur on   3

sûr(e) sure

  bien ~ of course   8

sûrement surely, definitely   14

surveiller to watch

sweat-shirt *m.* sweatshirt   4

TGV *m.* very fast train   7

tabac *m.* tobacco; tobacco shop   9

  bureau de ~ tobacco shop   5

table *f.* table   1

  à ~ at dinner, at the table   6

tableau *m.* chalkboard   CP

se taire to be quiet

  tais-toi! (taisez-vous!) keep quiet!   10

tant so much; so many   6

tante *f.* aunt   3

tard late   6

tarder to be a long time coming   13

tarte *f.* pie   8

tasse *f.* cup   2

taux *m.* rate

tchao bye   5

te you   10; (to) you   14

tee-shirt *m.* tee-shirt   4

téléphone *m.* telephone   1

  au ~ on the telephone   6

téléphoner (à) to telephone   6

télévision (télé) *f.* television   2

témoin *m.* witness   15

temps *m.* time   6; weather   4

  emploi du ~ *m.* schedule   4

  quel ~ fait-il? what is the weather like?   4

tendance *f.* tendency, trend

  avoir ~ à to tend to   12

tennis *m.* tennis   2

  jouer au ~ to play tennis   2

  tennis *f.pl.* tennis shoes   4

tentation *f.* temptation

terre *f.* earth   9

tête *f.* head   9

thé *m.* tea   2

théâtre *m.* theater

Tiens! Well! Gee!   3

timbre *m.* stamp   9

toi you   4

toilettes *f.pl.* restroom   3, 5

toit *m.* roof   5

tomate *f.* tomato   8

tomber to fall   2

ton, ta, tes your   3

tort *m.* wrong

  avoir ~ to be wrong; to be unwise   8

tôt early   6

toujours always   4; still

toupet *m.* nerve

tour *f.* tower   11

tour *m.* turn, tour   11

tourner to turn   7

Toussaint *f.* All Saints' Day

tousser to cough   9

tout/toute/tous/toutes *adj.* all; every; the whole   12

  tous les deux (toutes les deux) both   12

  tous les soirs every night   6

  toute la famille the whole family   11

  tout le monde everybody   CP, 4

  tout le week-end all weekend (long)   5

tout *adv.* completely; very   12

  ~ à l'heure a little while ago, in a little while   5

  ~ de suite right away   12

  À ~ de suite. See you very soon.

  ~ près very near   7

tout *pron. inv.* all, everything

  pas du ~ ! not at all!   1

train *m.* train   3

  être en ~ de to be in the process of   11

tranche *f.* slice   8

tranquille calm   10

travail (manuel) *m.* (manual) work   4

travailler to work   2

travailleur (travailleuse) hardworking   4

travers: à ~ throughout

treize thirteen   CP

tremblement de terre *m.* earthquake

trente thirty   3

très very 1
triste sad 4
trois three CP, 1
trompette *f.* trumpet 6
trop (de) too much, too many 3
trouver to find, to be of the opinion 2
  se ~ to be located
  où se trouve (se trouvent) …? where is (are) …? 5
  vous trouvez? do you think so? 2
truite *f.* trout 8
tu you *(familiar)* 1
tuer to kill 15

un(e) one CP, 1; one, a, an 3
union *f.*: **~ douanière** customs union
unique unique
  enfant ~ *m./f.* only child
université *f.* university 1
universitaire *(adj.)* university 5

vacances *f.pl.* vacation 6
  bonnes ~! have a good vacation! 6
  en ~ on vacation 6
vaisselle *f.* dishes 4
valeur *f.* value
valise *f.* suitcase
valoir mieux (il vaut mieux) to be better 10
valse *f.* waltz 6
vanille *f.*: **glace à la ~** *f.* vanilla ice cream 8
vaut: il ~ mieux que it is preferable that, it is better that 10
vélo *m.* bicycle 3
vendeur/vendeuse *m./f.* salesman/saleswoman 4
vendre to sell 9
vendredi *m.* Friday 5
venir to come 7

  ~ de … to have just … 7
  d'où venez-vous? where do you come from? 7
  je viens de … I come from … 2
vent *m.* wind
  il fait du ~ it's windy CP, 7
véranda *f.* porch 3
vérité *f.* truth 14
verre *m.* glass 2
vers toward 5
  ~ (8 heures) approximately, around (8 o'clock) 5
verser to pour 13
vert(e) green 4
veste *f.* sportcoat 4
vêtement *m.* article of clothing 4
veuf/veuve *m./f.* widower/widow 1
veux *(see* **vouloir)**
viande *f.* meat 8
victime *f.* victim 7
vie *f.* life 4
  c'est la ~ that's life 6
  gagner sa ~ to earn one's living
vieux/vieil (vieille) old 1
ville *f.* city 4, 5; town
vin *m.* wine 2
vingt twenty CP
vingt et un twenty-one CP
vingt-deux twenty-two CP
violet(te) purple 4
violon *m.* violin 6
visite: rendre ~ à to visit (a person) 9
visiter to visit (a place)
vite quickly 10
vitesse *f.* speed 10
  à toute ~ at top speed 10
vivement eagerly
voici here is; here are 3
voilà there is; there are 1
voir to see 14
  tu vas voir you're going to see 5

tu vois you see 11
voisin/voisine *m./f.* neighbor 11
voiture *f.* automobile 3
  en ~ by car 7
voix *f.* voice 7
vol *m.* flight 12
volant *m.* steering wheel 10
volontiers gladly 2
votre, vos your 1
vôtre: à la ~! (here's) to yours! (to your health!) 2
vouloir to want, to wish 10
  … veut dire … … means … CP, 6
  je veux bien gladly; yes, thanks 2
  je veux que I want 10
  je voudrais I would like 2, 10
vous you *(formal)* 1; (to) you 14
voyage *m.* trip, voyage 5
  chèque de ~ *m.* traveler's check 9
  faire un ~ to take a trip 5
voyager to travel 2
vrai(e) true 2
vraiment really 2

week-end *m.* weekend 5
  tout le ~ all weekend (long) 5
wolof *m.* Wolof *(language)* 5

y there 7
  allez- ~ go ahead 12
  il y a there is (are) 3
yeux *m.pl.* eyes 4, 9

zéro zero CP, 3
Zut! Darn! 12, 15

Vocabulaire

This vocabulary list includes only the active words and phrases listed in the *Vocabulaire actif* sections. Only those French equivalents that occur in the text are given. Expressions are listed according to the key word. The symbol ~ indicates repetition of the key word.

The following abbreviations are used.

adj.	adjective	*m.pl.*	masculine plural
adv.	adverb	*n.*	noun
conj.	conjunction	*pl.*	plural
f.	feminine	*prep.*	preposition
f.pl.	feminine plural	*pron.*	pronoun
inv.	invariable	*v.*	verb
m.	masculine		

a, an un(e)
able: be ~ pouvoir
about de; environ
  ~ 8:00 vers 8 heures
  ~ it (them) en
  hear ~ entendre parler de
absolutely absolument
accept accepter
accident accident *m.*
accompany accompagner
according to d'après
accordion accordéon *m.*
accounting comptabilité *f.*
acquainted: be ~ with connaître
activity activité *f.*
actor/actress acteur/actrice *m./f.*
address *n.* adresse *f.*
adore adorer
advance *v.* avancer
advertisement annonce *f.*
advice (piece of) conseil *m.*
afraid: be ~ avoir peur
after après
afternoon après-midi *m.*
  in the ~ de l'après-midi
again encore
against contre
age âge *m.*

ago il y a …
agree (with) être d'accord (avec)
  agreed entendu
ahead: go ~ allez-y
  straight ~ tout droit
air conditioning climatisation *f.*
airplane avion *m.*
airport aéroport *m.*
all *pron./adj.* tout (toute/tous/toutes)
  ~ weekend (long) tout le weekend
  not at ~! pas du tout!
allow permettre
  ~ me to introduce myself permettez-moi de me présenter
almost presque
alone seul(e)
  leave me ~! laisse-moi (laissez-moi) tranquille!
already déjà
also aussi
always toujours
  not ~ pas toujours
American *adj.* américain(e)
amusing *adj.* amusant(e)
anchovy anchois *m.*

and et
angry fâché(e)
  get ~ se fâcher
answer répondre (à)
anyone quelqu'un
  not ~ ne … personne
anything quelque chose *m.*
  not ~ ne … rien
apartment appartement *m.*
appear avoir l'air
appetizer hors-d'œuvre *m.inv.*
apple pomme *f.*
appointment rendez-vous *m.*
  have an ~ avoir rendez-vous
approximately environ; vers *(time)*
April avril *m.*
Arabic arabe *m.*
argue se disputer
arm bras *m.*
armchair fauteuil *m.*
around environ; vers *(time)*; autour de *(place)*
  ~ (8 o'clock) vers (huit heures)
arrive arriver
artist artiste *m./f.*
as aussi, comme
  ~ … ~ aussi … que

~ much autant (de)
ashamed confus(e)
ask demander
   ~ a question poser une
      question
asleep: fall ~ s'endormir
aspirin tablet cachet d'aspirine
   m.
assure assurer
at à
   ~ first d'abord
   ~ midnight à minuit
   ~ noon à midi
   ~ ... o'clock à ... heure(s)
   ~ the home of chez
athletic sportif (sportive)
attach attacher
attend assister (à)
attention: pay ~ faire attention
attentive attentif (attentive)
August août *m.*
aunt tante *f.*
automobile voiture *f.*
away: right ~ tout de suite
awful! berk!

baby bébé *m.*
back *n.* dos *m.*
back *adv.:* **go ~** retourner; rentrer
   ~ then à cette époque
   come ~ revenir
   give ~ rendre
back up reculer
bad mauvais(e)
   ~ driver chauffard *m.*
   that's (it's) too ~ c'est
      dommage
   the weather is ~ il fait
      mauvais
badly mal
bakery boulangerie *f.*
bald chauve
ball (dance) bal *m.*
bank banque *f.*
bar and café bistro *m.*
basement sous-sol *m.*
basketball basket-ball (basket) *m.*
bathing suit maillot de bain *m.*
bathroom salle de bain *f.*
be être
   ~ a long time coming tarder
   ~ able pouvoir
   **~ acquainted with, familiar
      with** connaître
   ~ afraid avoir peur

~ born naître
~ cold avoir froid
~ fed up en avoir assez
~ hot avoir chaud
~ hungry avoir faim
~ in the process of être en
   train de
~ interested in s'intéresser à
~ located se trouver
~ necessary falloir (il faut)
~ of the opinion trouver
~ probably, supposed devoir
~ right avoir raison
~ sleepy avoir sommeil
~ sore avoir mal (à)
~ sorry regretter
~ thirsty avoir soif
~ wrong, unwise avoir tort
beans haricots *m.pl.*
Beaujolais *(wine)* beaujolais *m.*
beautiful beau/bel/belle/beaux/
   belles
because parce que
become devenir
bed lit *m.*
   go to ~ se coucher
bedroom chambre *f.*
beef bœuf *m.*
beer bière *f.*
before avant
begin commencer
behind derrière; en retard
   right ~ juste derrière
beige beige
Belgian belge
Belgium Belgique *f.*
believe (in) croire (à)
   I don't ~ it! mon œil!
belong to être à
belt ceinture *f.*
   safety ~, seat ~ ceinture de
      sécurité *f.*
beside à côté (de)
best *adv.* mieux; *adj.* le/la
   meilleur(e)
   ~ friend meilleur(e) ami(e)
      m./f.
   I like ~ j'aime le mieux (le
      plus); je préfère
   ~ regards avec mon meilleur
      souvenir
better *adv.* mieux; *adj.*
   meilleur(e)
   it is ~ that il vaut mieux que
between entre

~ friends entre amis
beverage boisson *f.*
bicycle vélo *m.*
big grand(e), gros(se)
bill *n. (paper money)* billet *m.;*
   (restaurant check) addition *f.*
billion milliard *m.*
bird oiseau *m.*
birthday anniversaire *m.*
bistro bistro *m.*
black noir(e)
   ~ currant liqueur crème de
      cassis *f.*
blond blond(e)
blouse chemisier *m.*
blue bleu(e)
body corps *m.*
book livre *m.*
bookstore librairie *f.*
boots bottes *f.pl.*
Bordeaux *(wine)* bordeaux *m.*
boring ennuyeux (ennuyeuse)
born né(e)
   be ~ naître
borrow emprunter
boss patron (patronne) *m./f.*
both tous les deux (toutes les
   deux)
bother déranger
bottle bouteille *f.*
bowl *n.* bol *m.*
bowling: lawn ~ pétanque *f.*
box boîte *f.*
boy garçon *m.*
boyfriend petit ami *m.*
brake *v.* freiner
brand *n.* marque *f.*
brand-new neuf (neuve)
bread pain *m.*
breakfast petit déjeuner *m.*
bridge *(game)* bridge *m.*
Brie *(cheese)* brie *m.*
bring apporter
broccoli brocoli *m.*
brother frère *m.*
brother-in-law beau-frère *m. (pl.*
   beaux-frères)
brown brun(e); marron
brush *n.* brosse *f.*
   tooth ~ brosse à dents *f.*
brush *v.* se brosser
building bâtiment *m.*
burn brûler
business affaires *f.pl.,* commerce
   m.

mind your own ~! occupe-toi de tes oignons!
businessman/woman homme/femme d'affaires *m./f.*
busy occupé(e)
 be ~ with s'occuper de
but mais
butcher shop boucherie *f.*
 pork butcher's charcuterie *f.*
butter beurre *m.*
 peanut ~ beurre d'arachide *m.*
buy acheter
by par
 ~ car en voiture
 ~ chance par hasard
 ~ the way ... au fait ...
bye salut; tchao

café café *m.*, bistro *m.*
cafeteria cafétéria *f.*
cake gâteau *m.* (*pl.* gâteaux)
calculator calculatrice *f.*
call appeler, téléphoner
 your ~ from ... votre communication de ...
called: be ~ s'appeler
calm calme, tranquille
Camembert (*cheese*) camembert *m.*
campus campus *m.*
can *n.* boîte *f.*
can (be able to) *v.* pouvoir
Canada Canada *m.*
Canadian canadien(ne)
candy bonbon *m.*
car voiture *f.*
 by ~ en voiture
card carte *f.*
 credit ~ carte de crédit
 post ~ carte postale
cards (*game*) cartes *f.pl.*
care *n.* souci *m.*
 take ~ of s'occuper de
care *v.*: **I don't ~** cela (ça) m'est égal
carry porter
cartoon dessin animé *m.*
cat chat *m.*
cautious prudent(e)
centime centime *m.*
century siècle *m.*
cereal céréales *f.pl.*
certain sûr(e)
certainly tout à fait; certainement

chair chaise *f.*
chalk craie *f.*
chalkboard tableau *m.*
chance hasard *m.*
 by ~ par hasard
change *n.* monnaie *f.*
change *v.* changer (de)
channel: TV ~ chaîne (de télé) *f.*
charge: extra ~ supplément *m.*
charming charmant(e)
cheap bon marché *adj. inv.*
check chèque *m.*
 traveler's ~ chèque de voyage *m.*
 ~ (*restaurant bill*) addition *f.*
checkers dames *f.pl.*
cheese fromage *m.*
chemistry chimie *f.*
chess échecs *m.pl.*
chewing gum chewing-gum *m.*
chic chic *adj. inv.*
chicken poulet *m.*
child enfant *m./f.*
China Chine *f.*
Chinese chinois(e)
chocolate: hot ~ chocolat chaud *m.*
choice choix *m.*
choose choisir
Christmas Noël *m.*
church église *f.*
cigar cigare *m.*
cigarette cigarette *f.*
city ville *f.*
civil servant fonctionnaire *m./f.*
class cours *m.*, classe *f.*
 in ~ en classe
 in first ~ en première classe
classroom salle de classe *f.*
clean *v.* nettoyer
clean propre
close *adj.* près (de)
close *v.* fermer
closed fermé(e)
clothing (article of) vêtement *m.*
coat manteau *m.* (*pl.* manteaux)
Coca-Cola coca *m.*
coffee café *m.*
coin pièce (de monnaie) *f.*
cold (*illness*) *n.* rhume *m.*
cold *adj.* froid(e)
 be ~ avoir froid
 it's ~ il fait froid
collide entrer en collision
color couleur *f.*

what ~ is (are) ...? de quelle couleur est (sont) ...?
come venir
 ~ back revenir, rentrer
 ~ in! entrez!
 where do you ~ from? d'où venez-vous?
comfortable confortable
comic strip bande dessinée *f.*
commentary commentaire *m.*
commercial *n.* publicité *f.*
complete complet (complète)
completely tout *inv. adv.*; complètement
computer ordinateur *m.*
 ~ science informatique *f.*
confirm confirmer
console oneself se consoler
constant constant(e)
constantly constamment
contrary contraire *m.*
 on the ~ au contraire
cooking cuisine *f.*
cool: it's ~ il fait frais
corner coin *m.*
corridor couloir *m.*
cost *v.* coûter
cough *v.* tousser
could you ...? pourriez-vous ...?
country pays *m.*
course (*classroom*) cours *m.*; (*meal*) plat *m.*
 of ~ certainement, bien sûr
cousin cousin/cousine *m./f.*
crazy fou (folle)
 ~ person fou/folle *m./f.*
 in a ~ manner follement
cream crème *f.*
credit card carte de crédit *f.*
croissant croissant *m.*
cry *v.* pleurer
cup tasse *f.*
custom coutume *f.*
cut *v.* couper
cyclist coureur (cycliste)

dance *n.* bal *m.*
dance *v.* danser
dangerous dangereux (dangereuse)
darn it! mince!; zut!
date *n.* date *f.*; rendez-vous *m.*
date (someone) *v.* fréquenter (quelqu'un)

daughter fille *f.*
day jour *m.*
~ **after tomorrow** après-demain
have a good ~ bonne journée
New Year's ~ Jour de l'An *m.*
what ~ **is it?** quel jour est-ce?
dead mort(e)
dear *n.* chéri/chérie *m./f.*
dear *adj.* cher (chère)
death mort *f.*
debt dette *f.*
December décembre *m.*
definitely sûrement, certainement
delicatessen charcuterie *f.*
delicious délicieux (délicieuse)
delighted ravi(e)
demand (that) exiger (que)
department store grand magasin *m.*
departmental (local) highway départementale *f.*
departure départ *m.*
depend dépendre
it (that) depends ça dépend
depressed déprimé(e)
describe décrire
desk bureau *m.* (*pl.* bureaux)
dessert dessert *m.*
detective story roman policier *m.*
detest détester
die mourir
different original(e) (*m.pl.* originaux); différent(e)
dining room salle à manger *f.*
dinner dîner *m.*
at ~ à table
have ~ dîner
diploma diplôme *m.*
directions indications *f.pl.*
dirty sale
disappointed déçu(e)
discreet discret (discrète)
dish plat *m.*
dishes vaisselle *f.*
do the ~ faire la vaisselle
dishwasher lave-vaisselle *m.*
divorce *n.* divorce *m.*
divorce *v.* divorcer
divorced divorcé(e)
do faire
~ **the grocery shopping** faire les provisions

what am I going to ~? comment je vais faire?
doctor médecin *m.*, docteur *m.*
dog chien *m.*
dollar dollar *m.*
door porte *f.*
dormitory résidence (universitaire) *f.*
dozen douzaine *f.*
dress *n.* robe *f.*
wedding ~ robe de mariée *f.*
dressed: get ~ s'habiller
drink *n.* boisson *f.*
before-dinner ~ apéritif *m.*
drink *v.* boire, prendre
do you want to ~ **something?** voulez-vous boire quelque chose?; quelque chose à boire?
drive *n.*: **to take a** ~ faire une promenade en voiture   4
drive conduire
driver automobiliste *m./f.,* conducteur/conductrice *m./f.,* chauffeur *m.*
~ **'s license** permis de conduire *m.*
drums batterie *f.*
drunk *adj.* ivre
during pendant

each chaque
each one chacun(e)
ear oreille *f.*
early tôt, en avance
earn one's living gagner sa vie
earth terre *f.*
easy facile; simple
eat manger, prendre
~ **dinner** dîner
~ **lunch** déjeuner
economics sciences économiques *f.pl.*
education pédagogie *f.*
egg œuf *m.*
eight huit
eighteen dix-huit
eighty quatre-vingts
eighty-one quatre-vingt-un
eleven onze
embarrassed confus(e)
employee employé/employée *m./f.*
end *n.* fin *f.*

engaged fiancé(e)
engagement fiançailles *f.pl.*
engineer ingénieur *m.*
England Angleterre *f.*
English anglais(e)
enough assez
enter entrer
errands courses *f.pl.*
essential essentiel(le)
it is ~ **that** il est essentiel que
even même
evening soir *m.*
good ~ bonsoir
ever jamais
every chaque; tout (toute/tous/toutes)
~ **night** tous les soirs
everybody tout le monde
everything tout *pron. inv.*
exaggerate exagérer
exam examen *m.*
on an ~ à un examen
example exemple *m.*
for ~ par exemple
excellent excellent(e)
exciting passionnant(e)
excuse: ~ **me** je vous demande pardon; excusez-moi
executive cadre *m.*
exercise exercice *m.*
expensive cher (chère)
eye œil *m.* (*pl.* yeux)
my ~! mon œil!
eyeglasses lunettes *f.pl.*

fall *n.* automne *m.*
fall *v.* tomber
~ **asleep** s'endormir
false faux (fausse)
familiar: be ~ **with** connaître
family famille *f.*
famous célèbre
fantastic formidable
far (from) loin (de)
farmer fermier/fermière *m./f.*
fast rapide
fat gros(se), gras(se)
father père *m.*
father-in-law beau-père *m.* (*pl.* beaux-pères)
faucet robinet *m.*
fault faute *f.*
favorite préféré(e)
fear peur

February février *m.*
fed up: be ~ en avoir assez
feel sentir, se sentir
    ~ like avoir envie de
    ~ sorry (for someone) avoir
      pitié (de)
fever fièvre *f.*
few peu (de)
    a ~ quelques
fifteen quinze
fifty cinquante
film film *m.*
finally enfin
find *v.* trouver
fine bien
    I'm ~ je vais très bien; ça va
      bien
finish finir
first premier (première)
    ~ name prénom *m.*
    at ~ d'abord
    in ~ class en première classe
fish *n.* poisson *m.*
five cinq
flea market marché aux puces
    m.
Flemish flamand *m.*
flight vol *m.*
flight attendant *(female)* hôtesse
    de l'air *f.*
floor *(of a building)* étage *m.; (of a*
    room) plancher *m.*
    ground ~ rez-de-chaussée *m.*
florist fleuriste *m./f.*
flower fleur *f.*
flu grippe *f.*
fluently couramment
flute flûte *f.*
follow: ~ me par ici
following suivant(e)
food cuisine *f.*
fool fou/folle *m./f.*
foot pied *m.*
football football américain *m.*
for depuis; pendant; pour
foreign étranger (étrangère)
forget oublier
fork fourchette *f.*
fortunately heureusement
forty quarante
four quatre
fourteen quatorze
franc franc *m.*
France France *f.*
free libre

French français(e)
    ~ fries frites *f.pl.*
    in ~ en français
    in the ~ style à la française
    steak with ~ fries steak-frites
    m.
Friday vendredi
friend ami/amie *m./f.*
    make friends se faire des amis
from de
front: in ~ of devant
fruit fruit *m.*
fun amusant(e)
    have ~ s'amuser
funny amusant(e), drôle

game jeu *m. (pl.* jeux), match *m.*
garage garage *m.*
garlic ail *m.*
Gee! Tiens!
general: in ~ en général
generally généralement
generous généreux (généreuse)
German allemand(e)
Germany Allemagne *f.*
get obtenir, recevoir
    ~ along (with) s'entendre
      (avec)
    ~ angry se fâcher
    ~ dressed s'habiller
    ~ into monter
    ~ out of descendre
    ~ up, stand up se lever
    ~ washed, wash up se laver
ghost revenant *m.*
gift cadeau *m.*
girl fille *f.*
girlfriend petite amie *f.*
give donner
    ~ back rendre
gladly volontiers; je veux bien
glass (drinking) verre *m.*
glasses (eye) lunettes *f.pl.*
gloves gants *m.pl.*
go aller, rouler (in a vehicle)
    ~ across traverser
    ~ ahead allez-y
    ~ back retourner, rentrer
    ~ down descendre
    ~ into town aller en ville
    ~ out sortir
    ~ to bed se coucher
    ~ up monter
goat cheese chèvre *m.*

golf golf *m.*
good bon (bonne)
    ~ evening bonsoir
    ~ morning bonjour
    have a ~ day bonne journée
    have a ~ time s'amuser
good-bye au revoir
grade note *f.*
grains céréales *f.pl.*
grandchildren petits-enfants
    m.pl.
granddaughter petite-fille *f.* (*pl.*
    petites-filles)
grandfather grand-père *m.* (*pl.*
    grands-pères)
grandmother grand-mère *f.* (*pl.*
    grands-mères)
grandparents grands-parents
    m.pl.
grandson petit-fils *m.* (*pl.* petits-
    fils)
great formidable; chouette *(fam.)*
great-grandfather arrière-
    grand-père *m.*
green vert(e)
    ~ beans haricots verts *m.pl.*
grey gris(e)
groceries provisions *f.pl.*
    do the grocery shopping faire
    les provisions
guess deviner
grocery store épicerie *f.*
guitar guitare *f.*
gymnasium gymnase *m.*
gymnastics gymnastique *f.*

hair cheveux *m.pl.*
    hairbrush brosse à cheveux *f.*
half *adj.* demi(e)
    ~ past ... il est ... heure(s) et
    demie
hall couloir *m.*
ham jambon *m.*
hand main *f.*
handsome beau/bel/belle/beaux/
    belles
happen arriver, se passer
happy heureux (heureuse);
    content(e)
hard-working travailleur
    (travailleuse)
hat chapeau *m.*
hate *v.* détester
have avoir

~ an appointment, date avoir rendez-vous
~ a pain (in) avoir mal (à)
~ dinner dîner
~ fun s'amuser
~ just venir de
~ lunch déjeuner
~ pity avoir pitié (de)
~ to devoir
do you still ~ ...? il vous reste ...?
what do you ~ for (in the way of) ...? qu'est-ce que vous avez comme ...?
he *pron.* il; lui
head tête *f.*
health: (here's) to your ~! à votre santé!
hear entendre
~ about entendre parler de
heat chauffage *m.*
hello bonjour; bonsoir; salut
~ ! *(on the phone)* allô!
help aider
her *pron.* elle; lui
her *adj.* son, sa, ses
here ici
~ is, ~ are voici
hi! salut!
high-top sneakers baskets *f.pl.*
highway autoroute *f.*
departmental (local) ~ départementale *f.*
him *pron.* lui
his *adj.* son, sa, ses
hockey hockey *m.*
holiday fête *f.*
home maison *f.*
at the ~ of chez
go (come) ~ rentrer
homework devoirs *m.pl.*
honestly sans façon
hope espérer; souhaiter (que)
horrible affreux (affreuse)
hot chaud(e)
~ chocolate chocolat chaud *m.*
be ~ avoir chaud
it is ~ il fait chaud
hotel hôtel *m.*
hour heure *f.*
one ~ ago il y a une heure
one ~ from now dans une heure
house maison *f.*
at your ~ chez toi

housework ménage *m.*
do ~ faire le ménage
how comment
~ are you? comment allez-vous?; (comment) ça va?
~ do you say ...? comment dit-on ...?
~ do you spell ...? comment est-ce qu'on écrit ...?
~ long? pendant combien de temps ...?
~ many, much combien (de)
~ old are you? quel âge avez-vous?
~ ... he (she) was! comme il (elle) était ...!
hundred cent
hungry: be ~ avoir faim
hurry se dépêcher
husband mari *m.*

I *pron.* je; moi
ice cream glace *f.*
vanilla ~ glace à la vanille *f.*
idiot idiot (idiote) *m./f.*
if si
imbecile imbécile *m./f.*
impatience impatience *f.*
impatient impatient(e)
important important(e)
it is ~ that il est important que
in à; dans; en
~ a crazy manner follement
~ a little while tout à l'heure
~ exchange for contre
~ general en général
~ order to pour
~ the afternoon de l'après-midi
included compris(e)
incredible incroyable
indeed tout à fait
indicate indiquer
indispensable indispensable
inexpensive bon marché *inv.*
inform (se) renseigner
information renseignement *m.*
inside intérieur *m.*
~ of à l'intérieur de
insist insister
instrument instrument *m.*
insure assurer
intellectual *adj.* intellectuel(le)
intelligent intelligent(e)

interest intérêt *m.*
interested: be ~ in s'intéresser à
interesting intéressant(e)
interpreter interprète *m./f.*
introduce présenter
allow me to ~ myself permettez-moi de me présenter
invite inviter
Ireland Irlande *f.*
Israel Israël *m.*
it *pron.* cela, ça; il, elle
it is il est, c'est
is it ...? est-ce que ...?
~ better that il vaut mieux que
~ cold il fait froid
~ cool il fait frais
~ essential il est essentiel
~ nice out il fait beau
~ preferable il vaut mieux
~ raining il pleut
~ snowing il neige
~ windy il fait du vent
Italian italien(ne)
Italy Italie *f.*
its *adj.* son, sa, ses

jacket blouson *m.*
jam confiture *f.*
January janvier *m.*
Japan Japon *m.*
Japanese japonais(e)
jeans jean *m.*
jogging jogging *m.*
juice jus *m.*
orange ~ jus d'orange *m.*
July juillet *m.*
June juin *m.*
just: to have ~ ... venir de ...
just *adv.* juste

keep garder
key clé *f.*
kidding: no ~ sans façon; sans blague!
kilogram kilo *m.*
kind *n.* sorte *f.*
all ~s of things toutes sortes de choses
what ~(s) of ... quelle(s) sorte(s) de ...
kind *adj.* aimable, gentil(le)
kir kir *m.*

kiss *v.* s'embrasser
kitchen cuisine *f.*
knee genou *m. (pl.* genoux)
knife couteau *m. (pl.* couteaux)
knock frapper
know connaître, savoir
   I don't ~ je ne sais pas

laborer ouvrier/ouvrière *m./f.*
lady dame *f.*
language langue *f.*
lap *n.* genoux *m.pl.*
last dernier (dernière)
   ~ name nom de famille *m.*
   the ~ time la dernière fois
late tard, en retard
   be ~ être en retard
   it is ~ il est tard
lawn bowling pétanque *f.*
lay mettre
lazy paresseux (paresseuse)
leaf *(of paper)* feuille *f.*
learn apprendre (à)
least le/la/les moins
   at ~ au moins
   I like ~ j'aime le moins
leave laisser, partir
   ~ from partir (de)
   ~ me alone! laisse-moi
     (laissez-moi) tranquille!
   there's one left il en reste un(e)
left: to the ~ (of) à gauche (de)
leg jambe *f.*
leisure activity loisir *m.*
lemon-lime soda limonade *f.*
lemonade citron pressé *m.*
lend prêter
length *(of time)* durée *f.*
less moins
let laisser
   let's go allez-y, allons-y
letter lettre *f.*
library bibliothèque *f.*
license: driver's ~ permis de
   conduire *m.*
life vie *f.*
   that's ~ c'est la vie
lift lever
like *v.* aimer
   I would ~ je voudrais
like *conj.* comme
listen (to) écouter
liter litre *m.*
literature littérature *f.*

little *adj.* petit(e)
   ~ girl petite fille *f.*
little *adv.* peu (de)
   a ~ un peu (de)
live habiter
living room salon *m.*
long long (longue)
   a ~ time longtemps
   be a ~ time coming tarder
   how ~ ...? pendant combien de
     temps ...?
   no longer ne ... plus
look regarder; *(seem)* avoir l'air
   ~ after garder
   ~ for chercher
lose perdre
   ~ (one's) patience perdre
     patience
   ~ weight maigrir
lot: a ~ (of) beaucoup (de)
love *v.* adorer, aimer
   ~ each other s'aimer
lozenge pastille *f.*
luck chance *f.*
   good ~! bonne chance!
   what ~! quelle chance!
lunch déjeuner *m.*
   have ~ déjeuner

magazine magazine *m.*
mail *v.* poster
make *n.* marque *f.*
make *v.* faire
   ~ a request faire une demande
   ~ friends se faire des amis
mall centre commercial *m.*
man homme *m.*, monsieur *m.*
management gestion *f.*
manner façon *f.*
manners étiquette *f.*
many beaucoup
   how ~ combien
   so ~ tant
   too ~ trop (de)
map carte *f.*
map (city) plan *m.*
March mars *m.*
market marché *m.*
   flea ~ marché aux puces *m.*
   super ~ supermarché *m.*
marriage mariage *m.*
married marié(e)
marry se marier (avec); épouser
matter: what's the ~ with you?
   qu'est-ce que tu as?

May mai *m.*
may (be able to) pouvoir
   ~ I? vous permettez?, puis-je?
maybe peut-être
mayonnaise mayonnaise *f.*
mayor maire *m.*
me *pron.* me, moi
   ~ neither, nor I moi non plus
meal repas *m.*
   have a good ~! bon appétit!
mean *v.* vouloir dire
mean *adj.* méchant(e)
meat viande *f.*
medicine médicament *m.*
meet rencontrer
   to have met avoir connu
meeting réunion *f.*, rendez-vous
   m.
   have a ~ avoir rendez-vous
member membre *m.*
mention: don't ~ it il n'y a pas
   de quoi; de rien
menu carte *f. (à la carte)*; menu *m.*
   (fixed price)
merchant marchand/marchande
   m./f.
Mexican mexicain(e)
Mexico Mexique *m.*
midnight minuit
milk lait *m.*
million million *m.*
mind your own business!
   occupe-toi de tes oignons!
mine le mien/la mienne
minute minute *f.*
mirror: rearview ~ rétroviseur
   m.
miserly avare
Miss Mademoiselle (Mlle)
mistake faute *f.*
Monday lundi *m.*
money argent *m.*
month mois *m.*
moped mobylette *f.*
more encore, plus
   ~ ...? encore de ...?
   ~ to drink (eat)? encore à
     boire (manger)?
   there is no ~ il n'y en a plus
morning matin *m.*
Moroccan marocain(e)
Morocco Maroc *m.*
most (of) la plupart (de);
   the ~ le/la/les plus
mother mère *f.*

mother-in-law belle-mère (*pl.* belles-mères)
motorcycle moto *f.*
motorized bicycle mobylette *f.*
mouse souris *f.*
mouth bouche *f.*
movie film *m.*
  ~ theater cinéma *m.*
Mr. Monsieur (M.)`
Mrs. Madame (Mme)
much beaucoup
  how ~ combien
  not ~ pas grand-chose
  so ~ tant (de)
  too ~ trop (de)
museum musée *m.*
mushrooms champignons *m.pl.*
music musique *f.*
must devoir, il faut
  (someone) ~ not il ne faut pas
mustard moutarde *f.*
my *adj.* mon, ma, mes

naive naïf (naïve)
name *n.* nom *m.*
  family (last) ~ nom de famille
  in whose ~ …? à quel nom …?
  my ~ is … je m'appelle …
  what is your ~? comment vous appelez-vous?
named: be ~ s'appeler
nap sieste *f.*
  take a ~ faire la sieste
napkin serviette *f.*
nasty méchant(e)
nationality nationalité *f.*
  what is your ~? quelle est votre nationalité?
naturally naturellement
near près (de)
  very ~ tout près
necessary nécessaire
  it is ~ il faut, il est nécessaire (que)
need avoir besoin de
neighbor voisin/voisine *m./f.*
neither: me ~ moi non plus
nephew neveu *m.* (*pl.* neveux)
nervous nerveux (nerveuse)
never jamais (ne … jamais)
new nouveau/nouvel (nouvelle) (*m.pl.* nouveaux); neuf (neuve)
  ~ Year's Day Jour de l'An *m.*
  what's ~? quoi de neuf?

news informations *f.pl.*
newspaper journal *m.*
newsstand kiosque *m.*
next *adv.* ensuite, puis; *adj.* prochain(e); suivant(e)
  ~ door à côté
  ~ to à côté de
nice aimable, gentil(le)
  have a ~ day bonne journée
  it's ~ out il fait beau
  that's ~ of you c'est gentil à vous
niece nièce *f.*
night nuit *f.*
nine neuf
nineteen dix-neuf
ninety quatre-vingt-dix
ninety-one quatre-vingt-onze
no non
  ~ kidding! sans blague!; sans façon
  ~ longer ne … plus
  ~ more ne … plus
  ~ one ne … personne
nobody ne … personne
noise bruit *m.*
noon midi
nor: ~ I moi non plus
nose nez *m.*
  runny ~ le nez qui coule
not ne (n') … pas
  ~ anyone ne … personne
  ~ anything ne … rien
  ~ at all il n'y a pas de quoi, de rien; pas du tout
  ~ much pas grand-chose
  ~ yet pas encore
note note *f.*
nothing ne … rien
notice remarquer
novel *n.* roman *m.*
novel *adj.* original(e) (*m.pl.* originaux)
November novembre *m.*
now maintenant, actuellement
number nombre *m.*, numéro *m.*
  telephone ~ numéro de téléphone *m.*
nurse infirmier/infirmière *m./f.*

obey obéir
o'clock heure(s)
  at … ~ à … heure(s)
  it is … ~ il est … heure(s)
October octobre *m.*

of de
  ~ course bien sûr
office bureau *m.* (*pl.* bureaux)
  post ~ bureau de poste *m.*
officer: police ~ agent de police *m.*
often souvent
oh dear! oh là là!
okay d'accord
  if that's ~ si ça va
old âgé(e), vieux/vieil (vieille)
  how ~ are you? quel âge avez-vous?
omelet omelette *f.*
on sur
one *pron.* on
  no ~ ne … personne
one (*number*) un (une)
one-way: ~ street sens interdit *m.*
  ~ ticket aller simple *m.*
onion oignon *m.*
only *adj.* seul(e); *adv.* seulement; ne … que
open *v.* ouvrir
open *adj.* ouvert(e)
opening ouverture *f.*
opinion avis *m.*
  be of the ~ trouver, penser
  in my (your, etc.) ~ à mon (à ton, etc.) avis
opposite contraire *m.*
or ou
orange *n.* orange *m.*
  ~ juice jus d'orange *m.*
  ~ soda orangina *m.*
orange *adj.* orange *inv.*
order *v.* commander
order: in ~ to pour
ordinary *adj.* ordinaire
original original(e) (*m.pl.* originaux)
other autre
ouch! aïe!
our notre, nos
outgoing extroverti(e)
outside dehors
owe devoir
owner propriétaire *m./f.*

package paquet *m.*
pain: have a ~ (in) avoir mal (à)
pajamas (pair of) pyjama *m.*
pale pâle
pants (pair of) pantalon *m.*

paper papier *m.;* journal *m.*
  term ~ dissertation *f.*
pardon: I beg your ~ je vous demande pardon; excusez-moi
parents parents *m.pl.*
parents-in-law beaux-parents *m.pl.*
party boum *f.,* soirée *f.*
pass *(an exam)* réussir
pass *(a car)* dépasser
pastry pâtisserie *f.*
  ~ shop pâtisserie *f.*
patience: lose (one's) ~ perdre patience
patient *adj.* patient(e)
patiently patiemment
pavement chaussée *f.*
pay (for) payer
  ~ attention faire attention
peanut arachide *f.*
  ~ butter beurre d'arachide *m.*
peas petits pois *m.pl.*
people gens *m.pl.;* on
pepper poivre *m.*
per par
perfect parfait(e)
perhaps peut-être
period époque *f.*
person *(male or female)* personne *f.*
personally *adv.* personnellement
pharmacy pharmacie *f.*
photograph photo *f.*
physical physique
piano piano *m.*
picnic pique-nique *m.*
pie tarte *f.*
piece morceau *m. (pl.* morceaux)
pill pilule *f.,* cachet *m.*
pilot pilote *m.*
pink rose
pity pitié *f.*
pizza pizza *f.*
place *n.* endroit *m.,* lieu *m.*
  take ~ avoir lieu
place *v.* mettre
plain simple
plan to avoir l'intention de
plate assiette *f.*
play *n.* pièce *f.*
play *v.* jouer
  ~ a game jouer à
  ~ an instrument jouer de
  ~ sports faire du sport
  ~ tennis jouer au tennis

please s'il vous plaît (s'il te plaît)
  ~ do je vous en prie
pleasure plaisir *m.*
  with ~ avec plaisir
poem poème *m.*
point out indiquer
police officer agent de police *m.,* gendarme *m.*
politician homme/femme politique *m./f.*
politics politique *f.*
poor *adj.* pauvre
poorly mal
popular populaire
porch véranda *f.*
pork porc *m.*
  ~ butcher's charcuterie *f.*
post office bureau de poste *m.*
postcard carte postale *f.*
potato pomme de terre *f.*
pound livre *f.*
pour verser
practice répéter
prefer préférer
  I ~ that je préfère que
preferable: it is ~ that il vaut mieux que
prepare (a lesson) préparer (un cours)
pretty joli(e)
price prix *m.*
probably sans doute
process: be in the ~ of être en train de
program programme *m.*
  TV ~ émission (de télé) *f.*
promise promettre
  it's a ~ c'est promis
prudently prudemment
publicity publicité *f.*
punch (a ticket) composter (un billet)
pupil élève *m./f.*
purchase achat *m.*
purple violet(te)
put mettre
  ~ on attacher; mettre *(clothes)*
  ~ on weight grossir

quarter *m.* quart
  ~ past, ~ after et quart
  ~ to, ~ till moins le quart
question question *f.*
  ask a ~ poser une question

quickly vite; rapidement
quiet: keep ~! tais-toi! (taisez-vous!)

race course *f.*
radio radio *f.*
rain pleuvoir
  it's raining il pleut
raincoat imperméable *m.*
raise lever
rapid rapide
rapidly rapidement
rare *(undercooked)* saignant(e)
rarely rarement
rather assez
  ~ poorly assez mal
read lire
really vraiment; sans façon
reasonable raisonnable
recently récemment
recommend recommander
red rouge
  ~ -haired roux (rousse)
refrigerator réfrigérateur *m.*
regarding à propos de
relatives parents *m.pl.*
remain rester
remember se souvenir (de)
rent *v.* louer
repeat répéter
request *n.* demande *f.*
  make a ~ faire une demande
reserve réserver
reside habiter
responsibility responsabilité *f.*
rest se reposer
restaurant restaurant *m.*
restroom toilettes *f.pl.*
return retourner, revenir, rentrer
rice riz *m.*
rich riche
ride: take a ~ se promener, faire une promenade en voiture
ridiculous ridicule
right *n.* droit *m.*
right *adj.* droit(e); exact(e)
  ~ ? n'est-ce pas?
  ~ away tout de suite
  ~ behind juste derrière
  be ~ avoir raison
  that's ~ c'est exact
  to the ~ (of) à droite (de)
ring *n.* bague *f.*
road route *f.*

roast (of beef) rôti (de bœuf) *m.*
roll *v.* rouler
roof toit *m.*
room chambre *f.*; salle *f.*; pièce *f.*
   bath ~ salle de bain(s) *f.*
   bed ~ chambre *f.*
   class ~ salle de classe *f.*
   dining ~ salle à manger *f.*
roommate camarade de chambre
   m./f.
round-trip ticket aller-retour *m.*
rugby rugby *m.*
run courir
run a stop sign brûler un stop
run into heurter
runner coureur/coureuse
Russia Russie *f.*
Russian russe

sad triste
salad salade *f.*
   (green) ~ salade (verte) *f.*
salesman/saleswoman
   vendeur/vendeuse *m./f.*
salmon saumon *m.*
salt sel *m.*
sandwich sandwich *m.*
Santa Claus le père Noël
sardine sardine *f.*
Saturday samedi *m.*
sausage saucisse *f.*
saxophone saxophone *m.*
say dire
scarf foulard *m.*
schedule emploi du temps *m.*
school école *f.*
   high ~ lycée *m.*
science sciences *f.pl.*
   computer ~ informatique *f.*
season saison *f.*
second second(e), deuxième
   in ~ class en seconde
see voir
seem avoir l'air
-self(-selves) -même(s)
sell vendre
semester semestre *m.*
send envoyer
Senegal Sénégal *m.*
Senegalese sénégalais(e)
separate *v.* séparer
   ~ from each other se séparer
September septembre *m.*
series *(TV)* feuilleton *m.*

serious sérieux (sérieuse)
seriously sérieusement
service: at your ~ à votre service
set: ~ the table mettre la table
seven sept
seventeen dix-sept
seventy soixante-dix
seventy-one soixante et onze
seventy-two soixante-douze
she *pron.* elle
sheet (of paper) feuille *f.*
shh! chut!
shirt chemise *f.*
shoes chaussures *f.pl.*
shop *(clothing)* boutique *f.*
   tobacco ~ (bureau de) tabac *m.*
shopping courses *f.pl.*
   ~ center centre commercial *m.*
short petit(e)
shorts (pair of) short *m.*
shoulder épaule *f.*
show montrer
shower *n.* douche *f.*
shower *v.* se doucher
sick malade
since depuis
sincere sincère
sing chanter
singer chanteur/chanteuse *m./f.*
single célibataire
Sir Monsieur (M.)
sister sœur *f.*
sister-in-law belle-sœur *f.* (*pl.*
   belles-sœurs)
sit down s'asseoir
   ~ to eat se mettre à table
six six
sixteen seize
sixty soixante
skate patiner
skating rink patinoire *f.*
ski skier
skid déraper
skirt jupe *f.*
skis skis *m.pl.*
sleep dormir
sleepy: be ~ avoir sommeil
slice tranche *f.*
slippery glissant(e)
slow *adj.* lent(e)
slow down ralentir
slowly lentement
small petit(e)
smile *n.* sourire *m.*
smile *v.* sourire

smoke fumer
smoking (car) fumeur
   non- ~ non-fumeur
snail escargot *m.*
snow neiger
   it's snowing il neige
so alors, si
   ~ many tant
   ~ much tant
soap opera feuilleton *m.*
soccer football (foot) *m.*
socks chaussettes *f.pl.*
soda: lemon-lime ~ limonade *f.*;
   orange ~ orangina *m.*
sofa sofa *m.*
some *adj.* des, quelques; *pron.* en
someone quelqu'un
something quelque chose *m.*
sometimes quelquefois
son fils *m.*
song chanson *f.*
soon bientôt
sore: be ~ avoir mal (à)
sorry désolé(e)
   be ~ regretter
   feel ~ (for) avoir pitié (de)
sort of assez
so-so comme ci, comme ça
soup soupe *f.*
Spain Espagne *f.*
Spanish espagnol(e)
speak parler
specify préciser
speed vitesse *f.*
   at top ~ à toute vitesse
spell épeler
   how do you ~ ...? comment
     est-ce qu'on écrit ...?
   ... is spelled ... ... s'écrit ...
spend (a year) passer (un an)
spinach épinards *m.pl.*
spoon cuiller *f.*
sportcoat veste *f.*
spring *n.* printemps *m.*
stamp timbre *m.*
stand up se lever
start commencer; démarrer
   it's starting to get cold il
     commence à faire froid
state état *m.*
statue statue *f.*
stay rester
steak steak *m.*
   ~ with French fries steak-
     frites *m.*

steering wheel volant *m.*
stepbrother demi-frère *m.*
stepfather beau-père *m.* (*pl.* beaux-pères)
stepmother belle-mère *f.* (*pl.* belles-mères)
stepparents beaux-parents *m.pl.*
stepsister demi-sœur *f.*
stereo stéréo *f.*
still encore; toujours
stomach estomac *m.*
stop *n.* arrêt *m.*
  ~ sign stop *m.*
  bus ~ arrêt d'autobus *m.*
stop *v.* (s')arrêter
store magasin *m.*
  department ~ grand magasin *m.*
  grocery ~ épicerie *f.*
story histoire *f.*
  detective ~ roman policier *m.*
stove cuisinière *f.*
strawberries fraises *f.pl.*
street rue *f.*
  one-way ~ sens interdit *m.*
student étudiant/étudiante *m./f.*
studies *n.* études *f.pl.*
study *v.* étudier
stylish chic *adj. inv.*
succeed réussir
sugar sucre *m.*
suit *n.* complet *m.*
  bathing ~ maillot de bain *m.*
suitcase valise *f.*
summer été *m.*
sun soleil *m.*
Sunday dimanche *m.*
supermarket supermarché *m.*
  giant ~ hypermarché *m.*
supplement supplément *m.*
supposed: be ~ to devoir
surely certainement, sûrement
surprise surprise *f.*
  what a good ~! quelle bonne surprise!
swear jurer
  I ~ (to you) je te le jure
sweater pull-over (pull) *m.*
sweatshirt sweat-shirt *m.*
Sweden Suède *f.*
Swedish suédois(e)
swim nager
swimming pool piscine *f.*
Swiss suisse
  ~ cheese emmenthal *m.*

Switzerland Suisse *f.*

table table *f.*
  at the ~ à table
  set the ~ mettre la table
tablecloth nappe *f.*
tablet cachet *m.*
  aspirin ~ cachet d'aspirine *m.*
take prendre
  ~ a nap faire la sieste
  ~ a test passer (un examen)
  ~ a trip faire un voyage
  ~ a walk, a ride faire une promenade
  ~ place avoir lieu
talkative bavard(e)
tall grand(e)
taste goûter
tea thé *m.*
teach enseigner
teacher professeur *m.*
  ~ preparation pédagogie *f.*
team équipe *f.*
tee-shirt tee-shirt *m.*
telephone *n.* téléphone *m.*
  ~ number numéro de téléphone *m.*
  on the ~ au téléphone
telephone *v.* téléphoner (à)
television télévision (télé) *f.*
tell indiquer, raconter, dire, parler
  can you ~ me ...? pouvez-vous me dire ...?
  ~ a story raconter une histoire
ten dix
tend to avoir tendance à
tennis tennis *m.*
  ~ shoes tennis *f.pl.*
  play ~ jouer au tennis
term paper dissertation *f.*
test examen *m.*
thank *v.* remercier
thanks merci
  yes, ~ je veux bien
that *adj.* ce/cet, cette, ces; *conj.* que; *pron.* ce, cela, ça; *relative pron.* qui, que
the le/la/les
theater théâtre *m.*
their leur(s)
them elles, eux; les, leur
then alors, ensuite, puis
there là, y
  ~ is (are) il y a, voilà

  over ~ là-bas
therefore alors; donc
they *pron.* ils, elles, on, eux
thin mince
thing chose *f.*
think croire, penser, trouver
  do you ~ so? vous trouvez?
  I don't ~ so je ne crois pas
  what do you ~ of it (of them)? qu'en penses-tu?
  what do you ~ of ...? comment trouvez-vous ...?
thirsty: be ~ avoir soif
thirteen treize
thirty trente
this *adj.* ce/cet, cette, ces
  ~ way par ici
those *adj.* ces
thousand mille *inv.*
three trois
throat gorge *f.*
throughway autoroute *f.*
Thursday jeudi *m.*
ticket billet *m.*
  one-way ~ aller simple *m.*
  round-trip ~ aller-retour *m.*
  traffic ~ contravention *f.*
tie *n.* cravate *f.*
time temps *m.*; heure *f.*; fois *f.*
  ~ difference décalage horaire *m.*
  a long ~ longtemps
  at that ~ à cette époque
  on ~ à l'heure
  the last ~ la dernière fois
  what ~ is it? quelle heure est-il?
tired fatigué(e)
to à
  ~ the side à côté
toast pain grillé *m.*
tobacco tabac *m.*
  ~ shop (bureau de) tabac *m.*
today aujourd'hui
together ensemble
tomato tomate *f.*
tomorrow demain
  day after ~ après-demain
tonight ce soir
too aussi
  ~ many trop (de)
  ~ much trop (de)
  you ~ vous aussi
tooth dent *f.*
toothbrush brosse à dents *f.*

toothpaste dentifrice *m.*
tour tour *m.*
  ~ bus autocar *m.*
towel serviette *f.*
tower tour *f.*
town ville *f.*
  ~ hall mairie *f.*
trade ... for échanger ... contre
traffic circulation *f.*
traffic light feu *m.* (*pl.* feux)
train train *m.*
  ~ station gare *f.*
travel voyager
traveler's check chèque de voyage *m.*
trip voyage *m.*
trout truite *f.*
true vrai(e)
truly vraiment
  yours ~ amicalement
trumpet trompette *f.*
truth vérité *f.*
try essayer
  may I ~ ...? puis-je ...?
Tuesday mardi *m.*
turn *n.* tour *m.*
turn *v.* tourner
  ~ on (*the TV*) mettre
  ~ on the heat mettre le chauffage
turnpike autoroute *f.*
tuxedo smoking *m.*
twelve douze
twenty vingt
twenty-one vingt et un
twenty-two vingt-deux
two deux

ugly laid(e)
unbelievable incroyable
uncle oncle *m.*
under sous
understand comprendre
understanding compréhensif/compréhensive
United States États-Unis *m.pl.*
university université *f.*
unmarried célibataire
until *prep.* jusqu'à
unwise: be ~ avoir tort
up: get ~ se lever
us nous
useless inutile
usually d'habitude

vacation vacances *f.pl.*
  have a good ~! bonnes vacances!
  on ~ en vacances
vanilla vanille *f.*
  ~ ice cream glace à la vanille *f.*
vegetable légume *m.*
  raw vegetables crudités *f.pl.*
very tout; très
violin violon *m.*
visit visiter
  ~ someone rendre visite à qqn
voyage voyage *m.*

wait (for) attendre
waiter garçon *m.*, serveur *m.*
waitress serveuse *f.*
wake up se réveiller
walk *n.* promenade *f.*
  take a ~ se promener, faire une promenade
walk *v.* se promener
waltz valse *f.*
want vouloir, désirer, avoir envie de
war guerre *f.*
warning avertissement *m.*
wash laver; se laver
washing machine machine à laver *f.*
watch *n.* montre *f.*
watch *v.* regarder
water eau *f.* (*pl.* eaux)
  mineral ~ eau minérale
way route *f.;* façon *f.*
  by the ~ au fait
we nous
wear porter
weather météo(rologie) *f.*, temps *m.*
  the ~ is bad il fait mauvais
  what is the ~ like? quel temps fait-il?
wedding mariage *m.*
  ~ anniversary anniversaire de mariage *m.*
  ~ dress robe de mariée *f.*
Wednesday mercredi *m.*
week semaine *f.*
  per ~ par semaine
  two weeks quinze jours
weekend week-end *m.*
weight: put on ~ grossir

  lose ~ maigrir
welcome: you're ~ de rien, je vous en prie, il n'y a pas de quoi
Welcome! Bienvenue!
well *adv.* bien
  are you ~? vous allez bien?
  fairly ~ assez bien
  not very ~ pas très bien
Well! Tiens!
Well then ... Eh bien ...
what *pron.* qu'est-ce que/qu'est-ce qui, que; *adj.* quel(le)
  ~? comment?
  ~ am I going to do? comment je vais faire?
  ~ day is it? quel jour est-ce?
  ~ (did you say)? comment?
  ~ is (are) ... like? comment est (sont) ...?
  ~ is there ...? qu'est-ce qu'il y a ...?
  ~ is this? qu'est-ce que c'est?
  ~ is your name? comment vous appelez-vous?
  ~'s new? quoi de neuf?
  ~'s the matter? qu'est-ce qu'il y a?
  ~ time is it? quelle heure est-il?
wheel: steering ~ volant *m.*
weird bizarre
when quand
where où
  ~ are you from? vous êtes d'où?; d'où venez-vous?
  ~ is (are) ...? où se trouve (se trouvent) ...?
which *adj.* quel(le); *pron.* lequel
while pendant que
  a little ~ tout à l'heure
white blanc (blanche)
who qui
why pourquoi
  ~ not? pourquoi pas?
widower/widow veuf/veuve *m./f.*
wife femme *f.*
win gagner
  ~ the lottery gagner à la loterie
wind vent *m.*
  it's windy il fait du vent
windbreaker blouson *m.*
wine vin *m.*

winter hiver *m.*
wish vouloir; souhaiter
  I want je veux (que)
  I would like je voudrais (que)
with avec
without sans
witness témoin *m.*
Wolof *(language)* wolof *m.*
woman femme *f.*, dame *f.*
word mot *m.*
work *n.* travail *m.*
  manual ~ travail manuel *m.*
work *v.* travailler
world monde *m.*

worry *n.* souci *m.*
worry *v.* s'inquiéter
wounded *adj.* blessé(e)
wow! oh là là!
write écrire
wrong faux (fausse)
  be ~ avoir tort

year an *m.;* année *f.*
  school ~ année scolaire
yellow jaune
yes oui; si!
yesterday hier

yet encore
  not ~ pas encore
you *pron.* tu, vous; te, vous; toi, vous
young jeune
your *adj.* ton, ta, tes; votre, vos
  (here's) to yours! à la vôtre!
yuck! berk!
yum! miam!

zero zéro
zip code code postal *m.*

Index

In the following index, the symbol (v) refers to lists of vocabulary within the lessons. The symbol (g) refers to the sections titled *Il y a un geste* that explain gestures used with the indicated phrase.

à
+ definite article, 125
to express possession, 169
to indicate ingredients, 229
+ places, 141
rendre visite, 243
répondre, 243
réussir, 331
accent marks, 33
accepting, offering, and refusing, 40
accidents, 408
acheter, 251
activities, (v) 37
L'addition s'il vous plaît, (g) 219
adjectives. *See also* demonstrative adjectives; descriptive adjectives; possessive adjectives
agreement of, 15–16, 22, 68
of color, 100, 105
comparative of, 308, 310
gender of, 15–16, 95
invariable, 95, 101
of nationality, 18
position of, 106–107
superlative of, 311
adverbs
comparative of, 308, 310
formation of, 288
of frequency, 96
superlative of, 311
advice, (v) 281
agreement
of adjectives, 15–16, 22–23, 68
of past participles, 189, 394
aller, 127, 189
Comment allez-vous?, 34
conditional, 420
future of, 337
+ infinitive, 128
subjunctive, 366
alphabet, 4, 32
an, *vs.* **année,** 159
answering the phone, 322
apéritif, 31, 211

s'appeler, 13, 57, 360
apprendre, à + infinitive, 220
article. *See* definite articles; indefinite articles; partitive articles
s'asseoir, 360
past participle of, 363
assez, (g) 22
À toute vitesse, (g) 287
au, aux, 125
au pair, 91
au revoir, (v) 123, (g) 122
aussi, 308, 310
autant, 308
avoir, *See also* **il y a,** 60, 136
conditional of, 421
future of, 337
idiomatic expressions with, 55, 67, 227, 246
imperative of, 281
imperfect of, 301
passé composé with, 157–158
past participle of, 157
subjunctive of, 283, 367

beaucoup, 30, 222
bise, faire la, (g) 122
boire, 223
Encore à boire?, (g) 212
boissons populaires, (v) 44
Bonjour, 9, 12
Bonsoir, 12
boucherie, 250
boulangerie, 250
bravo, (g) 90

carte, *vs.* **menu,** 351
Ça va, (g) 34
ce, ces, cet, cette, 103
-cer verbs, 214, 302
c'est, ce sont, *See also* **être** 111, 169
+ stress pronouns, 169
c'est la vie, (g) 155
charcuterie, 250

cher, (g) 101
Chut!, (g) 272
classroom expressions, 2, (v) 5
cognates, 25, 91, 380, (v) 381
colors, (v) 100
combien, 69, 247
Comment?, (g) 5
answers to, 42
comparative, 308, 310
compliments, 31, 35
compter avec les doigts, (g) 3
conditional, 420–421
conduire, 287
connaître, 277
vs. **savoir,** 327
contact physique, (g) 10
contraction, 74, 125
countries, 141–142
cours, (v) 135
croire, 391

danser, 37
invitation à danser, (g) 274
days of the week, 133–134
de
choisir, 332
definite articles after, 74
finir, 332
+ infinitive, 396
after negation, 67, 71, 216
possession with, 73–74
possessive construction with, 73, 76
preposition of place, 195
after superlative, 311
vs. **des,** 107
definite articles, 41–42
à +, 125
after **avoir,** 105
after negation, 71
after superlative, 311
in dates, 134
de +, 74
use of, 42, 43
demonstrative adjectives, 103

depuis, 247

des. *See* indefinite articles

descriptive adjectives, 22–23, (v) 93, 95, 101, 106

désolé(e), (g) 239

devoir, 136, 413–414
    conditional, 421
    past participle of, 157

dire, 383
    vs. **parler,** 384

direct object pronouns, 226–227, 278, 387
    in imperative, 285, 358
    position of, 358

dont, 256, 395

dormir, 170

driving, 271, 408

du, de la, de l,' des. *See* partitive articles

écrire, 161
    choses à, (v) 162

en, 398

Encore à boire?, (g) 212

ennuyeux, (g) 94

envoyer, 171

épicerie, 250

-er verbs, 36–37
    conditional forms of, 420
    past participle, 157
    subjunctive, 283, 366

est-ce que, 46

etiquette, 351

être, 14, 136
    à + stress pronouns, 169
    c'est, ce sont, 111, 169
    conditional, 421
    future, 337
    imperative, 281
    imperfect, 301
    indefinite articles after negative, 71
    partitive articles after, 216
    passé composé with, 188–190
    past participle, 157
    + profession, 111
    subjunctive, 267, 283

Excusez-moi de vous déranger, 8–9

faire, 108–109, 136
    conditional, 421
    des achats, (v) 254
    expressions with, 108–109

future of, 337
    past participle, 157
    subjunctive, 367

false cognates, 49, 380–381

family, (v) 57–59, 298

feelings, expressing, (v) 397

fleurs, 240

flûte!, 322

fois, *vs.* **heure, temps,** 164

franglais, 91

frapper à la porte, (g) 2

future, 336–337
    aller + infinitive indicating, 128

gagner, (v) 338

games, (v) 167

gender, 4. *See also* agreement; definite article, 14, 41

-ger verbs, 37, 214, 302

good-bye, (v) 123

greetings, 9, 12

h-, initial, 14, 215, 273

health, (v) 246

hello, 8–10, 12, 123

heure, 130–131
    vs. **temps, fois,** 164

home, 70, 72, 154

hotels, 322, (v) 330, 329–330

illness, (v) 245–246

Il n'y a pas de quoi, (g) 350

il y a, 67
    + expression of time, 159

imperative, 139, 281
    direct object pronouns in, 285

imperfect, 301–302, 411
    reflexive verbs, 362
    si +, 423
    uses of, 301
    vs. **passé composé,** 304, 411

impersonal expressions, 5, 197
    future of, 337
    imperfect of, 301

indefinite articles, 59
    after negation, 71

indirect object pronouns, 385–387

infinitive, 36
    construction, 278
    constructions, 43
    de +, 396
    subjunctive +, 284, 367

s'inquiéter, 360

interrogative adjectives, 113, 392

interrogative pronouns, 112, 392–393, 414–416

inversion
    noun subject, 143
    subject pronoun, 46
    use of **-t-** with, 46

invitation à danser, (g) 274

-ir verbs, 331–332
    subjunctive, 366

ivre, (g) 409

j'ai eu très peur, (g) 409

j'ai oublié, (g) 155

jamais, 96

J'en ai assez, (g) 299

Je te le jure, (g) 379

Je vous en prie, (g) 184

jouer
    à, 167
    de, 167

languages, 42, 142

le, la, les. *See* definite articles; direct object pronouns

lequel, laquelle, lesquels, lesquelles, 392–393, 395

liaison, 11, 15, 37, 59, 60, 61, 64, 76, 124
    after **quand,** 143

lire, 161
    choses à, (v) 162

Madame, Mademoiselle, Monsieur, 9

marital status, (v) 16

marriage, 81, 298

McDo, 91

meals, 211, 215

meilleur, *vs.* **mieux,** 310

menu, *vs.* **carte,** 351

merci, 31, 211
    non, (g) 30

mettre, 353–354

Mince!, 322

moins, in comparative, 308, 310

Mon œil!, (g) 272

months of the year, (v) 197–198

musical instruments, (v) 167

nationality, 18

ne... jamais, 96, 157

ne... pas, 20, 157, 228, 285, 363

ne... personne, 417–418
ne... plus, 218–219
ne... que, 303
ne... rien, 162, 417–418. *See also*
    quelque chose
negation, 20
    definite articles after, 71
    imperative, 139, 285
    indefinite articles after, 71
    passé composé, 157, 417
    possessive adjectives after, 71
n'est-ce pas, 46
nettoyer, 171
nouns, plural of, 58
numbers
    cardinal, 3, 63–64
    gender of, 63
    ordinal, 285–286

object pronouns. *See* direct object
    pronouns; indirect object
    pronouns
offering, accepting, and refusing,
    40
offering flowers, 240
on, 14
orders, 281, (v) 283
où, 143
oublié, j'ai, (g) 155
oui, *vs.* **si,** 71

Pardon?, (g) 5
paresseux, (g) 94
parler, 36, 42, 136
    vs. **dire,** 384
partir, 170
partitive articles, 216
passé composé, 157, 188, 417
    with **avoir,** 157–158
    connaître, 277
    with **être,** 188–190
    negative form of, 157
    in questions, 158
    vs. imperfect, 304, 411
passer, + unit of time, 161
past, immediate, 200
past participle
    agreement of, 189, 279, 363
    avoir, 157
    devoir, 157, 413
    -er verbs, 157
    être, 157
    faire, 157

-re verbs, 243
pâtisserie, 240
payer, 253
    les achats, (v) 253
pendant, *vs.* **depuis,** 248
perdre courage, patience, 244
personne, 417–418
peu, 223
peur, (g) 409
pharmacie, 240
places, (v) 125–126
plus, in comparative, 308
plus-que-parfait, 412
possession, with **de,** 73–74
possessive adjectives, 68–69,
    75–76
    negation and, 71
politesse, 9, 322
pouvoir, 274
    conditional, 421
    future of, 337
    passé composé, 274
    puis-je?, est-ce que je peux?,
        325
    subjunctive of, 396
préférer, 230, 251
prendre, 220
prepositions
    of place, 138, 142, 195–196
    rien after, 163
present tense. *See also* individual
    verbs by name
    regular verbs, 36, 243, 331
prie, je vous en, (g) 184
professions, (v) 111, Appendix B
se promener, 360
pronouns
    en, 398
    interrogative, 112, 392,
        414–416
    object. *See* direct object pro-
        nouns; indirect object
        pronouns
    relative. *See* relative pronouns
    stress. *See* stress pronouns
    subject, 13

quand, 96, 143
    clauses and future, 338
quantity, expressions of, 222–223
que
    interrogative pronoun, 112,
        414–416
    relative pronoun, 256, 394

quel, quelle, interrogative adjec-
    tive, 112–113, 392
Quel imbécile!, (g) 409
Quelle histoire!, (g) 379
quelque chose, 162
quelques dates, (v) 198
Qu'est-ce que je vais faire?, (g)
    321
questions
    il y a in, 67
    with interrogative pronouns,
        414–416
    in the **passé composé,** 158
    yes/no, 45–46
qui
    interrogative pronoun, 112,
        414–416
    relative pronoun, 57, 256, 394
quoi, 414–416
    il n'y a pas de, (g) 350

raconter, *vs.* **dire, parler,** 384
reflexive verbs, 165–166,
    (v) 357, 357–358
    passé composé of, 190
refusing, offering, and accepting, 40
relative pronouns, 57, 256, 394
rendre visite à, 244, 386
-re verbs, (v) 243, 243–244
    past participle, 243
    subjunctive of, 283, 366
rien, 162, 417–418
rooms of a house, 70, (v) 72

Salut, 12, 122
Sans façon, 211
santé, à votre, (g) 30
savoir, 327
    conditional, 421
    future of, 337
    + infinitive, 327
    subjunctive, 367
seasons, (v) 197
second, *vs.* **deuxième,** 335
services, asking for, (v) 325
si, 246
    clauses and future, 338
    hypothetical, 423
    vs. **oui,** 71
sortir, 170
stress pronouns, 168–169, 308
subject pronouns, 13

subjunctive, 282–284, 365–367, 396–397
superlative, 311–312

tabac, bureau de, 240
Tais-toi!, (g) 272
table, 211
tard, *vs.* **en retard,** 356
téléphone, (g) 10, 322
  numéro de, 64–65
télévision, 380
temps. *See* time
  vs. **temps, heure, fois,** 164
terms of endearment, 271
time
  expressions of, 3, (v) 128, (v) 159
  stalling for, (v) 55
  telling, 130–131
  temps, heure, fois, 164
tomber, 36
tôt, *vs.* **en avance,** 356
tout, toute, tous, toutes, 333
traffic violations, 408

trop, 223
tu, *vs.* **vous,** 14, 55

un, une. *See* indefinite articles

vendre, 243
  subjunctive, 283, 366
venir, 194–195
  conditional, 421
  de + infinitive, 200
  future of, 337
  subjunctive, 366
verbs
  -er, 36–37
  + indirect object, (v) 386
  + infinitive construction, 43, 278
  -ir, (v) 331, 331–332
  negation of, 20
  -re, (v) 243, 243–244
  reflexive. *See* reflexive verbs
voici, voilà, 67
  direct object pronouns +, 278

voilà, (g) 54
voir, 391
vouloir, 274
  conditional, 421
  future of, 337
  je voudrais, 29, 275
  offering, accepting, and refusing with, 40
  passé composé, 274
  subjunctive of, 396
vous, *vs.* **tu,** 14, 55
weather expressions, 5, 197, 301, 337
will, (v) 365

y, 192
young adults, 298

zut!, 322

Permissions and Credits

The authors and editors wish to thank the following persons and publishers for permission to include the works or excerpts mentioned.

p. 49: © Besançon: Le Gab, Numéro 648.

p. 117: Jacques Prévert, «L'accent grave» in *Paroles*. © Éditions Gallimard. By permission of the publisher.

p. 148: Jean-Louis Dongmo, «Village natal». Reprinted by permission of Jean-Louis Dongmo from *Neuf poètes camerounais: Anthologie par Lilyan Kesteloot, Deuxième édition* (Yaoundé: Éditions Clé, 1971).

p. 174: © L'Alsace: Le Journal des enfants.

p. 175: tiré de *Les Plaisirs et les jeux* de George Duhamel. © Mercure de France, 1922.

p. 181: «Le Cadien/Cajun» par Christy Dugas Maraist. Reprinted by permission of the author.

p. 204: «Les femmes parlementaires européennes» par Elisabeth Schemla, *L'Express*, 6 juin 1996. Used by permission of The New York Times Syndication Sales Corporation.

p. 206: Jacques Prévert, «Refrains enfantins» in *Spectacle*. © Éditions Gallimard. By permission of the publisher.

p. 234: Jacques Prévert, «Déjeuner du matin» in *Paroles*. © Éditions Gallimard. By permission of the publisher.

p. 261: «Hystérie anti-tabac», *Le Point*, 31 août 1996, p. 15; «Les mesures du président», *Le Point*, 31 août 1996, p. 60.

p. 265: Bernard Dadié, «Je vous remercie mon Dieu» from *Bernard Dadié*, 1978.

p. 292: «La France au volant», Pierre Daninos, *Les Carnets du Major Thompson*, © Hachette, 1954.

p. 316: Marie-Célie Agnant, *La Dot de Sara* (Montréal: Remue-ménage, 1995). By permission of Les Éditions du Remue-ménage.

p. 347: Fatima Bellahcène, «L'Étrangère» from *La Littérature féminine de la langue française au Maghreb*, Jean Déjeaux, ed., 1994.

p. 372: © MCMXLVII by Enoch & Cie Paris. Tous droits réservés.

p. 401: © Télé Loisirs.

p. 428: «La France nucléaire», © *Le Point*, Numéro 761.

Photos

p.1, © Bruno De Hogues/Stone; p.6, © Owen Franken/Stock Boston; p.9, © Beryl Goldberg; p.19, © Owen Franken/Stock Boston; p. 28, © Owen Franken; p. 31, © Owen Franken; p. 52, © David Simson/Stock Boston; p.55, © David R. Frazier Photolibrary; p.60, © Jean-Marc Truchet/Stone; p. 61, © Owen Franken; p. 77,© Owen Franken; p. 84, © Reuters/Jim Young/Active Photos; p. 85, © Reuters/Vincent Kessler/Archive Photos; p. 86, © Dallas and John Heaton/Corbis; p. 86, © Imapress/The Image Works; p. 86, © Stephanie Ruet/Corbis Sygma; p. 87, © photo courtesy of Air France; p. 87, © Reuters/Stefano Rellandini/Archive Photos; p. 88, © Beryl Goldberg; p. 91, © Beryl Goldberg; p. 94, © Owen Franken; p. 109, © Kevin Galvin; p.120, © Bob Handelman/Stone; p. 123, © Beryl Goldberg; p.131, © Xavier Rossi/Liaison Agency; p. 148, © Siegfried Tauqueur/ eStock Photography (Leo de Wys); p. 151, © Owen Franken; p. 154, © Mark Burnett/David R. Frazier Photolibrary; p. 160, © Owen Franken; p. 172, © Eric A. Wessman/Stock Boston; p. 178, © Reuters/Jim Young/Archive

Realia

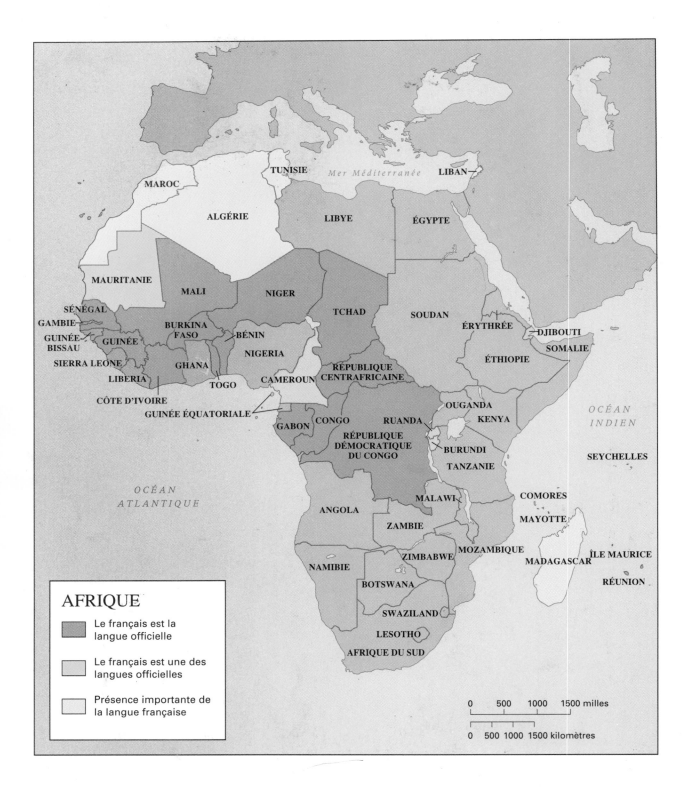

AFRIQUE

Le français est la
langue officielle

Le français est une des
langues officielles

Présence importante de
la langue française

MAROC
TUNISIE
LIBAN
Mer Méditerranée
ALGÉRIE
LIBYE
ÉGYPTE
MAURITANIE
MALI
NIGER
SÉNÉGAL
GAMBIE
TCHAD
SOUDAN
ÉRYTHRÉE
DJIBOUTI
BURKINA
FASO
GUINÉE-
BISSAU
GUINÉE
BÉNIN
SOMALIE
SIERRA LEONE
NIGERIA
ÉTHIOPIE
GHANA
LIBERIA
CAMEROUN
RÉPUBLIQUE
CENTRAFRICAINE
TOGO
CÔTE D'IVOIRE
OUGANDA
GUINÉE ÉQUATORIALE
KENYA
OCÉAN
INDIEN
GABON
CONGO
RUANDA
RÉPUBLIQUE
DÉMOCRATIQUE
DU CONGO
BURUNDI
SEYCHELLES
TANZANIE
OCÉAN
ATLANTIQUE
MALAWI
COMORES
ANGOLA
MAYOTTE
ZAMBIE
MOZAMBIQUE
ÎLE MAURICE
ZIMBABWE
MADAGASCAR
NAMIBIE
RÉUNION
BOTSWANA
SWAZILAND
LESOTHO
AFRIQUE DU SUD

0   500   1000   1500 milles

0   500 1000 1500 kilomètres